THE BIG BOOK OF

SCANDALOUS
AUSTRALIAN
Women

THE BIG BOOK OF
SCANDALOUS AUSTRALIAN
Women

KAY SAUNDERS

ABC
Books

The ABC 'Wave' device is a trademark of the
Australian Broadcasting Corporation and is used
under licence by HarperCollins*Publishers* Australia.

First published in Australia in 2014
by HarperCollins*Publishers* Australia Pty Limited
ABN 36 009 913 517
harpercollins.com.au

The Big Book of Scandalous Australian Women is a combined edition of Kay Saunders' previous books:
Notorious Australian Women (2011)
and *Deadly Australian Women* (2013)

Copyright © Kay Saunders 2011, 2013, 2014

HarperCollins*Publishers*
Level 13, 201 Elizabeth Street, Sydney NSW 2000, Australia
Unit D, 63 Apollo Drive, Rosedale, Auckland 0632, New Zealand
A 53, Sector 57, Noida, UP, India
77–85 Fulham Palace Road, London W6 8JB, United Kingdom
2 Bloor Street East, 20th floor, Toronto, Ontario M4W 1A8, Canada
195 Broadway, New York, NY 10007, USA

978 0 7333 3260 9 (pbk)
978 1 4607 0093 8 (ebook)

Cover design by Hazel Lam, HarperCollins Design Studio
Front cover images: (clockwise from left) Sydney underworld figure Tilly Devine,
SMH NEWS Picture by STAFF/Fairfax Syndication, FXJ200438; Portrait of Australian journalist,
Lillian Roxon, Sun Herald picture by Staff/Fairfax Syndication, FXJ36871; Martha standing at
the gate (MS 8296 Box 972/1 [b] Papers; Martha Needle. 1863–1894) courtesy State Library
of Victoria; Annette Kellermann in 1919, modelling her radical costume, Bain Collection,
Library of Congress, LC-B2-738-5.
Back cover image: Adela Pankhurst Walsh, standing on a chair in the street outside The Carrington
Press Printers, Sydney, 28 January 1941, SMH NEWS Picture by STAFF/Fairfax Syndication,
FXJ118453.
Typeset in 11.5/16pt Adobe Garamond Pro by Kirby Jones
Printed and bound in Australia by Griffin Press
The papers used by HarperCollins in the manufacture of this book are a natural,
recyclable product made from wood grown in sustainable plantation forests. The fibre source
and manufacturing processes meet recognised international environmental standards, and carry
certification.

Contents

Introduction

Our history is replete with rebels, rousers, eccentrics and plain bad girls: women – some even deadly – who have not received the sort of attention they rightly deserve. The two books in this compendium go some way towards addressing that.

Notorious Australian Women (first published in 2011) charts the lives of some 20 mavericks who defied the rigid cultural prescriptions of what it meant to be a woman in Australia. The scope of this book is wide, not just geographically and temporally but in the diversity of the women's cultural and class origins. Some of the women were born to privilege in Australia, others came from humble circumstances and from far-off European countries: Prussian-born brothel keeper Caroline Hodgson is profiled alongside cosmetic queen Helena Rubinstein, who rose up from plain beginnings in Poland; Sydney-born Annette Kellermann's parents were French and German classical musicians; Mary Cockerill was a teenaged Pallawah woman from the Hobart area who became a bushranger in 1815; and Walyer was a frontier freedom fighter in the northern area of Van Diemen's Land.

No matter where they came from and what their destiny held, each woman looked society's values squarely in the eye and went upon her own path regardless. Some flourished in their fame or infamy while others met inglorious and tragic ends. Their verve, courage and decisiveness deserve our applause and our admiration.

Deadly Australian Women (2013) showed that women could kill – sometimes within social contexts, but sometimes because they were by nature killers. There are women such as Donna Fitchett, who coldly murdered her two boys in 2005 in a bizarre revenge attack against her husband, and teenager Helen Moore who, in Sydney in the 1960s, set about killing and disabling children she was entrusted to babysit. A smaller but intriguing category of female serial killers includes Caroline Grills, a maternal Sydney housewife who found excitement in the early post-war years killing family members with the tasteless and odourless rat poison thallium.

The prevalence of infanticide and the abandonment of unwanted newborn babies throughout Australian history still have the power to shock. Many convicted murderers were imprisoned largely because of the roles they played in matters of reproduction and birth control in a time when women had limited choices. Abortionists such as Madame Harpur, an educated woman plying her trade in late-colonial Adelaide, made a fortune supplying terminations to often poor and desperate pregnant women. Sarah Makin and Alice Mitchell ran businesses providing care and shelter for ex-nuptial babies only to realise there was more money to be made in killing them.

Unhappily married women, with no option of an easy divorce, came up with deadly solutions to the problem of escaping unwanted or violent partners. Some husbands were dispatched for the insurance money, while others were eliminated through vengeful pacts with the new man on the scene.

The Big Book of Scandalous Australian Women takes readers into the hidden corners of our history, revealing women of audacity, courage and commitment alongside those who went beyond mere scandal into the realms of deadly action.

KAY SAUNDERS
Brisbane, January 2014

NOTORIOUS
AUSTRALIAN
Women

To
Louise Bass Saunders and Harolda Sizer,
my English great-grandmothers who fought valiantly in the WSPU
and
my granddaughter Gabriella Hilder who inherits their legacy

Contents

CHAPTER 1

Mary Broad Bryant

(1765–UNKNOWN)

*The highway robber and First Fleeter who rowed from Sydney
to Timor with her husband and two children.*

Mary Bryant was Australia's first authentic celebrity. The *Dublin
Chronicle* of 4 June 1793 brought fascinated readers up to date with
her remarkable story:

> The female convict who made her escape from Botany Bay,
> and suffered a voyage of 3000 leagues, and who afterwards
> was taken and condemned to death, has been pardoned
> and released from Newgate. A gentleman of high rank in
> the Army visited her in Newgate, heard the details of her
> life, and for that time departed. The next day he returned,
> and told the old gentleman who keeps the prison he had
> procured her pardon, which he shewed him, at the same
> time requesting that she should not be apprised of the
> circumstances. The next day he returned with his carriage,
> and took off the poor woman who almost expired with
> excess of gratitude.[1]

The description of Mary in the records of London's Newgate Prison
for the year 1792 reads: 'Mary Bryant, alias Broad, age 25 [sic], height
5'4", grey eyes, brown hair, sallow complexion, born in Cornwall,
widow'.[2] Neither this nor the *Dublin Chronicle* account reveal much of

7

the drama, courage and despair that characterised this young woman's life. Her extraordinary story might have been a sensation soon forgotten but for the advocacy of her benefactor, the Scottish aristocrat and barrister, also ninth Laird of Auchinleck and author of the famous *Life of Samuel Johnson*, James Boswell.

Mary Broad was born in Fowey, a small fishing village on the English Channel side of Cornwall, the daughter of mariner William Broad and his wife, Grace, and was baptised on 1 May 1765. Cornwall is a distinctive part of Britain, having far more in common with other Celtic regions in Brittany and Wales than the neighbouring English counties. Until the end of the eighteenth century, the Cornish spoke their own Celtic language, Kernewek. English language, customs, laws and ways of life were often seen as foreign impositions. Like the people in the maritime villages of nearby Devon, the Cornish were renowned for smuggling, which they regarded as a legitimate form of free trading. Looting and plundering wrecked vessels off the rocky coastline were also common practice. Indeed, the local economy along these coasts depended upon smuggling and looting luxury goods from France bound for the more urban centres of Bath, Plymouth and London. The historical novels by Daphne du Maurier, *Jamaica Inn* (1936) and *Frenchman's Creek* (1942), along with Winston Graham's *Poldark* series, capture the atmosphere of Cornwall at the time of Mary Broad's childhood.

As a mariner, William Broad would presumably have participated in smuggling, safe in the knowledge that this was a protected industry among his local community. However, Mary's biographer C. H. Currey has claimed the Broad family were also 'prominent sheep stealers'. Cornwall was an extremely poverty-stricken area of Britain in the eighteenth century, with little industry apart from fishing and smuggling. Stealing food and animals to sell was part of a folk culture that eluded the stronger claims of the law.

As a child, Mary spent many hours on her father's small vessel, learning the ways of the sea, an education that would later help preserve her life, but like girls of her class and region, she was illiterate. Free compulsory education did not arrive in Britain until a century after her birth. Despite her considerable nautical skills, life at sea, or as a smuggler, was not the province of a female, yet we do not know how she was employed once she was old enough to work. We can surmise that, like her sister Dolly – whose trade was mentioned much later in a letter of James Boswell – she was a domestic servant. Mary later worked as a cook in London after her escape from Botany Bay, so this might have been her occupation.

Mary came to public notice when she was convicted, at the Exeter Assizes in Devon on 29 March 1786, along with two female accomplices, of the highway assault of spinster Agnes Lakeman of Plymouth, the nearest large town to Fowey. They stole her cloak, bonnet and other personal items (presumably jewellery) to the value of £11/11s. It was a bold and daring crime, performed in broad daylight in full public view. Most transported convicts were found guilty of petty property crimes such as theft, selling stolen goods or pickpocketing, but this was an audacious assault and robbery. It was also conducted without much forethought and on the spur of the moment. Coming across the well-dressed woman of wealth and standing, who was without family or maid in attendance, Lakeman provoked envy among the three young women, whose lives were dictated by poverty and relentless hard work. But lacking discretion and cunning to successfully pull off such a bold move, they were easily apprehended.

All three young women were given a capital sentence, as thefts over the value of 40 shillings warranted the death penalty if undertaken with threats or violence. Mary would have felt terrified and alarmed – she had presumably only wanted to wear some beautiful clothes and jewellery, and soon she would be dead. Not only executed, but hanged in public to the shame of her family.

Fortunately, the sentence was later commuted to transportation for seven years (which was itself a fearful outcome). At twenty-one years of age, Mary was not a juvenile offender, so the comparative leniency of her sentence attests to her otherwise good character and disposition before the court. Certainly she had no previous convictions.

Nevertheless, transportation was the second most feared and severe punishment after execution. Introduced in 1717 – although suspended following the independence of the American colonies – transportation was devised to 'deter wicked and evil-disposed persons from being guilty of crimes'.[3] By 1786 the Secretary of State, Lord Sydney, had announced that transportation would resume in earnest, as places like Newgate Prison in London and the disused hulks of old sailing vessels moored in the waterways of England and used to house felons for years on end, were criminal training grounds rather than places of reformation.[4]

Mary was first confined in the decrepit and unsanitary hulk *Dunkirk*, off Plymouth. Convicts like Mary were sent from the hulks to work during the day, returning to the cramped, dank locations in the evening. But now as a member of the First Fleet, she was destined to be part of this new experiment, leaving the familiarity of Plymouth for an unknown destination at the end of the earth for a life of exile and compulsory, unremitting work.

The Governor of the new convict settlement at Botany Bay and commander of the First Fleet, Arthur Phillip, was at the end of a long but not particularly illustrious career. He was a man of probity, humanity and solid qualities. A professional naval officer who rose through the ranks, Phillip had seen action in the Seven Years' War and at Havana.[5] He also farmed successfully in Hampshire between bouts of active service, though this experience did not prepare him for the new conditions in the colony he was to establish. He commenced his complex and unique task of founding a colony with a surprising optimism and charity that seemed misplaced, considering his new charges were mostly habitual metropolitan criminals who preferred robbery and theft as a way of life.

Phillip spent the time between October 1786 and May 1787 preparing for the voyage and the establishment of the settlement. He penned his thoughts on the future direction of the settlement, wherein he imagined a robust civil society forming out of the Empire's criminal outcasts. His gift for level-headedness and sound administration can be appreciated in his dispatches.[6] He did not, however, provide for basic necessities, such as needles and threads to mend clothing, nor cutlery for the felons – hardly an inducement to reformation and manners. Yet, despite these oversights, he was a man of sympathy and humanity, unlike his deputy, Lieutenant Governor and Vice Admiralty Court Judge Major Robert Ross, who described New South Wales' felons as 'the outcast of God's works'.[7]

The First Fleet left Plymouth on 13 May 1787 for close to a nine-month journey.[8] Like other felons embarking into this unknown, Mary on board the *Charlotte* must have wept bitter tears of sorrow and fear as she lost sight of land and the fleet headed for the Azores – on their way to live among cannibals and monsters for all she knew. It would have been natural for her to assume she would never see her homeland or family again. She might die on the voyage from scurvy, or perish in a tempest, or languish in the new colony. Like most of the women felons, she was young, robust and healthy, a potential founder of new lines of residents in the penal colony, not that such thoughts of lineages, re-establishment and hope could have been much in their minds as they left behind all that was familiar.

Once underway on their journey, the convicts sought any comfort they could. Naval and civil officers decried the conduct of many of the convicts, particularly their sexual licentiousness, drunkenness and gambling, and sermons by the chaplain, the Reverend Richard Johnson, about penitence, reformation, the atonement of sins past and present and the perils of bad behaviour, were not heeded. This is hardly surprising given the character of the felons and the soldiers sent to guard them. Life on the transport ships was bleak and brutal; any pleasure that could be found could be seen as a small reward for life's precariousness and inequities.

Because of incomplete records, Mary Broad's name does not appear on Captain Arthur Phillip's list of transportees.[9] Her first official appearance in the New South Wales chapter of her life came when Surgeon John White, now remembered for his extraordinary zoological and floral depictions of the Antipodes, noted that 'Mary Broad, a convict, delivered of a fine girl at sea'.[10] The baby was named Charlotte, presumably in honour of the vessel on which they sailed, and given the surname Spence. There was a seaman on board named Spence, but he is undoubtedly not the father, as Mary would have been pregnant when she left Plymouth. Charlotte was baptised by the Reverend Johnson on 13 November 1787. If some officers despaired of these 'damned whores',[11] Mary was presumably not one of them. She was pregnant and then had the responsibility of tending to her new baby.

During the nine-month voyage to the new penal settlement, Broad met several other felons with whom her fate would be later entangled. Her future husband, William Bryant, a Cornish fisherman convicted of smuggling at the Launceston Assizes in March 1784, was originally sentenced to seven years' transportation to the American colonies. When the American War of Independence curtailed this outlet for the criminals of England, Bryant was sent to Botany Bay. Mary and William shared a lot in common as Celtic Cornish people from maritime villages. Their life experiences were very different from the majority of the convicts who came from large, overcrowded urban centres, such as London. Mary also met James Martin, an Irishman who stole from his employer Viscount Courtney; and James Cox, given a life sentence and exile through transportation, although the records do not reveal his crime.[12]

On board the *Charlotte*, Mary Broad also met Captain Lieutenant Watkin Tench, a veteran of the American War of Independence in which he was a prisoner of war of the American colonists for three months. His insightful and well-written *A Complete Account of the Settlement at Pt. Jackson in New South Wales* (1793) later brought the rigours of establishing a penal settlement in a hot, alien world sharply to life for readers on the other side of the world. His earlier volume, *A Narrative of the Expedition to Botany Bay* (1789), described the voyage of the First Fleet. A keen ethnographer and naturalist, Tench recorded his observations of the new world and the new arrivals with humanity rare among naval and military officers of the day. Later, he was the only senior officer who wrote kindly of Mary and William Bryant after their escape.

Among the people who disembarked at Sydney Cove in January 1788 were: 548 male and 188 female convicts, along with the civil and naval officers and their family members. There were nineteen officers, eight drummers, twenty NCOs, 160 privates, twenty-seven wives and thirty-seven children.[13] Arriving in the heat and glare of summer, we can assume Mary looked out from the *Charlotte* with deep apprehension; all she would have been able to see was wilderness, without a house, church or horse. Her only security lay in the familiarity of William Bryant's similar life experience. Indeed, Broad and Bryant married less than three weeks later in a mass ceremony with nine other couples, without the reading of banns – customary in the Church of England as a prelude to the ceremony of marriage – on 10 February 1788, conducted by the Reverend Johnson. Married felons received more privileges than single felons, such as their own hut with a garden rather than living in mass camps with no privacy and no degree of comfort, and these privileges may have been William Bryant's motive for undertaking a formal union.

In the new penal colony, the young couple was perhaps the most privileged of all the felons. William must have been well educated for his humble origins, for he signed his marriage certificate in a clear and confident hand. As a skilled sailor and fisherman he was placed in charge of the boats used for fishing to supplement the inadequate and mouldy rations brought from England and the Cape of Good Hope. Judge Advocate David Collins wrote in his book *An Account of the English Colony in New South Wales* (1798) that:

> From his having been bred for from youth to the business of
> a fisherman in the western part of England, William Bryant

was given the management and direction of such boats as were employed in fishing; every encouragement was held out to keep him above temptation; a hut was built for him and his family; he was always presented with a certain part of the fish which he caught ...

Mary kept busy with her baby and tending to her garden, a difficult undertaking in the hot and unfamiliar environment, but with a husband, she had some protection, unlike most of the convict women who were eagerly sought out by predatory men, both felons and the military.

But within two years William Bryant had abused the trust bestowed on him: he was caught trading some of the catch bound for the public store in exchange for liquor. His punishment was severe – 100 lashes and the loss of his hut and private garden. Mary and Charlotte thereby lost their privileged positions and extra fresh food. Collins again depicted the scene:

As, notwithstanding his villainy, he was too useful a person to part with and send to a brickcart, he was still retained to fish for the settlement; but a very vigilant eye was kept on him and such steps taken as appeared likely to prevent him from repeating his offence, if the sense of shame and fear of punishment were not of themselves sufficient to deter him.[14]

For Mary, William's punishment was harsh and humiliating. Her husband had risked all the family's comfort and necessities for his own pleasure in a drink of rum. Her feelings of anger and resentment must have been great during this period.

Meanwhile the early years of the colony progressed precariously in the extreme. The *Sirius* brought provisions from the Cape of Good Hope in May 1789. The following year it was lost at sea.[15] Another supply ship, the *Guardian*, was lost also when it struck an iceberg in

December 1789. Phillip was forced to cut the already lean rations as of November 1789. Tench noted that the struggling farms that had been established were hit by drought, describing them as 'in a wretched condition'.[16] Along with others in the colony, Mary must have wondered where the next meal was coming from. As starvation loomed, all the officers and even the chaplain were forced to go out fishing at night.[17] Amidst all this deprivation, Mary Bryant gave birth to a son, Emanuel, who was baptised by the Reverend Johnson on 4 April 1790.[18] Several weeks later the *Supply* sailed for Batavia (as Jakarta was then known) in the Dutch East Indies for food, and in June the *Justinian* arrived with provisions, unappetising as they were. The prospect of starvation was staved off for the present but could not have been far from everyone's mind for the future.

On 18 October 1790 the *Supply* returned to Sydney with provisions, and later in December the 350-ton Dutch vessel, the *Waaksamheyd*, under the command of Detmer Smit, hired by one of the NSW officers, a Captain Bell, arrived loaded with pork, beef, flour, rice and sugar. Smit was later recompensed with £100 from the English Treasury.[19]

Smit's arrival also provided an opportunity for escape for Mary and William Bryant. Judge Advocate David Collins, a man far less charitable in his judgments of human frailty than Tench or Phillip, recorded:

> Bryant ... was overheard consulting in his hut, after dark,
> with five other convicts, on the practicality of carrying off
> the boat in which he was employed [in late February 1791].
> The circumstances being reported to the Governor, it was
> determined that all his proceedings should be narrowly
> watched, and any scheme of that nature counteracted.[20]

What Collins and Phillip did not know was that William Bryant had obtained a compass, quadrant and nautical charts from Smit, along with two muskets and ammunition.

According to Collins, Bryant's escape was delayed by an accident when he was caught in a squall with the fishing catch and his fishing boat – and prospective escape – swamped, with the boat needing some repair. Interestingly, Charles Currey notes that Bennelong's sister and her three children were on board, perhaps helping with the fishing.[21]

We may speculate why a far more vigilant eye was not kept on William and Mary Bryant. We may also wonder why William Bryant wished to flee. His seven-year sentence was completed and he could return to England if he had the fare, though he would have had to wait until Mary finished her sentence in 1794 – regulations prevented jailers or their charges from abandoning legal wives and legitimate children. He may have been influenced by reports of Captain William Bligh's successful trip to Timor in an open boat after the *Bounty* mutiny. Detmer Smit may also have encouraged him in some way.

Even more interesting is to consider Mary's motives. William had already betrayed the trust placed in him and jeopardised the comfort and security of her family. Yet she bound her fate with his in the desperate undertaking of rowing to Batavia, thousands of kilometres away. Additionally she risked the lives of her two small children in this hazardous bid. Her faith in his nautical and navigational skills, along with her own, must have overcome any hesitation that this would destroy them all. But perhaps it was she who was the driving force behind the escape. After all, no one could be certain how long the supplies of food and clothing would last in the fledgling colony.

On 28 March 1791 the *Waaksamheyd* set sail for England, arriving in April 1792. That night, with *Waaksamheyd* gone and the *Supply* en route to Norfolk Island, and therefore no ships in the harbour, the party of eleven escapees departed under a moonless sky at 11pm in the Governor's six-oared open boat on which William Bryant had been working. One of the sailors in the settlement, John Eastey, left an account of the remarkable event in his diary, and perhaps provides a bit of an answer as to why the party risked all. He wrote:

> Between the hours of 9 and 12 it was supposed that they
> intended for Bativee but having no vessel in the harbour
> there was no Persuing them so thay got clear of but its a very
> Desparate attempt to go in an open Boat for a run of about
> 16 or 17 hundred Leags and in perticular for a woman and
> 2 Small Children the oldest not above 3 years of age but the
> thought of Liberty from Such a place as this Enoufh to induce
> any Convicts to try all Skeemes to obtain it as thay are in the
> same as Slaves all the time that thay are in this Country ...[22]

Tench, Collins and the Governor also recorded the escape. Sergeant James Scott noted in his journal that a party raised the alarm at 6am the next morning.[23]

Nine adults and two children escaped in the flimsy, uncovered craft. Each adult brought valuable skills to the enterprise. As Watkin Tench noted, William Bryant was an excellent sailor in charge of the vessel he stole. William Morton was a skilled navigator; James Martin, William Allen, John Butcher (aka Samuel Broom), James Cox, Nathaniel Lilley and John Simms (aka Samuel Bird) were experienced sailors. As a mariner's daughter, Mary was an experienced and proficient sailor. Tench also noted that Mary Bryant had gathered provisions and extra clothing for the voyage. In 1926 Ralph Isham found in the records of James Boswell a curious artefact labelled 'Leaves from Botany Bay used as Tea'. This was the only memento that Mary Bryant gave to her generous benefactor.[24] Undoubtedly it was the sole souvenir, if we could call it such, from her whole ordeal. The so-called 'sweet-tea' or 'sarsaparilla', *Smilax glyciphylla*, is a member of the eucalyptus family, used by the Eora people as a medicinal. Tench observed that '[t]o its virtues the healthy state of soldiery and convicts may be greatly attributed. It was drunk universally as "sweet-tea".'

The trip to the Dutch settlement at Koepang in Timor, a distance of 5240 kilometres, was a feat of navigational skill matching that of William Bligh. What is astounding is that the escapees were not trained naval officers like Bligh, who later expressed his admiration at their achievement.[25] With two small children aboard, and no sails for protection from the tropical sun and torrential rain, the voyage is even more extraordinary. Mary Bryant recounted her tale of endurance and suffering to the journalist who set down her story in the *London Chronicle* of 30 June–3 July 1792: 'During the first weeks of the voyage they had continual rain, and being obliged, in order to lighten the boat, to throw overboard all their wearing apparel. Etc, were for that time continually wet. They were once eight days out of sight of land.'

The rations Mary had so carefully garnered at great peril to her own safety in the penal colony were now ruined and inedible. For the other escapees, the children, who cried constantly in fear, driven by intense hunger and thirst, were excess baggage. Did thoughts of throwing them overboard ever surface? Yet all knew it was William's procurement of the vessel and the navigational instruments, and Mary's provision of the food, that had allowed them to undertake this hazardous enterprise in the first place.

They were kept from starvation by eating turtles and their eggs and calling into land at various places for water and whatever food they could obtain. Off Cape York they were attacked by Indigenous warriors and pursued by canoes filled with thirty to forty angry men. They survived one attack by firing their muskets. The narrative in the *London Chronicle* revealed they were 'much distressed for food and water … expecting every moment to go to the bottom'. While Bligh praised William Bryant who '… must have been a determined and enterprising man', he acknowledged that Mary and the children '… bore their sufferings with more fortitude than most among them'.[26]

William Bligh and his loyal *Bounty* seamen had found refuge at the Dutch settlement of Koepang two years before the escapees arrived. When Mary and her companions arrived, the decrepit and destitute band of convicts portrayed themselves as survivors of a whaling shipwreck, though the presence of a woman and two children should have raised some suspicions that this was not true. The Provincial Governor, Timotheus Wanjon, gave them hospitality, accommodation, and secured work for some of the men. James Martin stated that:

> We remained very happy in our work [in Timor] for two
> months till Wm Bryant had words with his wife, went and
> informed against himself, wife, children and the rest of us …
> We was immediately taken prisoner and was put [in irons] in
> the castle …[27]

What could explain this action? C. H. Currey, one of Mary Bryant's more reliable biographers, mentions William Bryant as never having seen the marriage as binding because no banns were read. Moreover, Charlotte was not his biological daughter. But he also quotes Watkin Tench's suggestion that one of them gave the party away when drunk.[28] For Mary, she had risked her children's safety and wellbeing on a journey of unimaginable horror and privation, only to be betrayed at the distant Dutch settlement.

On 7 September 1791, Captain Edward Edwards arrived in Koepang with some survivors of the *Pandora* wrecked off the Great Barrier Reef, along with a party of *Bounty* mutineers he had arrested in Tahiti. He added the convict escapees to his human cargo on 5 October, all to be dispatched to England for due process of the law. His memoirs cover these momentous events and provide some estimation of the fate of the convict escapees:[29]

> William Allen, John Butcher, Nath'l Lilley, James Martin and
> Mary Bryant were transported to HMS *Gorgon* at the Cape of
> Good Hope in March 1792; William Morton died on Board
> Dutch East India Com'y's ship, *Hornway*; William Bryant,
> died 22 December 1791, hosp'l, Batavia; James Cox (fell
> overboard), Straits of Sunda; John Simms, died on board the

Dutch East India Comp'y's ship, *Hornway*; Emanuel Bryant, died 1 December 1791, Batavia; Charlotte Bryant, died 5 May 1792 on board HMS ship, *Gorgon* (children of the above Wm and Mary Bryant).[30]

Mary Bryant lost her two children and her husband all within six months following the most gruelling deprivations of the journey to Timor. She must have reflected on the comparative safety of the convict settlement at Port Jackson. She had risked and lost everything – her liberty, her family, and her carefully won independence. All that faced her now, in her sorrow and grief, was further incarceration or possible execution. The account of her travails in the Irish and London newspapers only hinted at her suffering and despair. The report in the *Dublin Chronicle* of 4 June 1793 did not mention that her two children died, though her entry in the Newgate Prison records has her as a widow but not that she had lost her children. Written in the language of bureaucracy, her tragic personal story was hidden.

Newgate Prison, where she was sent on arrival in England, housed a series of famous felons including Jack Shepherd, Dick Turpin and Casanova, who described his surroundings there as 'an abode of misery and despair, a Hell such as Dante might have conceived'. Lawyer James Boswell earlier in the 1760s felt Newgate 'hanging upon my mind like a black cloud'.[31] Yet the escapees from Botany Bay '... thought this prison was a paradise, compared to the dreadful suffering they endured on the voyage [to Timor]'.[32]

Built originally during the reigns of King Stephen and Henry II, and situated on Newgate Street near the Old Bailey in the western part of the old city of London, Newgate housed prisoners, those awaiting execution, debtors, and the mentally ill. In the late eighteenth century there were over 200 capital offences, ranging from treason to murder and even impersonating an Egyptian. Children over the age of twelve could be executed. As late as 1772 the decapitated heads of two Jacobites (executed in 1746) fell off their spikes in public view at Temple Bar, near today's modern barristers' chambers. Tyburn, the site of public executions by hanging, was situated on Edgeware Road, where Marble Arch stands now. Some fifty public hangings occurred there every year in the 1770s. Boswell was addicted to the spectacle of the public execution with all its ritual, solemnity and horror. 'I had a sort of horrid eagerness to be there,' he admitted. His friendship with Richard Ackerman, the Keeper of Newgate, allowed him to watch many private executions conducted there from December 1783.Considering his fascination with death and the spectacle of execution, Boswell's later assistance towards Mary Bryant is both commendable and inexplicable.[33]

The first clue to historians concerning Boswell's interest in Mary Bryant was detected in a letter written by James Boswell to his brother David in November 1793:

> Be so good as to give Mrs. Bruce five pounds more and Betsy
> a guinea, and put into banking shop of Mr. Devaynes and Co.
> five pounds from you to the account of the Rev. Mr. Baron at
> Lostwithiel, Cornwall, and write to him you have done so. He
> has taken charge of paying the gratuity of Mary Broad.[34]

Mrs Bruce was Boswell's housekeeper and Betsy his daughter; but who was this mysterious Mary Broad? When Professor Chauncey Tinker of Yale University began his edition of Boswell's letters in 1922, he had no idea who she was and what her relationship with Boswell involved. The substantial collection of Boswell's records had not yet been retrieved from Lord Talbot at Malahide Castle in Dublin where they were stored. These were later obtained by the suave Anglo-American Ralph Isham in 1927 and purchased by Yale University in 1929.[35] When the papers were examined and catalogued, the mystery that had puzzled Tinker was solved. In his journals Boswell revealed his charity and beneficence towards Mary Bryant, whom he referred to by her birth name: Mary Broad. He also acted for her surviving co-defendants who had suffered the traumas of escape from Botany Bay to Timor.

Unlike William Bligh, who endured a comparable feat of navigation and deprivation on a voyage to Timor under challenging circumstances after the mutiny of the *Bounty*, Mary Bryant was illiterate and therefore unable to adequately present her case. She signed her marriage licence to William Bryant in February 1788 with an X. Bligh, on the other hand, was a prolific author and memorialist of his achievements and sorrows. James Boswell recorded in his diary entry of 12 October 1793 that 'I went to see her [Mary Broad] in the forenoon and wrote two sheets of paper of her curious account of her escape from Botany Bay.'[36] Unfortunately for later researchers, Mary's account in her own words was not found among Boswell's disordered manuscripts, journals and papers. The original report in the *London Chronicle* of 30 June–3 July 1792, where her case came to public attention, did not directly quote the survivors of the escape from Botany Bay and contained some inaccuracies.

Boswell wrote to his former college acquaintance George Dundas, the Secretary of State, about the 'adventurers from New South Wales, for whom I interest myself'. By using the term 'adventurer' Boswell began the process of romanticising Mary and her fellow escapees, though the term is a little jaunty for what they endured. The notorious highway robber and seafaring escapee was a free spirit in this scenario. He also approached Under Secretary of State Evan Nepean and the Chief Clerk, Mr Pollock.[37]

On 7 July 1792 Mary Bryant, James Martin, William Allen, John Butcher and Nathaniel Lilley went on trial at the Old Bailey and were ordered to complete their sentences. This was a particularly lenient punishment and no doubt owed much to Boswell's interventions on their behalf. As Nepean wrote to Boswell, 'Government would not treat them with harshness but at the same time would not do a kind thing to them, as they give encouragement to other escapees.'[38] Governor Phillip expressed similar concerns.[39]

There is a gap in Boswell's journal in early 1793, and researchers cannot track exactly what happened to Mary Bryant in Newgate. On

2 May 1793 Mary was given an unconditional pardon and settled in Little Titchfield Street between Great Portland Street and the less salubrious Tottenham Court Road in London, where the School of Law for the University of Westminster is now located. This was a pleasant area near Cavendish Square and both a spatial and symbolic distance from the St Giles' area near Oxford Street and the vice-ridden Rookeries where Mary might have found herself but for her benefactor. Boswell arranged and paid for her accommodation and found work for her as a cook to Mr Morgan in Charlotte Street, Bedford Square. As Mary, after her ordeals, found the work difficult, he arranged an annuity for her of £10 per annum 'as long as she behaved well, being resolved to make it up to her myself in so far as subscription should fail ...'[40] Boswell went to considerable trouble to reunite Mary with her sister Dolly, who was working as a domestic servant in a grand house in London. He showed an immense concern for her emotional wellbeing, confiding in his diary: 'I had a suspicion he [Mr Castel who knew Dolly Broad] might be an impostor ... It appeared he really did know her relations [in Cornwall] ... I cautioned Mary not to put any trust in anything he said until he had brought her sister. I sauntered restlessly ...' This said Castel alleged Mary's father, William Broad, had come into a great inheritance and this knowledge made Boswell protective and suspicious in case of fraud.[41] Mary's legacy may not have been a large sum to Boswell, but to someone of the Broad family's social rank even £200 would seem a great fortune. Mary was duly appreciative of all Boswell had done so unstintingly on her behalf, telling him, 'if she got a share [of the legacy] she would reward me for all my trouble'.

On 2 November 1793 the remaining escapees were freed by proclamation, due largely to Boswell's strenuous representations on their behalf. William Allen served on a warship against Napoleon; Nathaniel Lilley returned to work in London as a weaver; John Butcher joined the New South Wales Corps and received a land grant at Parramatta.[42] Mary Bryant's last correspondence with her benefactor, the Laird of Auchinleck, occurred in November 1794 acknowledging the receipt of her allowance. Boswell died the following May. Mary may have later married her childhood sweetheart, Richard Thomas, at St Bartholomew's Church at Lostwithiel.[43] A couple with those names married in 1805 when Mary Bryant would have been forty years of age and have lived in the area for some twelve years. The vicar in this village parish was the Reverend Mr Baron to whom Boswell entrusted the dispersal of her gratuity.

Few convicts were inclined or had the navigational skill to attempt such a hazardous undertaking as the Bryants and their fellow escapees did. Thomas Watling, the Scottish forger and artist briefly escaped en route to Port Jackson at Cape Town in 1791 but this was within an urban environment, hardly a difficult feat.[44] In November 1794 Molly Morgan escaped from Port Jackson on the store ship *Resolution* and got back to England. She next came to official attention when she was arrested for theft and resentenced to transportation in October 1803. Unlike Mary Bryant, Morgan became a wealthy landholder in Maitland.[45] The most spectacular escape, apart from Mary Bryant's, occurred among the Fenian political prisoners held in Western Australia in 1868. One of them, John O'Reilly, escaped on an American whaler, going first to Liverpool and then immigrating to Boston where he became a noted newspaper editor. His novel about his experiences as a convict escapee, *Moondyne* (1879), is perhaps too florid for modern tastes.[46] But none of these escapees enjoys the enduring notoriety of Mary Bryant.

CHAPTER 2

Mary Cockerill
(C1800–1819)

Walyer
(C1810–1831)

One daring outlaw and bushranger, and one frontier warrior.

Frontiers are deadly places with no rules or terms of engagement, but a complexity and flexibility that are at once profoundly unsettling and liberating. As two societies first encounter each other, the possibilities of mutual respect, wonder and accommodation, alongside negotiation, domination and violent struggle, are all present. Australian history has many stories about how Indigenous men and the invading British followed complicated paths of uncertainty, fear and aggression. In this narrative, women are often shadowy, hidden figures or the victims of male combat for supremacy over territory, resources and, ultimately, survival. Several Indigenous women in Van Diemen's Land in the years 1814 to 1831 defied these stereotypes of passivity, assuming new roles as bushranger, outlaw and warrior.

'Black Mary', as Mary Cockerill was often called in historical records, is a romantic figure of passionate loyalty, revenge and defiance, a young woman possessing remarkable intelligence, ingenuity and bush skills. Convict Thomas Worrall, in his contribution to *The Military Sketch-book* (1827), provided an image of Mary gained from an encounter in the 1810s that has been hard for later researchers to counteract:

We could hear the fellows [bushrangers] through the bushes, cursing, swearing and laughing. Some were cooking pieces of mutton, others lolling on the grass, smoking and drinking, a pretty, interesting-looking native girl sat playing with the long and bushy ringlets of a stout and wicked-looking man seated by her ... Her dress was neither Native nor European, but a very pretty sort of costume made of skins, feathers and white calico.[1]

Worrall could not have met Mary in the Tasmanian bush, as claimed, as she was captured in April 1817 and he only arrived in Hobart Town in October 1817.[2] We do know she was a notorious bushranger, the lover of Michael Howe, Van Diemen's Land's most famous early bushranger, the self-styled 'gentleman forester', and that, some time after Howe shot her when they were ambushed, Mary led the army to his hiding place deep in the forests of the Shannon River. Although one part of Worrall's account is inaccurate, he was with the party that captured and killed Howe.

We do not know Mary's real name, nor where or when she was born. There was no drawing made of her in her lifetime, or other images, as she lived before photography was invented. Mary most likely was a member of the Mouheneener band who lived near the Derwent River and Hobart in the southern areas of Van Diemen's Land, as Tasmania was called until 1855. She was born in the late eighteenth century, the latest probable date being 1800. Marcus Clarke, in his celebrated book *Old Tales of a Young Country* (1871), thought Mary was seventeen in 1817.[3] Written records about her adopted family, the Cockerells, are easier to locate. Their name also appeared in the 1818 muster (or census) spelled 'Cockerill'.[4] They were among the first white settlers who came to this outpost of the British Empire in 1804. Londoners by birth, William Cockerell and Mary Crisp were married in May 1787 at St Martin's in the Field Church. They decided to try their luck in the new settlement of Port Phillip in 1803, accompanied by their three children, Ann, William and Arabella, and niece, Sophia

Chivers. Setting sail from Portsmouth on the *Ocean* in early 1803, the family was full of hope that this dangerous adventure would reap them good fortune and prosperity.

Port Phillip was a disastrous experiment plagued by too few resources. Undeterred by the enormity of the tasks faced by the original colonisers, the Cockerells again joined the fleet of the *Ocean*, *Lady Nelson* and *Calcutta*, carrying the first batch of felons from England to the new settlement at Hobart Town. On 29 February 1804 the passengers, both free and in chains, left the vessels to start a new endeavour in Van Diemen's Land.[5] The Cockerells were granted 100 acres (40 hectares) at Stainsforth Cove (now New Town), on the western bank of the Derwent River.[6] For the Indigenous people of the island, isolated for thousands of years from the mainland, this was to prove the beginning of horror and near total destruction.

Initially, relations between the incomers and the traditional owners were amicable. In the 1860s the historian James Bonwick interviewed Salome Pitt, who as a child had been a neighbour of the Cockerells and their adopted daughter, Mary Cockerill. Salome recalled that she and her brother had tried to walk to Mount Wellington and, getting lost, were rescued by the Mouheneener, who treated them kindly and returned them to their home. She also visited their camp sites and played with the children there. British boys were often taken out hunting with the Mouheneener men, or 'the dark skins', as Pitt called them.[7] Mary was undoubtedly one of the children informally adopted into a white family. Like other dependent relatives of the time, she was expected to work for her keep. As the Cockerell children were no longer infants she would not have worked as their nursemaid but as a domestic. We know that she spoke excellent English, as her deposition in 1817 about her experiences as an outlaw was told in sound grammatical English. This would indicate she learned the language as a small child, a time that coincided with the arrival of the Cockerells.

Mary's life changed forever in late 1812 or early 1813 when she saw the handsome convict Michael Howe (1787–1818), who was assigned to John Ingle, a rapacious and rough wealthy merchant who had arrived with Lieutenant Governor David Collins in 1804.[8] Howe had been a deserter in both the British navy and army, though he was transported for highway robbery in 1812 from the York Assizes. Unrepentant in exile, Howe told Ingle 'he would be no man's slave' and promptly absconded.[9] Howe began a career as a robber and burglar, attacking the house of Richard Pitt, the Chief Police Constable of New Town and Salome's father. Mary first saw this handsome, proud man who called himself 'the Governor of the Ranges' when she was a child.[10] She most certainly saw him when he was employed by John Ingle as she lived nearby.[11] She did not, however, elope with him until late 1814 or early 1815.[12] This suggests that they had regular contact in the intervening couple of years. Presumably Mary had resisted returning to the Mouheneener for marriage, as would be expected in traditional Pallawah society, where the girls wed young, although such a marriage would not be consummated until the girl matured. It would also seem that Mary's defiant and headstrong ways were firmly established by the time she was thirteen.

In 1813 Howe absconded from his assignment, originally joining the Whitehead gang of twenty-nine army deserters and runaway felons at large around Hobart. He saw Dick Turpin as his hero and was described by the colonial historian J. E. Calder in 1873 as 'one of Byron's ruffian heroes'.[13] Though uneducated he had a 'taste for ceremony' and fine words, with a revolutionary turn of phrase. He 'borrowed' a dictionary from the farmhouse of Lieutenant Governor Thomas Davey, promising to return it.[14] Howe loved words, and the Old Testament in the King James Version of the Bible was a constant companion on his travels and adventures. It is no wonder that a beautiful, high-spirited young woman like Mary Cockerill found him irresistible. Howe was charismatic, charming when needed, quick-witted and audacious. These qualities mirrored Mary's own: she was articulate, brave and resolute, which, along with her personal beauty and physical stamina, made her an ideal partner for a bushranger.

The nature of bushranging in this period of Tasmanian history needs some explanation. The settlement was largely lawless, with the army hard pressed to maintain any sort of order. At first it was not conflict with the Indigenous people that made the society unstable but the presence of so many convict 'absenters' who became bushrangers.[15] The convict settlement was poorly provisioned, so from soon after the outset of British occupation in 1804, convicts and soldiers alike were armed with muskets and dogs and allowed to hunt kangaroos. A good hunting dog was a prized possession. The Reverend Robert Knopwood, the Anglican priest and magistrate of the convict settlement, offered a £10 reward, the equivalent of an English labourer's annual wage, in return for his bitch, Miss, who had been stolen by bushrangers.[16] By 1806 kangaroos were in short supply around Hobart Town and the New Norfolk area. The traditional owners, without dingoes to assist in hunting, had been careful harvesters of game, so the depletion of kangaroos and the superior weapons of the new arrivals meant far more conflict between the invaders and the Pallawah. It also meant that the British ventured further north into the island looking for game themselves.

'Bushranging' at first meant searching or ranging for food, often to sell. Indeed, the early bushrangers frequently saw themselves as canny traders rather than thieves and outlaws. When he robbed her family farm, Howe told one Mrs McCarty that 'we are bushrangers and freebooters, but not thieves'. A police magistrate in October 1814 reported to Lieutenant Governor Thomas Davey that the Howe gang '... were consummate bushmen, they dressed completely in kangaroo skins from cap to moccasin; they jokingly called themselves gentlemen foresters'. (The Pallawah also wore beautiful kangaroo capes to protect themselves against the cold winds from Antarctica.)[17]

These references to the English rural tradition of protest and resistance, like that of Robin Hood, were reinforced by the Howe gang's deployment of blackface, like protesters of England and Wales a century before. The *Waltham Black Act* (1722) specifically outlawed the practice with heavy penalties for any infringements. Blacking of the face in disguise was employed by the early convict bolters as early as 1807.[18] This deployment of potent symbols is not surprising; England was undergoing enormous transition with displacement and poverty caused by the Industrial Revolution as well as the prolonged wars with France and her allies. Many of the convicts, like Howe, exiled to the antipodean colonies were the direct casualties of these two massive social and economic dislocations.

Howe took this traditional symbol and gave it new meaning. He had enormous admiration for the Indigenous people, appreciating their bushcraft and ability to thrive in an often unforgiving environment. He meted out harsh punishment to anyone in his gang who mistreated the local people.[19] Howe was not alone in these alliances and attitudes. Sealer James Kelly in the north-east region reached an understanding with Indigenous leader Tolokunganah and his band, though this may have been to the detriment of the Indigenous man's kinswomen who were frequently traded to white men.[20] Bushranger Archibald Campbell made a home with his Indigenous wife and lived amicably with her kin.[21] Mary Cockerill's relationship with Howe, when considered in this context, is not so unusual; what marks it as extraordinary is her role as an armed and active bushranger, not just as a helpmeet and supporter.

Many settlers, whether former felons themselves or people employing former convicts, attempted to stay on amicable terms with the marauding bushrangers. Unlike later bushrangers, these gangs travelled on foot, as horses were a rarity in the early days of colonisation on the remote island. Military detachments were foot soldiers as well, thus, knowledge of the land and how to survive in it was a prerequisite for successful bushranging. Despite the hardships, the outlaw life on the island flourished. The difficulty of policing and cost of conducting trials in Sydney proved prohibitive for the tiny administration and defeated enforcement of the law.[22] By May 1814, the island was so infested with outlaws and absconders that Lieutenant Governor Davey was forced to issue an amnesty against their depredations.[23] Many of Whitehead's former gang took advantage of this amnesty and returned to Hobart Town. Michael Howe, however, wrote to Lieutenant Governor Davey detailing the specific terms of his amnesty. The letter was forwarded to Governor Macquarie who promised to dispatch it to the Secretary of State for the Colonies in London. Unfortunately, this bizarre document, written in kangaroo blood, has not been located.[24] There is no doubting Macquarie's word, for he acted with a degree of humanity and judiciousness unusual in colonial management.

With his demands as yet unmet, Howe continued his marauding, taking over the leadership of what remained of the gang and acting as its master strategist. He robbed homes in Hobart Town, attacking the home of the Cockerells' neighbour Richard Pitt, where he stole a book which was found in his kangaroo knapsack after his death. Called 'the Captain' by other members, Howe organised the gang with military precision, attempting to impose the discipline required by war. To inculcate moral virtue among his fellow outlaws he regularly read from the scriptures.[25]

Emboldened by his successes, Howe sent a challenge, again written in kangaroo blood, through the agency of the Reverend Knopwood to Lieutenant Governor Davey on 30 August 1814, reminding him that his troupe consisted of former soldiers who had seen active service in war, adding '… were we As Much Inclined to take Life As you Are … We could Destroy All the Partyes you can send out …'[26]

His fame spread, spoken of in whispers in the homes of the free settlers. No doubt Mary listened to the fears and anxieties expressed by the Cockerells, smiling secretly to herself as she thought about her own relationship with this audacious man. Howe had undoubtedly risked capture by visiting Mary on many occasions in 1813 and 1814. We do not know when Mary left the Cockerells, but presumably, given that the documents say she cohabited with Howe, she had left by the end of 1814. Despite the considerable age and cultural differences, Mary and Howe formed a strong alliance.

Howe's attacks on property, like the one against Police Magistrate Adolarias Humphrey at Pittwater on 24 April 1815 and on settlers at New Norfolk, became more daring. The 24 April attack is the first time the records mentioned 'a black native girl called Mary with whom Howe cohabited'. Mary took part in the attack on a Carlisle property in New Norfolk and the murder of Richard Carlisle, after the Pittwater robbery.[27]

The gang, including Mary, robbed Richard Pitt again in July 1816, taking his valuable hunting dogs, two muskets and ammunition.[28] This was territory that she had grown up in, and though kindly treated by her adoptive family and their neighbours, she had no hesitation in robbing and marauding her former neighbourhood. The thrill, danger and sheer audaciousness must have appealed to her wilful spirit.

Violence by the gang against settlers escalated, going from robbery with threats and burning of crops and buildings to cold-blooded murder, including that of James O'Berne, the captain of a vessel in the Derwent River.[29] The bushrangers also began roaming a wider territory, suggesting that they may have been aided by Mary's bush skills. Although she had lived with the Cockerells, it is more than likely she rejoined her band at various times, for she was an excellent bush woman and there were traditional routes and passageways that Mary must have known about from her own people or other friendly bands. Her relationship with the neighbouring Panninher, Pangeeninghe and Leenowwenne would also have assisted their progress. These 'Big River' bands kept on amicable terms with their neighbours and were the most travelled of all the Tasmanian clans.[30] Another possibility also presents itself. William James Cockerell, the son of William and Mary Cockerell, received a grant of land in 1813 at what is now Brighton, far closer to the Shannon River area than Hobart Town. Mary may have accompanied William and his bride, Mary Ann Peck, to their new home for a visit. This would have given her a familiarity with the wider region where Howe made his headquarters.[31]

Over the summer of 1816 and 1817 several members of the gang were waylaid and killed by soldiers of the 46th Regiment disguised as civilians. Mary led the bushrangers further along the Shannon River, where they established a base camp. Thomas Wells, Private Secretary to Lieutenant Governor William Sorell (who succeeded Thomas Davey in 1817), in 1818 wrote the first book published in Australia, *Michael Howe: The Last and Worst of the Tasmanian Bushrangers*. In it he stated that the 'site was chosen in taste, in an open undulating country, stretching to the western mountains: the spot was secluded from observation; was covered by large honeysuckle and on a rise sloping to the stream'.[32] Here the bandits corralled fifty-six sheep they had stolen with other provisions, and from this hideaway they continued their assaults into the Oatland, Jericho and Norfolk regions.

In the meantime, Howe was confident that Mary's bush skills and ability to negotiate with Indigenous bands, together with his military training, made him untouchable. He wrote a series of provocative letters to Lieutenant Governor Davey identifying himself as 'Lieutenant Governor of the Woods'. Mary, in this scenario, was hardly a Maid Marion – chaste, demure and wise – rather, she was active, aggressive and daring in these joint enterprises. In September 1816, Mary, Howe and the rest of the bandits raided Davey's farm of 3000 acres (1200 hectares), taking muskets, ammunition, tea, sugar, flour, needles and thread, as well as six bottles of fine wine from the cellar.[33] Just to annoy the Lieutenant Governor even more, the gang again raided his farm on Christmas Day 1816 and forced the servants and convict workers at gunpoint to dance and drink with them. They stole blunderbusses, pistols and ammunition, tea, 12 pounds of sugar and the overseer's trousers. Leaving the farm in a state of great excitement and intoxication, and shooting off their pistols, they headed for the nearby farms of Richard Troy and James Stynes to continue their terror.

Mary and another older Indigenous woman who is not named in the records were by this time core members of the gang. We do not know when this other woman joined the gang, as initial reports identified only one Indigenous girl, and Mary would have been at this time aged fifteen or so. A document of November 1816 records earlier horrific incidents during which some members of Howe's gang cut the throats of their confreres. According to this document Mary purportedly said to the chief perpetrator, 'Hillier, you killed my sister too!'[34] The two women were close, but 'sister' in the Western sense of the word may be too restrictive. This unnamed woman who apparently died a violent death at the hands of a fellow bushranger may have been Mary's putative sister, as Pallawah kin systems were highly complex, but she was a not a leader like Mary and this may account for her anonymity in the accounts. For Mary, this scene of one man dead with his throat cut, another severely wounded, and her sister dead, must have been traumatic in the extreme. Indeed, Van Diemen's Land society, both in its treatment of felons and conduct of the frontier war, was deeply violent and cruel.

The detailed deposition made by John Yorke, who was captured by the gang for a few hours on 27 November 1816, said the gang consisted of four men and two women. They informed him they could 'set the whole country on fire with one stick'. As mentioned, Howe conducted a strange prayer meeting where male gang members were made to swear oaths on the Bible. This behaviour, reflecting the dominant evangelism of the time, sits uneasily with his lawlessness and cruelty. Yet perhaps he took justification from many parts of the Old Testament that stressed violence, retribution and vengeance. Yorke believed they had recently forced settlers to render down the fat from the sheep they had stolen from various farms. This means that the bandits moved the sheep a considerable distance across the midland plains region of the island.[35] No doubt the dogs were useful as guards, hunters and herders.

The army increased its operations to locate and arrest the bandits. In March 1817 Mary and Howe decided to head out on their own with their hound, Bosun. In this desperate move, as the gang disintegrated amid rumours that the aforementioned Hillier had slit the throat of one of the men, the pair was more vulnerable to attack. Surrounded by the army and convicts armed with muskets, Mary and Howe tried to flee their pursuers. In the ensuing melee Howe shot Mary.[36] In early documents such as Thomas Wells' account, Mary was 'shot at by Howe ... receiv[ing], however, little injury'. Yet Worrall's account in *The Military Sketch-book* a decade later has her severely wounded in the shoulder and the back. K. R. von Stieglitz wrote Howe's official entry in the *Australian Dictionary of Biography* in 1966. In this Mary is said to have been heavily pregnant and severely wounded. This is entirely unlikely, as commentators at the time would have remarked upon her pregnancy, and the chance of surviving a gunshot wound and advanced pregnancy in 1817 was remote.

Wells and later authors were outraged with Howe, 'being hard pressed, in order to facilitate his own escape, he fired at this poor female companion, who, from fatigue was unable to keep pace with him ...'[37] Howe displayed a cruel cowardice towards his partner by leaving her wounded and at the mercy of the army to save his own skin. The treatment of bushrangers by the military was severe, and the soldiers might have raped, tortured or killed Mary, as she was an outlaw condemned in absentia for serious crimes. In June 1816 captured bushrangers were summarily executed and their bodies gibbeted on the wharf at Hobart Town. Executions and gibbeting also occurred at the Cascades where female convicts were housed.[38] It was rumoured that after his execution, the head of Whitehead, the former leader of Howe and Mary's gang, was impaled and put on public display. This had been common practice in England, though in 1746 two Jacobites supplied the last impaled heads shown at Temple Bar.

In 1871 Marcus Clarke wrote in his book that 'Mary relates that Howe was kind to her – after the manner of his sex – whenever "things went right for him"; but that if anything "crossed his temper he was like a tiger". He was very jealous of her, she says; when Edwards, one of the gang, gave her a shawl which he had stolen from Captain Tonnson, Howe pistolled him on the spot.'[39] How Clarke, writing almost sixty years after the events, could quote Mary Cockerill, remains unexplained. These words do not appear in any other records of the time though like Tasmanian colonial writers John West and Edward Curr, Clarke interviewed elderly people who remembered the events. This hint of domestic violence is consistent with Howe's cowardly, selfish behaviour in the moment of crisis when the army was upon him. He lost his valuable dogs and ammunition, but, most significantly, he lost Mary, his guide and confidante.

The *Hobart Town Gazette* of 12 April 1817, in a report on Captain Nairn's company of the 46th Regiment, stated that 'a Native Black Girl, named Mary Cockerill', having been wounded by Howe, led the soldiers deeper into the woods for 17 kilometres, where they found four huts which they promptly burned. Attempting to locate Howe and other gang members Geary and Septon, Mary now led the military search party. With her superior bush skills and knowledge of the area, she led the chase for two days until the trail weakened. But they recovered some of the sheep the gang had stolen from farmers. Mary later provided much information on the gang and its operations. This suggests she had been only slightly wounded, though her sense of outrage and betrayal at Howe's callousness spurred her on to wreak vengeance upon him.

Davey's earlier proclamation of martial law against the outlaws had not proven effective against the bushrangers, and was overruled by Governor Macquarie in Sydney. Davey's replacement, William Sorell, a man of moderate temperament and good sense, offered Howe a pardon for all his crimes bar murder, and a strong recommendation for clemency on that matter if he turned King's evidence. He also offered a considerable reward for the capture of the gang members still at large. Alone and vulnerable, Howe retreated further west. In his solitude he put to paper – made of fine kangaroo skin – his dreams and fantasies, penned in kangaroo blood. He wrote a message to his sister, alongside a list of the flowers and vegetables he wished to plant in his garden when he had done with bushranging. This expression of deep feelings and romantic longings perhaps gives us a clue as to what attracted him to Mary. Howe does not mention her in this strange and sad memoir,[40] nor does he say that he wanted to return to England, instead seeing his future in Van Diemen's Land. These writings were found when he was captured the following year.

For over a year Howe stayed on the run, forced to live in remote hideouts with no comforts or companionship. With Mary's assistance, he was captured, only to kill several of his captors. He was sent to Hobart Town, where he escaped again. On 21 October 1818, Howe was located and clubbed to death. He was decapitated and his head taken to Hobart Town where it was displayed as a moral lesson to other bushrangers.[41] Convict Thomas Worrall was pardoned for his role in Howe's capture and death.[42]

Mary Cockerill had been pardoned for her crimes as an outlaw in return for her cooperation and information. On her own request she went to Sydney, as she had no intention of rejoining any gangs. No doubt her own people did not want her to return to them, given her notorious reputation and criminal behaviour. Mary was fed, clothed and housed by the colonial authorities in Hobart Town before she left for Sydney. Once there, Governor Macquarie took a personal interest in her welfare, writing that 'I had a private decent lodging provided for her here ... and she is about to get some decent apparel ...'[43]

In Sydney Mary contracted pulmonary disease. She returned to Hobart Town and was admitted to hospital, where she died on 29 June 1819.[44] She did not record what she thought of Howe's demise and the indignity of his rotting and putrid-smelling head on public display. Mary was buried at St David's cemetery with a service conducted by the Reverend Robert Knopwood. Her burial with the full rites of the Church of England implies she was a communicant and raised in the Church.

The story of Walyer (or Tarenorerer, as she is sometimes called), a Pallawah warrior from the Plair-Leke-Liller-Plue band from Emu Bay on the north-west coast of Van Diemen's Land, reveals dramatically transformed race relations since the childhood of Mary Cockerill. Walyer was probably born around 1810, when few Europeans had ventured across the Bass Strait to live and work. Until the 1820s bushrangers were a far greater threat to stability and expansion by the pastoralists than the Pallawah.[45] In fact, Lieutenant Governor Thomas Davey had proclaimed martial law in 1816 – against the bushrangers, not the Indigenous peoples. By 1823 and 1824 this scenario had changed dramatically, with far more attacks by the Oyster Bay bands against stock keepers and pastoralists. The new Governor, William Sorell's successor, George Arthur, arrived in May 1824 after a posting in British Honduras, where he had ruled with a benign concern for the slaves. His attitudes to the Pallawah at first expressed this humanitarianism. Yet by 1826 they had hardened, as the original landholders refused to voluntarily relinquish their lands and embrace Christianity. On 26 November the Governor issued a notice allowing any settler to drive off Aboriginal 'intruders', using any degree of force. Moreover, the military could be summoned to assist in this process of dispersal and possible extermination.[46] Not altogether unsympathetic to the claims of Indigenous peoples, Arthur suggested that the north-east region, where pastoralists had not yet intruded, might be set aside as a permanent reserve. He saw this as a voluntary process whereby groups would enter the safety of the reserve of their own free will.

On 15 April 1828, the Governor divided the colony into the settled and unsettled districts, marked by the notorious Black Line. By this he meant, of course, settled by British occupation. Thus began the terrible Black War. As the violence escalated on the frontier, Arthur began to renounce his earlier moderation and declared a state of martial law on 1 November 1828. Reminiscent of the bounty parties that hunted bushrangers from 1815, military expeditions were now sent to find and destroy Aboriginal groups.[47]

This was the broad context within which Walyer operated. There were factors that exacerbated her situation. The sealers stationed in the islands of the Bass Strait frequently kidnapped women and forced them into raw and savage bondage. This process was aided by Pallawah men who caught Indigenous women from across northern coastal areas and sold them to the sealers. Walyer was one of those kidnapped and sold at a young age to work for the sealers and mutton birders. She was purchased for a few bags of flour and several dogs.[48] In 1828 she escaped from the island she was confined to and returned to the mainland of Van Diemen's Land, fired to wage war on the invaders. With her skills in using weaponry, particularly the use of firearms, she set about establishing herself as a warrior leader, teaching the men of the Emu Bay region how to use the British weapons. Walyer was the strategist of operations, directing some eight men, a boy and a woman to conduct raids against settlers. Often she called from a rise or hill, directing the manoeuvres and taunting the Europeans to come out of their huts and face spears and other weapons.

In June 1830 Walyer and her group met George Augustus Robinson, who had been commissioned by Arthur to conciliate with the Indigenous population and establish missions, as he was rounding up those Pallawah not dead or defeated. Robinson was taken aback by a woman warrior but believed that it was Walyer's aggressive raids that were causing a lot of the troubles west of the Tamar River.[49] In December 1830, Walyer was again captured by two sealers and taken to a small island in Bass Strait. She refused to work in any way for her captors, with intractable resistance. The sealers then proposed to isolate her on Penguin Island. On the way over she attempted to murder them and take control of the boat. For once the sealers were delighted to relinquish one of their captives to an emissary of Robinson.[50]

Robinson was a determined and methodical man who forced Walyer to go to the Swan Island Aboriginal Reserve, situated on a small island between Cape Portland and George Bay on the north-east coast. On Swan Island, Walyer was disruptive to Robinson's order as soon as she alighted from the boat. He then feared she would incite rebellion and revolt, so he determined to banish her. But her experience as a leader came to the fore and she warned the other internees that the soldiers would head out of the garrison at Launceston, perhaps to kill them all as had already happened to the Oyster Bay and Midlands peoples. She taught other women how to use firearms and conduct efficient warfare, and boasted of the many whites she had raided and killed. They were no doubt astounded, as women in traditional society never assumed the role of warrior or combatant. Walyer told an amazed Robinson that she liked *lutetawin* (white men) as much as she liked the black snake. She dealt with them in the same manner – death at all times when she was able.

Strangely, Walyer did not publicly denounce the Pallawah men who had originally sold her into servitude. Perhaps she did and it was not recorded, as the rhetoric of the frontier hardened the racial lines. Although a young woman, Walyer contracted influenza and died on 5 June 1831. Her role as a warrior and resistance fighter made her a notorious, indeed feared, woman. She broke every taboo about what it meant to be a woman, black or white. No other Indigenous woman in colonial Australia took on a similar leadership role to fight and resist the invaders.

Mary Cockerill and Walyer were products of the Van Diemen's Land frontier and both were aggressive, violent women who embarked upon crusades. For Mary, her role as a bushranger was entangled with her relationship with a white charismatic rebel and outlaw. For Walyer, her life in a frontier that had advanced and hardened in its resolve to subdue the Pallawah was dominated by capture, enforced slavery and servitude. Yet she too fought against the strictures of sexual and racial confinement, becoming a warrior and a challenge to all those who oppressed her.

CHAPTER 3

Eliza Fraser
(1798–1858)

The shipwreck survivor dressed in her fringe of leaves whose 'rescue' from Fraser Island continues to rock race relations in Queensland to this day.

Eliza Fraser remains the most intriguing and notorious woman in the Australian imagination. She has been immortalised in Patrick White's novel *A Fringe of Leaves*; as the crouching, naked figure, her hair falling over her face to hide her identity in Sidney Nolan's painting; as a disembodied head in a dark sky in artist Fiona Foley's depictions; and as an assertive voice in Barbara Blackman's libretto for Peter Sculthorpe's music-theatre piece *Eliza Fraser Sings*. In 1836 she survived a mutiny on board a ship under her husband's command and a shipwreck off the coast of what is now Queensland. She perhaps gave birth to a baby who died in a lifeboat, and she was reputedly 'captured' and tortured by 'cannibals' before being rescued by 'wild white men', escaped convicts who had merged into Indigenous societies, thus making them doubly 'savage' and vengeful. She was lionised in Sydney, the United Kingdom and the United States and was eventually revealed as an exaggerator, if not a liar, and reduced to giving public accounts of her ordeal for payment. Her life story holds no parallel for adventure and notoriety.

Eliza Fraser's version of her protracted ordeal magnifies the sensational aspects and makes it difficult to identify the central veracity of the events. She was at times courageous, resourceful, self-sacrificing, as well as manipulative, deceitful and hungry for celebrity and its attendant rewards. Even at her story's outset, the birthplace of Eliza Ann Slack is clouded in conjecture. Several versions appear in the historical records. According to one, Eliza was born in 1798 in Derbyshire in the English East Midlands, famously portrayed as the home county of Jane Austen's favourite hero, Fitzwilliam Darcy. The medieval centre of the lead-mining industry, Derbyshire was the first area to transform under the Industrial Revolution of the later decades of the eighteenth century.[1] Other sources suggest Eliza was born in the British settlement of Ceylon, now Sri Lanka. Colonised by Portuguese Jesuits in 1505, the Dutch in 1658 and the British East India Company in 1769, before recognition as a British colony in 1802, Ceylon was a beautiful, mysterious multicultural outpost of several European empires. Eliza's father may have been an officer in the British East India Company, as her birth date is consistent with the arrival of officers' families to the operation.[2] Eliza Fraser never publicly commented on her birthplace nor on her parents' origins. Rather, she kept her public pronouncements solely focused on her ordeal in the tropical hell of Great Sandy Island, now Fraser Island.

When she married Captain James Fraser at age twenty-one, he was already sickly and twenty years her senior. As an educated and articulate woman without family connections or her own money, few possibilities for independence existed for her at the end of the Napoleonic Wars. The life of a governess, in which she would reside in an ambiguous limbo between servant and accepted member of a rigidly hierarchical household, held little attraction for the spirited, intelligent young woman. But the marriage took her to an unlikely spot for someone of her character and inclinations. Stromness, in the Orkney Islands to the north of Scotland is a bitterly cold place blasted by the winds off the North Sea. Far more Norse and Danish than Celtic or Scottish – as the islands only came to Scotland in 1468 from Denmark – Stromness would have been a difficult home for a young woman from Ceylon, accustomed to the vitality, colour and heat of the tropics. With its small dark-stoned buildings, Stromness would have been made even worse by an older ill husband and a narrow-minded, strict Calvinist community.

When James Fraser was offered the chance to captain a vessel to Hobart Town, Sydney and Singapore in 1835, Eliza begged to accompany him. Despite the responsibilities of her three children, she felt he needed her reassuring presence. The captain had damaged the *Stirling Castle* in the previous year, which came on top of the loss of the *Comet* in the Torres Strait in 1830. This voyage was his last chance at professional redemption. No doubt he was filled with reservations, for women did not accompany the crew or officers on long, perilous voyages in small sailing boats. Convincing the island's stern Presbyterian minister to take care of her children, Eliza showed her first display of talented persuasion. In her rendition of the biblical story of Ruth and Naomi, she implored the minister to heed her cry: 'Whither thou goest, I will go; and where though lodgest, I will lodge …' What she did not pledge was the final part of the biblical pact of fidelity: 'Where thou diest, will I die …' Rather, like Job's unnamed wife, Eliza was forced to endure a journey of unimaginable travail, despair and loss.

Travelling down to London, Eliza delighted in the expensive shops in the handsome area of Mayfair around Regent and Old Bond streets. Gazing at the fashionable patrons in their finery, she felt a dowdy provincial in her bland, modest outfits appropriate for the Orkney Islands; Calvinist strictures there dictated plain garb, plain manners and a stoic demeanour.

Leaving London on 22 October 1835, the *Stirling Castle* initially made good progress to Hobart Town in far away Van Diemen's Land. The vessel brought new immigrants and manufactured goods to this distant British settlement at the edge of the known world. The boredom of so many days at sea and the even duller confined evenings were dispelled when she saw the beauty of Hobart Harbour and its brilliant light.

In Hobart Town the venture faltered. The *Stirling Castle* collided with another vessel on departure – in the eyes of the sailors an omen of disaster to come. Already they had little confidence in the sickly captain with his stomach ulcers, bad temper and erratic judgment, and they had heard rumours of his negligence on past voyages. Many of them left when the vessel reached Sydney. With the crewmen replaced, joining the captain's young nephew, midshipman John Fraser and Second Officer John Baxter, already on board, they set sail for Singapore. This should have been a calm passage, as the torrential rains and cyclones of summer off the east coast of Australia were long past, yet, on 21 May 1836, the brig was caught in a storm 500 kilometres off what is now Queensland.[3]

Eliza's report to Foster Fyans, the Superintendent of the Moreton Bay penal settlement, captured the panic of the shipwreck that ensued:

> [Captain Fraser] … gave orders [not to abandon ship] … the men however insisted … some of them said if he would not come they would leave him behind, he then consented. He now ordered beef, bread and water be brought up … some of the crew said that if he wanted it he could fetch it himself … They became very mutinous …[4]

Two lifeboats were launched. For Eliza in her skirts and petticoats, just to clamber into a tiny life raft was perilous. Women did not commonly wear underpants until later in the century and this would have been an embarrassment to overcome.

Without adequate food or water – though the captain took his charts and compass – the survivors headed southward to find Moreton Bay. After drifting for ten days, the mutinous crew departed in the faster lifeboat, taking with them the captain's nephew.[5] This left the Frasers with steward Joseph Corralis, first mate Charles Brown, second mate John Baxter, and the seamen Robert Darge, Henry Youlden, William Elliott, John Major, Michael Doyle, Robert Carey and Robert

Dayman in the lesser vessel. The mutineers were not fortunate and only one survived.

The Frasers' lifeboat took a month to find shelter on Great Sandy Island. How anyone survived this ordeal is a miracle. It is possible that Eliza also gave birth during this time. In 1838 reporter John Curtis gave an account of the event in his book *Shipwreck of the Stirling Castle* and claimed Eliza had given birth at sea. However, in the first two narratives she gave after her rescue – including the report to Foster Fyans at Moreton Bay – she made no mention of a pregnancy or birth. The humiliation for a woman to give birth among men in such cramped conditions can be imagined, and Eliza may have felt reticent about relating news of this to men. However, in her later versions of events, related in Moreton Bay and Sydney, she did mention it to the ladies who offered their support. She could have done so and not breached decorum. We can assume the story was a fabrication in the English press and in Curtis' book, and not one of Eliza's making. Interestingly, Olga Miller, a Butchulla elder, upon recounting the stories of her family, believed that Eliza had not given birth when her ancestors cared for her back in 1836,[6] and in an account seaman Henry Youlden published about his experiences some twenty years after the events no mention of a birth and death is made.

Youlden spared no sympathy for Mrs Fraser. He portrayed her as 'a very vixen … the most profane, artful wicked woman that ever lived, coming very near in my idea of the Devil'.[7] His vitriol is directed to the 'She-Captain' in an attempt to show her as a controlling female with a desperate and ineffectual husband who should have been there to command. Youlden failed to point out that Eliza had prepared food for the fourteen-month voyage, a difficult undertaking in Stromness. She had also insisted on the trunk of food going into the lifeboat along with her two trunks of clothing and china. Eliza also took turns at bailing out water when James was too ill to take his turn. In *Shipwreck of the Stirling Castle* Curtis paints her as a devoted companion, risking her own safety for her husband's welfare.

The party first landed on some rocky islands. In one of the illustrations in Curtis' book Eliza is depicted in her dress and shoes climbing rocks in search of water (hardly the activity of a woman who had recently given birth). What it does display is the pluck and resourcefulness that Youlden so despised. Continuing southward they spied Great Sandy Island. The crew insisted on going ashore, although Captain Fraser wanted to keep sailing to Moreton Bay. He had a morbid fear of cannibals, saying 'in all probability they would be eaten …'[8] Ironically, the only threat of cannibalism came from the British sailors: the seamen went so far as to threaten to kill and eat one of their number if he did not accede to their demands.

Landing on the northern end of Great Sandy Island with great difficulty in the high surf after a month at sea in the lifeboat, Eliza must have wondered if this was truly deliverance. Though spectacularly beautiful, there was little vegetation and sand dominated the landscape.[9] In the distance they spied some 'natives' waving spears at them. When no attack ensued, they focused on trying to mend their leaky boat, but without tools this proved impossible.

The local Butchulla clan approached the strangers with some trepidation. Could they be the return of the beings in long ships their ancestors had spoken about? Were they returning spirits of their ancestors, lost and bewildered to be on land again? Certainly they did not look like ancestors with their pale, reddened skins and strange adornments around their bodies and they already knew – from the nearby Kabi people – about strange beings with firearms that could kill or maim instantly. Offering some of their clothes for barter, Eliza was horrified to learn they merited only two mullets, and that she had virtually given away some precious protection against the sun. She had jeopardised the safety of the boat and incurred the wrath of the crew for two fish.

The landing had not yielded the safety or security the crew had hoped for, and this added substantially to the hostility among the group. Those who opposed the captain – Youlden, Dayman, Carey,

Elliott and Darge – set out to walk to the Moreton Bay settlement. The power struggle between the seamen and the now enfeebled commander reached its climax when the men took the party's muskets and ammunition by force. Realising that their safety lay in numbers, the others reluctantly followed. They left at night to avoid detection and began the 100-kilometre walk down the island. With only berries and pandanus fruit to eat, they were beset by 'flux' (diarrhoea), which further weakened their already depleted bodies. Even in winter the sun along the coast of Great Sandy (Fraser) Island is hot.[10]

Eliza had endured so much indignity, pain and humiliation since leaving Hobart Town, and now she was racked with diarrhoea, sunburn and dehydration. Her pale skin was blistered and sore. Walking along the seashore, the bedraggled party was met by Butchulla warriors who confiscated their clothes and weapons. Stripped of their clothes, the bodies of these strange beings were examined by the Butchulla, who marvelled at their colour and thinness. The standards of dress for a woman of Eliza's status in 1836 were rigid and modest. Her portrait in the State Library of Queensland shows her modesty of dress, with lace cap and her shawl hiding her contours. Eliza was mortified that these wild savages not only gazed at her body but had the audacity to touch her skin, feel her hair and examine the inside of her mouth as if she was an animal. This was a deep affront to her identity as a middle-class Englishwoman. Whatever her later embellishments to her story, the destruction of her modesty on the island must have been insufferable. According to Second Officer John Baxter, Mrs Fraser was left only with 'an article of underdress after this encounter'.[11] This was presumably a light chemise or petticoat. Along with the affronts she had already suffered, the group was deprived of their blankets, making the cool winter nights even harder to bear.

Moving slowly along the coast of K'gari, as the Indigenous owners called this territory, the castaways reached Hook Point on its southernmost extremity. Here the mainland was tantalisingly close, visible but difficult to get to without a raft in the shark-infested waters.

In any case, few people could swim in the 1830s. Seamen William Elliott and Michael Doyle later drowned when attempting to swim the channel to the mainland. By this time James Fraser and Charles Brown had become ill and exhausted. Strangely, Eliza became the most determined to survive the almost biblical afflictions. Whether she resorted to the lamentations of Jeremiah is not recorded, but her relative strength once again suggests that she had not recently given birth.

The Butchulla people, watching the pathetic strangers' slow progress down their lands, debated what course of action was appropriate. Clearly, if they were returning spirits they had completely forgotten how to survive even at the most elemental level. And if they were indeed these alien white beings they had heard about, they were not frightening in their power but weak and stupid. After much discussion, the Butchulla agreed to assist them. Henry Youlden and John Baxter later reported they were surprised to be offered food and water by the warriors, who seemed concerned for their welfare.[12] Their accounts of their treatment are completely different from Eliza's, who saw her time with the Butchulla as torture and hardship. Her account omitted that it was their many kindnesses that allowed her to survive.

The presence of these white beings presented a huge strain on the resources of the Butchulla. The island lacked good soil, and few fruits and berries grew in the sand. This was in contrast to the abundance on the mainland. But the territory did offer good fishing. The elders decided to divide the strangers into more manageable groups, so that a clan would be responsible for a few rather than one overwhelming group. With around seventy people in a clan and six clans on the island with prescribed territories, this was a sensible move.[13] In return, these reddened white men were expected to search for firewood and to fish.

Eliza was the odd one out in this arrangement. What should be done with a woman – this emaciated, burned wreck of a human being? When the Butchulla women conferred, they decided Eliza should join them in the women's area in the north-west of the territory at

Moon Point. A middle-class European woman accustomed to weak sunlight, always covered in protective clothing, Eliza had no defences against the subtropical sun. Her skin was raw and blistering. Her arms lay 'across her bosom, to shield her person as much as possible from the fierce oblique rays of the setting sun, which had a powerful effect, of course, upon a delicate skin so recently denuded of clothing'.[14] As an act of ritual cleansing, the Butchulla women threw sand over her body causing her excruciating pain. To heal the sunburn they applied charcoal and fat sealed with feathers, vines and twine to stop further penetration of the sun's rays and to offer a modicum of protection against the winter chill at night.

For Eliza these attempts to heal her spirit and her body were horrifying. In her eyes the Butchulla were trying to turn her into an uncivilised savage, naked, degraded and barbarous. Even more confronting was that she was expected, indeed forced, to dig in the dirt for roots and nuts, gather berries, care for babies and search for firewood. At Stromness she had a maid, as befitted her status as a captain's wife, and here in the wilds she was expected to work with her hands in the dirt and sand.

Eliza later reported to Superintendent Foster Fyans:

> During the whole of my detention among the natives I was
> treated with the greatest cruelty, being obliged to fetch wood
> and water for them and then constantly beaten when incapable
> of carrying heavy loads they put upon me; exposed during
> the night to the inclemency of the weather, being hardly ever
> allowed to enter their huts even during the heaviest rain.

It is interesting to note Eliza regarded her period as a castaway as a 'detention', without understanding she was incapable of leaving unaided and supporting herself with the basic elements of food, water and shelter. Indigenous societies contained small-scale hunting and gathering groups in which everyone had to work together, albeit in strictly gender-specific roles. No one had the luxury of leisure and not contributing to the communal effort.

James Fraser and First Officer Charles Brown were also made to gather firewood and undertake work they considered below their status as British officers. But as shipwrecked castaways their former identities and status were irrelevant. Why would the Butchulla care about what was in the past, or comprehend what an officer was, and why this person might merit special treatment? Butchulla elders were respected for their knowledge of law and religion, but even they worked. Fraser and Brown resisted this imposition to work, thereby angering their saviours. The ordinary seamen, accustomed to hard menial work, did not complain or resist, as we know from later testimony, and they coped far better and fitted in more easily to their radically new circumstances.

In her first report to Fyans, Eliza described her husband's condition:

> In consequence of these hardships my husband soon became so
> much weakened so as to be totally incapable of the work that was
> required of him, and being on one occasion unable through
> debility to carry a large log of wood one of the natives threw a
> spear at him which entered his shoulder just below the blade-
> bone. Of this event he never recovered and being soon seized
> with a spitting of blood he gradually pined always until his death
> which took place eight or nine days afterwards. During this
> time when he was laying on the ground incapable of moving,
> I was always prevented from approaching him or rendering him
> any assistance. When he died they dragged him away by the legs
> and buried him. [15]

Brown died also. In her testimony Eliza stated that he died a painful death. She acknowledged that his feet were so burned and torn that the bones showed through and his knees protruded through the skin. The Butchulla had attempted to heal his sunburn and wounds with clay heated by firebrands to seal the skin, but this was interpreted as gross cruelty. These wounds would have proven a challenge to heal in European society, as antiseptics did not then exist. Again, according to Eliza, she was prevented from helping Brown, reporting that when she tried to give him some cockles '... some of the natives came up, and taking them from me, they knocked me down and dragged me along the ground. After this I saw him no more ...'[16]

Baxter, who was not present at this incident, later told the London enquiry into the case that Brown was 'inhumanely tied to a stake and, a slow fire being placed under him, his body, after the most excruciating sufferings, was reduced to ashes'.[17] This report added to the already sensationalised account of the shipwreck survivors that had appeared in the *Sydney Gazette* of 17 October 1836. Far from being saviours, the Butchulla were portrayed as monsters who tortured and incinerated decent British men. Undoubtedly, the Butchulla did treat the men harshly and were exasperated at their feeble attempts at work, but theirs was a hard life and this was the punishment they meted out to their own for infringements of the rules of group survival. The Sydney newspaper article was the first public discussion of the men's deaths. Eliza further clouded the issue by saying the Butchulla were very friendly to Brown just before his death and concerned about his welfare. She interpreted this behaviour as cowardly, savage treachery.

In this second account of the deaths of Brown and Fraser, she embellished the gory details and used terms like 'savages' and 'cannibals', rather than 'natives'. She acknowledged that both men were already weakened and depleted from the ordeals of the shipwreck and its aftermath. Taking up this theme in her third rendition of the tale, in 1837, the image of the cannibal was firmly established. In an anonymous broadsheet ballad called 'Wreck of the *Stirling Castle* Horrib [sic] Treatment of the Crew by Savages', Eliza appeared in an accompanying illustration somehow miraculously fully attired in clean clothes, beset by stereotypical cannibals, replete with nose bones and surrounded by decapitated heads. Similarly, in an American pamphlet, 'Narrative of the Capture, Sufferings and

Miraculous Escape of Mrs. Eliza Fraser', Eliza, again fully attired with her hair neatly coiffured, is seen in the process of capture by the Butchulla who now are represented as Native Americans. This piece added to a substantial popular literature on captured white women taken by savage Indians, tortured, kept as slaves, raped and made to perform unspeakable indelicacies. It was a type of sensational forerunner to today's stories of outlandish and bizarre traumas seen in *The Enquirer* and the like.[18]

Eliza Fraser and the other survivors of the *Stirling Castle* were neither captured nor enslaved by the Butchulla people. These concepts were entirely foreign to Indigenous societies. The references to slavery were more relevant to current debates in the British Empire and the official abolition of slavery in 1833.

Taken in canoes to Butchulla territory on the mainland, Corralis, Darge, Dayman, Carey and Youlden decided to walk to the Moreton Bay penal settlement – if proof were needed that the group was not in captivity. Corralis and Darge stumbled across Lieutenant Charles Otter, who was out shooting game on Bribie Island. He recorded that he was astounded to see two 'black and perfectly naked' men coming towards him who spoke to him in English. Astonished, he realised they were not Indigenous people but castaways. They had been guided down this far by two Indigenous men who had spent a lot of time and effort passing through others' territory to assist the strangers. Youlden was resting nearby, unable to walk, as his feet were so torn. Isolated from the other men, Dayman and Carey were also resting at Lake Cooroibah on the Noosa River. An escapee from the detention centre in Moreton Bay, John Graham, who had lived with the Kabi people for many years, found Dayman and Carey 'in an abject state', naked, sunburned and deeply afraid.[19] On 19 August 1836, a search party was organised to find the rest of the survivors.

At this point it was thought that Baxter and Eliza Fraser still remained on Great Sandy Island. Graham, as an initiated man of a nearby tribe, made enquiries about their whereabouts and organised a search party with his friend and ally Gormondy, the only Indigenous person ever directly named in all the evidence and testimony. Near death, Baxter was found on the southern end of the island and rescued. Graham and Gormondy assumed Eliza was living in the women's camp on the far north. Returning to the mainland, after much negotiation and bartering they located Eliza's whereabouts at Fig Tree Point, 50 or so kilometres south of Great Sandy Island, at the northern tip of Lake Cootharaba, also attached to the Noosa River. When Graham located her Eliza was wandering around the huts at a large feast. Graham convinced the assembly that Eliza was the ghost of his dead wife and that he would assume control for her welfare. Taking her to his country at nearby Teewah Beach, he and four of his putative kin travelled in two canoes to the safety of a secluded beach where the party met up with Otter.

Graham recalled his first sight of Eliza:

On her head was a Southwester, the smell of the paint kept
the blacks from taking it. Around her loins were part of the
legs and waistband of a pair of trousers, which covered part of
her thighs, wound around with Vines twenty fold as well for
delicacy as the preservation of her marriage ring and Earrings
which she concealed in the vines.[20]

It was from this description that Patrick White wove his tale *A Fringe of Leaves*. Although we know all the castaways' clothes were confiscated on the trek, some may have been returned to Eliza. Graham had also previously been given clothing for Eliza in case she was naked.

Charles Otter provided an extraordinary picture of his first glimpse of Eliza after fifty-two days with the Butchulla:

You never saw such an object. Although only thirty-eight years
of age, she looked like an old woman of seventy, perfectly
black and dreadfully crippled from the sufferings she had

undergone. I went to meet her and she caught my hand and burst into tears and sunk down quite exhausted. She was a mere skeleton, skin literally hanging on her bones, while her legs were a mass of sores, where the savages had tortured her with fire-brands.

In just a few months, all the frail vestiges that marked her sex, class, marital status and nationality had disappeared, shrouded within the fringe of leaves and charcoal.

The group set out for Double Island Point, their progress hampered by Eliza's debilitated state. As they were without horses, she had to walk along with the men. They rested for a few days, and then left after some minor altercations with the local people, arriving in Brisbane on 21 August 1836.

Arriving at the penal outpost, where she gave her first short account, Eliza wept tears of joy at her deliverance, despite its rudimentary dwellings and convict population. Like Job's wife, she had survived her travails. She had lost her husband in tragic circumstances, but she still had her three children in Scotland who knew nothing of their parents' ordeals. With her mind focused on her husband's reputation and her children's welfare, she knew she had to compose herself and recover. Under the careful nurturing of the officers' wives for two months, she recuperated and transformed herself slowly back to a middle-class Englishwoman. These kind ladies provided her with clothes and money they could ill afford, before she set off to Sydney to be proclaimed a hero of the Empire.

By mid October 1836 Eliza was a *cause célèbre* in Sydney. As a guest of the Colonial Secretary, she repeated the story of her ordeal to thrilled and shocked audiences, embellishing each detail in the retelling. The surviving crew members were also in Sydney but receiving treatment different from Eliza's. A service in St James' Church in Macquarie Street – which Eliza did not attend – was held to raise funds for the survivors. During proceedings four of the seamen were forced to sit bare-chested in the aisle in some strange symbol of the shipwreck.[21] The crew was each given £5, held in trust for them until departure for England. Only after the intervention of the Governor was Second Officer Baxter given a new suit and passage home to England. These men all harboured deep resentments towards Eliza, whom they saw as unduly profiting from their shared trauma. To them the cause of their ordeal was her husband's gross incompetence, and they conveniently forgot their own insistence on landing on Great Sandy Island.

Eliza thus received both public acknowledgment and considerable largesse in Sydney. Her status as a respectable mother and widow who had suffered unimaginable hardship elicited deep sympathy and prurient curiosity. Yet there were whisperings undermining her reputation too. Was she molested by the 'cannibals' or the convict absconders who saved her? Charlotte Barton, a talented English gentlewoman separated from a brutal husband, wrote a curious book, *A Mother's Suffering to her Children* (1841), defending Eliza's reputation as a genteel victim. There were hints in Barton's narrative, and in the earlier book by Curtis, that Eliza Fraser was deranged from her ordeal. But more lasting in their consequences were Eliza's negative depictions of the Kabi and Butchulla peoples as 'savages' when in reality they had done their utmost to assist the survivors.

On 3 February 1837, only five months after her rescue, Eliza married naval captain Alexander John Greene. This was a shocking disavowal of her status as a respectable widow, for one year was the customary minimum of mourning expected before remarriage. How she met this new Scottish captain was a subject she kept to herself. The couple departed on the *Mediterranean Packet* on 16 February 1837, leaving Eliza's Sydney benefactors wondering about the honesty of the castaway. Had Eliza played the role of a docile, genteel woman driven to near insanity by her suffering to tug on their heartstrings and their purses?

Reports of the ordeal, including the questionable dead baby incident, preceded Eliza's arrival in Liverpool on 16 July 1837. Since this was before the invention of the telegraph and radio, news must have been prepared while she was still in Sydney and sent ahead on an earlier vessel to burst out sensationally on 3 July 1837. Greene was also a competent journalist who was fascinated by stories of women shipwreck survivors. He knew the details of Betty Guard and her two children who were stranded in New Zealand with Taranaki Maoris. A teenaged bride, Betty and her former convict husband, Captain John Guard, were shipwrecked in 1834. On returning to Sydney they recounted tales of torture and humiliation.[22] Tales of the even more horrific wreck and murder of survivors of the *Charles Eaton* in the Torres Strait had reached Sydney by 1836.[23] Curtis' book on Mrs Fraser also contained the story of this latter drama. Greene was thus entirely familiar with the narrative of the chaste, vulnerable Englishwoman thrown on the mercy of 'savages'. And so Eliza docked in Liverpool a fully created celebrity, again arousing much morbid curiosity and sympathy.

By the time Eliza Fraser – as she presented herself, with Greene merely as her agent – arrived at Liverpool docks, her story had been refined. She was a destitute widow with three children, cast upon wild and alien shores and subjected to unspeakable torture at the hands of 'cannibals'. Even when rescued, she alleged she battled on alone without resources or aid. This very understated nature allowed readers to flesh out their own details of sexual violence, torture and the eating of human flesh. That she travelled to London to capitalise on her fame, rather than rejoining her children in Scotland, gives a hint of her motives. Perhaps as she wandered the fashionable streets of Mayfair she saw herself in beautiful gowns and jewels now so tantalisingly within her grasp. A considerable subscription was taken up for her, with the support of the Lord Mayor of London. Feeding the appetite for sensation, lurid accounts of her ordeal appeared in the broadsheets: Eliza had been forever marked with hideous disfiguring tattoos; John Major was tortured, decapitated and eaten, his head forming a fine ornament for a war canoe.[24] In the United States, *Tales of Travelers*

(1837) fed the demand for sensational adventures. Yet, as the editor of the *Sydney Gazette* wrote on 25 January 1838, Eliza Fraser had been showered with money and gifts in Sydney. Middle-class Britons in the Antipodes were outraged that their generosity and kindness had not been acknowledged. She had been amply assisted in both Moreton Bay and Sydney. Indeed, she was now married to a naval captain and no longer a widow.

As other stories emerged the Lord Mayor withdrew his patronage and ordered an enquiry into the shipwreck of the *Stirling Castle* and the experiences on Great Sandy Island. He directed that all the subscription funds go to her children in Stromness. In 1838 John Curtis published his account, in which any discrepancies lay in Eliza's derangement from grief and torture. Eliza was depicted not as an impostor or perpetrator of a fraud but as an innocent victim of circumstances. An interesting sideshow to the affair was a performance in Hyde Park in which Mrs Fraser supposedly told her tale. The wealthy squatter and Old Etonian Henry Stuart Russell, who knew the convict renegades and other participants in the rescue, recorded in his memoirs that he had a handbill for the show.[25] Russell was a good researcher and documenter of his own life and the society around him. There was undoubtedly a sideshow; whether Eliza performed is unlikely. The strong constraints of her class and sexual identity suggest that the performer was an actor capitalising on Eliza's notoriety.

Yet Eliza was a manipulative embellisher of her tragedy as well as a strong, resolute and courageous woman. She revelled in publicity, seeing it as the means to a fortune. Eliza and Alexander Greene eventually migrated to New Zealand.

Eliza died in a carriage accident in Melbourne in 1858. Her complex notoriety also had diverse historical rewards; her story, with all its twists, turns, ambiguities, exaggerations and retellings, is the primary material for great art in the twentieth century.

CHAPTER 4

Lola Montez
(1818–1861)

The Irish-born grande horizontale *who destroyed
King Ludwig I of Bavaria through extravagance.*

In the year of revolution, 1848, Lola Montez was the most famous
and recognised woman in the world after Queen Victoria. Whereas
the later Empress of India and head of the British Empire grew
into the role of wise monarch and devoted wife and mother, Lola
was an infamous courtesan who ruined the life of the monarch of
Bavaria, on top of conducting other scandalous liaisons and entering
two bigamous marriages. Her notoriety far outlived her own time;
Aldous Huxley once remarked that every time he thought of Lola
Montez he thought of bedrooms – and this was nearly a century
after her death in 1861.

Lola's origins are clouded in uncertainty. She wrote in *The Times*
on 9 April 1847 that she was born in Seville in the year 1823: 'My
father was a Spanish officer in service of Don Carlos, my mother a
lady of Irish extraction … and married for the second time to an Irish
gentleman, which I suppose, is the cause of my being called Irish and
sometimes English, "Betsy Watson", "Mrs. James" etc etc. My name
is Maria Dolores Porris y Montez.'

There is little truth in this declaration, aside from the facts that her
mother was Irish and Lola was technically Mrs James. How did a young
Irish dancer of little talent, although an accomplished courtesan, come
to make such an important announcement in the press? By 1847 Lola

Montez was a household name across Europe and the English-speaking world. The Australian colonial press was already full of her doings, as she lurched from scandal to scandal. By the time she came to Sydney in 1855, she was the most notorious woman in the world.

Baptised Maria Delores Eliza Rosanna Gilbert, Lola was born in Limerick, Ireland, in 1818 to her fourteen-year-old mother, Elizabeth Oliver. Elizabeth, a milliner's assistant, was born in 1805 to Mary Green and Charles Silver Oliver, MP, a pillar of the Irish Protestant ascendancy and former sheriff of the County of Cork. This long-term alliance produced four children, before Charles Oliver married a woman of his own class background. He did, however, acknowledge his four illegitimate children and provided modestly for their welfare. Lola's father, Ensign Edward Gilbert, was a handsome young officer in the 25th Foot Regiment which had recently seen service in India. He met Lola's mother in Cork and they married on 29 April 1819 in Christ's Church, Cork, soon after Elizabeth discovered she was pregnant. Unlike her own mother, she was able to marry the father of her child, thus avoiding the stigma of illegitimacy that had affected her own life and chances.[1]

In 1823 the family went to India, where Edward was stationed with the British East India Company's troops. He died of cholera in September 1823, an event that was to change his young, high-spirited daughter's life forever. Her mother married a kindly Scotsman, Lieutenant Patrick Craigie, a scion of a bourgeois Montrose, Scotland, family. And it was only these two men that Lola ever truly loved, as her later life revealed. Sent home to Scotland, the young Lola was wild. She wrote in her autobiography, she was a 'queer, wayward, little East India girl' sent to the coldness of eastern Scotland.[2] Her book spoke at great length about the colours and vibrancy of India, so this exile, along with her beloved father's death, cast a terrible shadow over her spirits. After a brief period with her stepfather's sister in Durham, Lola was sent to Bath, where she attended the Misses Aldridge's Academy, and learned the graces and accomplishments of a young lady. This was an expensive exercise for Lieutenant Craigie to undertake.

The lessons in propriety and modesty were entirely lost on the stubborn teenager who had spurned the advice of her stepfather's friend Lieutenant General Sir Jasper Nicolls. Her extravagance and impetuousness were already apparent. In 1837 Lola saw her mother again after a six-year separation. Elizabeth proposed an arranged marriage with a 64-year-old widower, Major General Sir James Rutherford, a friend of her stepfather. Repulsed by this suggestion, Lola eloped with the handsome Lieutenant Thomas James, aged thirty-one. They were duly married by his brother, the vicar of a Protestant parish in Dublin. As Lola later wrote, '[r]unaway matches, like runaway horses, are almost sure to end in a smash up'.[3] The couple then went to Simla (now Shimla) in India, where Lieutenant James' regiment was stationed.

The nineteen-year-old bride, despite her childhood in India, was singularly unsuited to the constraints of an officer's wife in a tiny British outpost. The marriage faltered quickly. There is some speculation as to whether Lola or James abandoned the marriage, but evidence suggests that perhaps it was Lola who strayed from the marital bed, as she had an open affair on the ship returning to England. Caroline Marden, a female steward on this vessel, reported that 'I more than once saw Captain Lennox lacing up Mrs. James' stays.'[4] George Lennox was the aide-de-camp to Lord Elphinstone, and once in London Lola met with him in her hotel, again breaching the rules of decorous behaviour. By the age of twenty, Lola's life was characterised by scandal and notoriety – she had eloped and then abandoned her husband, and had now taken up publicly with another man. Meanwhile, Thomas James obtained a judicial separation in the Church of England's Consistory Court; divorce at this time was only by an Act of parliament.

Lola needed some way of supporting herself and by now she was estranged from her mother. The thought of working as a milliner's assistant, as her mother had done, never entered her head. Rather, Lola

– or Mrs Betty James as she was then called – needed to reinvent her whole identity. She went to the Fran Kelly Academy in Dean Street, Soho, to learn dancing, before taking a trip to Cadiz, Spain, to learn Spanish language and dances.[5] Lola later wrote in her autobiography that 'we poor women are such helpless creatures that we do not always have the choice of means. Often we are forced to achieve our goals by whatever is available to us, even if we recognized that we are thus put in an unflattering light.'

Billed as Donna Lolah Montez, Lola made her theatrical debut on 3 June 1843 at Her Majesty's Theatre in Haymarket, London, performing 'El Oleano', an early version of her famous Spider Dance. What reviewers remarked upon was not her proficiency in the art of dance but her spectacular appearance. With thick raven-black hair, intense blue eyes, a perfect porcelain complexion and superb figure, Lola was an extraordinary beauty.

The performance was marred by shouts of 'Betty James' when she was recognised from the audience. Her run at the theatre was short-lived. She fled to Hamburg and from there toured extensively in Germany, Poland and Russia, where she could be spared such ignominy and abuse. In early 1844 Lola met Franz Liszt, the Hungarian piano virtuoso with whom she conducted a barely concealed liaison, even scandalising the tolerant band of artists and intellectuals who populated the demimonde they inhabited. When the affair faltered, Lola went to Paris, armed with letters of introduction, to reignite her career. On 28 March 1844 she made her debut at the Paris Opera. Again the audience of men – ladies did not attend theatrical performances – admired her beauty and vivaciousness while lamenting her lack of talent and expertise in Spanish dancing.

After her limited artistic success, Lola did far better as a courtesan. Her first liaison in Paris was conducted with the young editor and owner of *La Presse*, Alexandre Dujarier. He died after a duel with Guadeloupe-born Jean-Baptiste Rosemond de Beupin de Beauvallon in March 1845. He left seventeen shares in the Palais Royal Theatre to Lola, and his horses and furniture to Alexandre Dumas *père* (author of *The Three Musketeers*). Lola then embarked on an affair with Dumas from whom it was rumoured she contracted syphilis.[6] She fitted in well into the demimonde of Paris, befriending Alphonsine Plessis, upon whom Dumas' illegitimate son, Alexandre Dumas *fils*, modelled his tragic *Lady of the Camellias*.

Lola set her sights beyond Paris and travelled to the fashionable health resorts at Spa in Belgium and Baden-Baden in Germany. She returned to Paris for the trial of de Beauvallon, following the duel, who was acquitted. Lola made a wistful figure in black, a colour she adopted henceforth. After the proceedings, she left Paris with Robert Peel, the eldest son of the former British prime minister. Arriving in Munich on 5 October 1846 for the Oktoberfest, she was presented to King Ludwig of Bavaria, who was smitten immediately by her beauty and vivacity. Pretending she was a Spanish noblewoman, Lola henceforth conversed with Ludwig in Spanish. We can presume his Spanish skills were limited as she fooled him completely. After seeing her perform her Spider Dance – a fast-moving spinning performance – Ludwig took his passion to another level and installed her as his official mistress. His generosity was almost boundless – he provided his new favourite with a house that was lavishly renovated and furnished, horses, carriages, clothes, jewellery, servants and a substantial income. Within a few months he had lavished upon her millions of dollars in today's currency.[7]

Not only did Lola entertain the besotted elderly King in the bedroom, but she took to advising him on politics. These years in the late 1840s were intensely volatile across Western Europe, with challenges to traditional monarchies and demands for more representative government. Lola allied herself with the university students and members of the Munich middle class, thereby alienating herself to Ludwig's aristocratic court and advisers. Still, on 10 February 1847 he made her a Bavarian citizen and, six months later, on his birthday, Ludwig elevated her to a peerage. She became the Countess Marie von Landsfeld and signed her last will in New York under this name.[8] Immediately upon this elevation Lola became far more formal and distant to her benefactor.

On 7 February 1848 riots against her influence spread through Munich, endangering her safety. Three days later merchants and other prosperous citizens who had previously formed the nucleus of her supporters, marched in their thousands on the King's residence in protest against her extravagance and political influence. Ludwig was forced to concede when presented with incontrovertible evidence that his darling Lolitta, as he called her, was an impostor. Even more humiliating was the detailed evidence of her affairs with handsome young students conducted while she was the King's mistress. With her house ransacked and her life in peril, Lola fled to Berne in Switzerland and her Bavarian citizenship was revoked. There she learned that not only had King Louis Philippe abdicated after riots in Paris, but her devoted Ludwig had also abdicated on 10 March. And after everything he had learned about her, Ludwig was still convinced of her affection and hoped to join her in his long exile.

In April 1848 a satirical play entitled *Pas de Fascination or Catching a Governor, or a Farce in One Act ... performed under the title of Lola Montez, or a Countess for an Hour* was premiered at the Theatre Royal in London. Its author, J. Stirling Coyne, did not enjoy an extended career as a playwright or satirist, but the ribald comedy was a success. News of Lola's exploits and affairs had spread across the world, albeit slowly. The Australian colonial newspapers followed the now notorious Lola's career with avid attention. She had returned to London at this time though no doubt she avoided Coyne's scurrilous farce. Lola had lost her house in Munich but she retained her annual income from Ludwig, and she rented a grand house in Half Moon Street, near Green Park in Mayfair.

On 19 July 1849 Lola went through a form of marriage to a wealthy 21-year-old former Etonian and Second Life Guards officer George Trafford Heald. In fact she went through two wedding ceremonies, one in the French Roman Catholic chapel in King Street, Westminster, followed by another ceremony that same day at the fashionable St George's Church of England in Hanover Square. Neither of the couple were Catholic and Lola was still legally married, although she described herself as one 'Maria de los Delores de Landsfeld, widow'. Protestant by baptism and an ardent anti-Catholic, as her later lecture tours and writings revealed, she was nevertheless a supposed Spanish noblewoman and forced into this pretence. She gave her place of birth as Seville, though later she admitted in her autobiography that she was born in Limerick.

George Heald's aunt Susanna Heald, suspicious of the beautiful 'widow', made her own investigations and confirmed that her naïve nephew had indeed married bigamously.[9] In August 1849 a warrant for Lola's arrest on the charge of bigamy hung over her head. The court case, commencing on 12 August 1849, was chronicled in *The Times*. Again reports spread across Europe and through the English-speaking world. At first she told the court she was divorced, and when this was proved incorrect, she pointed to the invalidity of the ceremonies because she had signed her declarations in a false name. Placed on bail at the enormous sum of £1000, which she didn't possess, Lola skipped bail for freedom in Paris, which was far more alluring than spending time in an English prison. She and Heald fled across the Channel, before going to Spain, their alliance soon descending into bickering, bitterness and separation. Heald bestowed on Lola an annual allowance of a mere £50, a pittance after the fortune lavished upon her by Ludwig.

Lola's response was to increase her demands on Ludwig for ever more money without the tediousness of cohabitation. Despite her new alliance, Lola had continued to profess her undying devotion in letters to the exiled Ludwig.[10]

Lola's relationship with Ludwig was now very useful. She possessed his passionate letters and had no hesitation in using them as a weapon for requesting further funds. Her former life in Bavaria was also to provide source material for future stage shows.

Lola Montez – or the Countess of Landsfeld – in the blossom of her youth. Lithograph by Sarony & Major; Library of Congress LC-USZ62-3913.

LOLA MONTES.
COUNTESS OF LANDSFELD.

Lola's first autobiography appeared in the journal *Le Pays* in 1851 and was also translated into German. Readers would have been greatly disappointed, however, as it dealt mostly with her reminiscences of her childhood in India.[11] Attempts to reignite her career in Europe were haphazard and, as it had for others before her, the New World beckoned.

Lola arrived in New York City in late 1851 to a blaze of publicity. The *New York Herald* of 30 December 1851 took up the promotion of the glamorous Countess. Lola decided that rather than relying on her Spider Dance, renamed 'Zapateado', she would lengthen her performances with the addition of a *corps de ballet*. Her shows were regarded as indecent; ladies not only did not appear on stage, they did not attend theatrical performances. Lola contributed to a benefit for the Fireman's Welfare Fund on 16 January 1852. American male audiences were fascinated by this supposed aristocrat in her own right who became a *maîtresse du roi*. Her beauty and fine figure were added attractions in this Puritan society.

Lola embarked on an extensive theatrical tour of the east coast of the United States, adding a new number entitled 'Lola Montez in Bavaria' in several sections – the *Danseuse*, the Politician, the Countess, the Revolutionary, and the Fugitive. Unfortunately, no printed copy of the bill for the show survives.[12] Always a rebel and groundbreaker, Lola was photographed with the Native American Cheyenne chief Light in the Clouds in Philadelphia, and with a cigarette in her hand on another occasion in Boston – the earliest known extant photograph of a woman smoking to survive.[13] More material was added to her repertoire, including something on the life of Charlotte Corday, the killer of Marat in the French Revolution, and 'Maritana, or the Maid of Saragossa', set in the Napoleonic Wars. The *New York Times* of 6 September 1852 reported how fetching Lola looked in male attire in this now forgotten work.

In the United States occurrences of her erratic and often violent outbursts became apparent. She was arrested for assault in the theatre in New Orleans where she was performing and jumped bail. Such behaviour was the first outward evidence, along with increasingly painful headaches and eye problems, of secondary syphilis. Meanwhile, adverse publicity about her was appearing across the world with increasing frequency. None was worse than accounts by *London Times* senior reporter William Russell, made famous later by his despatches on the Crimean War. In his novel *Mrs. Seacole's Adventures* (1858), he portrayed a thinly disguised Lola on her arduous trip across the Isthmus of Panama as:

A good-looking, bold woman with fine, bad eyes and collar turned down, determined bearing, dressed ostentatiously in perfect male attire ... she carried in her hand a handsome riding whip, which she could use as well in the streets of Cruces as the towns of Europe; for an impertinent American, presuming perhaps not unnaturally upon her reputation, laid hold jestingly on the tails of her long coat, and, as a lesson, received a cut across his face that must have marked him for some days ...[14]

Lola was upset by Russell's report and devoted some space in her second autobiography to his remarks.[15] She also added into this strange little memoir, so full of errors and reworkings of her past, that 'of Lola Montez's career in the United States there is not much to be said'.[16] The global press disagreed and her every move and performance was avidly followed. The *Maitland Mercury and Hunter River Advertiser*, for instance, had been keeping readers in its small regional area up to date with her career, starting around her time in Bavaria.

Arriving in San Francisco in May 1853, after an arduous trip by mule, coach and then sea, Lola set about trying to revive her allure on the stage. The gold towns of California were ripe for the pickings, in her opinion. On the voyage across she had met Patrick Purdy Hull, a young journalist and owner of the *San Francisco Whig*, who also committed himself to advancing her career. Within weeks of their meeting, on 2 July 1853, Lola entered into a marriage with Hull in a Roman Catholic ceremony. At this time, both James and Heald were still alive, so this was her second bigamous union.

Lola's acts on stage, supplemented with fare such as the role of Lady Teazle in *School for Scandal*, were welcomed by the culture- and leisure-starved miners. The price of admission at $5 a ticket was exorbitant compared to $1 in New York.[17] But the miners were far more discerning than she had anticipated and many appearances were marred by hissing and shouts of anger at her poor performances and lack of technical expertise. Lola countered this negativity by engaging in dialogue at the footlights with her detractors – something actors did not do – and managed to turn this into a form of theatre sport to which audiences flocked to see her ability to ad lib. By the standards of the day, Lola was a well-educated woman and her verbal dexterity was admired.

Lola Montez was clever in the way in which she capitalised on romantic notions of Spain, as noted by American writers Washington Irving and William H. Prescott. She appreciated the lengthy Spanish colonisation of California and the cultural heritage it bestowed. What was seemingly at variance with this admiration of *lo Español* was her increasingly frequent diatribes against the Jesuits; making claims they had tried to poison her with arsenic, that they shot at her on several occasions, and tried to kidnap her in Munich.[18] Such delusions may also have been caused by the spread of syphilis through her brain, with feelings of persecution and grandiose notions both appearing as the disease progressed.

Though seemingly isolated by distance from Europe, San Francisco was au fait with modern developments on the popular and traditional stage. Not only were *Hamlet* and *Romeo and Juliet* performed but also the farce *Lola Montez: or, Pas de Fascination*. Not to be outdone, local authors set about writing their own satires. One play, *Who's Got the Countess? Or, The Rival Houses*, played to capacity crowds. At another theatre a series of scurrilous songs were enthusiastically received. Publicly, Lola laughed, seeing these attacks as generating more publicity for her.[19] In California, public morality was not as strict as in London, from where she had fled several scandals earlier.

Her tours of the Grass Valley and Nevada City regions were eagerly reported as far away as the Australian colonies. An indulgent spendthrift who frittered away her constantly renewed fortune, Lola purchased a mine in northern California. With her 'marriage' abandoned within three months, she settled in the unlikely spot of Grass Valley where she kept a bear cub along with a menagerie of more domesticated animals and birds. She stayed in this rural retreat until early 1855, when she decided on a two-year grand tour of India, China and the Australian colonies.

Lola and her new company departed from San Francisco on 6 June 1855. On advice from her manager, the proposals to tour India and China were abandoned as too ambitious. A handsome young actor named Noel Follin (stage name Frank Folland) soon caught her eye. With his estranged wife and family in Cincinnati, he was free to embark on a tempestuous professional and personal relationship with the world's most notorious woman. It was a hasty decision he came to regret, as Lola's demands, rudeness, arrogance and irrational delusions appeared with ever more frequency.

Lola decided to test the Australian colonies with her new entourage. After a two-month voyage the *Fanny Major* disembarked in Sydney. The *Sydney Morning Herald* of 17 August 1855 reported its arrival but refrained from announcing the presence of Lola and her troupe. In her first engagement at the Victoria Theatre in Pitt Street, she performed 'Lola Montez in Bavaria'. After a performance in Melbourne, the *Argus* of 31 August 1855 informed readers that:

> [H]er appearance is good; but her voice, if not bad, deficient
> altogether in flexibility, and sweetness, at least when raised to
> a pitch calculated for the stage. She is sometimes graceful for a
> moment or two, but coarseness and vulgarity is sure to follow
> hard upon such glimpses of a better spirit. Her grand effect is
> as a 'postures'.

If this was harsh criticism, the critic went on: 'The Piece she played in ... is about the greatest piece of trash and humbug introduced before an English audience ...' Sydney's leading broadsheet remained entirely silent on her performance and, indeed, her presence in their city.

In Sydney Lola continued to suffer from headaches and ill health, a sign the syphilis was progressing rapidly. Curiously, while in Sydney with engagements still to come in Melbourne she dismissed the American company. When she attempted to jump bail for breaking her theatrical contracts in a farce involving an officer of the court trying to serve writs on the vessel *Waratah* bound for Melbourne, the *Sydney Morning Herald* finally got interested and reported the incident on 11 September 1855.

In Melbourne Lola played in her show, based on her adventures in Bavaria at the Theatre Royal with a far smaller company. Seweryn Korzelinski, an educated Polish miner who left a record of his time in Victoria, reported that Lola largely danced her Spider Dance to '… sailors [who] were duly impressed'.[20] By this, he rightly inferred this was low culture for an undiscerning male audience. Today she performance would appear innocent enough; in the mid nineteenth century, however, the public display of a woman's legs and ankles was regarded as immoral and lascivious. Melbourne, though a new city, possessed a substantial degree of high culture, with the *Messiah* a popular production and the Melbourne Philharmonic Society running 200 performances a year in 1860. Opera was appreciated, with Madame Carandini and Irish soprano Catherine Hayes great favourites there and on the goldfields. George Coppin, the owner of the Olympic Theatre, put on *Lucia di Lammermoor*, *La Sonnambula*, *Norma* and *Il trovatore*. For the town's elite, particularly the ladies, *soirées musicales* at home were the order of the day.[21]

During her time in Victoria, Lola continued to be plagued by headaches and illness, which affected her performances. The critic for the *Argus* on 20 September 1855 denounced the spectacle as '… a nuisance and … utterly subversive to all ideas of public morality'.[22] The Reverend John Milton went so far as to demand her arrest. With the Methodist and Presbyterian churches strong in the new colony, his opinion held weight.[23] She was also attacked by theatrical types themselves. George Coppin produced a satire in which he mimicked Lola's addresses to the audience. Lola had to endure all these less than flattering attacks.

From Melbourne Lola went to Adelaide, where she found respectability not enjoyed at any other point in her career. A vice-regal performance and a benefit for the widows and orphans of the 'heroes of Sebastopol' by 'Lola Montez, Countess of Landsfeld, Princess of Bavaria' added a hitherto elusive lustre to her name.[24] How she suddenly became a princess is a mystery. The *South Australian Register* of 9 December 1855 praised this 'clever *danseuse*'.

Lola's tour of the goldfields of Victoria also met with controversy. Korzelinski recorded that her charms were fading and her expectations that the 'miners [would] kiss her hand' were unfulfilled.[25] Far worse from a public relations point of view, Lola horsewhipped Henry Seekamp, the editor of the *Ballarat Times*, in the public bar of the United States Hotel. He attempted to punch her and pull her hair in retaliation. *The Age* of 23 February 1856 reported the altercation with great relish. Frank Folland threatened the hero of the Eureka Stockade – who defended the miners' rights in the press – with a pistol. News spread internationally.[26] The *Melbourne Punch* of 28 February 1856 wrote a long amusing poem in honour of the 'Battle of Ballarat'. Moreover, unrest within Lola's small company over payments escalated. Lola was horsewhipped herself by Mrs Crosby, the wife of her manager. When the whip broke, she pummelled Lola with her fists and pulled her hair.[27]

Lola returned to Melbourne in early March 1856, where her performances were greeted with hisses and boos. Undeterred, she and her troupe returned to the goldfields and performed in Bendigo and Castlemaine, the tickets now priced at only ten shillings. The *Bendigo Courier* of 10 May 1856 reported Lola as now thanking her audience for their attendance.

The troupe left Australia on 22 May 1856 on the *James A. Falkenberg* bound for San Francisco. Her relations with Frank Folland, her manager, and the rest of the ensemble had reached the depths of distrust, enmity and loathing. Worse was to come when Folland fell overboard between Fiji and Honolulu. There were doubts about whether this was an accident or suicide. For a self-centred woman Lola behaved admirably, selling her jewellery to benefit his children.[28] She was genuinely distraught, and sought comfort in spiritualism and mysticism for the last five years of her life. She never regained her insouciance and rebelliousness from this point.

Lola's career as an actor and dancer faltered. As she had done previously, she reinvented herself as a public speaker on topics such as beauty, the evils of Catholicism, and the women and wits of Paris, which included her old lover Alexandre Dumas. These lectures appear in her slim second autobiography.[29] Lola was greatly assisted in these endeavours by the Reverend Charles Chauncey Burr, with whom she had developed an unlikely friendship. Her advice on beauty, hair, deportment, diet and exercise showed her to be ahead of her times in its sensible instruction. One sad incident occurred in late 1857 when Lola, the great sexual temptress and lover, was duped publicly by Prince Ludwig Sulkowski, whom she went to France to meet, hoping for another marriage.[30] He was a married man with a family and this hoax was mere sport.

In November 1858 Lola and the Burr family went to Ireland to promote her lectures, where Lola had not been since her marriage in 1839. *The Times* on 16 January 1859 gave a full coverage to her lectures on American values and society. Returning to London and attempting to re-establish herself, Lola fell into debt trying to maintain an extravagant lifestyle. Leaving creditors baying, she fled to New York City, where she became increasingly interested in the reformation of prostitutes. She began attending the Methodist Church, now a repentant sinner and public reformer. Her last two years were spent in poverty and reflection on sins of the flesh. After a series of strokes and paralysis, Lola died on 17 January 1861, leaving money to the Magdalene Society. Her tombstone reads 'Mrs. Eliza Gilbert, died 17 January 1861 aged 42'. In her inscription there was just that modicum of truth she had so effectively eluded in life.

Lola Montez is fondly remembered in Australia. The Sovereign Hill Museum in Ballarat, in its proud retelling of the history of the gold rushes, features posters of her performances. The Australian Elizabethan Theatre Trust in Sydney, established in the post-World War II era to promote Australian high culture firmly following American and British trends, debuted a locally written musical about

Lola Montez on 22 October 1958. The national tour showed that Australian audiences were receptive to local material. Written by Alan Burke and Peter Benjamin with music by Peter Stannard, the musical sought to inspire Australian creative talents to engage with Australian culture.[31] Lola would no doubt have been amused to learn that a century after her sad, lonely death her life story was venerated as a vehicle of high culture.

CHAPTER 5

Ellen Tremaye
(Edward De Lacy Evans)
(1838–1901)

Marion ('Bill') Edwards
(1874–1956)

The women who challenged the gender order and became men.

Colonial Australia was a repressive place for women. With little formal education and few opportunities to earn a living beyond domestic service, bartending, prostitution and, later, factory and retail work, women were mostly constrained within the bonds of marriage and motherhood. Without inherited money, they could hope for little independence and autonomy. Yet some women broke the mould completely, choosing to forsake the rigid and restrictive gender roles and live as men. In the late nineteenth and early years of the twentieth centuries, Victorians Marion (Bill) Edwards and Ellen Tremaye lived, worked and wed as men. As Edward De Lacy Evans, Ellen entered into formal marriages not just once, but on three occasions.

This was not a case of cross-dressing or transvestism, but an entire gender realignment. In the late 1870s, when her story became public, Evans was the most notorious woman-man in the Australian colonies. Regarded as a medical freak to be studied and pitied, she was the subject of extensive newspaper speculation. Presented as a type of vanilla pornography, with its coded messages and seemingly bizarre practices, her case encouraged a furtive curiosity in unconventional sexualities and identities. Her former workmates, neighbours, shipmates and casual acquaintances volunteered their stories for publication in the newspapers. A modern celebrity, as we now know it, was created through the colonial press.

Marion (Bill) Edwards, on the other hand, was a cheeky larrikin who never suffered Evans' humiliations. Funny and resourceful, Edwards negotiated gender identities at will, with flair and a keen eye for publicity.

There were notorious cases in the colony earlier in the nineteenth century of women dressing and working as men, for convenience rather than identity. Catherine Henrys (c.1805–55), commonly known as Jemmy the Rover, was an Irishwoman from Sligo, transported to Van Diemen's Land in 1835 for stealing and robbery with violence. Assigned to haberdasher John Swan in Hobart in 1836, after unruly and disruptive behaviour she was returned to the Female Factory where she was put on bread and water for six days. Her next assignments were in rural areas but they were no more successful. At one stage in 1837, Henrys was assigned to Aboriginal Protector George Augustus Robinson on Flinders Island Aboriginal Reserve. Absconding from various masters, Henrys took to the bush, where she lived and worked as a man. She joined several male fugitives, though it is not clear whether they were bushrangers (like Michael Howe and Mary Cockerill in the 1810s). Attempts to incarcerate her failed. On several occasions Henrys escaped from custody with great initiative and aplomb. The *Launceston Examiner* remarked that this 'notorious woman' had a reputation as a pugilist and 'her masculine appearance was quite in keeping with her character'.[1] Henrys was an aggressive, combative personality who enjoyed the freedom bestowed by men's occupations and attire. Unlike Tremaye, she did not consider herself a man trapped in a woman's body.

Kitty Gallagher was another convict who dressed and worked as a man, though again she did not consider herself one. Born in rural Ireland in 1770s, Gallagher was a rebel leader in the White Boys, a terrorist agrarian organisation with Roman Catholic members. Formed in 1759 to protest against the enclosure of common lands, these activists joined the wider insurrection in 1798 when the Irish, with the help of French revolutionaries, attempted to overthrow English rule in Ireland.[2] Kitty and her husband, Frank Gallagher, were transported to New South Wales for their part in the so-called Wexford Rebellion. They later established a small cattle farm at Scone where they were attacked by bushrangers in 1839. Using her military skills, Kitty fought them off with muskets. After Frank's death she worked on pastoralist Henry Dangar's station droving cattle. Dressed as a working man, and armed with pistols, she smoked a clay pipe. Local historian William Telfer recalled 'this Amazon when i [sic] was a little boy in the year 1844'.[3] Her rural skills were considerable, especially her use of the plough. She died at the age of ninety-six.[4]

Ellen Tremaye, or Tremayne as she was frequently called in newspaper accounts, represents an altogether different category of women dressing and working as men. This was not for convenience and comfort in the process of undertaking hard manual work; rather, the male attire, haircut, masculine deportment and modes of speech were manifestations of her preference to live as a man with all the privileges it bestowed. Her life was filled with excitement, joy, disappointment, humiliation and public exposure, for she was psychologically a man trapped in a woman's body.

We know little about her early life or what brought her to migrate to Victoria just after the gold rushes, but she was most likely born in Waterford in Ireland in 1838 and came to Victoria in 1856 as a domestic servant.[5] On board the *Ocean Monarch*, other passengers later recalled that she was a strange young woman, dressed every day in an outfit of a sealskin coat over a green calico dress and men's undergarments. This was quite a feat given that voyages took many weeks through hot equatorial regions to reach the Australian colonies. Her luggage was marked 'Edward De Lacy Evans'. This name and the persona it implies – male, well connected and fancy – shows that Ellen had already begun to turn herself into Edward. To the other passengers it meant something else. Perhaps the person, Edward De Lacy Evans, who owned the unescorted luggage was the fiancé or brother of Miss Tremaye.

Certainly, rural Ireland in the 1850s was hardly a tolerant society conducive to gender realignments and grandiose fantasies. Eccentricity was for grand urban people in London and Paris. Tremaye's desire to become a man was, however, strong and undisguised on the voyage out. Remarkably, Tremaye shared her bunk with two women at various times en route to Melbourne. Though it was common for steerage passengers to be housed in close and cramped sex-segregated quarters, it was highly improper for two women to share the intimacy of a bunk. On board, Tremaye publicly declared her intention of marrying fellow passenger Mary Delahunty, an older educated woman who initially recorded her occupation as governess. Most of the female immigrants were illiterate or barely literate domestic servants, making Delahunty stand out as an educated lady by comparison.[6] One account by Miss Wain, a fellow passenger, reported that before the vessel left Portsmouth, Tremaye was anxiously awaiting a companion, whom they assumed was a man.[7] This suggests Delahunty and Tremaye may have known each other before embarkation and intended to 'marry', safe in the knowledge that they were unknown in the colonies.

When Ellen/Edward was exposed in the newspapers in late 1879, the accounts were sympathetic to her situation, speculating on her decision to leave Ireland. As one account ventured to suggest, she was an unmarried mother who decided to 'face the world and adopted the masculine garb for her better protection and support'.[8] This is an unlikely scenario; most unmarried mothers did not pursue the option of male disguise to hide their shame and later marry three women.

On disembarkation, Tremaye went to work as a domestic servant, initially at Melton, before she returned to Melbourne following her reinvention as Edward De Lacy Evans. Perhaps she began to experiment with this total gender inversion in Melton, for there she often slept with the publican's wife 'for company' when the husband was away on business. The publican, however, took a horsewhip to this interloper in his marital bed.[9]

It was at this point that Ellen decided to entirely relinquish her feminine appearance, denoted by clothes, hairstyle and demeanour, to become her alter ego, Edward Evans. She had constructed a grand lineage: the nephew of General De Lacy Evans, and scion of a wealthy French family.[10] Assuming grand identities was not uncommon in the colonies, where people could easily reinvent themselves. Whether others believed them was another matter. That Evans had no money, did not speak French, and was an uncultured person would indicate the identity was somewhat questionable.

Edward De Lacy Evans in 1879 dressed in both male and female attire. Photo: Nicholas White; State Library of Victoria H96.160/147.

Evans married Delahunty in Melbourne at St Francis' Catholic Church, but the marriage was not a success. Clearly, Delahunty knew Evans' real identity and circumstances and yet went along with the marriage.

It is also intriguing to consider why Evans and Delahunty returned to the district where he had worked as a female domestic servant before the horsewhipping incident saw him flee. Clearly he was known and recognised when he returned with a 'bride'. Perhaps colonial Victorians were more tolerant than might be assumed. Often people had fled their home countries and cities to forge out new identities and make new lives. Even so, gender realignment was not on the conventional list of personal transformations.

Certainly there was local gossip and scandal. Mr Ready, who had worked with Evans in 1857, recalled that he used to tease Evans and say he was a 'girl', as he had no facial hair. Evans flew into a 'passion' when called Polly and chased his tormentor with a knife. Perhaps this man thought Polly was a young homosexual. The informant also said he called Evans 'Mollie' and 'Mary Anne', slang terms used to identify gay men, though these terms were usually employed within the gay community.[11] The term 'homosexual' had not yet been invented; 'sodomite' was the more usual name. Yet clearly Edward Evans was not at all interested sexually in his miner workmates. Thus they no doubt assumed he was an effeminate man.

The marriage to Delahunty failed and Delahunty embarked on an open affair with a mining surveyor, Lyman Oatman Hart, scandalising the local district in Blackwood, but laughing it off by stating her 'husband' was really a woman. We may speculate why no widespread scandal erupted at this time. The case of a woman marrying another woman, one who was living and working as a man, and the other a supposed married woman conducting an illicit affair, had all the elements of a good international scandal. In 1862 Delahunty took the bold step of marrying Lyman Hart and moved to Daylesford.[12]

In 1862 Evans married again, in Sandhurst, declaring he was a widower. Like him, Sarah Moore was an Irish domestic servant. When Evans ran into a woman he had known in Ireland he begged her not to reveal his secret. Thinking that this might be concerning his sex, this woman was surprised to find out that Evans feared exposure to his second wife as originally a Roman Catholic who had changed religion to the Protestant faith.[13] In a society where sectarianism was rife, this was a real fear. Exposure as a woman married twice to women would seem to us to be far more compelling in its gravity than embracing Protestantism.

When Mr Ready moved from Melton to Blackwood and encountered Evans with his second wife, he remarked in the press later that Evans '… got into a huge rage, and threatened to kill his wife' when his wife realised he was a woman in disguise. The likelihood that the second Mrs Evans, Sarah Moore, had not realised she was married to a woman in men's clothing is implausible, even accepting the naivety and innocence of many women in the late nineteenth century. Little is known of this relationship and Moore died in 1867.

In 1863, however, a year after his marriage to Sarah Moore, Evans undertook a third marriage. This time to a pretty Frenchwoman, Julia Marquand, a dressmaker who had been friends with Moore's sister. Evans told Marquand he was a French widower from a rich family, though why she did not reject him with this obvious deceit is hard to fathom.[14] Not only did she know he was not French, a widower or wealthy, let alone a man, she went along for over a decade with the masquerade. This third marriage was not amicable, with frequent arguments and separations. Evans often left in search of well-paid work as a miner. The State Library of Victoria in Melbourne contains a curious photograph of the young couple; Evans is a short man in a three-piece suit, one hand jauntily in his pocket and the other in the conventional pose of protection on his wife's shoulder. Marquand is a tiny woman in a day dress with a brooch at her throat. An opened book lies in her right hand, indicating symbolically she is a cultured and educated woman.

Edward De Lacy Evans with Julia Marquand in a very traditional pose, around 1871. Photo: Aaron Flegeltaub; State Library of Victoria H29406.

In 1872 the couple reconciled after a split. Then in 1877 Marquand gave birth to a baby whom she named Julia Mary, after her mother. Clearly Evans was not the father. In a spectacular court case in 1879, Marquand charged her brother-in-law with failure to provide maintenance for his illegitimate child. Marquand had lived with her sister and brother-in-law, Jean Baptiste Loridan. He had 'seduced her' while Evans was away working. The affair had apparently continued for several months until Marquand found she was pregnant. Loridan had pursued his sister-in-law since she was a child, Marquand told the court in December 1879. He held enormous power in Marquand and Evans' lives, as he owned the Great Southern Mine where Evans worked. Loridan had also given them money for the house in which they lived.[15]

Even stranger was Evans' confession in his declaration in court that 'I am hurted', and that he had watched the couple in bed on many occasions from a back window. This destructive emotional voyeurism damaged Evans for the rest of his life. The whole scenario was full of humiliation for Evans, for now he was forced to reappear as Tremaye dressed in women's attire. Worse, Marquand described herself as a 'single woman', while Tremaye–Evans said, 'I know Julia Marquand. I used to live with her. She was stopping in the house with me.'[16] This is a sad and pathetic declaration after so many years of marriage, however stormy and unstable.

Evans had endured a nervous breakdown and had been admitted as an insane patient to hospital a few months before the maintenance case. When he was 'outed' as a woman, the colonial press had a field day of titillating and racy revelations, dubbing the affair the case of the 'male personator'. The *Hobart Mercury* of 29 September 1879 kept Tasmanians up to date on revelations. Likewise the *West Australian* of 19 September 1879 regaled readers with this strange case in Sandhurst. They noted Evans was simply not physically capable of the hard manual work of a miner. He was constantly teased about his 'effeminate appearance' and lack of strength by fellow workers. Often he was seen 'ruminating' after the birth of the baby.[17] As an Adelaide journalist wrote on Evans' death in August 1901, 'From that time, Evans was not to speak the same man … no heart in her work'.[18]

In hospital, Evans refused to eat and was threatened with force-feeding by the matron of Bendigo Hospital, Mrs Holt. Given only women's clothing to wear, Evans refused to dress and was thus forced to stay immobilised in bed. Transferred to Kew Lunatic Asylum for refusal to resume his biological and cultural identity as a female, Evans supposedly suffered from 'cerebral mania'. The symptoms of this vague disease were apparently 'her' mistaken belief she could become a man and marry women. Doctors were confident that this was not a permanent condition and could be cured quite rapidly.[19]

The following year the *Australian Medical Journal* provided a report by Dr Penfold who conducted an examination of Evans. It makes painful reading, as the doctor described how he probed Evans' vagina, while he was 'weeping and sobbing the whole time, but making no determined resistance'.[20] His genitals were described as 'shrunken' and 'childlike'. The whole tone of the article demonstrates an intense psychological violence as well as physical pain inflicted upon the 'male personator'. As a physician in Melbourne, Penfold had come to the hospital specifically to examine the 'freak'.[21]

Evans, now forced to reassume his identity as Ellen Tremaye, attended the maintenance hearing where he declared how he felt 'hurted'. The rest of his life was filled with sadness. The colonial magazine *The Bulletin* on 25 September 1880 contained an article about the man-woman on display in the Egyptian Hall. Sitting on a packing case in a shapeless dress, this figure looked bored except when tormented by small boys. This was hardly the beginnings of an enhanced career. He also was an exhibit in the Living Waxwork display in Bourke Street, again with a lack of success. This is unsurprising. People wanted to see a hermaphrodite, a strange creature existing in the space between the sexes. But all they saw was a defeated, middle-aged, masculine-looking, depressed woman. In February 1881 Evans applied for re-admission to the Lunatic Asylum in Melbourne, unable to find work or sustenance. As he was not insane, he was admitted instead to the Melbourne Immigrants Home where he remained for the next twenty years. This operated like an English workhouse which only the most indigent would enter. Now living as a woman, she refused to use the name of Ellen Tremaye and preferred to be called Mrs De Lacy Evans.[22] In her numerous obituaries around Australia in 1901, she was called Mrs De Lacy Evans. An uneasy amalgam of her various identities. She assumed the persona of a married woman in the title 'Mrs', yet attached it to her male persona of De Lacy Evans.

Marion Edwards presents a different style of cross-dresser – flamboyant, jaunty and keen for publicity. Born in 1871 in Murchison, Victoria, to a Welsh father, John Edwards, and a Scottish mother, Margaret

McKay, Marion claimed Welsh birth. She spent a lot of her youth at her uncle's farm on the Goulburn River, where she acquired many of her bush skills. In her picaresque memoir, *Life and Adventures of Marion-Bill-Edwards* (1907), she claimed to have refused several offers of marriage, a sensible move given her predilection for making 'hot love' to as many women as she could. In the mid 1890s she decided to take on a male persona, and dress and work like a man. Marion became Bill.[23]

On New Year's Day 1900, William Ernest Edwards married widow Lucy Minihan at St Francis' Catholic Church in Melbourne, the same church where Edward De Lacy Evans had married Mary Delahunty. As a widow, Lucy must have been aware that her new spouse was not a biological man. Marion–Bill Edwards later asserted in the colourful memoir that this was a marriage of convenience. This assertion begs more questions than it answers. Lucy was a small businesswoman with a boarding house and therefore did not need someone else's income. As

"MARION-BILL" EDWARDS.

Marion 'Bill' Edwards, as pictured in *Lone Hand*, 1 January 1908. State Library of Victoria MC_--MC 0529; 84.

a widow she had a respectable status in society. Was the convenience for Marion to firmly establish her masculine credentials as a married man? Whatever their motive for marriage, it did not last, though the two were good and loyal friends.

Their friendship was severely tested on 30 April 1905 when Bill, now a racehorse trainer, was arrested on a charge of burglary at the Studley Arms Hotel in Collingwood. His friend 'Jigger' Pollock was also arrested. Bill waited a week in the cells before contacting Lucy, who arranged his bail; Bill was now described as her 'boarder'. The considerable sum of £50 was posted as bail. When Bill failed to appear for his hearing, Lucy served a term of one month's imprisonment.[24] Assuming the name of William McKay – his mother's surname at birth – Bill skipped bail and went to Queensland. There he worked at many casual occupations before a former acquaintance informed the police that, not only was William McKay a fugitive from justice, but he was a woman. A media frenzy ensued with much publicity generated from the subsequent arraignments and trials.

'Billarion' was a particular hit in Brisbane and remains part of its contemporary folk culture. On 5 October 1906, the *Brisbane Courier* featured an article on 'Little Willie: or Billie the Girl-Man'. To the journalist, Bill was a fascinating, vibrant character: 'Wealthy girl, horse owner, roughrider, masquerader, alleged burglar, painter, varnisher, fighter, barman, yardman, labourer, and ingenious lover – all these roles she is rightly or wrongly credited with having filled' were listed as Little Willie's accomplishments. Even more astounding, the journalist went on to declare that '... two things stand out – the affection she has everywhere inspired, and to-day remains loyal to her when behind gaol doors, and the successful endeavour she has made to earn an honest living'. Brisbane women showered 'Little Willie' with gifts, *billets doux*, notes of support and affection. She was a role model they distinctly approved of in this highly male-dominated society. Her send-off back to the south from the wharves in Brisbane was spectacular, with a large adoring crowd of mostly women and girls waving and cheering.

To confuse her critics, Edwards turned up in female attire at the burglary trial in Melbourne.[25] Both Bill and 'Jigger' were found not guilty. Bill then found instant fame as a waxwork exhibit as 'The Far-famed Male Impersonator'. One incident nearly stopped dead this career – literally. As part of the show, Bill demonstrated his skills as a sharpshooter, and a member of the audience was accidently shot, though not seriously. If there was a time to persecute him it was now. Yet the press, quite enamoured of the Australian Annie Oakley or Calamity Jane, dismissed the incident at the entertainment venue Cylorama as a mere accident.[26] Bill's public revelations of the number of sexual affairs conducted with women drew interest rather than censure. The *Brisbane Courier* on 5 October 1906 had already signalled the press reaction to these confessions: 'She liked her own sex – and they liked her. In fact the girls ran after her, for she was a loveable man with nice ways …' Never was there a more damning indictment of Australian men's inadequacy in dealing with women's feelings and sexuality. On the other hand his former wife, now simply his boarding-house keeper, Lucy Minihan, told the *Truth* newspaper on 5 October 1906 that: 'As far as I know … EDWARDS IS A MAN. He has every appearance of a man and all the time I have known him I have taken him for a man.'[27] Supposedly to end confusion, Edwards granted an interview with the Melbourne *Herald*, published 18 October 1906, that simply created more speculation. When asked whether he preferred to be addressed as Bill or Marion, Edwards replied, 'Bill will do as well as Marion and Marion as well as Bill.' This gender play was taken as good fun, allowing the reader, then and now, to ponder the lines between identity, biology and cultural practices and conventions.

Edwards' autobiography has some correlations with Casanova's memoirs, though penned with far more delicacy, for it is largely an account of sexual conquests and affairs. There were stories of his days on the turf and of bar brawls, but largely it is a romantic and erotic journal. Cast often as flirtations, there is an ambiguity which requires the reader to add the details. The book garnered more attention for this folk hero.

The nationalistic magazine *Lone Hand*, of 1 January 1908, featured a long article, 'Marion Edwards. A Modern de Maupin', portraying Bill as an enterprising hero with a fluid sexuality and identity. The journalist Beatrix Tracey was a sympathetic recorder and interpreter of Bill's life. At one revealing point she reports Bill saying: 'I don't think the world is much of a place for women. They have the same tiresome graft day after day; the same tucker (what the old man and the kids can't eat!) … And no amusements. That sort of thing would have killed me if I'd fallen in to it.' Clearly, as Marion she had a very astute understanding of the limited lives most women endured, tied to the house and rearing many children. Unlike most of them, though, Edwards had fashioned an independent adventurous life on her own terms.

In 1916 Edwards was again charged with a criminal offence, this time for selling sly grog. The case hit the newspapers, but the court proceedings were far more concerned with sleeping arrangements in the house where Edwards lived than in the matter at hand. There are some hilarious moments in the case when the judge told co-accused Annie McClelland that he found it hard to believe she did not know if Edwards was a man or a woman, despite sharing a bed together. McClelland rather evasively replied: 'I never asked her.'[28] McClelland was found guilty and sent to prison, though here it might be inferred her conviction was for sexual deviance while the nation was at war, rather than criminal activity.

Bill fell off the newspapers' list of sensational characters after this case. *Smith's Weekly* of 3 September 1927 referred to his career as a horse and pony trainer in Melbourne. In men's clothes, Bill continued to work in foundries and as a bookmaker in Melbourne, though by this time he was getting too old for hard manual labour. He continued to wear men's clothes until the indignity of being forced to don women's bedclothes on his admittance to the Mount Royal Geriatric Home.

Edwards died in March 1956, described incorrectly on his death certificate as an actress. Edwards would have been both furious and amused after all the masquerade, charm, good humour and irreverence with which she conducted her life both as a man and as a woman. The 1984 play *In Male Attire*, staged at the St Martin's Theatre, Melbourne,[29] would have appealed to her good sense of humour and her unrivalled achievement as one of Australia's most notorious women.

CHAPTER 6

'Madame Brussels' Caroline Hodgson

(1851–1908)

The wealthy madam of Melbourne who catered for only the best gentlemen.

In the late nineteenth century, Australia's leading citizens went sex mad. In 1878 the eccentric Melbourne evangelist Henry Varley began a personal campaign against prostitution and other sexual transgressions. He published a book, *On the Social Evil*, and followed this in 1891 with *The War Between Heaven and Hell in Melbourne*. Madame Brussels, the famous owner of elite brothels in Melbourne from 1874 to 1908, who catered for the upper end of the sex trade – her clients were cabinet ministers and the wealthy men of property and business – was his personal bête noir.

With a high ratio of men to women in the colonies, late marriage was common and sex was often a commercial transaction. Without adequate contraception married women did not usually view sex with their husbands as a pleasure, rather as a path to conceiving children. And for respectable unmarried women, sex was unthinkable. Many men found these restrictions too limiting for their libidos. Streetwalking and hotels catering for prostitutes and their clients, alongside the brothels, were regular features in every town and city. For many women with few skills, education and opportunities, prostitution offered higher wages, greater freedom and a modicum of economic independence. For some, like Caroline Hodgson, an exclusive form of prostitution offered a lucrative income and friends in high places in Victorian society.

Born Caroline Lohman in 1851 in Potsdam, Prussia, little is known of her early life. Potsdam, 25 kilometres south-west of Berlin, was a sophisticated centre of culture and scientific endeavour, and the administrative centre of Prussia before German unification under Bismarck in 1870. A city of magnificent buildings, ornamental gardens and lakes, it offered a vibrant and refined way of life.

It is not known when Caroline left Prussia, but in 1871 she married Studholme Hodgson, the son of a wealthy and well-connected Hampshire landowner, in the registry office at Hanover Square in London.[1] The couple went straight to Melbourne after their wedding, arriving in July 1871, suggesting the union did not have the blessing of the groom's family. The following year Studholme Hodgson joined the Victorian police force and was sent to the country station of Mansfield. Here he was appointed sergeant, a surprisingly low rank for a man of his background.[2]

A country posting was hardly the life for a well-educated, cosmopolitan young woman like Caroline. Horrified at the thought of living in a rural hamlet far away from cultural pursuits and talented people, Caroline did not accompany Studholme to Mansfield, and the marriage was over by 1873, although they remained on amicable terms until Studholme's death in 1893.

In 1874, Caroline began running her first exclusive brothel in the red-light district of central Melbourne, at 32–34 Lonsdale Street. The streets between Bourke and La Trobe, bordered by Spring and Stephen (now Exhibition) streets contained many types of venues for commercial sex, from hovels to the luxurious surroundings of the establishment of Madame Brussels, as Caroline Hodgson was known professionally.[3] At the lower end of the thriving market, conditions for both the workers and clients were dire, but at the exclusive end of the market Madame Brussels offered a heavenly retreat.

Caroline's establishment viewed from the outside was 'discrete rather than stately', an unpretentious villa screened by lattice enclosing a beautiful manicured garden.[4] A private entrance off Little Lonsdale Street allowed special clients with a key to keep their comings and goings quiet. The well connected and wealthy used this method in preference to the more public entrance.

The interior of Madame Brussels' establishment resembled a grand French bordello with marble bathrooms, carpets 'like meadow grass' and lavish furnishings in ebony, buhl and ormolu, alongside marble and alabaster statues of buxom women. Erotic though tasteful paintings adorned the walls. For particularly favoured and affluent clients, the grand boudoir boasted a large rococo bed 'canopied like an Imperial Throne', for services costing the extraordinary sum of £2000.[5]

There is no direct evidence that Caroline worked as a courtesan before she opened her brothel. It is, however, unusual for a madam not to have worked in the industry first before going into the organisational and managerial aspects of the business. As a young woman Caroline was breathtakingly beautiful and graceful, described as 'a magnificent pink, white and golden-maned animal'.[6] She did not accompany her husband to Mansfield yet, in those two intervening years, she gathered sufficient capital, cash flow and contacts to establish a successful 'gentlemen's club'. Some of the money came from parliamentarian and solicitor Sir Samuel Gillott, who financed her mortgage in 1877. He was also Caroline's solicitor and went surety for her mortgages on her first establishment.

How Caroline obtained the pseudonym 'Madame Brussels' is speculative. Cyril Pearl, in his *Wild Men of Sydney* (1958), proposed that she was originally married to a Belgian engineer who came to work in Melbourne.[7] This is not correct. Madame Brussels does have, however, a far more enticing Francophile ring to it than Madame Prussia or Madame Potsdam, and it suggests an exotic background, a synthesis between French and Belgian cultures.

With the huge land boom in the 1870s and '80s and a fluid population of literate, highly skilled men, there was money to be made in the sex industry. Not that Caroline would have employed such a crude and unvarnished term. Rather, her establishments offered affluent, often married gentlemen, whether in the pastoral, commerce, legal or parliamentary fraternities, a taste of high French frivolity with beautiful, well-mannered, well-educated young women in opulent surroundings. The best quality champagne and food was served in the evenings, and for those gentlemen who stayed overnight, a hearty breakfast of bacon, eggs and coffee was provided. Guests could stay for a week if they chose. One wealthy western districts pastoralist, after a large sale, spent a week there at a cost of £150, the equivalent of eighteen months' wage for a skilled workman.

By the end of the 1870s, Madame Brussels owned the finest, most exclusive establishment in Melbourne and perhaps the whole of Australia. She soon owned eight brothels, and two houses purchased for £1300. These businesses employed over thirty carefully chosen women, some of whom went on to be the mistress or, it was rumoured, the wife of a client.[8] Caroline took over her pre-eminent position from Sarah Fraser, who had entertained Prince Alfred, the Duke of Edinburgh, on his visit to Melbourne in 1867. Mother Fraser, as Sarah was known, had a brothel in Stephen Street that was luxurious and discrete. The Prince had been introduced to the brothel by none other than the Chief Commissioner of Police, Frederick Standish, thus allowing Fraser to capitalise on royal patronage. With the 1880–81 International Exhibition held in Melbourne, Stephen Street – adjacent to the exhibition buildings – was sanitised with a new name and the brothels relocated.[9] There were also other salubrious and well-appointed establishments operating in suburbs such as St Kilda.[10]

Unlike Madame Brussels' operation, other forms of prostitution were crude and highly visible. The investigative journalist John Stanley James, 'The Vagabond', wrote extensively of Melbourne's demimonde. He meticulously described the 'saddling paddock' in the Theatre Royal where '[t]heir startling dresses and painted faces, without reference to their manner, stamp them as lorettes ... a positive nuisance and annoyance' during theatre performances as 'they flounce in and out of the stalls ...'[11] In this bar, the prostitutes were watched over by their pimps or 'cads'. James noted that in Paris or Berlin by the 1880s a gentleman might take his wife or daughters to the theatre and 'sit next to a notorious member of the demimonde and not know it'. There, courtesans were refined and discrete, though well known to gentlemen. In Melbourne their behaviour was far more audacious. One writer to the *Herald* of 14 August 1882, using the *nom de plume* 'A Mother', stated that at a theatrical performance the prostitutes offered 'winks, nods, and sly glances ... and speaking to every gentleman that passed, including those accompanied by ladies'.[12]

Madame Brussels' establishments stood out as the undisputed pinnacle of the vast network of the demimonde for over thirty years. Her clients came from the elite of Victorian society. The location of her central business in Lonsdale Street ensured easy availability to parliamentarians and cabinet ministers, able to meet in convivial surroundings. Caroline lived at the centre of political influence, albeit in a circumscribed and private way. No doubt her well-born first husband, now a member of the Victorian police force, was an entry card into police protection, but this did not stop her from being charged with brothel keeping in the 1890s, to which she was found not guilty.[13] In itself it was unusual for an elegant and well-connected madam to appear in court. The police usually hounded the older women and those on the street or in the 'saddling paddock'.[14] Her appearance may have been more a reaction to the public campaign against vice being mounted by the newspapers than about a conviction.

Associations with Madame Brussels sometimes proved dangerous for public figures. Solicitor David Gaunson, who acted for Caroline in addition to Samuel Gillott, was not the type you would expect to be taking care of a madam's legal affairs. His father, Francis Gaunson, was an elder in Dr John Dunmore Lang's Scots Church in Sydney.

In 1869 Gaunson began practising as a solicitor in Victoria, entering parliament in 1875 as a progressive Liberal aligned with the Premier, Graham Berry. Engaged as defence counsel for Ned Kelly, he was a leading force behind the petition supporting clemency for Kelly. Yet his argumentative and combative personality, along with suggestions he accepted bribes, tarnished his reputation. His position as Madame Brussels' solicitor did little to improve his public image. Depicted as Garside in Frank Hardy's novel *Power Without Glory* (1950), the gambling baron John Wren's legal adviser, Gaunson's shady reputation endured.[15] He had wandered far from his stern Presbyterian upbringing into the dens of iniquity and sin.

Caroline's name had already been attached to a parliamentary scandal in October 1891. In newspaper reports it was revealed that the mace of the Victorian parliament was removed illegally and taken to a bordello where MPs satirised parliamentary procedures in a lewd and undignified parody. A parliamentary enquiry later suggested it was not in one of Madame Brussels' brothels but in her rival Annie Wilson's house of assignation – Boccaccio. However, the press continued to point the finger towards the infamous Madame Brussels' establishment.[16]

An astute businesswoman who ran her empire with Prussian efficiency, Caroline still found time to enjoy her private life. In 1894 she returned to Germany and met Jacob Pohl, whom she married in December 1895 at St Patrick's Cathedral in Melbourne. By this time, Caroline was matronly in appearance, wearing gold-rimmed spectacles, and described as 'looking like a benevolent midwife'.[17] Like her first marriage, this one did not last, and they were divorced in 1906.

She also had a long-term affair with the composer Alfred Plumpton. The music director of St Patrick's Cathedral in Melbourne, Plumpton was an unlikely choice for a brothel madam. His international music career involved co-producing Gilbert and Sullivan's *Trial by Jury* with Howard Vernon in Singapore in 1876, he was the music critic for *The*

Age, and he composed the highly regarded Mass in G for the cathedral in 1881.[18] Apart from sacred music, he also composed popular tunes and light music. It was rumoured that together they had a daughter, Irene Hodgson, shortly before Plumpton's death in 1902 and while Caroline was married to Jacob Pohl. In a nasty exposé on 31 October 1903 *Truth* newspaper alleged that Madame Brussels kept Plumpton's photograph on her grand piano. 'When a female child was born the event was celebrated with a great orgie [sic]. All the "bloods" around town were invited and ... the child was "christened" in champagne and named "Syphilia".'

No birth certificate for Irene has been discovered. Caroline frequently called Irene her 'adopted daughter', including in her will. Referring to illegitimate children as 'adopted' was a common stratagem, especially when the mother was engaged in nefarious activities. It also prevented the child suffering the label of bastard. Managing to avoid the usual pitfalls of illegitimacy, Irene was well looked after by Caroline. She lived in the expensive suburb of St Kilda and was educated at an exclusive private school.

But times were changing for Madame Brussels. At the turn of the twentieth century, the rise of sensational newspapers such as *Truth*, with its determined manifesto to uncover and denounce sin and scandal, meant that the topic of illicit sex dominated the newspapers. However veiled the terms, the astute reader could be assured of titillating revelations and salacious exposés. John Norton, the editor and owner of *Truth* since 1896, not only attacked wowsers – a term he claimed to have invented and popularised – but also the objects of the wowsers' ire. Thus he had it both ways in moral debates. A campaign with such headlines as 'The Central Cattle Pen' and 'Unhappy Women Herded in Stinking Sty' put brothel keepers of all levels on notice.[19] And it did not exclude those like Caroline who catered for the crème de la crème.

In 1904–06 Norton was a councillor in the Flinders ward of the Sydney Municipal Council, winning the seat of Surry Hills in the

New South Wales Legislative Assembly. He had already exposed the operations of the Wind Club in George Street, Sydney, where worldly men met in a luxurious brothel, protected by police.[20] Not content with his Sydney domain, he set his eyes on a larger Victorian target for his next campaign. On 1 December 1906, *Truth*, under the headline 'Lechery and Lucre', directly addressed Sir Samuel Gillott, former Attorney General and Melbourne Lord Mayor, in the form of a letter accusing him of bankrolling brothels. A week later, more damaging allegations were printed concerning his professional alliance with Madame Brussels and her extensive empire of sin. To these allegations Gillott naively replied that he had been unaware of what sort of business she conducted on the various premises.[21] On 10 April 1907, *Truth* widened its concerns to include the relationship of brothel keepers and the police. Like Gaunson, Gillott had had dealings with John Wren, and in May 1906 was implicated in a gambling scandal and virulently attacked by the demagogue William Jenkins.[22] Deeply embarrassed, Gillott left the country soon afterwards.

The press offensive, along with these public outcries, resulted in the introduction of the *Police Offences Act* in 1907, whereby brothel keepers could be jailed and landlords who provided them with premises fined. This type of legislation had existed in the United Kingdom since 1885, but the colonial parliaments had been reluctant to take it on. By 1907 Caroline was seriously ill with diabetes and pancreatitis, and she closed everything. She died the following year and was buried next to her first husband, Studholme Hodgson, in St Kilda cemetery.

The era of the luxurious and decadent demimonde vanished with Madame Brussels' demise. In his autobiography, *The Pleasant Career of a Spendthrift* (1929), bohemian stockbroker George Meudell lamented the passing of the 'love palaces and their habitués. Where are they today? Gradually the Puritans annexed the money and power in the community ... and the joyousness of Melbourne night life was saliently squelched ...'[23]

CHAPTER 7

Helena Rubinstein
(1872–1965)

*The poor Polish girl who established a global beauty empire in
Melbourne and got ladies into make-up.*

Helena Rubinstein, one of the most talented and successful
businesswomen of the twentieth century, transformed women's
appearance through her cosmetics and skin-care products. It would
be fair to say that, along with fashion designer Gabrielle 'Coco'
Chanel, she crafted the appearance of the modern Western woman.
Her dictum that women needed to 'find themselves',[1] not just through
the products and beauty regimes she developed, but as autonomous
individuals, was revolutionary, and one that she practised herself.

The woman we know as Helena Rubinstein was born on Christmas
Day in 1872, in Krakow, Poland, then part of the Austro-Hungarian
Empire.[2] In her autobiography she describes her family as 'well to
do', residing in the charming medieval section of Krakow near the
university. She maintained that her grandfathers were wealthy mining
magnates and that her father 'had a passion for bibelots, antiques
and books', interests reminiscent of her cultivated and urbane first
husband, Edward Titus, a dealer in rare books. The reality reveals an
entirely different scenario.

Helena's birth name was Chaja, which she later anglicised to Helena.
Her father, Hertzel Rubinstein, was a modest kerosene dealer with no
business acumen. Her mother, Gitel Silberfeld, bore twelve children, four
of whom died in infancy. Helena's parents were not legally married. They

had undertaken the Jewish religious ceremony 'under the huppah', but had not legitimised their union in a civil service. They lived in the poor Jewish section of the ancient city.[3]

In her book, Helena states that she attended the local gymnasium, an elite secondary school, in preparation for entry into medical training at the University of Krakow – Copernicus' old university. Her assertion that she fainted on the first day of lessons in the operating theatre lacks credibility, as women were not admitted for medical courses to this university at this period, but it was a fabrication that established her claim to have been highly trained in modern science.

Some time in her teens, Chaja fell in love with a university student called Stanislaw, much to the horror of her parents who wished her to marry within the local Jewish community. With family tensions running high, Chaja left to live with her more sympathetic aunt, Rosalie Silberfeld Beckmann, never to return to her parents' home or secure their approval.[4] She later went to live with another aunt, Helena Silberfeld Splitter, in Austria. This Silberfeld sister had married well, her husband being a prosperous furrier. When the Splitters relocated to Belgium, Chaja decided to try her luck with another family who by this time had immigrated to Victoria.

Travelling as a 'tourist', 'Helena Juliet Rubinstein' left Genoa for Melbourne in 1896. 'I felt life in that part of the world sounded much more promising than in Krakow,' she declared in her autobiography. Already the romantic version of her life story was being constructed in her mind, with her Australian family branch described as wealthy, cultured people. Again the reality was rather different. Helena was headed for Coleraine, a small settlement some 300 kilometres west of Melbourne, where her uncle, Louis Silberfeld, owned the local grocery store.[5] Life in rural Victoria at the end of the nineteenth century would have been challenging for young Helena, who had no interest in rural pursuits, the weather and sheep prices – the usual topics of conversation – but she settled in and learned English, which she spoke forever with an exotic Polish accent.

Taking in her new surrounds, Helena was struck by the women of Coleraine with their 'sun-scorched, wind-burned cheeks'.[6] Helena abhorred the sun, which she rightly believed destroyed a woman's fresh complexion. By no means a beauty, she looked gorgeous compared to the women around her, with her exquisite complexion of clear white skin and her thick, glossy black hair. Petite, with a high forehead and upright posture, she was an imposing figure in her youth and later appeared fabulously gowned and bedecked in exotic jewellery as she prospered.

Helena claimed she also brought twelve pots of face cream from Europe with her, 'the cornerstone of my life', and it is possible she obtained some from her family in Poland to sell in Coleraine. Lindy Woodhead points out in her account of Helena Rubinstein that it was quite usual for Central European families to have their own recipes for protective creams, which they would have made at home.[7] Whether Helena could have obtained the ingredients in Coleraine is not clear, but as a merino sheep-raising area Coleraine abounded in one ingredient she would later use with great success: lanolin.

Any business projects which Helena was conducting, however, were interrupted when she moved to Queensland around 1900. Why she left Coleraine we do not know, although she later confided to her secretary, the urbane Patrick O'Higgins, that her uncle 'took liberties' with her, prompting her to flee.[8]

It is possible Helena first worked with the well-connected Fairburn family at Meltham, near Geelong in Victoria, and that this was where she was invited by a friend who worked with Lord Lamington, the Governor of Queensland, to join his staff.[9] Accepting the position, she moved to Toowoomba where she supposedly acted as governess and language tutor in French and German to the Lamington children. As the children were infants and Helena had not learned French at this time, the story seems doubtful, but having lived in Vienna, she did have the rudiments of German.[10] It is more likely that she worked as a nurserymaid in Toowoomba, where the Lamington family often resided to escape the heat of the coast. Helena had assisted in the care of her numerous siblings and although later a stern mother to her own two sons, she had a good rapport with children all her life. She perhaps felt children did not judge her as more worldly, sophisticated adults might do. Whatever the case, within the Lamington household, Helena had the opportunity to observe the aristocracy in the colonies at close quarters and gather material on etiquette and manners which she later used purposefully.[11]

After leaving the Lamingtons' employment, following Lord Lamington's appointment as Governor of Bombay in late 1901, Helena went to Melbourne in 1902 where she first worked at the Café Doré, followed by the Winter Garden tea rooms, frequented by the city's bohemians. Her start in cosmetics in a big way came from John Thompson, the manager of the Robur Tea Company, whom she met at the Winter Garden, and a supposed shipboard acquaintance, a Miss MacDonald, who loaned her money.[12] They may have regretted later that they did not invest more heavily in her beauty salons and products! With the arrival of her sister Ceska in Melbourne, the stage was set to put the pieces into place.

With all the attention Helena had received for her skin, and given her presumable knowledge of family or folk recipes, it was perhaps natural for her to venture into beauty products, but establishing a commercial enterprise took real pluck. Helena was assisted substantially by John Thompson, whose eye for advertising and publicity was modern and aggressive. It is possible that they were lovers, although sexual liaisons were never a priority for Helena at any time in her life. She was also aided by the sponsor of her naturalisation application for British citizenship (as was the practice in Australia at that time), Frederick Sheppard Grimwade, the proprietor of a pharmaceutical manufacturing company. From his company she may have obtained distilled pycnogenol from Australian pine bark. Helena later claimed she had been given the original ingredients of her skin protector in Poland through the actress Modjeska, a patient of a supposedly famous Hungarian chemist, Dr Jacob Lykusky. Whatever their source, she adapted the basic ingredients of oil of almonds and pine bark extract with Australian products and the resulting Crème Valaze became the mainstay of her business.

Originally Crème Valaze was a versatile potion for both cleansing and moisturising the skin. With the addition of peroxide, the preparation was advertised as also assisting in the bleaching of freckles. Zinc oxide provided another agent to whiten women's skin.[13] There were already respected cosmetic products on the market, such as Theron Pond's Golden Treasure, launched in 1846 in upstate New York, followed later by his cold cream in 1905, alongside many products of dubious origin. But it was Crème Valaze that began the modern facial product business, luxuriously packaged and fragrant, replete with promises of transformation.

In 1903 Helena rented rooms in 138 Elizabeth Street in Melbourne, where she provided skin treatments and products. Originally she advertised her product as the work of 'Dr Lykusky, most celebrated European Skin Specialist ...'[14] Protection of her product by patent, along with considerable press attention, resulted in the business taking off with extraordinary flair. However, a few mistruths were perpetrated in the advertisements. There were no rare herbs from the Carpathian Mountains, for example. Yet the product, in small glass bottles with tasteful labels, looked and smelt appealing and nourishing – just the luxury women needed to keep their faces fresh and smooth in the harsh Australian climate.[15] An early client, the famous actress Nellie Stewart, followed by the opera singer Dame Nellie Melba, lent endorsement to Valaze,[16] a marketing technique Helena perfected and used all her long career.

Helping to run the salon was her sister Ceska. Helena claimed in her autobiography that Ceska had studied chemistry with the famed Professor Joseph Kapp in Berlin, but Ceska had no more formal education than Helena, though she was an astute business manager and she ran the Melbourne salons for many decades.[17] Another of Helena's untrue claims was that Dr Lykusky himself came to Australia to assist her. Perhaps it was the chemists at Frederick Sheppard Grimwade's company who assisted in the scientific formulations of the product, but Helena was also an astute observer and practical researcher. She devised the system – now commonly used – of dividing women's skin into normal, oily and dry categories, each requiring different treatments. Later 'combination' and 'mature' formulations were added.

In early 1905 Helena left Melbourne and headed for Europe, where she briefly visited her mother in Krakow. Her mother may not have been pleased to see her 33-year-old daughter still unmarried and now embarked on a career in business. Whatever happened, the visit was cut short, with Helena claiming in her autobiography that she had to leave to undertake studies in dermatology in Paris with one Dr Berthalot and a Frau Dr Emmie List in Vienna.[18] She also visited a Dr Kapp at an exclusive spa at Wiesbaden, which proved to be a profitable relationship, for he kept her up to date for many years on various medical remedies for varicose veins and circulatory problems.[19] While in Europe surveying the various spa treatments available there, Helena also studied the new diet regimes that were fashionable and later adapted them for use in her clinics, along with a line of senna-based 'reducing' tablets, which were advertised as originating from King Edward VII's favourite spa at Marienbad.[20] An extensive section of her autobiography contains diet and nutrition schedules, but it is unlikely that she followed them herself. Helena's favourite foods were old Polish standards like crumbed chicken and fatty sausages.

Not content with surveying the latest European health and beauty treatments, Helena continued on to London where she sampled the treatments herself and visited Harrods and other department stores as possible vendors of her products. At this time such department stores did not sell cosmetics, which were still considered by respectable Englishwomen as paints for actresses and 'fallen women'. France was a little more advanced, with Guerlain producing lipstick as early as 1880, followed soon after by American Harriet Hubbard Ayer.[21] The Sears Roebuck catalogue of 1897 advertised 'lip rouge' but they did not sell well; in general they were too advanced for most women in the nineteenth century.[22]

Back in her expanded salon at 274 Collins Street in Melbourne's fashionable district, Helena proclaimed that with her two 'Viennese assistants', new equipment and face powders from Europe, she offered the most extensive treatments available in the country. The two Viennese attendants were her sister Ceska and cousin Lola. Helena called her clients 'patients' to emphasise the medical aspect of her business, and also offered massage treatments. Photographs of her dressed in a white laboratory coat reinforced the notion that her products were based on the latest scientific advances.[23]

Helena's business received considerable coverage in the fashionable Melbourne magazine *Table Talk*, established by fellow Jewish Pole Maurice Brodzky.[24] An exotic denizen of Melbourne at the time, Brodzky had served in the French army during the Franco-Prussian War in 1870–71; he was also language master at the exclusive Melbourne Church of England Grammar School. Brodzky later went to work for the Melbourne *Herald*, thus giving Helena access to influential journalists. The enthusiastic article about her new salon which appeared in *Table Talk* in December 1905 gushed at the beautiful carpets, ornate gilded chairs and modern equipment in her salon. Helena tactically offered the woman journalist who observed her premises a jar of her cream. In another article, Helena expanded on her scientific training, which now consisted of study with a Dr Pashki in Vienna, a Dr Lasaar in Berlin, a Dr Poitinoff in Paris and Dr Una in Hamburg, who had perfected the 'skin peeling' system for damaged complexions.[25]

Enthusiasm for Rubinstein skin products was not confined to Melbourne, or Sydney and Wellington in New Zealand where Helena had also opened salons. The provincial Hobart newspaper the *Mercury* regularly featured articles about her preparations. On 20 October 1909 an article entitled 'Beauty in the Making' advised readers they could purchase Mademoiselle Helena Rubinstein's book *Beauty in the Making*, translated from the original Russian, as well as purchase her

Valaze Herbal Soap and Blackhead and Open Pore Cure. How a book was written in Russian when her native tongue was Polish with some Yiddish reveals a true show-woman in action.

By this time Helena had ventured into the field of cosmetics: an article in the *Sydney Morning Herald* of 25 September 1909 marvelled at her 'lip lustre' which coloured and protected lips. A widespread acceptance of lipsticks, or lip rouge as they were frequently termed, was set to revolutionise respectable women's appearance – cosmetics were moving from the brothel and the stage to the vanity case of the middle-class woman. In her autobiography, Helena maintained that it was Margot Asquith, the British Prime Minister's wife, who '… had the courage to use it [lip gloss] openly'.[26] In Australia Helena's and other cosmetics received support with the claim they protected the complexion from the harsh elements. As well, Helena's products were subtle in appearance, which made them attractive.[27] Other rival products were often brash-looking and far too medicinal for comfort. Baroness d'Orchamps, in her book *Tous les Secrets de la Femme*, published in 1908, advised women on the use of a pomade for the lips made from camphor.[28] No wonder Helena's products were popular.

It was in Sydney that Helena met her future husband, the American-born Edward Titus, who, like her, was of Jewish and Polish heritage. They married in July 1908. Initially Helena had employed him to promote her products and design packaging. Titus was urbane, well educated and sexually adventurous. As the journalist Grace Davidson observed, '[m]ost of all … [Edward Titus] adored beautiful, sexy women'.[29] Helena was neither and her autobiography contains a revealing incident concerning their honeymoon on the Côte d'Azur where Helena saw Titus – as she always called him – flirting with a beautiful young woman. Enraged, Helena stomped off to buy some expensive pearls and went immediately to Paris. She added, '[b]uying "quarrel jewelry" is one of my weaknesses. Some women buy hats, but I am more extravagant in anger, as I am in most things.'[30] Her vast collection of expensive jewellery attests to the stormy incompatibility of the marriage.

Their relationship always worked best at the professional level, and Titus was instrumental in launching Helena's European career. She acknowledged his valuable assistance when she made him an equal shareholder in Helena Rubinstein Ltd in 1909 (her sister Ceska also owned six per cent).[31] Moving to London, Titus convinced her to purchase a lease on a Georgian mansion at 24 Grafton Street, where she established a luxury beauty salon. This time the salon was launched not as her other salons in Australia and New Zealand had been, with extensive promotion and advertising, but with the offer of free patronage for wealthy, often titled, women. Enlisting the support of Argentinean Baroness Catherine d'Erlanger, a favourite of Helena (who rarely had time for friendship), Helena learned to cultivate, flatter and pamper rich women, the core of her new image.[32] Soon treatments were costing Helena's clients an expensive £200 per annum, but rather than paying for each service individually clients received annual accounts.

Not content with this success, on Titus' urging Helena invested in a salon at 255 Rue du Faubourg Saint-Honoré in Paris. This time Helena purchased an established business with a good clientele, as well as the formulas of the previous Russian proprietor's skin creams. Here Helena offered her Australian range and the renamed products of the new business. A new product named Liquidine spread over the world. Thousands of kilometres distant from the exclusive enclave of Parisian fashion, the Hobart *Mercury* of 2 October 1912 would feature an article entitled 'Is Your Complexion Safe?', recommending this new remedy for red and blotchy skin. Helena's excellent marketing skills, honed by Titus, allowed her to launch the first global brand of the twentieth century owned and promoted by a woman.

Back in London with her husband Helena gave birth to a baby, Roy, born in 1909. Helena was now getting about in much smarter clothes. In Paris, she had favoured the designer Paul Poiret. His Grecian-style robe was flattering in pregnancy and later his well-cut outfits with superb fabrics flattered her short and increasingly dumpy figure. She remarked in her autobiography that 'I caused a sensation when I returned [to London from Paris] with Poiret clothes in 1908.'[33] Like Helena herself, Poiret was a self-made innovator who became a major collector of modern art.

Though never a bohemian, Helena made many alliances in the Parisian demimonde. Another Pole, Russian-born Misia Natanson Sert, provided Helena's entrée into the artistic world of Paris. Years later Helena spoke cautiously of her friendship with the unpredictable and eccentric Sert, though she did not acknowledge how she benefited from her introductions.[34] Through Misia, Helena began to purchase modern art, including some valuable African masks that she kept all her life. Always a leader and initiator, Helena began also to use modern and avant-garde designs in her salons. She also introduced a massage regime that used vibrators as part of the treatment. The novelist Colette, then the lover of Misia, declared that after one of these massages she was ready for anything, including seeing her husband, Willy![35] In the years before World War I and the doctrines of Sigmund Freud, vibrators were regarded as acceptable therapy tools.

Never one to be idle for long, Helena commuted to Paris every month and ventured back to Australia again in 1911. In May 1912 at the age of forty, she gave birth to a second son, Horace, in England, where the family was living in a beautiful large house in semi-rural Richmond. In late 1912 the family moved to Paris, where Titus' business as a rare book dealer was more secure. Helena benefited as well, as she began her studies in dermatology at the St Louis Hospital. This gave some measure of veracity to the scientific claims of her products.[36] Her sister Pauline ran the salon in Paris while the London operation was left in the capable hands of a non-family member, Rosa Hollay. This was a strange move, for Helena usually entrusted the management of her salons largely to her sisters.

The outbreak of war made the beauty business appear frivolous. In October 1914 Helena decided to leave Europe and travelled alone to the United States, aided by Titus' American citizenship. No doubt the marriage was in trouble yet again, though she did not refer to any animosities at this time in her autobiography. Six months later Titus and their sons, accompanied by her impressive art collection, joined her in New York City. There the mood was far more carefree, as the United States would not join the Allies in war until April 1917.

Helena wisely travelled around the country, estimating where she could be most successful, before eventually opening a salon in May 1915 on 15 East 49th Street, New York, in the exclusive Upper East Side. Condé Nast's fashionable magazine *Vogue* covered the opening with undisguised enthusiasm. In a nod to the war effort in Europe, it announced that Helena's businesses in London and Paris were supplying much-needed products for the Red Cross. This would have heartened many wealthy women in Francophile New York who joined the war effort as ambulance drivers on the front and would later become her clients.[37]

Helena's new salon in New York was a masterpiece of design. With her collection of Nadelman sculptures, mahogany furniture covered in rose silk, and walls with dark blue silk wallpaper, the atmosphere was immediately impressive. But unlike with her operations in Australia and New Zealand, Helena had stiff competition in this vibrant city.[38] Her rival and adversary, Elizabeth Arden (born Florence Nightingale Graham in Canada) had already established her beauty business on Park Avenue in 1910. Decorated with a red door, Arden's trademark, the interior was a heaven of gold, white and pink, and her products were beautifully packaged and desirable. Both women were hard-nosed business operators who had no advantages of birth, culture or education. They were ambitious, driven and single-minded in pursuit of excellence and success. Like Queen Elizabeth I and Mary, Queen of Scots, these rivals never met, but kept their enmity alive for decades. They waged war in the press and through advertising campaigns.

Helena realised that she could not operate salons in every major city in the United States – she had a limited number of sisters and cousins willing to work under her stern directions for meagre salaries – so she established a salon in San Francisco under the direction of her sister Manka, then in 1916 she set on a plan that would revolutionise the entire beauty industry. Rather than purchasing cosmetics and face creams at her salons, by mail or in selected pharmacies – as she had pioneered in Australia – she determined to sell them in department stores. Thus her expensive treatments became available in exclusive stores such as the Texan store Neiman Marcus and Marshall Field's in Chicago. There they were displayed on special counters with staff dressed in pretty uniforms and well trained by Manka and Helena in both promotion and beauty techniques. Helena, Manka and several assistants toured the country, spying out suitable locations for the Rubinstein range. Helena personally oversaw the introduction into each store, arranging ahead of time for publicity in newspapers.[39]

In 1918 with her business flourishing, her home life spiralled to an all-time low. Titus had more than an eye for gorgeous women; he was a libertine who saw marriage as no bar to his sexual adventuring. There came a point when Helena could no longer keep turning a blind eye. She hired a private detective and found out more than she might have wanted to know about her husband's infidelities. Armed with the report detailing an affair, Helena declared war, and from then on often conducted her relations with Titus through lawyers, employees and relatives.[40] They maintained civil business dealings but avoided each other as much as possible. They were not divorced until 1937.

For those twenty years, Helena tormented Titus with her hold over money and his financial security. His business as a rare book dealer evolved slowly and his ventures into publishing, with the establishment of the Black Manikin Press in Paris, were expensive initiatives he could not afford. For someone unreflective of herself, Helena made a startling admission in her autobiography that she had become 'more difficult to work with' and was on 'the verge of a nervous breakdown'.[41] At nearly fifty, she was tired, angry and deeply lonely.

At the end of World War I, Helena left the boys with Titus, who was an exemplary father, and the business with Manka, and returned to

Europe, where she consoled herself with massive expeditions to purchase art and jewellery. She purchased a beautiful apartment on the Quai de Béthune, which she filled with her expanding collection of art. She also acquired considerable commercial property in Montparnasse. Yet this reckless acquisition did not heal the pain of her estrangement from Titus. One of her hobbies, in her rare time off her work, was trawling through flea markets picking up bargains. This was a pastime she had enjoyed with Baroness d'Erlanger a decade earlier in London.

The post-war era launched a new approach to women's appearance and clothing. Influenced by Coco Chanel, clothes and hairstyles became streamlined and sleek, shown off best on thin, boyish figures. With the internationalisation of Hollywood films, new forms of cosmetics slowly became acceptable. Mae Murray and Clara Bow in the 1920s revelled in the new, coquettish modes for young women, with make-up, overt sexuality and fast lifestyles. Helena was always on top of new developments; indeed, she was ahead of them. She had earlier manufactured mascara for the silent star Theda Bara and devised a sophisticated silver eye shadow for her as well.[42]

Helena met this new challenge head-on with irrepressible energy and determination and new ranges of cosmetics. Her lipsticks, bright and long-wearing, were a far cry from the subtle dab of lip rouge of a generation ago. In some areas she remained steadfastly old-fashioned, though. She abhorred the new mode for sunbathing, made popular by Chanel. But with the boyish figure all the rage, Helena saw another opportunity for expansion. She added an exercise class in her new New York salon on 57th and Park Avenue; however, it was so exacting it failed. She also adopted the new styles, such as jersey pants, which hardly flattered her matronly figure. Always ahead of the game, Helena was an early client of designers Jeanne Lanvin and Elsa Schiaparelli.

Helena had an extraordinary eye for business. In December 1928 she sold out the US component of her business to Lehman Brothers, thereby avoiding the destructive forces of the Depression just a year ahead. She dissembled about this in her autobiography, claiming that she had wanted to be by Titus' side in Paris.[43] Part of her still wanted to be loved and cherished by her erring husband from whom she had been estranged for a decade, yet she did not tell him of her intending sale of the US business, or that she and their sons were going to Australia for a while. As she ventured from the United States, Helena was one of the wealthiest women in the country – and all by her own hands.

For a woman who was relentless in her pursuit of wealth and fame, this period in her life without her American business was depressing. She released a book, *The Art of Feminine Beauty*. It may have expanded on the first book she wrote in Australia in 1909, but it is now lost to researchers and we can only hazard a guess as to what was in it. Her relationship with Titus continued to obsess her. His affair with the writer of erotica Anaïs Nin so enraged Helena that she retaliated by removing Titus from their jointly held business dealings in Paris. She also bulldozed their property in Montparnasse, thereby destroying the famous Jockey Club.[44]

In 1934 Helena, who had taken on the persona simply of Madame, purchased back her US business at rock-bottom prices. She also ventured into the area of hormone rejuvenation, launching Hormone Twin Youthifiers, which did not pass the new Federal Drug Administration rules for cosmetics although her Ultrafeminine hormone crème was approved.[45] In response she expanded her cosmetics range. Her own rejuvenation came with marriage in June 1938 to forty-three-year-old Prince Artchil Gourielli-Tchkonia from Georgia, a year after her divorce from Titus. Both were pleased with the union – Madame was suddenly a princess, and he was connected to a wealthy woman who indulged his passions for gambling and an easy life. Living in a new apartment in New York, her business flourished – with the April 1939 *Vogue* cover featuring the Rubinstein Orchid Red lipstick. Her new waterproof mascara showed she was at the top of her game even as she approached seventy.

As the world entered World War II, avowed workaholic Helena

Helena Rubinstein (undated) about to embark on one of her many voyages. Bain Collection, Library of Congress LC-B2-6558-1.

began to find her husband's lifestyle a little too leisured, especially in wartime. Meanwhile, she had entered into the area of men's toiletries, opening the House of Gourielli in the St Regis Hotel lobby. This initiative simply sucked money out of her core business. With her extensive factories and supplies in the United States, Helena Rubinstein Inc. did not suffer unduly during the war years, but a shock to both Madame and her rival, Elizabeth Arden, hit suddenly in 1952 when Revlon launched the spectacularly successful Fire and Ice campaign. The following year Estée Lauder entered the skin-care market. The game had now clearly changed.

Yet Madame's greatest challenge at this time was personal. Gourielli died suddenly in 1955 while Helena was in Paris. His death was an event she could not have anticipated – he was so much younger than she was and never worked a hard day in his life. Too distraught to return to New York for the funeral, Helena was rich beyond her dreams, but now a lonely widow.

Taking two years to recover, in 1957 she embarked on an extensive trip which included Australia. There she was welcomed as a celebrity and continued her patronage of the arts. She established the Helena Rubinstein Art Prize in Sydney, and had her portrait painted by William Dobell and Graham Sutherland. These were more conventional portraits than earlier Surrealist-inspired ones by Dali and Dufy in the 1930s. What they captured was her imposing fortitude – she resembled an Easter Island stone monument in these renditions.

Towards the end of her life, though she was notoriously frugal with money (except on her art and jewellery), Helena invested heavily in philanthropy. The Helena Rubinstein Foundation was established in New York in 1953 and the Helena Rubinstein Pavilion for Contemporary Art in Tel Aviv was a generous gift to the new nation of Israel. In these last years, when work no longer consumed her, she travelled with an energy that belied her advanced years. When she did work, it was conducted from her lavish canopied bed, yet sadness and tragedy hit again when her son Horace died in April 1958.

In 1965, just before her death at the age of ninety-two, Helena published her autobiography, *My Life for Beauty*. Rather than setting the record straight, Helena codified her severely edited and fabricated version of her life, a story so extraordinary it needed no embellishments or fables. Instead she gave the fictionalised version of her family origins, her education, her training and expertise, making herself Madame Rubinstein, or simply Madame, a well-born Jewish woman from an educated and cultivated family, with scientific training, saviour of women's complexions worldwide. Helena was a notorious fabricator of her personal life, though never her substantial business achievements.

Helena Rubinstein died on 2 April 1965. In death she showed again her curious meanness. Faithful servants who had provided decades of service received pittances. For all those decades of striving and success, Chaja Rubinstein had never learned charity, kindness and generosity, thus diminishing the reputation of one of the world's finest business tycoons.

CHAPTER 8

Adela Pankhurst
(1885–1961)

*The rebel pacifist and socialist who became a fascist
and Japanese supporter in World War II.*

Adela Pankhurst was one of the most perplexing characters in Australian history during the world wars. She was a spirited suffragette and one of the founders of the Women's Social and Political Union (WSPU) in England, a militant socialist and pacifist during World War I and a founder of the Communist Party of Australia (CPA) in 1920. In the late 1920s, Adela switched to the right, and then to the extreme right in the Depression years, only to find herself in an internment camp during World War II as a supporter of the Japanese. At all stages of her public career, she attracted, in turns, notoriety, admiration and profound antagonism. Deeply emotional to the point of irrational devotion to various causes, Adela lived her life with passionate intensity. She took the motto of her father, lawyer Dr Richard Pankhurst, that 'life is nothing without enthusiasm' to such extremes that her actions and fundamental changes in beliefs were both bizarre and enigmatic.[1]

Adela's parents, Richard and Emmeline, were central figures of the English secular reform movement intent upon improving conditions in the mid Victorian age. Unlike earlier radical movements in the very early nineteenth century, such as the abolition and emancipation campaigners at whose core lay evangelical religion, the newer movements from the 1830s were more secular and political. The Chartists sought to establish the legitimacy of the working-class labour movement, while electoral reformers sought parliamentary representation for the emerging middle class.[2] In some senses, Richard Pankhurst straddled both these eras of English radicalism. His parents were fierce Baptists and devoted to political liberalism, a common combination in areas such as Stoke-on-Trent where Richard was born in 1834. As a non-conformist Protestant, he was unable to study at Oxford or Cambridge, which only admitted Anglicans, and so was educated at Owens College (later Manchester University) and the University of London, established by the utilitarian philosopher Jeremy Bentham. Both these institutions were renowned for their radical emphasis. On his return home to Manchester in 1868, Richard devoted himself to republicanism, women's suffrage and the abolition of the House of Lords and the established Church. His attempts to enter parliament were unsuccessful; his blunt approach and self-righteousness did not attract voters. His third daughter, Adela, possessed much of her father's heavy-handed style and inability to compromise, or even to listen to others' points of view.[3]

Emmeline Goulden Pankhurst always claimed she was born on Bastille Day in 1858 although she was actually born on 15 July that year. The daughter of a wealthy cotton manufacturer, her early life was privileged and secure. This was new money and security, and the family was not far removed from industrial poverty in the previous generation. Emmeline's mother, Sophia, had been an early feminist and supported Emmeline's education at an exclusive school in Neuilly, France. There her best friend was Noemie de Rochefort, whose father was banished for his activities in the Paris Commune in 1870–71.[4] When Emmeline returned to Manchester in 1878 she met Richard, a lawyer and fellow advocate of women's franchise rights. The pair married in 1879 and had five children: Christabel (1880–1958), Estelle Sylvia (1882–1960), Frank (1884–88), Adela Constantia Mary (1885–1961) and another Frank whom the family called Harry (1889–1910). Neither parent allowed their family to deter their intense political activities in the suffrage movement and the establishment of the Independent Labour Party (ILP). The children were left to the care of servants. Emmeline does not even mention Adela and Harry in her posthumously published autobiography, thereby writing her rebellious daughter out of her account of the suffrage movement. In any case, a sickly child with her legs in splints, Adela was rarely the object of her mother's affections.[5] An older father, Richard was often gruff and incomprehensible to his children, although he was more attentive than Emmeline.

In their new home in Russell Square in London in July 1889, a fortnight after Harry's birth, Emmeline, along with Richard, established the Women's Franchise League. Four years later the family returned to northern England where the girls were sent to the exclusive Manchester Girls High School. Much of their life education was spent watching their parents' involvement in radical social reforms, particularly for women and children. In 1898 Richard died at the age of sixty-three, leaving the family almost destitute. Adela was taken from Manchester Girls and sent to a local boarding school, then to the Disley Road School as an apprentice teacher.[6] Surprisingly, Emmeline was not entirely in favour of rigorous studies for girls, an attitude seemingly at odds with her militant feminism. However, Christabel was permitted to undertake law studies at Manchester University.

During the Boer War (1899–1902), Adela took her first independent steps towards political action. Both she and young Harry decided they were pacifists. Her deep hatred for British Imperialism stemmed from this period, as well as her distaste for financiers and Jews. With a mélange of views that were often contradictory, so began the pattern of Adela's political life: deeply held convictions, expressed with emotional vehemence, regardless of internal consistency and logic. Despite her secular upbringing, she also embraced a naïve, fervent fundamentalist Christianity. Adela's time as a pupil-teacher intensified both her incipient socialism and Christianity. Her pupils were desperately poor and ragged, even by the standards of industrial slums. Their poverty, malnutrition and poor health had a lasting impact on the young Adela. When she later moved to the far right during the Depression in Australia, she recalled the plight of these damaged children.

The WSPU was formed in October 1903 in the Pankhursts' front parlour, as a breakaway women's lobby group from the male-dominated ILP, but it was not Emmeline's efforts alone that established this new aggressive vehicle for political action. The movement crossed class boundaries, although most of its leaders were middle-class women with the time to devote to meetings, writing pamphlets and, soon, engaging in fierce demonstrations. Aged eighteen Adela was always more concerned with the rights of working-class women, especially those burdened with large families. Many of her talks were aimed at working-class women, whereas her mother and Christabel focused on middle-class women.[7]

In June 1906, Adela was arrested for disrupting a Liberal Party meeting and sentenced to seven days in prison. She had tasted the thrill of extreme defiance and now found herself hooked. The discipline required in teaching disadvantaged children taxed her emotionally, whereas the spotlight of public meetings, the camaraderie of a struggle, and the intoxication of fighting for a moral cause were far more seductive and appealing.

Adela moved to London in October 1906, where the feminist movement was larger and more active, and she threw herself headlong into militant advocacy. Along with others, she was arrested for being part of a demonstration in the House of Commons lobby, and spent time in Holloway Prison. This was a turning point in the WSPU campaign. From there on it escalated its confrontational tactics, causing much consternation within the ILP. By 1909, damage to 10 Downing Street, violent demonstrations in Trafalgar Square, London, Manchester and other northern centres, alongside hunger strikes by imprisoned suffragettes, marked the movement's transformation into a radical challenge to English democracy. Adela's capacity to understand the nature and limitations of working-class women's lives made her tours to provincial areas successful. The work was unrelenting and gruelling, and Christabel, in her memoir, generously praised Adela for her efforts in this area.[8]

In 1910 Harry died from poliomyelitis at the age of twenty. He had been Adela's confidant and comrade-in-arms throughout their childhood and adolescence and her health deteriorated due to exhaustion and stress in the wake of his death.[9] In many regards this was her breaking point with the suffragette cause. Along with her sister Sylvia, Adela had become increasingly devoted to socialist causes, and the split with Emmeline and Christabel, who were concerned with more conservative politics and were anti-socialist, was brutal and irrevocable. Surprisingly, Adela later said she thought the vote had been won by the more conservative methods of the National Union of Women's Suffrage Societies.[10] In a letter to former leading suffragette Helen Fraser Moyes, she wrote:

> I never regarded the militant tactics as more than a drum
> which attracts attention and brings up the crowd to hear the
> message. I had time to realize [in 1910] that militancy was out
> of control ...[11]

Her activities almost ceased when she undertook, at her mother's insistence, studies in agriculture in Warwickshire. Emmeline wanted to get Adela out of the spotlight, but this was hardly a suitable career move for a feisty young woman and she failed to complete her studies. She then worked as governess to Alec and Betty Archdale in Switzerland in 1912, and agreed to accompany them to Australia.

Adela was packed off to Australia with a meagre £20 in her purse, a letter of introduction to women's suffrage campaigner Vida Goldstein, and some knitted woollen clothes.[12] She arrived in Melbourne in March 1914 and was met by Vida Goldstein and the pacifist singer Cecilia John.[13] Vida was the first woman to run for parliament, after Australian women had won the right to vote in federal elections in 1902, twenty-six years before Britain. Adela's fame by association preceded her and she was no doubt less than pleased to be recognised as 'Miss Adela Pankhurst, daughter of the noted English suffragette'. Her play *Betrayed*, written in 1917, channels many of the emotional traumas she experienced through her mother's ruthless tunnel vision and favouritism towards Christabel.[14] It was reminiscent of a Victorian melodrama, with the black sheep of the family dispatched to the distant colonies, although its political themes – the dangers of a Chinese invasion and a military dictatorship if conscription was introduced – masked Adela's personal wounds.

In Australia, Adela the militant suffragette and passionate socialist was a star and did not have to compete for attention with her mother and sisters. She was famous as an orator and campaigner for working women's rights. Her first speech in May 1914 to an enthusiastic crowd in Melbourne, in a hall festooned with the purple, green and white colours of the WSPU, was highly praised in the socialist press. In July she gave an impassioned speech highlighting the plight of English women factory workers who earned one penny an hour,[15] yet the intense and uncritical adulation she received sowed the seeds of her eventual undoing. She loved the spotlight, the roar of the crowd, and the urgency of discussing radical issues in public. Her talks across south-east Australia were highly emotional and intense, as she castigated the British Liberal government under David Lloyd George for its inhumane treatment of women activists.[16]

These forays gave her the attention she desired but had a limited shelf life. In order to progress her reputation, Adela needed to find an Australian theme to interest her audience. The outbreak of war in August 1914 presented her with the opportunity to shine. Recalling her pacifism during the Boer War, which sat alongside a dangerous admiration for Germany, Adela revived her commitment to peace. Closely aligned with Vida Goldstein, who had visited England in 1911 to address the WSPU, Adela took on pacifism with an alarming fervour. With women split over the issue of Australia's participation in the war, the battle lines were drawn. Adela accepted the role of secretary of radical activist group the Women's Political Association in early 1915, while maintaining her membership of the Australian Peace Alliance. The war years were the highpoint of left-wing activism in Australia, with anarchists, socialists, Bolsheviks, anti-conscriptionists and various anti-war activists clamouring for attention to turn around militarism – although there were some Melbourne activists, such as Lizzie Ahern, who were militant socialists, not pacifists.[17] Adela's pamphlet 'Put up the Sword!' published in November 1915, sat firmly in the pacifist camp – at least for the moment.

In July 1915 Vida Goldstein and Cecilia John renamed the Women's Political Association the Women's Peace Army (WPA). This pre-emptory move alienated many progressive but mainstream feminists, as a militant pacifist and anti-conscription organisation ran counter to the beliefs of many supporters. Adela was among its first members. Her pronouncements often seem illogical. She pointedly asked a female audience to remember that 'Women! You have a duty to Humanity, to God', as she discussed the dangers to British womanhood of civilisation crumbled and women resorting to prostitution for survival.[18] At this Bijou Theatre performance in Melbourne her speech on 'The War and the White Slave Traffic' missed its mark, for the central concern of the audience was involvement in the war.[19] The origins of her move later to extreme right-wing politics and women's role in the family can be detected in these emotional pleas. Her activities were not always confined to polemic and public declaration, she had strong practical skills as well. Adela and Cecilia established a farm at Mordialloc to earn much-needed cash, as well as a women's employment bureau at 229 Collins Street, Melbourne. Adela also involved herself in the consumer issues of the day, as prices soared and wages fell.

The Socialist, a journal of the Victorian Socialist Party (VSP), proclaimed: 'Adela the star. Is she not the most popular woman in the world? And such a young thing too. Wherever did she pick up all that knowledge?'[20] This patronising praise only fuelled the beginnings of a desperate and ongoing need for public adulation. The referendum on conscription in 1916 gave her the perfect opportunity to expand her repertoire of activism. Labor Prime Minister Billy Hughes needed a positive vote in the referendum on the issue of compulsory military conscription for overseas service to overcome the *Defence Act* of 1909, which provided only for (male) conscription in the event of war on Australian soil. Deeply committed to the Imperial war effort, Hughes – knowing that the Allies were not doing well, especially after the Battle of the Somme in July 1916 – wanted to commit more troops. Adela exhausted herself with vehement anti-conscription protests as she toured Australia and New Zealand (where conscription was already a reality).

This arduous tour brought her into the orbit of Tom Walsh, a sympathiser of the anarcho-syndicalist organisation the Industrial Workers of the World (IWW). He had already clashed with former union leader Billy Hughes and aligned himself with the radicals. Walsh was elected New South Wales Secretary of the Federated Seamen's Union of Australasia in 1912.[21] There was trouble brewing; his union was anti-conscription but pro-war. This mirrored many allegiances in the labour movement in Australia. The Labor Party split everywhere except in Queensland, where the socialist government under T. J. Ryan was able to maintain unity. Adela undertook a tour of regional Queensland, New South Wales and then Adelaide in support of the 'No to Conscription' vote in July and August 1916. She showed herself to be tireless, charismatic and defiant.

Signs of later developments in Adela's thinking were on display at her performance at a rally in Melbourne on 27 September 1916. Criticising the Imperial tie, she demanded 'Australia for the Australians'. The gathering took on the atmosphere of a religious revival meeting.[22] In October 1916 Adela shared an open-air platform with later prime minister John Curtin and trade unionist Jennie Baines. With the arrest of the key members of the IWW on conspiracy charges that month, and increased state surveillance and intimidation of anti-war activists, Adela was on an emotional high. After a WPA meeting in Melbourne, she was carried on the shoulders of her supporters to much acclaim.[23]

On 28 October the 'No' vote to conscription prevailed all over the country, except in Victoria. Loyalties and old friendships were torn asunder by ideological rancour as the first conscription referendum was lost. Adela and Vida Goldstein too found they had less in common as Adela moved more towards radical politics with male colleagues. In early 1917 Adela resigned from the WPA and joined the VSP as an organiser, touring Western Australia with John Curtin to argue against Australia's commitment to the Allied war effort. To mark the occasion *The Socialist* advertised a 'plastic bust of Miss Pankhurst' on sale for three shillings and ninepence.[24] The government considered charging her with sedition but a wiser course was taken, although not one to Adela's liking: the press was forced to largely ignore her speeches through intense official censorship.

Adela lost the close ties of emotional warmth and support of her new maternal figure Vida and went to stay with Ethel and Robert Ross – generous socialists who had been caring for Tom Walsh's three daughters following his wife's death in 1914. Cut loose from Vida's more calming influence, Adela undertook a series of aggressive direct actions. With constant arrests, she spent a lot of time in court defending herself. The authorities tired of her almost hysterical harangues against the Prime Minister, and other federal parliamentarians decided to increase their pressure on her. She was sentenced to six months' imprisonment for leading a demonstration against rising food prices in September 1917, although she was released on appeal. Fed up with what he saw as her disruptive antics, Hughes called her a 'little devil' and considered her deportation. Earlier a series of IWW radicals had been deported, often illegally. Adela was a different category of rebel: she commanded too many supporters in England and Australia, and she was a woman.[25]

In late September 1917, dressed in her grandmother's remodelled silk petticoat, Adela suddenly married Tom Walsh. The service was conducted in Melbourne by reforming parson the Reverend Frederick

Sinclair, with Tom's daughter Hannah Walsh as bridesmaid.[26] Adela sometimes claimed that she undertook this marriage to the much older Irish widower because she was threatened with deportation,[27] but their union was stable and happy, and the one enduring emotional calm in her life. No sooner were they wed than Adela was sent to prison for four months in November 1917 for leading a demonstration banned under national security regulations. This was not a good time for extreme antagonism towards the government. There had been a series of long, bitter strikes in 1917 in Australia, and a second conscription referendum had been lost. At the extended battle of Passchendaele in Belgium, lasting from June to November 1917, the Australian Imperial Forces lost many men to the savage brutality of trench warfare. But it was the success of the Bolsheviks in Russia that alarmed liberals and conservatives alike. The fear of communism was to dominate Australian politics for the next sixty years.[28]

On her release from prison, Adela resigned from her position in the VSP, largely in order to assist with editing the *Seamen's Journal*, from its base in Sydney to where she and Tom moved. In November 1918 she gave birth to Richard, the first of her five children. Like earlier feminists, Adela did not believe in contraception, seeing it as against nature. For a short time her life became more contained within the domestic sphere. However, with the seamen's strike in early 1919 and Tom in the spotlight, Adela again entered public life. This was a period of intense industrial and ideological struggle in Australia, with frequent clashes between ex-servicemen and radical workers, who were more and more inclined to Bolshevik doctrines. Adela took on the new ideology with her usual intense enthusiasm, but her activities were limited by the arrival of another baby, Sylvia, in late 1920. That year she and Tom had joined the new CPA as founding members. Her first article in the journal *Australian Communist* attempted to balance family and the revolution, a theme she would pursue more ardently as a fascist in the 1930s.

Adela was hardly a theoretical Marxist or doctrinaire in her approach; rather, her methods and loyalties were based on emotion. The new party, with its subservient devotion to the Comintern in Moscow, was scarcely aligned with the needs of a charismatic and iconoclastic woman like Adela, and she and her husband left the party within a few years. By this time they had three small children.

Adela and her family relocated to Melbourne for Tom to find work. Now the war was over, Adela found there were no longer the burning issues that had previously consumed her time. For someone who needed public attention, these were stultifying years. For Tom, too, they were hard years as he moved more to the right, antagonising many in his fiery union. He favoured arbitration, as well as tactics delaying ship departures, to secure his members better conditions. Employers successfully applied to deregister the seamen's union in June 1925, and the new conservative Prime Minister Stanley Bruce moved swiftly to introduce legislation banning certain radical organisations, with deportation provisions aimed at decimating the union leadership of its 'foreign' – non-British born – leaders like Irish-born Tom Walsh. Amendments to the *Crimes Act* provided the government with a powerful weapon to target radical unions. Tom and his deputy, Jacob Johnson, were arrested on charges of inciting workers to strike and sent to Garden Island in late 1925.[29] Adela, pregnant once again and with four children to look after, worried how they would cope if Tom was banished. For the Walshes there was personal tragedy when their new baby, Faith, died in January 1926. Adela retreated from public life to home and family to recover her spirits and strength.

Tom successfully appealed against his deportation, but his experience of the force of state power caused him to re-evaluate his position on industrial militancy. He lost the presidency of the union in 1928. That year, also, Adela made an extraordinary move to the right, founding the Australian Women's Guild of Empire, despite her earlier hostility towards the British Empire. She had made a cautious peace with her mother, who died in June 1928. For all her previous opposition to Emmeline's and Christabel's moves to more conservative positions, like supporting the Imperial war effort in World War I, she followed the same path from militancy to intractable conservatism.[30] She was a firm supporter of the conservative new Industrial Peace Union, and became now a determined enemy of communists and radical labour supporters. When Tom lost his earning capacity within the union movement, their resentments grew in wild profusion. Both of them supported themselves through casual journalism for magazines such as *Pioneers* and *Empire Gazette*, a considerable feat with seven children to support. Later the Guild provided a meagre wage on which the family survived.

Like earlier nineteenth-century feminists who preached the doctrine of domestic feminism to reinforce women's security in the home but worked tirelessly outside their own homes, Adela exhorted women to become better mothers. Yet she retained her interest in industrial peace and militancy, speaking frequently on these issues to often bewildered listeners who could not comprehend how her views had so dramatically turned around. She was not alone in such about-faces. Sir Oswald Mosley in England went from Labour MP in 1931 to founder and leader of the British Union of Fascists in 1932; and former suffragette Norah Dacre Fox also became a fascist.[31] The largest mass movements in Australia in the 1930s were organisations in Sydney such as the proto-fascist paramilitary New Guard. The worldwide Depression left parliamentarians, economists, trade unionists and citizens struggling with solutions to cope with this devastating dislocation so soon after the war. Communists may have been feared in Australia but they were few in number, unlike the extreme right-wing organisations.

The Guild's activities in the years 1933–34 were reminiscent of a Christian charity: supplying food to the needy, providing clothes and toys for children, and free entertainment for the families of unemployed workers. Expanding as the despair and poverty of the Depression escalated, the Guild attracted many well-connected women to its ranks, including architect Marion Mahoney Griffin. How Adela found her niche amid all this knitting and pouring of cups of tea in the streets is puzzling, as it was a domain far from suited to her adversarial nature. Her new doctrine was the destructiveness of industrial strikes and she pushed her views on former comrades-in-arms from the left, then she would dash off to a factory and preach to the entirely unconverted.

As the Guild's momentum slowed, in 1937 Adela expressed yet another developing passion – for Germany. Since the time of the Boer War she had despised British Imperialism and identified with the Boers (whom she had mistaken for Germans). She later sympathised with the Germans and lamented how harshly the Allies had treated a defeated Germany in the Versailles Treaty of 1919. By 1937 she took to arguing that the Nazis had been democratically elected and brought industrial peace to a troubled nation. With the maverick businessman William Miles funding the incendiary journal *The Publicist*, from July

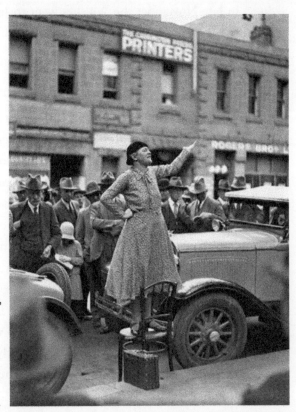

Adela Pankhurst Walsh, standing on a chair in the street outside the Carrington Press Printers, Sydney, 28 January 1941. SMH News picture by Staff; Fairfax Media 2362105.

1936, she was provided with a channel to convey her increasingly pro-German and pro-Japanese views.[32] That she reconciled these views with the presidency of the Women's Guild of Empire is remarkable.

Adela was ahead of her time in realising that Australia was not 'Britain in the Antipodes' but a nation in the Asia-Pacific region. Yet to support a brutal, militaristic regime like Japan in the late 1930s, especially given her earlier pacifist views, was almost incomprehensible. Her public denunciations against Jewish financiers, whom she believed 'caused' the Depression, constituted yet another instance of her extreme right-wing views. After war was declared in August 1939 but before Japan was yet involved, Adela struggled with poor mental health, ranting in public and crying in the Guild's offices. When deposed from its leadership, she was almost violent in her anger.[33] Even more worrying was her meeting with the Japanese Consul in Sydney. In late November the Walshes went to Japan as guests of the government. On their return Adela published 'Conditions in Japan' and 'What You Should Know about the Orient'.

In early 1940 Adela established the pro-Japanese People's Guild with a tiny membership. Its newsletter, *Voice of the People*, also attracted few readers. She stood for the Senate in the September 1940 federal elections, garnering few votes. Undeterred, she spent her Saturday afternoons proselytising in Sydney's Domain to bewildered and hostile onlookers. For someone so accustomed to adulation and support, this was a devastating blow. She seemed unable to realise this was not a popular cause, like opposing compulsory overseas conscription. When this new Guild failed, she joined forces with Percy Stephensen in the ultra-nationalist, anti-Imperialist Australia First Movement. Stephensen was a Rhodes Scholar from the University of Queensland who travelled from the far left to the far right in the inter-war years. This strange extreme nationalist group was also financed by the quirky businessman William Miles.[34] Violently anti-British hatred was hardly a view popular in World War II, when Australian troops were fighting in the Middle East.

When Japan entered the war on 7 December 1941, Adela's fate was sealed. After the Fall of Singapore in February 1942, Australia itself seemed at risk of a Japanese invasion. Security forces rounded up enemy aliens including Italians – most of whom were intensely anti-fascist – and groups such as the Australia First Movement, as potential fifth columnists. Adela was taken into custody on 20 March and interned in Liverpool camp. Tom was far too ill to warrant detention. Adela unsuccessfully demanded to appear in court in a public hearing, which was not permitted under the *National Security Act 1939–40*. Threatening to go on a hunger strike, she was released. Her military intelligence dossier makes sad reading, for Adela spoke warmly of her dying husband, her children at home and son Richard on active service, without any understanding of what had brought her to this final humiliation.[35] Tom died on 5 April 1943. Adela subsequently retired from public life altogether. Before her death in 1961, she converted to Roman Catholicism.

CHAPTER 9

Annette Kellermann

(1886–1975)

The Sydney 'Million Dollar Mermaid' who got women out of corsets and into the water in togs.

Annette Kellermann was a rebel who revolutionised women's dress at the commencement of the twentieth century. Like Coco Chanel, Kellermann took a male item of clothing, in her case the swimming costume, and fashioned it into a practical garment that allowed women freedom to swim and enjoy water sports. She also dared to bare her legs in order to swim in public, and this act alone tore down the restrictions of Victorian prudery that had confined women within, through both psychologically and physically restraining clothing.

Annette's notoriety made her an extremely wealthy woman, and she carved out the life and career she wanted on her terms. Her talents were manifold: she was Australia's first international film star and the first star of any film with a million-dollar budget in the United States; she was the world's highest paid female theatre act for nearly two decades, during which she performed dangerous diving and swimming routines on stage to packed audiences; she appeared on the New York stage imitating Pavlova, not in a skit but as a credible dancer. Yet after all her success, she died on the Gold Coast in 1975 in poverty and obscurity, a sad relic of an age that had forgotten those women who challenged and destroyed the boundaries of female restriction.

Australia produced several other women who boldly broke conventions. Isabel Letham (1899–1995) was the first Australian to ride a surfboard when she was chosen to ride in tandem with Duke Kahanamoku to show the Hawaiian surf riding technique in Sydney in 1915. At the young age of fifteen, Isabel, in that one ride, revolutionised women's participation in water sports. She went on to an international career in swimming instruction and was appointed director of swimming for the city of San Francisco.[1]

A contemporary and friend of Kellermann, Fanny Durack (1889–1956) was Australia's most notable woman swimmer for many decades. A New South Wales champion, she perfected the new stroke of Australian crawl or freestyle. Fanny's path to fame was not easy. Her father was a publican in Balmain, a rough area full of prostitutes and SP bookmakers, and as a working-class girl she had few opportunities for leisure.[2] Durack trained with Mina Wylie, whose father built and operated Wylie's Baths at Coogee, in Sydney, and who permitted the girls to train with leading male swimmers. In 1912 Durack represented Australia in the Olympics after much controversy about women's participation in the Games. She won the gold medal in the freestyle event, and Wylie took home a silver.[3]

Born in Sydney in 1886, Annette Kellermann came from a well-educated and cultured family. Her mother, Alice Charbonnet, was a concert pianist, trained by the illustrious Madame Paule Gayrard in Paris, before moving to the Paris Conservatoire to study with Cecile Chaminade. Alice was born in 1860 in Cincinnati, into a sophisticated and cosmopolitan family; her mother was American while her father, Amable Charbonnet, was the Chief Justice of the French Possessions and Colonies in the South Pacific.[4] Alice arrived in Australia in 1880 as part of the French government's contribution to the International Exhibition in Melbourne, where she demonstrated the Pleyel and Erard pianos.[5] She met Australian-born Frederick Kellermann, a talented violinist, though his background was not quite as illustrious as her own. His grandfather and father, also Frederick Kellermann, owned a shop in Sydney. They sometimes anglicised their name to Kellerman, though Annette was frequently called by both versions of her surname. Her book *How to Swim* (1918) uses the name Kellermann.

Alice and Frederick married in 1882 and established their own Conservatoire de Musique at 43 Phillip Street in Sydney, as well as the Sydney Orchestra Society.[6] They attracted talented students, among them Kellermann recalled a Helen Mitchell, later known as Nellie Melba, Australia's first internationally acclaimed opera singer. The young couple were the centre of musical excellence in Sydney, as well as popular hosts.[7] In recognition of her international career and training, Alice was known always as Madame Charbonnet.

The Kellermanns had four children: Maurice (1885), Annette (1886), Marcelle (1887) and Frederick (1891). Despite an affluent home life, young Annette contracted rickets, a disease often associated with poverty. Confined to a strict diet and with constant medical attention, her legs were encased in heavy calipers at the age of six.[8] She later recalled the humiliation of being thought of as a cripple.[9] One advanced medical practitioner, Dr David Cope, recommended that eleven-year-old Annette take up swimming to strengthen her weak legs.[10] In her later book *Fairy Tales of the South Seas* (1926), illustrated by her sister Marcelle Wooster, Annette explained that 'I was awfully scared of the water and did not learn to swim quickly, but Mr Percy Cavill, who was my teacher, never frightened me, so I lost all fear.'[11] Percy Cavill was largely responsible for developing the Australian crawl stroke.[12] Later Annette wrote: 'With strength came hope, and hope, reacting, gave more strength, and presently my legs began to take on normal shape.'[13] She had the good fortune to practise swimming with the future champions Snowy and Frank Baker. She swam at Farmer's Baths at Farm Cove aged fifteen where she learned 'overarm stroke'.[14] The water was not her only milieu; Annette took up other activities and became a proficient ballet dancer, as well as a champion tennis player.

Annette began competing in swimming carnivals in 1902 with the full support of her father, who, as her success grew, became her guide and manager. Fred Kellermann also began organising carnivals for women competitors at the St George Baths in Redfern. These were supplemented with displays of graceful underwater ballet routines. In March 1902 Annette competed against Mina Wylie and Fanny Durack, winning the 100 yards event in 1 minute and 26.5 seconds.[15] What made this competition unusual, apart from the women's events, was the presence of male spectators watching the girls. The display was considered an outrageous breach of public conventions on proper attire for a mixed audience.[16] Some of Annette's fiercest opposition in competitive swimming came from Rose Scott, the famous feminist and president of the New South Wales Ladies Amateur Swimming Association, who totally opposed 'mixed bathing' and went so far as to denounce male spectators at women's events. By the standards of today, the girls' heavy woollen costumes were cumbersome. Yet at the turn of the twentieth century, women often wore corsets, stockings and shoes in elaborate bathing ensembles. Indeed, Edwardian strictures even forced men to wear skirts over their bathing costumes at Manly Beach.[17]

In 1902 the Kellermanns made the decision to relocate to Melbourne, where Madame Charbonnet obtained a position as music mistress at Simpson's School, now Mentone Girls Grammar School. Annette and Marcelle attended the school, where Annette was an indifferent and uninterested student.[18] She began giving swimming lessons and public performances as a mermaid at the Princes Court entertainment centre and the Melbourne Aquarium. In 1903 she undertook a role in the play *The Breaking of the Drought*, at the Theatre Royal.[19] Her sister, Marcelle, later wrote that: 'She was being whirled around and towards the big [water] outlet, her arm already in a pipe, when a stage hand saw the danger and turned off the water ... Nothing daunted her if it was in the script.'[20] It was this daredevil courage that later caused Annette to be seriously injured and temporarily crippled with a long road to recovery during her film star years.

When her father, Frederick, suffered his first heart attack in Melbourne in 1903, Annette realised she had to earn a living to help support her family. Competing in marathon races up the Yarra was the start of her long-distance swimming career.[21] Today, long-distance competitions are often the preserve of men, but unusually in these early days of the sport, the conventions were more flexible. With her father as manager and chaperone, Annette transferred her career to London in 1905, after a tour of the Australian states. Within the dynamics of the Kellermann family, Fred sided with his athletic elder daughter, much to the dismay of the creative and refined Madame Charbonnet. By this time, however, Annette was a mature and confident nineteen-year-old. Her journey from colonial swimming star and aquatic performer to international star is a revelation in the construction of modern celebrity, albeit, in this case, one with immense drive and talent. Not that it was easy. Swimming was not as popular in England and promoters did not want the expense and trouble of erecting a pool on stage 'just to see a woman make a fish of herself'.[22]

Annette understood that fame meant a strong and active engagement with the mass media. For a cultured middle-class woman, her choice was both clever and surprising. She aligned her public career with the down-market *Daily Mirror*, the first newspaper to incorporate pictorials, thereby revolutionising newspapers and widening the readership. This newspaper, developed by the canny Lord Northcote, made sensation and deviance a core feature of its fare, although it also advocated a more liberal attitude to the place of women in society.[23]

In collaboration with this paper, her first feat was to swim 42 kilometres of the Thames River in 3 hours and 54 minutes. On 1 July 1905 the *Daily Mirror* reported on the immense crowd that watched Annette dive from Putney Bridge in her blue swimming costume, 'her youth and beauty alone have won all hearts; her pluck and skill require equal admiration'. She fitted very neatly into the racial and cultural construction of the lanky, robust Anglo-Australian – though in fact she was of European extraction – brimming with health, strength and vitality, the best of the British Empire. This swim in the Thames was hardly a doddle – it was cold, rainy and blustery that day. She arrived in the East End wharves covered in mud and debris from the dirty water to the acclaim of thousands of spectators cheering her exploits.

Her next stratagem, which is now mandatory for today's stars, was to endorse a product – Cadbury's Cocoa, promoted heavily through the pages of the *Daily Mirror*. Then she did something even more daunting. For the thirtieth anniversary of Captain Matthew Webb's Channel swim, Annette decided that she would be the first woman to successfully swim that body of water. Organised by the *Daily Mirror* and sponsored by Cadbury's, Annette, covered in porpoise fat to keep warm, attempted the crossing on 24 August 1905 but was unsuccessful. She tried again on 7 August 1906. Then *Paris Match* sponsored a swim in the Seine, passing by all twenty-four bridges. Scheduled for 10 September 1905, Annette came equal third with a male competitor.[24] What is most remarkable is that she made these attempts so close together. The *Daily Mirror*, dubbing her the 'Australian Mermaid', coined the term by which a considerable part of her future career depended – the half-woman, half-mythical creature with extraordinary powers, more at home in the sea and water than on land. Not only were her athletic accomplishments reported in the newspapers, but the *Daily Mirror* began to describe and show photographs of her in her swimsuit. This marked a fundamental shift in news coverage – a middle-class woman displaying her legs and torso was being scrutinised in public. Such notoriety breached all Victorian conventions of modesty and restraint – Annette was a lady by her birth and training, but she was a foretaste of the modern independent woman.

There was no scandal, however, for the Prince of Wales (later George V) attended a Royal Command Performance at the Bath Club. Annette also performed her aquatic act in front of Queen Alexandra.[25] In June 1906 she beat the first woman to attempt a Channel cross, Viennese Baroness Isa Cescu, in a 22 mile (36 kilometre) race down the Danube from Tulu to Vienna.[26] Annette was severely cut on rocks and bruised during this swim.[27]

Her attempts at cracking the music hall circuit in England with a season at the London Hippodrome were not so successful.[28] She also decided to pursue a theatrical career, but in consultation with her father, she decided to relocate to the United States, where vaudeville could incorporate her type of indoor performance. Her first engagement at Chicago's White City Amusement Park was hardly set among uplifting, genteel entertainment: she competed with a Filipino 'headhunter' for her audience. Called 'The Lady Dolphin' in the Chicago papers, the initial reaction was lukewarm. As crowds improved, the performance proved extremely well paid. For her fifty-five short shows a week, including eighteen on the weekends, Annette earned the extraordinary sum of £2000.[29] This was at a time when a working woman in Australia earned about £2 per week if she was fortunate.

In Chicago, Annette met a friend of her brother Maurice, Jimmie Sullivan, a former boxer who had become a successful theatrical entrepreneur. This was a business relationship fully endorsed by her father and Maurice. But in the meantime, her father, Frederick, was ailing, and unable to continue managing his daughter. He died in the USA in 1907.

In 1912 Annette and Jimmie married and remained together until Jimmie died in 1972. In their relationship, Annette was always the 'star' at home and in public, although she would not have attained her fame in the United States without his careful management of her career. But Jimmie was not a good business manager of her earnings. Rather than investing her considerable earnings in property, they were largely frittered away on extensive first-class travel, relocating across continents or half-hearted ventures that fizzled out.

The most famous incident relating to the early part of Kellermann's career, after she relocated to the Wonderland Park in Boston, concerned a banning for public indecency when she appeared in a man's swimming costume at Revere Beach, the first public beach in the United States. Most commentators on her life and career take her word, which is reiterated in her unpublished autobiography, that she caused a scandal and appeared in court, however, her talent for publicity and other research suggests she may have embellished the account. Marcelle's notes on her famous sister also maintain Annette was arrested 'for having bare legs in the water'. The incident forms a dramatic moment in her 1952 biofilm, *Million Dollar Mermaid*, starring Esther Williams, where the incongruously cast Victor Mature as Jimmie arranges a stunt to garner publicity.[30] The Australian biography *The Original Million Dollar Mermaid* (2005) reiterates this central image in the history of women's liberation and modernity.[31] Yet careful research by Jacqui Donegan in the court records and contemporary newspapers in the United States did not uncover the story.[32] The Boston papers sang her praises:

> No more Gibson bathing girl
> Shall Grace the Newport summer whirl
> Annette declares her garment's wrong
> At both ends too extremely long.[33]

Her fame spread further when, after examining the statistics of over 10,000 women, the eccentric Harvard professor Dudley Sargent, a former circus performer turned instructor in physical education, identified her as the 'perfect woman', in line with Venus de Milo.[34] Annette's athletic body heralded a change in standards of female beauty from the soft, curved Edwardian ideal to the modern, streamlined, trim and fit form. From Sargent's declaration onwards, Annette had the publicity tag for the rest of her career. Yet as she aged, it became a millstone around her neck.

The issue of how women should dress on the beach or when swimming advanced through Annette's advocacy of sensible, appropriate attire. In her autobiography she wrote: 'How could these women swim with shoes – stockings-bloomers-skirts-over-dresses with puffed sleeves in sailor collars – in some cases tightly fitted corsets?

Annette Kellermann in 1919, modelling her radical costume. Bain Collection, Library of Congress LC-B2-738-5.

But then no one went swimming ...'[35] Annette's ensemble – a man's costume plus leggings – were commonly referred to as 'Annette Kellermanns'. She often ripped her swimming costume with scissors on stage to demonstrate she was not wearing a corset. This was a sensational act for a respectable woman to perform in public. Her father would certainly not have approved and doubtless her mother suffered the indignities of her daughter's performances when she learned of them back home in Melbourne. By now, though, Annette was a rich woman, commanding the highest fees for any female performer in vaudeville.[36]

In her revised and more glamorous stage act entitled 'On the Beach at Boulogne', she wore a lighter costume. On 25 November 1908, she opened at B. F. Keith and F. F. Proctor's Fifth Avenue Theatre, performing in a 25,000-gallon pool to huge crowds, including middle-class women, a new addition to audiences. This was despite reservations in some quarters about her attire and its lack of modesty. *Variety* assured potential patrons 'there is nothing shriekingly loud about her act ...'[37] Annette also performed in the new Paradise Roof Garden Theatre, known also as Hammerstein's, built on top of a new invention, the skyscraper. Charlie Chaplin had also appeared there.[38] Annette widened her repertoire, adding a high-wire act, fencing and boomerang throwing, as well as diving from great heights. Her incorporation of ballet techniques underwater later gave rise to whole new genres of performance – water ballet and synchronised swimming.

Annette's reputation after her father's death was verging on unseemly. She was cited in a divorce case in March 1909, although she strenuously denied any wrongdoing. Her frequent arrests for speeding in her new white Buick she viewed as evidence of her modernity and carefree spirit; others saw it as dangerous behaviour, and some regarded her as a spoilt show performer who thought she was above the law. At the same time, Annette also made some serious errors in her career. When she went over to a new agency, William Morris, in 1909, Keith and Proctor immediately sued. Morris had challenged the Keith and Proctor monopoly two years before, and won the case. Stealing contracted artists was impudent, ambitious and illegal. The judge ruled that Keith and Proctor had developed Annette's new act and promoted her career, thereby making a landmark ruling in entertainment law.[39] Annette was forced to stay with Keith, in a frosty relationship that endured for the next two decades.

The lengthy case did allow Annette to branch out into new fields of endeavour. She first tried to enter the world of opera with the help of her mother – who now lived in Paris – and Dame Nellie Melba, but nothing came of this late start. There was always an emotional tension between Annette's original training in the high arts of music and ballet and her commercial career based on athleticism, and motion pictures presented another challenge. She decided to launch into the new medium of cinema, then regarded as a rather low-class entertainment. Her first role, in 1909, was in *The Bride of*

Lammermoor, followed by three other short films in the same year, all produced by the Vitagraph Company. In her first major film, *Neptune's Daughter*, Annette was billed as 'The Perfect Woman'. Directed by Herbert Brenon, the film was spectacular, with Annette performing her own stunts. She was severely injured at one stage and spent six weeks in hospital, and she carried the scar on her forehead for the rest of her life. Before filming started she suffered the loss of her mother in 1914. Filmed in the Caribbean under trying and primitive conditions, the film contained provocative scenes of Annette swimming naked. Strangely, this did not cause a scandal when it was released in 1915; presumably the audience understood mermaids did not have much reason to wear clothes.[40] A huge hit, the film ran for seven weeks in New York City.

Flushed with success, Annette made another extravaganza, *A Daughter of the Gods*, filmed in Jamaica in 1915, with producer William Fox and Brenon as director, although he was later replaced. Annette trained the 'mermaids' herself. This film was a cinematic landmark with its lavish sets, scenery and million-dollar budget. There was disharmony on the set, however, with rumours that Annette had more than a professional interest in her director. Jimmie baulked at his secondary role in her life, but it was beyond his control in the theatres of New York. The film opened to enthusiastic crowds in October 1916. With its expert tinting, photography and stunts, the film, now lost, was a rival to D. W. Griffith's and Cecil B. DeMille's great shows.[41] William Fox, who had founded the Fox Film Co., was a master of publicity. He realised that Annette was a commodity he could push to its limit, and arranged for a life-sized cut-out of Annette to be placed outside cinemas. Women could then use a tape measure to see how closely they resembled the 'perfect woman'.[42]

Annette was enjoying a busy professional period. Since 1909 she had endorsed a series of American products, just as she had done in London in 1905. They ranged from Buick cars and Du Pont raincoats to Black Jack Chewing Gum, which supposedly assisted with the

Frederic Shipman Enterprises present Annette Kellermann, 'The Perfect Woman'. David Elliott theatrical postcard collection, National Library of Australia, nla pic-an22948275.

prevention of coughs and colds.[43] She had also kept her stage career happening. In London in 1912, she appeared on stage in *Undine*, an 'idyll of forest and stream', followed later by a stint at the Winter Garden in New York, where Al Jolson also performed.

Her career stalled after a serious horseriding accident in 1918 when on location in Maine for her new film with Fox, *Queen of the Sea*. Paralysed and confined to bed, Annette showed true courage as she fought her injury. She began the slow process of recovery and learning to walk again. For someone who had been crippled as a child, this was a terrible nightmare to endure once again. It took a year for Annette to recover. Jimmie's steadfast support cemented their marriage, and from then on there were no rumours of infidelity. Later she pledged support to Sister Elizabeth Kenny's revolutionary methods of assisting patients with polio, and the principal's office at the Women's College at the University of Queensland is named in honour of Annette's support for the emerging profession of physiotherapy.[44]

In *Queen of the Sea* Annette swam and dived naked. The first director of the film, Lois Weber, was one of the pioneer women directors in the film industry, although she was replaced by G. Adolfi.[45] The critics and public were not so enthusiastic about this formula film. Critics found the film unconvincing and contrived, noting its weak plot and rehashing of previous efforts and stunts.[46] In Annette's following film, *What Women Love* (1920), she played a flapper; yet again it rested upon familiar, now hackneyed themes and scenes.[47] Her last major film, shot in New Zealand, *Venus of the South* (1924), directed by her husband, was also a flop.

Annette decided not to sign a five-year contract with William Fox, preferring instead to re-ignite her career in vaudeville and follow her aspirations for legitimate theatre as well. In her autobiography she revealed that in 1917 her performance of classical ballet, doing an impersonation of Anna Pavlova in Saint-Saëns' *Swan*, under the baton of Arturo Toscanini at the New York Metropolitan Opera House, was the 'biggest thrill of my whole career ...' On the same program Caruso sang arias from *Madama Butterfly*, and violinist and composer Fritz Kreisler also appeared. She later danced with Pavlova and military march composer John Philip Sousa in the Hippodrome. Annette was particularly proud that Pavlova's time was severely cut to allow more of her own performance on stage. She also revived her aquatic act, performing the diving scene from *A Daughter of the Gods*.[48]

With her stage career now a little passé, and despite spectacular stunts such as jumping out of a plane without a parachute and diving into the sea, Annette needed to reinvent herself yet again. With her brand as a marketable commodity, Annette Kellermann Inc., established in 1909, was launched in earnest with her book *How to Swim* in 1918. It is a curious book, with the first section focusing on her own life and its challenges, and the second an instructional manual. Capitalising on her depiction as the world's 'most perfect woman', Annette released another book in 1918 on health, beauty and fitness – *Physical Beauty: How to Keep It.* Having already patented her swimwear design in 1910, Annette began major production in New York with her own manufacturing company in 1920.[49] Her invention of a women's one-piece suit, made for comfort and speed, revolutionised women's apparel into a more streamlined design than men's. She capitalised on the mail order market, and from her Broadway office sold another book – now lost – *The Body Beautiful*, which also canvassed her struggles from disability and deformity as a child to 'the most perfect woman'. A firm believer in yoga and good breathing, Annette preached holistic routines of diet and exercise.[50] Articles by her that appeared in physical culturist Bernarr Macfadden's journal *Physical Culture* reached out to new audiences. Annette could be brutal in her advice to women. Her enemy was flab and fat. She advised lying on the floor naked with the legs rolled up to gauge fat deposits. This was surely a strike against Victorian prudery. How women responded to this test remains unknown.[51] Syndicated in the Hearst newspapers, her advice was widely read across the United States.

Annette was part of the revolution that saw the ideal of physical perfection and the use of health regimes directed from small coteries of believers to a mass audience, begun in earnest with Dr John Harvey Kellogg (1852–1943) and his strict food and exercise program at the Battle Creek Sanitarium in Michigan. A Seventh Day Adventist, Kellogg brought his religious principles into his medical practice in the hope of eliminating diseases caused by poor diet. Annette, like Kellogg, had been a long-term vegetarian and teetotaller. In 1909 she planned an 800-room health resort for women and children in Pennsylvania, but nothing came of it.[52] Her next attempt involved a ranch for women and children – the Kellermann Country Club, located north of Los Angeles, opened in 1925. The club was far in advance of then current practice, with facilities for disabled children, pools and gymnasiums. It was based on Kellogg's idea but vastly expanded.[53] This venture did not last long and went out of business. Later, in the 1950s, Annette opened a health food store in Los Angeles, which also proved to be too far ahead of its time to be profitable.

In some ways Annette managed her stardom well, but by branching out into so many areas she dissipated her core vision. She possessed the energy and foresightedness to understand what might work, but the constant juggling act between various parts of her commercial empire made them all, at times, precarious. Resuscitating her vaudeville career, just as that whole institution was at the point of decline, was not sensible. In 1921 she toured Australia and New Zealand, staying for two years. Adept at languages, she learned Danish and Dutch in order to be able to tour to Denmark and Holland and speak with the locals. She also knew some Swedish.[54] In London in 1925 she introduced a new high-wire act at the Coliseum, where she had moving dolls of Mary Pickford, Buster Keaton and Charlie Chaplin dance on the wire with her. A serious fall on stage did not stop her run.[55] How she could hope to manage her country club and sanitarium in California at the same time showed a confidence and energy that was sometimes out of step with reality.

Always apolitical, Annette went to Germany in the mid 1930s to preach her brand of athleticism. This showed a curious lack of judgment on her and Jimmie's part. But her views on bodily perfection and discipline resonated with Aryan ideology. She was also very proud of her German and French heritage. Nothing much is known about the three years she spent in Germany.

In 1937 Annette returned to the United States, where she met President Franklin Roosevelt and advised him on diet and exercise to assist with his polio. Returning to Australia in 1939, she lived on Newry Island, off Mackay, where she took an interest in the Great Barrier Reef. By this time, her sister, Marcelle, and Marcelle's husband had joined Jimmie and Annette permanently. During World War II, Annette engaged in a considerable degree of war work for the Red Cross and created a show called *We're All In It*, performed with 200 swimmers at the North Sydney Olympic Pool to raise money for the organisation.

Her performing career was virtually over by 1945. On her return to the United States, she continued working for the Red Cross, often visiting rehabilitating soldiers to whom she played the piano accordion and reminisced. Her parents would have been mortified to see their daughter perform on a folk instrument in public.[56] Suddenly, in 1951, plans were afoot for a film biography of her cinematic career, but Annette was aghast that an uneducated American from humble circumstances – Esther Williams – was to portray her. Even at the age of sixty-five she felt she could do the role much better,[57] and if not her, she requested the role be filled by a fellow Australian. The film, *Million Dollar Mermaid*, was panned by critics who found the story line unconvincing and thought Busby Berkeley's choreography was merely an echo of his great days in the 1930s. Yet the image of a heavily made-up Esther Williams smiling underwater made a lasting impression on many baby boomers. Williams also starred in a remake of *Neptune's Daughter*.

However, the public no longer remembered Annette Kellermann, who was now referred to as the 'Esther Williams of her day'. This was the woman celebrated in F. Scott Fitzgerald's *This Side of Paradise* (1920) as the essential modern woman and exemplar of the jazz age, but by the end of her life, Annette had become conservative. Her contributions to public debate, such as her criticisms of the bikini in the 1950s, seemed old-fashioned and prudish. She took the position of: 'My goodness, things have changed since my day,' without recognising the irony that she was the very person who successfully challenged Victorian strictures of dress for women.[58] Relocated to a poor area of the Gold Coast and living in a fibro shack, Annette became a relic of an earlier time, swimming every day in gaudy costumes and doing high kicks in public. The house she lived in was owned by her Brisbane relatives Mervyn and Ede Clarke. She kept much of her memorabilia in the tiny dwelling, a poignant and constant reminder that once she had been the highest paid woman in American theatre. Signed photographs of Lucille Ball, Grace Kelly and John Wayne adorned her walls.[59]

With Jimmie in declining health, she spent her days caring for him, until he died in April 1972. An arresting item appeared in the *Sydney*

Morning Herald in March 1975: 'Movie Star, Retired to Gold Coast, No Longer Had Need of Mink Coat',[60] describing how Annette's coat, sold to a woman for $600, was worn to the opening of the Sydney Opera House.

Annette was thrilled to be inducted into the International Swimming Hall of Fame in Florida in 1975, but she was too feeble to attend the ceremony.[61] Admitted to a Gold Coast nursing home, where she exercised every day, including doing high kicks, she died on 6 November 1975. Funeral rites were conducted in the Catholic faith of her childhood. Her sister, Marcelle, her faithful companion through all the heights of success and lows of her travails, undertook Annette's last wish that her ashes be scattered over the Great Barrier Reef waters that she loved so much. Annette's papers, costumes and memorabilia were initially donated to the archive of the Sydney Opera House, though they were later dispersed and some sold at public auction. Annette would be both amused and delighted to learn that her name and image are the central features on a series of murals painted by Wendy Sharpe, adorning the Cook and Phillip Park Aquatic Centre in Sydney.

CHAPTER 10

Lady Maie Casey
(1891–1983)

The bohemian artist, writer and chatelaine of Yarralumla who met the who's who of the world.

Maie Casey was a most unlikely bohemian. Born into the Australian upper class in 1891, she was a talented artist and writer whose work was constrained by the demanding career of her husband, Lord Richard Casey. Appointed the inaugural Australian Ambassador to the United States, Governor of Bengal, a cabinet minister in Australia, member of the British House of Lords as Baron Casey of Berwick and Westminster, and, lastly, Governor-General, the demands of Richard Casey's public life always came first in this close but puzzling relationship. Despite that, Maie maintained several intense, long-term romantic relationships with women and in some ways she resembled the character of Princess Margaret or Lady Edwina Mountbatten – bohemian, adventurous and unconventional at one level, but deeply status conscious, snobbish and demanding of reverence on another. She moved in the highest international circles, a confidante of Gandhi, Churchill, Noël Coward, Dame Judith Anderson and Eleanor Roosevelt. Her book, *Tides and Eddies* (1966), reads like a rollcall of the rich, famous and powerful of the mid-twentieth century.[1] Maie also had much in common with the effervescent Dame Zara Holt (1909–89) who mixed in similar circles. Unlike Maie, who was cool and often cutting in conversation, Dame Zara possessed a warm personality, good business intelligence and sincerity that made her a popular international and national figure.[2]

Both sides of Maie's family quickly rose up the newly established hierarchy in Victoria in the 1850s. Her maternal grandfather, a Protestant Irishman named Theodotus Sumner, was a merchant, who entered into partnership with businessman Richard Grice in Melbourne in 1855.[3] The business owned a shipping line, well-appointed pastoral properties in several colonies and a guano plantation on Malden Island in the Central Pacific.[4] A public-minded philanthropist, Sumner was on the board of the Royal Women's Hospital in Melbourne from 1856 to 1870, a member of the Victorian Legislative Council and also of the Melbourne Club.[5] Theodotus purchased the family home, Stony Park, at Brunswick for his bride, Sarah Peers, the daughter of a Welsh builder who had made his fortune first in Van Diemen's Land in the 1830s and later in Melbourne from 1838.[6]

Maie's mother, Alice Elfrida, was, by Maie's account, a self-absorbed beauty who made her feel anxious as a child. She realised at the young age of seven or eight that '[my mother] ... had a tall beautiful body that moved with grace ...'[7] For the rest of her life Maie was haunted by her own dissatisfactions with her appearance, teased by her aunt Maud Nash that 'Maie is stumpy, like the Ryans [her father's side of the family]!'[8] As Maie herself remarked, 'I did not admire myself at all: a depression settled on me every time afterward that I saw myself in a mirror.' Certainly she was no beauty – her face was broad and square with a strong chin. Her forceful character and her talent were, she would come to realise, far more important.

Her father, Sir Charles Snodgrass Ryan (1853–1926), was a charismatic, handsome man of adventure. His Protestant father, Charles Ryan, arrived from Ireland in 1840, marrying Marian Cotton. The Cottons in London were a wealthy family connected with Sir Joshua Reynolds.[9] Born on Killeen Station in Victoria, Charles was educated in medicine at the University of Melbourne. He undertook postgraduate studies at Bonn and Vienna before working as a military surgeon in the Turkish army during the Turko-Serbian and Turko-Russian Wars in 1876–78. Charles later wrote an interesting account of these years in his book, *Under the Red Crescent* (1897). Returning to Melbourne in 1878, he set up as a surgeon with a large commitment to poor patients.[10] Charles was a well-connected young man about town before his marriage, and Maie recalled in her book on Nellie Melba that as a child she visited a society dressmaker who asked about 'Charlie'. She recalled thinking this was 'a strange way not to say your papa'.[11]

The Ryans were a cultured family. Charles' sister, Ellis Rowan (1848–1922), was a distinguished botanical artist.[12] Another sister, Ada, married Lord Charles Scott, the younger brother of the sixth Duke of Buccleuch and eighth Duke of Queensbury. In her family memoir, Maie recalled discussing this marriage with Queen Mary, who joked about the dangers of marrying Australians in the nineteenth century.[13] The story reveals that Maie mixed in the highest circles of the British aristocracy and that Australians were formerly perceived as descendants of convicts.

In July 1883 Alice Sumner married Charles Ryan at Christ Church, Brunswick. Maie wrote in her memoir that she was born at home at 37 Collins Street, Melbourne, 'opposite the Melbourne Club'.[14] She was actually born in her Grandmother Sumner's house, Stony Park. Her birth names, Ethel Marion Sumner, display the mark of family lineage. Yet from early childhood she became 'Maie', an altogether more charming name than Ethel. Like many privileged children, Maie was not reared primarily by her parents but by a Swiss nurse, Berthe Tissot, whom she later wrote was the 'real pivot of my life'.[15] Although Berthe was Swiss and spoke French, Maie's mother insisted she take 'proper' French lessons from 'Madame Princep who exhaled Eau de Cologne; Mlle Maillard, a poor sad disarming woman with chilblained fingers like bunches of bananas; the beautiful goggle-eyed Madame Hossendoff'.[16] From these descriptions, which breathe life into her teachers in a short phrase, Maie's creative talent can be appreciated.

Along with Grandmother Sumner, her mother and Berthe, Maie went to England at the age of five. She was privately educated with the daughters of the Australian barrister Sir Edward Mitchell, KC, before attending St George's School at Ascot in England at the age of sixteen. This had been Winston Churchill's old prep school.[17] During her holidays she spent time with her aunt, Lady Scott, in Northamptonshire, and with her brother, Rupert, who had been sent to the exclusive Harrow School.[18] Maie completed her education at a 'finishing school' in Paris. She did not attend university, despite her ability and intelligence, on advice from a family friend, Sir Richard Stawell.

Maie returned to Melbourne in 1910 to the life of a privileged young woman but was back in England in 1914 to be presented at court to King George V and Queen Mary, the epitome of acceptance for a young Australian hoping to scale the social heights. That same year both Rupert and Charles volunteered for war service and Maie began work for the war effort as a housemaid at the Home for Wounded Officers in Park Lane, an unusual choice for such a well-placed young woman. In 1915 she joined the Australian Wounded and Missing Enquiry Bureau established by Vera Deakin, daughter of the former Australian prime minister.[19] Maie recalled the trauma of the war: 'we were afraid to read the casualty lists in the morning newspapers'.[20]

On her return to Melbourne, Maie and her friend Joan Weigall (later Joan Lindsay, and now better remembered as the author of *Picnic at Hanging Rock* [1967]) set about studying art. In 1921 she accompanied Rupert to Coblenz, Germany, where he worked for the Inter-Allied Rhineland High Commission. Some of his colleagues, including Josslyn Hay, son of the High Commissioner, Lord Kilmarnock, were distinctly bohemian in their attitudes. Later, as the Earl of Erroll, Hay was murdered in mysterious circumstances in Kenya in 1941, a central figure in the sexually promiscuous and drug-taking 'Happy Valley' set. Along with Hay's sister, Rosemary, Maie experimented with opium in Germany.[21] At this time cocaine was also a popular drug among the fast-living and privileged.[22] By some accounts Maie was seriously attracted to the vivacious young Rosemary and encouraged her far more sedate brother to pursue Rosemary, and indeed in 1924 they were married.[23]

In October 1923 Alice died. Maie's account of her mother's death is brutal: '[she] ... dropped dead while staying with Rupert ...'[24] but what resentments she harboured towards her mother were never fully explained in her published works. In early 1924, Maie relocated to London, sharing a flat with journalist Lady Kitty Ogilvie Vincent, later the eccentric author of *Two on a Trip: With Sledge Dogs in Canada* (1930). At a wedding that year, Maie met Richard Casey, a man she had vaguely known in Melbourne.[25] Born in Brisbane in 1890, Richard studied engineering at Trinity College, Cambridge, before serving in World War I. He was part of the first landing at Gallipoli in 1915. Awarded the Distinguished Service Order in 1918, Richard worked in Melbourne first before going to London as Australia's liaison officer. His close relationship with conservative Prime Minister Stanley Bruce (later Lord Bruce), opened many doors for Richard, then and in the years to come.[26]

Maie and Richard were married on 24 June 1926 in St James' Church in Piccadilly. At the age of thirty-five, Maie was an older bride for the time. She had intended wearing black taffeta before her friends convinced her that ivory was a more suitable bridal colour.[27] They returned to Melbourne the following year, briefly, before settling in London. Their daughter Jane was born in October 1928, much to Maie's horror, as she had wanted a son.[28] Their son, Donn, was born in 1931, yet she was equally as cold and demanding towards him. This set the tenor of her relations with both her children for the rest of her life.

Maie and her family returned to Melbourne that year as Richard intended to stand for federal parliament. He won the seat of Corio in late 1931 for the conservative United Australia Party.[29] Living in the tiny capital of Canberra after her sophisticated life in London was a challenge for Maie, made more palatable by horseriding and gardening. In 1932 she took on the responsibility for her nephew Patrick, Rupert's son. This was hardly a good move for Patrick, abandoned by one mother and placed into the care of a frosty aunt. In 1934 Maie's Aunt Winifred died, leaving Maie and Rupert – along with two relatives who were bought out – her beautiful house and estate, Edrington, at Berwick in the Dandenongs. There was some suspicion in the family that Maie had induced this bequest while tending to her dying aunt.[30] This was unlikely; but undoubtedly it shows that even her family regarded Maie as ruthless and manipulative. The property proved to be a bolt-hole for Maie.

In 1933 Richard was appointed deputy federal treasurer, although Maie did not see it as incumbent upon her to be the dutiful public wife engaging in political networking and entertaining. This was a surprisingly independent stand; Maie was devoted to Richard, not to his career. She decided to learn art properly, enrolling with George Bell, a former official war artist. Bell had a sound lineage, as he studied with Fred McCubbin and also in Paris.[31] A decided Modernist, he was just the mentor that Maie needed, as her work was highly individual, frequently focusing on Aboriginal themes.[32] Through the school, Maie later met Sali Herman and Russell Drysdale.

In 1937 Maie ventured out of the bohemian art world to attend the coronation of King George VI. Among other duties, Richard accompanied the king when he went trout fishing with Neville Chamberlain, whose career was soon to be discredited with his unfortunate 'peace in our time' pronouncement. And Maie purchased a Picasso painting, *Le Repos*.[33] This was the first Picasso to arrive in Australia. Another passion was also indulged. Since World War I Maie had been fascinated by aircraft. She purchased a Miles Whitney Straight, commencing lessons for her licence when she returned home.[34] Soon she could fly from Edrington to Canberra to be with Richard. The children were left totally in the care of nannies and governesses.

Maie kept up her passion for painting, meeting Cynthia Reed (later Nolan) for whom she developed a passion, if an unrequited one. Cynthia reported to her sister-in-law, Sunday Reed: 'Maie is over and has brought a Picasso painting. I was having a mild flirtation until it made me sick and I got out.'[35] This behaviour, perhaps acceptable in the bohemian world, was at odds with Maie's position as the wife of a potential prime minister. When Prime Minister Joseph Lyons died suddenly in April 1939, Maie thought Richard might step up to the role. She flew immediately to Canberra to discuss Richard's chances against his rival, Robert Menzies, who described her as a 'Lady Macbeth'. This was not to be, as Richard was not a capable networker, and favoured the return of Stanley Bruce from London. Richard's decision displayed a considerable lack of political judgment, as Bruce had lost his seat while prime minister in the 1928 election and now sat in the House of Lords.[36]

As a consolation prize, Casey was appointed as the inaugural Ambassador to the United States. At the time Australian foreign policy was totally reliant upon that of the United Kindom, so this was a highly audacious move. But it was a role far more suited to his skills and personality. On the way to Washington, Maie met a woman who was to become significant in her life for many years. Pat Jarrett was a champion swimmer and journalist, assigned to sports writing, then an unusual role for a woman.[37] The two found themselves travelling by ship to the United States together, where Pat taught the children to swim and Maie to dive. Maie asked Pat to act as her secretary but this was not quite what Pat had hoped for in her journalism career in America, so she declined. Capitalising on her connections with Pat's employer, Keith Murdoch, Maie arranged for Pat to come to Washington for a trial run of two months. Pat realised even then how cold and manipulative Maie could be, a warning she should have kept in mind for their future dealings.[38] The pair became increasingly close after a trip to Connecticut in July 1940, Maie happy to throw off the restrictions of marriage and her role as an ambassador's wife. Pat later recalled these were some of the happiest days of her life.[39] Reading between the lines suggests that they were lovers and that Richard was aware of the affair.[40]

Maie was a talented hostess in diplomatic circles, although frustrated by the strict protocols and boring people she had to endure. Her life had always been much freer. There was some compensation though: she met Noël Coward, already a friend of Richard's, and they became firm, enduring friends. Richard invited him to visit Australia in 1940.[41]

At this time the United States was not yet involved in World War II. Richard undertook the role of selling the Allied cause to the Americans.[42] Maie also took on the role as advocate of the Allied war effort. She travelled a lot in this endeavour, sometimes flying. One of her chief delights during her time in the States was her association with the exclusive Ninety-Nines, the original women's pilots' association that counted Amelia Earhart and Amy Johnson among its members. When the States entered the war in December 1941, Maie continued her intense war work.

Her life changed abruptly again when Winston Churchill appointed Richard as the British minister in Cairo in March 1942. This was a sensitive appointment, with northern Africa and Lebanon under the Vichy French, Libya under the Italians, Spanish Morocco under neutral Spain, and Egypt and Palestine under strong British influence. With the desert campaigns in progress this appointment was an enormous task.[43]

For Maie again, life became highly restricted. She was guarded by Gurkhas, who took their duties seriously, and she was not permitted any idle tourist activities. Maie busied herself by contributing to the war effort, working with blind servicemen at St Dunstain's Hospital and travelling with the Hadfield–Spears Mobile Hospital. Visitors provided some distractions. Maie met Cecil Beaton, who later revelled in a story that when Maie was presented to Queen Farida, she ignored the strict protocol and showed her mosquito bites to an astonished royal party.[44]

Fortunately Queen Farida was a fellow artist and an ardent feminist, so she took this enormous breach calmly.

Other guests included Noël Coward, who was then engaged in troop entertainment. More importantly, Churchill stayed with the Caseys in December 1943 as part of the Allied heads' meeting with President Roosevelt and General Chiang Kai-shek. Richard did not entirely enjoy the confidence of the British government, as senior minister Harold Macmillan regarded him as 'weak' and 'not ... very clever. Mrs Casey is, however'.[45] Richard was clever in his own profession of engineering, but he lacked cunning and guile as a diplomat.

At the same time as this important event, the children arrived from America, where they had been left in the care of the Squire family. This was hardly an auspicious arrival for Maie. Not only had she not seen the children for some time, but they were both seriously ill, and her attention was taken away from her important guests.

When Richard was appointed as Governor of Bengal in November 1943, Maie was again presented with new challenges. Richard went without a title, after turning down the offer of a British peerage, as this would not go over well in Australia, where he still maintained political ambitions for the future. Pat Jarrett was once again released from her duties with the Murdoch press in the United States to act as Maie's personal secretary.[46]

Maie arrived in Calcutta in early 1944, fully aware that her knowledge of India was negligible. Her informality caused distinct tensions in the rigidly run Government House. The snooty staff were accustomed to British lords and ladies in the vice-regal role. Initially Maie was left to cope with her new role alone, as Richard contracted dysentery. Worse for the status-conscious staff was Maie's decision to have Cecil Beaton as an extended house guest. His effete ways were never a hit with them, or with Richard. When Pat arrived on 4 March, Maie's life was made far easier and more pleasant, especially when the children were sent to Hallett, a boarding school for British children in

India. They were now distinctly Americanised, much to their mother's disapproval. Fortunately for Donn and Jane, Pat proved to be a wise friend and supporter for the rest of her life, providing a bulwark against their parents' aloofness.[47]

Maie was not entirely self-absorbed, however. She worked remarkably hard for Indian Red Cross efforts to gather supplies for the terrible famine that had earlier ravaged Bengal. She and Richard were surpassingly egalitarian in Bengal, at least in comparison to the British. Both were strong advocates of Indian independence after the war.[48] Their relative informality found warm acceptance among the Bengalis. Maie's work to enhance the status of women and to encourage education was particularly appreciated. The Australian press made much of her diligent reform activities on her return to Melbourne.[49] In further recognition Maie was appointed a Commander (Dame) of the Order of St John of Jerusalem. This was an ancient order; in its modern mode it was fiercely religious and anti-communist. She was also awarded the Imperial Gold Kaisar-i-Hind medal for her work in India.

Maie and the family returned to Australia in early 1946, fully expecting that the Liberal Party would fall at Richard's feet. This did not occur overnight; he waited until the next year before he became party president, and then entered federal parliament by winning the seat of La Trobe in 1949. By then Maie was active as a speaker and as an artist, lending many of her own paintings – including her Picasso – to an exhibition at the National Gallery of Victoria. She was the patron of luminaries such as Sidney Nolan, purchasing a painting of his in 1949 and writing the introduction to the catalogue of a Sydney exhibition. She also used her formidable international network to promote his work.

In 1951 Maie again met Frances Burke, another artist with whom she developed a long and passionate relationship. They had originally been students together in George Bell's school in the 1930s, but their lives had taken different trajectories. Like Florence Broadhurst,

Frances was an important innovator in arts and design in Australia.[50] She established the first major screen-printing business as early as 1937. Taking orders from Frances Burke Fabrics, Maie displayed these innovative designs in Washington and in Calcutta. Unlike Maie, Frances was open about her sexual relationships with women, and was called 'our resident lesbian' when they were students together.[51] Pat had returned from New York in March 1947, and by this time she was working on, of all things, the women's pages of the Melbourne *Sun News-Pictorial.* From the early 1950s she lived in Berwick near Maie, for several decades on part of Edrington Maie had given to her, though this was hardly convenient for her work as a journalist.[52] Given Maie's public reticence and the gaps in her papers, we do not know for certain how her relationship with Pat evolved after Frances became Maie's great source of womanly affection. Very soon Maie and Frances went away for weekends together at Anglesea, with Richard's approval. They dined frequently at the Lyceum Club in Melbourne.

Maie found a new enthusiasm for her career when she collaborated with leading artists such as Daryl Lindsay, the husband of her old friend Joan Weigall, on a project named *Early Melbourne Architecture, 1840–1888* (1953). Acting as editor and compiler, Maie worked tirelessly on an innovative assessment of buildings that included the grand and humble.[53] She was passionate about preserving Australia's colonial heritage and was far ahead of her time in this. In 1953 she also took part in the inaugural all-women air race.[54] Her life was also filled with overseas travel as she accompanied Richard in his role as Australia's External (now Foreign) Affairs Minister. Maie continued her own career, researching and writing her family history, *An Australian Story, 1837–1907* (1962), which she illustrated beautifully. Her gifts in portraiture and landscape were fully realised in this charming memoir. The following year she introduced the exhibition of her aunt Ellis Rowan's botanical illustrations in London.

Her life changed dramatically in 1960 when Richard was appointed a life peer, the second Australian after Stanley Bruce to accept this

Imperial honour. This appointment was entirely in keeping with the Caseys' world view, but it was totally out of touch with modern Australia. His title, Baron Casey of Berwick and Westminster, attempted to reconcile his dual loyalties. From now on Maie was known as 'the Lady Casey', and the title was not lost on her assertive public interactions with women. She made a play for a young woman in the Lyceum Club in 1962, until told by a friend, 'Lay off, Maie, she's married.'[55] This is an interesting observation; what if the object of her desire had been single and unattached?

Maie's literary career continued. Her self-published book of poems, illustrated by Frances Burke, was a far more personal undertaking.[56] Yet she allowed Margaret Sutherland to set some of the poems to music in 1964. She and the distinguished composer further collaborated in 1965 on the opera *The Young Kabbarli*, about the life of Daisy Bates, whom Maie had met in 1934. A limited edition of this rare work was published in 1972. Maie was fascinated by this strange relic of the Edwardian era who had lived in the desert like a prophet for so many decades. Far more competent was her memoir of her public life, *Tides and Eddies* (1966), which was necessarily tactful about many eminent personages still alive. The opium and other drug-taking in Germany in the 1920s with the future Earl of Erroll was discreetly omitted.

In 1965 Richard was appointed Governor-General. Maie was perhaps the most eccentric and fascinating of all the spouses of this high office. As highly decorous but reserved conversation bored her, her dinner *bons mots* could be provocative and racy. She made new friends, including the waspish Patrick White. Her invitation list to Yarralumla included many artists and creative people, and never before were so many gays and lesbians entertained by the governor-general. After four years Richard retired from this office, pleased to be recognised as a Knight of the Order of the Garter. In 1970 he was named Australian of the Year, a somewhat surprising honour given his deep commitment to the United Kingdom. Life for both the Caseys in retirement was an anti-climax after decades of fascinating public service. During this period both Richard and Maie relied upon Pat Jarrett's support and practical skills.[57]

When Richard died in 1976, Maie was inconsolable and deeply depressed with grief. One of the strangest manifestations of Maie's self-centredness occurred at Richard's funeral. After decades of loyalty, service and affection from Pat, Maie decided she was not welcome at the funeral. What Pat did to deserve such shabby and insensitive treatment remains unclear, since Maie destroyed most of the correspondence between them. Yet it demonstrates Maie at her most selfish and manipulative. Pat left Berwick and settled in Mount Eliza.[58] Maie's treatment of her children had always contained these elements of disapproval and ruthlessness. She was hard, self-serving and callous beneath the superficial charm and humour.

When Maie died in 1983 her tributes were fulsome, especially from the Australian Women's Pilots' Association. Her beloved Edrington was sold by her daughter, Jane. Previously Maie proposed leaving the property to four grandchildren.

CHAPTER 11

Florence Broadhurst

(1899–1977)

*The girl who came from poverty in Mount Perry in Queensland
and conquered the worlds of haute couture and wallpaper design.*

Florence Broadhurst was a highly accomplished woman as well as an extraordinarily bold, determined liar, and notorious self-promoter and mythmaker. Born into humble circumstances at Mount Perry, a tiny hamlet inland from Bundaberg in Queensland in 1899, she later purported to be an English aristocrat, invited to Princess Elizabeth's wedding in 1947. A good seamstress who learned needlework from her mother, in the 1930s Florence adopted the persona of Madame Pellier, trained in Paris, and established a *maison de couture* and was appointed a court dressmaker in Mayfair. With a lot of courage and cheek she carried it off successfully. Although she had left school at thirteen, Florence declared she had studied to a high level at the Trinity College of Music and the Slade School of Fine Arts in London, as well as studying art for ten years in Paris.[1] Yet later in life she had a brilliant career as a wallpaper designer and manufacturer that required no dissembling and fudging of the truth. Unable to celebrate her own rise from rural hardship at the beginning of the twentieth century to international recognition, she presented an incongruous figure, full of bravado, talent and deep insecurities. Her brutal murder in 1977 ended the life of one of Australia's most fascinating and talented women.

Florence Maud Broadhurst was born on Mungy Station near Mount Perry, population 250. Her father, William, was a drover, promoted to team leader before he purchased a modest property of his own, 'The Oakes', in 1902. Bill later became a favourite publican when the population of Mount Perry grew to 3675 after the copper smelter brought wealth to the community. Her mother, Margaret Crawford, was a quiet homemaker, fond of needlework and the arts. Florence attended the local state school where she obtained a basic education. As a young teenager she had penned her ambitions to '... do great things', a document she kept for the rest of her life.[2] She was to take the ambition and drive inherited from her father, and her mother's craft skills, to forge several illustrious careers as an adult.[3]

Under Margaret's influence, Florence studied singing and dancing in Bundaberg, necessitating a long 95-kilometre drive on unsealed dirt roads from their small hamlet. Bundaberg was a wealthy sugar town with beautiful wooden Queenslander homes owned by the sugar planters, such as the Crann Brothers and Angus Gibson. Later renowned for Bundaberg Rum, the town was a thriving provincial centre. Gladys Moncrieff was born there in 1892. Her mother, Amy Wall Moncrieff, had been a professional singer in Melbourne before her marriage and encouraged the musical development of the town, as well as of her young daughter. Gladys went on the stage at the age of six, touring around north Queensland, before her spectacular rise to an international career in musical comedy and light operetta. By the time Florence began her lessons in Bundaberg, Moncrieff had already paved the way for a girl from Bundaberg to sing professionally.

Florence's career took another path: she began with the local music festivals, most notably the well-regarded Queensland eisteddfod. In August 1918, after success at the eisteddfods, Florence performed at the Princess Theatre in Toowoomba for a patriotic concert. She had joined a group called the Smart Set Diggers, known for their renditions of popular patriotic songs and sang 'Beyond the Dawn'. Florence befriended the female impersonator Ralph Sawyer, a key performer in the Smart Set Diggers. Through his invitation, she joined the troupe. At this time a female impersonator was more like the Barry Humphries' character Dame Edna Everage, rather than code for a transvestite and the genre of the male-as-female revue was popular among troops in World War I. Two months later at a fundraiser, Florence gained attention when she sang the well-known 'Still as the Night'.[4]

The highlight of her amateur career came when she sang with Dame Clara Butt, in 1921, at St John the Evangelist Anglican Cathedral in Brisbane.[5] Dame Clara had studied at the Royal College of Music in London, and Queen Victoria had paid for her training in Paris. A woman of great presence and stature – at 6 feet 2 inches (189 cm) – she is now remembered for the 'Sea Pictures', composed for her by Sir Edward Elgar.[6] To be chosen to accompany such an internationally renowned singer was high praise for the young woman from Mount Perry. But a career in the classical and operatic repertoire did not appeal to Florence, who was far more modern and racy in attitudes than the redoubtable Dame Clara.

In 1922 the Smart Set Diggers were renamed the Globetrotters and embarked on a fifteen-month tour of South-East Asia and India.[7] For Florence this was the opportunity to leave the bush forever and embark on the first chapter of her international careers. From this point until the end of her life, she would rewrite the areas she felt ashamed of and wished to ignore. Mount Perry was eliminated firmly from her biography. In this regard she was unlike Gladys Moncrieff, who never pretended she came from anywhere but Bundaberg. Such honesty was no hindrance to long runs on the West End stage in London.

The Globetrotters consisted of Ralph and Charles Holt, both female impersonators; Richard Norton and Dick Crichton, the comedians; and Wallington Tate as pianist. In line with this ensemble, Florence became the 'boy' of the group and was renamed Miss Bobby Broadhurst. A flapper in full flight and costume, Florence left Brisbane on the *Montoro* bound for Singapore in December 1922.[8] Though not a typically beautiful woman, she had dazzle and vivacity aplenty – a sharp wit and a predilection for wisecracks, abundant energy, an open mind and plenty of talent equipped her first steps to success. At her age many young women in rural Australia had already married, their ambitions hemmed in by narrow expectations and opportunities. This was not for Florence – ever.

The tour was a successful undertaking, ambitious in its scope as it ventured through Singapore, Bangkok, Kuala Lumpur, Penang, Delhi, Karachi, Hong Kong, Shanghai, Tientsin (now Tianjin) and Peking (now Beijing). Modern, flippant and very gay in its approach, the ensemble entertained local elites and expatriate colonials in these distant outposts of Imperial influence. Somerset Maugham, international bestselling author and spy, travelled through China and Hong Kong in 1920 gathering material for his book of short stories *On a Chinese Screen* (1922). His version of colonial life was not the frivolous light-hearted world of the Globetrotters, but in some way their worlds did intersect with their gay subtexts. This was a world recovering from the devastation of the Great War, and for many, the years of suffering and anxiety had not ended with the war. For young people who never went into combat or lost family in the global conflicts, the new jazz age, as F. Scott Fitzgerald dubbed it, was fast, exhilarating and dangerous. They were tired of sorrow, grief and tearful melancholic renditions of 'Abide with Me'. Fast cars, fast lives throwing off Victorian and Edwardian prudery, new sexual mores, and even drugs made for a dramatic change in the 1920s. Even in the early novels of Agatha Christie, such as *The Murder of Roger Ackroyd* (1926) and *Death in the Clouds* (1935) 'Bright Young Things' snorted the odd line of cocaine.

For Bobby Broadhurst, it was a heady taste of the high life, in which she was courted by rich and powerful men. In 1924, Florence and the troupe went to India. The Maharajah Amer Kashif fell desperately in love with her after seeing her performance and shot a tiger in her honour.[9] The troupe went to Shanghai, the most sophisticated, decadent city in Asia, which had been divided up into Western European sectors under American, French and British control. Shanghai grew in the 1920s when White Russians, loyal to

The nearly all-boy review. Florence is the one dressed in the top hat. Mitchell Library, State Library of NSW PXE 937_no8.

the tsar – or at least opposed to the new Bolshevik government – fled to this cosmopolitan city. Many Russian Jews, often highly educated and formerly wealthy, were a part of this wider European community. The exotic and dangerous atmosphere of Shanghai was captured in the film *Shanghai Express* (1932), directed by Josef von Sternberg and starring Anna May Wong and Marlene Dietrich.

Florence entered into this heady world at full throttle. Performing at the ritzy Carlton Club, the Globetrotters was a popular act. Florence – or Bobby – also performed with other groups such as the Broadcasters, Carlton Follies and Carlton Sparklers, leading to extensive press coverage of her singing and Charleston dancing.[10] When the original troupe disbanded, Florence decided to capitalise on her popularity and establish her own business. In February 1926 she opened the Broadhurst Academy Incorporated School of the Arts, which gave instruction in violin, piano, singing, banjolele, modern ballroom dancing, ballet, musical culture and journalism.[11] She employed experienced tutors such as Madame Boulueva who studied at the Dresden Conservatorium in pianoforte and Boulueva's daughter, a classical dancer from the Imperial Russian theatre.[12] With extensive publicity in the local and English-speaking press, the academy got off to a good start.

Unfortunately, though, this was not a particularly stable or secure time to be in Shanghai. With civil war raging between the communists and the Kuomintang forces, the city was a target for both combatants who opposed Western influence and control of Chinese territory. On 12 February 1927 a general strike erupted. A fierce conservative and Anglophile, Florence defied the fearful atmosphere of the city, and hosted a fundraiser for the British troops stationed there two weeks later. On 12 April 1927 the Kuomintang forces entered the city, looted property and massacred residents, particularly those suspected of being communists. Six weeks later, Florence brazenly and publicly celebrated Empire Day.[13]

With civil war at her very doorstep, Florence had no alternative but to abandon her business and return to Australia. She visited her family in Mount Perry, having not seen them for nearly five years. She had left as a local country girl with high ambitions and returned a glamorous international celebrity, a worldly, sophisticated and confident woman. In July she was involved in a car accident in her father's Studebaker and sustained injuries to her back, destroying any possibility of her returning to the stage.[14] After recuperating, Florence decided to try her luck in London. Clearly the confines of her childhood were far too narrow, and even Sydney seemed small and tame after glamorous, menacing and decadent Shanghai.

Florence left Australia in October 1927 and arrived in London little more than a year after the horrors of the General Strike. Florence was not deterred by the continued calls for class warfare and the tense atmosphere. Hit hard by the enormous casualties of World War I, with men destroyed forever by combat, and massive war loans crippling the economy, London contained elements of deep poverty and depression. This was not a world in which Florence had any intention of inhabiting. Her aspirations were far more concerned with conquering the world of the supposedly carefree upper class, so wittily satirised by Evelyn Waugh in his debut novel *Decline and Fall* (1928). It was upon the world of gay, quick repartee and graceful living that Florence set her ambitions.

With her formidable skills in dressmaking and embroidery, she went to work for the couturier Madame Corot at 33 Old Bond Street, London. At this time women couturiers such as Madeleine Vionnet, Coco Chanel and Elsa Schiaparelli extended the tradition set by the design houses Callot Soeurs and Jeanne Lanvin. Madame Paquin opened a couture house at 39 Dover Street in London in 1902, while Scots-Canadian Lucile (Lady Duff Gordon) was another successful society dressmaker in London in the early years of the twentieth century.[15] These women maintained a leading role in a profession that was later transformed after World War II by such men as Christian Dior, Hardy Amies, Hubert de Givenchy and Cristóbal Balenciaga.

Florence then went to work for W. W. Reville-Terry, the prestigious Grosvenor Square couture house which, like Norman Hartnell, was among a number of other establishments that made court presentation clothes.[16] Florence's experience in the finest haute couture establishments in London gave her invaluable skills for her subsequent careers. While there she also designed film and theatre costumes.[17]

In June 1929 Florence married stockbroker Percy Kann at Brompton Oratory, an exclusive Roman Catholic church, in South Kensington. They set up house in St John's Wood, a charming, leafy suburb not far from the London Zoo. In 1933 Florence, with Percy as a director of the company, established Madame Pellier Ltd Modes et Robes at 65 New Bond Street in Mayfair. There was already a Madame Pellier in the St James Building in George Street in Sydney,

Florence Broadhurst on her wedding day. Mitchell Library, State Library of NSW PXE 937_no1.

who brought Parisian sophistication and chic to women in Australia.[18] To use the name of a well-established identity, albeit one in Sydney, was a daring move.

But in her new venture Florence was first intent upon taking away business from her former employers. From 1935 to 1937 her *maison de couture* was listed as a court dressmaker. The salon was expensively outfitted in silvery grey and adorned with fresh flowers daily. At this end of the market, the clientele may not have felt the cold winds of the protracted Depression.[19] Even riskier was Florence's decision to pretend she was a French woman who had trained in Paris. Here was a young woman with little formal education from a bush school in Queensland, now inventing herself as a French *grande dame*. Other contemporary London couturiers, such as Captain Edward Molyneux, had couture houses in both France and England, but he didn't assume a French identity, although he was fluent in the language and familiar with the customs. Yet with pluck and steely nerves she pulled off this

Florence Broadhurst with her husband Percy Kann. Mitchell Library, State Library of NSW PXE 937_no6.

persona. No doubt many of her clientele were aware of the charade, but she made damn fine clothes!

The Kann marriage did not endure Florence's commercial and creative success. In 1937 Florence, now aged thirty-eight, met 23-year-old Leonard Lloyd Lewis who later went under the surname of Lloyd-Lewis. A diesel engineer by trade, Leonard was Florence's partner in life and business for decades to come. They never formally married, yet, after Leonard left her in 1961 Florence presented herself as a divorced woman.[20] Her only child, Robin (Robert) Lloyd-Lewis, was born on 3 April 1938. Suddenly Madame Pellier disappeared entirely, as the new 'Mrs Lewis' went to live in the stockbroker belt suburb of Banstead in Surrey. (Banstead is now remembered for its location in H.G. Wells' 1895 novel *The Time Machine*.) This undertaking was an extraordinary move for an ambitious, successful woman to contemplate, let alone execute; to abandon her hard-won independence, financial security and prestige to become a housewife of sorts. Evidence did not suggest Florence was particularly maternal – as later her son was sent to boarding school in Australia when his parents lived in London. In the summer holidays Robert was sent to various camps.[21]

During World War II, the family had a safe haven in semi-rural Barnstock, as it was not a target for the Luftwaffe. Never one to sit still, Florence joined the Australian Women's Voluntary Services which provided amenities and entertainment for Australian soldiers on leave.[22] After the war, the family moved to Worthing in Sussex. Perhaps Florence had gone there as an entertainer in the war, as this seaside town accommodated and trained several Allied divisions preparing for the D-Day landing in 1944. Near Chichester, Worthing is famed for its sailing. Florence, always alert to acquiring new skills, obtained her fishing and professional passenger boat licences.[23] A resolute anti-Labour stalwart, Florence joined the Art Women's Movement Against Socialism.

A theatrical costume designed by Madame Pellier. Mitchell Library, State Library of NSW PXE 937_no37.

Post-war England was a sad and deprived society, and full rationing remained in force until 1954. Florence and her family decided to move to Sydney. They arrived in 1949 and Florence set about reinventing herself. Having triumphed in her theatrical career and as a couturier, she decided that conquering the art world would be her next challenge. The Lewises settled near the seaside again, in Manly. Florence visited her family, whom she had not seen since 1927 when she left Australia for London. After Florence's return from Mount Perry, she decided to undertake an extensive tour of the continent to get inspiration for her new career. In two years she produced some 114 paintings. In 1954 she held an exhibition in Sydney at David Jones department store gallery, followed in 1955 by a show at Finney's department store in Brisbane.[24] Other venues were more down-market, such as her showing in Bathurst.[25] Her declarations in the press about her aristocratic heritage, her training at the Slade and in Paris were distressing for her family in Queensland to endure.[26]

Leonard also had to be recast and glorified in this process of self-aggrandisement. But far from being a 'financier', as Florence had claimed he was in the press,[27] Leonard opened a car and truck yard, where Florence also worked, in Crows Nest, Sydney. But some of her public representations were correct: she *had* been a court couturier and an international performer.

Florence saw an opportunity to engage in high-level charitable activities as the means by which her aspirations could be attained. She joined the Royal Arts Society, a rather old-fashioned organisation even in the 1950s. What the society did have were connections with Sydney's elite. She was invited to a reception at Government House in January 1958 and was associated with Nola Dekyvere, the president of Sydney's elite Black and White Charity Committee, and the Countess d'Espiniary.[28] Florence was a superb networker, even if she was too pushy and aggressive in her manner. With a flair for publicity and good organisational skills, she got things done and she was noticed; not something these genteel institutions were known for.

Her big chance came in early 1958 when the Queen Mother undertook a tour of Australia. Invited to Government House and to several other regal functions, Florence unexpectedly landed her indisputable entrée into Sydney high society. The Queen Mother came forward to Florence at a gathering and asked how she was doing in Australia. Florence had previously told various ladies in Sydney that she had attended Princess Elizabeth's wedding in 1947, and now the Queen Mother recognised her in public![29] This act corroborated her fanciful stories. More likely, Florence and Robert were spectators along the road to Westminster Abbey to see the bridal party in the royal coach. Yet the royal family may have patronised Madame Pellier in its brief existence in the 1930s. No matter why the Queen Mother recognised her, from then onward, Florence was set up for the rest of her career in Sydney.[30]

Florence carefully mounted her campaign to be a Sydney society *grande dame*. She lacked a title, her husband lacked a knighthood and she was neither new nor old money. In essence Florence was a pushy, outrageous parvenue who had conquered other worlds seemingly more impenetrable than the eastern suburbs of Sydney. With determination, skill and single-mindedness Florence began her new offensive by making herself indispensable on the Australian Red Cross Fundraising Committee. Her most influential coup occurred when she assumed the mantle of president of the Black and White Ball Committee. This charity work, however, had many uses apart from the contacts she made. Florence was placed in charge of assembling the decorations for the 1964 *Die Fledermaus* Opera House Ball.[31] Alongside the role of organiser for the United Nations Association of Australia International Ball Committee in 1966, Florence was a member of the Sydney Opera House Appeal and a foundation member of the Art Gallery of NSW.[32] Her interest in opera and music was genuine, and she brought an extraordinary range of skills to her roles in these prestigious organisations.

The reality was that Florence worked with Leonard in the truck and car business until it was sold to TNT. Their relationship finally faltered in Sydney; her insistence on a lifestyle far above their means and his different expectations of cultural fulfilment made for constant conflict. Their lives were for a long time joined by the business and its obligations. In October 1958 Robert married and this was the first step in Florence and Leonard's final separation. But more devastating for Florence was Leonard's affair with a young woman whom he later married. There was nothing she could do about it. They never legally married so there were no messy divorce proceedings.[33] No doubt Leonard was tired of playing second fiddle to Florence, whose fantasy world of privilege and titles was hard to sustain both emotionally and financially.

Before the permanent rift with Leonard, her companion since 1937, Florence began tentative moves towards the career that secured her international fame. Like the couturier Paul Poiret, who had established a successful wallpaper enterprise in 1912 with a store at 15 Baker Street in London,[34] Florence moved into interior décor. In 1959 she established a small wallpaper business called Australian (Hand Printed) Wallpapers Pty Ltd at the rear of the trucking business shed. This brought together a series of elements in her life: first her tours through Asia in the 1920s, where she was inspired by delicate Chinese and Japanese drawings, especially of birds and flowers and second, her artistic talents in composition which had floundered in the 1950s. She was never destined to become a famous artist such as Sidney Nolan, Joy Hester, Judy Cassab or Margaret Olley, as painting was not the right medium for her expansive talents. The production of high class wallpaper allowed her skills in craft, construction and design to come together. There is controversy about what role Florence played in the designs that she claimed as her work.[35] A more accurate assessment suggests that Florence had the ability to choose highly competent, loyal designers who could execute her vision. As a couturier in London in the 1930s she hardly cut out and sewed every garment she sold; yet they were her designs, and her talent brought her clientele to her *maison de couture*. Again, with her increasingly poor eyesight, she needed artisans with perfect sight to undertake the complex task of making luxury wallpaper.[36] She secured a loan of £5000 to finance the business in August 1960.[37]

Certainly Florence learned to screen print from Phyllis Sholto and relied on artists John Long, Peter Leis and David Bond. The production of finely crafted wallpapers required a series of skills far beyond the design. The patterns had to match exactly, not an easy task with intricate designs, especially those of her geometric forms. Like Poiret, who pioneered modern bold patterns, Florence was also innovative, steering away from the Sanderson English floral chintz tradition so beloved in Mayfair and more conservative homes in Australia. Her patterns contained vibrant colours, textures and production innovations like printing onto metallic surfaces and vinyl finishings. The latter were particularly useful in hotter subtropical climates where mould presented innumerable problems with traditional paper.[38] The magazines *Australian House and Garden* in April 1965 and *Australian Home Journal* in February 1968 both featured flattering and informative stories of the achievements of this new endeavour. *Vogue Living*, in 1972, prominently assessed Florence's contribution to Australian design.[39]

In 1969 the expanding firm changed its name to Florence Broadhurst Wallpapers Pty Ltd, with the slogan 'the only studio of its kind in the world'. This referred to the airy and spacious new premises in Paddington that were a far cry from the hot, cramped operation in the car yard in Crows Nest. Florence sold her wallpapers to the top interior decorators in Sydney, such as Leslie Walford, Barry Little and Yvan Méthot. Walford was a crucial advocate of her products; a well-educated Englishman with wide cultural and intellectual interests, he catered to the crème de la crème of Sydney society. Far from a stuffy traditionalist, Walford was a promoter of new talents and creative expressions, but also had a formidable knowledge of more traditional modes. This was the beginning of international interior decoration conducted by highly trained professionals. Australia never produced an Elsie de Wolfe, although decorators like Marion Best conducted successful businesses from the 1930s in Sydney.[40]

Florence's business expanded after the move to trendy Paddington. She secured contracts in Kuwait, Los Angeles, Peru, Norway, Paris and the United Kingdom. The refurbishment of the Raffles Hotel in Singapore was a particularly prized assignment. And her career as a singer and dancer was launched in Singapore in 1922, so she had fond memories of the place.

Florence's appearance became more stylised as she grew older. She was one of the first recipients of a facelift in Sydney and in 1973 she underwent cell therapy in England in the hope of rejuvenation.[41] Her brightly hennaed hair, strikingly bold clothes and large items of chunky, antique jewellery made her a memorable figure in Sydney society. Rather than settling for one partner, she conducted many affairs and sexual adventures of varying durations. For a woman in her seventies such behaviour was risqué and confronting.[42]

Florence's life came to an end in the most brutal of circumstances when she was murdered in October 1977. The person may have known the premises; the police were convinced the building had not been forcibly entered. She suffered two massive head wounds, as well as the indignity of being placed head first in a toilet bowl after death. Her funeral was held at St Mark's Church at Darling Point on 20 October 1977.

In death Florence's reputation grew, albeit slowly. Robert attempted to run the business, but in the end sold the collection of patterns and designs to Wilson Fabrics, later owned by James Hardie Industries. In 1999 David and Helen Lennie purchased Florence's library of over 530 designs when they assumed control of Signature Prints, the artistic arm of Wilson Fabrics. Celebrities such as Carly Simon, Marc Jacobs and Stella McCartney have all adorned their homes with Florence's designs. The Japanese-trained designer Akira Isogawa used her prints when he undertook a commission for the Sydney Dance Company in 1999. The following year he used her designs for his Chelsea and

Nagoya clothing range. Karen Walker and Nicole Zimmermann employed Broadhurst designs for their women's clothing lines, Funkis used her motifs for homeware, while Customwear Carpets and Rugs produced carpets à la Broadhurst.[43] The Powerhouse Museum in Sydney owns a substantial collection of Broadhurst's oeuvre.

Few Australian women born at the end of the Victorian era had the opportunity, tenacity and flair to have three substantial international careers, all of which she directed with aplomb and an often cavalier disregard for the truth. As Leslie Walford remarked after her death in 1977: '[Florence Broadhurst] was a red-hot character; a red-hot manner, bright-eyed and flame-haired. She was fierce and determined with sassy sex appeal, still having affairs into her seventies.'[44] Talented, notorious and quixotic, Florence Broadhurst was a remarkable achiever and innovator.

CHAPTER 12

Pamela Travers

(1899–1996)

The creator of Mary Poppins who hid her Queensland origins
but delighted the children of the world.

The celebrated author of the *Mary Poppins* series, P. L. Travers, spent her life reconstructing her identity. The trauma of her father's death when she was only eight years old left her forever determined but emotionally vulnerable. Born Helen Lyndon Goff in Maryborough in coastal Queensland, she became a famed literary *grande dame*, more English than the English as she evolved into her persona, Pamela Lyndon Travers. In the *Dictionary of Literary Biography* her nationality is still listed as 'English'.[1] During her lifetime she was sometimes called a New Zealander,[2] and one encyclopedia entry lists her as an Irishwoman.[3] In 1966 she simply said that she was born in 1907 in the 'British Commonwealth'.[4] She later remarked: 'I grew up and was nurtured on the Celtic Twilight, Yeats and all. Therefore Australia never seemed to be the place I really wanted to be. My body ran around in the southern sunlight but my inner world had subtler colours …'[5] Even more revealing was her contention that '… sorrow lies like a heartbeat behind everything I write …'[6] This flight from her origins made her a notorious dissembler throughout her adult life.

Pamela was related to the wealthy Queensland pastoralist and parliamentarian Boyd Dunlop Morehead. Like many children who are thrown down the class system through family financial disasters, Pamela never lost her resentment that her entitlements had been stolen

Travers Goff in the late
1880s. Mitchell Library,
State Library of NSW PX*D
334/no20.

from her. When she died in April 1996, her obituary in the *Guardian* incorrectly stated that her grandfather was the founder of the Colonial Sugar Refining company.[7] All her life she confounded the truth, weaving stories of lost glories and distinguished lineage, maintaining a false privacy that deterred too ardent an interrogation of her origins and tribulations. Yet, as with many of the women in this book, her achievements as the creator of one of the most enduring characters in literature, the redoubtable Mary Poppins, belied any need for fabrication and dissembling.

In many ways it was her charming, but less than truthful, father, Travers Lyndon Goff, who made the mould of how she was to live her life. Pamela maintained her father was a younger son of the Irish gentry from Wexford, but in fact he was born in Deptford, London, to a ship's agent and chandler. This working area on the south bank of the Thames was renowned for the Royal Docks established under Henry VIII. There were no grand houses with gravel drives in Deptford. Goff initially went tea planting in Ceylon before arriving in Queensland in 1891. This was hardly a propitious time to establish a career; the sugar industry had gone bankrupt in 1889 and the colony was in the grip of a depression with class wars erupting in the pastoral industry.[8] Travers went into bank management. His first major post in 1898 was in the beautiful subtropical city of Maryborough as manager of the Australian Joint Stock Bank, with a salary and allowances of £300 per annum.

Pamela's mother, Margaret Morehead, came from far more exalted stock. She was a niece of Boyd Dunlop Morehead, a wealthy pastoralist and former inspector for the Scottish Australian Investment Company. His Scottish father, Robert Morehead, had established and managed this large enterprise alongside an impressive portfolio of other industries. A fervent laissez-faire Liberal, Boyd Morehead was a parliamentarian in Queensland from 1871–96, and served as premier in 1888–90.[9] The family residence in O'Connell Street, Sydney, was opulent. Margaret's father, Robert, died early from tuberculosis, and when her mother, Maria, remarried in 1870, Margaret went to live with her grandfather and unmarried Aunt Helen, later known as Aunt Ellie. Margaret received an inheritance from her father, which was left under the control of her uncle Boyd, however, the tangle of wills and legacies left a lasting impression on her, and was later transferred to her daughter. In the *Mary Poppins* series the drive for prosperity at 17 Cherry Tree Lane, London, and the mysterious world of the father, Mr Banks, reflects much of the anxieties in the Morehead and Goff households.

Margaret met Travers Lyndon Goff in Sydney and married him in the Anglo-Catholic church All Saints in Brisbane in August 1898. This was, in itself, unusual, for the Moreheads were socially prominent in Sydney. Possibly the young bride wished to signal her connections in the Queensland ruling class by this choice. Her Uncle Boyd gave her away. Little did she suspect he had also frittered away her inheritance in dubious investments. Nine months after the wedding, Helen Lyndon Goff was born, named after her mother's guardian –

Aunt Helen – and her father. In childhood she called herself 'Lindy' or 'Ginty'. These were Gaelic words for water and stone.[10]

Though Goff was an amiable and congenial companion, who told tales of mystical Ireland, he was also an alcoholic. When Margaret realised this is uncertain, but she spent part of her early marriage back home with Aunt Ellie in the comfort of an ordered home with servants. Thus, young Lyndon (or Lindy) was initially reared in comfortable luxury, which later fed her aspirations and sense of dissatisfaction as an adult. Often absorbed in daydreams, in which she imagined she was a hen sitting on a nest, she was developing her creativity.[11] Back in Maryborough life was far sparser, but for Lyndon there was the delight of her father's company and his tales of long ago in Ireland.

While Goff drifted into the ethereal world of Gaelic spirits and spiritualism, Margaret was practical, replete with maxims for every occasion. Later, these were given to Mary Poppins in her attempts to bring order to the Banks' household. Margaret needed this steadfastness; in 1905 Travers was moved to another office, no longer the manager. His salary was cut and his pride shattered. In July Lyndon was sent to live with Aunt Ellie again, as Margaret coped with two new arrivals, Moya and Barbara. Later, Lyndon re-created those days in her book *Aunt Sass* (1941). When Goff was moved to the bank at Allora, young Lyndon returned to her family. This was Goff's chance for reformation, but unfortunately he was demoted again in early 1907. He died of pneumonia on 8 February 1908. The following week Margaret and the children went to live in the security of Aunt Ellie's world, before relocating to Bowral to reside with Great-Aunt Christina Saraset.[12]

For the times, Lyndon was well educated, attending the Sydney Church of England Girls Grammar School in Bowral and later a private school in northern Sydney when she moved back to Aunt Ellie's. Some of the characters she later developed were based on local identities in Bowral, which now claims to be the home of Mary Poppins.[13] Lyndon faced indignity as a poor relation, and after completing her schooling at Normanhurst Aunt Ellie insisted she begin work as a secretary at the Australian Gas Lighting Company in 1916.[14] She later recalled that, as the eldest daughter, she felt the burden to support her mother.[15] Without money, she would need to marry well or pursue a career. So, in 1920, with financial security in mind, Lyndon took to the stage, to the horror of the Morehead ladies.[16] Her first performance was in a pantomime, *Sleeping Beauty*, as a dancer. Her next role, in *The Merry Wives of Windsor* with Allan Wilkie's Shakespearean Company, was met with greater approval in the Morehead household, thanks to the Shakespearean element. For Lyndon, this new career, however tentative, heralded a change in her persona and she became known as Pamela Travers. Her new identity didn't meet with immediate success and she toured the regional circuit with a small troupe from the company. Pamela's first major role was as Titania in *A Midsummer Night's Dream* in April 1922 in Sydney.[17] She performed in *Othello* the

Pamela Travers as a professional actor, Sydney, 1922. Mitchell Library, State Library of NSW PX*D 334.

Pamela Travers on stage in Sydney, 1922. Mitchell Library, State Library of NSW PX*D 334_folio26.

following year, where press notices called her 'the budding poetess'.[18] With her fair hair, beautiful skin and piercing eyes, she was a gorgeous ingénue.

In 1923, touring New Zealand, Pamela again transformed herself. She fell in love with a journalist and began writing slightly erotic poetry to express these new feelings. Emboldened by her newfound creativity, she submitted them for publication and they appeared in *The Triad* and the *Christchurch Sun*. For a new author to publish in the leading arts journal *The Triad* was a coup.[19] Launched in Sydney in 1915 after a successful period in New Zealand, the journal published leading writers such as Katharine Susannah Prichard, Vance Palmer, Dorothea Mackellar, Eleanor Dark and Dymphna Cusack.[20] Pamela's poetry was also accepted by *The Bulletin*. But it was Frank Morton, the editor of *The Triad*, who guided and nurtured her early career. He introduced Pamela to theosophy and mysticism, which she took up more consistently in the next decade. She began working in the journal's Sydney office as a columnist in May 1923, just months before Morton's death.[21] Her columns were often witty, with the wry sense of humour that she later developed in her Poppins novels.

With Morton's death, Pamela felt little tied her to Sydney. Despite some reservations, Aunt Ellie paid for her passage to Southampton and she departed in February 1924. Pamela listed her occupation as 'actress' for the ship's records, rather than journalist or writer. Unlike most Australian writers who sought recognition overseas, Pamela was emotionally located in Ireland, set to rediscover her father's legacy of enchantment and fantasy. London culture had moved on considerably since her father's adoration of William Butler Yeats and the Irish Revival. Poetry was sharp and modern – with Americans Ezra Pound and T. S. Eliot in vogue – and sat alongside the varied artforms of the Ballets Russes, Michael Arlen, Virginia Woolf, Edith Sitwell, Noël Coward, and jazz. There were few sweet longings for old Eire here. That dreamy world had been shattered by the horrors of World War I. The most prominent Irish writer was the exile James Joyce, whose gritty narratives hardly accorded to the tenets of Yeats' 'Sailing to Byzantium'. Still, Pamela managed to keep herself financially afloat by continuing her contributions to Australian and New Zealand publications.

Determined to make her name, she sought a mentor and patron. George Russell, or 'AE' – from the Greek word for distant time as well as the mystic notion of power from the Divine Being – an Irish writer and painter, had been involved with the Irish Revival with Yeats and theosophy. Born in 1867 he was, like Frank Morton, another father figure. Certainly there was no sexual attraction: in his late fifties, AE was corpulent, with dark, discoloured teeth from his pipe smoking, and badly dressed. He was, however, generous, charismatic and charming. As the editor of the *Irish Statesman*, he was an influential figure in literature and the politics of authorship.[22] His reputation now is overshadowed by that of Yeats, although a character in Samuel Beckett's 1938 novel *Murphy*, reads from Russell's *The Candle of Vision* (1919).

Pamela first made contact with Russell through writing letters of devotion. The standard praise he issued to aspiring authors beckoned her to Dublin, where she was not disappointed with his welcome. Promises of publication added to her joy. Her discovery of her Wexford relatives, however, was far less jubilant, as they were nothing like the mystic Irish her father had portrayed. After the flurry of letters, AE came to visit Pamela in her London flat, assuring her he had met her in a previous life.[23] On this visit he gave her a gift, an inscribed copy of one of his books, which was exhilarating.[24] Her papers in the Mitchell Library reveal her lifelong devotion to him. By 1926 she was publishing her lyrical, old-fashioned poems in the *Irish Statesman*. Yet she maintained her contributions to the *Christchurch Sun*, detailing much of her day-to-day life in London, such as her move to 14 Old Square in Lincoln's Inn.[25]

This year, 1926, also saw the burgeoning of the character of Mary Poppins. Although Pamela later claimed that the characters and story suddenly appeared to her in 1934, there had been hints of the dreamy world of children and their hopes and fears at least a decade previously in *The Triad* of December 1924.[26] She later also refuted the notion that she wrote for children.[27] Like other great writers of children's books, such as A. A. Milne and Frances Hodgson Burnett, her stories can be read at different levels by young and old. A story published in the *Christchurch Sun* on 13 November 1926, 'Mary Poppins and the Match Man', introduced the Banks family, Mary with her parrot-headed umbrella and white gloves, and Bert the pavement artist and match seller.[28] Pamela was later horrified when the Walt Disney film production of *Mary Poppins* suggested a romance between Mary and Bert with the song 'It's a Jolly Holiday with Mary'. Julie Andrews was also far too saccharine and pretty for the plain but mysterious and sharp-tongued Mary.[29]

Pamela's emotional and creative life was caught up with AE. She went on holidays with him to Donegal in north-western Ireland. The cold, wet and boggy country was still not the mystical Ireland of her childhood imagination.[30] Surveying AE's beautiful paintings, such as *Carrying Driftwood, Girls Playing in a Forest* and *Mystical Figures*, it is clear that Pamela, with her halo of fair hair and dreamy eyes, must have seemed like an apparition straight out of these works. Set in verdant soft landscapes, the young, chaste women figures in these paintings glide through the air in a manner reminiscent of the English Pre-Raphaelites decades earlier.

In 1927 AE travelled to New York where he was regarded as a prophet of the new independent Ireland.[31] His absence left a vast emptiness in Pamela's life. Even more pressing was the urgency of rent. Her income from journalism was meagre. Though she liked privacy, Pamela took on a flatmate, Madge Burnand, the daughter of Sir Francis Burnand, a prolific playwright and editor of *Punch*.[32] Born in Ireland, Madge maintained many literary friendships with Irish writers, which was an important attraction for Pamela. The exact nature of the relationship remains in contention. In the 2009 Sydney play *The Knowing of Mary Poppins* Madge and Pamela are lovers.[33] A photograph of Pamela bare-breasted taken by Madge suggests an intimate relationship, but Pamela's papers in the Mitchell Library contain little about her. Certainly there seemed to be no young men in Pamela's life. All her close male associates and friends were older men with whom she maintained a platonic relationship more in keeping with acolyte and master.

By the late 1920s Pamela began travelling, on some occasions to improve her health. She always complained she suffered poor health, although she lived for nearly a century. Holidays in 1928 with Madge to Spain and Italy were for leisure; others, like her visit to the USSR, were for professional reasons.[34] To afford to travel more, Pamela and Madge moved to a smaller flat in Woburn Square near Euston Station, an area on the fringe of Bloomsbury. They moved again before eventually relocating in 1930 to the rural peace of Pound Cottage near Mayfield in Sussex, with Tunbridge Wells the largest town in the vicinity. The house was old and charming, but lacked modern conveniences. Not that that concerned Pamela too much,

Pamela at Pound Cottage with her mentor 'AE' George Russell. Mitchell Library, State Library of NSW MLMSS5341_ITEM6_.

for she left the cooking and all practical daily matters to Madge. However, the location was vastly inconvenient, being fifteen minutes or so by car to Mayfield. This move to the country was brought about by several events in Pamela's life. Her mother had died in November 1924, leaving her with only a modest estate. Pamela continued to fret about her health and feared she would be struck down with tuberculosis like her grandfather – a real concern in the '20s and '30s, before the advent of penicillin in 1944. She had several prolonged stays in sanitariums due to lung problems.[35]

In the early 1930s AE moved into his mystical stage of life, selling his possessions after his wife's death. He left Ireland, satisfied that his contribution to the Irish Revival was complete, and settled in Sussex Gardens near Paddington Station in London, often visiting Pamela and Madge in the country. AE introduced his protégée to Alfred Orage, the influential Yorkshire editor of the *New English Weekly*. Pamela and Orage were colleagues and friends for only a year before

Orage's death in 1934.[36] His biography was reviewed in Melbourne in 1937 with no mention of his connection to a distinguished Australian author.[37] Orage's influence on Pamela's development was substantial, however, for he introduced her to the thoughts and teachings of Armenian-born George Ivanovich Gurdjieff. These were a mixture of Indian mysticism and the works of Madame Helena Blavatsky, the founder of theosophy. With the challenge of Darwin's ideas to conventional Christianity in the mid-nineteenth century, various forms of mysticism became popular. Spiritualism and Eastern religions, without their emphasis on Judeo-Christian monotheism, alongside the post-Freudian notion of self-improvement and self-development through an inner spiritual quest, attracted many followers. The charismatic cult leader Gurdjieff required obedience and subservience from his followers, in whom he induced self-doubt.[38] He claimed to have studied Tibetan mysteries and Indian wisdom. His acolytes were often rich and well connected, but despite this he lived on meagre rations.

When AE was ailing in 1934 and Orage had died, Pamela was left without a creative master to worship. Gurdjieff filled the need to devote herself again to a dominant older man.[39] Yet this was Pamela's most creative period, for in 1934 she published her first novel in the Mary Poppins series, dedicated to the memory of her mother, which was strange, given her devotion to her father. The book is set in Edwardian London before the destruction of that orderly society by the Great War. Like Agatha Christie's great creation Hercule Poirot, Mary and all the other inhabitants of Cherry Tree Lane never age. The five children – Michael, Jane, Barbara, John and Annabel – and Mr and Mrs Banks along with the rest of the household, the maid Ellen, the cook Mrs Brill and the handyman Robertson Ay, live in chaos before the arrival of the tart-tongued Mary Poppins. She brings order and magic into their closed little world. Published by Gerald Howe in London and complemented by the wonderful illustrations of Mary Shepard, the book was an instant hit.

Pamela's relationship with her illustrator does not show her in a positive light.[40] Mary came from a distinguished line of illustrators. Her father, Ernest Shepard, illustrated A. A. Milne's *When We Were Very Young* (1924) and *Now We Are Six* (1927), as well as the series beginning with *Winnie-the-Pooh* (1926); her mother, Florence Shepard, was also an artist. Pamela had wanted to collaborate with Ernest but he was unavailable. Madge knew Mary Shepard and recommended Pamela take a chance with her. Pamela had seen a Christmas card drawn by Mary, who at twenty-three was fresh out of art school, and reluctantly she took on Ernest's daughter as her illustrator. Mary always knew she was second choice, a situation hardly conducive to a good working relationship. An equal relationship had never been Pamela's intention, for the books were always *her* work in her mind. She did not understand that great partnerships derive from mutual respect.

Though AE was seriously ill in early 1935, he was able to help Pamela with suggestions to market her book. While in the United States, he had given a copy of *Mary Poppins* to the head buyer of Marshall Field's, a Chicago department store. Published through Reynal and Hitchcock, it was initially advertised in the Chicago press and soon became an American bestseller.[41] AE returned to London terminally ill. He died in July 1935 with his friends around him. His body was returned to Ireland where he was accorded a state funeral attended by President Eamon de Valera and Yeats. For Pamela, this was a period of deep grief and introspection, compounded by the death of her Aunt Ellie, also in 1935.

The year did not end badly, however. Pamela completed *Mary Poppins Comes Back*, which was also published in the States. Aunt Ellie had left her a handsome share portfolio and real estate in Sydney, which supplemented her journalism and book royalties to provide a period of financial security. With this assurance she purchased Pound Cottage and hired a maid, Doris Vockins. The power balance between Pamela and Madge shifted with her newfound independence. After a romantic disappointment in 1935 with the Irish poet Francis

Macnamara, Pamela began another deep emotional attachment with Jessie Orage, her mentor's widow, staying with her and her children when in London. In early 1936 Jessie and Pamela went on holidays to Switzerland. They became friends with American Jane Heap, the editor of *The Little Review* and a devotee of Gurdjieff, and her lover Margaret Anderson, who had founded the magazine. Indeed with Jessie, Pamela met the master, Gurdjieff, at the Café de la Paix in Paris in March 1936.[42] The alarm bell should have rung, for he demanded money from all his disciples. They were always an exclusive, talented group, numbering among them T. S. Eliot – despite his attachment to Anglo-Catholicism – Katherine Mansfield and Georgia O'Keeffe. Timothy Leary was a later devotee.

By the following year, Pamela's relationship with Madge reached breaking point. Madge went to the United States and never returned to live at Pound Cottage. Then Pamela took the extraordinary step of enquiring whether she could adopt her young maid, Doris, one of seven children. When Doris' parents refused, Pamela sacked Doris on the spot. She had observed how Jessie adored her children and fixed on the idea that a child would be her perfect love object. In 1939 she adopted John Camillus Hone, one of twin boys, from a distinguished Irish literary family and a cousin of Francis Macnamara. Ironically, it was Madge who knew the Hone family and their impoverished circumstances. The family urged Pamela to take both boys, but on her initial visit to Dublin she went away empty-handed. She obtained a horoscope for the twins which decided her upon Camillus. Pamela took to wearing a wedding ring, for it was unusual for a single, middle-aged woman to adopt a child in 1939.[43] This decision to separate the twins so carelessly was to have long-term repercussions. Young Camillus did not know he was a twin until he was seventeen.

With the Blitz starting, Pamela and Camillus evacuated to Canada. Her task was even more daunting, for she chaperoned otherwise unaccompanied children from Tunbridge Wells. For a self-absorbed, neurotic woman, always a hypochondriac and fussy, the sudden responsibility of a baby and strange children was terrifying. Fortunately, Pamela met the sculptor and wood engraver Gertrude Hermes on the boat, who not only assisted with the children, but formed a strong bond with Pamela. Little is known about this intense relationship, as references to Gertrude were excised from Pamela's papers. Moving to East 52nd Street in New York in 1940, Pamela resumed her writing career. She published *I Go By Sea, I Go By Land* and *Aunt Sass* in 1941, followed by *Ah Wong* in 1943. That same year *Mary Poppins Opens the Door* was released in the United States and published in London the following year.

In 1944 Pamela was offered a trip to New Mexico by the Commissioner of Indian Affairs, John Collier. Like D. H. Lawrence, US arts patron Mabel Dodge Luhan and artist Georgia O'Keeffe before her, Pamela fell in love with the stark, pink beauty of the desert landscape. She had already travelled there the previous year with Camillus to visit Jessie Orage, who had moved to Santa Fe after their relationship ended. From Jessie's diaries, it appears that Pamela was full of despair about her deteriorating relationship with Gertrude.[44] Pamela took to wearing a version of the south-western costume with floral shirts and turquoise jewellery, reminiscent of Frida Kahlo.

In March 1945 Pamela and Camillus returned to England, buying a Georgian house in Smith Street in Chelsea. When Camillus went away to board at Dane Court preparatory school in Pyford, Surrey, Pamela was lonely and dissatisfied. She resumed contact with the London Gurdjieff group and visited the master in Paris in 1948. He died the following year, having survived the war, supported by his many disciples. Pamela joined the vigil over Gurdjieff's body. He was buried with a Russian Orthodox service at Alexandre Nevski Cathedral in Paris. Pamela was emotionally distraught and physically ill from grief. The next few years passed in a blur for her. In 1952 *Mary Poppins in the Park* was published, perhaps the most mystical of all the series, and reflects some of her beliefs garnered from Gurdjieff's teachings.

Through a chance meeting in a pub, Camillus met his twin in 1956. His confusion and anger were explosive and he never forgave Pamela her deception and separation from his 'other half'. For several years Pamela carried the legacy of her deceit, suffering depression. This lifted in 1959 when she was asked to sell her rights to the *Mary Poppins* series to Walt Disney Productions. What seemed delivery from eking out a modest but comfortable living, however, had its pitfalls, as the American company could and would develop the story in its own way.

Pamela travelled to Los Angeles, staying at Disney's expense at the Beverly Hills Hotel. She met Walt Disney at his studio in South Buena Vista Street, Burbank, where they discussed the *Mary Poppins* project. The new script by Bill Walsh and Don DaGradi substantially revised her script, which had been an adaptation of seventeen episodes from the first three books. The Disney script concentrated on three stories only, 'East Wind', 'The Day Out' and 'Laughing Gas', with new material and different interpretations to the original themes. Pamela was horrified by the incorporation of American slang into her Edwardian England setting

Pamela in later years. Mitchell Library, State Library of NSW PX*D 334_ folio28.

and chirpy songs by Richard M. Sherman and Robert B. Sherman, although during the filming of *Mary Poppins* Pamela corresponded with the lead actress Julie Andrews.

To accompany her professional anxieties along came the news that Camillus had been sent to jail for drink driving in 1960. After his release in 1961, Pamela decided to sell her home in Smith Street and purchase a new home in Shawfield Street, Chelsea.

In 1963 Pamela made a short trip back to Australia where she was less than forthcoming in interviews, and then went to Japan to study Zen Buddhism. She travelled to Los Angeles for the 27 August 1964 premiere of Disney's *Mary Poppins* at Grauman's Chinese Theatre on Hollywood Boulevard. Walt Disney ignored her and concentrated on the lead actress Julie Andrews. In a further insult, she was acknowledged in the credits as merely a 'consultant'. In small type it read, 'Based on the stories of P. L. Travers'. At the London premiere on 17 December 1964, Pamela was presented to Princess Margaret and Lord Snowdon, standing in line with cast members Julie Andrews, Hermione Baddeley and David Tomlinson. The film went on to win five Oscars in 1965.

After her less than perfect experience with the Disney film, Pamela decided to take up a writer-in-residence sojourn at Radcliffe College in Boston in 1965–66, but this was not a success.[45] Pamela was distressed that she was now known only for the Disney film and not, as she believed, for her own creativity. Searching for another guru to follow, she became devoted to Krishnamurti, the Indian mystic who claimed many rich followers in Hollywood.[46]

In 1975 she wrote to her Swedish translator and the author of a book on her work, Staffan Bergsten, that she declined to write an autobiography or consider an authorised biography as 'All that matters to me is the story of a soul and I am not going to wear that on my sleeve for the general public. And one little life – what is that?'[47] A notorious dissembler and chameleon all her life, Helen Lyndon Goff, who became Pamela Lyndon Travers, always hoped she could find true peace and security in the mystical fairytale world her father bequeathed to her.

Pamela spent the last decades of her life largely as a recluse in her Chelsea home. She was delighted to receive an OBE in 1977, but from this point on her life revolved increasingly around mysticism and meditation. She did, however, prepare a version of her own obituary which mentioned little of her life and nothing of her origins. She died at her Shawfield Street home in April 1996, and no dates or details were included on her tombstone in St Mary the Virgin Church in Twickenham.[48]

CHAPTER 13

Enid, Countess of Kenmare

(1892–1973)

The daughter of the winemaking family, who married into the aristocracy and took many lovers but never forgot her Australian beginnings.

Over the last century, several Australian women notably married into the higher echelons of European aristocracy. 'A high society beauty', Sheila Chisholm from Woollahra, Sydney, in 1915 married the son of the fifth Earl of Rosslyn, known as 'the man who broke the bank at Monte Carlo', then in 1928 Sir John Peniston Milbanke, and lastly Prince Dimitri Romanoff in 1954. A member of Edward, Prince of Wales' fast London set in the 1920s, Sheila was a cultured woman who was great friends with novelist Evelyn Waugh.[1] Born in Melbourne in 1948, fashion journalist Dale Harper married Lord Tryon in 1973 and was a favoured mistress of Charles, Prince of Wales before he met Camilla Parker-Bowles. Even more spectacularly, Tasmanian Mary Donaldson married Crown Prince Frederik of Denmark in 2004.

Perhaps the most notorious among those select few who married so well was Enid Lindeman from Sydney, who ended her days as the Countess of Kenmare, but was viciously dubbed 'Lady Killmore' after she was widowed four times. When she was depicted by author Dominick Dunne as a cruel, drug-addicted social climber in *Vanity Fair* in March 1991, Enid's reputation was shredded. In 2004 the autobiography of her daughter Pat Cavendish O'Neill, *A Lion in the Bedroom*, shed further light on Enid's life by presenting a frank account of an extraordinarily sexually promiscuous woman. Yet Enid's kindness to her three children and stepson reveals a complex woman who charted the dangerous waters of the upper echelons of British society for much of the twentieth century.

Enid was born into the distinguished Lindeman family, which established the wine industry at Cawarra near Gresford in the Hunter Valley in New South Wales. Dr Henry Lindeman studied viticulture in France and Germany after finishing his medical degree at St Bartholomew's Hospital in London. Lindeman claret won prizes in Bordeaux in 1882.[2] His son Charles assumed control of the business in the late 1870s and established a family. Daughter Enid was born in 1892, preceded by three brothers from whom she learned to ride horses, shoot and fish. This stood her in good stead later when she participated as an equal with her lovers and husbands in such sports. Rather than sit on the sidelines, Enid was accomplished and determined to win.[3]

As with many well-born girls of her day, Enid's education was to prepare her for marriage and domestic life rather than a career or an active role in the family business. At the age of nineteen, Enid met the shipping magnate Roderick Cameron in Sydney. He was twenty-four years older than she. His father, Canadian-born Sir Roderick Cameron, established the Australian Pioneer Line in 1852, carrying supplies from the United States to the Australian goldfields. (Lola Montez and her troupe arrived in Sydney in 1855 on one of his vessels.) Sir Roderick owned a magnificent estate, Clifton Berley, on Staten Island in New York, as well as a sixteen-storey skyscraper in Manhattan.[4] Like his father, Roderick Jr was a good judge of horse flesh and perhaps this is how young sports-mad Enid first met him. Enid and Roderick married in 1913 and went to live at Clifton Berley. Tragedy struck when Roderick died of cancer the following year, leaving Enid with a baby son, Roderick, always known as Rory.

Not one to mourn for long, Enid started an affair with financier Bernard Baruch, thereby scandalising New York society – not so much by the speed of the liaison but by Bernard's being Jewish. Dominick Dunne alleged that Enid had an affair with Bernard before her marriage when she was sixteen. Like so many other issues in his coverage this is incorrect; at that time Enid was a schoolgirl in Sydney.[5] Bernard and Enid remained lifelong friends.[6] Enid showed few of the prejudices of her times; she was later criticised for mingling with all sorts of guests, from royalty to jockeys, at her magnificent home, La Fiorentina on the Côte d'Azur. One notable socialite from that era, Elvira de la Fuente, claimed Enid was just as happy sitting next to a prince or a waiter. At her lunch parties at La Fiorentina, the Duke of Veduna and Greta Garbo might sit with 'people no one had ever heard of'. Thus, an unusual democracy prevailed at her gatherings.

Leaving for London in 1915, Enid took on a role as a *grande horizontale*, having affairs with such powerful men as Group Captain Walter Wilson and the Minister for War, the Earl of Derby, before marrying the impoverished, handsome aristocrat Brigadier General Frederick 'Caviar' Cavendish, the second son of the fifth Baron Waterpark in Paris in June 1917. In the early twentieth century the social code for a wealthy young widow was to marry and then pursue whatever life she wished. The Cavendishes are one of England and Ireland's most distinguished aristocratic families. They are related to the Dukes of Devonshire, Dukes of Marlborough and the Spencer family, thereby making 'Caviar' a relative of Diana, Princess of Wales, and Sir Winston Churchill. Georgiana Cavendish, Duchess of Devonshire in the late eighteenth century, the renowned beauty painted by Gainsborough, was a notorious ancestor who gambled away a large fortune. Frederick's relative Richard Cavendish married Kathleen ('Kick') Kennedy, daughter of the US Ambassador to the Court of St James, Joseph Kennedy, and sister of President John F. Kennedy. This was also a scandalous marriage, as the Kennedys were Irish-American Catholics who gained their fortune in dubious circumstances.

All this was a far cry from Enid's family of solid professional and business entrepreneurs in Australia. Her grandfather and her brother, Grant Lindeman, were respected physicians and wine makers, and she was never allowed to forget her origins as she moved into the aristocracy. At one time the famed beauty Daisy Fellowes, daughter of the third Duc Decazes et Glücksbierg and Isabelle-Blanche Singer, heir of the Singer sewing machine fortune and niece of Princess Edmond de Polignac, described Enid as 'an Australian with a vague pedigree'. When Enid remarked in conversation 'people of our class', Fellowes raised her hand and stopped her midsentence: 'Just a moment, Enid. Your class or mine?'[7] Enid's retaliation to this snobbery was to tell elaborate yarns about her family's convict origins, embellishing sordid details as she went along. Unlike many Australian women who did well in England and hid their origins, such as Pamela Travers, Enid was fiercely proud of her Australian identity and her family's wine business in which she later invested heavily.[8] Her intended humour and attempts to deflate the pomposity and snobbery of many of her European acquaintances later rebounded on her. She often joked she had murdered all her husbands. An Australian audience would understand this as an immensely dark jest, a form of the tall tale in dubious taste. The British did not.

Enid was a firm supporter of the Allied war effort and her ability to drive a car, a rare feat for a woman in those days, was put to good use. She served on the front line of the battlefields as an ambulance driver. This was a particularly dangerous operation. Her son, Rory, recalled in his memoirs that his mother, when not in uniform, wore fabulous dresses by the couture house of Worth. All the officers fell madly in love with her.[9] Her splendid war work counted for not much against the story that on a bet she supposedly bedded all the officers in her new husband's regiment. With a taste for the high life and his polo ponies, Frederick was dependent on her capital from Cameron's will to maintain his lifestyle and in no position to complain. Her whole style was outrageous and confronting. When Frederick was transferred to Egypt, Enid dressed as a man and played in a band in the officers' mess, thereby challenging both the gender and class codes of the time. Frederick had received the French Legion of Honour, a rare honour for an Englishman, and served on Marshal Foch's staff, so Enid's public behaviour dented his heroic reputation.

Enid was never mercenary in her dealings with rich men, though decidedly high-handed to those without a fortune, as Frederick could attest. When another admirer, Group Captain Walter Wilson, died, he bequeathed to her the fortune he had accumulated from his investments in the White City Stadium in London. Enid generously gave half to the woman with whom he lived for many years. Her daughter, Pat, joked that her mother spent much time with lawyers going over the wills of various lovers and admirers who left her fortunes.[10] Not that Enid needed money. She was, after all, remarkably wealthy from her first marriage. Her life in Mayfair, London, was luxurious in the extreme; her freshly ironed sheets matched her negligee each night. Her bedroom was sprayed with Patou's expensive perfume 'Joy' every evening. Yet Enid was not entirely self-absorbed. She often visited poor and injured ex-servicemen to take them and their families food and money, in her chauffeured car. This highlights two aspects of her character: she thought of others who were not as fortunate as herself, yet she never compromised her standards or patronised anyone under any circumstances.

The Cavendishes were not well suited, but then Enid needed only the façade of a marriage in order to pursue her chosen lifestyle of pleasure, sport and sex. They had two children: Patricia ('Pat'), born in June 1925, and Frederick Caryll, born fifteen months later. Both parents were devoted to their children. Pat fondly remembers her father teaching her to ride in steeplechases and picking her up from her ballet classes. Frederick died in December 1931 when Enid and the younger children were at Biarritz. The injuries he sustained on the front in World War I shortened his life.

By this time Enid had assumed the character that fascinated many and repelled others. No one denied that she was a striking beauty with a perfect oval face. Her fair hair went sleek silver at age twenty-eight in 1920 after a bout of illness. With her green eyes and perfect complexion her appearance was distinctive. One unnamed person from her days in Kenya in the 1930s thought she had 'cold cold, cruel eyes'.[11] Her acutely snobbish first sister-in-law, Anne Cameron Tiffany, remarked that Enid's beauty made the 'cars [in New York City] come to a halt the better to view this vision of perfection'.[12] Pat claimed incorrectly that at least five men committed suicide over her mother, including the distinguished scientist Franz Meissner and Peter Coats, the talented garden designer.[13] And this was only during the time she was married to Viscount Marmaduke Furness.

Enid was not widowed for long. She met Marmaduke 'Duke' Furness and married him in August 1933 without introducing him to her children. Duke hated children including his own, Richard (Dick), Averill and William – known as 'Tony the bastard', hinting that the Prince of Wales was his biological father. His first wife, Daisy, died at sea on board his yacht in 1921 and rumours followed that he had murdered her. Unlike the Cavendish family, the Furness fortune and title was extremely recent. His second wife, Thelma Morgan Converse, whom he married five years after Daisy's death, remarked in the autobiography she wrote with her twin, Gloria Morgan Vanderbilt, that Duke had a strong north Yorkshire accent and was a well-tailored plain man with red hair. His mother was an old-fashioned Yorkshire woman who longed for life to go back to the certainties of the Victorian age when, she imagined, life was stable and good.[14] Later Thelma experienced his vile temper, excessive drinking and jealousy. Enid discovered his less desirable character traits all too soon during their marriage.

Duke Furness was one of England's richest men. His family had originally owned collieries then went into shipbuilding. His father, Sir Christopher Furness, was an astute but hard-nosed, aggressive magnate with no pretensions to good manners or culture. His only concession to cultivated society was his decision to name his son Marmaduke.

He did not think much of his son or his abilities. Duke did not originally inherit the business, which went to his cousin, Stephen. When he acquired the business empire after Stephen's sudden death in 1914, Duke showed a rare acumen for all sorts of dealings and improvements. He was elevated to the peerage for his substantial contribution to the war effort. In 1926 when he married the actress and socialite Thelma Converse, who had been reared in Europe where her father was a distinguished diplomat, he was a much-feared and disliked man. Thelma recorded that she mixed with people in the Prince of Wales' set at the Embassy Club, among them Australian-born Sheila Milbanke (née Chisholm) and the Duke and Duchess of Westminster.[15] This may have been a warning sign of incompatibility, for it was Thelma who had the introductions into royal circles not the nouveau riche businessman Duke Furness. The marriage broke down when Thelma began an affair with the Aly Khan and was the acknowledged mistress of Prince Edward before he married Wallis Simpson. Thelma and Duke were divorced in 1933; Thelma retained the title of Thelma, Viscountess Furness. They were eventually on good terms after an early period of intense acrimony.

Duke married Enid soon after his divorce. He was already a troubled and deeply suspicious man, embarrassed by being a public cuckold. His background from the upper middle class of northern England did not encompass the aristocratic amorality allowing affairs for married women. Rather than take pride in Thelma's royal liaison he was hurt and angry. A man like Frederick Cavendish would have been proud to be the husband of the mistress of the future monarch. Enid's daughter, Pat, reported that Furness was very cold and distant to Enid's children and housed them in separate quarters with their own staff at his home, Burrough Court, near Melton Mowbray in Leicestershire. His son, Dick, a cavalry officer, was charming to both Pat and Caryll, in contrast to his father's behaviour. Dick was disinherited by Furness in one of his tyrannical outbursts; he later died a hero at Dunkirk, trying to save the men under him. In turn,

Enid was solicitous for the welfare and emotional state of her stepson, little Tony, whom she regarded as abandoned and neglected. Her treatment of the various children in her life showed Enid at her best – warm, solicitous and amusing.[16]

At first the marriage went well. Each morning Duke and Enid went out riding with a pack of hounds when they were resident in Burrough Court. Enid, attired in a top hat and veils, rode side-saddle with speed and accuracy. A warning should have been signalled when Duke always went out with a silver hip flask. His vile language at even the slightest annoyance also indicated a nasty temperament. His second wife, Thelma, had found these outbursts worrying and tiresome.

By the time of her third marriage, Enid had acquired, among her domestic animals like her pet hyraxes – always called Tikki – and fifty poodles, two silver foxes, several porcupines and a cheetah. This glorious animal had long featured as the ultimate status symbol. Charlemagne had a pet cheetah and the Mughal Emperor Akbar the Great kept over a thousand of these extraordinary animals. In the twentieth century, avant-garde aristocrats such as Nancy Cunard and the Marchesa Casati each appeared in public with a cheetah on a lead in an elaborate jewelled collar. Usually Enid was accompanied by a pet crow and the current Tikki, including at the dinner table.

With the Furness fortune, Enid travelled better than royalty on ships, aeroplanes and in the best cars. When she moved to one of her favourite spots such as Le Toquet or Biarritz, her maids and valets had the unenviable task of assembling the entire luggage and menageries of wild and domestic animals ready for travel. Enid, meanwhile, was oblivious of the chaos and stress this manoeuvre entailed. Often sixty trunks were included in her personal luggage, not counting that of the children, their governesses, nurses and servants.[17] In Kenya, where she spent the winter months, Enid kept a leopard named Chui. While all this sounds pretentious, Enid always had a deep respect and love of animals. In later life when all the husbands and lovers were put aside, she devoted herself to animals.

Their winter months in Kenya were luxurious in the extreme. Duke was dubbed 'Champagny Lordy' for his display of wealth, which included Lord Allenby's Rolls Royces from World War I and maintaining a retinue of local and English servants dressed in the Furness livery. Life among the 'Happy Valley' aristocratic set in Kenya in the 1930s was decadent and opulent. Enid and Duke stayed with Lady Idina Sackville, the famed 'bolter' who abandoned her children and husband, Charles Gordon, when she ran off with Josslyn Hay – later the Earl of Erroll – in 1923. The spoilt rich aristocrats Danish Baron Bror Blixen and American Alice de Janzé led lives of promiscuous abandon, in which cocaine and sometimes morphine were the party drugs-of choice. In his *Vanity Fair* article Dominick Dunne alleged that Enid was a drug addict who enticed others into abusive behaviour. While she certainly took prolonged prescribed medication for a serious back injury sustained when she fell from a horse at Burrough Court – this kept her in hospital for months on end – she was not part of the inner circle of the sex- and drug-addicted coteries within the Happy Valley set. For one thing, she was closely watched by Duke who took to setting private detectives on her tail to report her every move.

Tensions between Duke and Enid reached a crescendo when he suspected she was having an affair with the Duke of Westminster, England's richest man and a senior royal. He threatened that he would not attend the coronation of King George VI with her in 1937; she retaliated by threatening to attend with Westminster. They had one last trip to Kenya in 1938. Then Enid took the younger children to meet her former relatives, the Camerons, in New York. On board the *Queen Mary* they met Gary Cooper who was charming to the children, unlike many celebrities who put on the charm only for adults. Later they met William Randolph Hearst and his mistress Marion Davies in California and attended the 1939 World's Fair in New York. While she was away Enid decided she would have a facelift. She chose the New Zealand-born surgeon Sir Archibald McIndoe, who was shocked when he entered her recovery room to find a cheetah happily ensconced there.

Enid left for France soon after her operation. She had made friends with P. G. Wodehouse, the author of the Bertie Wooster and Jeeves stories, and his wife at Le Toquet. Duke was jealous even of this innocent friendship. As war approached, Enid went to her villa on the Bay of Beaulieu on the Côte d'Azur, La Fiorentina. When war was declared and shortages were felt even among the rich in France, the ever-resourceful Enid got a herd of goats from which the villa residents obtained both cheese and milk. Other guests, including an unnamed Belgian countess, brought other less welcome habits like severe drug addiction. Enid dealt with this situation quickly, sending the poor woman to the local asylum.[18] She also apparently hid Allied airmen on the run in her home, dressing them as maids but the Germans were not in the South of France so this may have been a fanciful contribution to the war effort.

Back in England Enid decided to assist the war effort by working in a factory to which she ventured in her Chanel and Schiaparelli gowns. She learned how to weld and practised in her London residence until she reached an admirable proficiency. Burrough Court was taken over by Allied airmen, who carelessly burned it down. Duke, by this time, was terminally ill from decades of heavy drinking. Enid nursed him at La Fiorentina but he died on 5 October 1940. Enid was devastated despite the eruptions in their marriage. In her autobiography, Thelma Furness hints that it was she who nursed her former husband.[19] She tried unsuccessfully to have Enid charged with murder. This was nonsense; had Enid wished to she could easily have divorced Duke – there was no need to resort to murder. The Australian press followed developments between the two Ladies Furness with some glee, clearly on side with the local girl done well.[20] Enid's career and fabulous lifestyle were avidly reported, though curiously in the Sydney press she was usually termed 'sister of Dr Grant Lindeman'.[21] Somerset Maugham's quip that Enid was 'Lady Killmore' was cruel, especially given her kindness to this crusty and difficult man. She hid Maugham's valuable art collection in her home and spent many hours playing bridge with him.[22]

Enid married Valentine Castlerosse, the Irish Earl of Kenmare, in February 1943. He was a direct descendant of Mary Tudor, Henry VIII's sister. They made a strange pair. Born in 1891, Castlerosse was enormously fat by the 1920s. He served in the Irish Guards without much distinction during World War I; he was a man hardly suited to the discomfort and athleticism required to endure war. He was, however, proud to have served and worshipped the men and officers of his old regiment with a strange devotion all his life. Though his mother was a Baring of the banking fortune, Valentine was virtually penniless. Well educated at Cambridge, he was a bon vivant and aesthete without the income to finance his lifestyle, and after the war he went to Paris to live as a dandy. He took the extraordinary measure of writing a gossip column in the *Sunday Express*, one of Lord Beaverbrook's popular newspapers. This was a remarkable move in 1926 for an aristocrat, albeit an impoverished one. He was successful in his new career: witty, erudite and far less catty than gossip columnist Godfrey Winn. Divorced from actor Doris Delavigne in 1938, he married Enid at Brompton Oratory Church in Kensington, London. This too was a strange move for a devout Catholic; divorce was hardly condoned by the Church. Enid and Valentine went to live in her house in Lees Place, just behind Park Lane and Marble Arch.

They moved to a suite in Claridge's Hotel when bombing intruded into their home. The Earl died suddenly of a heart attack on his estate in Killarney some six months after his marriage. Enid was then in London.[23] Over 7000 people attended his funeral in Ireland, from the poorest tenant farmer and worker to the grandest in the land. At this time Enid was fifty-one but she claimed she was pregnant with his child. Her daughter Pat maintains that Enid, in consultation with her mother-in-law, the Dowager Countess of Kenmare, decided that an abortion was necessary. This seems implausible as women of fifty-one can rarely conceive and the Dowager Countess was a devout Roman

Catholic who would hardly countenance abortion, a mortal sin. Rather, it appears to have been a strange delaying tactic. Kenmare's bachelor brother Gerald inherited the title and the estate.[24]

By this time Enid's son Rory Cameron had joined the newly formed American Office of Strategic Services, the forerunner to the CIA, and was engaged in high-level operations. With his proficiency in languages and his contacts among the wealthy and well connected in both Europe and the United States, he could pretend to be an idle man of leisure while conducting espionage. He worked often in England with the distinguished historian Hugh Trevor-Roper. Pat was now a young woman, rather shy and reticent despite her beauty and kind temperament. From this time, although there were to be a few romances in the late '40s and '50s, Enid's sexual encounters with men were largely over. Pat believed Enid never really fell in love with any of her myriad lovers or husbands. Despite spending a good deal of her enormous energy pleasing them, she was largely indifferent – her children were her real emotional attachments.[25] Yves Vidal, the distinguished Parisian art collector who spent a lot of time at La Fiorentina, remarked that '[b]efore anything else Enid was a mother. Most of the things she did, marrying all those men, were for the children more than herself.'[26] Though perhaps not as close to Caryll, who spent his formative years at Eton, Enid adored Rory and Pat.

In 1948 the three of them went to Australia for an extended visit. Enid displayed quite surprising elements of her personality; she was eager to meet Daisy Bates, who resided with the Indigenous desert peoples along the Nullarbor Plain, and she was interested in wider questions of Indigenous culture and welfare.[27] Enid also spent time with the old Australian gentry families such as the Jamiesons in South Australia and was shocked that they had to chop their own wood. She was delighted to catch up with a Sydney grand seigneur, Ernest Watt, who had introduced her to Roderick Cameron in 1912. Watt was a wealthy grazier and shipowner, a man of deep culture and wit.[28] Enid undoubtedly kept in touch with her friends and family in Australia, despite infrequent visits home.

In her final widowhood Enid lived at first with Rory at La Fiorentina where they entertained lavishly. Increasingly, the guests were invited by Rory, with Enid a reluctant hostess, often late for dinner and silent. Rory was a cultured man of wide learning and talents. His various books show his extensive, sometimes arcane, knowledge. He particularly treasured his friendships with older beauties like Emerald Cunard, Nancy's mother, to whom he saw a direct link back to the eighteenth century before the prudery of the Victorian age.[29] Strangely, Enid was shocked to learn that Rory was gay; he was in his forties when he told her. For all her knowledge of men she had not perceived the most fundamental aspect of her son's character.

Theirs was a privileged world. Enid was invited to the twenty-fifth anniversary of Prince Louis of Monaco's reign. She hoped that his son, Rainier, would marry Pat, a rather fanciful wish since she was not a Roman Catholic. The family was invited to his wedding to Grace Kelly. Enid had contributed much to the economy of Monaco over the years, since she was an avid gambler in the deluxe casinos in Monte Carlo. When she went there with Furness, Enid on one occasion wore a beautiful Molyneux dress with lace flowers into which was sewn a real diamond. She wore the Furness tiara with pear-shaped diamonds, setting off her silver hair, which was always dressed by the famed Alexandre. Apparently the tables were silent as she made her way through the rooms.[30]

By 1950 Enid began to spend a lot of time in her bedroom painting, surrounded by numerous animals. She had been introduced to Nassau in the Bahamas by her sister-in-law Anne Tiffany and now spent several months there every year. She also purchased a Kenyan property, Ol Orion, for Caryll for £10,000 in the '50s and spent several months there each year as well. Enid still dressed formally for dinner but the extravagances of her life in Kenya with Duke Furness in the 1930s were over. The days of Happy Valley had ended with the murder of the Earl of Erroll in 1941 – as Kenya moved towards independence such decadence was no longer tolerated. Rather she increased her interest in animals, adding chimpanzees and lions to her menagerie.[31]

By her sixties Enid was suffering from a heart condition that slowed down her usually energetic lifestyle. When Pat moved to South Africa, Enid accompanied her with all their wild animals. Her interest in horseracing went from being a spectator to breeding and training with the assistance of the Australian trainer Tommy Smith. Enid employed Beryl Markham, the famed pilot and hunter from Kenya, but this was not a happy match between two independent and strong women. With Enid a wealthy widow and Markham impoverished and with her glory days behind her, the differences in the women's lives at this point were in stark contrast. Yet Enid admired Beryl's achievements by her own efforts.

Enid Lindeman led a life that reads like a fairytale – although perhaps an X-rated one, so replete was it with notoriety, sex, gambling and drugs. Many envied the rise of the middle-class Sydney woman to the very heights of British nobility and American money, yet she suffered much sadness in the deaths of various husbands. She also battled with severe chronic pain from the riding accident in the '30s. Her reputation as a black widow who killed all her husbands for money is entirely undeserved. At the centre of this fabled and almost unbelievable life lay a deep devotion to her children and sympathy for those less fortunate than herself. Unlike many sacred monsters, she truly did have a heart of gold, even if its reach remained personal and close to home.

CHAPTER 14

Tilly Devine
(1900–1970)

*From London streetwalker to wealthy Sydney madam
and standover merchant.*

Alongside her long-standing rival Kate Leigh, Tilly Devine occupies a unique position in Australian history. Both women led notorious gangs of pimps, prostitutes and drug sellers. Both were audacious and ran enduring criminal enterprises. American bank robber Bonnie Parker operated with her partner, Clyde Barrow, while Kate 'Ma' Barker was a support to, not a leader of, the Barker gang; other figures such as actor and chorus girl 'Texas' Guinan in New York ran a famous speakeasy; but none organised their own criminal networks, oversaw its operations with standover men and police protection, or took part in public violence. American gangsters were ruthless men – Al Capone, 'Bugs' Moran, Hymie Weiss and 'Big Jim' Colosimo – whose empires ran on ethnic and religious lines. Women in their world were 'molls', 'dames', prostitutes, wives, mothers and daughters, not cunning leaders and entrepreneurs. In this regard, Australia struck an early blow for gender equality, albeit in the underworld of terror and violence.

Tilly Devine and Kate Leigh were not well-educated madams like Caroline Hodgson ('Madame Brussels') in late Victorian Melbourne, or crusading prostitutes like Shirley Brifman in the 1960s or Kim Hollingsworth in the 1990s; rather, they were tough, savage and merciless criminals.[1] Tilly and Kate formed the basis of the composite character Delie Stock in Ruth Park's novels set in the slums of Surry Hills *The Harp in the South* (1948) and *Poor Man's Orange* (1949).[2] Tilly's reputation has been sanitised in some quarters in the forty years since her death. She featured in an Australian War Memorial exhibition as an example of a World War I bride, and a café in Canberra is named in her honour. The authoritative Australian Women's Register calls Tilly 'colourful', a euphemistic term for this ferocious and formidable woman.[3] Peter Kenna's play *The Slaughter of St Teresa's Day* (1973) was more in keeping with her notoriety, and a 2009 exhibition at the Justice and Police Museum in Sydney attempted to rectify the surprising sentimentality about this vicious criminal.[4] The inner eastern suburbs of Sydney, including notorious 'Razorhurst' (Darlinghurst) – as described by the salacious newspaper *Truth* on 23 September 1928 – of the inter-war years, with its armed gangs, executions of rivals, drug-running and prostitution, has now been gentrified, except for the former bohemian enclave of Kings Cross.

Matilda Mary Twiss was born at 57 Hollington Street, Camberwell, near Southwark in South London. This area, mentioned in the Domesday Book, had been a rural idyll, but by 1900 it was an area infested with noxious factories, the so-called 'stink industries' banned from across the Thames, crime and slums, the misery relieved by many music halls.[5] George Gissing's novel *The Nether World* (1889) conveyed the 'evil smells' of the district. Charles Booth, the reforming author of *Life and Labour of the People of London* (1903), depicted this area in his maps of London in 1898–99 as inhabited by 'savages' and criminals existing in the haze of permanent alcoholic overindulgence.[6] The Twisses lived in 'one of the vilest slums in the whole of London'.[7] Tilly's father, Edward Twiss, was a bricklayer, often out of work, and the family lived in poverty so relentless and destructive that it is now hard to imagine.

Like other children of the slums, Tilly left school barely literate at the age of twelve or so, and was sent to work in one of the local factories, where conditions had not changed since Charles Dickens wrote *David Copperfield* in 1850. She soon left this employment for a far more prosperous one as a streetwalker along the fashionable Strand, where the Savoy Hotel was built in 1889. Tilly was a pretty, solidly built young woman, with a foul temper and the street cunning and manners of Camberwell. Her earnings as a prostitute were substantial. At the age of sixteen, she met James Devine from the 4th Tunnelling Company of the Australian Imperial Forces. Like many servicemen on the lookout for bright company in boisterous Soho, he told Tilly he owned a kangaroo farm back home.[8]

Their relationship from the outset was filled with violence, combative anger and boozing. Tilly and Jim married in the Church of the Sacred Heart of Jesus in Camberwell in August 1917. Strangely for a young married couple, Jim insisted Tilly earn a good income as a prostitute and acted as her 'protector'. Even at the young age of fifteen, Tilly had accumulated a substantial police record for offences ranging from assault to theft and prostitution. In October 1918, she was arrested for soliciting on the Strand and paid a fine of forty shillings rather than go to jail. By that time she had also had two children, a girl who died at birth and a son, Frederick, whom she left with her mother when she sailed to Australia in 1919. Jim had already embarked for home with his fellow Diggers.[9] The Devines lived in his rented flat in Glenmore Road, Paddington, now an exclusive enclave but then a seedy area of the inner eastern suburbs. Tilly soon returned to her old job as a streetwalker.

She was highly successful. With her beautiful, pale complexion, buxom figure, and 'deep, husky, fascinating voice', she charged ten shillings for a half-hour encounter, then a top price.[10] Tilly chose to work on her own with Jim, rather than enter a brothel where police protection money was paid and harassment of sex workers was far less. Jim expanded his activities as a drug dealer – at this time only cocaine and opium were listed as illegal, dangerous drugs in Australia – and as a chauffeur and a standover man. Tilly earned so much that soon she and Jim were able to drive around in a Cadillac; often she entertained clients in the back seat of this luxury vehicle, cutting the cost of a hotel room and allowing a quick get-away.[11] She also purchased a fruit shop in Bondi Junction for Jim so he could appear to have a legitimate source of income.

Between 1921 and 1925 Tilly was arrested on seventy-nine occasions for prostitution-related offences and she spent several terms in Long Bay Prison, where she was dubbed 'Pretty Tilly'.[12] Along with another woman, Elsie, Tilly was arrested in 1923 for attempted robbery of a client. (This may have been the commencement of her activities as a manager rather than a worker in the sex industry.) That year Tilly and Jim were involved in a shooting incident at a party where guests' wallets and purses were stolen. This departure from the *modus operandi* indicates that the Devines were now part of an emerging criminal gang network.

Several big changes in legislation ensured the vibrancy of an underworld culture selling drugs and sly grog. In 1916, after years of agitation from Protestant reformist groups such as the Women's Christian Temperance League, the hours when it was legal to sell alcohol in a hotel were curtailed. The days of the 'six o'clock swill' – when patrons rushed to the bar before six o'clock closing to swill as much alcohol as possible – were ushered in with some rapidity.[13] Rather than curb consumption of alcohol, the legislation produced sly grog dealers like Kate Leigh.[14] Following the American and British lead, soon after World War I prohibitions were also enacted to ban the importation of opiates and cocaine.[15] Opium, since the 1660s in England, had been widely used in teething syrups for infants, as a sleeping draught, and as a remedy against diarrhoea. Many respectable citizens, especially women, who were prohibited from consuming alcohol in public venues, became addicted to laudanum from patent medicines. Cocaine had originally been used in the soft drink Coca-Cola as a pep-me-up. Throughout the 1920s and 1930s cocaine was a popular party drug used by wealthy socialites through to streetwalkers. Prohibition created a lucrative source of income for gangsters in Sydney by the early 1920s.

Tilly was part of this shift. Given that her days on the streets of London and Sydney had left her with numerous scars on her face, chest and arms – police photographs of her taken in 1925 reflect her fading beauty and disfigurements, all part of her occupation's hazards – she seized on a loophole in the New South Wales *Police Offences (Amendment) Act* (1908) that made it an offence for a male to operate a brothel or act as a pimp, and like Madame Brussels in Melbourne in the late nineteenth century, Tilly saw her opportunity to run her own business. She purchased a derelict house in Palmer Street, Surry Hills, and refurbished it, adding the distinctive red light outside. She proved to be a benevolent dictator, generous in her payment to workers but ruthless with those who concealed their earnings. By the end of the decade she owned eighteen brothels, largely in the Surry Hills, Darlinghurst, Woolloomooloo and Paddington areas. With the substantial earnings from these bordellos, she bought a house for herself and Jim in middle-class Maroubra. The Devines were hardly welcome neighbours, with their raucous parties, loud quarrelling and domestic violence.[16]

In May 1925 Tilly was convicted of slashing a man with a razor and sentenced to two years' imprisonment. She had walked into a barber's shop and slashed him as he sat in the chair, uttering the words, 'This is for Mary.' Presumably this was a revenge attack on a customer who had injured one of her girls. Tilly always commanded great respect and admiration, tinged with a modicum of fear, from her stable of prostitutes. Yet if one was abused or injured she took decisive action on their behalf.[17] She did her best to protect them from the incursions of her rival Kate Leigh's drug pushers, often with immense force and violence.[18] Unlike the United States, where gangsters flourished in the wake of Prohibition and used machine guns as their weapon of choice, Sydney gangs favoured the razor. The *Pistol Licensing Act* (1927) made it harder to possess pistols and other weaponry. The razor was easy to conceal and made no noise, a great advantage in killing or wounding by stealth. It could also be used simply to maim or identify a rival.

Tilly Devine in Sydney in the early 1930s. SMH News picture by Staff; Fairfax Media 5085583.

In 1927 the sensationalist tabloid newspaper *Truth* in a series of exposés chronicled the rise and extent of the razor gangs. The tabloid coined various terms – 'Razorhurst', 'Gunhurst', 'Bottlehurst', 'Dopehurst' – to characterise their theatre of activities.[19] On 1 January 1928 it proclaimed 'Razor Terror' in Sydney's inner eastern suburbs. By this it meant three gangs in particular: Kate Leigh's, Tilly and Jim Devine's, and, until recently, Norman Bruhn's. Bruhn was murdered in June 1927, shot in a laneway in Darlinghurst.[20] The mainstream *Sydney Morning Herald* of 28 June 1927 also employed the term 'razor gangs'. American terms such as 'racketeers' and 'gangsters' had also entered common parlance, even before popular Hollywood films such as *The Public Enemy* (1931) appeared.

In 1929 with bipartisan support for the New South Wales *Vagrancy (Amendment) Act*, with its draconian 'consorting clause', the police formed a consorting squad to target madams like Tilly and Kate Leigh, as well as their standover men and pimps. Under this new Act, Leigh was sentenced to a prison term and then another for cocaine dealing.[21] Tilly enjoyed a modicum of police protection, as well as employing manoeuvres to undermine the letter of the law. For instance, in her brothels she rented out rooms to respectable tenants so she could maintain the charade of operating as a landlady.[22] But this did not stop her street fights and brawls. In early 1929 she was arrested for her involvement in a fight with Elsie Kaye and Vera Lucas in the courtyard off the Central Criminal Court, in which she nearly severed one of her opponent's fingers. All three women were fined.[23] Tilly also threatened a butcher who sold her rotten meat, poking his chest with a knife and saying, 'Give me my fucking money back, or I'll put this knife through your fucking chest.' The case did not end up in court.[24] Kate and Tilly, accompanied by members of their gangs, brawls often conducted brawls outside one or the other's brothels. Guns were used when forty mobsters fought in Kellett Street, Kings Cross, in mid 1929. Victims were slashed with razors, though none made a formal complaint to the police for fear of retribution.[25] On 5 September 1929 the police confiscated all the weaponry held at the Devines' home.

In 1930 the *Crimes Amendments Act* was passed, allowing for six-month jail terms and a flogging for unlawfully possessing a razor. Tilly's luck ran out when she was charged with consorting, riotous behaviour and assaulting a police officer in January 1930. She was defended by an ex-Labor mayor of Sydney, R. D. Meagher, who promised that Tilly would leave the country for two years if released.[26] Tilly told an amazed court that she had to return to London to tend her ailing mother and see her son whom she had abandoned in 1919. As she wrote in *Truth* of 29 June 1930, '[m]y dear mother is very sick at this time and I am nursing her back to health ...' Most of the letter was a diatribe against Kate Leigh, who was then serving yet another lengthy jail term.

Though ordered to stay out of the country for two years, Tilly returned in January 1931 after only nine months' absence. At their home in Maroubra she found Jim entertaining a strange woman he claimed was the new housekeeper. In a rage, Tilly hit him. He retaliated with a threat to shoot her with a rifle. When they ran out onto the street screaming and cursing, neighbours called the police, who arrested Jim for attempted murder and possession of an unauthorised razor. At the trial, which began on 16 January 1931, Tilly refused to testify against him and the case was dismissed. What the incident signalled was the deep rift between Tilly and Jim. Two months later, Jim was attacked with a knife when he opened the door.[27] He later earned the nickname 'Scarface Big Jim Devine'. Jim's violence, alcoholism and erratic temper became a liability to Tilly's enterprises and her personal safety.

A few weeks later Tilly was in court charged with stealing £2 from George Hudson. In court she let fly with abusive language and insults to the magistrate, who sent her to jail for a month.[28] Stealing and risking further imprisonment when she was already a wealthy woman shows a lack of critical judgment on her part. Yet the Depression hit Tilly's cash flow, for her wealth resided in her property investment. With mass unemployment, evictions and unprecedented poverty in Sydney, the money for sly grog, visits to prostitutes and gambling was curtailed for many men. In early 1932 Tilly was sentenced to six months' imprisonment on charges of consorting. In an outburst in *Truth* of 7 February 1932, Tilly let fly with accusations of dope peddling against Kate Leigh. Yet a NSW Police Report in 1933 believed that the cocaine rings of the previous decades had largely been eliminated.[29]

Always alert to market forces, Tilly ran a three-tiered system of prostitution. At the top, her well-educated, more refined girls catered to politicians, businessmen and senior police officers out of decorous Darlinghurst terrace houses replete with bars, or their clients visited them in their own homes. Earning as much as £5 as well as tips and presents, these women could reap financial rewards unobtainable to professional women. Many were not full-time call girls but young women supplementing their meagre earnings from legitimate employment. On the next tier were housewives trying to feed their families, low-paid workers, single mothers and women from the bush. Tilly often provided food and accommodation, as well as banking a proportion of their earnings for them. At the bottom operated the 'boat squad' who catered to the dockside crowd. They were in the front line of the game, where savage beatings, robbery and even murder lurked.[30] Tilly also engaged some women as shoplifters in department stores Mark Foys and David Jones, and then sold the stolen goods.

By the mid 1930s Tilly and Kate Leigh realised that their public campaigns against each other, played out in the pages of *Truth*, were detrimental to both of them. They decided on a truce, each carving out her own specialty in criminality without interference or the chance of the police being informed. At the same time, their incomes were undermined by the way the entertainment industry was changing. Nightclubs in Sydney after 1936 were permitted to sell alcohol after 6pm, thereby ruining the fortunes of sly grog dealers. At the outbreak of war in September 1939 many customers enlisted in the armed services, causing even more financial strain on Kate and Tilly.

Yet it was war that saved their criminal enterprises. With the arrival of American servicemen from early 1942, suddenly there was a surfeit of customers for sex, gambling, drinking and drugs. Kate took care of the drinking and drugs, leaving Tilly to the sexual services arena. They were by no means alone in these activities, and sharp new operators entered the rich field. Tilly was still not immune from prosecution: in June 1943 she was charged with owning a 'disorderly house'.[31] She was also arrested for maliciously wounding one of her prostitutes, Ellen Grimson, who was an alcoholic cocaine addict. Appearing before Mr Justice Street, Tilly explained that Grimson was often drunk and forgot to turn out lights. Tilly took a knife to her face after repeated warnings about the blackout and saving electricity. She got six months' imprisonment for this offence.

Tilly's personal life had also reached a turning point. In March 1943 she filed for divorce from Big Jim, tired of his beatings and abuse, his promiscuity with young, more attractive, women, and his alcoholism.[32] They had not lived together since 1940, after Jim was sentenced to yet another jail term for stealing. He continued to harass her for money, often using violence to obtain it. Tilly had naively thrown a party for their twenty-fifth wedding anniversary in August 1942 despite their separation. Jim disgraced her by turning up hours late, drunk and ready to pick a fight, then he paraded his latest girlfriend in front of Tilly and all her guests. Jim finished off the party by fracturing Tilly's skull. She was admitted to St Vincent's Hospital and required weeks of recuperation.[33]

Despite her personal and professional challenges, in some ways the war years gave Tilly a new lease of life. She hosted parties for servicemen, not riotous sexual and drinking binges, but simply good old-fashioned fun. A keen supporter of the British and Australian war effort, she donated thousands of pounds to veterans' welfare associations. She also gave generously to children in hospital.[34] In some ways, Tilly saw herself as a benevolent matriarch, dispensing largesse and kindness through her Surry Hills domain. In her own mind, her violence and revenge on those who crossed her was always justified.

After her release from prison, Tilly met Eric Parsons, a seaman and barman a few years younger than herself. They started an affair in 1944 and Parsons moved in with Tilly fairly quickly. The relationship was tempestuous, to say the least. In February 1945 Tilly let fly with her temper and shot Parsons after he had been drinking heavily. The police were called to the house after neighbours heard a row and gunshot. Parsons denied he had been injured. At St Vincent's Hospital he said he had no idea who had shot him. After some intense interrogation he admitted that indeed Tilly had pulled the trigger over a fight about Mrs Mary Parsons, or, as Tilly put it, 'over a bit of a yike over his missus'. Tilly was arrested and charged with attempted murder. Parsons refused to testify and she was released.[35] They married on 19 May 1945. Tilly wore all her diamond rings, a powder-blue outfit and blue ribbons in her blonded hair, as well as far too much make-up. His nephew George later recalled that on his marriage, Eric ceased to be an independent man but was now a Flash Harry.[36]

In 1948 Tilly sailed first class to England to visit her ailing father. On her arrival in Southampton, she called a press conference to keep up her reputation back in Sydney. Her use of a chauffeured Daimler as transport was in stark contrast to the slum her father still lived in. On her return, Tilly put on an elaborate party for her fiftieth birthday. *Smith's Weekly* of 23 September 1950 covered the 'Lobster Spread', at which Tilly gave renditions of her favourite music hall numbers from her youth. By this time she was nicknamed 'Diamond' Tilly Devine, the 'tough peroxide blond from Camberwell Green ... [who] is probably one of Sydney's wealthiest citizens ...'[37] Tilly was annoyed that the *People* article elicited many requests for money from her old home stamping ground, Camberwell.

Tilly went to the Melbourne Cup in 1951, a rather risky move, as she had jumped bail in Melbourne in 1934. This time she was arrested for consorting at Flemington Racecourse. She wore a fur coat despite the heat and diamonds on every finger, so she was hardly inconspicuous. She told the magistrate she had cancer. Sentenced to twelve months' imprisonment, she served only five weeks.[38] Not one to harbour grudges, Tilly went again in style the following year to enjoy the Melbourne Cup. In 1953 she decided to return to London to witness Queen Elizabeth's coronation. Tilly and Eric watched from a vantage point on their allocated seats on Pall Mall, near where Tilly had walked the streets in 1915 and 1916.[39]

This was perhaps Tilly's last hurrah. Eric had to have an eye removed in London, and on her return the Australian Taxation Office besieged her. In 1955 she owed £20,000 in back taxes, which required a serious sale of her property assets to cover the huge amount.[40] Eric died of cancer in November 1957, leaving Tilly devastated and alone. By 1959 she owned only one brothel, in Palmer Street. Like Al Capone, she may have colluded with corrupt police, but the tax investigators were relentless and eager to recover lost taxes. As the

NSW Royal Commission into Crime revealed in 1961, the nature of organised crime was rapidly changing, with longer opening hours in hotels and legal off-course betting.[41]

In January 1964 Kate Leigh died, after years spent as a recluse in her little flat in Devonshire Street, Surry Hills. Tilly attended Kate's funeral at St Peter's Catholic Church, Surry Hills. Many old acquaintances, police and former customers came to pay their respects to someone they had seemingly forgotten in her twilight years.

From this time Tilly was increasingly thin and frail, suffering chronic bronchitis.[42] Her rivals and associates had all died, leaving her as a relic from another age, out of step in the new world. She closed her last brothel in 1968 after a series of threats from new crime entrepreneurs such as Joe Borg. A firebomb was thrown into the brothel and her house was ransacked. Even for Tilly, who would have fought back with more violence in her heyday, this was terrifying. Once one of Sydney's wealthiest women, who had earned her money by her own hand and not through inheritance or marriage, Tilly lived in poverty on the old age pension. In 1969 she went to the Sacred Heart Hospice in Darlinghurst when she was diagnosed with stomach cancer. One nun, Sister Mary St Joseph, who grew attached to Tilly, arranged for visits and outings on her behalf.[43] She died in Concord Repatriation Hospital on 24 November 1970, and was cremated after a Catholic requiem mass to a tiny congregation.

Unlike the tributes to Kate Leigh, those to Tilly were harsh and unforgiving. One journalist went so far as to say she was 'a vicious, grasping, high-priestess of savagery, venery, obscenity and whoredom'.[44] No doubt this was all true. But Tilly Devine, one of Australia's most notorious gangsters and madams, had simply outlived her time of glory.

CHAPTER 15

Sunday Reed
(1905–1981)

Born into the Melbourne Baillieu family, Sunday snared Sidney
Nolan and helped create Australia's best art.

Sunday Reed was a renowned patron of the arts in Australia. Along with her husband, John Reed, she supported artists such as Sidney Nolan – with whom she conducted a passionate affair for many years – Joy Hester, Albert Tucker, John Perceval and Charles Blackman. Born into the wealthy Baillieu family, Sunday was a rebel, feisty and determined to make her mark in a male-dominated world. Her notorious love affairs, her commitment to art with Australian themes and her challenges to conventional morality mark her as a woman of flair, intelligence and determination.

The Baillieu family arrived in Victoria in 1853, when James Baillieu jumped ship by swimming ashore to Queenscliff. His antecedents were a fascinating lot. Etienne Baillieux fled to England from Liège early in the French Revolution. The family were lacemakers and embroiderers, creative endeavours of which Sunday was remarkably proud. Etienne's son, Lambert Baillieu was a dancing master and musician. Welsh-born James was the third of Lambert's fifteen children. Once in the colonies, James found employment as a boatman in the health service in Queenscliff. In 1858 he married Emma Pow from Somerset. Not content with his lowly job, in 1881 James built a hotel, where the Victorian governor holidayed. His second son, William Baillieu, was the financial genius behind the family's spectacular rise to wealth. The family company, Mutual Trust, employed six of the Baillieu brothers, with the daughters marrying close associates of William.[1] Family loyalty was placed at a premium, a value instilled in Sunday as a child.

William built a vast commercial empire based upon real estate. When he narrowly avoided bankruptcy by some dazzling financial manoeuvres in the depression of the early 1890s, his reputation was impugned. Undeterred, he went into mining in Maryborough, Victoria, armed with British capital. Within a decade, he and some of his brothers were astoundingly wealthy. Sunday's father, Arthur Sidney Baillieu (1872–1943) built his own fortune upon real estate. Her mother, Ethel Ham, was also Australian-born. Arriving in Victoria in 1849, Ethel's father, David Ham, made money as a miner at Ballarat, then as a stockbroker with business interests in Queenscliff.[2] His reputation was secured when he was appointed to the Victorian Legislative Council in 1880. Ethel was a gifted painter whose professional aspirations were severely limited by marriage. Like her daughter later, she was a prominent patron of the arts, supporting Frederick McCubbin and Arthur Streeton.

When Sunday – Lelda Sunday Baillieu – was born in October 1905, the family had not yet overcome the odium caused by their business dealings in the previous decade. They were rich, but newly rich, unlike respected old families such as the Hentys, the à Becketts, or the Cunninghams.[3] There was a taint of the sly, ruthless and recently-made-good hanging over them. The Baillieu men were simply not yet gentlemen. This polite appellation awaited William's elevation to the House of Lords in 1936. Sunday always felt the intense masculine camaraderie of her family. She had two elder brothers, Jack (known as King) and Darren, and a younger brother, Everard. Unlike many wealthy parents, Ethel and Arthur were close to their children, with Sunday particularly close to her father, a far more sensitive and imaginative man than his rambunctious brothers.[4]

Sunday's early life was secure and privileged. When she was five, her parents moved to Balholmen in Toorak, then a small exclusive enclave.[5]

Grand houses were surrounded by hectares of beautiful lawns and gardens, allowing a high degree of privacy for residents. The Baillieu boys were sent to Geelong Grammar School, leaving Sunday in the care of governesses. She was not destined for a career, so she learned domestic skills at home. Her one outlet was gardening. At the age of fifteen she attended St Catherine's School in Toorak.[6] At this time, the school operated as a finishing school rather than an academically orientated institution such as Presbyterian Ladies College, where Nettie Palmer, Ethel Florence (Henry Handel) Richardson, Nellie Melba and Dame Jean McNamara were educated. At school, Sunday felt out of place and was viewed as a mere parvenue with disreputability still hanging over the family's reputation. Her maid, Clare Pitblado, was her best friend, an indication of her isolation and lack of friends.[7]

Holidays as a teenager were spent at the family home, Merthon, at Sorrento, now immortalised in Arthur Streeton's paintings *Nocturne* (c. 1920) and *Point King, Sorrento* (1920).[8] As it was for many wealthy Melbournians, the holiday period was extended and leisurely, commencing in November and terminating around Easter. Entertainment was kept within the family. There Sunday felt at ease and relaxed.

Like Maie Casey, Sunday was expected to make her debut at a court presentation. The Baillieus had many business and social connections in London, so her path to the royal event was smooth. By 1924 the dress expectations for ladies had slightly relaxed, though they were still elaborate and expensive, requiring ostrich plumes and a white evening dress often with a four-metre train. Sunday wore a beautiful shift with a string of pearls.[9] Attractive, slim and athletic from her years of swimming, she looked magnificent. After this rite of passage, Sunday was considered a young woman rather than a girl, and allowed far more freedom. What she did with this new freedom was to mark the rest of her life.

Sunday went to Paris where she gained a sophisticated elegance in her dress. Chic modern clothes looked perfect on her. She favoured white, cream and pale blue in tailored clothes, a style she maintained all her life. She did not rush into cropping her hair, though by the time she returned home the following year she had an Eton crop, a short hemline and smoked cigarettes. She also learned to drive early. This was not quite what the Baillieu family anticipated from Sunday's expensive presentation. Then her life changed when she met handsome and debonair Leonard Quinn in Sydney, sometime in 1925. Affecting the persona of a rich young American, Quinn was a petty thief accustomed to living on his wits. He was entirely unsuitable for Sunday as he represented everything her family would hate – a Boston Roman Catholic and a charlatan. Moreover, her mother Ethel, had become a Christian Scientist, an American religion popularised by Nancy Astor in England.[10] When her beloved brother King died suddenly of typhus in 1926, Sunday was besieged by grief, an emotion that Leonard was quick to manipulate.[11]

Sunday's engagement was announced just before her twenty-first birthday. The wedding took place at St Mary's Star of the Sea Catholic Church in Sorrento, unlike the usual society events for young ladies from Toorak. Her parents hosted a modest reception at Merthon, where Leonard disgraced his bride by becoming drunk very quickly.[12] Sunday was assured of a comfortable allowance from her father, which permitted her and Leonard to travel to Europe and live without worrying about work. They headed for Paris after the wedding, where Sunday moved in an outer ring of the Hemingway circles. Her French lessons paid off and she could behave like an accomplished participant rather than a wealthy cultural tourist. As with another fashionable couple, Zelda and F. Scott Fitzgerald, Sunday and Leonard also moved to the Côte d'Azur where Sunday luxuriated in the beach life. Coco Chanel had made a healthy tan fashionable so this choice was even more palatable, and Sunday was particularly taken by the absence of sharks.[13]

The Quinns moved to England for the years of 1928 and 1929 and settled in the picturesque village of Broadway in the Cotswolds. They moved back to Paris as the marriage disintegrated. Sunday was devastated to learn that she had contracted gonorrhoea from Leonard and required an immediate hysterectomy. He simply abandoned her to her grief of dashed dreams and lost children. At the young age of twenty-five, Sunday was thrown into the bewildering symptoms of a sudden menopause, which was not at that time treated with hormone therapy. Her parents were neither hostile nor reproving, and she spent her long recuperation with them in Melbourne before returning to Paris. When Sunday was painted by Agnes Goodsir, an Australian artist long resident in Paris, she had lost her freshness and soft features.[14] Life in Paris alone held no appeal for Sunday, and she returned home in 1931.

On her return, Sunday was fortunate to met John Reed, a sensible, good-looking young solicitor, born into wealth and privilege in northern Tasmania. He and his sister, Cynthia Reed, hated the strict, Non-conformist Church Wesleyan piety that dominated their upbringing.[15] Reed was a quiet, reflective man who found solace in nature. Educated at Cheltenham College in England, Geelong Grammar, and Gonville and Caius College, Cambridge, John was a far more appropriate match for Sunday. He was introduced to modern art by artist and journalist Clarice Zander, the owner of the New Gallery in Melbourne.[16] Clarice's acquisition of the exhibition of British Contemporary Art in 1933 was a masterly coup. John shared an apartment with engineer Fred Ward, an influential Modernist furniture designer whose collection is now housed in the Powerhouse Museum in Sydney.

Sunday and John met at a tennis party in Toorak in 1931 and he was immediately smitten by her vitality and beauty. She was also attracted to the rather stiff and formal solicitor, whose background matched her own. Even at the outset of their affair, Sunday's sexual appetites vastly ran ahead of John's, though it was all well managed when they later married. Her libido simply went elsewhere. During their engagement John came to know her moody self-absorption, her tendency to retreat to the sickbed at any sign of stress and her myriad minor physical ailments, yet he was not deterred. Rather like Leonard Woolf's care for Virginia, John was the devoted attendant to a highly strung, demanding and selfish woman of talent.[17] Like those famous denizens of Bloomsbury, Sunday and John entered into a virtual *mariage blanc*.

Sunday's parents were delighted with this appropriate choice of partner while the Reeds were notably less enthusiastic. A divorcee was perfectly fine in a sophisticated Lubitsch comedy in Hollywood, but it was certainly out of the question in Australia in the 1930s. Sunday was, after all, a woman who was sterile because of an unmentionable disease. And she was not even divorced, but technically still a married woman. Most likely Arthur Baillieu paid Quinn off in order to release his daughter, who was formally divorced in June 1931. Sunday and John were married in St Paul's Anglican Cathedral on 13 January 1932 in a small side chapel, not before the central altar. This was the Church's concession, in view of the status of a divorcee remarrying with a former husband still alive. But the marriage did not appear in the cathedral's records, given the Anglican strictures on divorce. Sunday signed her certificate 'Sunday Baillieu Quinn' then crossed out 'Quinn'.[18] The new couple honeymooned overseas.

On their return to Melbourne later in the year, Sunday began her commitment to modern art in earnest. She purchased a painting by Adrian Lawlor, an emerging artist and writer, with articles in the progressive literary journals *Vision* and *New Triad*.[19] Associating with artists George Bell and William Frater, she mixed in the same art circles as Maie Casey. Sunday and John also met another of Casey's colleagues, Sam Atyeo, who had a far more profound influence upon their tastes and sensibilities. Born into a working-class family in Melbourne, Sam exhibited at Fred Ward's gallery and at Cynthia Reed's shop at 367 Little Collins Street in June 1933. In the 1940s he became a diplomat.[20] He and Sunday conducted a passionate public affair with John's approval in 1933. (Thirty years later, in 1963, John curated an exhibition of Atyeo's work for George's Gallery.) What Atyeo's partner, Moya Dyring, felt or thought of the affair at the time was irrelevant to Sunday, blown away by her own needs and desires. Dyring, nevertheless, later collaborated on projects at Heide, John and Sunday's future home, which they opened to a wide circle of artists.[21] Perhaps in response to their partners' affair, John and Moya engaged in a tepid liaison. Sam also had an affair with Sunday's sister-in-law, Cynthia; all in all, a highly incestuous little group. Moya later painted both Sam and Cynthia, the latter in a most unflattering light. These claustrophobic couplings were to become a core feature of Sunday's life.

Sunday was beset with grief when her mother, Ethel, died after a long illness in late 1932. The overwhelming masculine ruggedness of her family was even more apparent after her mother's death. That year Sunday enrolled in the George Bell–Arnold Shore School in Bourke Street.[22] The only Modernist school in Melbourne, it taught potential artists as well as dabblers and Toorak matrons.[23] Students such as Sunday and Maie Casey wanted to become serious artists, but the demands of their social lives and class, plus their limited ambition, relegated them to the ranks of the gifted amateur. Sunday had the foresight to realise she would never become a professional artist and destroyed most of her work, gauged less than perfect and original by her own exacting standards.

While their personal lives were caught up with Sam, Cynthia and Moya, John and Sunday also became serious art collectors, commencing with Sam's works.[24] They were facilitators, not patrons, they frequently protested; friends of artists, not simply their financial supporters.[25] Yet their patrician upbringing and their financial abundance, along with their deep need to be involved in creativity, rendered them archetypal patrons, albeit in a modern Australian setting. For Sunday, her childlessness and her failure as an artist required a direct imaginative expression. In 1935 the couple moved to their new home, Heide, in Heidelberg. Perhaps no location represents more communal creativity and transformation than Heidelberg, for it was here in the later 1880s that Tom Roberts, Frederick McCubbin and Arthur Streeton captured the beauty of the Australian environment.

The house was in keeping with its artistic and cultural heritage. Balholmen provided a source of substantial furniture, at odds with the Modernist paintings Sunday collected. She also included her mother's old Streeton and McCubbin paintings. The house was surrounded by a decaying garden, but Sunday oversaw its restoration, along with the help of friends, as a creative outlet. Guests recalled they were expected to pitch in with chores in the garden, whether they liked it or not. This was despite the employment of domestic and garden staff to do the basic work of maintaining the property in the initial stages.[26] Strict dietary rules were rigorously enforced upon guests, long before the raw food regime was popularised.

That year a major change occurred in Sunday's life. John, a partner in the prestigious law firm of Blake and Riggall, was asked to resign after an alleged affair with his secretary. He then made the dubious move of entering the Baillieus' commercial networks, which meant a financial dependency upon Sunday and her family. John did not inherit from his own family until 1956. By the mid 1930s the Baillieu empire, under the banner of the Collins Group, invested heavily in the Tasmanian pulp wood industry, real estate and mining ventures associated with BHP and formerly Mount Morgan. Sunday's Uncle William had been dubbed 'Australia's Money King' and was successful in outbidding the Australian government agent's tender for a major loan in London. William's son Clive maintained his father's business acumen, later becoming a chairman of Rio Tinto.[27]

The impact of John's new circumstances and her tempestuous affair with Sam began to take their toll on Sunday's health. Along with her old servant, Clare, she went to the United States in 1937 to recuperate and gain some distance from her problems. By 1938 her spirits and energy had revived and, back in Australia, she suddenly had a new focus for her life. Sunday met young Sidney Nolan through John initially, when Nolan brazenly asked for £50 to finance his hoped-for overseas training.[28] John later recalled, 'Nolan ... was a kind of wild-cat spirit, unformed, uncertain of his destiny, but arrogantly confident that the fates were on his side …'[29] Working for Fayfield Hats as a signwriter, Nolan spent a lot of his day studying Modernism from books. A series of casual jobs left him despondent. He pondered whether he should become an artist or a writer. It was this connection to literature that sealed his initial bond with Sunday. He entered the world of Heide where he was surrounded by money, a high European aesthetic and the Modernism of artists like Atyeo. For Sunday, this was her chance to nurture a great talent to her own designs, at least initially.

On the spur of the moment Nolan married Elizabeth Patterson, a student at the Gallery School. Rather than existing solely in the world of art and creativity, Nolan also ran a little pie shop in Lonsdale Street, before landing a commission with the de Basil Ballet Company to design sets for their productions in Sydney. When compared to the attractions of Heide, the marriage fell apart despite the birth of a daughter, Amelda, in 1940. Yet at this artistic refuge, the management of a ménage à trois had difficult logistics to surmount, not that this bothered Sunday in the slightest; she had located her potential genius and he was her life work for the moment. Conscripted into the army in April 1942, Nolan reluctantly left the security of his new home. For his art, the dry Wimmera landscape, where he was stationed, ignited his imagination and led him to produce his first paintings in his own style. The letters Nolan wrote to Sunday in this period are cool and intellectual, concerned with Kierkegaard, Dylan Thomas, William Blake and André Gide. Reading them gives no indication they were lovers or so much as intimate friends.[30] Nolan always detested the accusation he was a 'kept man'.[31] Back at Heide, Sunday prepared his canvases, mixed paints and purchased books.[32] She would have been well advised to note the dispassionate tone of his correspondence. The consequences of all this assistance were to explode later over the ownership of the finished works after he left for London in 1951.[33]

Sunday was not solely preoccupied with Nolan, however. The artist Joy Hester was increasingly drawn into the Heide set, which also included Arthur Boyd, Albert Tucker and John Perceval.[34] Joy found inspiration within this domain, drawing *Gethi in a Tree*. The image referred to Sunday's doll, Gethsemane, which she treated as a substitute child. There is an added poignancy, as later Sunday adopted Joy's baby son, Sweeney, when Joy was struck down with Hodgkin's disease. As the men went to war, Sunday and Joy consolidated their friendship through their mutual interests in art and literature.

When Arthur Baillieu died in 1943, Sunday inherited a considerable estate, though not the family house, Merthon.[35] That year, John left work as a solicitor at the Baillieu company. In his new liberation he founded the avant-garde magazine *Angry Penguins*, with poet and critic Max Harris, as well as the publishing company Reed and Harris. The capital, however, came from Sunday. The Ern Malley hoax in 1944, in which poets James McAuley and Harold Stewart created the fictitious Ern Malley and his impressionistic poems to prick the Modernist pretensions of the Angry Penguins movement, was a *succès de scandale* and largely finished the magazine.[36] For Sunday this was a disappointing outcome for her literary hopes. She had little time to fret over it, however, for Nolan was commencing his series of Ned Kelly paintings. *Ned Kelly*, *The Encounter* and *The Chase* were all painted in 1946. In the process of representing the Kelly legend, Nolan transformed post-war Australian painting. Nolan and Sunday fed each other's creativity. Later, he wrote to John Reed, 'I do not ever feel that the Kellys belong to anyone other than Sun.'[37] Nolan left for Brisbane when he completed the series in 1947. Outwardly, Sunday was dignified, as letters from Joy Hester indicate; her inner turmoil, grief and anger were kept largely at Heide.[38] Joy innocently reported that she visited Cynthia at her home in Wahroonga, Sydney, in January 1948, just before Cynthia's affair with Nolan, and later socialised with the new couple.[39]

Sunday was apprehensive about the longevity of her affair and artistic collaboration with Nolan, yet her life took on a new challenge when she adopted Sweeney, the son of Joy Hester and Albert Tucker. Joy declared that she saw herself primarily as a painter and was glad to have a wealthy couple take over the care of her young son. When Joy moved to Sydney to live with artist Gray Smith, she welcomed the opportunity to go alone.[40] For Sunday, Sweeney was the child she had been unable to conceive and nurture. Her longing for Nolan had not ceased however, and she fretted and became more depressed over a relationship she correctly feared was over. What she did not realise was that Nolan had begun living with her sister-in-law Cynthia in Sydney. Cynthia had largely alienated her entire family with the recent publication of a toxic portrayal of them in *Daddy Sowed a Wind!* (1947). When she and Nolan married in March 1948, they decided to see the Reeds straight after. This was hardly a conciliatory gesture and Sunday's sense of double betrayal was overwhelming and enduring. Later in 1971, Nolan's savage collection of poems *Paradise Garden* tore through his relationship with Sunday and John in the 1940s.[41]

The Reeds sought solace in travel, venturing to Paris, Belgium, England and Italy. They took some of the Ned Kelly series with them, their faith in Nolan's genius remaining steadfast. But Sunday no longer felt the same ease with sophisticated Parisian life as she had in the 1930s, and even as they stayed on, they felt alien and provincial. Sweeney was sent to a family in Tours, making his life even more chaotic and insecure. During this childless time, Sunday and John negotiated for a short exhibition of Nolan's work to be shown at the Maison de l'UNESCO.

When the Reeds returned to Melbourne in 1949, the focuses of their cultural aspirations – Nolan, Arthur Boyd and John Perceval – had moved away. Brisbane-born bookseller and librarian Barrett Reid guided the Reeds in their new period of patronage. Through him they met and nurtured Charles and Barbara Blackman, Robert Dickerson, Nadine Amadio, George and Mirka Mora, as well as Judith Wright.[42] John kept in touch with Albert Tucker, informing him about this new pool of talented artists.[43]

Like Nolan and Hester before them, this group was as passionate about literature as art. Life at Heide took on a new dimension as

Sunday decided to home-school Sweeney, perhaps not a good idea for a child already so indulged and neglected at various times. At the age of nine, after years of frustration on both sides, he was sent to Geelong Grammar as a boarder, a tremendous change for a child who had not been encouraged to learn self-discipline.[44] The arrival of Peregrine and Fern, the children of his mother and Gray Smith, as half-siblings hardly assisted his sense of security.

In 1953 John re-established the Contemporary Arts Society (CAS).[45] By 1956 it was the premier gallery showing contemporary Australian art in Melbourne. This was a momentous year for John as he finally inherited his estate, the family sheep farm at Deloraine and was now free of his financial dependency upon Sunday. He could afford to indulge his passions with his own money. Often profligate with funds, the newly renamed Gallery of Contemporary Art (GCA) was a financial hole into which he poured his money.[46] Through the influence of artists Ian and Dawn Sime, Sunday and John were introduced to American Abstract art. This movement was hardly to their taste and it remained a fleeting interest. Far more important to Sunday was the restoration of the house and the construction of her Heart Garden.

Within a year the GCA was losing money at a speedy rate. Because of a certain inflexibility the Reeds would find themselves surpassed in the fickle, bitchy world of art. In the very week the GCA was launched, John Perceval chose to open an exhibition at the Australian Galleries in Collingwood. Cocooned by decades at Heide, neither Sunday nor John were accustomed to the more aggressive world of the open art market and its critics.[47] When the gallery was reopened as the Museum of Modern Art of Australia (MoMAA) in June 1958, Sunday relocated much of her collection at Heide to this new enterprise. Waging war against the Melbourne *Herald*'s art critic Allan McCulloch was hardly a smart move. But McCulloch's assessment that the Reeds were far too isolated and introverted in their patronage and tastes had a strong ring of truth.[48] They should have called it the Museum of Contemporary Melbourne Art, such was their parochialism.

The vexed question of the Nolan paintings remained. In 1957 the Whitechapel Gallery in London organised a Nolan retrospective. The paintings at Heide were not included, despite Nolan's entreaties. Sunday '... became hysterical with grief' at the mere thought of relinquishing them.[49] To do so meant abandoning her hopes for reconciliation with him. Seven years later, Fred Williams was asked to conserve the paintings, many of which had been damaged by Sunday's cats' urine. Subsequently, the paintings went into a bank vault. Pamela Warrender, the chairman of the MoMAA, undertook the emotionally fraught role of accompanying the paintings to a 1964 exhibition in London, where she had to deal with Nolan and his anger over the paintings kept at Heide. John accused Nolan of behaving like 'an executioner' towards both him and Sunday, whom he believed had provided enduring love and support.[50]

While Sunday continued to feel a searing, relentless attack on her very being regarding Nolan, she was able to support other emerging artists such as Charles Blackman, purchasing his *Golden Alice* from the Alice in Wonderland series. When Nadine Amadio went to live at Heide, her first impression of the house was the beauty of this painting.[51] The Reeds' coterie, however, was rapidly diminishing. They did not purchase new works by Arthur Boyd or John Perceval, as they had moved out of the Heide circle. In 1959 Russian painter Danila Vassilieff died at Heide, while the following year in Prahran, Joy Hester finally succumbed to Hodgkin's lymphoma. Another major change occurred when a second Heide was built. Everything in the original house, including the piano, books and furnishings, was abandoned, left to fester along with Sunday's increasing bitterness over her lost cultural domains. Yet it also produced renewal. Instead of Victorian comfort, Sunday now moved to cool clean 1960s design – a beautiful building designed for displaying art brought much pleasure back into her life.

In May 1965 John's life changed radically once more when he resigned from MoMAA.[52] The museum closed that year after tottering financially for a decade. The construction of the new Heide was more than enough to fill John's time, since the process went on for several years. Yet, in the end, Sunday's vision for her new enterprise, Heide II, was rewarded. In this fresh environment she adopted new tastes, including brightly coloured plastic bowls from Finland. Even in her sixties she felt all the enthusiasm of a teenager for Beatlemania.[53] It is hard to imagine the Toorak patrician attending a Little Richard concert, yet she absorbed all the latest popular music and art with gusto. Her next project was a bookstore in Exhibition Street, Melbourne. Barrett Reid warned her of the financial pitfalls of this enterprise but, never one to listen, Sunday learned the hard way.

An even harder lesson came with the release of Nolan's collection of poems, paintings and drawings *Paradise Garden* in 1971. In it Nolan portrayed himself as a Candide seduced by a 'subtle tart'. Sunday was mocked and humiliated for her infertility and her age, while John was a knowing, weak cuckold. The poems made painful reading. Sunday told her friend Jean Langley that she was 'quite blind with sadness. I would die and be lost forever if I tried to repress these thoughts …'[54] She certainly did not deserve this vicious public treatment, which detracted from Nolan's own reputation. Sunday also had to endure more sadness, as Sweeney grew up an irresponsible and wild young man, trying this and that before failing and trying something else, squandering his parents' money.

In 1972 Sunday decided she would donate her Nolan paintings to the nation.[55] In 1977 she finally relinquished the Nolan oeuvre she possessed to the National Gallery of Australia. Cynthia Nolan had committed suicide in November 1976, perhaps making the decision easier. Yet with this long-standing rival gone, Sunday was distressed to learn that in January 1978 Nolan married her friend Mary Boyd Perceval, whom she had supported when she left the alcoholic John Perceval.[56] When Mary and Sidney Nolan visited Melbourne later that year, Mary went to Heide II and her husband sat in the car. A phone call to Nolan soon after was so distressing that Sunday burned his entire correspondence going back into the late 1930s. Yet the demon of her obsession for forty years did not die.[57] Further horror was to come when John was diagnosed with cancer and in March 1979 Sweeney committed suicide. He left no farewell note to his parents. John wrote months later '... our world has fallen apart ... It is hard at our age to learn to live without him.'[58]

When the Victorian government purchased Heide II to use as an art gallery, Sunday and John moved back to the original Heide, a painful relocation full of traumatic memories. Sunday did not attend the opening of the gallery. John's health deteriorated rapidly.[59] He died on 5 December 1981. For Sunday, the loss of her life companion and champion was too overwhelming to endure. She committed suicide ten days later. Her ashes were scattered among the trees of Heide.

CHAPTER 16

Rosaleen Norton
(1917–1979)

The Kings Cross resident witch and satanic artist.

Rosaleen Norton holds a unique place in Australian history. An artist who depicted hermaphrodites, women coupling with panthers at a witches' sabbath, penises evolving into terrestrial serpents and seductive Lucifers, she was dubbed the nation's most notorious and well-known witch. The pagan themes of her art went far beyond the sexually alluring depictions produced by Norman Lindsay; they entered into the darkest places of the psyche, where disorder, alien lust and supernatural forces rule. In the repressed years of the 1950s, her appearance alone marked her as a woman dancing to the beat of a different drum from conventional suburban or even bohemian ones. With jet-black hair and naturally pointed ears, Rosaleen wore heavy red lipstick and wildly coloured clothes, an intricately carved cigarette holder her perpetual prop. She also possessed a 'third breast', a thin strand of flesh that hung from armpit to waist, the sign of the demon and witch in medieval cosmology.[1] With her arched eyebrows and steely, unflinching gaze she was the definition of a woman totally at odds with the society around her. She lived for her art, rejecting any form of economic security, in abject poverty in Kings Cross.

Little in her childhood predicted Rosaleen's destiny. Born in the stern and rigid Scottish-settled city of Dunedin, New Zealand, her early environment was highly repressive. Her later art explored the murky moral imperatives very distant from the certainties of the

Calvinism practised in New Zealand's southern city. Her father, English-born Albert Norton, was a master mariner employed by the New Zealand Steam Company. His family contained gifted creative people – the distinguished composer Ralph Vaughan Williams was a cousin. Albert was said to possess his cousin's charm and dark good looks with sad magnetic eyes. Rosaleen adored her often absent father. Her mother, Beena Salek Aschman, was born in New Zealand. Her life work was her home and role as mother to daughters Cecily, Phyllis and the much younger Rosaleen. Spoilt and pampered by her mother and sisters from an early age, Rosaleen became accustomed to getting her own way. The family followed the practices of the Church of England, though without any apparent devotion or conviction. Rosaleen later recalled her mother as 'a very difficult woman, hysterical, emotional and possessive'.[2] This revealed a lack of insight into the fact that, with her husband at sea, Beena was left for extended periods on her own to raise the family.

In 1925 the family moved to Lindfield in Sydney, where Rosaleen went to the Church of England Girls School in nearby Chatswood, which she found restrictive and conventional. Even as a child, Rosaleen baulked at discipline and convention. At home she insisted on living in a tent in the backyard and she soon came to admire the world of spiders, toads and lizards. Her parents were obviously far more tolerant and relaxed than she ever gave them credit for. At the early age of three, Rosaleen had begun drawing ghosts, otherworldly creatures and dragons.[3] This, in itself, is remarkable, for most children of this age draw their house, pets and family members. In 1957 she explained that her childhood dreams fuelled her art. At seven she knew she possessed the sign of the witch by several blue marks on her knees. In adolescence her depictions of the macabre and Gothic alarmed her teachers. At fourteen she was expelled from school, the teachers fearing her 'depraved nature' would corrupt other pupils.[4] When she was twelve, she had experimented sexually with a boy, although she did not repeat the painful experience for another five years. Her sexuality, enjoyed with both men and women, ventured into the realms of sado-masochism: she enjoyed being tied up and beaten by men.[5]

Rosaleen enrolled at the East Sydney Technical College in Paddington, studying under the distinguished English sculptor Rayner Hoff. He had arrived in Sydney in 1923 and soon became friends with the artist Norman Lindsay. Known for his controversial war memorial sculptures, as a former soldier in World War I Hoff believed he understood the nature of war better than his critics.[6] Hoff was a fortunate choice of mentor for the rebellious Rosaleen, who had not yet decided on her ultimate career path. She wavered between art and writing, having published stories in the popular conservative journal *Smith's Weekly* at the age of fifteen. Rosaleen's signature theme in her first published work was already fully developed. Editor Frank Marien later recalled that: '[n]ever have we discovered a juvenile author so obviously gifted as Rosaleen Norton'.[7] He had an uncanny ability to spot the talents of cartoonists and pen-and-ink artists such as Stan Cross, Mollie Horseman, and Emile Mercier.[8]

Rosaleen wrote of the macabre, the supernatural and the world-beyond-knowing. Marien offered young Rosaleen a cadetship at the newspaper, although she soon wanted to transfer to the art department. Her unusual imagination did not fit within the strictures of a newspaper so she left at the age of eighteen. With her mother's death around the same time, she also left home somewhat impulsively, heading for the Ship and Mermaid Inn in the Rocks area.[9] Known as 'Beggary Barn' or 'Buggery Barn', it was both 'arty' and decrepit. Jack London and Joseph Conrad had stayed there on trips to Sydney.[10] To support herself, Rosaleen took casual jobs in kitchens and hotels, as a telegram messenger and as a model for Norman Lindsay. These jobs allowed her time to start studying the Jewish Kabbalah and Greek mythology.[11]

In 1935 Rosaleen met seventeen-year-old Duco sprayer Beresford Conroy, whom she married in 1940. When he enlisted for active service, he effectively ended the marriage. Meanwhile, Rosaleen revived her artistic career submitting sketches to the innovative journal *Pertinent*, edited by Leon Batt.[12] It published leading writers of the time such as Dulcie Deamer, Kylie Tennant, George Farwell and Ian Mayleston Mudie.[13] Rosaleen's first drawing was published in October 1941, a study entitled *The Borgias*. In a later issue that year, she published drawings of Merlin, ghouls and goblins, as well as a centaur. Surrealism was a popular mode for young avant-garde artists in the inter-war years but Rosaleen took no influence from this movement; rather, her work stepped back into medieval and earlier pagan themes and representations.

During the war Rosaleen continued with her art, though she waited until 1947 before her notorious work was exhibited at Pakies Club at 219 Elizabeth Street in Sydney. A critic for the *Sydney Morning Herald* described her erotic drawings as 'artistic maladjustment'. Rosaleen also experimented with self-hypnosis as a means of gaining access into the darker terrains of her psyche. These methods were not unique; worldwide there had been an upsurge in spiritualism after World War I, when the grief-stricken tried to contact their lost loved ones. Later the Surrealists in France employed similar techniques. Sir Arthur Conan Doyle was a practitioner of the paranormal, particularly after his son died in the war. With the publication of the work of Swiss psychoanalyst Carl Jung, exploring fundamental archetypes in human consciousness and dreams as a vehicle into the subconscious mind, psychic investigations were widely undertaken by intellectuals and artists. This was not common in Australia, however, which was far less exposed to the new thoughts of Freud, Jung and writers like James Joyce than the United States and Europe in the inter-war period. Rosaleen cited the significant influence of Jung in her book *The Art of Rosaleen Norton* (1952).[14] Jung had few followers in Australia, and it is unlikely that Rosaleen read the more accessible books of his Australian disciple Dr William McCrae.[15] She seems to have read the original texts.

Surrealists Salvador Dali, André Breton and Joan Miró all practised automatic writing and art as a means to enter the subconscious, with varying degrees of success.[16] Rosaleen also practised this form of creativity. She spoke at length about this process with psychologist Professor L. J. Murphy at the University of Melbourne in 1949, recalling that: 'I had a feeling (intuitional rather than intellectual) that somewhere in the depths of the unconscious, the individual would contain, in essence, the accumulated knowledge of mankind ...'[17]

Her research into mystic texts in the 1940s and '50s led her to study the works of Madame Blavatsky, the Ukrainian founder of theosophy. Incorporating beliefs from Eastern mysticism, with an emphasis on intuition, mystical revelations and reincarnation, theosophy was popular with many distinguished individuals in the later nineteenth century.[18] The movement was moderately popular in Australia – Prime Minister Alfred Deakin was its most noted exponent.[19] Australia was a comparatively secular culture without an established Church. The loose doctrines of theosophy found a ready audience in people wanting some spirituality without the conventions of formal religion.[20]

Rosaleen's other sources of mystical knowledge came from modern European movements devoted to spiritualism and inner revelation. Eliphas Levi – born Alphonse Constant – had originally studied for the Catholic priesthood in Paris in the 1830s. Abandoning this call as he felt he lacked sufficient vocation, Levi went to England where he was influenced by the popular novelist and politician Sir Edward Bulwer-Lytton[21] and Rosicrucianism. Levi later wrote books on magic and other ancient occult practices destroyed by Christianity. Many of his ideas were incorporated into his disciple and translator Arthur Edward Waite's English version of the tarot cards, still in use today. Rosaleen probably did not read Levi but those who succeeded him.

She certainly read the works of the Welsh mystic Dion Fortune – née Violet Mary Firth (1890–1946) – who had visions of Atlantis at the age of four.[22] Trained as a psychotherapist in London, Fortune was also attracted to mysticism. A follower of the Temple Alpha et Omega in London in 1919, she then went over to the Stella Matutina, a magical order.[23] Such organisations are often fragile in structure, with members cohering around charismatic leaders. They often fail and evolve into new sects. The Temple Alpha et Omega was a breakaway from the original Hermetic Order of the Golden Dawn, founded in England in 1888. Fortune later formed the Fraternity of the Inner Light. She was a prolific novelist and early exponent of the Wicca religion. Her work on the Kabbalah was well received in mystic circles in the 1930s. Such movements were attractive to women as they allowed leadership roles denied them in conventional Christian and Jewish religions.[24]

Another major influence was Aleister Crowley – born Edward Alexander Crowley in Leamington Spa in England in 1875 to devout Exclusive Brethren parents. This alone made him an outsider in Victorian England. His father, however, was acquainted with Aubrey Beardsley, an early influence on young Aleister. Crowley studied at Trinity College, Cambridge. Independently wealthy as a young man after the death of his father, Crowley was able to indulge his passions for occultism, the study of magic, chess and bisexuality. He studied mysticism with Arthur Waite and W. B. Yeats before he left the Hermetic Order of the Golden Dawn to pursue his interests in yoga and Buddhism. In 1920 he co-founded the Temple of Thelema in Sicily. He was a heavy drug-taker, believing this to be a means of entering into the mystic portals of consciousness.

Crowley's influence was profound and enduring in many areas; an image of him appeared on the cover of the Beatles' *Sgt. Pepper's Lonely Hearts Club Band* (1967). For Rosaleen, his interest in the god Pan was particularly significant. His poem *The Hymn to Pan* (1929) was widely admired.[25] His work was well known in Australia through the publications of P. R. Stephensen, later to end up interned during World War II, with suffragette and co-founder of the Communist Party of Australia Adela Pankhurst, for his strange beliefs.[26] Crowley's works were collected in Australia as *The Spirit of Solitude; An Autohagiography Subsequently Christened the Confessions of Aleister Crowley* (1929). They were not mainstream interests for Australians, who did not have the

English tradition of mysticism and modern magic. Where Rosaleen struck others as deviant and odd in her homeland, she might have been regarded merely as eccentric in England. In some ways she was simply ahead of her time; by the 1960s many of these ideas and practices had entered mainstream Western youth culture.

Rosaleen was not simply interested in pagan beliefs; she wanted a soulmate to share them with. In 1949 she became reacquainted with the young Adelaide poet Gavin Greenlees, who also published with *Pertinent*. She may have met him some years earlier in Sydney, but given the difference in age – he was born in 1930 – the friendship was initially casual. In August they hitchhiked from Sydney to Melbourne to locate a venue for her first major exhibition, which demonstrates just how poverty-stricken they were. Her exhibition was launched in the Rowden White Library of the University of Melbourne, perhaps not the most congenial location for such provocative and unusual works. Forty-six were shown, introduced by the prominent academic Professor A. R. Chisholm, a major scholar both of Rimbaud and Australian poetry. Uproar occurred when the police raided the exhibition, removing four works: *Witches' Sabbath*, *Lucifer*, *Triumph* and *Individuation* were declared to be obscene. Complaints had been made that the works were 'lewd and disgusting'. The case went to court; Rosaleen's solicitor pointed out the charge had been lodged under legislation passed in 1836. With support from the University of Melbourne, the case was dismissed with all costs awarded to the police.[27]

Rosaleen did not sell her paintings and drawings at the exhibition, since most of the visitors were poor students. She and Gavin returned to Sydney to live in a flat at 179 Brougham Street in Kings Cross, the underworld hub of drugs and prostitution. The tiny flat was a squalid, cluttered mess, with a welcoming sign proclaiming 'Welcome to the house of ghosts, goblins, werewolves, vampires, witches and poltergeists'. Artist Dulcie Deamer, the so-called 'Queen of Bohemia', had lived in the area since the 1920s. She and Rosaleen were kindred spirits and friends, although Deamer had a more conventional past as the mother of six children.[28] Other prominent artists, such as sculptor Loma Latour and painter Sir William Dobell, had also lived there at some time.[29] Rosaleen showed her work at various coffee shops, including the Californian Coffee Shop, Kashmir Café and the Arabian Café.[30] Paintings rarely sold, but they added atmosphere to these modest establishments.

Although Rosaleen and Gavin had a roof over their heads, they were arrested for vagrancy in 1951. They were offered work in a most unlikely place – *The Pastrycook's Review* – by its editor, Wally Glover, a returned soldier. He had heard of their arrest for vagrancy and offered them a respectable source of employment. They were to assist with the production of images. Rosaleen made the mistake of allowing Glover the right of ownership of all her work in return for financial support. With this sudden windfall they were able to concentrate on their creative projects for a major book, *The Art of Rosaleen Norton with Poems by Gavin Greenlees* (1952). Copies were beautifully bound in red leather and printed on Glastonbury Antique paper. Both Glover's and Rosaleen's fathers died suddenly on the same day of the advance copies' release. When the book was finally released, Rosaleen was ambitious for her work and sent copies to Professor C. S. Lewis, the author of the *Narnia* series, to Dame Edith Sitwell and, even more bizarrely, to Albert Einstein, then at Princeton University. The release was dogged by controversy and legal intervention. Glover was charged in August 1952 with producing an obscene publication and fined £5. The United States Customs officials burned copies on entry to America. In 1957 Glover was declared bankrupt largely because of the financial strain of this unusual publication and copyright was transferred to the Official Receiver of Bankruptcy.[31]

By the time of the book's release Rosaleen was already dubbed 'The Witch of Kings Cross', an epithet she carried for the rest of her life. Rather than attempt to understand her art, it was far easier to assign a conventional label to this eccentric woman. Nevertheless, her paintings and drawings went on permanent display at the Apollyon Café, a rendezvous for tourists wanting a taste of the occult and the bizarre at a safe distance. She was regarded as an exotic animal exhibit to be scrutinised. Newspaper reports that she conducted black sabbaths, however, severely damaged her reputation as a serious artist. The curious went to her flat in the hope of witnessing the occult at first hand or taking away some souvenir from her premises.

In September 1955 a mentally ill woman named Anna Hoffman claimed she had attended a black mass at the flat, accompanied by 'sex orgies and parties', which led to charges against Rosaleen. The judge dismissed Anna Hoffman's allegations, considering her to be 'a menace', nevertheless, the extensive coverage in newspapers damaged Rosaleen's reputation even further.[32] Another dramatic case hit the headlines in October after the vice squad raided Rosaleen and Gavin's flat. The police alleged that two men had photographs of a black mass, with Rosaleen and Gavin engaged in 'an unnatural sexual act'. The

One of Rosaleen's fascinating sketches, *Self-portrait with Devil*. Mitchell Library, State Library of NSW P3/211.

photographs had been taken at a ceremony devoted to the god Pan, and then stolen from their flat. The culprits were sentenced to four months' imprisonment for theft.[33] The case did not go altogether well for the couple. Rather than dressing conventionally, Rosaleen attended court in leopardskin shoes, a sign of her deviancy in conservative Sydney. More alarming was her obvious stupor from the drugs methedrine and dexedrine, which left her incoherent and unable to concentrate. These drugs became more popular later in the '60s. Rosaleen and Gavin were released on £100 bail.

At the same time David Goodman, the proprietor of the Kashmir Café where Rosaleen showed her paintings, was charged under the *Obscene Publications Act*. He was fined £5.[34] The court was particularly offended by the *Witches' Sabbath* – retitled *Black Magic* – depicting a muscular young woman copulating with a black panther, with a figure satirising the Virgin Mary watching. Where Rosaleen's hatred of Christianity came from is a mystery, since the Church of England does not generally provoke such strong emotions. Aleister Crowley's rejection of his repressive and doctrinaire Exclusive Brethren upbringing is far more understandable.

For all her notoriety, Rosaleen had famous friends within the establishment. Sir Eugene Goossens, the internationally famous conductor of the Sydney Symphony Orchestra (SSO), struck up a 'rather indiscreet friendship' with her dating from around 1952.[35] At that time his rehearsal studios in Darlinghurst were close to her flat. Described in his obituary as 'urbane and civilised', Goossens was a protégé of Sir Thomas Beecham and an early supporter of Diaghilev's Ballets Russes in England.[36] Moreover, he championed the young office worker Joan Sutherland in her first major performance. But this sophisticated man was far too cosmopolitan for local tastes in the 1950s. Goossens appreciated that both Rosaleen and Gavin were serious researchers and artists. He proposed that they collaborate on a project using Edgar Allan Poe's *The Fall of the House of Usher* as inspiration. Earlier, Claude Debussy had attempted a musical score based on this macabre and Gothic tale.[37] Nothing came of the Goossens–Norton collaboration. Goossens was a participant in many of the rituals dedicated to Pan and conducted in the Brougham Street flat.[38]

Goossens' reputation was ruined when Australian Customs arrested him in March 1956 for possession of over a thousand 'obscene' photographs, books and pamphlets. Today, much of this material would not raise an eyebrow, but in 1956 it was viewed as deeply depraved, wicked and threatening. Masks destined for use in rites to Pan were regarded as particularly offensive to good public morality.[39] The distinguished conductor did not appear at his hearing in the lower court, pleading guilty through his solicitor. His contract with the SSO was not renewed, and thereafter no major engagements came his way. As the *Sydney Morning Herald* of 23 March 1956 predicted, '[t]he end of his career has been pitiful beyond measure'.

Gavin was also affected by this series of revelations in the newspapers. In October 1955 he was admitted to Callan Park Hospital for the Insane in Sydney's Rozelle. Two psychiatrists, Dr S. G. Sands and Dr R. J. Kierly, believed he suffered from schizophrenia with attendant symptoms of hearing voices and delusions. He was emaciated as well. His conversation was almost exclusively about sex.[40] Rosaleen continued to support Gavin, visiting him often and talking about her projects. She showed herself to be kind, loyal and supportive, an image far different from her public one. In the *Australasian Post* of 20 December 1956, an article entitled 'I Am a Witch' depicted her in the thrall of dark satanic forces. The accompanying photograph, which no doubt she found amusing and satirical, was nevertheless damaging. Rosaleen wore a child's witch's hat and was surrounded by a ritual dagger, a phallic snake's head and her pet cats, which she called her 'familiars'. This was followed by a series of exposés on her life and career. Her attempts at explaining her world view and beliefs were lost on a prurient public eager for salacious details of depravity. Rather foolishly she stated that 'If Pan is the devil, then I am indeed a devil worshipper.'[41]

Since her art did not often sell, Rosaleen decided that she would trade on her reputation as a witch by making and marketing charms and performing hexes for selected clients. Her art became increasingly repetitive as she recycled old images of the black sabbath, devils, and Pan. When Gavin was released from psychiatric treatment, his condition had not improved. His behaviour deteriorated to the extent that he threatened Rosaleen with a knife in January 1964. When the police were called, rather than summon medical assistance, they arrested both Gavin and Rosaleen as vagrants, even though they were living in a house in East Sydney. Gavin was jailed for what was perceived as a domestic violence dispute. Clearly he should not have been released from Callan Park Hospital.[42] He died in 1983.

As the East Sydney house was owned by Gavin's parents, Rosaleen next moved in with her sister Cecily Boothman, who lived comfortably in Kirribilli overlooking Sydney Harbour. This was a far more restful and tranquil world than Kings Cross. With her sister's care and sympathy, Rosaleen tried to put Gavin's savage attack on her in the past. In 1967 she moved back to Kings Cross to a decrepit room in Bourke Street. She again constructed an altar to Pan and covered the walls with her paintings.[43] By this time, with the rise of the alternative youth movements, hippies and anti-Vietnam protests, Rosaleen's art, persona and notoriety were all rather passé. She seemed as contemporary as a flapper or a bobby-soxer. Undeterred, she attempted to recapture the public spotlight with an interview in February 1969 with journalist Nan Javes, in which she described herself as a 'Coven Master'.[44]

The attendant publicity sparked controversy within the evangelical wing of the Church of England in Sydney, which called for a wider investigation. By the early 1970s, readings from tarot cards, runes and the I Ch'ing had become widespread. Teenagers and university students held ouija board parties simply for fun rather than with any devotional intent. Rosaleen's influence was totally overestimated; she alone was hardly responsible for this renewed global interest in reading tarot cards. The Church instigated a commission of enquiry into the occult – it was the sole Protestant Church ever to attempt such a move. More significant might have been the influence of two popular films, *Rosemary's Baby* (1968) and *The Exorcist* (1973). The report was handed down in August 1975. The conventional religion came under criticism for not providing for the spiritual needs of modern Australians, yet it condemned the use of tarot cards and ouija boards, hardly items to rock the moral foundation of any society.

The press was not moderate in its coverage of the enquiry's findings, dwelling on a few sensational aspects. Journalists rather predictably headed to Rosaleen for comment. She was now living near Rushcutters Bay on the less fashionable edges of the eastern suburbs. She agreed with Anglican Dean Shilton's belief that amateurs should not meddle with dark forces. The photograph that accompanied her interview portrayed a haggard, tired-looking woman with dyed-black hair and startlingly pointed, heavy black eyebrows. She looked far older than her years. She held in her hand a three-pronged table fork that presumably denoted the devil's symbol.[45]

By this time Rosaleen's public notoriety had began to diminish. She spent most of her time alone in her flat, listening to classical music, painting or tending to her cats. She had unwittingly become the stereotype of the lonely older woman lavishing love on her cats. In late 1978 she was diagnosed with colon cancer. A year later she entered the Sacred Heart Hospice in Darlinghurst where she was tended by the nuns. She died on 5 December 1979. Her paintings went on sale at auction in early 1980, alongside works by Sir Arthur Streeton and Arthur Boyd. Few sold. Interest was revived when Wally Glover re-released *The Art of Rosaleen Norton*. He produced a supplement in 1984. By this time, although her paintings were not fashionable, she had begun to be mythologised and was the subject of a play entitled *Rosaleen: Wicked Witch of the Cross* by Barrie Lowe.[46] It was no more frightening than Frank Baum's character the Wicked Witch of the West, who alarmed young Dorothy from Kansas. Rosaleen's life, so full of rebellion and fuelled by an enduring determination to live out her own vision of herself, was reduced to bathos, yet just thirty years earlier, she had been depicted as Australia's most notorious and dangerous woman.

CHAPTER 17

Charmian Clift
(1923–1969)

The poor New South Wales countrywoman who fought her way to fame and, in the process, destroyed herself.

Charmian Clift was a surprising writer. Her modest background from the New South Wales seaside town of Kiama, her initial public attention as a beauty queen, and her limited education at Wollongong High School were not the prototype for a successful travel writer and popular *Sydney Morning Herald* columnist. At the age of eighteen, she relinquished a baby daughter born out of wedlock. Her life with husband, novelist George Johnston was stormy, competitive and often aggressive, with vitriolic, alcohol-fuelled fights. The grinding poverty in which they lived with their three children in their modest home in Greece, and the nurturing of career aspirations, always made their relationship volatile and often destructive. Charmian's later role as breadwinner for the family, as Johnston's health deteriorated with tuberculosis, was not conducive to a happy marriage, while in the 1960s tough gender expectations allowed little initiative for talented married mothers. Her suicide in 1969 was a profound loss to Australian literature and journalism.

Charmian was born in the small New South Wales coastal town of Kiama near Wollongong in 1923. The area was developed by British squatters in the 1840s for its abundant supply of cedar trees. These squatters were often not gentleman pastoralists but rough, aggressive men intent upon attaining wealth and upward social mobility.[1] In

Walk to the Paradise Gardens (1960) Charmian used her birthplace to great effect. Her unfinished autobiography, 'The End of the Morning', developed her almost photographic ability to recall landscapes and characters of the hilly seaside village.[2] The fictional Lebanon Bay, a tribute to the old cedar forests long gone, was portrayed from the viewpoint of both the insider and the wiser, more sophisticated observer from outside. Her attempts to psychologically flee the restrictions and narrow vista of her early years, long after her physical removal, remained a complex process throughout her life.

Charmian's father, Sydney Clift, was born in 1887 in Huntington in windswept East Anglia. Her grandfather had been born in Benares (Varanasi) in India, where his father was stationed as a sergeant in the 7th Division Grenadiers. For Charmian this exotica felt like part of her DNA. Sydney trained as a fitter and turner in Derby before immigrating to Australia in 1909. Charmian's mother, Amy Currie, was born in Inverell in 1886, the daughter of a coachbuilder. In her autobiography, Charmian claimed her grandmother was a delightful 'beautiful Irish Jewess' and her grandfather of mixed French and Scottish origins. Her paternal grandmother was also Jewish.[3] In her essay 'Portrait of My Mother', she maintained that even 'skivvying for a boarding house in King's Cross' did not dim Amy's glow.[4] For Charmian this heritage took her soaring above the mundaneness of a more typical Australian heritage, providing her with a fanciful romantic mythology to cultivate in her imagination. She freely admitted her family of origin were 'tremendous embroiderers', without fully understanding that she was the most accomplished weaver and embroiderer of them all.[5]

Her parents married in Christ Church Saint Laurence in George Street, Sydney. As a bastion of Anglo-Catholicism in Sydney, this seemed an unlikely site for two professed agnostics. The marriage was at one level content, although her mother's dissatisfaction with the confines of her life later swept through Charmian's psyche, propelling her to success in the wider world. Both her parents, despite their rudimentary education, were lovers of serious books and interested in ideas. She later wrote that her father made her read Laurence Sterne, Rabelais, Balzac and Cervantes, as well as children's books such as *The Wind in the Willows*.[6]

Life in Kiama was not all concerned with the heavy canon of Western literature; the beautiful environment was an important influence of young Charmian, who recalled in her first travel book, *Mermaid Singing* (1956), that '[m]y own Australian childhood had been wild and free'.[7] Her love of swimming came from days at the dangerous beaches surrounding the hamlet. Life with her school mates, often from the rough communities around the nearby quarries, displayed her independent mind, nurtured by literature and fantasy in her home, and made her an uneasy, odd companion. Clever and talented, she was a delight for teachers unaccustomed to children with aspirations beyond the mundane world.

When she was twelve Charmian won a scholarship to Wollongong High School, which provided educational opportunities lacking in Kiama. Despite her talents, she left after two years, returning to Kiama and engaging in odd part-time jobs.[8] Her life then spun into anguish when she was raped by an unnamed family friend. The impact of this ordeal was to haunt her the rest of her days.[9] She now wanted to escape Kiama at all costs. In 1941 she entered a beach glamour competition for the populist magazine *Pix*, which had been established three years before. Noted for its covers featuring voluptuous young women, the magazine was racy yet oddly prurient in its approach to life. But for Charmian, winning that competition was her ticket out of obscurity into the cosmopolitan world of Sydney.

The distinguished novelist Ruth Park later described the youthful Charmian: 'Her walk, carriage, quick glancing expressions, radiant health and vitality were what drew the eye.'[10] This vitality and zest for living life to the full as a young woman were noted by others. Alan Ashbolt's obituary in the *Sydney Morning Herald* in 1969 appreciated the 'sort of pagan vitality or inner glow of mischief which illuminated her whole personality …'[11] Her stunning beauty and fine physique, honed by many years at the beaches around Kiama, were legendary.

Both men and women were dazzled by her physical perfection, her wit and her good humour, at least in the early days.

Her dreams of an altogether different life were initially limited by her employment as an usherette at the Minerva theatre in Potts Point. The manager David Martin insisted his female staff don evening frocks which were to be worn with grace and refinement. He was a canny entrepreneur with a rare flair for glamour.[12] For Charmian relocation to the big city brought temptations, affairs with married men, and, even more disastrously, an unwanted pregnancy. At the age of eighteen she was not in a position to keep the little girl she bore at the Women's Hospital on Crown Street, Surry Hills. Her parents and older sister, Margaret, would not tolerate the shame for one thing, and there was little provision in the 1940s for single mothers.[13] Her daughter, Suzanne Chick, has written movingly of discovering that Charmian was her birth mother.[14] Like other relinquishing mothers, Charmian never got over the loss of her first child to adoption.

Charmian Clift, winner of the *Pix* beach glamour competition, 1941. Private collection.

Charmian and Margaret joined the Australian Women's Army Service in April 1943. For many young women the war offered the opportunity to expand their horizons and to contribute in a way that was unthinkable during the previous world war. Charmian was quickly identified as officer material. She later claimed she was the youngest woman officer appointed.[15] Relocated to Broadmeadows in Melbourne in 1944, she undertook the training with verve. She was fortunate that her new duties included editing a magazine for the Ordnance section. Charmian met an influential mentor, Bruce Kneale, a former journalist for the Melbourne *Argus*, who encouraged her fiction writing. With his support she placed a short story, 'Other Woman', in the *Australia National Journal* in 1945.[16]

Through Kneale, Charmian met George Johnston, Australia's first accredited war correspondent. A rendition of their introduction at the Hotel Australia restaurant in May 1945 concluded his semi-autobiographical novel *My Brother Jack* (1964), with his alter ego David Meredith meeting the beautiful young Lieutenant 'Cressida Morley'. At the outset, Charmian and Johnston found each other amusing company. Nothing came of it, however, for he was a married man with a baby, and off to China for another dangerous assignment. Charmian was also emotionally unavailable. She had announced her engagement to Leo Kenny, the scion of a wealthy, well-connected Victorian Catholic family. She was later dismissive of this liaison, remarking that 'I did like flashing that half-hoop of family diamonds around the barracks for a while, and was reluctant, really, to have to give it back.'[17] Their backgrounds were too different to ever endure a long-term involvement.

Charmian was not demobilised until May 1946, from when she went to work as a journalist for the *Argus*. Running into Johnston in the lift of the newspaper offices, their mutual attraction was re-ignited. Yet Johnston did not seem a good prospect, initially, for such a lively and ambitious young woman. He was born in 1912 in eastern Melbourne where his father, John Johnston, had risen from the lowly occupation of labourer to an engineer on the tramway. His mother, Minnie Wright, came from a far more cultured and affluent background in Bendigo. Johnston had been apprenticed as a lithographer before accepting a cadetship at the *Argus* in 1933. Five years later he married Elsie Taylor; their daughter, Gae, was born in 1941. His career as a war correspondent in both the Pacific and European fronts was distinguished. Johnston witnessed the signing of Japan's surrender on the warship *Missouri*. The numerous books he published during the war captured the immediacy of combat on several fronts.[18] On his return to life as a civilian journalist in October 1946 he was a celebrity.

For Charmian, it was not simply professional admiration; she fell deeply and suddenly in love with Johnston. He represented much she desired – an older, more experienced man, successful by his own efforts in rising from the limitations of his background, well known, and offering her an escape from a dreaded suburban non-existence. For him, Charmian offered a comrade with literary ability, aspirations that mirrored his, as well as a physical beauty and sexuality that was at once enticing and youthful. In an early draft of his novel *Clean Straw for Nothing*, Cressida/Charmian '… represents the unobtainable prize, something more than he can ever hope to have achieved'.[19]

Their hot affair was soon noticed by office colleagues – and Elsie Johnston. Charmian and Johnston went to live as a couple in the Post Office Hotel in inner Melbourne in 1946, much to the surprise and indignation of many who had seen his former affairs fizzle out quickly. They were portrayed as the 'koala version of the Mailers or the Fitzgeralds', as travel writer Colin Simpson later acerbically remarked.[20] Yet this was not to be the case – Charmian was a talented journalist and writer, not a driven figure like Zelda Fitzgerald, who could only rely on her beauty and charm. Even during the heady, lust-fuelled first stage of their romance, Charmian was extending her professional range with articles and short stories.

Adultery in 1946 was a serious matter, especially between two workmates. Even though Johnston was the married party in question,

Charmian was summarily sacked. Johnston handed in his resignation, which was accepted. For both of them, these events were disastrous professional setbacks, filled with disbelief and shame. They were thus thrown together in a way that might not have evolved in more temperate circumstances. They moved to Sorrento on the Mornington Peninsula in the off-season, where their relationship was tested. Johnston was jealous and possessive, a point that perhaps Charmian should have taken more notice of right at the start. In *Clean Straw for Nothing*, his alter ego proclaimed, 'And she is his. The most precious thing he ever owned. To lose her would be to lose everything ... For Cressida is Golden Boy's real laurel.'[21] This is dangerous talk – it is the language of the domestic violence perpetrator who views his partner as personal property. For Johnston had also sacrificed his promising career, perhaps in haste.[22] But his 'prize' – Charmian – carried a heavy burden and obligation through the marriage.

A new start was needed. The couple moved to Manly in Sydney where they married on 7 August 1947. Their collaboration on a joint enterprise, a novel entitled *High Valley* (1948), went well for two writers with such different methods of putting words to paper. It won the *Sydney Morning Herald*'s literary prize for 1948. The prize money of £2000 was an enormous amount at a time when post-war austerity still ruled.[23] In November 1948 Charmian gave birth to their son, Martin. Before her confinement, she painted her toenails different colours. Not that it helped – the birth was painful, like being 'in a torture chamber'.[24] Whatever joy she attained in her new role as a wife and mother, she was nevertheless relegated to this status while Johnston's career began to flourish. In 1948 there were no public debates about work–family balance. A mother's place was firmly in the home. Charmian's one outlet was the parties they hosted. Yet even these attracted intense suspicion later on. Ruth Park wondered whether Charmian and Johnston were really professional writers, or merely poseurs who talked about writing at parties, yet got down to little.[25] Park is unfair and perhaps jealous that she and her partner

D'Arcy Niland did not attract the same amount of public attention and popularity. Niland later wrote the bestseller *The Shiralee*, so this enmity is surprising.[26]

Charmian began writing radio scripts for the Australian Broadcasting Commission (ABC). These paid poorly but allowed her to hone her craft. With two children now, after the birth of daughter Shane, the couple needed to work at jobs perhaps not as congenial to creativity as they might have liked. In 1951 Charmian's life suddenly changed when Johnston was appointed as the bureau chief of the Associated Newspaper Services' London office. Ruth Park recalled their jubilation at a lunch attended by actor Peter Finch. Charmian proclaimed, 'We've got the world by the scruff' – quite a different sentiment from having the world at your feet.

For Charmian, London offered a window on to a more sophisticated world, though the possibilities were curtailed by domesticity and two children. She and Johnston worked collaboratively on a novel, *The Piping Cry*, a situation fraught with tension as he maintained his day job as a reporter and her slower, more private methods of creation clashed with his. More often Johnston's was a day and evening job, since he had to telephone copy at 2am to reach the Melbourne office. Unfortunately, the manuscript was rejected by publishers. Along with this rejection Charmian had to bear hints that Johnston was repeating the pattern of his first marriage with shallow sexual liaisons.

All was not grim, however. The family went on a pleasant holiday to Italy and France in 1952. This infatuation with old Europe was to sustain Charmian for the rest of her life, as it did indeed for Johnston, who relied on Charmian's travel diary for material in *Clean Straw for Nothing*.[27] In mid 1952 they embarked on another collaboration set in seventeenth-century China entitled *The Big Chariot*. For Charmian it was a disaster. She was a slow, deliberate writer, not a journalist like her husband, accustomed to high-speed production in noisy environments. She was relegated to the role of a research assistant for this endeavour and for his novel *Pagoda*. Her own book *Mermaid Singing* outlines her feelings of resentment and her fears that she was disappearing into domesticity.

With Johnston plagued by pneumonia, the family went to Greece in April 1954. This holiday was pivotal to a new phase in their lives. Johnston published the novel *The Cyprian Woman* (1955) about the holiday, in which the Charmian character is not shown in a positive light but as a woman on the lookout for sexual intrigues. Despite her indignation at the fictionalised portrayal, Charmian held her resentments in check. They decided to relocate permanently. For Charmian the sunny islands offered freedom for the two children to play and dream as she had done in Kiama. For Johnston and herself she imagined a life devoted to writing full-time. This was a highly risky business. Even with a low cost of living in Greece compared with London, the expectation of earning a living from creative writing was at best optimistic.[28]

There were other motives that propelled the move. Charmian knew of Johnston's affair with a colleague and wanted to take him away from the daily temptation of attractive young women eager to score with a famous war correspondent. On the other hand, the core motif that runs through his autobiographical novels is the persistent and flagrant infidelity of Cressida. Johnston's behaviour and hypocrisy, though not uncommon in that era, showed the inherent difficulties for a woman with children to maintain her independent existence. Motherhood placed an iron-bound cage around any woman's body and psyche in the 1950s.

The family left London in cold and blustery November 1954, settling in warm, and initially inviting, Kalymnos. *Mermaid Singing* revealed Charmian's almost childlike delight in the heat, the beautiful bright colours and the sea. The ochres, bright pinks and azure blues contrasted dramatically with the shadowy greyness of London, with its constant drizzle and impenetrable skies. The rocky island was famous for its sponge divers whose seasonal stint finished just as the family arrived. This made the small communities on Kalymnos appear far more lively, carefree and happy than usual. It was a deceptive and temporary charm that encircled Charmian. The children were less than enthusiastic, though; suddenly they were in an alien environment, away from their friends and surrounded by children who did not speak English.

Charmian and Johnston published *The Sponge Divers* in 1956. Its production had again caused the build-up of considerable tensions and resentments. The release of *Mermaid Singing* produced jubilation, for it showed she was not just the beautiful, talented wife of a famous writer and journalist, but an artist in her own right. Unfortunately, despite positive reviews, it did not capture the popular imagination and sales were poor. Because of where they were living, she was not able to arrange publicity and conduct interviews with influential reviewers. This was a severe handicap. Charmian's decision to change publishers from Faber to Collins certainly did not help.

In August 1955 the family relocated to the more populated island Hydra, which had the misfortune to be right on the tourist track. They went ahead and purchased a house, making their life in Greece more tangible and permanent. Yet a more immediate issue for Charmian was her realisation that she was again pregnant. Her hopes for professional advancement and esteem seemed to be slipping out of her reach, as another baby would enmesh her even more firmly in domesticity. Jason was born in April 1956, an event she recalled in her travel book *Peel Me a Lotus* (1959). The employment of a nurse, Zoe, certainly assisted her to find some time to think and write. Impelled by financial urgency, however, Johnston started publishing detective stories under a pseudonym – Shane Martin. He, too, had legitimate gripes that supporting a family and hack work took him away from his serious endeavours.

Charmian nevertheless found time for another diversion. By 1958 her affair with a young French artist, Jean-Claude Maurice, had given an explosive edge to an already tense marriage. That Johnston had conducted affairs in London hardly mattered; double standards applied.

In Greece in the 1950s, they were even more rigid. The local and expatriate communities marvelled at the lovers' doings, much to the humiliation of Johnston.

Charmian's work was not going well despite her romantic interest. The path to publication of *Peel Me a Lotus* was tortuous and slow, with rejection, rewriting and all its attendant anxieties. With never-ending financial worries and continued illness, Johnston became far more withdrawn. His chest problems were diagnosed as tuberculosis. Around this time, he and Charmian ceased their sexual relationship.[29] This was not good timing. Johnston brooded upon these resentments, magnifying them until they spilled out into his fiction with disastrous effects. In *Clean Straw for Nothing*, not only is Cressida/Charmian portrayed as a faithless wife deserting her husband at his greatest time of need, but he also strips her of her professional identity.

It wasn't all gloom, however. The Canadian poet and later international singer Leonard Cohen stayed with them in Hydra and he later wrote affectionately about Charmian.[30] Her and Johnston's time in Greece was marked substantially by boozy confrontations, wounding arguments more ferocious than those in *Who's Afraid of Virginia Woolf?* With a constant stream of visitors and hangers-on, all of whom witnessed this publicly performed domestic carnage, Charmian's creativity shrank. Ruth Park, who '… deplored the public soap opera of her life with George Johnston …' went so far as to call her a 'failed writer … this flashing, faulty woman'. More kindly, journalist Valerie Lawson felt that 'the balance in the marriage was not right'.[31] Scarce funds were channelled into entertaining strangers and purchasing prodigious amounts of alcohol. Charmian began to lose her vitality, health and emotional balance; her beauty was damaged by emotional stress, haphazard nutrition and excessive alcohol.

In mid 1960 Johnston and Charmian met a wealthy young English couple, Peter and Didy Cameron, who proposed a house swap, with the advantage for the Johnstons of a splendid country house for weekends. Within months the family had relocated to a small village in the Cotswolds. The younger children, who had not really been brought up in an English-speaking environment, were shell-shocked, while Charmian was now resentful, cold and rightly wondered whether this hasty move to a drizzling climate assisted Johnston's recovery. Funds were precarious despite a few royalties from various publishers.[32] For Charmian the publication of *Peel Me a Lotus* (1959) and *Walk to the Paradise Gardens* (1960) did not provide the satisfaction she expected. The family returned to Hydra in April 1961.

In 1962 Charmian began her novel *Honour's Mimic*, published in London in 1964. This was a new departure, for it was a novel of which she was the sole author and also not a travel memoir. The subject, an unlikely romance between an Australian woman and an illiterate Greek sponge diver, was a bleak assessment of love and loyalty. She began an autobiographical novel, 'The End of the Morning', set in Kiama, which was never completed.[33] In September 1962 her mother died, causing Charmian intense grief and periods of guilt. Amy had not seen her wayward daughter in over a decade, and had had no personal contact at all with her three grandchildren brought up in distant Greece. Charmian fell into a period of what is so dismissively called 'writer's block', a devastating condition for any professional writer who depends on creativity and its uncertain ensuing funds. Around this time her passionate affair with the English biographer Anthony Kingsmill flourished, especially when Johnston went home to Australia in February 1964 to publicise his novel *My Brother Jack*.[34] Her young lover moved into the marital home and lived with her and the children until they returned home to Australia six months later.

For the children this move was a total change from their upbringing; for Charmian, it was professional obliteration. Johnston's novel was hailed as a masterpiece, while her publications lay obscured and forgotten. She was relegated to the role of the 'literary wife'. Old friends were shocked at the physical and emotional transformation from the beach beauty to a haggard, prematurely aged woman, captured later in Ray Crooke's portrait. She was no longer the trophy

Johnston had won in Melbourne – he was now the star, around which all wanted to revolve. Johnston leased their new home in Mosman, Sydney. Charmian later told her friend Grace Edwards that she was 'a low-life prole', one of the 'great unwashed', unsuited to the life in snobbish north shore Mosman.[35]

Yet all this was to change. Charmian was offered a column writing for the women's pages of the *Sydney Morning Herald*. Her subjects ranged over all sorts of topics of daily life to the meaning of life, and everything in between. In the foreword to a selection edited by Johnston after her death he wrote that, 'Above all she was an implacable humanist. Her great gift was her ability to reach all types of people, and on all levels, young as well as old, rich and poor, men as well as women ... with her undeviating insistence on the simple and ancient verities and values of being ...'[36] Her ongoing generosity to his creativity was not in doubt. Charmian adapted *My Brother Jack* for a television play on the ABC, where she showed 'a true, vivid talent for that medium'.[37]

There were other traumas to absorb in her relocation. Her brother Barre died and Johnston's health deteriorated, exacerbated by chronic depression and moodiness. She remarked that he was also 'often pretty heavily drugged',[38] making life at home frequently intolerable. Charmian now had to earn a living for her family, yet this caused immense resentment. Johnston had old-fashioned ideas about being the breadwinner in his family. Certainly, too, the public attention given to Charmian's column did not allow him to express gratitude or admiration. Rather, he was resentful as she sped out in taxis, went to openings and other events important to her work, and of the obligations to her employer, which she took seriously.[39] Charmian blossomed in her new role and her appearance mirrored this new confidence. New clothes, hairdo, make-up and even stiletto heels after years of sandals and bare feet in Greece, all contributed to her new professional persona. Not that producing a column was easy: it required strict discipline that she had not practised since her army days a quarter of a century earlier.

Johnston spent much time in hospital and underwent major surgery in 1966 and 1968.[40] He worked on *Clean Straw for Nothing*, his sequel to *My Brother Jack*, which had won the Miles Franklin Award in 1964. For Charmian, this prospect filled her with dread, as she wondered how her alter ego, Cressida, would be portrayed and what would be revealed. She also quarrelled constantly with their daughter, Shane, now in her late teens, perhaps jealous of her beauty and youth, with all its attendant possibilities.[41] Charmian fretted over the lost potential of her earlier unpublished work; she drank heavily, and was often depressed and melancholy. The award of a Commonwealth Literary Grant in late 1968 gave her the money and thus the time to devote herself to her fiction.[42] Yet it did not allay her deep anxieties. The turbulence of her marriage took a huge toll on her spirit and energy; the impending publication of Johnston's new novel, which she believed dramatised her numerous love affairs, was the final blow for this defiant woman. Her shadow identity as Cressida Morley in Johnston's books vanquished the real woman both literally and symbolically. What is even more worrying is that the persona of Cressida Morley was invented by Charmian as her fictional alter ego, and this was appropriated by Johnston for his semi-autobiographical novels. Not only did he cannibalise her life for his books but he took her fictional identity as well.

Ever present was the thought of exposure in Johnston's new novel. She later said she had not read *Clean Straw for Nothing* (1969), though clearly she had read some passages about herself which she regarded as less than flattering. She penned an extraordinary article early in 1968 in which she put her fears into the public domain, declaring that '[nothing] could force me back into the old side-stepping role. Nor all my professionalism could lure me into listening dispassionately.'[43] Overall, his portrayal is not as bitter and vicious as it could have been, given the soap opera of their lives in Hydra.[44]

On 8 July 1969 Charmian took a fatal dose of barbiturates, having asked a friend the evening before to accompany her on an extended holiday to get away from her life in Sydney. She had been drinking heavily all that fatal day and arguing with Johnston about her excessive drinking. Charmian wrote a sad but recriminatory letter of farewell to Johnston:

> Darling, Sorry about this. I can't stand being hated — and you
> hated me so much today — I am opting out and you can play
> it anyway you choose from now on. I am sure you will have a
> distinguished and successful career ... I will cease upon the
> midnight and no pain — isn't that something?[45]

This was a terrible legacy to leave anyone, with its charges of fault and neglect. The horror in the family continued, as Johnston died the following year, and both Shane and Martin ended their own lives.

CHAPTER 18

Lillian Roxon
(1932–1973)

*A refugee from the Nazis who came to Brisbane and eventually
defined the world of rock'n'roll journalism in New York.*

When Germaine Greer published her provocative treatise *The Female
Eunuch* in 1970, she dedicated it to Lillian Roxon, a fellow member of
the libertarian Sydney Push, 'whose energy has never failed despite her
anxieties, and her asthma, and her overweight'. The words were both
flattering and deeply cruel.[1] The most prominent early rock journalist
besides Lester Bangs in the United States, Lillian was a charming,
combative and influential writer in a new genre that was edgy, defiant,
and rebellious.[2] Her publication, *Lillian Roxon's Rock Encyclopedia*
(1969), proudly proclaimed her own construction of the discipline,
attributing to raw popular music a respectability that it previously lacked.
In turn, Lillian was called the 'mother of rock and roll journalism'.[3] Her
life as an independent, assertive and confident woman was often lonely
in a world dominated by hard, swaggering and rambunctious men, both
on stage and at the typewriter. She died alone after a massive asthma
attack in her home in New York City in 1973.

Lillian Roxon's early life was full of turbulence and travel. Born
Liliana Ropschitz in Savona, Italy, she changed her name and her
identity as she moved through her life. Her parents were well-educated,
cultured Poles from Lvov (Lviv) in Galacia. Established in 1256, Lvov
was an important academic and cultural centre now incorporated
into Ukraine. Passing through the control of various powers over

the centuries, this area was attacked by the Red Army in 1920. For Jewish residents like Liliana's family this event was significant, for the Russians were virulently anti-Semitic. Her father, Izydor, was prevented from studying medicine in his homeland. Instead, he studied at the esteemed University of Padua, established in 1222 with such distinguished alumni as Galileo, Casanova and William Harvey. On graduation, Izydor established a fashionable practice at Alassio on the Italian Riviera. Her mother, Rosa Breitman, was an intelligent woman whose life was centred on the family and home. Liliana's brother Milo was ten years older. In 1936 her younger brother, Jacob (Jack), was born.

The family was initially privileged and able to spend their holidays in Vienna and the Polish resort town of Zakopane, near Slovakia. This came to an abrupt end with the German–Italian pact in 1938. Liliana's parents decided to emigrate and arrived in Australia under Polish passports in July 1939 aboard the *Dunera*, which brought refugees from Nazism to Australia.[4] Izydor and the family relocated to Queensland, where he was able to practise medicine. They settled in the inner-city suburb of New Farm, a beautiful and once wealthy multicultural area, and anglicised their name to Roxon. Liliana became Lillian. Though Brisbane was a provincial city in the '40s, it was soon alive to the beat of American jazz and the jitterbug. General Douglas MacArthur planned strategies for the war in the Pacific from July 1942 in the AMP Building in Queen Street. The city and surrounding areas were inundated with nearly 100,000 American service personnel among a population of just 345,000.[5] Dance halls like the Trocadero and the grand ballroom of the City Hall buzzed with American dances and songs, seen before only in films. New Farm Park by the river was a favourite trysting place where sex was often fast and furious.

In 1944 Lillian was sent to board at St Hilda's School at Southport. Founded in 1912, St Hilda's was the most exclusive girls school in Queensland, catering largely for the wealthy pastoralist families. Although her background was far removed from those of her fellow pupils, she excelled academically. She later claimed she was expelled, and in 1947 she enrolled at the elite, selective Brisbane State High School.[6] Students during the war produced the innovative magazine *Bajai*, which nurtured writers Thea Astley and Barbara Patterson (later) Blackman and arts administrator Charles Osborne.[7] Judith Wright published with this talented group of students. With her cultured European upbringing, again Lillian stood out, forming friendships with teachers like Rhyl Sorensen. At this time Lillian fell in love with a young actor, Peter Munro, who later died of cancer aged twenty-two. This was a harbinger for her subsequent unlucky romantic life.[8]

Lillian's social life centred around the Pink Elephant Café, a bohemian meeting place frequented by a gay and creative crowd, where waiters dressed in full drag. Located in upper Queen Street near the beautiful Customs House, the café had been financed through Donald Friend's coterie. The owners of the Ballad Bookshop, Barrie (later Barrett) Reid and Laurie Collinson, who became part of the Reeds' Heide circle in Melbourne, were core members of this refuge from conservative Queensland society.[9] Lillian attended Charles Osborne's twenty-first birthday party at the café, along with the troupe from the visiting Ballet Rambert.[10]

In 1949 Lillian decided to attend the University of Sydney, boarding in a guesthouse in Bondi. Anne Coombs, the chronicler of the Push, described Lillian as 'a bright, naïve, middle class girl' in 1949.[11] At university Lillian soon met the faster crowd inhabited by people such as Margaret Elliott (later film producer Margaret Fink) and Aviva Canton (later Layton). She was drawn into the Sydney Push, a group of anti-materialist, anti-careerist rebels and libertarians who met in the Royal George Hotel in Sussex Street and the Tudor Hotel in Phillip Street, as well as the Lincoln coffee house.[12] Some of the members were exceptions – such as CSIRO physicist Dr Gilbert Bogle, now famous for his mysterious death with lover Margaret Chandler in 1963.[13] Dominated by educated men who had dropped out of the privileged world of university studies, when that was available to very few in the '50s, the Push nurtured elements of nihilism and unproductive disillusionment. The hard drinking and casual sex, in an era before oral contraception, demanded far more from its women members than its men. Nor were its men, in particular, in the league of the French existentialists, who produced major philosophical and cultural works.[14] Insider Neil C. Hope characteristically remarked, '[t]he Push was not a repository of dedicated thinkers drawn into its vortex by an inexorable logic. It was an atmosphere, congenial to like temperaments, a refuge, a fireplace and a home ... a union of outsiders ...'[15] David Malouf recalled that: '... that world ... used people up very quickly ... people were brilliant at the age of twenty-three or twenty-four. But hardly a single one of them ever came to anything.'[16]

Lillian's entanglement in the Push represented a rejection of bourgeois femininity with its aspirations of a 'good' marriage and children. She said in a letter to Aviva Layton around 1959: 'If I do not marry Glenn I'm going to travel around the world and have fun and settle down when I am thirty with a nice American with dough ...'[17] Her unpublished novel set in this period captures the mood of a young, voluptuous and beautiful woman who opts for independence. The description of an illegal abortion illustrated the pain that might accompany the freedom.[18] In contrast with other Push members, Lillian had had strong career aspirations since her days at St Hilda's; she sent in her first article to *Woman* (later *Woman's Day*) when she was fourteen.[19] She merely took from the Push what she needed. There is an apocryphal story that young men in a Christian college at the University of Sydney were sung a song, the refrain of which proclaimed, 'Beware Karl Marx, Professor John [Anderson, the prophet of libertarianism] and Lillian Roxon.'[20]

Despite the hedonism around her, Lillian was still a virgin in 1950, a plight she discussed in a letter to her friend Barbara Blackman. Not that offers were not frequently forthcoming to this witty, exuberant, plump and delectable young woman. She chose an architecture student, George Clarke, for her initiation in sexual experience, her 'happy release from that wretched condition'. They began living together, still called 'living in sin' until the late '60s, in Windsor House in Jamison Street, Sydney, along with her brother Milo. Fortunately, the landlady lived off the premises, allowing bohemian residents more freedom than usual. Clarke later went on to become one of Australia's leading town planners.[21]

Other friends from that time included David Malouf, then a retiring young student from the University of Queensland, and Zell Rabin, later a famous journalist working for Rupert Murdoch in New York.[22] Lillian disarmed Malouf by offering him, on first acquaintance, a copy of Magnus Hirschfeld's *Sexual Anomalies and Perversions* (1944). Her party game was his test of sophistication.[23] He passed splendidly; to such a degree that Lillian later introduced him to her parents.

Lillian graduated from the University of Sydney in 1955 and in January the following year her father died. Lillian made a visit to New York City to try her luck and this saw the beginning of her career as

Lillian Roxon, 10 January 1972, when she was on the Sydney *Sun Herald* staff. Picture by Staff; Fairfax Media 10980070.

a rock journalist. Zell Rabin was already established there, so she had a friend who could lead her through the maze that was cosmopolitan New York. She tracked down such luminaries as Woody Guthrie, the initial inspiration of young Bob Dylan. However, she returned to Sydney before long and her mother purchased a flat in Double Bay for her. This signalled a massive cultural and social step away from the Push, with its bare and decrepit lifestyle. She began working on Frank Packer's racy magazine *Weekend*, edited by Donald Horne, in January 1957.[24] This offered an unsurpassed apprenticeship with a master craftsman as mentor and adviser. *Weekend* was a precursor to tabloid celebrity magazines so common now. Articles included one with the intriguing title, 'Why Queensland Will Become a Second Hollywood'.[25]

In 1959, Lillian got the opportunity to return to New York to stretch her cultural and professional horizons. She first worked for Murdoch's *Daily Mirror* under the direction of its bureau chief, Zell Rabin. She found a small apartment in Hudson Street in West Greenwich Village, a good location to pursue the emerging music scene as it changed from folk music and beatniks to protest and rock genres. But dissatisfied with the type of subject given to her as a 'woman' journalist, Lillian headed for London for the summer as part of the *Sydney Morning Herald* team. On her return to New York in October 1960, the pace of change in the United States was accelerating, with the election of the young and charismatic John F. Kennedy as president. Donald Horne, now the new editor of *The Bulletin*, attempted to lure her back to Sydney, but Lillian instinctively felt that destiny had brought her to New York. As she reported to her mother: 'New York is hot and exhausting, a sort of huge Brisbane, but I don't mind. I love it with a tireless and quite uncritical devotion.' What she had seen in Brisbane to compare it to the pace of New York remains a mystery.[26]

Lillian moved to the Lower East Side on East 11th Street, to live in a cheap, rundown old Irish neighbourhood. After several years of insecure freelancing, she began working for the *Sydney Morning Herald* in 1963. She celebrated her new security by moving to East 21st Street near Gramercy Park and the Flatiron district. Lillian scored a professional coup when she got a few words from Sybil Burton, the humiliated wife of Richard Burton, during his affair with Elizabeth Taylor, for *Woman's Day*. This popular Australian women's magazine sent her on assignment to the Mexican film location of *Night of the Iguana* starring Ava Gardner, Richard Burton and Deborah Kerr. The following year she wrote an insightful piece on Jacqueline Kennedy. Her work also covered the race riots and civil rights movement.

In early 1965 Lillian returned to Sydney, primarily to visit her mother who was emotionally lost without her daughter. Rosa died soon after Lillian's return to New York. She pondered her mother's closed life full of bitterness and regret, making her even more enthusiastically determined to embrace life with all its disappointments and joys. Her old Push buddy Neil Hope had died in a car accident the year before and in the following year Zell died of melanoma at the age of thirty-four.[27] Lillian was devastated. Her confidante in New York had been such a solid presence in her life.

Lillian's professional career prospered. She was right at the centre of the new 'happenings'. She wrote to Aviva Layton in May 1965 that she went to '… an Oldenburg happening in Al Roon's Steam Baths [located in the Riverside Plaza Hotel on West 75th Street]', a black tie party in honour of hairdresser Vidal Sassoon and 'cocktails with Miss bloody Australia at QANTAS … Thursday, *Seventeen* magazine is having a happening. Erk. I have been to half the bloody avant-garde theater groups in town …' She also reported that she witnessed an impromptu performance by the artists Robert Rauschenberg and Roy Lichtenstein another time at Al Roon's pool. Andy Warhol was also present.[28]

In May 1966 Lillian went to London to catch up on the fashions, and she was delighted with the Biba boutique and the styles along Carnaby Street and King's Road. She met up with old Push friends John Taylor, Ruth Biegler and journalist Paddy McGuinness, now the unofficial leader in London. Always at the right spot at the very right time, Lillian went to the Beatles' last performance in the UK.[29] Previously she had interviewed Brian Epstein, the manager of the Beatles, asking him '… are you a millionaire?' signalling the realisation that rock music had become a huge industry, where vast fortunes could be made and lost.[30] This was her breakthrough interview in a career that was to define her enduring reputation. Danny Fields, the editor of *Datebook*, a teenage magazine, recognised her potential with this interview. She also encountered Linda Eastman, a young photographer for the snobbish magazine *Town and Country*.[31] The synergy of these new friendships came together as Fields later wrote Linda McCartney's biography.[32] The three of them covered the Rolling Stones' first visit to New York in 1966. Lillian was fascinated with Linda Eastman, the beautiful blonde journalist, Jewish and ambitious like herself. Nor did Lillian forget her Australian background, supporting the Easybeats on their first trip to the States in 1966.[33] She also had a brief fling with lead singer Stevie Wright.

Lillian had an instinct for pinpointing the next trend, writing about the emergence of the hippies in San Francisco in early 1967, months before the 'Summer of Love' was documented.[34] She embarked on her personal summer of love with teenaged Canadian drummer David Wynne, who started working for her. He later returned to his more conventional origins, becoming a senior diplomat.[35] For Lillian, this relationship, though brief, was important. She felt dispirited and defeated by her constant battles with her weight, ever mindful of her father's cruel remarks in her girlhood.

Her professional ambitions widened when she conceived a project to systematically document the rock scene. Rock was slowly being taken seriously. Lillian wrote that Norman Mailer, Timothy Leary and Allen Ginsberg 'all settl[ed] raptly ringside the night The Byrds first played [in New York]'.[36] Beginning in 1968, she researched all the personalities and genres for her magnum opus, *Lillian Roxon's Rock Encyclopedia*. Her celebrity status at Max's Kansas City, a club at 213 Park Avenue, ensured she had access to anyone who was anybody in the rock world. This venue, described by Andy Warhol as '... the exact spot where Pop Art and Pop Life came together in the sixties ...', drew celebrities and the talented from the arts and music in a fertile cross-mix. Raunchy, decadent and influential, Max's Kansas City lured all the luminaries and wannabes.[37] Lillian reported that '[I]t looked pretty sleazy, at least it would have to an outsider, but in that crowded cellar any night there was more money and more power than the rest of Tin Pan Alley put together.' Limos waited outside the venue until 4am to take the rich and famous away to who knows what.[38] At the centre Lillian held court. She knew the entire Warhol Factory crowd, Leonard Cohen, Jim Morrison, Janis Joplin, Lou Reed, Philip Glass and the Velvet Underground.[39] Lillian wrote that '[G]oing to a Warhol party (I really mean this) currently rates higher than being asked to Jackie Kennedy's for brunch.' At one party at Warhol's The Factory, Tennessee Williams, Rudolf Nureyev, Montgomery Clift, and Judy Garland all laughed with habitués and other guests.[40]

Lillian's fame and reputation as a journalist were acknowledged when she was asked by the Beatles to cover the Lennon–McCartney tour in New York in May 1968. Her article entitled '101 Hours' was a *tour de force*. It appeared in the September 1968 issue of the popular culture magazine *Eye*, where Lillian was a contributing editor. At the same time, Linda Eastman renewed her friendship with Paul McCartney. By the end of the stay they were lovers and Linda left for England.[41] Lillian never saw or spoke to her 'closest friend' again, as Linda's life ascended into the pop stratosphere. Lillian was devastated not to be invited to their wedding in March 1969. She did, however, write a positive article in *Woman's Day*; but her anger simmered slowly and relentlessly. Lillian had her revenge, taken sweetly in 1973, when she reviewed a McCartney TV special in the New York *Sunday News* of 22 April.[42] This assessment is still regarded as one of the most dismissive pieces ever written by a major journalist. Lillian wrote pointedly: 'I can tell you right now ... [Linda] did not marry a millionaire Beatle to end up in a Liverpool saloon singing "Pack up your troubles in your old kit bag" with middle-aged women named

Mildred ...'[43] Linda was devastated to learn of Lillian's death, and was racked with guilt at her sudden departure and abandonment of her American friends so effortlessly.[44]

Lillian went on to make other combative friendships with powerful women. The most notable was with '... the big G, Germaine Greer in London ... She is seven feet tall and a bully and about the only female I know who is NOT a eunuch ...'[45] They had met in 1959 when Melbourne was abuzz with the filming of *On the Beach*. Lillian was amazed to meet Greer, who then had purple hair and wore red stockings. Their reacquaintance in London in 1968 was full of fun. Lillian was particularly impressed by Greer's knitting pattern for a 'cock sock', her column in the provocative underground Dutch magazine *Suck*, and her celebrity status, confirmed by a photograph by Lord Snowdon.[46] Greer first visited New York City in late 1968, when Lillian was exhausted from reporting on the presidential elections. Trouble arose over Lillian's choice of accommodation and things got worse from there. Lillian was trying to write her book, however, she went out of her way to show her visitor around Max's Kansas City and its famous habitués.[47] Greer, who described herself at the time as 'superwhore, supergroupie ...', wrote a vitriolic account mentioning Lillian, for London *Oz* in February 1969. Another article in *Suck* advised readers, 'Anyone who wants group sex in New York and likes fat girls, contact Lillian Roxon.'[48] This public ridicule was cruel, especially since Lillian's weight had ballooned from her use of cortisone medication for her severe asthma. Her phone number was listed in the New York directory and endless telephone calls from prospective sex partners followed this piece, distressing Lillian.

Lillian's professional status prospered despite this ignominy. In 1969 her book, *Lillian Roxon's Rock Encyclopedia*, was released to tremendous praise. Using careful research, she estimated the career and significance of various performers and genres, viewed through her lens not just as passing ephemeral wonders but often as legitimate artists. She was more sure-footed in her appraisals of those she had heard and met, rather than the early rock'n'rollers of the 1950s. Motown was clearly not much on her radar either. For all its limitations, *Lillian Roxon's Rock Encyclopedia* was a monumental achievement which carved out an entire discipline. It has been rather forgotten now.

Nik Cohn's *Pop from the Beginning*, also published in 1969, was essentially English in its tone, and lacked the immediacy of Lillian's interaction with many major players. Enduring magazines, like *Rolling Stone*, established in 1967, have kept their momentum by their very conspicuous presence. Lillian and her friend, journalist and later contributing editor to *Vanity Fair* Lisa Robinson nurtured the talents of other rock journalists, including Lester Bangs, Jon Landau, Richard Meltzer and Lenny Kaye. The salon at Max's Kansas City, where they discussed ideas and methods, were high-testosterone duelling matches, tempered by Lillian's good interpersonal skills and ability to listen carefully to others. When she died, the group fell apart.[49]

Lillian's pace of recreational and professional achievements was conducted at a high-powered level. Considering that she worked full-time for the Fairfax press, as a contributing editor to *Eye* and freelanced for various other publications while researching a major reference book involving long hours at Max's Kansas City, it is no wonder her health began to deteriorate. She did not have the support of a committed partner who could provide solace and love. She was an independent woman with many friends but no one special in her life, and a celebrity in her own right after the extraordinary success of her book, feted in newspapers and on television shows. Yet, as she confided to Richard Neville, the editor of *Oz* magazine in London, she had made no money out of its success.[50] She had naively signed a less than satisfactory contract, an altogether familiar story for first-time authors. This lack of financial largesse could never detract from the monumental achievement and the accolades accorded her by her peers, usually so dismissive of women's capabilities. She lamented: 'True, I've been offered ten books but they are all dreadful. The worst was called "Under Thirty".'[51]

Lillian was not simply attuned to fashions and shifts in the music industry, she was a first-class journalist with a strong antenna for social change in its earliest manifestations. She recorded the historic march of 25,000 women down Park Avenue to celebrate the jubilee of women's suffrage in the United States. The march is commonly regarded as the beginnings of second-wave feminism, but this overlooks a blow which occurred five years earlier in her home town of Brisbane when three women chained themselves to the bar of the Regatta Hotel to protest against discrimination against women in hotels.[52] A march like this was an important historic moment that was widely publicised. Lillian wrote a long and incisive article entitled 'There is a Tide in the Affairs of Women' for the *Sydney Morning Herald* of 28 August 1970, in which she spoke of her own excitement and disappointment that many women spectators jeered the marchers. Some even carried placards proclaiming '"M-O-M" for "Men Our Masters"' and 'actually scuffled with their marching sisters …' She ended this appraisal by writing: 'If the idea of change makes you uncomfortable, don't worry. You're not alone. All of us ladies agree that this time getting there is not going to be half the fun. But being there is going to be an important part of a brave new world.' She also reported on the drug arrests of Robert Kennedy Jr and Robert Shriver, noting how drug issues affected not just the poor and marginalised.[53] Her friend Danny Fields summed up the era when he remarked that '… people look back on those speed [amphetamines] years and they think, "Did I spend those years wallpapering an apartment with stamps when I could have written a play?"'[54]

In the two years before her death, Lillian's asthma became progressively worse, despite treatment. Her letters to an always sympathetic Aviva Layton began to deal far more with Zen diets (and why they did not work), her medication, which made her obese, and her battle with asthma. One happy occasion during this time was when she went to a fancy dress party dressed as Dame Nellie Melba and took first prize.[55] She contemplated leaving New York as it is '…

brilliant and glittering and hard and ruthless, a terrible cheat and a liar, but it is also full of tender little surprises, and if it's in a giving mood, it has a lot to give ...'[56] She thought of Italy, London, or even returning to Australia 'before I have no eggs left – with a nice, mythical man called Kevin'.[57] Lillian's frantic lifestyle was the very opposite of what was needed to manage her life-threatening illness. Her drive for professional success did not abate. A daily radio program called 'Lillian Roxon's Discotheque' went out from March 1971 to over 250 stations. The show ran for six months. This alone would have constituted a full-time job for most people. She also ran a column in *Mademoiselle* magazine entitled 'The Intelligent Woman's Guide to Sex' from March 1972 and she took on more assignments for new rock magazines, such as the short-lived *Fusion*. All this extracurricular activity and her fame caused ructions at the Fairfax office.

In 1973 Lillian returned to Brisbane, meeting up with old friends from school with whom she had always corresponded. This shows a generous side to her character, an unexpected loyalty from a woman feted in New York. She admitted to Rhyl Sorensen, 'New York is killing me, but I can't live without it.'[58] Her addiction to this city was as lethal as heroin. She and Richard Neville caught up with Mick Jagger in Sydney. Lillian was amused by Jagger's description of Linda and Paul McCartney as 'the lovely couple'.[59] Lillian saw many of her old Push friends now on the Whitlam government bandwagon of arts boards, with mortgages and private schools for their children. In the Push they had been temporarily absent from the bourgeois origins of their youth but had now slipped back, however awkwardly.

When Lillian returned to New York, her health had not improved. Subject to mood swings from her illness and medication, along with feelings of deep insecurity, she was no longer the amusing, witty companion of old. Her last days were poignant, in retrospect. She argued with her boss, Derryn Hinch, about what he paid her when he suggested that she needed an air-conditioned apartment.[60] She spent her last evening at Max's Kansas City supporting a friend of Danny Fields, dressed in a long black gown with an Iggy Pop badge positioned on her chest. As a person who constantly talked on the phone to her friends, an alarm went out two days later when her phone went unanswered. Lisa Robinson and Danny Goldberg called the police who broke into her apartment, finding her dead.[61] The *New York Times* of 12 August was extravagant with praise in its obituary, though the *Sydney Morning Herald*, for whom she had worked for decades, was restrained and brief. At her funeral many rock journalists were present and respectful of their great pioneer and champion.[62] Her brother, Jack Roxon, and some friends established the Lillian Roxon Memorial Asthma Research Trust.

In New York City she had carved out an enviable career as a journalist and rock chronicler, producing the inaugural encyclopedia of the genre. Intensely loyal and loving to all her family, Lillian did not take the vituperative path of Germaine Greer, who castigated her mother in public. Her generosity with her time, advice and connections helped many young artists, and she was loving, sympathetic and nurturing, despite her notorious reputation. Yet Lillian's poor health and immense drive to work and accomplish great things took a lethal toll. To die alone, with no one to help her, was far from what this courageous woman deserved.

Acknowledgments

All too often the people who get your manuscript to a beautiful book on the bookstore shelves are a small afterthought in acknowledgments. At HarperCollins all the team offered me warm support as well as invaluable and spirited guidance.

I should like to thank all those librarians who assisted me in my intense labours to bring my twenty 'bad girls' to life – most notably Dr Jeff Rickert at the Fryer Library at the University of Queensland (UQ) and Trudy Johnston and Diane Byrne at the John Oxley Library in Brisbane. The librarians at the Mitchell Library, State Library of New South Wales assisted me with all the collections I read and aided with illustrations. Rebecca Carter, the Document Delivery Librarian at UQ helped me track down rare books, articles and pamphlets. Once on the hunt nothing deterred her mission to get those items to me as quickly as possible. I simply could not have written the book without her help. No challenge was too much for her, indeed she welcomed it.

Mark McGuiness, historian and obituarist, made many welcome suggestions and once again rendered generous support. Shirleene Robinson, with whom I have written more academic work, also read drafts and provided invaluable comments.

Carol Brill, a direct descendant of the Cockerell family in Hobart Town, allowed me access to records and her own work, engaging in an active conversation about the history of Van Diemen's Land and Mary Cockerill in particular. Her generosity is much appreciated.

Barbara Tucker kindly allowed me access to photographs in the Albert Tucker Collection. Her insights into the Heide groups were fascinating.

No doubt all my friends are very pleased to hear of something else apart from Sir Samuel Griffith and his achievements (another recent project). My Zonta group hosted a lunch where a selection of entries had their first public run. In particular thanks to Susan Davies, Rhonda Irwin-Davison, Barbara Kent, Julie Mannion, Iris Scott, Allison Williams and Jennifer West, along with Christina Coles, Bruce Hawker, Tess Livingstone, Andra Muller, Anthe Philippides, Janet Prowse and Lesley Synge, who regularly heard dispatches from the war room of research.

Lastly and most importantly to Donald James, my heart's delight, who supported and encouraged me even though enduring a life-threatening illness and severe pain. He has never wavered as my number one cheer leader and inspiration. When things got tough, he always says, 'You can do it, Kitty.' And so I do.

Endnotes

Chapter 1 Mary Broad Bryant

1   Reprinted in *Historical Records of Australia* (*HRA*), 1915, vol. 2, pp. 809–810.

2   C. M. H. Clark, *A History of Australia*, vol. 1 (MUP, 1969, first published 1962), p. 91.

3   *Ibid.*

4   *Ibid.*, p. 69.

5   B. H. Fletcher, 'Phillip, Arthur (1738–1814)', http://adb.anu.edu.au/biography/phillip-arthur-2549.

6   Arthur Phillip's undated memorandum to the Secretary of State is contained in *Historical Records of NSW* (*HRNSW*), vol. 1, part 2, pp. 50–54.

7   Fletcher, *op. cit.*

8   C. H. Currey, *The Transportation, Escape and Pardoning of Mary Bryant* (Sydney, Halstead Press, 1986, first published 1963), p. 1.

9   *The Voyage of Governor Phillip to Botany Bay; with an Account of the Establishment of the Colonies at Port Jackson and Norfolk Island* (London, 1789).

10 John White, *Journal of a Voyage to New South Wales* (ed. A. H. Chisholm), (Sydney, Angus & Robertson, 1962, first published J. Debrett, London, 1790), p. 88.

11 *Journal of Ralph Clark*, 21 June 1787, cited in Clark, *op. cit.*, p. 84.

12 Refer to Currey, *op. cit.*, pp. 1–3, for more details.

13 Refer to *HRNSW*, vol. 1, part 2, p. 79. There is much discussion among historians and demographers as to the exact number. I have tried to balance the numbers in my estimation.

14 David Collins, *An Account of the English Colony in New South Wales*, vol. 1 (London, T. Cadell Jr & W. Davies), p. 55.

15 Watkin Tench, *Sydney's First Four Years: A Narrative of the Expedition to Botany Bay and a Complete Account of the Settlement at Port Jackson, 1788–1791* (printed by the Library of Australian History, 1979), pp. 149–150.

16 *Ibid.*, pp. 165–166.

17 Phillip to Lord Sydney, 11 April 1790, *HRA*, series 1, part 1, p. 168.

18 Currey, *op. cit.*, p. 9.

19 Secretary Charles Long to Governor Phillip, 27 June 1792, *HRA*, vol. 1, series 1, p. 359.

20 Collins, *op. cit.*, p. 153.

21 Currey, *op. cit.*, p. 11.

22 John Eastey, *Memorandum of the Transaction of the Voyage from England to Botany Bay, 1788–1793* (Sydney, Trustees of the Public Library of NSW with Angus & Robertson, 1965), p. 127.

23 James Scott, *Remarks on a Passage to Botany Bay, 1787–1792* (original ms in Mitchell Library, Sydney, Trustees of the Public Library of NSW with Angus & Robertson, 1963), p. 62.

24 Frederick A. Pottle, *Boswell and the Girl from Botany Bay* (London, William Heinemann, 1938), p. 27. These sarsaparilla leaves were presented by Yale University to the Mitchell Library in 1956.

25 William Bligh, *Remarks on Log Book of HMS* Providence, *1792–93*, p. 236 cited in Currey, *op. cit.*, p. 26.

26 *Ibid.*, p. 22.

27 *Ibid.*, p. 28.

28 *Ibid.*, p. 3.

29 Edward Edwards, George Hamilton and Basil Thomson, *Voyage of HMS* Pandora *Dispatched to Arrest the Mutineers on the* Bounty *in the South Sea, 1790–91* (reprinted London, Francis Edwards, 1915).

30 'A list of Convicts, Deserters from Pt. Jackson, delivered to Captain Edward Edwards, of HMS ship, *Pandora* by Timotheus Wanjon, Esq., Governor of the Dutch Settlement at Timor, 5 October 1791', *HRA*, series 1, part 1, p. 369.

31 This material is cited in Peter Ackroyd, *London: The Biography* (London, Chatto & Windus, 2000), p. 250.

32 *Dublin Chronicle*, 21 July 1793 reprinted in *HRA*, vol. 2, pp. 800–802.

33 www.oldandsold.com; Ackroyd, *op. cit.*, pp. 290–302.

34 C. B. Tinker (ed.), *The Letters of James Boswell*, vol. 2 (Oxford at the Claredon Press, 1924), p. 426.

35 Frederick A. Pottle, *Pride and Negligence: The History of the Boswell Papers* (New York, McGraw-Hill, 1982), pp. 83–86, 182.

36 Cited in Pottle, *Boswell and the Girl from Botany Bay*, *op. cit.*, p. 26.

37 *Ibid.*, p. 23.

38 *Ibid.*

39 Governor Phillip to Lord Grenville, Dispatch no. 1, 5 November 1791, *HRA*, series 1, vol. 1, p. 269.

40 Cited in Pottle, *Boswell and the Girl from Botany Bay*, *op. cit.*, pp. 27–28.

41 *Ibid.*, p. 25.

42 Entry in A. W. Jose, *Australian Encyclopedia* (Sydney, Angus & Robertson, 1927), p. 211.

43 Jonathan King, *Mary Bryant: Her Life and Escape from Botany Bay* (Sydney, Simon & Schuster, 2004), p. 276.

44 Rex Rientis, 'Watling, Thomas (1762– ?)', http://adb.anu.edu.au/biography/watling-thomas-2776.

45 Elizabeth Guilford, 'Morgan, Molly (1762–1835)', http://adb.anu.edu.au/biography/morgan-molly-2480.

46 Wendy Birman, 'O'Reilly, John Boyle (1844–1890)', http://adb.anu.edu.au/biography/oreilly-john-boyle-4338.

Chapter 2 Mary Cockerill and Walyer

1 Cited in Glenn Howroyd, *Sun Herald*, 28 June 1986.

2 Carol Brill, 'Flights of Fancy – The Legendary Bushrangers Michael Howe and Mary Cockerill', unpublished paper kindly forwarded to me with permission to quote. Ms Brill is a direct descendant of the Cockerell family which employed Mary in the 1810s.

3 Marcus Clarke, *Old Tales of a Young Country* (Melbourne, Mason, Firth, McCutcheon, 1871), chapter 6, read as an electronic book 16 November 2009.

4 Information supplied by Carol Brill in email to Kay Saunders, 24 October 2009.

5 'Heaven and Hell Together', www.heavenandhelltogether.com/, Cockerell family site.

6 Kim Pearse and Susan Doyle, 'New Town: A Social History' (Hobart City Council, 2002), cited in Carol Brill, 'Mary Cockerill aka Black Mary and

the Cockerell Family', unpublished ms in possession of the author by kind permission of Ms Brill.

7   James Bonwick cited in James Boyce, *Van Diemen's Land: An Environmental History* (Melbourne, Black Inc., 2008), p. 32.

8   K. A. Green, 'Ingle, John (1781? –1872)', http://adb.anu.edu.au/biography/ingle-john-2260.

9   John West in *The History of Tasmania* (ed. A.G.L. Shaw), (Sydney, Royal Australian Historical Society and Angus & Robertson, 1971, first published 1852), p. 359.

10 *Ibid.*, p. 360.

11 'Heaven and Hell Together', *op. cit.*

12 *Ibid.*

13 J. E. Calder, 'Early Troubles of the Colonists', *Hobart Mercury*, 17–27 November 1873.

14 Alan Atkinson, *The Europeans in Australia. A History. Volume Two: Democracy* (Melbourne, Oxford University Press, 2004), p. 69.

15 *Ibid.*

16 Boyce, *op. cit.*, p. 55.

17 *Historical Records of Australia (HRA)*, 3, no. 2, pp. 80, 703.

18 L. L. Robson, *A History of Tasmania Volume 1: Van Diemen's Land from the Earliest Times to 1855* (Melbourne, Oxford University Press, 1983), p. 86.

19 J. E. Calder, *Some Accounts of the Wars, Extirpation, Habits etc. of the Native Tribes of Tasmania* (Hobart, Fullers Bookshop, facsimile edition, 1972, first published 1875), p. 46.

20 Robson, *op. cit.*, p. 69.

21 James Bonwick, *The Lost Tasmanian Race* (London, Sampson Low, Manston, Searle & Rivington, 1884), p. 41.

22 Robson, *op. cit.*, p. 81.

23 Governor Macquarie's Proclamation, 14 May 1814, *HRA*, 1, no. 8, pp. 262–265.

24 Robson, *op. cit.*, p. 90.

25 West, *op. cit.*, pp. 359–360.

26 Rev. R. Knopwood to Davey, 30 August 1814, *HRA*, 3, no. 2, pp. 77–79.

27 Edward Curr, *An Account of the Colony of Van Diemen's Land to 1824* (Hobart, Platypus Press, 1967, first published 1824), p. 180.

28 *Hobart Town Gazette*, 27 July 1816.

29 Robson, *op. cit.*, p. 85.

30 Lyndall Ryan, *The Aboriginal Tasmanians* (Sydney, Allen & Unwin, 1996, first published 1981), pp. 23–29.

31 Carol Brill to Kay Saunders, email, 24 October 2009.

32 Thomas Wells, *Michael Howe: The Last and Worst of the Tasmanian Bushrangers* (Hobart, Andrew Bent, 1818), reproduced in Curr, *op. cit.*, p. 190.

33 Davey to Macquarie, September 1816, *HRA*, 3, no. 2, pp. 591–592, 603–604.

34 Sworn statement of John Yorke reproduced in Curr, *op. cit.*, pp. 187–188. In the account in the *Sydney Gazette* of 20 May 1815 there was nothing about the murder of a woman, only the cold-blooded killing of a man.

35 Report in *Sydney Gazette*, 25 January 1817 and Yorke deposition in Curr, *op. cit.*

36 Lieutenant Governor William Sorell to Governor Macquarie, 30 June 1817 and 11 September 1817, *HRA*, 3, no. 2, pp. 238, 262–263, 276–277.

37 Wells, *op. cit.*, pp. 188–190.

38 *Hobart Town Gazette*, 8 June 1816.

39 Clarke, *op. cit.*

40 Calder, 'Early Troubles', *op. cit.*

41 Sorell to Macquarie, 18 November 1818, *HRA*, 3, no. 2, pp. 363–364.

42 *Hobart Town Gazette*, 24 October 1818.

43 Bonwick, *The Lost Tasmanian Race*, *op. cit.*, p. 31.

44 *Hobart Town Gazette*, 3 July 1819.

45 Robson, *op. cit.*, pp. 80–101.

46 Ryan, *op. cit.*, pp. 88–94; see also N. J. B. Plomley (ed.), *Friendly Mission: The Tasmanian Journals and Papers of George Augustus Robinson, 1829–1834* (Hobart, Tasmanian Research Association, 1966); Cassandra Pybus, *Community of Thieves* (Melbourne, William Heinemann, 1991).

47 Ryan, *ibid.*, pp. 110–113.

48 *Ibid.*, p. 141.

49 Julia Clark, 'Walyer' in Heather Radi (ed.), *200 Australian Women* (Broadway, Women's Redress Press Inc., 1988), p. 11; see also Henry

Reynolds, 'The Black War: Tasmania's First Land Rights Movement',
Island Magazine, 2, no. 1, 1988, pp. 104–107.

50   Ryan, *op. cit.*, p. 150.

Chapter 3 Eliza Fraser

1   Elaine Brown, 'Fraser, Eliza (1798–1858?)', http://adb.anu.edu.au/
biography/fraser-eliza-anne-12929.

2   Yolanda Drummond, 'Progress of Eliza Fraser', *Journal of the Royal
Queensland Historical Society*, 15, no. 1, 1993, p. 16.

3   Kay Schaffer, *In the Wake of First Contact: The Eliza Fraser Stories*
(Melbourne, Cambridge University Press, 1995), p. 4 for more details. This
is the most impressive account of the entire Eliza Fraser story. Readers are
directed to this study for a more complex rendition of her stories and their
interpretation. See also Raymond Evans and Jan Walker, '"These Strangers,
Where Are They Going?" Aboriginal–European Relations on Fraser Island
and the Wide Bay Region 1770–1905', *Occasional Papers in Anthropology*,
vol. 8, 1977, pp. 39–105.

4   The whole first narrative of Eliza Fraser is reproduced in Barry Dwyer and
N. Buchanan, *The Rescue of Eliza Fraser* (Noosa, Noosa Graphics, 1986),
appendix 7.

5   Evidence of Robert Hodge cited in John Curtis, *Shipwreck of the Stirling
Castle* (London, George Virtue, 1838), pp. 31–32.

6   Olga Miller, 'K'gari, Mrs. Fraser and Butchulla Oral Tradition' in Ian
McNiven et al, *Constructions of Colonialism: Perspectives on Eliza Fraser's
Shipwreck* (London, Leicester University Press, 1998), p. 34.

7   Henry Youlden, 'Shipwreck in Australia', *The Knickerbocker*, vol. 41, no. 4,
1853 cited in Schaffer, *op. cit.*, p. 36.

8   Curtis, *op. cit.*, p. 33.

9   An excellent summary is found in Elaine Brown, 'Eliza Fraser: An
Historical Record' in McNiven et al, *op. cit.*, pp. 19–20; Schaffer, *op. cit.*,
chapters 2 and 3.

10   Curtis, *op. cit.*, pp. 220–240.

11   Cited in Brown, 'Eliza Fraser: An Historical Record', *op. cit.*, p. 20.

12   Cited in Schaffer, *op. cit.*, p. 87.

13   Miller, *op. cit.*, pp. 30–31.

14 Curtis, *op. cit.*, p. 143.

15 See Dwyer and Buchanan, *op. cit.*

16 *Ibid.*

17 Reported in Curtis, *op. cit.*, p. 79; see also Brown, 'Eliza Fraser: An Historical Record', *op. cit.*, pp. 22–23.

18 Refer to Schaffer, *op. cit.*, pp. 45, 47, 49–60.

19 Curtis, *op. cit.*, p. 181; see Brown, *op. cit.*, pp. 19–22.

20 Cited in Brown, *ibid.*, p. 25.

21 Schaffer, *op. cit.*, p. 42; Michael Alexander, *Mrs. Fraser on the Fatal Shore* (London, Michael Joseph, 1971, reprinted 1976), p. 106.

22 Don Grady, 'Elizabeth Guard (1814–1870)', www.teara.govt.nz/en/biographies/1g23/guard-elizabeth.

23 Schaffer, *op. cit.*, p. 44.

24 *Ibid.*, pp. 43–49.

25 H. S. Russell, *The Genesis of Queensland* (Sydney, Turner & Henderson, 1888), p. 250. I discussed his depiction of the Mrs Fraser story at the Clem Lack Memorial Lecture at the Royal Queensland Historical Society on 21 August 2009.

Chapter 4 Lola Montez

1 Bruce Seymour, *Lola Montez* (New Haven, Yale UP, 1995), chapter 1. This is the most reliable and well researched of the considerable literature on Lola Montez.

2 Lola Montez, *Autobiography and Lectures* (London, James Blackwood, n.d.), p. 8.

3 *Ibid.*, p. 11.

4 Horace Wyndam, *The Magnificent Montez: From Courtesan to Convert* (London, Hutchinson, 1935), p. 45.

5 Her autobiography makes some references to these events.

6 Michael Cannon, *Lola Montez: The Tragic Story of a 'Liberated Woman'* (Melbourne, Heritage, 1973), p. 10, and 'Montez, Lola (1818–1861)', http://adb.anu.edu.au/biography/montez-lola-4226.

7 The material on Paris and Bavaria is taken largely from Seymour, *op. cit.*, chapters 8–17.

8 *Ibid.*, p. 147.

9   Cannon, *Lola Montez: The Tragic Story of a 'Liberated Woman'*, *op. cit.*, p. 12.

10 Seymour, *op. cit.*, p. 259.

11 *Ibid.*, pp. 273–282.

12 *Ibid.*, pp. 293–294.

13 *Ibid.*, pp. 295–300.

14 Cited in Cannon, *Lola Montez: The Tragic Story of a 'Liberated Woman'*, *op. cit.*, p. 47.

15 Montez, *op. cit.*, p. 49.

16 *Ibid.*

17 Janet R. Fireman, 'Lola Montez' in Glenda Riley and Richard W. Etulain (eds.), *By Grit and Grace: Eleven Women Who Shaped the American West* (Golden, Col., Fulcrum Press, 1997), p. 58; see also J. F. Varley, *Lola Montez: The Californian Adventures of Europe's Notorious Courtesan* (Spokane, A. H. Clark, 1996), and Seymour, *op. cit.*, chapters 24 and 25.

18 Fireman, *op. cit.*, pp. 58–59.

19 *Ibid.*, pp. 59–60.

20 S. Korzelinski, *Memoirs of Gold-Digging in Australia* (translated and edited by S. Robe), (St Lucia, University of Queensland Press, 1979), p. 148.

21 Geoffrey Serle, *The Golden Age: A History of the Colony of Victoria, 1851–1861* (Carlton, Melbourne University Press, 1963), pp. 363–364.

22 *The Age*, 22 September 1855.

23 Serle, *op. cit.*, pp. 341–343.

24 E. H. Pask, *Enter the Colonies, Dancing: A History of Dance in Australia 1835–1940* (Melbourne, Oxford University Press, 1979), p. 35.

25 Korzelinski, *op. cit.*, p. 57.

26 Weston Bate, *Lucky City: The First Generation at Ballarat, 1851–1901* (Carlton, Melbourne University Press, 1989), pp. 109–110.

27 Seymour, *op. cit.*, p. 344.

28 *Ibid.*, pp. 348–352.

29 Montez, *op. cit.*

30 *Ibid.*, p. 366.

31 Richard Waterhouse, '"Lola Montez" and High Culture: The Australian Elizabethan Theatre Trust in Post-war Australia', *Journal of Australian Studies*, March 2001, www.highbeam.com/doc/1G1-20152561.html.

Chapter 5 Ellen Tremaye (Edward De Lacy Evans) and Marion ('Bill') Edwards

1   For more details see Lindy Scripps, 'Jemmy the Rover' in Heather Radi (ed.), *200 Australian Women* (Broadway, Women's Redress Press, 1988), pp. 7–8.

2   *Columbia Encyclopedia*, sixth edition, 2008, accessed 26 November 2009.

3   William Telfer, *The Wallabadah Manuscript; The Early History of the Northern Districts of New South Wales* (ed. Roger Milliss), (Kensington, UNSWP), 1980, p. 103. The manuscript was written around 1901.

4   Jillian Oppenheimer, 'Kitty Gallagher' in Radi, *op. cit.*, p. 3; The Australian Women's Register entry www.womenaustralia.info/biogs/AWE3691b.htm. The Register is not correct on her birth date. She was already married in 1798 so she could not have been born in 1785.

5   The best single source for this chapter is Lucy Chesser, *Parting With My Sex: Cross-dressing, Inversion and Sexuality in Australian Cultural Life* (Sydney, Sydney University Press, 2008).

6   *Ibid.*, pp. 6–11.

7   'The Male Impersonator', *Herald* (Melbourne), 8 September 1879.

8   *Bendigo Advertiser*, 5 September 1879 cited in Chesser, *op. cit.*, p. 20. The references from the Bendigo newspapers are taken from Chesser.

9   *Ibid.*; *Bendigo Independent*, 6 September 1879.

10 *Ibid.*, p. 200.

11 *Argus*, 6 September 1879.

12 Chesser, *op. cit.*, p. 11.

13 *Ibid.*

14 *Argus*, 27 August 1901.

15 Chesser, *op. cit.*, pp. 28–29. The material on the affair is taken from Chesser's account.

16 *Bendigo Advertiser*, 6 December 1879.

17 *Bendigo Advertiser*, 8 September 1879.

18 *Adelaide Advertiser*, 29 August 1901.

19 *Bendigo Independent*, 5 September 1879.

20 O. Penfold, 'A Case of Man-personation by a Woman', *Australian Medical Journal*, 2, no. 4, 1880, p. 147.

21 Chesser, *op. cit.*, p. 27.

22 *Ibid.*, p. 31; see also Gail Reekie, 'She Was a Loveable Man: Marion/ Bill Edwards and the Feminisation of Australian Culture', *Journal of Australian Feminist Lesbian Studies*, vol. 4, 1994, pp. 43–50.

23 Mimi Colligan, 'Edwards, Marion (Bill) (1874–1956)', http://adb.anu.edu. au/biography/edwards-marion-bill-12901.

24 *Ibid.*

25 Chesser, *op. cit.*, pp. 238–270.

26 *Argus*, 22 October 1906.

27 Cited in Chesser, *op. cit.*, pp. 247–248.

28 *Ibid.*, pp. 266–267.

29 Colligan, *op. cit.*

Chapter 6 'Madame Brussels' Caroline Hodgson

1   Philip Bentley, 'Hodgson, Caroline (1851–1908)', www.adb.anu.edu.au/ biography/hodgson-caroline-12986.

2   John Sadlier, *Recollections of a Victorian Police Officer* (Ringwood, Penguin, 1973, first published 1913), pp. 176–178; see also Paul de Serville, *Pounds and Pedigrees: The Upper Class in Victoria, 1850–80* (Melbourne, Oxford University Press, 1991), pp. 41–51; his death notice referred to his illustrious family.

3   Chris McColville, 'The Location of Melbourne Prostitutes, 1870–1920', *Historical Studies*, vol. 19, no. 74, 1980, pp. 86–97.

4   Cyril Pearl, *Wild Men of Sydney* (London, W. H. Allen, 1958), p. 202.

5   *Ibid.*, p. 203.

6   Bentley, *op. cit.*

7   *Ibid.*

8   Raelene Frances, *Selling Sex: A Hidden History of Prostitution* (Sydney, Allen & Unwin, 2007), pp. 134–135.

9   Philip Bentley, 'Edifices of Venereal Renown and Gilded Palaces of Sin' (BA Hons thesis, Monash University, 1993), pp. 36–37.

10 J. Parsons, *Thirty Six Years Among Criminals* (1906) cited in Graeme Davison et al, *The Outcasts of Melbourne: Essays in Social History* (Sydney, Allen & Unwin, 1985), p. 100.

11 John Stanley James, *The Vagabond Papers* (ed. Michael Cannon), (Melbourne University Press, 1969), pp. 231–232.

12 Davison et al, *op. cit.*, p. 80.

13 Frances, *op. cit.*, p. 157.

14 Andrew Brown-May and Shurlee Swain (eds.), *The Encyclopedia of Melbourne* (Melbourne, Cambridge University Press, 2005), p. 575.

15 Geoffrey Serle, 'Gaunson, David (1846–1909)', http://adb.anu.edu.au/biography/gaunson-david-3599.

16 Pearl, *op. cit.*, p. 204.

17 *Ibid.*, p. 203.

18 Geoffrey Cox, 'Music at St. Patrick's Cathedral: A Profile', www.cam.org.au/cathedral/music/recording-of-the-music-of-the-choir-3html.

19 *Truth*, 18 December 1900, 23 September 1900, 5 July 1900.

20 Judith A. Allen, *Sex and Secrets: Crimes Involving Australian Women Since 1880* (Melbourne, Oxford University Press, 1990), p. 74.

21 Pearl, *op. cit.*, p. 202.

22 David Dunstan, 'Gillott, Samuel (1838–1913)', http://adb.anu.edu.au/biography/gillott-sir-samuel-6390.

23 George Meudell, *The Pleasant Career of a Spendthrift* (Melbourne, Robertson & Mullen, 1929), pp. 274–275. Another version was released in 1935; see Diane Langmore, 'Meudell, George Dick (1860–1936)', http://adb.anu.edu.au/biography/muedell-george-dick-7564.

Chapter 7 Helena Rubinstein

1 Helena Rubinstein, *My Life for Beauty* (Sydney and London, Bodley Head in Australia, 1965), p. 118; M. Fabe, *Beauty Millionaire: The Life of Helena Rubinstein* (New York, Thomas Cromwell, 1972), p. 17; Maxene Fabe's biography is full of mistakes and perpetuates many myths about the life of Helena Rubinstein, for instance that Helena's father wanted her to study medicine.

2 Lindy Woodhead, *War Paint: Elizabeth Arden and Helena Rubinstein: Their Lives, Their Times, Their Rivalry* (London, Virago, 2004, first published 2003), p. 441. Woodhead undertook research in Poland and located the original birth certificate, thereby refuting Rubinstein's *Australian Dictionary of Biography* entry which has her born in 1870.

3 *Ibid.*, p. 30.

4 *Ibid.*, pp. 32–33.

5   J. R. Poynter, 'Rubinstein, Helena (1870–1965)', http://adb.anu.edu.au/
     biography/rubinstein-helena-8293. This entry contains many errors that
     have been rectified in Woodhead's book.

6   Rubinstein, *op. cit.*, p. 28.

7   Woodhead, *op. cit.*, p. 25.

8   Patrick O'Higgins, *Madame: An Intimate Biography of Helena Rubinstein* (New
     York, The Viking Press, 1971), p. 146. This is a delightfully candid book.

9   *Ibid.*; Poynter, 'Rubinstein, Helena'. Poynter's family came from Coleraine
     and he possessed considerable family knowledge of Helena's early time in
     Victoria. See also Helena Rubinstein, *The Art of Feminine Beauty* (New
     York, Victor Gollancz, 1930), p. 12. In her later autobiography she said she
     worked for Lord Hopetoun, Australia's first governor-general; Peter and
     Sheila Forrest, *All for Queensland: The Governors and the People* (Darwin,
     Shady Tree Press, 2009), pp. 125–141.

10   Woodhead, *op. cit.*, p. 43.

11   *Ibid.*, pp. 44–45.

12   *Ibid.*, pp. 46–47; Rubinstein, *My Life for Beauty*, pp. 26–27; O'Higgins,
     op. cit., p. 149 contains the most frank account of Rubinstein's time in
     Australia in her own words.

13   Woodhead, *op. cit.*, p. 49.

14   Advertisement in *Table Talk*, March 1903.

15   Woodhead, *op. cit.*, p. 52.

16   Rubinstein, *My Life for Beauty*, pp. 30–31.

17   *Ibid.*, pp. 27–29.

18   *Ibid.*, p. 32.

19   Woodhead, *op. cit.*, p. 70.

20   *The Australasian*, 30 January 1909, interview with Helena Rubinstein.

21   Maggie Angeloglou, *A History of Make-Up* (London, Studio Vista, 1970),
     pp. 99–107.

22   M. C. Cohen and K. Kozlowski, *Read My Lips: A Cultural History of
     Lipstick* (San Francisco, Chronicle Books, 1998), pp. 17–19.

23   *Table Talk*, December 1905.

24   M. Cannon, 'Brodzky, Maurice (1883–1973)', http://adb.anu.edu.au/
     biography/brodzky-maurice-5365.

25   *The Australasian*, 30 January 1909, interview with Helena Rubinstein.

26 Rubinstein, *My Life for Beauty*, p. 43.

27 *Argus*, 3 November 1911; *Sydney Morning Herald*, 25 September 1909; *Adelaide Advertiser*, 6 March 1912.

28 Cohen and Kozlowski, *op. cit.*, p. 23.

29 Woodhead, *op. cit.*, p. 78.

30 Rubinstein, *My Life for Beauty*, pp. 39–40.

31 *Ibid.*, p. 81.

32 Rubinstein, *My Life for Beauty*, pp. 44–45.

33 *Ibid.*, p. 48.

34 *Ibid.*, p. 53.

35 *Ibid.*, p. 54; Woodhead, *op. cit.*, pp. 89–91.

36 *Ibid.*, p. 58.

37 Woodhead, *op. cit.*, pp. 103–109.

38 *Ibid.*, p. 110.

39 *Ibid.*, p. 118.

40 *Ibid.*, pp. 119–121.

41 Rubinstein, *My Life for Beauty*, p. 74.

42 *Ibid.*, p. 62.

43 *Ibid.*, pp. 71–74.

44 Woodhead, *op. cit.*, pp. 170–177.

45 *Ibid.*, p. 230.

Chapter 8 Adela Pankhurst

1 Verna Coleman, *Adela Pankhurst: The Wayward Suffragette, 1885–1961* (Carlton, Melbourne University Press, 1996), p. 1. Readers are advised to consult this text. It is the most comprehensive study of Adela's life.

2 F. F. Rosenblatt, *The Chartist Movement* (London, Taylor & Francis, 2006).

3 David Mitchell, *Queen Christabel: A Biography of Christabel Pankhurst* (London, Macdonald & James, 1977), pp. 14–19; Coleman, *op. cit.*, pp. 3–4; see also Emmeline Pethick-Lawrence, *My Part in a Changing World* (London, Gollancz, 1938); E. Sylvia Pankhurst (introduced by Richard Pankhurst), *The Suffragette Movement: An Intimate Account of Persons and Ideals* (London, Virago Press, 1977, first published 1931) provides excellent accounts by participants. A solid overview is contained

in David Mitchell's *The Fighting Pankhursts: A Study in Tenacity* (London, Cape, 1967).

4   Coleman, *op. cit.*, p. 5.

5   Emmeline Pankhurst, *My Own Story* (London, E. Nash, 1941); June Purvis, *Emmeline Pankhurst: A Biography* (London and New York, Routledge, 2002). Sylvia also complained in her autobiography of her mother's lack of affection and neglect of her children. Emmeline was callous when Harry was ill with poliomyelitis. He died at the age of 20.

6   Susan Hogan, 'Pankhurst, Adela Constantia Mary (1885–1961)', http://adb.anu.edu.au/biography/pankhurst-adela-constantia-9275.

7   Coleman, *op. cit.*

8   Christabel Pankhurst, *Unshackled: The Story of How We Won the Vote* (ed. L. Lord), (London, Hutchinson, 1959).

9   Coleman, *op. cit.*, pp. 46–48.

10 E. Sylvia Pankhurst, *op. cit.*, p. 588.

11 Letter to Helen Fraser Moyes, undated cited in Mitchell, *Queen Christabel*, p. 175.

12 Mitchell, *The Fighting Pankhursts, op. cit.*, p. 55; Hogan, *op. cit.*

13 Patricia Gowland, 'John, Cecilia Annie (1877–1955)', http://adb.anu.edu.au/biography/john-cecilia-annie-6849 and J. N. Brownfoot, 'Goldstein, Vida Jane Mary (1869–1949)', http://adb.anu.edu.au/biography/goldstein-vida-jane-6418.

14 Adela Pankhurst, *Betrayed: A Play in Five Acts* (Melbourne, Fraser & Jenkinson, 1917). A copy of this turgid drama is held in the John Oxley Library in Brisbane.

15 *Sydney Morning Herald,* 22 July 1914.

16 *The Woman Voter*, 15 September 1914.

17 A good account of these years can be found in Raymond Evans, *Loyalty and Disloyalty: Social Conflict on the Queensland Homefront, 1914-1918* (Sydney, Allen & Unwin, 1987); Joy Damousi and M. Lake (eds), *Gender and War: Australians at War in the Twentieth Century* (Melbourne, Cambridge University Press, 1995). See also Geoff Hewitt, 'Ahern, Elizabeth (1877–1969)', http://adb.anu.edu.au/biography/ahern-elizabeth-lizzie-4977.

18 Coleman, *op. cit.*, pp. 64–65.

19 Mitchell, *The Fighting Pankhursts, op. cit.*, p. 55.

20   *Ibid.*, p. 66.

21   Hogan, *op. cit.*

22   C. M. H. Clark, *A History of Australia: Volume 4: The Old Dead Tree and the Young Tree Green* (Carlton, Melbourne University Press, 1987), p. 40.

23   Coleman, *op. cit.*, pp. 72–74.

24   Mitchell, *The Fighting Pankhursts, op. cit.*, pp. 58–59.

25   L. F. Fitzhardinge, *The Little Digger, 1914-1952: A Political Biography of William Morris Hughes*, vol. 2 (Sydney, Angus & Robertson, 1979), p. 277.

26   Coleman, *op. cit.*, pp. 79–80.

27   Hogan, *op. cit.*

28   Stuart Macintyre, *The Oxford History of Australia*, vol. 4, *1901–1942: The Succeeding Age* (Melbourne, Oxford University Press, 1986), and his book, *The Reds: The Communist Party of Australia from Origins to Illegality* (Sydney, Allen & Unwin, 1998).

29   Clark, *op. cit.*, pp. 239–255.

30   Coleman, *op. cit.*, pp. 107–109; Mitchell, *The Fighting Pankhursts, op. cit.*, pp. 213–226.

31   James Barnes and Patience Barnes, *Nazis in Pre-War London, 1930–1939* (Brighton, Sussex Academic Press, 2005).

32   Chris Cunneen, 'Miles, William John (1871–1942)', http://adb.anu.edu.au/biogs/A100489b.htm.

33   Coleman, *op. cit.*, pp. 146–150.

34   Craig Munro, 'Stephensen, Percy Reginald (1901–1965)', http://adb.anu.edu.au/biography/miles-william-john-7576; Cunneen, *op. cit.*

35   Kay Saunders and Roger Daniels (eds.), *Alien Justice: Wartime Internment in Australia and North America* (St Lucia, University of Queensland Press, 2000).

Chapter 9 Annette Kellermann

1   Nikki Henningham, 'Letham, Isabel (1899–1995)', www.womenaustralia.info/biogs/AWE2231b.htm.

2   'Sarah Frances "Fanny" Durack (1889–1956)' and 'Annette Kellermann (1886–1975)' in Susanna de Vries, *The Complete Book of Great Australian Women* (Sydney, HarperCollins, 2003), p. 2.

3   'She's Game: Women Making Australian Sporting History: Fanny Durack' in www.womenaustralia.info/exhib/sg/durack.html.

4   Emily Gibson with Barbara Firth, *The Original Million Dollar Mermaid: The Annette Kellerman Story* (Sydney, Allen & Unwin, 2005), p. 5. This book relies a lot on Kellermann's papers which are lodged in the Mitchell Library.

5   *Ibid.*, p. 6.

6   *Ibid.*, pp. 6–7.

7   Jacqui Donegan, 'Banned in Boston: A Biography of Annette Kellerman (1886–1975)' (BA Hons thesis, University of Queensland), p. 12.

8   G. P. Walsh, 'Kellermann, Annette Marie Sarah (1886–1975)', http://adb. anu.edu.au/biography/kellermann-annette-marie-sarah-6911; refer also to John Lucas, 'Making a Statement: Annette Kellerman Advances the World of Swimming, Diving and Entertainment' in *Sporting Traditions*, vol. 14, no. 2, 1998, pp. 25–35.

9   Annette Kellermann, *How to Swim* (London, William Heinemann, 1918), pp. 12–15.

10   *Ibid.*; Marcelle Wooster, 'A Résumé of Annette Kellermann', unpublished manuscript, Fryer Research Library, University of Queensland, 1975.

11   Annette Kellermann, *Fairy Tales of the South Seas* (London, Sampson, Low, Marston, 1926), p. 11.

12   Kay Saunders, 'James Freeman Cavill (1867–1952)' and 'Sir Henry Sydney Williams (1920-2003)' in *Queensland: 150 Years of Achievement* (Sydney, Focus Books, 2009), p. 161.

13   Annette Kellermann, 'How I Swam into Fame and Fortune' in *American Magazine*, 1917, quoted in Donegan, *op. cit.*, p. 16.

14   Donegan, *op. cit.*, pp. 15–17.

15   *Sydney Morning Herald*, 26 March 1902.

16   Veronica Raszeja, 'Bathing Costumes Controversy' in *Oxford Companion to Australian Sport* (Melbourne, Oxford University Press, 1994, 2nd edn), p. 58.

17   *Ibid.*

18   Donegan, *op. cit.*, p. 21.

19   Walsh, *op. cit.*

20   Wooster, *op. cit.*

21   Gibson, *op. cit.*, pp. 16–19.

22   Annette Kellermann, 'How I Swam into Fame and Fortune', *op. cit.*, p. 28.

23 Hugh Cudlipp, *Publish and Be Damned: The Astonishing Story of the Daily Mirror* (London, Dakers, 1953).

24 Gibson, *op. cit.*, pp. 39–41.

25 *Ibid.*, p. 46.

26 Walsh, *op. cit.*

27 Donegan, *op. cit.*, p. 36.

28 Gibson, *op. cit.*, p. 45.

29 *Ibid.*, p. 38; Kellermann, 'How I Swam into Fame and Fortune', *op. cit.*, pp. 82–83. Her ADB entry calculates she earned $1250 per week.

30 www.classicfilmguide.com/indexef48.html, *Million Dollar Mermaid*.

31 Gibson, *op. cit.*, pp. 58–60.

32 Jacqui Donegan undertook extensive research in the USA and failed to locate records verifying this event; refer to Donegan, *op. cit.*, pp. 41–46.

33 *Boston Post*, 7 November 1908, cited in Donegan, *op. cit.*, p. 46.

34 Donegan, *op. cit.*, pp. 51–52; B. L. Bennett, 'Dudley A. Sargent – A Man for all Seasons', *Quest*, vol. 29, 1978, pp. 33–45.

35 Cited in Gibson, *op. cit.*, p. 89.

36 Donegan, *op. cit.*, p. 53.

37 Gibson, *op. cit.*, pp. 66–72.

38 *Ibid.*, p. 85.

39 Donegan, *op. cit.*, p. 55.

40 *Ibid.*, pp. 57–58; Gibson, *op. cit.*, pp. 107–122.

41 Gibson, *op. cit.*, pp. 128–149.

42 *Ibid.*, p. 46.

43 Donegan, *op. cit.*, p. 50.

44 *Courier-Mail* (Brisbane), 14 July 1945.

45 Gibson, *op. cit.*, pp. 155–161.

46 *New York Times*, 2 September 1918.

47 Donegan, *op. cit.*, pp. 63–64.

48 Gibson, *op. cit.*, pp. 169–172.

49 Donegan, *op. cit.*, p. 68.

50 Gibson, *op. cit.*, p. 95.

51 Gibson, *op. cit.*, pp. 175–176.

52 *Ibid.*, p. 90.

53 Donegan, *op. cit.*, pp. 70–71.

54   *Woman's World* (Australian edition), 1 April 1933.

55   Gibson, *op. cit.*, pp. 182–185.

56   *Ibid.*, pp. 192–203.

57   Esther Williams and Digby Diehl, *The Million Dollar Mermaid* (New York, Simon & Schuster, 1999), pp. 213–215.

58   *Sunday Telegraph* (Sydney), 16 March 1975.

59   *Ibid.*

60   Gibson, *op. cit.*, p. 218.

61   Walsh, *op. cit.*

Chapter 10 Lady Maie Casey

1   Maie Casey, *Tides and Eddies* (Penguin, 1966). This is a record of her public not private life.

2   Zara Holt, *My Life and Harry: An Autobiography of Dame Zara Holt* (Melbourne, Herald Books, 1968); P. A. Pemberton, 'Holt, Dame Zara Kate (1909–1989)', http://adb.anu.edu.au/biography/holt-dame-zara-kate-12652. Dame Zara's personal papers in the National Library of Australia reveal many sexual peccadilloes in the higher echelons of society in the 1960s. Never judgmental or cruel, she was a witty observer of life.

3   Maie Casey, *An Australian Story, 1837–1907* (London, Michael Joseph, 1962), pp. 23–24.

4   J. S. Legge, 'Grice, Richard (1813–1882)', http://adb.anu.edu.au/biography/grice-richard-3669.

5   www.thewomenshistory.org.au/history/guides/general/provlist.htm. The Royal Women's Hospital, Melbourne, Provenance – Creators and Custodians. It was then termed the Melbourne Lying-in Hospital and Infirmary for Diseases of Women and Children; refer also to his entry in Paul de Serville, *Pounds and Pedigrees: The Upper Class in Victoria 1850–80* (Melbourne, Oxford University Press, 1991), p. 401.

6   Casey, *An Australian Story, op. cit.*, pp. 27–31.

7   *Ibid.*, p. 33.

8   *Ibid.*, p. 34.

9   *Ibid.*, pp. 78–94.

10 F. M. C. Forster, 'Ryan, Charles Snodgrass (1853–1926)', http://adb.anu.edu.au/biography/ryan-charles-snodgrass-8311.

11 Maie Casey, *Melba Revisited, 1861–1931*, privately printed by the author, 1975. A copy resides in the Fryer Library, University of Queensland. It is beautifully illustrated.

12 'Marian Ellis Rowan (1848–1922)' in Kay Saunders, *Queensland: 150 Years of Achievement* (Sydney, Focus Books, 2009), p. 34.

13 Casey, *An Australian Story, op. cit.*, p. 76.

14 *Ibid.*, p. 115.

15 *Ibid.*, pp. 151–157. The chapter entitled 'The Stranger' concerned her early life with Berthe Tissot, of whom she writes far more warmly than her mother, who was designated 'The Wife'.

16 *Ibid.*, p. 152.

17 Diane Langmore, *Glittering Surfaces: A Life of Maie Casey* (Sydney, Allen & Unwin, 1997), p. 19. This is a well-researched biography and readers are advised to consult this for more details on Casey's life.

18 Diane Langmore, 'Ryan, Rupert Sumner (1884 –1952)', http://adb.anu. edu.au/biography-ryan-rupert-sumner-11593.

19 John Rickard, 'White, Vera Deakin (1891–1978)', http://adb.anu.edu.au/ biography/white-vera-deakin-12014.

20 Casey, *Tides and Eddies, op. cit.*, pp. 27–30.

21 Langmore, *Glittering Surfaces, op. cit.*, p. 31.

22 Langmore, 'Ryan, Rupert', *op. cit.*

23 Casey, *Tides and Eddies, op. cit.*, pp. 43–45.

24 *Ibid.*, p. 45.

25 Joan Lindsay, *Time Without Clocks* (Melbourne, Cheshire, 1963), p. 205.

26 Saunders, *op. cit.*, p. 12; W. J. Hudson, *Casey* (Melbourne, Oxford University Press, 1986), pp. 1–75 for his early life and career; W. J. Hudson, 'Casey, Richard Gavin Gardiner (Baron Casey) (1890–1976)', http://adb.anu.edu.au/biography/casey-richard-gavin-gardiner-9706.

27 Langmore, *Glittering Surfaces, op. cit.*, p. 38.

28 *Ibid.*, p. 40.

29 Hudson, *Casey, op. cit.*, p. 76.

30 Langmore, *Glittering Surfaces, op. cit.*, pp. 47–49.

31 Fred Williams, 'Bell, George Frederick Henry (1878–1966)', http://adb. anu.edu.au/biography/bell-george-frederick-henry-5192.

32   Maie Casey, 'George Bell in Bourke Street' in *Art and Australia*, vol. 4, no. 2, 1966, p. 166.

33   Christie's sale of estate of Peter Purves Smith, www.christies.com/ LotFinder/lot_details.aspx?intObjectID=4205918. The Caseys hung this painting in their home in Washington, along with Russell Drysdale, Rupert Bunny, George Bell, Peter Purves Smith and Mary Cecil Allen. For more details refer to Audrey Tate, *Fair Comment: The Life of Pat Jarrett 1911–1990* (Carlton, Melbourne University Press, 1996), p. 58.

34   Casey, *Tides and Eddies*, *op. cit.*, p. 66.

35   Cited in Langmore, *Glittering Surfaces*, *op. cit.*, p. 58.

36   Hudson, *Casey*, *op. cit.*, pp. 105–108.

37   Audrey Tate, 'Jarrett, Patricia Irene Herschell (Pat) (1911–1990)', http:// adb.anu.edu.au/biography/jarrett-patricia-irene-pat-12694; Tate, *Fair Comment*, *op. cit.*, pp. 58–9.

38   *Ibid.*, pp. 57–60.

39   *Ibid.*, p. 62.

40   Langmore, *Glittering Surfaces*, *op. cit.*, pp. 73–74.

41   Kay Saunders, *Between the Covers: Revealing the State Library of Queensland's Collections* (Sydney, Focus Books, 2006), p. 82.

42   Hudson, *Casey*, *op. cit.*, pp. 119–136.

43   Hudson, 'Casey, Richard', *op. cit.*

44   Cited in Langmore, *Glittering Surfaces*, *op. cit.*, p. 90.

45   Hudson, *Casey*, *op. cit.*, p. 145.

46   Tate, 'Jarrett, Patricia', *op. cit.*

47   Tate, *Fair Comment*, pp. 96–97.

48   Hudson, *Casey*, *op. cit.*, pp. 167–170.

49   Langmore, *Glittering Surfaces*, *op. cit.*, p. 126.

50   Grace Cochrane, *The Crafts Movement in Australia: A History* (Kensington, UNSW Press, 1992), pp. 83–86, 174–180; *Argus*, 17 January 1945; *The Age*, 17 August 1949.

51   Cochrane, *ibid.*, p. 148.

52   Tate, 'Jarrett, Patricia', *op. cit.*

53   Maie Casey (editor and compiler), *Early Melbourne Architecture, 1840–1888* (Melbourne, Oxford University Press, 1953). The book was reissued twice more.

54 *Argus*, 24 October 1953.

55 Langmore, *Glittering Surfaces, op. cit.*, pp. 130–131.

56 Maie Casey, *From the Night*, illustrated by Frances Burke (self published, n.d.). A copy is held in the Fryer Library, University of Queensland.

57 Tate, *Fair Comment, op. cit.*, p. 160.

58 Langmore, *Glittering Surfaces, op. cit.*, pp. 225–226; Pat's biographer, Audrey Tate, provides a different version of this decision, saying it was amicable and does not comment on Richard's funeral; refer to Tate, *Fair Comment, op. cit.*, p. 160.

Chapter 11 Florence Broadhurst

1 *Sydney Morning Herald*, 1 April 1954.

2 Resolutions, in Notebook, n.d. (but an earlier version in her handwriting indicates she was about fifteen years old), in Florence Broadhurst papers, ML box 2, 4145/2.

3 Helen O'Neill, *Florence Broadhurst: Her Secrets and Extraordinary Lives* (Prahran, Hardie Grant Books, 2006), pp. 1–5; Siobhan O'Brien, *Life by Design: The Art and Lives of Florence Broadhurst* (Sydney, Allen & Unwin, 2004). Readers are advised to consult these two excellent books for more details on Florence's life. Her papers in the Mitchell Library (ML) are fascinating, as she kept a detailed record of her professional life. Even when issues show her to be deceitful and negligent in paying her bills she kept them for posterity. There is, however, little on her personal life.

4 *Ibid.*, p. 5; Anne-Marie Van den Ven, 'Broadhurst, Florence Maud (1899–1977)', http://adb.anu.edu.au/biography/florence-maud-12812; the Florence Broadhurst papers in the ML box 2, 4145/2 contain many clippings from this period.

5 *Ibid.*, p. 5; *The Queenslander*, 19 November 1921.

6 See Winifred Ponder, *Clara Butt: Her Life Story* (London, George Harrap, 1928, reprinted 1978) for a comprehensive study of her remarkable career and life.

7 There are extensive newspaper clippings from the tour in her papers in the ML box 2; refer specifically to *The Eastern Mail*, Delhi (n.d.), *Penang Gazette and Straits Chronicle* (n.d.), *Malay Mail*, 17 February 1923, *Bangkok Daily Mail*, 26 March 1923. All articles were enthusiastic about her talents.

8   O'Neill, *op. cit.*, pp. 9–10.

9   *Ibid.*, p. 15.

10   *Ibid.*, pp. 15–18; Van den Ven, *op. cit.*

11   Van den Ven, *op. cit.*

12   Brochures of the Broadhurst Academy are contained in her papers, ML box 2, 4145/2, as well as newspaper coverage which highlighted the talents of the staff in each discipline.

13   O'Neill, *op. cit.*, pp. 22–23; refer to extensive coverage of the events in China in the *Bundaberg Daily Mail*, 23 July 1927, contained in her papers, ML box 1, 4145/1.

14   An anonymous newspaper clipping proclaimed 'Queensland Actress Seriously Injured. Car Overturns', *ibid.*

15   Lindy Woodhead, *War Paint: Elizabeth Arden and Helena Rubinstein: Their Lives, Their Times, Their Rivalry* (London, Virago, 2004, first published 2003), pp. 83–84; Cecil Beaton, *The Glass of Fashion* (London, Weidenfeld & Nicholson, 1954), p. 32. Beaton is catty and snide about Lucile's clothes which he saw as far too feminine and flouncy. Her sister was Elinor Glyn the bestselling author.

16   Letter W. W. Reville-Terry to Florence Broadhurst, 24 January 1929. She worked on commission as indicated in this letter in her papers, ML box 1, 4145/1.

17   The letterhead of Mme Pellier states 'Design and Dress Consultant to Film and Stage', contained in Florence Broadhurst papers, ML box 1, 4145/1.

18   *Sydney Morning Herald*, 1 September 1936, an article by Mme Pellier on the subject of silk fabric; refer also to 'Tambour Beading Frame and Hook', www.powerhousemuseum.com/collection/database/?irn=9725.

19   O'Neill, *op. cit.*, pp. 35–37; Van den Ven, *op. cit.* Cecil Beaton surveyed this world in depth in his memoir *The Glass of Fashion*. In his account it would be hard to ever imagine that two world wars and the Depression cut swathes through wider society outside this wealthy, often titled, enclave of privilege.

20   O'Neill, *op. cit.*, p. 40.

21   *Ibid.*, p. 58.

22   Letter Christina Duncan, Australia House, to Florence Broadhurst, 5 December 1945, in her papers in ML box 1, 4145/1.

23 Licence to operate Slow Passenger Boat is contained in her papers, ML box 1, 4145/1; Van den Ven, *op. cit.*

24 Finney's Catalogue of Exhibition, 13–24 July 1954, Broadhurst papers, ML box 3, 4145/3; *Canberra Times*, 6 September 1954.

25 O'Neill, *op. cit.*, pp. 52–58.

26 There are numerous newspaper clippings in her papers in the ML stating she was English. The *Daily Telegraph*, 1 April 1954, described her as an English woman who discovered Australia.

27 *Sydney Morning Herald*, 18 May 1954; article by Andrea in *Truth*, n.d., contained in Florence Broadhurst papers, ML box 3.

28 Material is contained in the Florence Broadhurst papers ML, box 1, 4145/1. She organised the preview of Mme Lamotte's Winter Collection in Mrs George Falkiner's home in Bellevue Hill on 31 January 1968.

29 *Daily Telegraph*, 21 January 1958.

30 O'Neill, *op. cit.*, p. 62.

31 *Sunday Mirror*, 28 June 1964, noted Florence was the set decorator; refer to her papers, ML box 3, 4145/3.

32 Van den Ven, *op. cit.*

33 O'Neill, *op. cit.*, pp. 65–66. Some authors like Van den Ven and O'Brien write that she was married and divorced; O'Neill's research shows however that Broadhurst and Lewis were a de facto couple.

34 Palmer White, *Poiret* (London, Studio Vista, 1973), pp. 119–122. Poiret's business was far more comprehensive with rugs, carpets, furniture and fabrics.

35 O'Neill, *op. cit.*, pp. 72–73.

36 *Ibid.*, pp. 72–90; Van den Ven, *op. cit.*

37 Loan agreement between Florence Lewis [sic] and Hooker Finance, 17 August 1960, Florence Broadhurst papers, ML box 1, 4145/1.

38 *Ibid.*

39 Van den Ven, *op. cit.*; see also the numerous articles in Florence Broadhurst papers in ML box 1, 4145/1, for a fuller coverage.

40 Catriona Quinn, 'Best, Marion Esdale Hall (1905–1988)', http://adb.anu.edu.au/biography/best-marion-esdale-hall-12205; Penny Sparke, *Elsie de Wolfe: The Birth of Modern Interior Decoration* (London, Acanthus Press, 2005).

41   Letter Peter Hepham Clinic, London, to Florence Broadhurst, 2 May 1973, Florence Broadhurst papers, ML MSS box 3, 4145/3.

42   O'Brien, *op. cit.*, pp. 204–208.

43   'Go with the Flo', *Sydney Morning Herald*, 10 November 2004.

44   O'Brien, *op. cit.*, p. 15.

Chapter 12 Pamela Travers

1   Patricia Demers, 'P. L. Travers', *Dictionary of Literary Biography*, www.bookrags.com/biography/pamela-lyndon-travers-dlb; refer also to her biography, *P. L. Travers* (Boston, Twayne, 1991). Demers cites Travers' nationality as born in Australia; 'Pamela Lyndon Travers (1899–1996)' in Kay Saunders, *Queensland: 150 Years of Achievement* (Sydney, Focus Books, 2009), p. 176.

2   *Sydney Morning Herald*, 10 October 1940.

3   http://conservapedia.com/Mary_Poppins.

4   Valerie Lawson, *Out of the Sky She Came: The Life of P. L. Travers, Creator of Mary Poppins* (Sydney, Hodder, 1999), p. 191.

5   Cited in *ibid.*, p. 18; refer also to P. L. Travers papers, Mitchell Library (ML), Sydney, ML MSS 5341/2: Personal Papers. Her papers constitute an extensive archive accessible now to researchers on microfilm.

6   Janet Graham, 'The Cup of Sorrow in Every Woman's Life', *Ladies' Home Journal*, vol. 84, no. 2, 1967, p. 68, cited in Demers, *P. L. Travers, op. cit.*, p. 2.

7   Cited in Lawson, *op. cit.*, p. 6.

8   Raymond Evans, *A History of Queensland* (Melbourne, Cambridge University Press, 2007), pp. 118–130; Kay Saunders, *Workers in Bondage: The Origins and Bases of Unfree Labour in Queensland, 1842–1916* (St Lucia, University of Queensland Press, 1982).

9   D. S. Macmillan, 'Morehead, Boyd Dunlop (1843–1905)', http://adb.anu.edu.au/biography/morehead-boyd-dunlop-4240.

10   P. L. Travers, *New York Times* interview, 20 October 1962.

11   Jonathon Cott, *Pipers at the Gates of Dawn: The Wisdom of Children's Literature* (Sydney, Random House, 1983), pp. 215–216. Cott interviewed Travers for this publication.

12   Demers, *P. L. Travers, op. cit.*, p. 7.

13 *Southern Highland News*, 17 July 2009.

14 Lawson, *op. cit.*, p. 50.

15 P. L. Travers, interview with Michele Field, *Publishers Weekly*, 21 March 1986, p. 41.

16 Roy Norquist, *Conversations* (Chicago, Rand McNally, 1967), pp. 426–427. Pamela remarked to him that 'This was quite impossible in my kind of family at that time.'

17 *Ibid.*, pp. 52–60.

18 *Sydney Morning Herald*, 26 November 1923.

19 P. L. Travers papers, ML MSS 5341/14: Poems 1920s.

20 Roger Osborne, 'Vance Palmer: Short Fiction and Magazine Culture in the 1920s', *Journal for the Study of Australian Literature*, vol. 6, 2007, pp. 49–56. This article provides a solid overview of publishing in Sydney in the 1920s.

21 For more details on this remarkable man refer to B. G. Andrews and Martha Rutledge, 'Morton, Frank (1869–1923)', http://adb.anu.edu.au/biography/morton-frank-7667.

22 L. R. McLennan, 'Our Writing Grows Virile', *Sydney Morning Herald*, 22 April 1939. The most comprehensive study of her poetry is contained in Demers' 1991 biography, especially chapter 2, 'Apprenticeship as a Poet'.

23 P. L. Travers papers, ML MSS 5341/18.

24 Lawson, *op. cit.*, pp. 72–88.

25 P. L. Travers papers, box 2. She has several boxes devoted to his writings; refer to P. L. Travers papers, ML MSS 5341, add on 2130 1(2).

26 P. L. Travers papers, ML MSS 5341/22, item 21, interview with Janet Graham; 'Mary Poppins Chooses an Author', *Women's Mirror*, 19 June 1965, and *Saturday Evening Post*, November 1964.

27 P. L. Travers, 'On Not Writing for Children', *Bookbird: International Periodical on Literature for Children and Young People*, vol. 6, no. 4, 1968, contained in P. L. Travers papers, *ibid.*, item no. 8.

28 Lawson, *op. cit.*, pp. 90–93 has a good coverage of Mary's evolution.

29 P. L. Travers, writing from the Beverly Hills Hotel in 1961, reproduced in http://nationaltreasures.nla.gov.au/index/Treasures/item/nla.int-ex6-s28; material relating to Walt Disney MSS 5341/9. This includes letters from Julie Andrews.

30 P. L. Travers papers, ML MSS 5341/3 material relating to AE (George Russell) 1926–1982.

31 R. M. Kain and J. H. O'Brien, *George Russell (AE)* (Lewisburg, Pa., Bucknell University Press – Irish Writers Series, 1976).

32 *New York Times*, 15 February 1906, covered his resignation from *Punch* in some detail. He was an entry in the 1911 edition of the *Encyclopaedia Britannica*.

33 Review by Jason Blake, *Sydney Morning Herald*, 26 May 2009; see also Chelsea Cain, 'The Nanny Diarist', *New York Times*, 22 October 2006.

34 *Sydney Morning Herald*, 23 June 1934, noted her book *Moscow Excursion* (New York, Reynal & Hitchcock, 1934).

35 P. L. Travers papers, ML MSS 5341/3 material relating to AE (George Russell) 1926–1982 contains letters on her health.

36 C. Zilboorg, 'Orage, Alfred Richard (1873–1934)', www.oxforddnb.com/index/35/1101035322.

37 (Melbourne) *Argus*, 29 May 1937, review of Philip Mairet's biography of A. R. Orage (New York, University Books, c1966).

38 C. S. Nott, *Teachings of Gurdjieff: The Journal of a Pupil: An Account of Some Years with G. I. Gurdjieff and A. R. Orage* (London, Routledge & Kegan Paul, 1961).

39 P. L. Travers papers, ML MSS 5341/19, especially item 31.

40 Correspondence of Pamela Travers and Mary Shepard, Pamela Travers papers, ML MSS 5341/8.

41 Lawson, *op. cit.*, pp. 161–163.

42 *Ibid.*, pp. 173–175; P. L. Travers papers, ML MSS 5341/19 papers relating to Gurdjieff.

43 Lawson, *op. cit.*, pp. 178–183.

44 *Ibid.*, p. 200.

45 Radcliffe College presented Pamela with a beautifully bound album of photographs as a memento of her stay. These are kept in her extensive papers in the ML 5341: Add On 2130 2(3).

46 Lawson, *op. cit.*, p. 307.

47 *Ibid.*, p. 348.

48 Letter to Dr Staffan Bergsten, 24 January 1988, P. L. Travers papers, ML MSS 5341 Add On 2132 1 (2) item 1. This series contains all her correspondence with Bergsten.

Chapter 13 Enid, Countess of Kenmare

1 Caroline Simpson, 'Chisholm, Margaret Sheila Mackellar (1895–1969)', http://adb.anu.edu.au/biography/chisholm-margaret-sheila-9742.

2 Frank L.Woodhouse, 'Lindeman, Henry John (1811–1881)', http://adb.anu.edu.au/biography/lindeman-henry-john-4022.

3 Pat Cavendish O'Neill, *A Lion in the Bedroom* (Sydney, Park Street Press, 2004).

4 *New York Times*, 20 October 1900.

5 Dominick Dunne, 'Memento Mori', *Vanity Fair*, March 1991, p. 169.

6 O'Neill, *op. cit.*, pp. 18–20.

7 Dunne, *op. cit.*

8 O'Neill, *op. cit.*, pp. 34–35.

9 Roderick Cameron, *My Travel's History* (London, Hamish Hamilton, 1950), p. 207.

10 O'Neill, *op. cit.*, p. 22.

11 James Fox, *White Mischief* (London, Vintage, 1998, first published 1982), p. 60.

12 O'Neill, *op. cit.*, p. 15.

13 *Ibid.*, p. 21.

14 Gloria Vanderbilt and Lady Thelma Furness, *Double Exposure: A Twin Autobiography* (London, Frederick Muller, 1959), pp. 126, 186–187.

15 *Ibid.*, p. 174.

16 O'Neill, *op. cit.*, pp. 38, 71–74.

17 *Ibid.*, pp. 46, 69, 81.

18 *Ibid.*, pp. 112–113.

19 Vanderbilt and Furness, *op. cit.*, pp. 305–307.

20 *Argus, Sydney Morning Herald*, 18 July 1941.

21 *Sydney Morning Herald*, 16 July 1936. Her marriage to Viscount Furness was extensively covered in 1933.

22 Robert Calder, *Willie: The Life of W. Somerset Maugham* (New York, St Martin's Press, 1989), pp. 209, 284.

23 G. M. Thomson, *Lord Castlerosse: His Life and Times* (London, Weidenfeld & Nicholson, 1973) gives a full account of this remarkable man's life.

24 O'Neill, *op. cit.*, pp. 141–161.

25 *Ibid.*, p. 20.

26 Cited in Dunne, *op. cit.*

27 Cameron, *op. cit.*, p. 220.

28 Martha Rutledge, 'Watt, Ernest Alexander Stuart (1874–1954)', htpp://www.adb.anu.edu.au/biogs/A120456b.htm.

29 Cameron, *op. cit.*, pp. 3–10.

30 O'Neill, *op. cit.*, p. 16.

31 *Ibid.*, pp. 305–350.

Chapter 14 Tilly Devine

1 Phil Dickie, 'Brifman, Shirley Margaret (1935–1972)', http://adb.anu.edu.au/biography/brifman-shirley-margaret-9580; 'The Queen of the Cross', *Sixty Minutes*, 18 April 2010, produced by Sandra Cleary.

2 Joy Hooton, 'Ruth Park: A Celebration', www.nla.gov.au/friends/ruth/award.html; Bruce Moore, 'Niland, D'Arcy Francis (1917–1967)', http://adb.anu.edu.au/biography/niland-darcy-francis-11242.

3 See 'Fifty Australians – Tilly Devine', www.awm.gov.au/exhibitions/fiftyaustralians/15.asp; Australian Women's Register, www.womenaustralia.info/biogs/AWE2105b.htm.

4 Pauline Askin, 'Ruthless, Real: Sydney Showcases its Criminal Women', www.reuters.com/article/2009/03/17/us-exhibitions-criminals-women-idUSTRES2G0W020090317.

5 Peter Ackroyd, *London: The Biography* (London, Chatto & Windus, 2000), pp. 691–692.

6 Refer to the London School of Economics, Charles Booth Online Archives, 'Poverty Map of London' section for more information, http://booth.lse.ac.uk.

7 Cited in Larry Writer, *Tilly Devine, Kate Leigh and the Razor Gangs* (Sydney, Macmillan, 2001), p. 19. This publication is an excellent reference for the larger story of these two women's careers in gangland.

8 *Ibid.*, p. 22.

9   *Ibid.*, pp. 22–25; Judith Allen, *Sex and Secrets: Crimes Involving Women* (Melbourne, Oxford University Press, 1990), p. 168.

10   *Ibid.*, p. 26.

11   Allen, *op. cit.*, p. 169.

12   Writer, *op. cit.*, p. 29.

13   Lucy Hughes Turnbull, *Sydney: Biography of a City* (Sydney, Random House Australia, 1999), p. 352; there had been earlier reforms like the *Amended Vagrancy Act* of 1905, the *Gaming and Betting Act* of 1906, the *Police Offenders Act* of 1908 and all contributed to a rise in criminal networks that police could not control or monitor. See also Alfred W. McCoy, 'Two Cities and Their Syndicates: A Comparative Urban History of Organised Crime' in Jim Davidson (ed.), *The Sydney – Melbourne Book* (Sydney, Allen & Unwin, 1986), pp. 104–105; and his book *Drug Traffic: Narcotics and Organised Crime in Australia* (Sydney, Harper & Row, 1980), chapters 1 and 2.

14   Judith Allen, 'Leigh, Kathleen Mary Josephine (Kate) (1881–1964)', http://adb.anu.edu.au/biography/leigh-kathleen-mary-kate-7164.

15   David Pennington, AC, 'The Need for a Rational Policy on Illicit Drugs', http://museumvictoria.com.au/lectures/read/980602/rational%20 policy%20transcript%20140799x.pdf.

16   Writer, *op. cit.*, pp. 30–31.

17   Allen, *Sex and Secrets, op. cit.*, p. 170.

18   *Ibid.*, p. 171.

19   *Truth*, 23 December 1927.

20   McCoy, *op. cit.*, p. 107.

21   *Ibid.*; Allen, *Sex and Secrets, op. cit.*, pp. 172–173.

22   Writer, *op. cit.*, p. 95.

23   *Ibid.*, p. 97; Jim Devine was charged with the murder of fellow gangster Gregory Gaffney in August 1929. He was found not guilty on the grounds of self defence and protecting the life of his wife and the sanctity of his home.

24   *Ibid.*, p. 98.

25   *Ibid.*, pp. 113–114.

26   Allen, *Sex and Secrets, op. cit.*, p. 173. Meagher came to prominence when he defended George Dean who was convicted of poisoning his wife in 1895; refer to Martha Rutledge, 'Dean, George (1867–1933)', http://adb.

anu.edu.au/biography/dean-george-5929. There was a royal commission conducted into the case.

27 Writer, *op. cit.*, pp. 154–159.

28 *Sydney Morning Herald*, 23 April 1931.

29 Cited in McCoy, *op. cit.*, p. 107.

30 Writer, *op. cit.*, pp. 199–201.

31 *Sydney Morning Herald*, 18 June 1943.

32 *Ibid.*, 31 March 1943.

33 Writer, *op. cit.*, pp. 260–261.

34 *Ibid.*, pp. 255–257.

35 *Sydney Morning Herald*, 21 February 1945; (Melbourne) *Argus*, 31 March 1945.

36 Writer, *op. cit.*, p. 267.

37 'Study in Scarlet: An Uncrowned Queen of Slumland Drips with Diamonds and Charity', *People*, 15 March 1950.

38 *Canberra Times*, 7 November 1951, and *Sydney Morning Herald*, 7 November 1951.

39 Writer, *op. cit.*, pp. 300–303.

40 *Ibid.*, p. 311.

41 McCoy, *op. cit.*, p. 112.

42 Judith Allen and Baiba Irving, 'Devine, Matilda Mary (Tilly) (1900–1970)', http://adb.anu.edu.au/devine-matilda-mary-tilly-5970.

43 Writer, *op. cit.*, pp. 329–330.

44 *Ibid.*, p. 332.

Chapter 15 Sunday Reed

1 J. R. Poynter, 'Baillieu, William Lawrence (1859–1936)', http://adb.anu.edu.au/biography/baillieu-william-lawrence-5099.

2 Janine Burke, *The Heart Garden: Sunday Reed and Heide* (Sydney, Knopf, 2004), p. 13.

3 Paul de Serville, *Pounds and Pedigrees: The Upper Class in Victoria 1850–80* (Melbourne, Oxford University Press, 1991), pp. 269, 289, 304–305.

4 Burke, *op. cit.*, p. 12.

5 E. M. Robbe, *Early History of Toorak and District* (Melbourne, Robertson & Muller, 1934).

6   www.stcatherines.net.au/110-years.

7   Burke, *op. cit.*, p. 29.

8   Ann E. Galbally, 'Streeton, Arthur Ernest (1867–1943)', http://adb.anu. edu.au/biography/streeton-arthur-ernest-8697; see Ann E. Galbally, *Arthur Streeton* (Melbourne, Landsdowne, 1973, revised edn) for more details.

9   Burke, *op. cit.*, pp. 32–34.

10 J. P. Wearing (ed.), *Bernard Shaw and Nancy Astor* (Toronto, University of Toronto Press, 2005).

11 Burke, *op. cit.*, pp. 41–42.

12 *Ibid.*, p. 48.

13 *Ibid.*, p. 51.

14 Frank Cusack, 'Agnes Goodsir', www.daao.org.au/bio/agnes-goodsir. Goodsir painted portraits of Tolstoy, Mussolini and Bertrand Russell.

15 Sally O'Neill, 'Nolan, Violet Cynthia (1908–1976)', http://adb.anu.edu. au/biography/nolan-violet-cynthia-11251.

16 Christine France, 'Alleyne Clarice Zander', www.daao.org.au/bio/alleyne-clarice-zander. She was later Will Dyson's long-term lover after her husband's death from injuries sustained in World War I.

17 Burke, *op. cit.*, p. 91.

18 *Ibid.*, pp. 94–95.

19 Gavin Fry, 'Lawlor, Adrian (1889–1969)', http://adb.anu.edu.au/ biography/lawlor-adrian-7112. Lawlor was later appointed the art critic for the Melbourne *Sun* and *Art in Australia* after a bushfire destroyed his home and his collection in 1939.

20 Daniel Mandel, 'Atyeo, Samuel Laurence (Sam) (1910–1990)', http://adb. anu.edu.au/biography/atyeo-samuel-laurence-sam-12154. Cynthia, who did not enjoy an allowance from the stern Henry Reed, first worked for Ward before establishing her own business. Refer to O'Neill, *op. cit.*

21 Juliet Peers, 'Dyring, Moya Claire (1909–1967)', http://adb.anu.edu.au/ biography/dyring-moya-claire-10085. She married Sam Atyeo in 1941.

22 R. Dedman, 'Shore, Arnold Joseph Victor (1897–1963)', http://adb.anu. edu.au/biography/shore-arnold-joseph-victor-8423. John Reed in his interesting assessment, 'Artobiography', published in *Overland*, no. 101, 1985, wrote enthusiastically about the influence of George Bell and the original Contemporary Arts Society.

23 Mary Eagle and Jan Minchin, *The George Bell School: Students, Friends, Influences* (Melbourne, Deutscher Art, Sydney, Resolution Press, c. 1981), p. 174; M. E. Eagle, 'Purves Smith, Charles Roderick (1912–1949)', http://adb.anu.edu.au/biography/purves-charles-smith-roderick-8135.

24 Refer to Richard Haese, *Rebels and Precursors: The Revolutionary Years of Australian Art* (Ringwood, Penguin, 1991).

25 Burke, *op. cit.*, p. 133.

26 *Ibid.*, chapter 6 for more details; refer also to Brian Adams, *Such is Life: A Biography of Sidney Nolan* (Sydney, Vintage, 1989), pp. 38–39.

27 Poynter, *op. cit.*

28 Adams, *op. cit.*, p. 37.

29 Reed, 'Artobiography', *op. cit.*, p. 58. This is an invaluable article with a firsthand perspective on the creativity in art in the 1930s and 1940s.

30 Letters Sidney Nolan to Sunday Reed, September 1942, 8 November 1942, 29 March 1943, 2 August 1943, contained in Nancy Underhill (ed.), *Nolan on Nolan. Sidney Nolan in His Own Words* (Ringwood, Viking, 2007), pp. 113, 122–126.

31 Adams, *op. cit.*, p. 88.

32 Reed, *op. cit.*, p. 60.

33 *Ibid.*, pp. 40–46; Susan Wyndham, 'Was Sunday Reed the Hidden Hand behind Sidney Nolan?', *The Age*, 2 October 2004.

34 Janine Burke, 'Hester, Joy St Clair (1920–1960)', http://adb.anu.edu.au/biography/hester-joy-st-clair-10493.

35 Burke, *The Heart Garden*, *op. cit.*, p. 239. Her brother, Everard, inherited the property.

36 Michael Heyward, *The Ern Malley Affair* (London, Faber & Faber, 1993); Adams, *op. cit.*, pp. 75–80; letter John Reed to Max Harris, 25 February 1941, proposing the establishment of *Angry Penguins* in Barrett Reid and Nancy Underhill (eds), *Letters of John Reed: Defining Australian Cultural Life, 1920–1981* (Ringwood, Viking, 2001), pp. 200–201; letter John Reed to Max Harris, 30 March 1943, pp. 207–208; letter 21 June 1944 referred to the concoction of the poems, p. 325.

37 Cited in Burke, *The Heart Garden*, *op. cit.*, p. 256.

38 In a letter to Joy Hester in December 1947, Sunday wrote casually, '[D]id you hear from Nolan?' In January 1948 Joy reported that 'Nolan

seems to love Sydney and says she must have been blind when he was here before …' Janine Burke (ed.), *Dear Sun: The Letters of Joy Hester to Sunday Reed* (Melbourne, William Heinemann Australia, 1995), pp. 134, 143.

39 *Ibid.*, p. 143.

40 'Joy Hester and Friends' exhibition in the National Gallery of Australia, 2001, www.nga.gov.au/Hester.

41 Adams, *op. cit.*, p. 233; Andrew Sayers, *The Oxford History of Australian Art* (Melbourne, Oxford University Press, 2001), p. 164.

42 Burke, *The Heart Garden*, *op. cit.*, p. 299; Reid and Underhill, *op. cit.*, pp. 461–464.

43 Letters John Reed to Albert Tucker, 23 July 1953, 9 December 1954, 15 March 1956, in Reid and Underhill, *op. cit.*, pp. 487–492, 501–504, 507–510.

44 Letter John Reed to Hugh Montgomery (Master at Timbertop, Geelong Grammar School), 28 June 1960, *ibid.*, p. 534; Burke, *The Heart Garden*, *op. cit.*, pp. 317–320.

45 Reid and Underhill, *op. cit.*, pp. 3, 17–19, 462.

46 Letter John Reed to Michael Sharland, December 1956, *ibid.*, p. 514.

47 Burke, *The Heart Garden*, *op. cit.*, pp. 340–344; Reid and Underhill, *op. cit.*, pp. 12–18, 512–513, 528–533.

48 Letter John Reed to Editor, *Herald*, 1 July 1959, Reid and Underhill, *op. cit.*, pp. 528–529.

49 Burke, *The Heart Garden*, *op. cit.*, p. 351, quoting an interview with Barrett Reid.

50 Letters John Reed to Pamela Warrender, June 1964 and John Reed to Sidney Nolan, 12 October 1964, in Reid and Underhill, *op. cit.*, pp. 600–602, 616–619.

51 Burke, *The Heart Garden*, *op. cit.*, p. 357.

52 Letter John Reed to Elwyn Lynn, 21 August 1965, in Reid and Underhill, *op. cit.*, pp. 650–651. This letter outlines John's grievances on the matter.

53 Burke, *The Heart Garden*, *op. cit.*, pp. 378–380.

54 Cited in *ibid.*, p. 404.

55 Letter John Reed to James Mollinson, Director of the NGA, 27 January 1972, in Reid and Underhill, *op. cit.*, p. 765.

56   Reid and Underhill, *op. cit.*, p. 681. Mary Boyd married Perceval at the age of fifteen.

57   Burke, *The Heart Garden, op. cit.*, pp. 419–420.

58   Letter John Reed to Mary Christina Sewell, 27 August 1979, in Reid and Underhill, *op. cit.*, pp. 850–855.

59   Letter John Reed to Mary Christina Sewell, 4 December 1981, in Reid and Underhill, *op. cit.*, pp. 869–870.

Chapter 16 Rosaleen Norton

1   Nevill Drury, *Pan's Daughter: The Magical World of Rosaleen Norton* (Mandrake of Oxford, 1993, first published 1988), p. x. This volume is the most comprehensive assessment of Norton's life and career.

2   This 1949 psychological profile of Rosaleen is quoted in *ibid.*, p. 5.

3   Rosaleen Norton, 'I Was Born a Witch', in *Australasian Post*, 3 January 1957.

4   Drury, *op. cit.*, p. 11.

5   *Ibid.*, p. 47.

6   Noel S. Hutchinson, 'Hoff, George Rayner (1894–1937)', http://adb.anu. edu.au/biography/hoff-george-rayner-6696; see also Earl of Beauchamp et al, *Sculpture of Rayner Hoff* (Sydney, Sunnyside Press, 1934).

7   George Blaikie, *Remember Smith's Weekly* (London, Angus & Robertson, 1967), p. 88.

8   Kay Saunders, *Queensland: 150 Years of Achievement* (Sydney, Focus Books, 2009), p. 41, entry on Jim Case and Mollie Horseman.

9   *Sydney Gazette and NSW Advertiser*, 5 July 1842. The inn was already remarkable by this early date.

10   Lindl Lawton, 'Conrad in Australia', *Signals*, no. 81, December 2007–January 2008, pp. 11–12.

11   Drury, *op. cit.*, p. 17.

12   Leon Batt, *Not for Fools* (Sydney, W. Farrell, 1945).

13   Martha Rutledge, 'Deamer, Mary Elizabeth Kathleen Dulcie (1890–1972)', http://adb.anu.edu.au/biography/deamer-mary-elizabeth-kathleen-dulcie-5928; Stuart Inder, 'Farwell, George Michell (1911–1976)', http://adb.anu.edu.au/biography/farwell-george-michell-10159; Philip Butterss, 'Mudie, Ian Mayleston (1911–1976)', http://adb.anu.edu.au/biography/mudie-ian-mayleston-11192.

14 Rosaleen Norton and Gavin Greenlees, *The Art of Rosaleen Norton* (Sydney, Walter Glover, 1952). A supplement was issued in 1984.

15 Marion Dixon, 'McRae, William Alexander (1904–1973)', http://adb.anu. edu.au/biography/mcrae-william-alexander-11027.

16 Jemma Montagu, *The Surrealists: Revolutionaries in Art and Writing* (London, Tate Publications, 2002), p. 15.

17 Interview between Professor L. J. Murphy and Rosaleen Norton, 27 August 1949, cited in Drury, *op. cit.*, p. 30.

18 S. L. Cranston, *Helena Petrovna Blavatsky: The Extraordinary Life and Influence of Helena Blavatsky, the Founder of the Modern Theosophy Movement* (New York, Putnam, 1994).

19 A. J. Gabay, *Messages from Beyond: Spiritualism and Spiritualists in Melbourne's Golden Age, 1870–1890* (Carlton, Melbourne University Press, 2001).

20 Jill Roe, *Beyond Belief: Theosophy in Australia* (Kensington, UNSW Press, 1986).

21 Refer to Margaret Drabble (ed.), *The Oxford Companion to English Literature* (New York, Oxford University Press, 2000), p. 147.

22 Nevill Drury, *Dictionary of Mysticism and the Esoteric Traditions* (Bridgeport, Prism Unity, 1992).

23 Alan Richardson, *The Magical Life of Dion Fortune* (Aquarian Press, 1991).

24 See Mary K. Greer, *Women of the Golden Dawn: Rebels and Priestesses* (Rochester, VT, Park Street Press, 1995, first published 1985) for more details.

25 John Symonds, *The Great Beast: The Life of Aleister Crowley* (London, Rider, 1951).

26 P. R. Stephensen (with new introduction by Stephen J. King), *The Legend of Aleister Crowley* (Enmore, Helios Books, 2007, first published 1935). Biographer Nevill Drury believes that Rosaleen was particularly influenced by Fortune and Crowley, as these were the works available before the *Witchcraft Act* was repealed in the UK in 1951. Drury, *Pan's Daughter, op. cit.*, p. 137.

27 Drury, *Pan's Daughter, op. cit.*, pp. 38–47.

28 Rutledge, *op. cit.*

29 Mary Eagle, 'Dobell, Sir William (1899–1970)', http://adb.anu.edu. au/biography/dobell-william-10025; Jan Roberts, 'Latour, Loma Kyle (1902–1964)', http://adb.anu.edu.au/biography/latour-loma-kyle-10788.

30 Drury, *Pan's Daughter*, *op. cit.*, p. 54; refer also to *The Art of Rosaleen Norton* (introduced by Nevill Drury), (Sydney, Walter Glover, 1952, 1982 edn), pp. 9–11.

31 Drury, *Pan's Daughter*, *op. cit.*, pp. 55–70.

32 *Ibid.*, pp. 81–83.

33 *Daily Telegraph*, 7 October 1955.

34 Drury, *Pan's Daughter*, *op. cit.*, p. 87.

35 David Salter, 'Goossens, Sir Eugene Aynsley (1893–1962)', http://adb.anu. edu.au/biography/goossens-sir-eugene-aynsley-10329.

36 *The Times*, 14 June 1962.

37 Gary R. Thomson, *Great Short Works of Edgar Allan Poe* (Sydney, HarperCollins Australia, 2004) for more details.

38 Drury, *Pan's Daughter*, *op. cit.*, p. 86.

39 Gavin Greenlees reported this to Nevill Drury, in *ibid.*

40 Drury, *Pan's Daughter*, *op. cit.*, p. 88.

41 Rosaleen Norton, 'Witches Want No Recruits', *Australasian Post*, 10 January 1957.

42 Drury, *Pan's Daughter*, *op. cit.*, p. 94.

43 *Ibid.*

44 *Ibid.*, p. 96.

45 *Sunday Mirror*, 17 August 1975.

46 Drury, *Pan's Daughter*, *op. cit.*, pp. 102–108.

Chapter 17 Charmian Clift

1 Alan Atkinson, *The Europeans in Australia: A History: Volume Two: Democracy* (Melbourne, Oxford University Press, 2004), pp. 210–212, 304–5.

2 Nadia Wheatley, *The Life and Myth of Charmian Clift* (Sydney, Flamingo, 2001), p. 14. This is by far the most comprehensive account of Charmian Clift's life.

3 *Ibid.*, pp. 23–34.

4 Charmian Clift, 'Portrait of My Mother' in George Johnston, *The World of Charmian Clift* (Sydney, Ure Smith, 1970), pp. 80–81.

5 *Ibid.*, p. 32.

6 *Ibid.*, p. 85.

7   Charmian Clift, *Mermaid Singing* (London, Michael Joseph, 1958, first published 1956), p. 75.

8   Nadia Wheatley, 'Clift, Charmian (1923-1969)', http://adb.anu.edu.au/biography/clift-charmian-9764.

9   Wheatley, *The Life and Myth of Charmian Clift*, *op. cit.*, pp. 106–107.

10   Ruth Park, 'Nothing but Writers', *Independent Monthly*, September 1989, included in Donna Rath papers, ML MSS 6498/2.

11   Alan Ashbolt cited in Johnston, *The World of Charmian Clift*, *op. cit.*, p. 9. The original is in *Sydney Morning Herald*, 12 July 1969.

12   Martha Rutledge, 'Martin, David Nathaniel (1898–1958),' http://adb.anu.edu.au/biogs/A150372b.htm.

13   Wheatley, *The Life and Myth of Charmian Clift*, *op. cit.*, pp. 130–133.

14   Suzanne Chick, *Searching for Charmian: The Daughter that Charmian Clift Gave Away* (Sydney, Macmillan, 1994).

15   Wheatley, *The Life and Myth of Charmian Clift*, *op. cit.*, p. 153.

16   *Ibid.*, p. 155; it was republished in Connie Burns and Marygai McNamara (eds.), *Feeling Restless: Australian Women's Short Stories, 1940–1969* (Sydney, Collins, 1989).

17   Charmian Clift, 'Betrothing a Daughter' in Johnston, *The World of Charmian Clift*, *op. cit.*, p. 78.

18   Garry Kinnane, 'Johnston, George Henry (1912–1970)', http://adb.anu.edu.au/biography/johnston-george-2277. Kinnane is the author of an authoritative biography of Johnston published in 1986, *George Johnston: A Biography* (Melbourne, Nelson, 1986).

19   Cited in Wheatley, *The Life and Myth of Charmian Clift*, *op. cit.*, p. 190.

20   Cited in Park, *op. cit.*

21   This is taken from the manuscript of the novel and cited in Wheatley, *The Life and Myth of Charmian Clift*, *op. cit.*, p. 199. Underlining in the original document.

22   Kinnane, 'Johnston, George Henry', *op. cit.*

23   Ibid; Wheatley, 'Clift, Charmian', *op. cit.*

24   Cited in Wheatley, *The Life and Myth of Charmian Clift*, *op. cit.*, p. 212.

25   Park, *op. cit.*

26   Bruce Moore, 'Niland, D'Arcy Francis (1917–1967)', http://adb.anu.edu.au/biography/niland-darcy-francis-11242.

27 Refer to Kinnane, *George Johnston, op. cit.*, for this issue from Johnston's point of view.

28 Wheatley, *The Life and Myth of Charmian Clift, op. cit.*, pp. 275–288.

29 *Ibid.*, p. 379.

30 Max Brown, *Charmian and George: The Marriage of George Johnston and Charmian Clift* (Dural, Rosenberg, 2004), p. 89.

31 Valerie Lawson, 'A Place in Mind', *Sydney Morning Herald*, 4 May 1991.

32 Kinnane, 'Johnston, George Henry', *op. cit.*

33 Wheatley, *The Life and Myth of Charmian Clift, op. cit.*, pp. 420–423.

34 John Hetherington, 'An Australian Author Returns to His Native Land', *The Age*, 8 February 1964.

35 Brown, *op. cit.*, p. 215.

36 George Johnston, *The World of Charmian Clift, op. cit.*, p. 10. When I occasionally read her columns as a young woman working in the Department of the Army in Canberra in the mid 1960s, I entered an adult world that Charmian helped explain.

37 Park, *op. cit.*

38 Charmian Clift, 'My Husband George', *Pol*, no. 9, 1968, p. 85, contained in Rath papers, ML. *Pol* was a racy women's magazine edited by Richard Walsh that addressed important issues just before the resurgence of feminism. It was my secular bible for the new ways of thinking and living in the late 1960s.

39 Brown, *op. cit.*, pp. 196–197.

40 Kinnane, 'Johnston, George Henry', *op. cit.*

41 Chick, *op. cit.*, pp. 329, 341.

42 Wheatley, 'Clift, Charmian', *op. cit.*

43 Charmian Clift, 'My Husband George', *op. cit.*

44 Gary Kinnane believes that Charmian did not read the manuscript. He is at pains to show how Johnston gave a positive account of Cressida's doings. Kinnane, *George Johnston, op. cit.*, p. 273.

45 Wheatley, *The Life and Myth of Charmian Clift, op. cit.*, p. 616.

Chapter 18 Lillian Roxon

1 Lillian Roxon later stated that 'Germaine Greer and her double-edged dedication changed my life and is she proud of herself? She's braver,

crueller and bawdier than I'll ever be, also more generous and patient,'
cited in Anne Coombs, *Sex and Anarchy: The Life and Death of the Sydney Push* (Ringwood, Viking, 1996), p. 218.

2   Jim Derogatis, *Let it Blurt: The Life and Times of Lester Bangs, America's Greatest Rock Critic* (New York, Broadway Books, 2000).

3   Yvonne Sewall-Ruskin, *High on Rebellion: The Underground at Max's Kansas City* (New York, Thunder's Mouth Press, 1998).

4   Robert Milliken, *Lillian Roxon: Mother of Rock* (New York, Thunder's Mouth Press, 2005, first published 2002), pp. 13–17.

5   Libby Connors, Lynette Finch, Kay Saunders and Helen Taylor, *Australia's Frontline* (St Lucia, University of Queensland Press, 1993).

6   Milliken, *op. cit.*, p. 29.

7   See Barbara Blackman, *Glass After Glass* (Ringwood, Penguin Books, 1997); Kay Saunders, *Queensland: 150 Years of Achievement* (Sydney, Focus Books, 2009), p. 177; Patrick Buckridge and Belinda McKay (eds.), *By the Book: The Literary History of Queensland* (St Lucia, University of Queensland Press, 2007), pp. 60, 80; Charles Osborne, *Giving It Away* (London, Secker & Warburg, 1986).

8   Milliken, *op. cit.*, pp. 31–33.

9   Clive Moore, *Sunshine and Rainbows: The Development of Gay and Lesbian Culture in Queensland* (St Lucia, University of Queensland Press, 2001), pp. 121–133.

10   Milliken, *op. cit.*, pp. 38–39.

11   Coombs, *op. cit.*, p. 26.

12   See James Franklin, *Corrupting the Youth: A History of Philosophy in Australia* (Sydney, Macleay Press, 2003), chapters 2 and 8.

13   Cameron Hazlehurst, 'Bogle, Gilbert Stanley (1924–1963)', http://adb.anu.edu.au/biography/bogle-gilbert-stanley-9534; refer also to the section in Coombs, *op. cit.*, for more details, pp. 162–164.

14   Coombs, *op. cit.*, for more details.

15   Cited in Coombs, *op. cit.*, pp. 202–203; see also Milliken, *op. cit.*, pp. 53–55.

16   Cited in Milliken, *op. cit.*, p. 70; refer also to other assessments. Gerard Henderson, 'Left Right out of the Radical Push', *Sydney Morning Herald*, 4 June 1996, and Judith White, 'The Push for Freedom', *Sun-Herald*, 2 June 1996.

17   Letter Lillian Roxon to Aviva Layton, circa 1959, Aviva Layton papers, ML MSS 7869. Apart from the Layton papers, Roxon's archive in the ML is on closed access. My attempts to gain access during my research trip there in May 2010 were unsuccessful.

18   This novel is contained in Lillian Roxon's extensive papers in the Mitchell Library, Sydney.

19   Robert Milliken, 'Roxon, Lillian (1932–1973)', http://adb.anu.edu.au/biography/roxon-lillian-11577; Barbara Lemon, 'Lillian Roxon', www.womenaustralia.info/exhib/cal/roxon.html.

20   Coombs, *op. cit.*, p. 73.

21   Papers of George Clarke, 1932–2005, are contained in the Mitchell Library, Sydney. He was one of the authors of the City of Sydney Plan.

22   Kay Saunders and Julie Ustinoff interviewed his sister, Milly Goldman, in July 2004, researching a book on the Miss Australia Quest. Mrs Goldman spoke at length about her brother and his tragic early death. She and her husband, Dr David Goldman, named one of their sons in his honour. The family was from Lithuania and fled persecution as Jews in 1939. Like many other Jewish refugees they were well-educated professionals. He studied at the University of Queensland where he was editor of the student magazine, *Semper Floreat*. He later worked for the *Courier-Mail*.

23   Milliken, *Lillian Roxon, op. cit.*, p. 73.

24   Donald Horne, *Portrait of an Optimist* (Ringwood, Penguin Books, 1988).

25   Milliken, *Lillian Roxon, op. cit.*, p. 89.

26   *Ibid.*, p. 108.

27   Milly Goldman interview with Kay Saunders and Julie Ustinoff.

28   Letter Lillian Roxon to Aviva Layton, 27 May 1965, Layton papers, ML MSS 7869.

29   Letter Lillian Roxon to Aviva Layton, May 1966, Layton papers.

30   Danny Fields, *Linda McCartney: A Biography* (Los Angeles, Renaissance Books, 2000), p. 11.

31   www.sfmuseum.org/hist6/lindabio.html.

32   Fields, *op. cit.*, pp. 6, 11, 78.

33   Glenn A. Baker, 'Easybeats', http://nla.gov.au/nla.cs-ma-NAMO-3422.

34   *Sydney Morning Herald*, 4 March 1967.

35   Cited in Milliken, *Lillian Roxon, op. cit.*, pp. 147–148.

36 Lillian Roxon, 'Will Success Spoil Lillian Roxon?', *Quadrant*, January–February 1971, p. 60.

37 Tony Weinburger, *The Max's Kansas City Stories* (New York, Bobbs-Merrill, 1971).

38 Roxon, *op. cit.*, p. 61.

39 M. J. Taylor (ed.), *The Downtown Book: The New York Art Scene, 1974–84* (Princeton, Princeton University Press, 2006), p. 43.

40 Steve Watson, *Factory Made: Warhol and the Sixties* (New York, Pantheon Books, 2003), p. 206; refer also to Wayne Koestenbaum, *Andy Warhol* (London, Phoenix Books, 2001).

41 Fields, *op. cit.*, pp. 78–96.

42 www.economicexpert.com/a/Paul:McCartney:and:Wings.htm; *Sunday News*, 22 April 1973. I happened to see Wings on their Australian tour and concur with Roxon. The band was ill-assorted and Linda McCartney was not a musician but a strange figure that appeared uncomfortable on stage.

43 Fields, *op. cit.*, p. 171.

44 *Ibid.*, p. 172.

45 Milliken, *Lillian Roxon*, *op. cit.*, p. 179.

46 Lillian Roxon, 'The Other Germaine Greer: A Manicured Hand on the Zipper', *Crawdaddy*, 4 July 1971.

47 Lillian Roxon, *Woman's Day*, May 1971, cited in Milliken, *Lillian Roxon*, pp. 184–185.

48 Cited in Milliken, *Lillian Roxon*, *op. cit.*, p. 191.

49 *Ibid.*, p. 166.

50 *Ibid.*, p. 171.

51 Roxon, 'Will Success Spoil Lillian Roxon?', *op. cit.*, p. 63.

52 Saunders, *op. cit.*, p. 7.

53 *Sydney Morning Herald*, 4 October 1970.

54 Cited in Watson, *op. cit.*, p. 152.

55 Undated letter circa 1971 to Aviva Layton, Layton papers, *op. cit.*

56 Cited in Milliken, *Lillian Roxon*, *op. cit.*, p. 206.

57 *Ibid.*, p. 207.

58 *Ibid.*, p. 216.

59 *Ibid.*, p. 217.

60 *Ibid.*, pp. 220–221.
61 *Ibid.*, pp. 221–222.
62 Fields, *op. cit.*, pp. 172–173.

DEADLY
AUSTRALIAN
Women

*To
Donald James,
a brave, lion-hearted man*

Contents

Author's Note

In 1836 Charlotte Anley, a protégé of the prison reformer Elizabeth Fry, undertook a tour of the convict colonies of Australia to determine the condition of those transported and exiled. Her cousins William and Henry Dumaresq were prominent free settlers, with William initially serving as private secretary to New South Wales's Governor Ralph Darling and later appointed as a Legislative Councillor.[1] On her tour of the Parramatta Female Factory, which was used to incarcerate recidivists and women deemed too unruly to work as assigned servants on farms, Anley encountered two young prisoners who had been sentenced to life imprisonment for contributing to the death of their master, Captain Charles Waldon, a wealthy landholder and father of twelve children. They were, to the visitor, 'young and extremely pretty', though prison officials later told her they were 'both among the most refractory and violent' of the inmates. The encounter between Anley and Mary Maloney reveals many of the enduring Western cultural preconceptions concerning women and criminality, especially murder and killing. As Anley recounted:

> She and her companion [Sarah McGregor] were always
> pointed out as *murderers*, and they thought it hard that they
> could have no peace, but were 'hunted like wild beasts' for a
> crime they had never committed. I was afraid to irritate her
> by direct contradiction, but I ventured to say, that so serious a
> charge would hardly have been brought against them without
> some grounds. She repeated her denial of the deed, adding 'I

am *not* a murderer, for I never meant to kill the man. I was in liquor when we beat him as we did, but we couldn't help it that he died ...'

I replied 'I could readily believe an act of murder to be of awful passion, and not a premeditated crime.' Here she interrupted me, looking up with an expression of deep emotion, such as I shall never forget, and exclaiming, 'Then you do believe that' – 'Yes' I replied, 'I could scarcely think otherwise of a woman.'[2]

Anley maintained the belief about the essential nature of women that, regardless of their status or class, they were inherently incapable of murder and premeditated violence. This was not simply the mistaken belief of an evangelical reformer; rather, Anley articulated far wider cultural patterns of gender differentiation and their inherent characteristics.

By the following year, with the ascension to the British throne of young Queen Victoria, those notions of women's essential passivity, goodness, virtue and empathy assumed far more power and scope. By 1854 these beliefs were enshrined in the term 'the angel in the house', taken from a poem by Coventry Patmore. The picture was of dutiful and devoted wifehood and self-sacrificing loving motherhood located within the security of marriage, where gender roles were rigidly delineated.[3] The separate spheres which had developed from the Industrial Revolution were now exclusive territories; men and women came together only within the patriarchal home. This construction of the ideal bourgeois family was an immense distance from the lives of countless poor women, who struggled to exist. Even for many privileged women within the confines of the home where servants undertook menial domestic labour, the ideal of a loving and beneficent husband was also altogether absent. Reality was reflected in the law, which provided only limited options to sever the marital bond and deprived married women of property rights and custody of their children.

Despite its origins as mostly a series of convict colonies, these ideas flourished in colonial Australia, where notions of upward mobility and respectability took hold after the gold rushes of the 1850s. Thanks to the general level of comparative affluence, more settler women were located within the home. This development occurred despite other potent cultural and social forces. First, many women were poor and dependent upon arduous labour, often as domestic servants in the homes of other women. Second, without reliable female-controlled contraception until the advent of the oral contraceptive in the early 1960s, unwanted pregnancy and its consequences pervaded the lives of women of all classes.

Women's reproductive functions harboured the potential for calamity and ruin, especially for single women who found themselves pregnant. A network of underground entrepreneurs sprang up to address these individuals' adversities. Abortionists – often with little or no medical training – established lucrative practices, often under the guise of midwives. For backstreet women abortionists in particular, although the legal risks they ran were high, the remuneration and low overheads made up for it. Police attention to these illegal activities was largely concentrated upon those terminations that resulted in the patient's death, usually from blood poisoning. These illegal operations continued until the later twentieth century, when laws were changed to allow legal abortions under certain prescribed conditions.

Some desperate women who went through with an unwanted pregnancy later resorted to other drastic options. For the single young woman experiencing the stigma of unmarried motherhood and the inability to earn a living, infanticide could seem to be a viable option. It was not uncommon for domestic servants to be impregnated by the master or sons of the house and then left to face an uncertain future. Such illegitimate babies might be smothered or left unattended at birth, to be disposed of when the opportunity arose. As many of these births were unassisted and surrounded by secrecy, the possibility of discovery was diminished. One of the first cases in this book revolves around infanticide in Hobart in 1817. To bring the stories recounted in *Deadly Australian Women* full circle, the most recent major criminal trial examined in the narrative concerns Keli Lane, who in 2010 was found guilty of the murder of her newborn baby, Tegan Lane. This recent conviction harks back to nineteenth-century practices, when young unmarried women committed desperate acts that they hoped were invisible and undetectable.

For those vulnerable young colonial women who killed their babies and were caught out, should the law deem the act one of murder, the maximum penalty was execution. In reality this occurred haphazardly, and the lesser offence of 'concealing a birth' tended to be prescribed. Both the law and all-male juries often understood that the perpetrator was herself a victim of her circumstances.

By the later nineteenth century, the rise of a strong, organised feminist movement seeking to protect the rights of women and children ensured that public attention was directed to the plight of the young and unmarried filicide. The pronouncement of death sentences now caused public outrage as too harsh – especially when the absent father of the newborn escaped recriminations and prosecution. By the twentieth century, courts were taking into account biopsychiatric opinion about whether underlying medical issues contributed to the neonatal killing.

Before the introduction in the interwar years of legal adoption processes in Australian states, the practice of baby farming offered another solution to the unmarried mother who could not raise her baby. Many practitioners were caring married women who took in babies and small children to supplement their meagre household income. Others saw the opportunity to benefit financially from other women's misfortune. Babies and young children could be left in the care of a baby farmer, who would normally take a fee and a weekly subsistence allowance. That weekly stipend could be continued long after the baby had died either from gross neglect or from direct actions that resulted in death. Australia's most lethal multiple-killer, Alice

Mitchell from Perth, was responsible for the deaths of over thirty-five babies left in her care in the first decade of the twentieth century.

For mothers who killed older children, the law held no ambiguity. This was not infanticide – a category encompassing only babies. Killing one's own children, alongside killing parents, is the strongest taboo in Western culture. For a woman to kill her children defies every cultural notion of caring and nurturing. The image of the vengeful Medea, who murdered her children to take revenge on her husband, is a classic cultural depiction of the female monster who violates parental duty and accountability. Donna Fitchett, who was convicted of the murder of her two sons in Melbourne in 2005, gave a modern suburban twist to this archetypal portrayal. Recent research, however, suggests that many of these killers could not account for their motivation and described their actions as 'senseless'.[4] Their own traumatic childhoods, mental illness and substance abuse in many cases point to more complex explanations than evil or pure revenge. Since the mid-nineteenth century, firstly in the United Kingdom and subsequently in the Australian colonies, medico-legal expert opinion has been sought to determine the question of whether a convicted violent prisoner was mad or simply bad.

Other children have been killed by carers or babysitters entrusted with their welfare. Take sixteen-year-old convict nursemaid Mary Sullivan, who murdered an infant in her care in Hobart in 1852. The case was both repugnant and aberrant; Sullivan offered no explanation apart from her dislike of children. In 1980 Patricia Moore, an eighteen-year-old Sydney woman, was convicted of the murder of three children, including her own half-brother, and the attempted murder of two others.[5] After substantial if conflicting psychiatric evaluation was offered during her trial, the jurors decided she was simply bad, not mad.[6]

Husbands and domestic partners emerge as leading categories of victim, after infants and children. Reasons are varied. Before no-fault divorce was introduced in Australia in 1975, some individuals simply wanted to be rid of inconvenient spouses and inherit the marital property. Others, tired of their domestic situation and having met an attractive lover, conspired to kill the now redundant husband. The instance of Elizabeth Scott, the first woman executed in Victoria in 1863, concurred with this pattern.

Yet for other women in this book, the violence within their marriage coupled with the seeming impossibility of escaping their tormentor led to desperate acts. Despite the dramatic changes to women's legal, economic and political status from the late nineteenth century to the present day, the issue of domestic violence and what has come to be called the 'battered woman syndrome' persists. Power relations within the domestic unit have scarcely altered. Some women only escape when they eventually kill their domestic abuser. In 1991 this concept was first tested in an Australian jurisdiction in the Runjanjic and Kontinnen cases in South Australia.

The notion of women's essential goodness and innate nurturing capacity persists as a cultural image. Marsha Clowers, in her entry on 'Women Who Kill' in the *Encyclopedia of Crime and Punishment*, concludes that 'women and murder are [terms seen as] mutually exclusive. Females are expected to be victims, not victimizers.' Women commit far fewer murders, manslaughters and other unlawful killings than men. Their patterns also do not conform to the male model of the accidental 'pub brawl' death, where the victim and the assailant are complete strangers. Women rarely kill strangers, historically or in the present day. They overwhelmingly kill intimates, and often within the direct family circle.

Women who kill use firearms or fists far less frequently than men do. They are typically portrayed as stealthy killers, more likely to use poison within the domestic setting to achieve their deadly purpose. Plato suggested that, by nature, all women were given to secrecy and stealth. What he may have identified is a response to the powerlessness of women's familial role, whether in fifth-century BCE or in twentieth-century Australia. As Melinda Page Wilkins proposes: '[The female killer] is deceitful, nearly invisible to her would-be victims and the surrounding culture, and cloaked in the raiment of her gender.'[7] Her invisibility in the home going about her domestic activities, her sheer ordinariness, often hides a darker reality.

Several high-profile legal cases in the nineteenth century resulted in the execution of women convicted of poisoning their spouses. Louisa Collins, executed in 1889, was the last woman hanged in New South Wales, while Elizabeth Woolcock was the only woman ever executed in South Australia.

Martha Rendall was executed for the murder by poisoning of her three stepchildren in Perth in 1908. She was accused and found guilty of administering poison while pretending to render treatment for serious illness. Serial poisoner Caroline Grills, a motherly Sydney housewife, in the late 1940s and 1950s murdered three relatives and seriously harmed others by the use of thallium, which she dispensed in food and cups of tea. In the secrecy surrounding ordinary domestic rituals Grills killed over a number of years, her outward appearance of caring decency and motherly goodness belying her activities. She did not become rich from her crimes; she apparently simply enjoyed the power she had over her unsuspecting victims.

This book addresses the multiple ways in which women in Australia have killed others. *Deadly Australian Women* is not a book just about murder, which encompasses a legal definition of unlawful and wilful killing of another person with intent. The case of Audrey Jacob in Perth in 1925 shows the difference between killing and murder. On Wednesday 27 August 1925, with their fundraising ball at Government House in full swing, the organising committee of the St John Hospital was delighted with their social and financial success. Around 1am, in front of dozens of witnesses, Jacob shot and killed her sexually roaming fiancé. She did not deny killing Cyril Gidley, which would have been a rather difficult manoeuvre given the number of revellers who had watched her stride across the dance floor, pull out a revolver and shoot him. In her subsequent trial the jury found her not guilty of *wilful* murder and she was discharged. Her defence that this was an accident that she had neither planned nor intended was accepted by the all-male jury.

Rather than constituting a rarity, there are numerous instances where women in Australia have killed other people. I have canvassed cases from the earliest written records from the 1810s right up to the present day. As well as various historical periods, I have attempted a wide geographic coverage.

A vast array of primary sources is now available. Colonial newspapers from the earliest publication until 1954 are available online from the National Library of Australia's resource, Trove. Court proceedings were frequently reported almost verbatim and form an important depository of information. The case of Mabel Ambrose, whose body was discovered in a trunk in the Yarra River in 1899 – after she had been disposed of when her abortion proved fatal – was reported in detail not just in Melbourne but across the country. Some details were censored, however, as they were deemed not fit for public consumption.

The Macquarie University online series of colonial legal cases, while it repeats much newspaper coverage of earlier crimes, is another valuable resource. The Tasmanian State Archives provides an online service to researchers free of charge to investigate their files. Repositories such as state archives hold many files open to researchers. I used the Queensland State Archives to read depositions and follow the progress of a number of significant legal cases.

In this book, the changing legal and judicial framework in which trials were conducted is an important factor. Criminal trials until 1839 were held with military juries, after which male property-holders were allowed to act as jurors. Only in the mid-1950s did women come to sit on juries in criminal cases. Until the late nineteenth century, few defendants could testify in their own defence, even for capital offences. Earlier, in 1830, convict Mary McLauchlan was tried and convicted of murdering her newborn son without the benefit of counsel or legal representation. Her military jury unsuccessfully recommended mercy.

Later, defendants relied upon the services of barristers appearing for them pro bono. Not until the early years of the twentieth century did the states provide public legal counsel for poor defendants. With generally fewer financial resources than men, women accused of serious crimes were doubly disadvantaged. For, as Kathy Laster reminds us, often women were treated more harshly simply because they had not lived up to the ideals of stereotypical womanhood. 'Precarious politics, not law, determined their fate.'[8]

While a considerable literature on female killers and murderers is concerned with well-known cases, such as those of Scotswoman Madeline Smith and Myra Hindley in England, Lizzie Borden and Aileen Wournos in the United States and Jean Lee and Martha Rendall in Australia, I have not confined my attention so narrowly to celebrity murderers. This canon, much of it constructed in the 'true crime' genre, is highly illuminating within the scope of its particular parameters. Notwithstanding these examples of deadly women, many of those convicted of killing or murder were ordinary women and girls caught up in desperate situations that seemed insoluble except through violent action. While criminologists have attempted to categorise them within analytical frameworks, such as Black Widows, Angels of Death, Thrill Killers, Child Killers, Revengers, Missionaries, Profiteers, Quiet Killers (mostly poisoners) and Team Killers (with a sub-genre the Couple Killer),[9] many fall into the category 'unexplained'. Killing is both a personal and a public act which does not readily fall into analytical categories.

Recent commentators Lindy Cameron and Ruth Wykes, in their book *Women Who Kill: Chilling Portraits of Australia's Worst Female Murderers* (2010), propose that 'Trying to understand why women kill is … well, it's pointless. Women kill for many of the same reasons that men do – and sometimes it can be explained, and sometimes it can't.'[10] Motives for killing are indeed varied. As this book proposes, the consequences of women's familial roles when they become distorted and extreme are the triggers for many lethal encounters. Killing unwanted babies, trying to cope with children while in a mentally precarious state and retaliating against violent domestic partners all appear explicable once the individual's circumstances are interrogated. But many others, such as thrill killing, poisoning family members just for the pleasure of watching them suffer or killing children in one's care, are less easy to interrogate for motive.

Unlike popular novels and television series would appear to suggest, those convicted of major crimes like murder do not willingly confess. Indeed, authors such as Judith Knelman argue that in the nineteenth century women convicted of murder in Britain were far less likely to repent or confess than male offenders.[11] Even on the gallows, convicted murderers such as Mary Sullivan and Mary McLauchlan did not repent; the prospect of being judged harshly in the next world did not elicit a response from them in their silent stoicism. The modern-day case of Keli Lane, who although convicted of murder has never confessed to any wrongdoing, is no different. Such cases remain bewildering and impenetrable. The common-law legal system, which we inherited from England, requires the prosecution to prove its case 'beyond all reasonable doubt', not for the defendant to prove her innocence. Even today, defendants are not obligated to testify in their own defence.

My own interest in women who kill goes back to 1981, when I was appointed as an official visitor and advocate for long-term women prisoners in the Women's Prison at Dutton Park in inner-city Brisbane. Ironically, the prison sat next to the Queensland State Archives, where I had spent several years undertaking research for my doctoral thesis. As a divorced young mother and academic, entry into the world of a prison was confronting. Nothing prepares a middle-class woman for the experience, albeit even as a visitor who leaves. I admire the courage of Charlotte Anley back in 1836.

One of the inmates was serving a sentence for infanticide. Her hopes of marriage with the baby's father had been sadly unfulfilled. Many of the long-term prisoners were in for drug-related offences and had been prostitutes who started taking illegal drugs then selling them to support their habit. To a woman, they all despised the filicide, whom they simply termed 'the baby-killer'. She was never referred to by her name and she was excluded from the bonds of friendship and camaraderie that characterised prison life. Unlike a male prison, where 'thuggery and buggery' dominate the internal culture, a women's prison is run along emotional lines of inclusion and exclusion. To be excluded and shunned made prison life even more unendurable. This woman never sought my company or advice, though she could have done so readily. Nor did she approach the two cheerful Sisters of Mercy who ministered to the inmates. I have often pondered this woman's sad desperation and wondered what happened to her.

The Queensland prison service also contained the so-called 'Lesbian Vampire Killers' in Brisbane, from 1991, and Valmae Beck, convicted of raping and murdering a young girl in tandem with her partner, Barry Watts. Cases like these are not included in this volume – they require another volume to examine their motives, exploits and trials.

Emerita Professor Kay Saunders AM,
Official Historian,
Bond University

CHAPTER 1

Lethal Abortion in the Nineteenth Century

Sex has long been a lucrative business for entrepreneurial women, one way or another. Even during the supposedly puritanical decades of the Victorian era, courtesans and madams could earn fabulous sums selling sexual favours. But in the nineteenth century in England and the developing colonies of Australia, sex formed the basis of other more squalid business.

There has, of course, always been a flip side to the sex industry. Without reliable forms of contraception and with only a hazy idea of the reproductive cycle, unwanted pregnancies were not uncommon in the lives of nineteenth-century women of all classes. And the way of dealing with them depended also on class. An upper-class woman – or even one from the middle classes who had enough money and knew where to go – could, through the hushed network of whispered gossip, find a doctor who would be willing to help her. Acquiescent medical practitioners were able to offer more sanitary environments, the benefits of medical training and, later, anaesthetics such as ether or chloroform to dull the extreme pain of a termination.

But if a doctor refused to perform a termination, even affluent women had little recourse but to approach those nurses and midwives known to perform abortions, even though the risks of death were higher. Word of mouth or even carefully coded advertisements in newspapers could lead to these abortionists. Affluent women consulted the new 'male midwives', or accoucheurs – trained medical practitioners with more knowledge of anatomy and access to devices such as the speculum.

Poorer women, on the other hand, were forced to rely upon the age-old remedies of traditional midwives – the use of abortifacient herbs such as pennyroyal – or to run the risk of back-room poisons or implements of dubious safety to obtain abortions. Given the laws, practices and morals of the time, not only prostitutes but any woman who found herself pregnant had limited options open to her, particularly if she was unmarried. Unskilled wages were so low that it was often virtually impossible to raise a child as a single mother, let alone face the opprobrium attached to such a pregnancy. Terminating the pregnancy by one means or another was often the only answer to a desperate situation. Death was a frequent consequence of both childbirth and abortion.

In just one morning, a busy abortionist could earn the equivalent of several years of a domestic servant's wage. A working-class woman with little education or training and few skills could set herself up with almost no overheads. The risks were high, since the desperate women and girls who came to her might die from the effects of negligence, gross incompetence and filthy, unsterile instruments in dirty surroundings. Yet, despite the considerable hazards of this form of domestic entrepreneurship, the temptations to run an abortion business were great.

Procuring an abortion was initially not a common-law offence, and did not even enter the English statutes until 1803. Until the beginning of the nineteenth century, English cultural attitudes emphasised the importance of male reproduction. Anxiety passed from men's sexuality to women's reproduction. Whereas the law had no place in the bedroom to monitor the mechanical functioning of male ejaculations, suddenly women's reproductive capacity became the focus of harsh laws, repressive ideological imperatives and interventions because pregnancy provided a tangible physical and symbolic reality that sperm ultimately lacked.

Initially the new law against abortion did not receive widespread endorsement in legal or social practice. It took twenty years for the first case to be prosecuted in the Old Bailey.[1] The courts were not primarily concerned with the crime of procuring an abortion as such – instead, attention focused on whether the mother died following the procedure.

Then, in 1828, new legislation made the significant distinction between women who were 'quick' with discernible foetal movement – in which instance abortion was an offence – and those who were not. The House of Lords debate on the new Act was fully reported in New South Wales.[2]

Medical knowledge grew rapidly during the nineteenth century, and with it changes to relevant legal thinking, especially in the area of medical jurisprudence. For the first time the ethics of abortion – the harm to the foetus as well as to the woman – were taken into consideration. As early as 1823 Theodric Beck's *Elements of Medical Jurisprudence* addressed the issue, as did Alfred Swaine Taylor's 1836 *Manual of Medical Jurisprudence*, which contained sections not just on criminal abortion but also on concealment of birth. William Guy, Professor of Medicine at King's College, London, and a leading statistician, first referred to the term 'foeticide' (or criminal abortion) in his landmark and enduring treatise, *Principles of Forensic Medicine* (1844).

In 1861 the British Parliament enacted another *Offences Against the Person Act* whose provisions were followed in the Australian colonies (updating the Acts of 1828 and 1837), but the emphasis was on the use of poison and instruments to procure an abortion – both of which were far more dangerous, indeed lethal – rather than on the traditional swallowing of herbs. From this time, women who attempted to give themselves an abortion could now be prosecuted with a possible penalty of life imprisonment.

Despite these increased legal strictures, the justice system did not witness a sudden influx of cases under these provisions. The *British*

Medical Journal launched a spirited campaign against criminal abortion in 1868 to no avail.[3] The following year, Pope Pius IX issued his *Apostolicae Sedis Moderationi*, in which abortion was equated with murder. This had been an early Christian belief, but it had been reversed from the fifth century when St Augustine argued that an unborn child could not have a soul. Pius IX's 1869 papal bull radically changed over a thousand years of official Church thought. Even then, this represented a moral and theological conceptualisation and not a legal proscription in common-law jurisdictions such as the Australian colonies.

After 1828, with the enactment of the *Australian Courts Act*, all the laws of the United Kingdom were upheld before the tribunals and courts of the young Australian colonies. From the mid-nineteenth century, as self-government and elected representation began in the colonies, greater autonomy in the interpretation of the laws was accepted. This explains why penalties for performing an illegal abortion in the Australian colonies could be more severe than in England and Wales.

The first notable case to appear before the Australian courts relating to abortion with death as a result of negligence occurred in December 1882 when Elizabeth Taylor, a widowed abortionist from Richmond in Melbourne, was named in the inquest into the suspicious death of Mrs Margaret Robertson of West Melbourne. Initially, Mrs Robertson had visited Dr James Beaney. Known for not removing his diamond rings when performing terminations, 'Champagne Jimmy', as Beaney was also known, had been charged twice with the murder of a young woman in 1866 caused by an inept abortion. Though acquitted, Beaney's reputation as an abortionist persisted.[4] When Beaney refused to become involved in Margaret Robertson's case, Robertson consulted Taylor, whose abortion business was thriving.

On the day that Robertson sought her services, Taylor's house was full of patients, each paying some £20 for a termination; this fee was a domestic servant's wage for ten months. On returning home, Robertson was seriously ill. Dr Samuel Peacock was urgently summoned for a consultation. He was a noted wealthy abortionist who also charged £20 or more, depending on the financial circumstances of the client,[5] conducting his own women's hospital in East Melbourne. But there was little he could do for this patient, who was dying of gangrene.

In an obvious attempt to disguise the illegality of the situation before her death, Robertson told Peacock she had suffered a miscarriage, and that 'Mrs Smith' (the name she used for Taylor) was her nurse. Robertson's common-law husband cooperated with police, however, and identified Taylor as the abortionist who had caused his wife's death.

In her testimony at the inquest Taylor said she had run into Robertson, an acquaintance, in the Royal Arcade – off Collins Street in Melbourne – and Robertson had mentioned seeing Taylor's advertisement offering her services as a nurse and midwife: 'Elizabeth Taylor, Practical Midwife, Ladies' Nurse, consulted 10 to 4, 1 Waxman's Cottages, Bridge Street, RICHMOND.'

The inquest jury decided that Taylor was guilty of manslaughter and should stand trial. They also recommended that doctors submit accurate death certificates.[6] Despite the verdict at the inquest, at her trial in February 1883 – with no witnesses, no confession and a practice conducted in secret – Taylor was found not guilty of manslaughter after attempting to procure an abortion.

Mrs Taylor was again in the national news in 1886 with the coverage of her trial following the death of twenty-one-year-old Julia Warburton. Warburton, an actress, had recently finished an engagement at St George's Hall in Bourke Street. She and her siblings were orphans and her late father, Percival Warburton, a well-known theatrical manager, had left the family in straitened circumstances. The three younger children had been sent to the Home of Hope, a private institution for destitute children in Collingwood, and their stepmother worked as a nurse and companion to an invalid in Royal Park. With her stepmother's approval, Julia rented a room in a 'small and ancient cottage' in Young Street, Fitzroy, in preparation for her termination. The owner, Rose Calloway – known as Mrs Hamilton[7] – supplemented her meagre income by cooperating with Taylor in her illegal abortion business. Hamilton's compensation was low for she believed that she took very few risks.

Julia Warburton underwent an abortion on 20 July 1886. Within six days she was seriously ill, and on 27 July she died without having seen a doctor.

Mrs Taylor, when she went to check on Julia at Mrs Hamilton's house, claimed that the girl had died from blood poisoning after extensive drug-taking. Her immediate problem was how to obtain a legal death certificate signed by a consulting medical practitioner. Dr Samuel Peacock had been summoned but refused to produce the certificate – for an enlarged liver – that Mrs Taylor requested from him.[8] When notified of the young woman's death, police immediately became suspicious of the circumstances and arrested Taylor within twenty-four hours.

Taylor's solicitor was Samuel Gillott, later Lord Mayor of Melbourne and Victoria's attorney-general. With a large police court practice, he was also solicitor to Caroline Hodgson, 'Madame Brussels', the proprietor of two of the city's exclusive brothels on Lonsdale Street.[9] It is a testament to Taylor's earning capacity as an abortionist that she could enlist Gillott's services.

Professor Allen of the University of Melbourne conducted the autopsy on the now blackened corpse and declared that Warburton had succumbed to blood poisoning after an 'illegal operation'. When she heard the report of the autopsy, Taylor became desperate. She declared to her neighbours: 'I'm innocent. I knew of nothing wrong.'[10]

Taylor's protestations of innocence were rejected. Melbourne's coroner, Dr Richard Youl, hastily convened an inquest at Pepper's Victoria Parade Hotel. Born in Van Diemen's Land in 1821, Youl had trained in London and Paris, becoming Melbourne's coroner in 1854.[11]

At the inquest, details of the operation of Taylor's lucrative abortion network emerged.[12] Mrs Hamilton (aka Rose Calloway), the resident of the cottage in Young Street, feigned ignorance of Taylor's business and said that she regretted having rented out a room to Taylor for her clients' use. She testified that Taylor had asked her not to reveal anything when Dr Peacock was called in to attend her 'patients'. Taylor had told her that she would ask Dr Peacock to certify Warburton's death as rupture of the liver, paying him £50 for his services. He refused.

The inquest also heard that Taylor had tried to enlist the support of Dr Peacock, declaring that 'the girl is just dead. She has actually poisoned herself with drugs.' This was hardly feasible when Warburton died from gangrene. Peacock had warned her not to attempt to bribe him, which raises the question: had this occurred in the past? Peacock would certainly not have wanted to get involved with a midwife whose 'patient' had just died from an abortion. He had his own lucrative business to protect.

For her part, Taylor claimed that Warburton had gone to her (Taylor's) house in Richmond simply for a consultation with her as a nurse. As Taylor had never trained through the hospital system, this was unlikely; nor was she recommended by a doctor.

A neighbour, Annie Walton, told the inquest that on the day of Warburton's death Taylor had asked her to run a message, explaining: 'I am in trouble.'

After deliberations the jury decided that the injuries Warburton had suffered were not self-inflicted. Furthermore, Elizabeth Taylor had performed an illegal operation, the result of which caused the young woman's death. She was committed for trial after the inquest declared that she was guilty of murder.

Taylor was indicted for murder and the case was heard in September 1886 before Justice Edward Dundas Holroyd, who had trained at Trinity College, Cambridge, and at Gray's Inn, and was recognised as a jurist for his fairness and impartiality.[13] She was found guilty of murder, a crime that carried the death sentence.

In an appeal in late November to the Full Court, consisting of Justices Holroyd, Thomas à Beckett – nephew of former Chief

Justice William à Beckett – and Hartley Williams,[14] the case revolved around the distinction between murder and manslaughter. Taylor was represented by James Liddell Purves QC, who had studied both medicine and law in London,[15] and who, with instruction from Sir Samuel Gillott, formed an enormously expensive legal team.[16]

After considerable deliberation, Taylor was found guilty of manslaughter. With the jury's recommendation for mercy taken into consideration, she was sentenced to two years' hard labour. This was a light punishment, given that this was a case where death had resulted from gross negligence, which could have attracted life imprisonment or even the death penalty.[17]

It appears that despite her punishment, Taylor was undeterred on release. The profits from her enterprise must have been too high to be dismissed because of any moral qualms or fears of conviction. In June 1891 she again appeared in the Supreme Court – before Mr Justice à Beckett, who had heard her earlier appeal. She was indicted for the murder of Mrs Eliza Carter from Ballan, a small settlement 80 kilometres from Melbourne, following an abortion in May 1891. By word of mouth, Taylor's reputation as an abortionist had reached far beyond the boundaries of urban Melbourne into the rural districts.

In his testimony before the Royal Commission to Enquire into the Fall in the Birth Rate in 1903, pharmacist George Stevens testified that not only did women frequently consult him in search of abortifacients, but he was aware of the informal women's networks in rural areas that spread the identity and location of urban abortionists.[18]

The jury again found Taylor guilty, their recommendation of mercy no doubt reflecting an understanding of the desperation that drove women to call on her services during the decade-long Depression in the 1890s, when banks and businesses collapsed and unemployment was high, and even those who still had a job were forced to accept lower wages. Despite this recommendation, Taylor was convicted and sentenced to death.[19] On appeal, the sentence was reduced to fifteen years' hard labour.[20] Taylor was allowed early release.

In September 1898 she was arraigned once more on charges, this time before Justice Holroyd, concerning the death of a young woman named Mathews. Whether struck by remorse or guilt after her termination, this daughter of a local schoolteacher had committed suicide by hanging herself in the family home. Her mother, Mrs Walters, was now chronically depressed as a result. Taylor was found not guilty of the various offences pertaining to Mathews' death.

Justice Holroyd remarked with some sarcasm: 'You are an exceedingly unfortunate and very indiscreet woman. You know what I mean. You can go.'[21]

Taylor never again appeared in court. Perhaps the prospect of finding herself on the end of a noose was an incentive to close her once-lucrative enterprise.

Every capital city in the colonies contained a network of well-known abortionists. Some businesses were highly organised. In Sydney, for instance, an outfit in Elizabeth Street calling itself the British Medical Institute was the front for an elaborate termination clinic in the 1890s. None of the male and female abortionists had any medical knowledge or training.[22] On 3 October 1892 a detailed advertisement appeared in the *South Australian Register* alerting readers to the practice of Madame Melissa Harpur, a 'Lady Doctor' with extensive training and professional experience in England, Wales, Ireland, France, Germany, Scotland and America, as well as in New South Wales 'where no doctor has set foot'. At her consultation rooms, the advertisement continued, at North Terrace in Adelaide, she specialised in 'diseases of women' and could supply 'corrective pills' (code for supplying drugs to produce abortion). She also treated 'palpitations of the heart, restlessness at night, despair of recovery, anxiety, fear of death, nervous irritability, sluggish liver, epilepsy, coated tongue, varicose veins and consumption'.

Madame Harpur was not a registered medical practitioner in the colony and her long list of supposed areas of expertise was simply

'Madame Harpur' was just one of many aliases used by abortionist Melissa Harper. She became well known to the justice system because over the years several of her patients died. Image: *Barrier Miner*, 6 March 1897.

part of her cover as an abortionist. She went under various other names: Melissia Fairburn, May Fairbairn and Melissa Fairbairn. She was assisted in her practice by her untrained daughter, Elsie. Her husband, Dr Brierley Fairburn, *was*, however, a registered medical practitioner and on occasion collaborated in her practice. Additionally, he had had considerable legal training so he knew how to evade any police prosecutions.[23] He was regarded by his peers as unscrupulous and disreputable. He conducted abortions with Harpur on several occasions that came to police attention.[24]

Harpur made an excellent living out of her practice, often performing five abortions in a morning.[25] Five years passed without her attracting official notice. In March 1897, however, 'May Fairbairn, known professionally as Madame Harpur', was charged with the murder of Mrs Frances Blain from blood poisoning following a late-stage abortion. Blain was a married woman of thirty-four whose husband had gone to seek his fortune in the Western Australian goldfields. She sought assistance from Fairbairn when she was advanced in an adulterous pregnancy. Blain had suffered a wound in her uterus which became infected.

The accused was represented by the distinguished and expensive barrister and parliamentarian Sir John Downer QC, a notable conservative who nevertheless was a strong advocate of women's rights.[26] The Crown case acknowledged that murder had not been the intent but rather the death was the consequence of illegal procedures. Discrepancies in the evidence of Fairbairn's servants, even about the date of Mrs Blair's consultation, substantially aided her case.[27]

Expert testimony was given by Dr William Ramsay Smith, a Scottish physician and forensic medical specialist who came to South Australia as a pathologist and in 1899 was appointed city coroner.[28] He suggested that the deceased had died as a result of a wound from an incorrectly inserted catheter.

Presided over by Chief Justice and Privy Councillor Samuel Way, the trial was notable for Downer's expert cross-examination of the prosecution's witnesses. The court was overflowing with eager and curious visitors in the gallery, including many well-dressed women, some of whom spilled out into the wide corridors.

Way's explanation to the all-male jury of the distinction between murder and manslaughter was concise and erudite. After twenty-five minutes' deliberation, the jury returned a verdict of guilty of manslaughter. Mr Justice Way pointedly told the prisoner that she had escaped the penalty of a capital offence. He made particular mention of the fact that Fairbairn had not 'brought in a medical man' when the patient was obviously infected. Nevertheless, Fairbairn received a lenient sentence: three years' hard labour.[29]

In April 1903 Fairbairn was again committed for trial in the South Australian Supreme Court after an inquest into the death of a hotel cook Annie Holmes, the mother of a six-year-old child who lived in Victoria. The coroner, again Dr William Ramsay Smith, was aided in his deliberations by the presence of the attorney-general,

J. M. Stuart KC. In the nineteenth century, attorneys-general were active participants in cases before the courts.

The first witness was horse trainer Alexander Miller, a friend of the deceased. His testimony was somewhat contradictory. He said that Holmes had told him she had used this particular service several times previously. Madame Harpur's business had run for the previous two years from a house in Flinders Street; a prominent notice in the window advertised her services. Even though Miller advised Holmes not to 'have anything to do with Madame Harpur', he did, however, make inquiries on Holmes's behalf and, in fact, went to see Harpur.

Holmes was weak and ailing soon after her termination when she and Miller met at the Globe Hotel in Glenelg, where she worked and he resided. During their conversation Holmes admitted she had bled profusely although 'everything has come away'. Fairbairn had used an instrument which, for some unknown reason, Holmes took home with her and thus could later be used as evidence in the trial.

Nurse Bertha Stacey testified that she looked after Holmes at the hotel before taking her to the Adelaide Hospital in an ambulance. Local practitioner Dr A. P. T. O'Leary attended Holmes, who by then was haemorrhaging and suffering a high temperature. Further testimony from Dr A. E. Shepherd, the honorary gynaecologist at the Adelaide Hospital, confirmed her parlous condition, which had required more surgery.[30] But in the absence of antibiotics, there was little he could do for his patient.

Fairbairn was arrested on 19 March 1903 while Holmes was still alive in hospital. On the order of Mr Justice William Bundey, a former parliamentarian with a successful practice in criminal law, Fairbairn was escorted to the dying woman's bedside for a positive identification. Holmes died soon after. The inquest jury returned a verdict of death from septic peritonitis, caused by an abortion during which a catheter had been used by Melissa Fairbairn, otherwise known as Madame Harpur.

Judicial action was challenged by the prisoner's defence counsel, Rupert Ingleby, on several grounds. In the first instance, he argued, a hospital was not a site within the justice system; further, the prisoner did not have to incriminate herself; plus, the identification visit occurred on the Lord's Day, Sunday, 22 March 1903. In a hearing *in banco* – that is, with the full bench – consisting of the chief justice, Mr Justice James Boucaut, and Mr Justice Bundey, the matter was reviewed. The picture that emerged was one of judicial and administrative bungling.

Mr Justice Bundey made the revelation that he had been ill in bed when he was visited by the Crown solicitor, who urged him regardless to issue an order on the grave matter of Holmes's botched termination and impending death. This in itself was an extraordinary action, suggesting how keen the Crown was to prosecute. The Crown solicitor filed the required affidavits. The learned judge remarked that he had doubted even at the time of the Crown solicitor's visit whether it would be to good effect, since Sunday was not a day set aside for court business.

Dr Helen Mayo, the University of Adelaide's first female medical graduate, was a young intern in the Adelaide Hospital and charged with the care of Holmes. When the police rang her requesting she permit a 'visit' from the prisoner, she informed them that her patient was critically ill and declined the request. Dr Mayo's concerns were overruled; the police took Fairbairn to the hospital for a positive identification.

As a result of the legal technicalities raised by Ingleby, the matter against Madame Harpur did not proceed to trial, despite the inquest's findings and recommendations.

In spite of her narrow escape from formal prosecution in 1903, Melissa Fairburn (aka May Fairbairn) was the centre of another coronial inquiry in April 1908, once more headed by Ramsay Smith. Laura Tucker, a poverty-stricken twenty-three-year-old woman, died following a termination at the hands of Madame Harpur. Tucker's mother had been dead for many years and her blind father resided in a benevolent institution for the impoverished, so she had been self-sufficient from an early age, working as a domestic at the Adelaide Hospital. She had a young, illegitimate child, who was boarded out with a Mrs Harriet Markham.

The last time Markham saw her alive was on 7 April 1908, when she took an obviously unwell Tucker to the Wright Street residence of a Mrs Billingham, presumably Tucker's landlady. Miss Jean Mills, the supervisor of the Lady Victoria Buxton Girls' Club, an Anglican charity, was consulted for advice since she was an authoritative middle-class woman. She advised that Tucker was in urgent need of medical attention.

In her testimony at the inquest, Miss Mills said that she had asked the other women to leave the room so she might speak to Tucker in private. The stereotype of innocent spinster certainly did not apply to Mills, who showed herself determined and knowledgeable about the 'troubles' that beset women who became unwillingly pregnant. No doubt other such cases passed through her club. Tucker only admitted to having fallen heavily and denied being 'in a certain way'. Mills knew this to be a lie. Seeing that Tucker was desperately ill, Mills summoned a district nurse to attend her, and also made urgent inquiries for further medical attention.

As she was being readied to go to hospital, Tucker confided in the nurse, Theodora Sweetapple, that Madame Harpur had performed an abortion by using an instrument 'which she left in for a few days'. She had charged five guineas for the service, although the inquest revealed Tucker had only paid £3/3/-. When Tucker first became seriously ill she had stayed with Harpur and her daughter, Elsie, for several days before she was turned out, literally onto the street. Harpur warned her not to say anything about what had happened to her, and her parting words were: 'You go to your lodgings and you will get along all right.' Unlike Elizabeth Taylor, who attended to clients who became ill as a result of their abortions, Fairburn took care not to be directly implicated.

At the inquest the police stated that when they interviewed Tucker on her deathbed she was rambling from the effects of her fever. Inspector Edward Priest testified that the dying woman admitted she had been pregnant and had sought a termination at 'a certain place' where a woman and her daughter 'helped her'. She maintained that 'Madame' and her daughter had 'been kind to me', despite forcing her to leave the house and abandoning her near the cemetery. Tucker told the police that Cyril Jackson was the father but she had no idea where he lived or how to contact him.[31]

Immediately, a warrant was obtained for the arrest of Melissa and Elsie Fairburn. Inspector Priest returned to the hospital later in the evening with James Gordon, a stipendiary magistrate, and William Hall, the clerk of the Adelaide Police Court, who were there to record Tucker's testimony in the presence of medical staff. Tucker stated that she had procured an abortion at Madame Harpur's place, adding that they 'tried to burn my eyes out'. As her fever intensified, Tucker's narrative became even more confused and rambling and the doctor in attendance, Edgar Wells, stopped the proceedings. Elsie and Melissa Fairburn were arrested soon after, but both strenuously denied having any knowledge or acquaintance with Laura Tucker.

Dr Wells testified that he knew Laura Tucker because she was a maid on the wards at the hospital. He had questioned her when she was admitted and she told him she had been to see Madame Harpur. Tucker told him that she hoped to 'get well soon'. And she sang him a song. When the coroner questioned Dr Wells, he testified that he thought the deceased had very little idea of the court proceedings at her bedside, but that she had positively identified Madame Harpur.

The coroner reported the jury's decision that Melissa Fairburn and Elsie Fairburn were guilty of wilful murder, and both were committed for trial. At the conclusion of the inquest, the defendants' counsel, Rupert Ingleby, identified certain inconsistencies in the bedside vigil. Clearly, the deceased's accusations that her eyes were burned out indicated some level of confusion.[32]

The trial was set for 1 June 1908 in the Supreme Court presided over by Justice Robert Homburg, who had studied under Sir James Boucaut and Sir John Downer. However, in preparing their case, the police concluded that the prosecution did not have sufficient direct evidence to substantiate a charge of murder and so the trial was abandoned. This was the last time that Madame Harpur – under any of her names – appeared in the judicial system.[33]

A short time before Christmas 1898, the body of a young woman was found at South Richmond floating in a trunk in the Yarra River. Three boys out boating sounded the alarm after they opened the box, which had been tied up with rope and weighted down with a large stone. A decomposing body, 'quite nude' and with a shaven head, had been shoved downwards into the trunk.[34] The 'Body in a Trunk' was an immediate public sensation. The government offered a reward of £50 for information leading to identification of the corpse and a further £500 for information leading to a conviction of the killer(s).[35] A free pardon was offered to any accomplice deciding to provide queen's evidence.

The police decided to take the unusual step of decapitating the corpse and preserving the head in spirits to offer for inspection. Several dozen families ventured to the morgue to determine whether this was the remains of missing daughters. In addition, thousands of people, including parents with small children, also visited the morgue eager to view the gruesome spectacle.[36] A local satirical magazine, *Melbourne Punch*, published a photograph of the woman's pickled head and an accompanying article on 12 January 1899, a decision of poor taste and judgment unrivalled in the annals of Australian journalism.

That same day, Olga Radalyski, Travice Tod and Thekla Dubberke were arraigned in the Melbourne City Court in connection with the suspicious death of Mabel Ambrose, the girl in the trunk, whose mother had identified her head. Mabel had been just seventeen years old and had lived in South Yarra. A large crowd milled around Russell Street court during the arraignment, anxious to hear any salacious revelations about the mystery that had gripped the city over the summer. Three police officers had to be stationed to prevent the public galleries overflowing. Seven honorary magistrates sat on the bench, a mark of the importance of the case.

Thekla Dubberke, described as a pale young woman in a simple black frock with a gold cross at her throat, was the star witness; she had provided the police with vital evidence, denying that her motive was to obtain a reward. Constable Organ in South Yarra had made local inquiries, which led to Dubberke's involvement in the investigation. She was remanded for a week. Next, an older woman, 'Madame Olga', who was both deaf and nearly blind and looked 'wretchedly ill', and Tod, a young man in his twenties, were remanded in custody. Dubberke was taken under police escort to 73 Osborne Street, South Yarra, to assist the police with further inquiries.[37] The alleged perpetrators of the crime had been foolish enough to leave a card with this address in the box with the body. It was where Thekla Dubberke and Madame Olga lived.

That same day, 12 January 1899, a medical practitioner with rooms in the Prell Building in Collins Street was mentioned in the confession Tod supplied to police. Dr William Gaze MD LSA LMCP London MRCS was a principal in the Polypathic Medical Institute. Dubberke (or Beatrice Jamison, as Gaze knew her), he first alleged, asked him in mid-December to accompany her to a house in Osborne Street, South Yarra, where her 'step half-sister ... Madame something or other', was caring for a girl who was 'very ill'. He told her he never made home visits. Further conversation with his visitor revealed why the girl was dying. Gaze stated to police that he '... never had anything to do with cases of this sort'.

After consulting with an unnamed colleague, Dr Gaze visited the house in South Yarra, by which time the 'patient' was dead. Dubberke told him a local doctor had issued a death certificate. Gaze also told police that Tod, the deceased's lover, who had been present during his visit, had arranged to pay for the funeral expenses.[38]

The following day Gaze supplied another statement, in which he said he had had a conversation with Dr James Neild, a medical colleague he had never previously met, on the subject of the crime. This in itself was odd, since James Neild was a distinguished forensic pathologist lecturing on the subject at the University of Melbourne since 1864.[39] It was then that Gaze admitted that the 'patient' was not simply dead when he went to the house in South Yarra but already decomposing. The body lay on a bed covered in blankets and hot water bottles. He saw that she had been dead for at least a day and he believed that the ruse to keep her warm was to make him think the girl had just died.[40]

The police further interviewed Gaze, who now claimed he visited the premises in South Yarra merely as 'a personal favour to Dubberke' – this despite previously denying that he knew her well. He then elaborated to say that he had met her when she accompanied Madame Olga to his consulting rooms. Gaze further stated he did not consider these circumstances 'suspicious'. The *Argus* on 16 January noted that Gaze had opened his practice in Melbourne only two years previously, after moving from New Zealand, and had taken over the rooms of the former coroner, Dr Youl, a close colleague of Dr Neild. The police discovered that Gaze, reportedly, had been a notorious abortionist in Westport, New Zealand, where he also 'kept' a number of women.[41]

The Radalyski house in Osborne Street was soon a destination for thousands of curious onlookers, who crowded onto the street and footpath. Some went to look at the real-estate agency – located in the same street – where Tod was employed, as well as the home of Mabel Ambrose's mother, Mrs Ambrose (or Dissratia, as she was also known), in Grosvenor Grove. The public was so gripped by the case that the *Argus* continued to report on events occurring even 'within the last 2½ hours', especially as statements made by Dr Gaze showed him increasingly drawn into the web of accomplices.

On 16 January, Gaze finally admitted that he had indeed known Dubberke 'for some time' and that she had brought Mabel Ambrose to him for a consultation to determine whether she was 'in a certain condition'. This seems to suggest that such a visit was a regular occurrence, thus implicating Gaze in Madame Olga's abortion racket, although perhaps not as a surgical abortionist.

In a press statement issued on 16 January 1899, Gaze confirmed that Ambrose was pregnant when she consulted him the first time, but said he only saw her again when she was dead.[42] Gaze now admitted that in retrospect it was 'foolish not to have reported the matter to the police'.

Dubberke's testimony at the inquest further alleged the doctor had supplied an abortifacient and recommended the internal injection of Condy's crystals.[43]

The officer in charge of the investigations, Superintendent Brown, was keen to obtain a conviction. Police had had Madame Olga primarily in mind when they began their investigations after the corpse was discovered on 17 December 1898. She was already a well-known palm reader and fortune-teller in Melbourne, and women in this line of work were often a source of information for clients who wanted to obtain an abortion.

Madame Olga's Russian pseudonym belied her origins as Elizabeth Elburn, the daughter of the licensee of the National Hotel in Essendon. She had married a career criminal, Charles Boswell, who – on release from prison – established himself in August 1894 in Launceston as a masseuse and 'medical electrician' – another euphemism for abortionist – under the improbable name of Carlo Adolph de la Lebedur. He was in fact an abortionist, with Madame Olga acting as his 'nurse'. Neither had any medical training or knowledge. They relocated to Dunedin in southern New Zealand and set up as abortionists again, but Madame Olga returned to Melbourne in December 1896 with her daughter, Mary, after her husband went off with another woman.[44] At the time of her indictment in January 1899, Madame Olga had never been implicated in performing abortions in Victoria, although the police had had their suspicions.

On 20 January, Dubberke accompanied the police to the city morgue, where she identified the trunk in which Ambrose's body had been abandoned and the handwriting on the card bearing the address as hers.[45] This was the vital piece of evidence the police needed to link the body to the perpetrators. That the handwritten card had accidentally been left in the trunk was remarkable, but that it had then somehow survived the immersion was extraordinary.

Events moved swiftly as the inquest was convened on 25 January 1899 under the watchful and experienced eye of coroner Dr G. C. Morrison. It was a comprehensive inquest, with Crown prosecutor C. A. Smyth, Dr Neild as the forensic pathologist for the Crown, and barristers representing the three key witnesses. The *Argus* continued to relate proceedings in immense detail for the entire case. According to the report of 26 January 1899, 'Madame Olga ... was the only one who looked the part in the drama that was to be enacted'. She appeared depressed, staring into space, while her co-accused Travice Tod, the father of Ambrose's unborn child, appeared not to realise that this grave matter concerned him. Dubberke, on the other hand, smiled and seemed insensitive to the situation, 'an interested observer rather than the central figure in the case'.[46]

The deceased's mother, Mrs Dissratia, as she was now known to be, testified that her daughter had met Tod, their house agent, through her. Tod's counsel, H. S. Cole, immediately attacked Dissratia, who admitted that Mabel had been wayward and often absent from home. Later testimony revealed that her daughter was known as 'Dirty Mabel' and was a habitué of inner-city hotels – with the implication that she was a young woman of loose sexual morals. Worse was to come when Dissratia's younger daughter, only ten years of age, told the inquest that Tod had given Mabel a card on which were printed the words '73 Osborne Street'. This was the card in Dubberke's handwriting that had been found in the trunk. The girl gave her testimony with no understanding of the importance of this evidence.

The Crown now had the sequence of evidence to link the three suspected perpetrators, although it was not explained how Tod had contacted Dubberke, the chief instigator of the tragic events.

Undoubtedly local knowledge had been readily available on the whereabouts of abortionists.

Thekla Dubberke was next called to the witness box. The *Argus* dramatically reported that 'a strained silence which had prevailed from the first was, if possible, deepened and interest was intensified'.[47] Dubberke was only twenty years of age, yet, as the report continued, 'she demeaned herself as if she were twice that age'. She was favourably compared to experienced expert witnesses: 'calm, self-possessed, decided, keen to grasp the purpose and direction of every question, with a well-modulated voice, a correct and even refined articulation, a ready command of well-chosen words ... She might easily have been taken for a well-educated lady.' It turned out that she was an uneducated woman from rural Victoria, born to immigrant German parents.

Unfortunately, the newspaper did not print her direct evidence, as it was deemed to be too 'gruesome'. At the time, there was no such thing as a court reporter to take down the proceedings in shorthand as a court record. Thus, newspaper accounts were the most comprehensive public record of trials.

As the drama unfolded there was clearly going to be someone defined as an ogre and someone who would seem to be an almost innocent bystander, although, as events revealed, the persona changed. Dubberke portrayed herself as an upright citizen who waived her right to remain silent during police interrogations, anxious only to assist. The thought of the £550 reward and immunity from prosecution of course did not enter her head. Her composure in court remained 'unruffled', calm and persuasive.

Readers were assured that Dubberke had indeed identified the sequence of events undertaken by young Mabel Ambrose with such fatal consequences. Once more assuming the role of bystander, Dubberke described how she heard 'terrible screams which drew her to the room in time to see the dying girl laid back on the bed. Tod had left the house an hour before.' Her role, she claimed at first, was passive and at a distance.

Dubberke provided damning evidence against Tod, who she alleged had purchased two chains with which he intended to weigh down the trunk destined for the river. Several days later, 'Thekla' as she was now dubbed in the papers, had taken an emotional Madame Olga 'to the spot on the river bank where the trunk was despatched, hopefully never to emerge'. She went further and identified Dr Gaze of the Polypathic Institute as an accomplice.

According to Dubberke, 'Madame Olga' took up residence at 73 Osborne Street on 22 November 1898 when she leased the house from a builder, William Dixon. His later testimony at the inquest was that Madame had been accompanied by 'a young girl', whom he identified as Thekla Dubberke. Another 'girl' he could not identify had stayed there for around three weeks. This was undoubtedly Mabel Ambrose, who had been asked to perform household duties while undergoing procedures to effect an abortion. Another male acquaintance of both Radalyski and Dubberke could not positively identify Ambrose as the third woman he had seen them with.

When Dubberke (or Vera Orloff or Beatrice Jamison, as she variously called herself) returned to the witness box, she continued her role as the star of the proceedings. She said that she was a domestic servant who had known 'Madame Olga', then a palm reader, for only six months. Ambrose had come to see the palm reader seeking treatment for 'her certain condition'. Dubberke stated that Ambrose told her that Travice Tod was the father. He had promised to marry her, even though he was engaged to be married to a respectable young lady. Tod also supplied 'dangerous' drugs which caused Ambrose 'great pain' and uncontrollable retching. Dubberke, under cross-examination later, told the inquest she had advised Ambrose to consult an unnamed, well-known abortionist who was a medical practitioner, but Ambrose refused.[48]

Dubberke also attempted to obtain drugs from a pharmacist – initially unnamed – at the Royal Alfred Hospital to ensure an abortion for Ambrose. The pharmacist was familiar with the operations of 'Madame Olga'.[49] This implies that the latter had been practising as an abortionist, but until now no one had died as a result and thus she was unknown to the courts.

When the inquest reconvened on 2 February 1899, Edward Fisher, the dispenser at the Royal Alfred Hospital, stated that Dubberke had come to see him saying she had infected gums and needed drugs. He told her to consult a dentist.[50] He denied supplying ergot, a well-known purgative used to assist abortions.

Another witness, Robert Gabriel, an assistant at a 'Eucalyptus Oil Depot' in Chapel Street, Prahran, also testified that Tod had come to the business asking for ergot, admitting that it was to procure an abortion. 'Madame Olga was going to do the trick with a battery,' he confided, but this was the backup. Gabriel purchased ergot from Felton Grimwade and Co., a firm that manufactured chemicals. Tod returned several days later saying that 'it has not worked'. But all was well, he informed Gabriel, as Ambrose had run off with an unnamed man from South Australia.[51]

With no results after three weeks, 'Madame Olga' asked Dubberke to take Ambrose to consult Dr Gaze in order to get 'more drugs'. Gaze originally said he had refused, advising Ambrose to stop her 'treatments' with 'Madame Olga'. After this Ambrose was subject to an operation with the electric battery 'which caused her great pain'. When she died on 13 December, the ruse to obtain a medical certificate the following day from Dr Gaze was perpetrated. Clearly, Tod was desperate to get rid of his problem with Ambrose, using as many methods as possible to effect his desired outcome.

When no death certificate was forthcoming, the accomplices decided to dispose of Ambrose's body. Tod offered to bury it in the bush, but had to abandon the plan when he encountered difficulties hiring a suitable buggy. He then decided to dump it in the river. Dubberke and Tod placed the body in the trunk and then disposed of it in the river without realising that it would float to the surface. Concerned, Dubberke visited Dr Gaze the following day, under the name Vera Orloff, and told him what had happened. He told her that gases in the body would probably make it rise to the surface.

Under cross-examination from Gaze's barrister, Dubberke was forced to admit she was 'kept' by a man whose identity she refused to reveal. He did, however, have an office in the Prell Building, the same building in which Dr Gaze's rooms were located. It was delicately implied that the star witness might be a prostitute. Her positive portrayal in the press came to an abrupt end as more was revealed of her life and circumstances.

Dubberke was actually kept by three different men, each of whom thought he was her sole protector. She also admitted that she had sexual intercourse with other men. Gaze may have been a client since she revealed he sometimes 'gave me money'. Laughter broke out at the inquest when Dubberke then added: 'He said he might have me taught dispensing and typewriting.' She also stated he had given her unspecified 'medicine' (presumably an abortifacient) on one occasion.

Returning to the issue of the disposal of the body, Dubberke reluctantly revealed to the inquest that she had 'contemplated' cutting off Ambrose's hair and had suggested knocking out her teeth to prevent further identification. The body had had several lower teeth knocked out and had been shaven.

'Madame Olga's' defence counsel, Mr Levy, with a certain desperation after these revelations, suggested that Ambrose may have succumbed to an epileptic fit, which explained the use of the battery. Why it would have been deployed for epilepsy in Ambrose's uterus was left unanswered.

At the conclusion of the inquest Dr McInerney, William Gaze's counsel, added that his client had indeed supplied a 'harmless remedy in the case of a slight irregularity'.[52] This was the term used in abortionists' advertisements – they did not perform abortions, rather they simply relieved menstrual irregularities. The evidence pointed to Gaze as an unethical medical practitioner involved in the lucrative abortion business.

The jury retired to consider its verdict for just seven minutes. Ambrose had died of 'suffocation' at the hands of 'Madame Olga

Radalyski', with Dubberke, Gaze and Tod accessories before the fact. They were all committed for trial at the Victorian Supreme Court. This was despite Dubberke's cooperation with police inquiries and her belief that she was therefore protected from prosecution. The police were commended for their strenuous efforts. Senior Constable Davison was praised for his foresight in preserving the decapitated head in spirits.[53]

The trial before Chief Justice Sir John Madden (1844–1918) began on 22 February 1899, with the gallery packed with well-dressed women fanning themselves in the heat. Radalyski was charged with wilful murder, and Tod and Gaze as accessories. Dubberke was the star witness for the Crown. Her evidence reiterated that given at the inquest and was again described as 'unrepeatable' for public broadcast.[54] No new testimony or evidence was supplied after the comprehensiveness of the inquest. Dubberke, however, asserted that she did not want 'Madame Olga' imprisoned for 'concealing a body' if Tod escaped prosecution. This had been her motive for turning queen's evidence.[55]

At the conclusion of the trial Gaze was acquitted, although his medical practice was now ruined. He had hired Sir Frank Gavan Duffy,[56] who was to be appointed in 1913 as Justice and in 1931 as Chief Justice of the High Court. He was an outstanding orator in the courtroom, a service for which his clients paid dearly. Radalyski and Tod were found guilty of murder, with a recommendation from the jury for mercy since the defendants had not intended to kill Ambrose. Chief Justice Madden was not a sentimental man. He ignored the jury's plea for mercy and sentenced the defendants to death.[57] A week later Dubberke, now living with a Lutheran pastor's family, claimed the reward of £500. Constable Organ of the South Yarra Police Station also contemplated applying for the reward.[58] The matter was referred to the Colonial Secretary.

In the end it was Mr C. S. Pratt from the Prell Building in Collins Street who received the generous reward. He initially gave information to the police that led to their identification of Dubberke. No details regarding Pratt's source of information were forthcoming.[59] There was speculation that he was one of the unnamed men who 'kept' Dubberke. On 13 April 1899, the *Argus* reported that Charles Seymour Pratt had vacated his office and left the colony.

On 26 April 1900, the marriage of Thekla Regina Dubberke to an unnamed 'old admirer' was conducted in an unnamed Church of England parish. According to the newspaper account, dressed all in brown, Dubberke had two Anglican deaconesses as witnesses. The only other members of the congregation were 'two girlfriends and an elderly man'. Dubberke had sought refuge in the 'Deaconesses Home' and was now, as the Reverend Canon Charles Godby, rector of St George's, Malvern, revealed, 'truly penitent'.[60] What was not reported was that Dubberke had been admitted to the Anglican nuns' House of Mercy in Cheltenham, which had begun life as a home for wayward girls in Lonsdale Street.

For Tod and Radalyski, life did not proceed so promisingly. Radalyski wrote to her father on 27 February 1899: 'I may never see you again in life. Better had it been last year than I should have lived through this disgrace and horror. God comfort you my father and pray for your unfortunate girl and forgive me …'[61] The disgrace she referred to was clearly the death of Ambrose and the subsequent inquest and trial rather than her occupation as an abortionist. Radalyski's parents petitioned the governor to extend mercy, blaming her marriage to her criminal husband for all her misfortunes.

The Victorian cabinet considered the capital sentences on 19 March 1899. After extensive debate a recommendation was forwarded to the Executive Council asking that Radalyski's sentence be commuted to ten years' hard labour and Tod's to six years' imprisonment. Both condemned prisoners were told their good news as they sat in their cells awaiting the dawn on the day they were to be executed. Radalyski heard the news through an ear trumpet into which the prison governor shouted loudly. From that moment onwards, she disappeared from the public gaze.

CHAPTER 2

Lethal Abortion in the Twentieth Century

Australia entered the twentieth century a society obsessed by sex – or at least the results of it. Influenced by the Depression of the 1890s, there was a dramatic decline in the birth rate in Australia from 1891 – when married women typically gave birth to seven or more babies – to 1901 – when the number had fallen to five, a fact that prompted intense debate. Politicians, clergymen, journalists and medical practitioners fumed about 'racial decay' and 'race suicide' as they envisaged scenarios of a thinly populated bastion of British civilisation 'swamped' by the 'hordes from the north'. In cartoons and illustrations of the day, the new nation was frequently depicted as a nubile if modest young woman whose virtue was under siege from nefarious Asian interlopers intent upon rape and plunder. This collective anxiety reached its crescendo in 1903 when the New South Wales government established a Royal Commission to inquire into the decline in the birth rate.

Australian women were the targets of the commission's criticisms: it argued they were selfish in their desire to limit their families, initially by the use of contraception. The often hidden spectre of abortion and maternal death also moved from the shadows into the full light of public inspection and discussion.

In 1905 two sensational cases brought the issue into widespread public scrutiny again. In the Hobart Police Court on 30 August 1905, Dr Bingham Crowther, the scion of one of Tasmania's most illustrious scientific and medical dynasties,[1] was charged with the murder of Winifred Luttrell. His colleagues, Dr P. J. Godfrey and nurse Sarah Knight, also stood condemned. The postmortem revealed Luttrell had undergone an abortion a few days before her unexpected death. In the Supreme Court trial, heard before Tasmania's Chief Justice, Sir John Dodds (1848–1914), in September 1905, all the plaintiffs were found not guilty after the jury deliberated for just twenty minutes.[2] Given Crowther's background (his father, Dr W. L. Crowther, was well known as a surgeon and parliamentarian in Tasmania, and had briefly – in 1879 – been the premier), the finest and most expensive legal counsel represented the trio.

In the second notable case, the defendant was *not* a well-connected medical practitioner. Margaret Jackson, an elderly unqualified 'nurse', was arraigned on the charge of the murder of a young woman, Sidney Hanlon, who died of peritonitis after undergoing an abortion in Sydney. William Hanlon, the husband of the deceased, was found guilty of manslaughter for supplying the fee for the procedure, and sentenced to two and a half years' imprisonment and a self-recognisance of £100 upon release.[3]

At her trial the police produced evidence of extensive advertising by Jackson, with hundreds of pamphlets and cards offering abortifacients as well as other 'midwifery' services for 'irregularity'.[4] Margaret Jackson was found guilty of manslaughter and sentenced to six years in prison – with 'light labour', a concession to her advanced age.

When Jackson appealed her sentence, justices Henry Cohen, Sir William Owen and Robert Pring, all of whom were considered fair and humane jurists, quashed her sentence on technical argument.[5] At a time when public and official concern was focused on maternal deaths and the falling birth rate,[6] this was an unpopular decision. The Crown in turn appealed, taking the case to the new High Court of Australia, even though this august institution had primarily been established to determine constitutional issues. This appeal was heard by Chief Justice Sir Samuel Griffith and justices Edmund Barton and

LADIES!

The Special Diseases incidental to young, middle-aged, and old ladies.

IRREGULARITIES treated with entire confidence and success.

FEMALE PILLS,

for Irregularities and Obstructions. 10s. and 20s. per Box (extra strong). Guaranteed.

29 York-st, Wynyard-sq.;

Box 920 G.P.O., SYDNEY.

Dr. CARTWRIGHT'S

FEMALE TABLETS

Nothing causes Girls and Women so much Worry and Distress as Irregularities and Delays. These Newly-Discovered Tablets are a Positive Cure, even in the most obstinate cases of Obstruction.

Price 10s and £1 per Box (extra strong). Call or Write.

29 York Street, Wynyard Square, Sydney.

Bulletin, 7 November 1896.

Advertisements for so-called cures for menstrual irregularities – the 'cures' were really abortifacients – offered hope for women dealing with unwanted pregnancies.

Richard O'Connor, and the original conviction against Jackson was upheld.[7] In his opening remarks, Griffith did observe that criminal appeals from the Crown were unsuitable for his court's jurisdiction.

The matter did not end there, however. Jackson's counsel, Wilfred Blacket, moved for a *rule nisi* on the grounds of habeas corpus due to the defendant's re-confinement in Darlinghurst jail.[8] Subsequently, the Full Court of New South Wales ruled that she could be released, even though the Chief Justice had declared that Jackson had indeed been fortunate in the first instance not to be found guilty of murder as charged.[9] This was not in any way a precedent for lenient treatment of cases where a death occurred after an illegal abortion; rather, it was a ruling based on points of law.

In 1906 the New South Wales government established an inquiry into the operation of private and unregulated 'lying-in' hospitals, where so many illegal abortions were conducted. That year Octavius Beale, a commissioner on the 1903 birth-rate inquiry, funded a federal commission into the sale of secret cures, drugs and foods; abortifacients were clearly a target.[10] Undeterred by what he perceived as official hesitation, Beale continued his campaign, publishing an alarmist polemic, *Racial Decay*, in 1910.

Such admonitions from community and government leaders hardly deterred the lucrative abortion industry. The *Adelaide Register* of 4 December 1908 featured an article entitled 'Women and Tragedies', which dealt with one case of a lethal abortion and another of infanticide and domestic violence.

Florence Hope, 'a fashionably dressed woman of about forty years of age', was taken to the Melbourne watch house at midnight on 3 July 1908. She had been arrested in connection with the death of Bertha Whitford, a twenty-seven-year-old domestic servant, at The Hospital for Women in Melbourne on the previous 30 November. The daughter of farmers in rural Victoria, Whitford had gone to see Hope at her home in the expensive bayside suburb of Sandringham several days before her death.[11]

The inquest conducted at the city morgue was presided over by an experienced coroner, Dr Robert Cole. The famed pathologist Crawford Mollison had conducted the postmortem and he testified that Whitford had died from blood poisoning. Represented by Percy Ridgeway, a solicitor with nefarious connections and reputation, Hope was released on bail to appear in the Supreme Court in February 1909.[12]

The crucial evidence in the trial heard before Justice (later Sir) Leo Cussen concerned testimony taken by police at Whitford's bedside when she knew she had no hope of recovery. Apart from testimony from Whitford's sister, this constituted the only substantive evidence for the prosecution. Dying declarations in the case of homicide have a special place in English law and were (and still can be) regarded as the equivalent of a sworn oath. This exception to hearsay evidence law rested on the unfairness of secret offences going unpunished.

Hope was found guilty and sentenced to death despite the jury's recommendation for mercy. She appealed immediately with the Full Court of Victoria, which upheld the original sentence. Still determined, Hope appealed to the High Court on the grounds that the dying statement of the deceased was inadmissible evidence. The case was heard in the High Court of Australia by Chief Justice Griffith and justices Barton, O'Connor, Isaac Isaacs and Henry Higgins in March 1909. Hope was represented by William Schutt, who had been an associate of Isaacs and was later appointed to the bench of the Supreme Court of Victoria.[13] A majority indicated that the appeal should be denied.[14] Hope's only chance to avoid the noose lay with the Victorian Executive Council, which deliberated on 19 March 1909. The Chief Justice, Sir John Madden, in his role as lieutenant-governor of the state, presided at the meeting; the outcome was a recommendation that Hope's sentence be reduced to ten years' hard labour.[15]

✳

On 7 May 1910 police discovered the body of a 'neatly dressed girl' in O'Connell Street, North Melbourne. Isabel McCallum was not a girl but a domestic servant from Geelong, aged in her early twenties, who had died from haemorrhage, shock and peritonitis following an abortion. At the inquest conducted on 22 May, her fiancé, a blacksmith named James McCarthy, testified that he had wanted to marry McCallum and had pleaded with her not to undergo an 'illegal operation'. He said that, despite this, he had accompanied her to a house in Stanley Street, Collingwood, on 4 May. There he met Minnie Yee Lee, a herbalist from Ballarat, who assured him his fiancée was 'in good hands'. Present also was a 'heavily veiled', disguised woman, later revealed to be Clara Pennington. When he visited the house again on 7 May he was informed Isabel was dead and that he should 'keep his mouth shut or it will cause terrible trouble'. The abortion had cost £10/10/-. McCarthy was distressed not just by his fiancée's death but also by the apparent theft of her engagement ring.

Although they did not perform the lethal operations, Yee Lee and Pennington were sisters and both involved in an abortion business that clearly operated through regional centres and was linked into Melbourne. Yee Lee stated that she had given McCallum herbs at her practice in Ballarat[16] and, when questioned by police, both women admitted they had taken McCallum to the house of 'nurse' Elizabeth Downey on 4 May, and had then gone back to Pennington's home to have 'a cup of cocoa' before returning to Downey's later in the evening. They alleged that the deceased had asked them to return her engagement ring to her 'sweetheart'.

The coroner found Yee Lee, Pennington and Downey guilty of murder and committed them for trial. Clara Pennington's husband, Henry Pennington, was arrested as an accessory. Police Magistrate Cresswell granted the defendants bail.

Charges were dropped against Henry Pennington but Yee Lee, Downey and Clara Pennington stood trial on 20 June 1910 before Justice Sir Joseph Hood. He was the first Melbourne-born and -educated justice in Victoria, appointed in 1890 to the bench, and regarded highly as fair and logical in his judgments.[17]

Downey was represented by George Maxwell, considered the foremost advocate of the criminal bar in Victoria, whose fee matched his reputation and expertise.[18] James Purves KC and L. B. Cussen appeared for the sisters. Both were highly experienced, able and expensive counsel.

The Crown rejected arguments that Downey should be tried separately. Indeed, the prosecutor, Mr Woinarski KC (later Judge Woinarski), informed the jury that this was not a case of wilful murder where malice or revenge was involved.

Downey stated she had not performed an illegal operation and had merely taken McCallum into her home as 'an act of charity'. But McCarthy's testimony revealed how the unfortunate series of events occurred. He had written to Yee Lee at 6 William Street, Ballarat, although he did not explain how he knew she was an abortionist who could 'bring things right'. The 'medicine' was ineffective, so he inquired about 'an operation', which he was informed would cost £10/10/-. When he replied that he did not favour this action, Yee Lee wrote back that 'this was a great injustice to the girl'. McCarthy accompanied his fiancée to Pennington's home in Melbourne. Here he was reassured that Yee Lee had 'dealt with thousands of cases like this and had a doctor behind her'. Yee Lee telegrammed him initially that all went well. The use of letters and telegrams – albeit that they could be later used as tangible evidence – suggests that the abortionists were confident and highly experienced. When McCarthy returned to Melbourne, however, Clara Pennington informed him that 'your young lady's dead. She took a bad turn at nine o'clock, and died at eleven.' Some time later, McCallum's engagement ring was actually returned to him.

Justice Hood pointed out to the jury that while the operation was performed by Downey, the other two defendants were equally involved as accomplices. The jury found all guilty of murder, with a recommendation for mercy for Pennington. All received the death sentence and were admonished for 'carrying on an abominable trade for some time'. Many women in the gallery burst into tears when they heard the sentence, some even becoming hysterical.

It turned out that Downey had been in court on abortion charges eight times previously. On one occasion she had been found guilty and sentenced to death; the sentence was later overturned on a technical point on appeal to the full bench.[19]

Eventually, cabinet recommended that Downey serve life imprisonment, with Yee Lee given fifteen years' hard labour and Pennington ten years.[20] Downey died in prison in April 1912 after a stroke.

On Saturday 13 January 1923, newspapers contained a tiny item about thirty-one-year-old Frank Bonfiglio, who had been shot in the left arm and the back at 2 Burnley Street, Richmond, in Melbourne. The police discovered other bullet marks in the wall of the house. Bonfiglio was admitted to St Vincent's Hospital, where he was questioned by police.[21] His former wife, Hannah Elizabeth Mitchell, aged forty-five, had shot him, he alleged. Police arrested her.

These were the only details initially released. That a woman shot a man with a pistol was an unusual event in Australia at the time since women rarely used firearms here or elsewhere. Despite this, the tone of the article was very matter-of-fact. According to later newspaper reports, an unnamed woman had rung the Richmond police saying: 'I have just shot a man.' In Burnley Street they found Frank Bonfiglio, who had crawled to the next-door neighbour's house, from where Nurse Ilma Walters called the police.[22]

Walters was not the assailant. When Detective Frederick Piggott interviewed him as he lay in St Vincent's Hospital, Bonfiglio revealed that 'Nurse Mitchell' had shot him. Subsequently, Hannah Mitchell was arrested for attempted murder and then released on bail.

The lead-up to the story was complicated. It seemed that Bonfiglio and Mitchell had planned to remarry in November 1922, but Bonfiglio decided instead to go to Western Australia to re-establish himself as a marble cutter. While he was in Perth, Bonfiglio admitted, he had tried to extort money from Mitchell. Then, when he returned to Melbourne on 12 January 1923, he had 'come to her and asked for £500',[23] an exorbitant amount.

Aspects of the story seemed strange to the investigating police. Why would Mitchell be so eager to marry for what would be her fourth time? By law, however, spouses could not be forced to testify against each other in court proceedings. Exactly what Bonfiglio had over his former wife was not revealed …

Then the national newspapers of the weekend of 3 February 1923 were dominated by a story that was both gruesome and fascinating. In a feature entitled 'Body Thrown from Bridge', the *Sydney Morning Herald* carried the eyewitness account of Harold Sharkey-Boyd of West Melbourne, who had seen what he believed to be a body dumped into the Yarra River at 11pm the previous Thursday. A car stopped at Anderson Street Bridge, and 'two figures … emerged from the shadows, carrying a heavy object'. After apparently satisfying themselves that no one was watching, or so they thought, the pair dumped their cargo in the water and the car then sped away towards Richmond. Sharkey-Boyd was unable to recall the number plate. Within hours police were dredging the river, and eventually a heavy bag was discovered.

By this time hundreds of spectators had lined the bridge to watch. Their curiosity was rewarded: inside the bag Detective Sydney McGuffie and Detective Sergeant Taylor found the putrefying corpse of a young woman. Police reported that 'the legs were bent up' to fit into the corn sack. Inside there was another smaller bag, with the logo 'Victorian Portland Cement Company, Cave Hill, Lilydale'. Upon opening this, the police found a woman's skull, its brown hair slimy and entangled with ferns. This suggested that initially the body had been buried, then later thrown into the river.

Brisbane's *Courier Mail* that weekend emphasised that the body was naked as well as headless. Comparisons were drawn to the case of Mabel Ambrose (see pages 28–38) some twelve years before: could this be another instance of a lethal abortion?

On 2 February forensic pathologist Dr C. H. Mollison conducted the autopsy on the headless corpse, announcing it was impossible to ascertain the cause of death due to the severe decomposition of the body. Pupa casings caught in the dead woman's hair were an important finding. He noted, too, that the skull had no teeth.

This gave police an important lead in identifying the victim. A woman previously reported missing, Bertha Coughlan, had had all her teeth extracted by a dentist three years earlier, in 1920.

Based on the findings of the forensic examination, the police suspected that the woman's body had first been dumped in a gully in Coldstream, near Healesville.

Swiftly, Hannah Mitchell, a nurse from Richmond, was charged with Coughlan's death. The shooting of Frank Bonfiglio and the discovery of the young woman's body now began to seem connected. Newspapers ran the two items concerning Nurse Mitchell as one feature, even though reporters were yet to unravel the relationships and violent actions surrounding her.

From then on events moved rapidly. On Saturday 3 February 1923, Melbourne's city police court was crowded with spectators eager to follow the arraignment of Nurse Mitchell, her daughter Margaret (known as 'Queenie'), and Mitchell's sister, Margaret Milward, for the murder of Bertha Coughlan on or about 18 November 1922. It was Bonfiglio's allegations while in hospital the previous month that had ultimately led to the arrest of the three women; he was granted immunity from prosecution.

Detective Piggott submitted to the court that on or about 17 November, Coughlan had gone to Mitchell's house in Burnley

Street, Richmond. The following day, Mitchell and 'a man named Bonfiglio' went to Carlton to obtain a car. Two days later the car was driven to Coldstream in the Yarra Valley.

'The accused were smartly dressed and composed in their demeanour during the proceedings,' major newspapers reported. The local *Richmond Times* went even further, giving fashion details: 'Mrs Mitchell wore a frock of biscuit-coloured *crepe de chine* with a smart grey fur and a small hat decorated with oriental colours.'[24]

Despite their smart clothes and property in Carlton and St Kilda, the Mitchell women were aggressive and coarse. It was reported that Hannah Mitchell's daughter, Queenie, a nineteen-year-old student, threatened to shoot Bonfiglio – 'if you do any harm to my mother ... and I will shoot your son' – when he suddenly appeared on their doorstep on 12 January 1923. He returned later that night and joined Nurse Mitchell in bed for the evening. She shot him the following morning when he attempted to blackmail her. Journalists also noted that longtime residents of Richmond were standing across the road from the courthouse to watch Mitchell's appearance in court.[25]

Police had located the car, in which bloodstained carpet was found. It was owned by one of Mitchell's sons-in-law, although this individual was not implicated in any wrongdoing.

Mrs Milward admitted that she had been in the car when the body was dumped and had assisted her sister and Bonfiglio. At this point in the proceedings, Mitchell's solicitor, the notorious Percy Ridgeway, demanded to know if Milward was the police informant. This was overruled by the police magistrate.

Mitchell was remanded in custody while her accomplices were each released on £500 bail, guaranteed by Ridgeway.[26]

By Monday the Melbourne *Argus* of 5 February was able to fill in some gaps in the story, confirming that the corpse belonged to Bertha Coughlan, for whom police had been searching since 13 January 1923. (She had in fact been missing since 18 November 1922.) Coughlan was the twenty-eight-year-old unmarried daughter of a farmer, John

Coughlan of Hinnomunjie near Omeo. Her engagement to the local grocer had recently ended – the break-up triggered by the revelation that she was pregnant to a married farmer.[27] Relatives reported that Bertha had taken her broken engagement badly. She shredded her wedding dress and hid the remains in a drawer. Her former fiancé had left the tiny township suddenly.

Detective Piggott along with his team, including Dan and Warry, two black trackers, were searching bushland to try to match the ferns found in the sack. They were also trying to locate a gold brooch with the word 'Coughlan' engraved upon it. This was a treasured keepsake given to Bertha by the residents of Omeo in memory of her elder brother, James, who had died in the Great War. Bertha always wore this brooch.

The lengthy inquest into the death of Bertha Evelyn Coughlan, held in the Melbourne morgue under the direction of coroner Dr Robert Cole, began on 1 March 1923. Detectives Piggott and Edmund Ethell were key witnesses for the prosecution of the case. Piggott refused to divulge his informant's identity, although it could only be Bonfiglio and/or Milward. He told the court he had been informed that the body of the deceased had been moved several times, with the head removed from the body at a time unknown. The accidental finding of the headless body in the bag off the Anderson Street Bridge was 'a complete fluke', thanks to Harold Sharkey-Boyd.

Frank Bonfiglio was the star witness at the inquest. He recounted how his former wife, Hannah Mitchell, had come to visit him unexpectedly at Palamara's Richmond fruit shop on 18 November the previous year, asking him to accompany her to Caulfield racetrack. He reported he was not entirely comfortable about going with her since Mitchell had falsely charged him with 'cruelty' during their marriage. Her lover and solicitor, Percy Ridgeway, had collaborated on the charge, and Bonfiglio was convicted and imprisoned.[28]

Nevertheless, he did go to the races with Mitchell that afternoon – and she won £600, a considerable sum. He later returned to Mitchell's town house in Richmond, at around 9.30pm.

As usual, the downstairs bedrooms were filled with women, often four to a bed, crying and moaning – all Mitchell's patients who had undergone abortions. Unlike many abortionists, Mitchell provided accommodation and care after any procedure. In the sitting room, Bonfiglio got into conversation with a man, Horace Solly, whose wife was a patient. They simply could not afford a sixth child, he confided, saying Nurse Mitchell was their only hope.[29]

Suddenly Mitchell appeared, demanding Bonfiglio assist her to get a patient 'who has taken very bad' to the bathroom. In an upstairs bedroom a young woman lay in a pool of blood on a bed. With some difficulty, he and Milward got the seriously ill woman ready for another procedure. Mitchell performed a dilation and curettage on her without any painkillers or anaesthetic. Milward's son was asked to fetch the girl some brandy after forty-five minutes. Mitchell continued her work. Her next-door neighbour, Nurse Walters, came in at some time during the proceedings, the inquest revealed, and heard a 'glug of blood forming in the girl's womb'. The patient began to haemorrhage and was put back to bed. Mitchell was so exhausted that she retired to bed, telling Bonfiglio to keep her sister company.

At the inquest Bonfiglio stated that he asked Mitchell why she did not call a doctor. 'A doctor can do no more than I did to her,' she responded.

Milward continued giving the patient brandy, although it was clear she was dying. She told Milward she belonged to the Church of England and her name was 'Coug...' before she died. She was distressed that 'her boy' was not present. Her last words were: 'I feel so cold. Could you rub my hands, please? You are kind; you are so good to me ... I am dying.' Milward then went into the kitchen and had a cup of coffee with her friend, Mrs Florence Spicer.

Bonfiglio claimed he tried to wake Mitchell from her slumbers when he learned of the death. When she asked him later to help dispose of the body, Mitchell made it clear to Bonfiglio that she had successfully disposed of dead patients in the past with the assistance of unnamed accomplices with cars.[30]

Throughout the inquest, more came to light about the series of events that led to this terrible death. John Coughlan said he had reported his daughter missing in November and was not surprised to learn she had died. He could not remember her birthday but thought she was 'about twenty-seven or twenty-eight'; nor could he give a good description of her appearance. All he could really say was: 'She had not a baby face.'

Bertha had travelled to Melbourne seeking treatment for persistent earaches, and had stayed with her aunt. She learned of Mitchell's services through a network of men from her own district, including the local train driver and another, who paid for her confinement. This man was presumably the unnamed father.

It was startling how Bertha had learned of Mitchell since in other cases it was generally a tight women's network of information that was at work. Evidently men had their own network when needed.

The morning after Coughlan died, the inquest heard, Mitchell went to Nurse Laura Gidley's private hospital next door and spoke to Nurse Walters. On occasions, Mitchell passed on her clients. She told Walters that a patient with a *placenta praevia* (where the placenta expels before the foetus) had died. This was untrue – both Milward and Queenie Mitchell had seen the evidence on the blood-soaked bed. This was Mitchell's ruse to deflect any suggestions of incompetence or a failure to call a doctor.

When Mitchell returned home, she asked Mrs Spicer to locate a particular man she knew to be a 'fixer', who would dispose of the body for £300 or £400. The task proved fruitless since the unnamed man refused on this occasion to engage in any illegal activities.[31]

It was later that Mitchell borrowed her son-in-law's car and dumped the body at Coldstream, with the assistance of Milward, Bonfiglio and her daughter. They covered the stiff corpse with leaves and ferns but made no attempt at burial. Mitchell's only comment, as reported in the press, was that 'she will be eaten by some animal in a few days, and it will not be known who she is when they find her'.[32] At dawn they returned to Richmond and set about destroying all traces of Coughlan's presence, trying to decide what to do with her gold brooch and her engagement ring. Mr Solly was still waiting for his wife in the sitting room, unaware of the drama that had unfolded.[33]

A Mrs Lillian Mueller, described at the inquest as the person who had originally brought Coughlan to Mitchell's place, suddenly turned up to take Coughlan back to her home. She did not persist when told Bertha had already departed. It would appear that Mueller was acting as an agent for abortionists.

Another crucial witness, Mrs Emily Tucker of Prahran, told the inquest that Bertha Coughlan had stayed with her before going to Mitchell's place. Mitchell had turned up on her doorstep asking her to say that Bertha had been at her home on 20 November. As an incentive to change her story Mitchell offered her £500 as the 'other two would try to lay the blame on me'. Tucker refused.[34]

More sensationally, Margaret Milward's testimony confirmed Frank Bonfiglio's. Her chief point of difference was to emphasise that Coughlan had suffered a 'premature confinement', not an abortion. She also testified that she told her sister she felt guilty and would tell the police what had happened. It was after this that Mitchell arranged for three unnamed men to pick up the body from the gully and dump it into the Yarra River.[35]

Young Alfred Milward also testified at the inquest, reiterating his mother's account of the events that led to the death of Bertha Coughlan. Florence Spicer gave damning evidence, testifying that Mitchell had told her: 'Keep your mouth shut. You know people who talk can be silenced.' That was the last time she spoke to Mitchell, who was well connected in the Melbourne underworld.

On Friday 9 March, the coroner concluded the hearings, stating first that there was no possible doubt the body was that of Bertha Coughlan and, second, that Hannah Mitchell was guilty of murder, with Margaret Mitchell and Margaret Milward accessories to murder.[36] Within a few days, though, all charges against Margaret

Milward and Margaret Mitchell were withdrawn after they fully cooperated with the police.[37]

Despite this, in the hearing at the city police court on 12 March, all three women stood accused. R. Knight acted as police magistrate, with a bench of six justices of the peace. The police restated their willingness to withdraw the charges against the accessories. Hannah Mitchell was ordered to appear before the Supreme Court of Victoria on 22 March.

The Supreme Court case was heard before Justice Frederick Mann, who in 1935 became Chief Justice of Victoria. He was noted for his scholarly knowledge of the law and his sense of justice.[38] Mitchell was represented by L. B. Cussen, instructed by Percy Ridgeway. Cussen's defence was canny; he called Dr Richard O'Sullivan to testify that, given Coughlan's persistent poor health, she might have died 'from a natural mishap'. Precisely how ear infections were relevant to her death was not explained. Nurse Mitchell, in this scenario, was merely assisting a patient in difficulties.

Mitchell elected not to testify under oath but took the extraordinary measure of addressing the jury from the dock for over an hour.[39] Even with three participants giving evidence for the prosecution, she was found not guilty – a surprise, given the finding at the inquest that she was guilty of wilful murder.

Undeterred by her narrow escape from a possible death sentence or life imprisonment, Mitchell continued her lucrative business. She appeared in court again in September 1923, charged with performing an illegal operation on a single woman, Beryl Moreno. The case did not proceed.[40] In early November that year she was in court once more, charged this time with the murder of Mabel Hodgkinson, a married woman with three children, who died after an abortion on 28 October 1923. Ridgeway again appeared for her defence in the police court. Senior Detective Davey informed the court that he had interviewed Mrs Hodgkinson in the Women's Hospital. He had been accompanied by Mitchell, who was identified as the person who had performed the abortion that had turned septic. Mitchell was allowed bail of £1000 as well as a personal surety of £500.

At the inquest, Owen Hodgkinson, a house painter from Brighton, testified that he had not been in favour of his wife's course of action, although he had accompanied her to Nurse Mitchell's place in Burnley Street. Mitchell said she would help and would charge £15 as 'he is a poor man'. This amount was still more than a male worker's pay for a month. After the procedure Mabel Hodgkinson went to her sister's house. When her condition deteriorated, a medical practitioner was consulted and she was admitted to hospital. The coroner found Mitchell guilty of wilful murder and committed her for trial in the Supreme Court of Victoria on 15 February 1924.[41] At the trial, yet again she was found not guilty.[42]

A year later, Mitchell was once more charged with wilful murder. Eva Pitt, a married woman with a family, died after undergoing a procedure. She had provided the police with a statement identifying Mitchell as the person who had conducted her abortion. By then, Hannah Mitchell had become well known to readers across the nation. The *Brisbane Courier* on 10 March 1925 announced: 'Hannah Mitchell Again In Trouble'. At the inquest heard before the city coroner, Frederick Pitt testified that his wife, Eva Pitt, the mother of six children – the youngest of whom was only seventeen months old – had undergone an abortion performed by Mitchell on 29 January. The coroner pronounced Mitchell guilty of murder but allowed her bail of £500.[43] By 25 March, the Crown prosecutor had dropped all charges for this offence.[44]

On 11 January 1928, George Rosser, a young draper from Cowra in New South Wales, reported his wife, Inez Rosser, missing. He told the police he had accompanied her to a house in Richmond, where she had undergone an illegal operation. They had married on Boxing Day, even though she was pregnant to another man. In relation to this matter, Hannah Mitchell was arrested for 'using an instrument'. She denied the charge, although she did admit that she had met George Rosser.[45]

Rosser further told police that he last saw his wife on 2 January at Mitchell's house and she was 'seriously ill'. When he returned three days later, he was informed his wife had left after lunch and she was 'all right'. When he demanded to know what had happened to Inez, Mitchell simply told Rosser to go to the police if his wife was missing.[46] The police announced they would drag the river near Richmond.[47] Despite rigorous efforts, nothing was discovered.

After Rosser made his missing person's report, the police also searched the house in Burnley Street. No trace of Inez Rosser was found. A full description of the missing woman and the clothes she was last seen in was released. A week after that, the Victorian government offered a reward of £250 for information leading to the whereabouts of Inez Ada Rosser, 'dead or alive'.[48]

Initially, newspaper accounts of Rosser's disappearance were vague, referring to a missing woman 'with foul play suspected'. Soon, though, Nurse Mitchell's name was in the news[49] when, by February 1928, reporters discovered that Mitchell was again under suspicion for the death of a young married woman.

In the hearing before the Richmond Court, Mitchell was ordered to appear in the Supreme Court on charges of malpractice.[50]

The case was heard in November 1928 before Judge Williams, in a courtroom packed with enthusiastic spectators. Mitchell was represented by a former journalist, the successful and expensive barrister Thomas Brennan, only that year appointed as a KC. This time she chose not to use Ridgeway as her instructing solicitor but rather J. Barnett. It was a hard case to prosecute successfully with no eyewitnesses to the procedure and with no body. The jury deliberated for only an hour and found Mitchell not guilty as charged.[51] This proved to be her last appearance in the Supreme Court.

It can only be speculation that Inez Rosser died on the premises at Burnley Street and that her body was disposed of more efficiently than that of Bertha Coughlan. It was clear she had not joined her former lover, a naval officer. A year after the trial, police investigated reports that a young woman's body had been dumped in a mine at Korumburra in the Gippsland district; they got nowhere.[52] The whereabouts of Inez Rosser were never discovered.

By the late 1920s, attitudes to sex, at least to marital sex, were undergoing significant transformation. Dr Marie Stopes's publications *Married Love* and *Wise Parenthood*, both published in 1918, commended a new frankness. A palaeobotanist by training, Stopes was part of the movement that favoured planned parenthood and marital sexual compatibility, not simply for the benefit of the individual family but for the wider eugenic health of Western society. The eugenics movement, which was popular in the early decades of the twentieth century, believed that planned reproduction would ensure that preferred characteristics were strengthened in the human population, while less desirable ones were bred out. Followers believed that the poor simply bred too many sickly, malnourished children – as enlistments in the armed services had so starkly revealed during the recent global war. Although Stopes's books were initially banned by Australian Customs,[53] during 1928 the film of *Married Love* was shown across the nation. In Brisbane it played at the Lyceum Cinema on a double bill with Charlie Chaplin's *The Circus*.[54]

The first indications that such ideas might have an effect on the liberalisation of legal attitudes to abortion were evident in the United Kingdom when Justice Sir Henry McCardie applauded a grand jury at the Leeds Assizes in December 1931 for throwing out a case against a woman who had performed a lethal abortion. The deceased had three children already. The judge said that he could not 'think that any woman should bear children against her will'. This was a revolutionary concept for the times. He then proceeded to criticise the law that prosecuted lethal abortion with a charge of murder.[55] This 'era of savagery' should end, he concluded. McCardie was a prominent member of the Eugenics Society in the United Kingdom.[56]

Even though Australia's laws were still influenced by those of Britain, McCardie's rebellious opinion was not immediately echoed in the Australian judiciary or statutes.

In 1933 the Racial Hygiene Association of New South Wales opened its first family planning clinic in Sydney, designed to cater to women with a family history of hereditary medical problems and those in poverty. Its founder, Lillie Goodisson, had been married to a syphilitic man later confined to a lunatic asylum.[57] The society upheld eugenicist principles of racial fitness and national vitality, which – it believed – were diminished by the evils of syphilis, 'mental retardation' and 'inferior stock'.

The clinic of course could hardly prevent all Sydney's unwanted pregnancies. This was a service performed from the mid-1940s onwards by Dr Reginald Jones, a Macquarie Street gynaecologist, reputedly with a lucrative abortion practice. A well-known racetrack identity, he also owned the Four Hundred Club, where many underworld figures gathered. Attempts to prosecute him proved fruitless.[58] Medical practitioners had long been preferred for such services by those who could afford their fees. Only doctors could legally use chloroform, a bonus during such a traumatic and dangerous procedure.[*][59]

The birth rate fell dramatically during the 1930s with the impact of the Depression, during which there were fewer marriages and more abortions. To mark King George V's silver jubilee, in 1935 a subscription fund was set up by the federal government, with an initial £50,000 government grant announced by William (Billy) Morris Hughes, the federal Minister for Health, who regarded maternal welfare as a national priority.[60] The King's Jubilee Gift Fund for Maternal Welfare supported reforms to improve child and maternal welfare along the lines of the provisions that had already been instituted in Queensland since 1922.

---

[*] In 1915 Dr Thomas Hodgson in Brunswick Street, Fitzroy charged £35 for a procedure conducted under chloroform and £15 with none. He was prosecuted that year.

That year the distinguished gynaecologist, obstetrician and lecturer at the University of Sydney Dame Constance D'Arcy delivered the Anne MacKenzie Oration at the Institute of Anatomy in Canberra, where she addressed Australia's alarmingly high maternal mortality rate: one in 180 women died in childbirth and it was estimated that up to 20 per cent of women who obtained illegal abortions died as a direct result of the procedure. As a young medical practitioner, she had been called to give evidence in a lethal abortion inquest, and the experience confirmed her antagonism to this procedure.[61]

Dame Constance was not the only influential person who campaigned against abortions and their perpetrators. Tragedy hit the family of Billy Hughes when in 1937 his daughter, twenty-one-year-old Helen Hughes, died from an illegal abortion in London. She had attended the coronation of King George VI with her parents.[62] The details of Helen's death were kept secret but no doubt fuelled Hughes's campaigns against abortion and its often lethal consequences. And rumours had circulated in Victoria in the 1920s that the police commissioner, Thomas Blamey, was hard on abortionists because a former girlfriend had died at the hands of Dr Albert Bretherton.[63] Death from a mishap during an abortion could strike women from all classes, not just those who consulted unqualified local women trying to earn a living.

In 1938 Professor Marshall Allen, an academic and obstetrician from Melbourne, followed up his earlier groundbreaking, empirical research into the incidence of maternal mortality, claiming that one-third of maternal deaths were due to abortions.[64] That same year, Dr H. H. McClelland, a senior gynaecologist at the Women's Hospital in Brisbane, also publicly decried the incidence of lethal abortion, blaming 'degenerate doctors and nurses' as well as 'the decay of chivalry'.[65]

Despite a landmark case in England in 1938 that changed the principle of British law for almost the next thirty years – R v Bourne, in which gynaecologist Dr Aleck Bourne was acquitted after prosecution under the 1861 *Offences Against the Person Act* for performing a therapeutic abortion on a fourteen-year-old rape victim – and a 1929 amendment that allowed for 'preserving the life of the mother' when done in good faith, such defences of lethal abortion did not immediately follow to Australia, where earlier strict precepts were maintained.[66]

World War II saw a spate of prosecutions for illegal abortions where death resulted. The influx of a million young American servicemen into Queensland, Sydney and Melbourne challenged more traditional moral values. Sexual behaviour for many young Australian women changed dramatically.

In February 1943, Vera Humphries stood trial before Chief Justice Sir William Webb in the Queensland Supreme Court on the charge of murder. On 6 January that year, Detective Inspector Frank Bischof had accompanied Humphries to the Brisbane General Hospital, where Laura Mowat lay dying from toxaemia and gangrene of the uterus; she died five days later. A clerk at the GPO in Brisbane, Mowat had become pregnant to Corporal Patrick Hill, a soldier in the 2nd Australian Imperial Force, who she thought would marry her. But – it emerged at the trial – he was already married, and Mowat was not his only lover.[67] So, instead, he located an abortionist for her. Hill stated that: 'Somebody gave me the number J 3914 ... And I told [Humphries] I had a girl in trouble and she said she would fix her for £12/10/-'.[68] Humphries visited Mowat at home when she became ill, reminding her and Hill: 'If you get a doctor, mention no names, nor anything that has happened.'

Humphries was an unusual abortionist. She was well educated and had been a governess on a property before her marriage in 1920 to a farmer in Cairns. She ended the marriage after seven years of domestic violence. Later she worked at the Goodna Mental Hospital and had been an abortionist for a number of years when she married Petty Officer Thomas Humphries of the Royal Australian Navy in 1942.[69]

The jury deliberated for some time before finally delivering a verdict of guilty. She was sentenced to life imprisonment with hard labour, upheld on appeal.[70]

Concern for the falling birth rate was again expressed in public policy when the federal Labor government in 1944 established another inquiry to investigate this 'national decay'. The federal parliamentary Labor Party now contained many more Roman Catholics than previously, leading to a renewed hardening of attitudes towards any form of birth control. Arthur Calwell, the Immigration Minister in Chifley's government from 1945, suggested in a parliamentary debate that Australian laws should be similar to those of Nazi Germany and Italy.[71] In 1943, providing an abortion to an Aryan woman became a capital offence, and Mussolini not only outlawed abortion but banned contraception. That Australia had been at war with these nations seemed to escape Calwell's notice. Australian attitudes to illegal abortion were also reinforced. In South Australia three justices of the Supreme Court in 1944 proclaimed their dismay about this 'dangerous modern trend against the natural increase of the population' as well as criminal abortion.[72]

Several post-war cases exemplified the renewed determination to punish lethal abortionists. In February 1946, a housewife in inner-city Brisbane, Amelia Dow, was charged with the murder of Mrs Freda Bevan. Dow had no medical training – she simply 'wanted to help all these girls'. Bevan had left her war-time job and marriage in Sydney, relocating to Brisbane in 1943, where she engaged in sexual affairs with American servicemen. She obtained work at the Oriental Café in Fortitude Valley, close to the city centre, and with another woman set up in a flat in the nearby inner suburb of New Farm in March 1945. Her friend Sheila Malone stated that Bevan had '… kept company with a US serviceman', who had returned home. Pregnant and alone, Bevan had arranged to have an abortion with Amelia Dow for the sum of £16. Dow also cared for six state-fostered children, a fact which no doubt made her more aware of the fate of unwanted children.

Bevan came to seek her help via the networks that surrounded abortion practices. She arrived at Dow's inner-city home in Brisbane at a time when Dow's husband was working an extended shift on the tramways. Initially, Dow told Bevan that she was 'tired of doing this sort of thing'. She relented, unfortunately for Bevan. Dow admitted performing an abortion, stating that Bevan got up and left after the procedure. Mrs Bevan was found the next morning fully dressed and dead in Plunkett Street, Paddington, with £16/17/3½ in her purse and ants crawling all over her body. The trial revealed that Dow's adult son, Jim Dow, had arrived home at 9pm when Bevan was already dead. He took her body and dumped it in a nearby street.

Dow's main concern was not the fate of her deceased client but for her husband, who she said, '... knows nothing about all this business ... This will kill poor old Dad.' Despite the case being heard before Mr Justice Benjamin Matthews, a judge particularly sympathetic to ordinary people,[73] the jury had no hesitation in finding Dow guilty, with a recommendation for mercy. Nevertheless, she received a life sentence.[74] On appeal before the Full Court, her sentence was reduced to five years' imprisonment, largely because the trial judge had not sufficiently explained to the jury the distinction between murder and manslaughter.[75]

In Melbourne in March 1949, Gladys Brown and Kathleen Brian were convicted of the murder of Brian's sister, Mrs Joan Brady, on 8 December 1948. She died from suffocation when hands were held over her mouth to prevent the noise of her screams being heard, her counsel alleged. The postmortem revealed Brady died from heart failure when an instrument was plunged into her uterus. There was no suggestion that Brown had any medical training. Brian, an unskilled process worker from West Brunswick, had taken her sister to Brown for the procedure.

Brian was defended by the leading criminal barrister of the day, Jack Cullity KC. The case was heard before Mr Justice Duffy, who condemned Brown for conducting 'a horrible trade' but also lamented the harshness of the law concerning this sort of case.[76] The defendants were found guilty and sentenced to death, despite a recommendation for mercy from the jury.[77]

In dramatic circumstances, the Full Court of Victoria upheld the original decision, with a reduction in the sentence to three years' hard labour. The appeal rested on the point that the trial judge had taken the jury away from a general verdict by the direction of his remarks. The jury should have been able to return another verdict, such as manslaughter. Their Honours Justice Martin, (Sir) Charles Lowe and (Sir) John Barry also pointed out that this harsh legal regime had not been in force in England for fifty years. In that country, juries were allowed to distinguish between murder and manslaughter, for which there was no anticipation of death. Justice Barry was also less than happy that Kathleen Brian's confession might have been made under police duress.[78] For the prisoners, this was a reprieve beyond anything they could have imagined as they sat in the cells in Pentridge Prison awaiting imminent execution.[79]

Another sensational case in Melbourne occurred when Edna McDonald, aged twenty, died following an abortion. Her partly clad body was found dumped in a rubbish tip. George Cowen, Fred Cranella and Harold Plummer were charged with illegally disposing of a dead body.[80] Varna Patterson, the mother of six children, and Lillian Cohen were charged with McDonald's murder. Patterson had urged McDonald not to undergo the procedure, even offering to adopt the child herself.[81] Both judge and jury took note of this offer and she was released on a bond, while Cowen was sentenced to eighteen months' imprisonment for manslaughter.

In 1948, Ruth Park's prizewinning novel *The Harp in the South* was criticised for including a scenario in which a character, Rowena Darcy, contemplates having an abortion, although her Catholicism prevents her undertaking the procedure. Though newspapers had for decades reported on the underworld of abortionists and those who died at their hands, the subject had not yet entered the realms of literature. Park's novel is set in poverty-stricken Surry Hills in Sydney, and in many ways depicted a disappearing world.

By the 1950s, medical practitioners with access to the new drug penicillin, as well as to painkillers, were favoured as abortionists. The female 'backyard' abortionists had by no means disappeared, but the days when those convicted for murder after a lethal abortion were given sentences of death or life imprisonment were over.

CHAPTER 3

Baby Killers in the Nineteenth Century

Life for the newborn, as Charles Dickens wrote in *Oliver Twist* in 1838, was all too often '... unequally poised between this world and the next'. In some cases their mothers assisted their journey. Without effective contraception, British women had long resorted not only to abortion but also to infanticide to deal with unwanted pregnancies. In the years from 1803 to 1828, 107 women were publicly executed in Great Britain and Ireland. Seventeen were hanged for 'murdering a bastard child' and another nine for murdering an older child – nearly 25 per cent.[1] But by the twentieth century infanticide and child murder had become the most common crimes for which English and Welsh women were sentenced to death. In the years 1900 to 1950, 102 female prisoners were given a capital sentence out of a total of 130 for baby and child murder.[2] In New South Wales at the end of the nineteenth century 80 per cent of women charged with murder were indicted for killing their newborn baby.[3]

Three sensational infanticide cases occurred in Van Diemen's Land (later Tasmania) in the earliest years of the colony, and each demonstrated an extraordinary range of responses and outcomes for the perpetrators of this desperate crime.

In 1817 Lily Mackellar, a single woman who lived in Hobart with her sister and affluent brother-in-law, gave birth to an illegitimate baby, an 'almost perfect child' later found buried with his umbilical cord tied around the neck. Dr Edward Luttrell (1756–1824), the aristocratic and reportedly negligent principal surgeon of the colony, declared the boy had bled to death.[4] He should have been more suspicious since Mackellar had previously asked him for calomel, a product used at that time to produce an abortion. A request he'd refused.[5]

At the inquest another surgeon was asked if the baby had been born alive or stillborn. His answer was that 'it [sic] may have died at birth'. He was unlikely to have known any better. In 1817 the disciplines of forensic science and jurisprudence were in their infancy. A paper entitled 'On the Uncertainty of the Signs of Murder in the Case of Bastard Children' by a surgeon and 'male midwife', the late William Hunter, was presented to the Medical Society in London in 1784. Hunter's research was only preliminary but he had identified the presence of air in the lungs as a sign of life, although he had conceded that a newborn could die soon after.[6] His approach was sympathetic to desperate mothers driven to commit infanticide, laying the blame upon their seducers.[7] This short treatise was not printed, however, until 1818.

The imprecise nature of forensic principles at the time, therefore aided Mackellar's case. At the inquest a servant told the court that she had never seen 'Miss Mackellar making baby linen', an indication that Lily had never intended keeping the baby alive. Mackellar never admitted she was pregnant until the evidence of the dead baby appeared. She did, however, make a confession in which she admitted that 'at 5.30 the child was born. I took the child up and laid it in my arms. It was a male child, [and] it was alive. I fainted and when I came to myself it was dead ... '[8] Her position as a middle-class woman clearly helped Mackellar evade legal penalty. Her reputation, however, was irredeemably damaged.

The case of Mary McLauchlan thirteen years later could not have been more different in its progress and outcome. Born in the ancient fishing village of Saltcoats, near Glasgow, she was a twenty-six-year-old worker from Glasgow who had been convicted of 'theft by housebreaking' in April 1828 at the west circuit of the High Court of Justiciary. Many items had been stolen, suggesting that more than one person was involved in the robbery.[9] There is evidence that she protected her husband, William Sutherland, from the forces of the harsh law. In the original investigation he had been the primary suspect. A respectable relative of her father also provided her with a credible alibi. Sutherland worked at home as a weaver, an old occupation under significant threat from the Industrial Revolution. Mary McLauchlan was employed from dawn to dusk as the supervisor of ten children who worked in William Dunlop's cotton mill in the Barrowfield Road as cotton pickers.[10] This area, near the Clyde Iron Works established in 1786 by James Dunlop at Tollcross, formed the heartland of the new industrial economy.

McLauchlan had no previous convictions before her transportation to Van Diemen's Land for fourteen years. This was a severe sentence given that Scottish Roman-based law was generally more liberal than its counterpart in English common law. The jailkeeper at Tollbooth prison wrote of her: 'Connexions respectable and former course of life good.'[11] This suggested that the economic downturn of the late 1820s, which had hit Scotland hard, affected normally law-abiding people such as McLauchlan and her family. Mary McLauchlan was transported on the *Harmony* from a southern English port, arriving in Van Diemen's Land in January 1829 after a voyage of nine months.

On disembarkation in Hobart, the women from this voyage of the *Harmony* became the first group to be sent to the new Female Factory at the Cascades in south Hobart rather than to the original Factory beside Hobart Town jail. Female Factories were a form of workhouse, where production such as spinning took place, as well as a temporary residence for female convicts who were kept there before being assigned to an employer. The Factory at the Cascades held the women away from the more populous areas of Hobart and, as a purpose-built structure, made sure the women were contained; there had been frequent escapes from the Hobart Town Factory. The group from the *Harmony* disembarked at 4am to prevent any commotion likely to be caused by the presence of 100 women in a male-dominated convict settlement.

There, Principal Superintendent of Convicts James Gordon and the Convict Muster Master Josiah Spode took down details of the newly arrived felons in order to record their details for Governor George Arthur's Black Book, and to assess their prospects for work with settlers. McLauchlan was described as 5 foot 3½ inches (161 centimetres) tall, with an oval face, dark hair and complexion, and hazel eyes. She had one missing tooth in her lower jaw.[12] The women in the group were also examined by surgeon James Scott, a Scotsman who had trained at the University of Edinburgh. He was also permitted to conduct a lucrative private medical practice and was given extensive land grants.[13] In this small community he was a powerful man.

After eight days of assessment each woman was given a fresh set of clothing, consisting of a brown serge jacket, a petticoat, a linen shift, a pair of worsted stockings, a pair of shoes and a neck scarf. McLauchlan was assigned to a merchant, Charles Ross Nairne, who lived with his sickly wife, Katherine Stirling, and their young son on a farm on the Coal River near Hobart.[14] The Nairnes, from Paisley in Scotland, had arrived in the colony on 1 March 1822.[15] McLauchlan was intended as a domestic servant, an occupation quite unlike her previous industrial employment.

Within two months of her assignment McLauchlan was pregnant, a not uncommon situation for female convicts. Sexual services all too often comprised part of the duties expected of assigned domestics. Most of the convict women sent to the Female Factory at the Cascades returned from service pregnant or with a baby.[16] McLauchlan never revealed the identity of the father although many suspected her employer, whose wife was then eight months' pregnant. The marriage was turbulent and not destined to survive the scandal of McLauchlan's fate.

When McLauchlan was five months' pregnant Nairne sent her back to Hobart, charging her with unspecified forms of 'misconduct'. Unrepentant, McLauchlan told Spode, now the Principal Superintendent of Convicts, that she had not been given her new clothing allowance. She was despatched to the House of Correction (the Female Factory) while Spode then made inquiries about the matter. The official record stated that he requested Katherine Nairne to provide further evidence concerning McLauchlan's allegations. Mrs Nairne refused. This was unusual since employers invariably gave at least the appearance of cooperating with the authorities to ensure a continued supply of convict workers. Katherine Nairne's refusal was possibly connected to her knowledge of the parentage of McLaughlan's child. McLauchlan was placed in a cell on a diet of bread and water for six days awaiting further investigation.[17] Governor Arthur had published the rigid new regulations concerning offending convicts in the *Hobart Town Gazette* on 3 October 1829.

At the House of Correction, McLauchlan was placed in C class – for criminal women – along with her former shipboard companions Mary Cameron and Sarah Bromley. Another woman, Mary O'Donnell, had recently been found 'not guilty' of infanticide at her trial in the Supreme Court. The work and diet regime in the House of Correction was thought harsh even by colonial standards. McLauchlan gave birth to a baby boy on 1 December 1829. His body was found in the privies. Mary Cameron had given assistance while other women stood outside. One of the inmates, however, reported the matter to Superintendent Esh Lovell and Matron Anne Lovell.

An inquest was ordered. Court records of this proceeding and for the Supreme Court trial that followed were not kept. Court reporters in Australian jurisdictions did not exist until the 1920s; Pittman's shorthand was not invented until 1837. Any information to be found comes, as it mostly did during this period in Australian history, from accounts in local newspapers. Such trial reports tend to give broad outlines of proceedings rather than minute accounts of testimony; moreover, many events such as the murder of a baby or a spouse were deemed simply too gruesome and unsavoury for extensive reportage in the press.

Joseph Hone (1784–1861), formerly a barrister at Gray's Inn in London, was appointed as the coroner to the inquest. He had arrived in the settlement in 1824, taking on the role of Commissioner of the Court of Requests and Master of the Supreme Court, as well as Commissioner of the Quarter Sessions for the island. He was conscientious, although 'universally looked upon as only a few degrees removed from an idiot'.[18] The facial twitch he suffered made him seem even worse. Even more detrimental to McLauchlan's case was that Hone had business interests in the Derwent Steamship Navigation Company with Charles Nairne. These fellow businessmen and respectable settlers had strong bonds of loyalty and self-interest.

On 15 April 1830, Mary McLauchlan's trial in the Van Diemen's Land Supreme Court began. Established in 1823, this was the first superior court in Australia. Chief Justice Sir John Pedder (1793–1859), who had trained at Cambridge and Middle Temple, presided. Given the difficulty at the time of finding enough suitable free men to make up a jury, the legal system allowed for military juries to act in this capacity. In McLauchlan's trial the jury consisted of six officers and one ensign of the 63rd Foot Regiment, two of whom had already served at Mary O'Donnell's trial. Captain Pery Baylee, commandant of convicts at the feared Macquarie Harbour penal station,[19] headed the jury. He was considered to be severe but fair.

The legal system in this brutal outpost of the Empire was particularly vicious – runaway outlaws and bushrangers were decapitated on capture and their heads displayed on pikes around what is now Salamanca Place in Hobart. There were over 200 offences deemed as capital, which meant the number of public executions for such a tiny population was high. Most were for the theft of sheep and cattle. Some 103 men were executed in the year 1826–27, their bodies often left for the carrion to feed upon as a reminder to everyone who saw them to obey the law. Twenty-two prisoners were executed in a single day, on 3 May 1830.[20]

McLauchlan was not represented by counsel at her trial. This was not uncommon, given how few barristers and solicitors there were at the time – and even fewer rights for felons. Nor were prisoners able to speak on their own behalf until the late 1890s. The basis of law was for the prosecution to prove its case rather than the defence to demonstrate innocence. Trials were generally short in duration, even in capital offence hearings, but in McLauchlan's case a large number of witnesses were called. Surgeon James Bryant was the most important witness. He was described in the newspapers as a gentleman,[21] no doubt to distinguish him from 'barber–surgeons' and apothecaries who were also able to act as medical practitioners before the profession was regulated in 1844. He had arrived in Van Diemen's Land in November 1828 along with the new attorney-general and later Supreme Court judge, Algernon Montagu (1802–80), the illegitimate grandson of the Earl of Sandwich.

Bryant already knew McLauchlan since his duties included the inspection of inmates at the House of Correction and other government facilities. He was young and inexperienced, and in constant conflict with his superior Dr James Scott. The older man was better qualified, but had not been born a gentleman – and such distinctions counted. Scott, however, had the advantage of training at the University of Edinburgh in the new discipline of medical jurisprudence, which had been formally established in 1807.[22] This had greatly aided the outcome of Mary O'Donnell's trial for which he had been the principal medical and forensic witness.[23]

Despite the growing body of forensic knowledge, an autopsy was not carried out on the dead infant to determine whether air had entered his lungs. This was highly detrimental to McLauchlan's case since evidence from an autopsy was vital in cases of infanticide where there could be doubt as to the cause of death. McLauchlan was found guilty and ordered to be publicly executed and her body dissected after her death. The court did not charge her for the lesser offence of 'concealing a birth', even though the particular circumstances warranted such an indictment.

Just two years later, in 1832, the eminent Scottish legal commentator Sir Archibald Alison provided a sympathetic analysis of the plight of unmarried pregnant women, who, he argued, should be pitied and helped rather than being given the death sentence:

> Their distress of mind and body deprives them of all
> judgement, and they are delivered by themselves ... and
> sometimes destroying their offspring without being conscious
> of what they are doing. Accordingly, it is a principle of law,
> that mere appearance of violence on the child's body are not
> *per se* sufficient, unless some circumstances of evidence exist
> to indicate that the violence was knowingly and intentionally
> committed.[24]

The secrecy and lack of expert assistance that surrounded illegitimate births like McLauchlan's always made the investigation and judgment of neonatal deaths problematic. But, given her circumstances, McLauchlan was never going to be granted the benefit of doubt or any sympathy. She was a convict in a pitiless prison system. In England, women who killed their newborns might find themselves incarcerated in a lunatic asylum, such as Bethlem in south London, or one of the many private 'madhouses' for the more affluent. These institutions did not exist in the convict settlements in Australia.[25]

McLauchlan's was the first female capital sentence in the settlement, although women convicts had been executed in Sydney for crimes such as armed robbery. The Executive Council, chaired by Governor Arthur and including Chief Justice Pedder, Colonial Secretary John Burnett and Colonial Treasurer Jocelyn Thomas, reconsidered her punishment. Thomas was a well-born Irishman who had arrived in Van Diemen's Land in 1824, driven to leave his native Ireland after the failure of a land reclamation venture; the Scotsman, Burnett, was the first colonial secretary of the settlement but was soon recognised to be a man of limited ability and vision.[26] Pedder and Burnett actively disliked each other, disagreeing on all matters.[27] Governor Arthur was not clear where his authority exactly lay within the Executive Council and yielded 'in every *doubtful* matter'.[28] The Executive Council met on the Saturday following the trial and then again on the Sunday. Clearly, there was dissent. Thomas and Burnett were inclined to leniency, believing McLauchlan could have been forced into her actions by pressure from the well-to-do father, Charles Nairne. Pedder, on the other hand, stood by his sentence.

While her fate was being decided, McLauchlan was visited by the Reverend William Bedford (1781–1852), the Anglican chaplain who had worked diligently on behalf of prisoners since his arrival in Hobart Town in 1821.[29] The governor of the Hobart jail, John Bisdee (1796–1862), was also regarded as a 'just and humane man'.[30] His wife Ann attended McLauchlan with considerable devotion.[31] Despite their ministrations, McLauchlan did not immediately confess to her crime, nor did she reveal the father of the baby. Reverend Bedford suspected McLauchlan might denounce her 'seducer' on the gallows, where prisoners were permitted final words. It is telling that her master Charles Nairne did not make entreaties for mercy on her behalf to the governor, a common practice in capital cases. McLauchlan did, however, reveal his identity to Mary Cameron, her fellow felon, who aided her at her confinement.

An extraordinary event occurred on the Monday, the day before her scheduled execution and dissection. A letter arrived from Captain Baylee, the jury foreman, who revealed that all the jurors believed that McLauchlan had been '… driven to commit the crime by a sense of degradation and shame from the fear the birth of her child would become known to her relatives at home'.[32] As a married woman with children this was far more shameful than had she been single. All members of the military jury had been impressed by her demeanour and courage during her trial. Governor Arthur immediately asked Joseph Hone to speak to McLauchlan to determine her motive and the identity of the father. She had no reason to confide in this powerful man: not only was he an ally of Nairne, but he was also the coroner who should have demanded a proper autopsy at the inquest, and the master of the Supreme Court. She said nothing to save herself.

The *Tasmanian and Austral–Asiatic Review* provided the most extensive coverage of the execution on Monday 19 April 1830, noting that McLauchlan wore a long white gown 'and appropriate underclothing'. She was composed and silent as the Reverend Bedford, Bible in hand, assisted her on her last walk. On the previous evening she had finally confessed her story and the identity of the father of her child to him. The Presbyterian minister, Mr McArthur, also attended the young Scotswoman. A newspaper later printed Nairne's name in capital letters to remind readers of the name of her employer and implied 'seducer'. McLauchlan refused to confess in public and did not beg for forgiveness for the crime of murdering her baby. Her last words on Earth were a poignant 'Oh, My God!' as the hangman, John Dogherty, kicked aside the peg on the scaffold and the drop opened.

The press took up McLauchlan's case with some degree of fervour, particularly after her execution. The *Tasmanian and Austral–Asiatic Review* of 23 April 1830 denounced her 'seducer' and his escape from justice, reminding readers that in England such a case would more likely have been prosecuted under the lesser charge of 'concealing a birth'. The penalty for that was two years' imprisonment. The *Colonial Times* was uneasy about the execution and subsequent dissection given the ambiguity about whether the baby had been stillborn. The *Hobart Town Courier* was not quite so favourable to McLauchlan's case.

In the Tasmanian State Archives there is a bizarre final mention of the case, composed by Edward Cook, the convict clerk of records, who drew a little gallows with a hanging figure in a dress alongside his incorrectly dated entry: 'Executed for the Murder of her Infant'. This was Mary McLauchlan's last entry in the official record.

Yet McLauchlan's punishment did not end in death. Under Imperial legalisation dating from 1752, those executed for murder were given to medical practitioners and surgeons to 'anatomise'. These procedures in hospitals and mortuaries were frequently public events. Prisoners often feared this additional penalty far more than death itself. Even for those not religiously inclined, the thought of not being able to mount intact into heaven on the Day of Judgment, as foretold in the New Testament, was terrifying beyond measure.

The dissection of murderers was banned in England in 1832 under the *Anatomy Act* which instead allowed unclaimed bodies, particularly deceased inmates of workhouses or prisons, to be 'anatomised' by surgeons. This legislation was widely reported in the Australian press.[33] Regardless, Tasmania maintained dissection for murderers until 1857 when Alex Cullen was despatched to St Mary's Hospital in Hobart after his execution for the murder of Elizabeth Ross.[34] Three murderers were dissected in Melbourne as late as 1864 when Professor George Halford wished to examine their brains for signs of congenital insanity.[35]

Dr James Scott conducted McLauchlan's dissection in the Hobart Town Hospital, which was likely to have been witnessed by notable but unnamed men of the colony as well as medical students. The convict surgeon Francis Hartwell, John Dawson, a surgical instrument-maker, and artist Thomas Bock, who drew other dissected felons, were probably in attendance.[36] Surgeon Edward Bedford, the son of the Reverend Bedford, would have been present since he was a student of Scott. The colonial auditor, George Boyes, who kept records of his impressions of the colony, had previously attended medical dissections and private anatomy lessons in London, and may also have been present.[37] McLauchlan would have been laid naked on the table since the hangman was permitted to keep the clothing of those executed. The dissection of a healthy young woman was a rare event, an invaluable lesson for medical practitioners and students who in that era were not permitted to examine the bodies of living women.

After the surgeon and students had completed their task, the remains of Mary McLauchlan were buried in the Parish of Hobart Town.

Just five years later another extraordinary case of infanticide occurred in Van Diemen's Land. We know far less about the case of Sarah

Following Mary McLauchlan's execution for the murder of her newborn son, her burial was duly recorded in the Parish of Hobart Town's register. Image: Tasmanian State Archives and Library, RGD34-1.

Masters since she was found not guilty, and therefore no execution – with its attendant records, publicity and public discussion – took place. On Friday 8 May 1835, Mrs Sarah Masters appeared in the Supreme Court before Justice Algernon Montagu, indicted on the charges of 'bringing forth a male child alive, and afterwards making an assault upon the body of the said child, by smothering it in a blanket, by which act of the mother the child instantly died … '. The military jury was sworn to secrecy and reconvened the following day.[38]

Masters pleaded not guilty on all counts. Her circumstances differed greatly from those of Mary McLauchlan. First, she was a free woman, not a felon, and lived with her husband most of the time. Joseph Masters had gone away for some six months in search of work. While he was away she became pregnant to another man. The deceased baby was the product of this union. The boy was '… not entirely of European origin … from the appearance of the face, the width of the nostrils, and the thickness of the nose and lips; the hair was jet black, and thick; much thicker than children's hair normally is; the face was very dark; there was a woolly appearance on both sides of the face …' reported Surgeon F. J. Park, the medical practitioner who conducted the autopsy on the dead boy. Joseph Masters, Park assured the court, was certainly not black. The father was likely to have been an Indigenous Palawa man, who remained unnamed. This was a scandal of the highest order in colonial society, breaching every rule of propriety. How Sarah Masters met this man and how they conceived a child together was not discussed in the trial.[39]

One witness, Catherine Fenwick, who had been serving four days in Oatlands jail for misbehaviour, told the court that she was released to assist with the birth. The labour was prolonged, Fenwick recounted. Sarah Masters returned to bed, telling her husband to go out all day with the children and 'let her not be disturbed'. She took some gruel and went to sleep. After several hours, Masters asked for Fenwick to help her again, saying 'she was very bad'. Fenwick claimed she did not know what was wrong, thus contradicting herself. After making the children's bed and attending to Masters' soiled bed linen, Fenwick gave her half a pint of brandy, a remedy to alleviate pain in the absence of anaesthetics, which were not discovered until 1847. After this Masters declared she had given birth to a stillborn baby but insisted that her husband was not to be told. Instead, he was to be informed his wife had suffered a painful miscarriage.

Fenwick claimed the baby was stillborn with the 'natal string round its neck'. The dead infant was placed in a box and covered by a blanket, Fenwick continued. Masters suddenly laughed, declaring the baby was not her husband's and that it was conceived during his absence. She was anxious the truth not be revealed to her husband as it would be 'the cause of [their] parting and she loved her husband and two children, as she loved her life'. Masters also revealed that 'it was the first time she had been guilty of such a crime [adultery] since her marriage'. When Joseph Masters returned, Fenwick informed him his wife had suffered a miscarriage and was feeling very ill.

A few days later Fenwick removed the body in secret with the help of Henry Soby, the cook at the local public house. There was no imputation that he was the father. He testified he had been given '… a bucket with Mrs Masters' miscarriage and threw it into the lagoon'. Why he undertook this unpleasant task and what his relationship was to the two women was not revealed in the testimony. A few days later he returned with another man named Salmon and retrieved the body. During this recovery he noticed a baby's leg protruding from the bundle. Evidently his conscience had been bothering him and he wanted a witness to his actions.

When Salmon was asked to give evidence, he testified that what was wrapped in the quilt was a dark, fully formed baby 'with very large features'. Surgeon Park was present at the discovery of the body, dissecting the remains afterwards. In his testimony Dr Park stated that the results of his autopsy led him to believe the boy had been born alive since the lungs and liver were buoyant when placed in a bowl of water. He further gave his opinion that the baby had been strangled and the umbilical cord had not been cut and tied properly. At this point newspaper reports state that no more of the doctor's extensive and detailed evidence would be published given its graphic and offensive nature. Dr Edward Bedford, now highly qualified after studying in London, gave expert opinion that in some rare instances respiration could occur during birth, with a resultant death.[40] Dr James Scott told the court that he could offer no opinion apart from the observation the child could have died from natural causes. Neither Scott nor Bedford was present at the autopsy, but this opinion from the colonial surgeon would certainly have helped Masters' defence.

Several important legal points were made by the judge concerning provisions within the 1828 *Offences Against the Person Act*. First, in the case of 'concealing a birth' and 'disposing of a dead body', the concealment of the birth had to be undertaken by the mother herself. The attorney-general pointed out that the concealment of a birth by the mother could be regarded as evidence of murder, the penalty for which was death. But in this case others had disposed of the body and they had not been charged with the offence. The jury, no doubt swayed by the opinion of Dr Scott, came back with a verdict of 'not guilty'. Justice Montagu was not altogether pleased with this verdict, clearly believing that Masters had killed her baby and got others to dispose of the body. He closed the court by remarking that the defendant could have been charged with manslaughter in the first instance, a point dismissed by the attorney-general. Sarah Masters was discharged from the proceedings, her life and marriage ruined by the revelations of the case.

With the emergence of medical specialisation and professional training in British hospitals from the 1820s, new textbooks became available. Gynaecology and obstetrics emerged as a new discipline for male medical practitioners, rendering traditional female midwives less qualified and authoritative. Edinburgh-trained Dr Robert Gooch (1784–1830), a pioneering 'man-midwife' and lecturer in midwifery at St Bartholomew's Hospital in London from 1812, published the influential text *On Some of the Most Important Diseases Peculiar to Women* in 1829 and, posthumously, the following year, *Observations on Puerperal Insanity* in which he coined the term 'puerperal insanity' to describe postpartum psychosis, a serious affliction that could cause a newly delivered mother to kill her baby. This was the commencement of biopsychiatric understanding of the disease.[41]

In 1861 the British parliament passed a new *Offences Against the Person Act*, which provided clauses to extend legal penalty to males assisting in infanticide or in concealing the body of a newborn baby. The Royal Commission inquiring into capital punishment in 1864 reviewed these penalties. As the distinguished jurist Baron Bramwell suggested, it is difficult to secure a conviction against a person who does not have to testify against herself: if a birth is conducted in secret, there are often no witnesses; and when does birth in fact occur – before or after the separation of the umbilical cord?[42] The penalty for the conviction of the wilful murder of an older child remained the same – death by hanging.

These more liberal views did not immediately translate into practice in the Australian colonies. In New South Wales, the Bathurst Circuit Court on 23 October 1867 heard two separate cases of infanticide. In one, Elizabeth Coppock was found not guilty of the murder of her infant daughter. The second case was far more convoluted and profound in its effects. Harriet Short and her mother, Mary Williams, were indicted for the murder of Short's illegitimate three-week-old daughter in Bathurst on 11 September 1867. They were defended by Edward Lee, a court-appointed barrister. Senior Sergeant Waters testified how he had recovered the body of a baby in a well near Williams's restaurant. He removed the body, dressed in a frock, chemise and flannel bandages, and took it to the local hospital for a postmortem.

William Wells, a carpenter from Bathurst, told the court that his children played near the well. One day he saw the lid was not secured correctly, and on investigation he noticed what he first thought was a child's doll in the water, until he realised it was a baby. The most damaging testimony came from a neighbour, Ellinor Johnson, who reported that Mrs Williams, whom she hardly knew, came to her house and started lamenting the fate of the 'baby in the well', declaring: 'Oh, the wretch of a mother, whoever she is, wants to be hanged.' She continued: 'It's no odds; it will never see God, for it never was christened.' As an Irish Roman Catholic, Williams was implying that the infant would stay for eternity in limbo. The following evening she returned late to again decry what had happened. She suddenly blurted out: 'It's a pretty mess that Harriet has got herself into ... she couldn't keep it; she has nothing to keep it with, as she has nothing to maintain the ones she has.' When Johnson asked her why she had not given the child into care, Williams replied that '... she wants to hide her shame as much as she can'. Williams then admitted she had urged her daughter to 'chuck it into the well'. When she was unable to, Williams told Johnson, she had said to her daughter: 'Then give it to me and I will.' When probed further Williams admitted that she had 'indeed chucked it in the well'. Johnson immediately informed the police.

The putative father, Charles Atkins, swore under oath that 'I am not the father of Mrs Short's infant' and that he hardly knew her, even as a casual acquaintance. Other evidence, however, did in fact suggest he was indeed the father. Without the support of Charles Atkins, Harriet Short's options were very limited, as her mother had told Ellinor Johnson. At the time there were no foundling hospitals in the colonies and church orphanages tended to admit children rather than babies.

The case received widespread publicity especially when both women were found guilty and sentenced to death for wilful murder. The final public execution for infanticide in England had occurred in 1849 when Rebecca Smith was executed outside the Devizes House of Correction in Wiltshire. She had killed seven of her eleven children by arsenic poisoning. Since the colonies tended to follow metropolitan precedents, it was unlikely that the death sentence would occur in this particular case. To date, only Mary McLauchlan in Hobart in 1830 had been executed for this type of murder.

Mary Williams appeared to be brutal and pragmatic in her treatment of her little granddaughter, whom she regarded as simply a thing to be disposed of after some initial delay. But this was not an uncommon response to illegitimate babies at the time – although it was usually the mother who killed the baby and hid the body. Williams herself had had a fraught life as an abandoned infant sent to a foundling hospital in her native Ireland. She had survived against the odds for such children and had arrived in New South Wales in 1835 on the *Duchess of Northumberland.*

The judge had also had a troubled and chaotic life that impinged upon his judgments. John Fletcher Hargrave (1815–85) came from a modest merchant family in London and was educated at Trinity College, Cambridge, and Lincoln's Inn. He was unstable and volatile to such an extent that his wife had him committed to a private mental asylum in 1849. He arrived in Sydney eight years later, and became a foundation judge of the new District Court. Driven by resentment for his wife, he determinedly decided against female defendants and plaintiffs. The local bar boycotted his swearing-in as a Supreme Court judge in 1865 because he was erratic in his behaviour and judgments. He spent much of his time on the regional circuits of the court before he was overwhelmed by permanent insanity.[43]

Hargrave did not recommend mercy in his correspondence with the colonial governor about the trial. This was unusual in a case of infanticide. He pointed out that the act had been premeditated and designed for concealment. He was particularly concerned with what seemed to be a spate of infant and child murders in Bathurst and pressed for execution for all 'domestic crimes of aggravated guilt'. The governor, however, chose to ignore Hargrave's suggestion and extended mercy to Harriet Short, who served ten years' imprisonment, while her mother was given a life sentence.

The story of Harriet Short had one final twist in the tale. A month after her initial capital sentence was announced the history of her marriage was revealed. A Dr Hayley, who had a practice in Queanbeyan, New South Wales, told newspaper reporters of the death of one his patients, Alfred Short. A brief account had already appeared in the local newspaper in July 1867 concerning the death of 'a stranger' from consumption (tuberculosis). He had come into the township looking for work as a private tutor. Unlike most rural itinerants, Short was a highly educated man whose father was a wealthy solicitor residing in the exclusive area of Regent's Park in London. In Short's pockets Dr Hayley found a letter from a firm of solicitors informing Short that he had been left a considerable inheritance. Further investigation revealed that Short had married Harriet Williams in the Church of St Michael and St John in Bathurst on 28 December 1859. How such an educated man came to marry a poor unschooled woman was not revealed. The couple had two children before they separated. The drowned infant was not his child.[44] As his wife, Harriet Short and her legitimate offspring would have inherited his estate had circumstances not brought her to the killing of her illegitimate baby.

The colonial courts dealt harshly with sane married women indicted and found guilty of killing an unwanted newborn. A former domestic servant, Annie Magann Judge, had been married for three months and was living in a 'humpy' at Sandy Creek near the mining settlement of Clermont in Queensland. Her husband Michael Judge could barely earn a living. Jane Brown, a neighbour, testified before the preliminary hearing in the Police Magistrate's Court in Clermont that in December 1884 Judge had complained she had sore eyes and 'a bad cold'. She was agitated that she was unable to meet the train to get meat for her husband's meal that evening. She also said that she had taken a fall and that she was bleeding. Brown fetched the local midwife, Mrs Parsons, from Clermont as she had already noticed that Judge 'was in the family way'. Dr Apiridion Candiotti testified that he was summoned by the police to examine Judge two days later and confirmed she had recently given birth. He also found the body of a newborn boy wrapped in a silk handkerchief and a towel in a box. Working under a gum tree he conducted a postmortem investigation that revealed the boy had been born alive and died of suffocation. His testimony was detailed, although it was not published in the newspapers. When he returned to the humpy Judge was 'composed but crying'.

Mary Anne Parsons, the midwife, an illiterate but highly articulate witness, informed the proceedings that Judge told her she had suffered a miscarriage and thrown away the child. Pressing further, Parsons insisted the baby be found. A trail of ants leading to a box eventually led her to the body. Still Judge refused to admit she had just given birth. When her husband returned later she also refused to confide in him, saying simply that she 'would tell Mrs Parsons what happened'. Parsons refused to identify the father of the baby.

Judge was indicted on 15 December 1884 in the Queensland Supreme Court in Rockhampton before Justice George Harding (1838–95) on the charge of wilfully murdering her newborn son with malice aforethought. Educated at Magdalene College, Cambridge, Harding was far more comfortable in the lofty heights of equity cases than in sordid criminal matters.[45] Even though this was a capital case, Judge was undefended during her trial because 'she is too poor to procure counsel'. No solicitor or barrister oversaw the case to protect her interest, which was not unusual in this type of trial. The Crown prosecutor, Patrick Real, was a highly able barrister who later became a judge of the Queensland Supreme Court. He had risen from humble circumstances in the mining town of Ipswich and was noted for his sympathy for the poor.[46] Yet in this instance it was notably absent.[47] The jury, however, recommended mercy given her youth and a suspicion that she had been insane at the time of the killing. Under these circumstances Annie Judge could have been judged guilty but insane and sent to the lunatic asylum near Ipswich. But she was given the death sentence.[48]

Although Judge was a married woman who had killed her illegitimate baby and clearly tricked her husband into marriage when she knew she was pregnant to someone else, the Queensland public was sympathetic to her plight and outraged that the death sentence had been passed. Petitions to plead for clemency, signed mostly by men, were assembled in Brisbane and Rockhampton.[49] Although there is nothing to confirm this in the records, it is probable that Judge was able to mount an appeal thanks to public generosity. For the appeal to the Full Court, Judge was represented by a barrister, Edward Mansfield, who came from a distinguished English legal family. He was later appointed as a District Court judge as well as an Acting Justice of the Supreme Court. His peers believed he always acted with 'fairness and common sense'.[50] Mansfield argued that the prosecution had not established its case, although an impartial reading of the evidence confirms it had. The court then went off at a tangent about what constituted 'legitimate issue', given that the baby was born in wedlock. In the final point, Mansfield emphasised that the appellant had been undefended in her original trial.[51] This constituted a far more reasonable argument, especially in a capital case. Her sentence was commuted to penal servitude for ten years.

The later 1880s and 1890s witnessed a period of intense concern over the falling birth rate and national vitality. Members of a select committee that convened in New South Wales in 1886 to investigate the registration of births and deaths expressed their alarm at the irregularities that surrounded illegitimacy and stillbirth. It was known, for example, that some mothers forged the signature of a midwife to register the death of a child they had killed.[52] The New South Wales Coroner's Annual Report for 1891–1892 listed a depressing catalogue of abandoned dead babies – some starved, and others drowned, mutilated or otherwise subjected to violence.[53] Dead babies were found in privies, in parks, mineshafts, secluded streets, rivers, beaches, gardens and dumps, with no indication who they were – they were simply unwanted refuse to be disposed of in secret. The *Argus* newspaper editorialised that there was 'a very army of murderesses within our midst'.[54] Only a small number of these cases ever went to court. Often no mother was found to prosecute.

When Maggie Heffernan, an unmarried domestic servant from Gundowring in rural Victoria, fell pregnant to her longtime boyfriend, she anticipated he would marry her. When he refused she went to Melbourne – the big city allowing her to escape the opprobrium she would have been forced to endure if she had remained in her small community. She gave birth on 29 December 1899 in the hotel where she worked before being transferred to the Melbourne Women's Hospital. After six days she went to a church refuge run by Mrs Cameron in Armadale. A week later Heffernan unsuccessfully tried to find accommodation in several boarding houses. Desperate, with nowhere to go, Heffernan wandered around the Treasury Gardens. A Mrs Taylor asked her if she needed assistance, clearly concerned by Heffernan's appearance and agitated manner. She took Heffernan and the baby to two institutions in search of accommodation, only to be told they did not admit women with babies. Heffernan eventually found a room above a coffee shop for 1/6-. The next morning the landlady gave her a cup of tea and a slice of toast, the only food she had consumed for over twenty-four hours. But as she didn't have enough money, Heffernan had to leave.

Heffernan then purchased a newspaper to look for employment where she could take a baby. There was none. After tramping the streets for hours, tired and increasingly desperate, Heffernan discovered her milk had dried up. Walking down to the river, she again tried to feed the baby but when this proved unsuccessful she threw him into the Yarra, where he drowned. As she walked back to Flinders Street Station she noticed she still had baby clothes on her arm, and she began crying: 'Oh God! What have I done to my baby?' No one came to her assistance or asked why she was so upset.

Soon after, Heffernan found work as a wet nurse in Hawthorn, but she was dismissed because her work was unsatisfactory, presumably because she had no milk. Heffernan was arrested for wilful murder on 20 January 1900, but was not cautioned by police. A lady, presumably her employer, visited her in jail and secured a leading barrister to represent her. When the sheriff suggested she accept Sir Bryan O'Loghlen, she did so thinking he was the person arranged for her. Irish-born O'Loghlen (1828–1905) trained at Trinity College, Dublin, and was called to the Victorian bar in 1862. He became a QC and practised criminal law for fifteen years before going into parliament in Victoria, where he was known for his liberal views.[55] During his political career, O'Loghlen was premier for one term and attorney-general three times. When he took on Heffernan's case he was seventy-two and had retired from politics.

The trial was a disaster. Heffernan's parents were not informed until just a few days before proceedings began, and could not attend. Her weak intellect,[56] former good character and her attempts to support her child were not used as mitigating evidence. Nor was the story of her absconding lover who'd left a bogus forwarding address. The trial judge, Justice Sir Henry Hodges (1844–1919), while known to be capable of humane sentencing, was considered sarcastic and temperamental.[57] When medical witness Dr (later Sir) Richard Stawell, who had trained in paediatrics at the Great Ormond Street Hospital for Children in London, was asked whether Heffernan suffered from puerperal fever, he simply replied 'no', and both Hodges and O'Loghlen left it at that.[58] In such a case, a gynaecologist conversant with puerperal fever and problems of newly delivered mothers would have given supportive expert testimony. Stawell, however, had specialised in paediatrics at Great Ormond Hospital for Children in London. But unlike medical experts in other Victorian cases, he believed that a woman suffering from puerperal fever would be 'unable to give a distinct account of her actions'.[59] Unlike Maggie Heffernan.

Heffernan was found guilty and sentenced to death.

Public opinion and feminist organisations swung behind her, since her sentence was so manifestly unfair under the circumstances.

The influential Sydney feminist Rose Scott worked tirelessly on her behalf alongside women's organisations in Melbourne. Huge public protests were held in Sydney and Melbourne, arguing the Crown had spent little on her defence and allowed the father of the child to go unpunished. A petition with some 15,000 signatures was forwarded to the Executive Council. The citizens of her hometown and district sent a long petition begging for mercy. The *Argus* newspaper on 22 January 1900 pleaded for justice for this young woman who was 'in the shadow of the gallows'. After consideration, the Victorian cabinet commuted Heffernan's sentence to four years' imprisonment. She was finally released on the signature of the solicitor-general, Agar Wynne, in December 1901.[60]

CHAPTER 4

Baby Killers in the Twentieth Century

On a Monday morning in March 2009 the crew assigned to the water treatment plant at Pinkenba in Brisbane was confronted by an operational disaster. Among the human waste they found the decomposing body of a newborn baby girl.[1] This was by no means a singular event; in 2008 workers at the Jacks Gully Waste Disposal Centre at Narellan in New South Wales found the body of a newborn baby boy who had been placed in a rubbish bin near Camden.[2] These events could just as easily have been played out a hundred years earlier, when unwanted babies were routinely abandoned. It wasn't until the 1920s, when adoption legalisation was introduced, that the children of single mothers could be given up to a new family, creating a way out other than taking drastic measures. In 1973 the federal government introduced the supporting mother's pension, which provided a basic allowance for single women to care for their children, somewhat reducing the level of economic hardship. Yet despite shifts in legislation, public opinion and more liberal social attitudes, the stigma of unwanted pregnancy and birth has endured.

Despite the pro-natalist fervour of the early twentieth century, the courts could sometimes deal sympathetically with mothers who killed their unwanted babies. Sydney resident Emily McDonald was charged with the wilful murder of her eighteen-month-old daughter, Thelma, by crushing a box and a half of phosphorus match heads into a drink of water in January 1901. She had afterwards tried to kill herself by also ingesting the poisonous match heads then throwing herself from a window. McDonald's husband and sister-in-law attested that she had been depressed since Thelma's birth. The jury at her trial in February delivered a verdict of not guilty, adding that they believed she had not been of sound mind when the acts were committed. She was held under observation in an asylum at the governor's pleasure.[3]

Agnes Ferry, described as a 'young, unmarried girl', was charged with the wilful murder of her daughter in the sittings of the Supreme Court of Victoria at Horsham on 4 March 1913. Born into a poor family in the rural district of Dimboola, Ferry had little education and few skills. The baby, already in an advanced state of decomposition, was found in an outhouse (toilet) located in a laneway in the township. A lace from a corset was wound tightly around the baby's neck. Ferry told the court that she had no memory of the birth, or of killing the baby or disposing of her body. Her testimony was consistent with a newly delivered woman suffering from severe postpartum anxiety disorder where the mother is confused, dissociated from her actions and often suicidal.[4] With the additional factors of an undisclosed and unwanted pregnancy, and an unassisted birth, the factors leading to neonatal killing are high.[5] Medical research as early as 1830 had identified this syndrome, although it was not referred to in Ferry's case.[6]

Ferry was represented by the leading criminal barrister in Victoria at the time, George Arnot Maxwell (1859–1935).[7] A man of strong Presbyterian convictions he was also sympathetic and devoted to the legal causes of the poor, especially those like Agnes Ferry. Sir Thomas à Beckett (1836–1919), the scion of Victoria's leading legal dynasty, presided over proceedings. His forte was equity, although he was calm, resolved and patient in criminal cases.[8] The jury returned a verdict of guilty but recommended mercy. His Honour had no alternative but to sentence Ferry to death as demanded by law. On hearing this Ferry collapsed and required medical attention. No appeal was heard. When the Executive Council reviewed the capital sentence it recommended that she be detained at the governor's pleasure thus setting no limits for release.[9]

In 1915 Emma Lonsdale was arraigned in the Supreme Court of Victoria for the murder of her newborn son, George. She was a seventeen-year-old unmarried mother who had given birth in a nursing home in Carlton. On 20 March 1915 a nurse went to Lonsdale's room to check on the baby, only to find him unconscious on the bed. She immediately called for the local doctor. George had been poisoned with Lysol, a strong disinfectant, and later died in agony in the Children's Hospital. Lonsdale told the court she did not know 'what came over her' nor did she realise the consequences of her act – she merely wanted him to stop crying. She was also distraught that her parents had abandoned her. Her defence team, again led by George Arnot Maxwell, argued that she was suffering from puerperal mania. The jury was not convinced, returning a guilty verdict.[10] In sentencing her to death, the chief justice, Sir John Madden (1844–1918), took into consideration her youth and circumstances, although he admonished her for the terrible way she had killed George. He added that he would recommend mercy to the governor on her behalf. Her sentence was duly commuted to 'the pleasure of the governor', something that could mean life imprisonment.[11] Emma Lonsdale's was the last case of neonatal murder in Australia where the death sentence was recorded.

Nellie Spiers, a domestic servant living in the exclusive suburb of Clayfield in Brisbane, appeared in court in June 1924 on the charge of 'concealing a birth'. The gardener, Arthur Clarke, testified that he found the decomposing body of a baby boy in a paper bag in the garden where he was digging. His employer, retired bank manager Arthur Noyes, called the police around 7pm on 10 May 1924. He testified he did not notice that Spiers was pregnant and nor did she complain of being ill at any time. He added that he left all the management of the servants and the house to his wife, Susan Noyes.

As soon as the body was discovered Susan Noyes questioned Spiers, who readily admitted that she had given birth in secret and buried the baby. Spiers, twenty-six, made a long statement to the police in which she revealed that she was from Charleville and had come to work in Brisbane thirteen years before, after her parents had died. She had been employed by the Noyes family for over ten years. During the war, she said, she 'kept company with soldiers but nothing happened to [her] then' and that she had 'much misconducted [sic] [herself] with them'. Later she 'kept company' for nearly a year with a returned serviceman, Jack Williams, a scrub cutter from Nanango. She was distressed that he left for Melbourne without telling her of his intended departure.

Spiers also admitted she was 'keeping company with two other men ... and used to meet them different nights during the week'. She only knew them as 'Ernie' and 'Bill'. They never went out on dates; rather, they simply had sexual encounters in secluded but public places. When she realised she was pregnant, Spiers could not identify who the father might be. Not that such knowledge was likely to have led to a proposal of marriage.

With no other choice, Spiers kept working despite illness and nausea. She stated that the baby was suddenly born in the lavatory: 'I was half silly at the time but the baby was not alive as it did not move ...' After wrapping the body in paper she then buried it. Later in her statement Spiers referred to 'her miscarriage', although the baby was full term. She outlined the shame, fear and confusion about what she should do, and the secrecy that she felt had to surround the birth even though her parents were dead and she did not live in her hometown. Spiers was at pains to inform the police that she had never taken any 'medicine to get a miscarriage'.[12]

The trial was heard before Justice Lionel Lukin (1868–1944), the first Queenslander to be appointed to the bench, and the autopsy conducted by the distinguished physician Dr Espie Dods (1875–1930), who had served in the Boer War and at Gallipoli.[13] He reported that there were no signs of violence upon the body, to which the umbilical cord was still attached. With the decomposition he could not say whether the baby had been stillborn or born alive. With this medical testimony Spiers was found guilty of the lesser offence of 'concealing a birth'. Lukin dealt sympathetically with Spiers in his sentence of twelve months' imprisonment, suspended on the payment of a £100 good behaviour bond. As this sum was far beyond her limited means, no doubt her employers paid it. Whether she remained in their employment was not recorded.

Legal adoption had been well embedded into social policy and law in the states since the 1920s, but an article in January 1952 on the Berry Street Foundling Hospital (the former Victorian Infant Asylum and Foundling Hospital, established in 1877) revealed that babies were still abandoned in Melbourne in 'rubbish bins, hedges and somebody's front lawn'. A baby boy had been found in Royal Park wrapped in a newspaper. Matron Elizabeth Fry pointed out that the centre provided 'a sanctuary' for 'unmarried girls' who found themselves pregnant and alone. Care was extended for three months.[14] For those mothers who concealed their pregnancy and gave birth in secret, the public acknowledgment of their 'shame' by taking their baby to the foundling home was too dreadful to contemplate. This type of response continued right into the twenty-first century. Lauren Curnow, a seventeen-year-old student from Ballarat, gave birth in her bedroom unassisted in August 2004, having managed to conceal the pregnancy from her parents. Curnow punched the boy soon after birth, resulting in his death. After extensive forensic psychiatric evidence and testimony she was sentenced to five years' imprisonment, immediately suspended by Justice Bernard Bongiorno in the Victorian Supreme Court.[15]

Many cases of neonatal killing defy any suggestion of broad categorisation. The arrest in October 1951 of Alwyn Atkinson, a farmer from Kimba in South Australia, throws light on an issue rarely discussed in public. The father of twelve children, Atkinson had committed incest with one of his daughters for three years. She became pregnant in October 1950, giving birth to a baby boy in June 1951. No one knew that the child was the result of an incestuous union. Somewhere between Port Augusta and Buckleboo the infant was smothered and then buried in the bush.[16] At the trial before Justice Sir George Coutts Ligertwood (1888–1967) in the Supreme Court of South Australia only Alwyn Atkinson was arraigned. He received a light sentence of four years' imprisonment for each of the offences of manslaughter and incest.[17] Since he pleaded guilty, the full circumstances of the case remain undisclosed. However, this highlights the possibility in other cases that infanticidal young mothers may be victims of incest but remain silent to avoid the shame and notoriety.

Other cases of neonatal killing have occurred within domestic settings that appeared outwardly normal and suburban. One of the most complex and disturbing cases of serial murder in modern Australia involved infanticide that went undetected until four infants had died at the hands of their mother, Kathleen Megan Folbigg. Her own early life, full of trauma and abuse, had an impact on her ability to nurture her four babies. The full extent of the horror she had herself experienced as an infant only came to public light when she was sentenced in the Supreme Court of New South Wales in October 2003.[18]

When Folbigg was just eighteen months old, her father killed her mother, stabbing her more than twenty times. Folbigg entered the foster system. In 1970, when she was three, she was fostered by Neville and Deidre Marlborough and led an apparently unremarkable childhood. She left school at fifteen and went to work as a cash register operator in a local service station. Kathleen Marlborough found out some details of her early life and adoption two years later when she met her half-sister. The following year she met Craig Folbigg, a worker from the local BHP Steelworks. They married in 1987 and set up home in the suburb of Mayfield, becoming more financially secure with Craig Folbigg's change of career to car sales.

Caleb Gibson Folbigg was born on 1 February 1989, a healthy baby except for a 'floppy larynx', a minor condition that caused some difficulties in feeding. Folbigg underwent an epidural delivery with forceps that precluded stable walking for a month, a trying situation for a vain young woman proud of her figure and appearance. She decided not to breastfeed since it made her feel uncomfortable. When he was two weeks old Caleb was taken to see Dr Barry Springthorpe, a leading paediatrician at the Royal Newcastle Hospital, to investigate the feeding problems that were connected to difficulties breathing through his nose. Two days later Craig and Kathleen Folbigg took Caleb with them to a family barbeque. That night Caleb ate well and went to sleep without difficulty.

Caleb took his early morning feed at 2am on 20 February 1989 without any difficulties and went to sleep straight away. Kathleen Folbigg attended to Caleb some hours later, although he was not due for another feed and did not wake her crying. When she entered his semi-lit room, she recalled: '... you can hear babies breathing. They are very definite in how they take a breath. So when I ... didn't hear that, that's when I thought, what have you done? Have you rolled over or something? ... And I just placed my hand on his chest and didn't feel it ... rise ... I don't remember exactly what happened next ... I was just callin' out to Craig, which I had to do three times as he is a sound sleeper ... and back then we didn't know about CPR ... So it was a case of us both pretty much panicking on what we were supposed to be doing ... and we just rang the ambulance.'[19]

Craig Folbigg's version differed in some details concerning whether Caleb was in his bassinette. He stated that he grabbed the still-warm baby from the bassinette, noting that his lips were blue. He attempted CPR until the ambulance arrived. Ambulance officers David Hopkins and Richard Baines, who arrived at one minute before 3am, were unable to resuscitate the boy, and Hopkins recorded, 'Sudden Infant

Kathleen Megan Folbigg, pictured leaving court in 2003, supported by Salvation Army chaplain Major Joyce Harmer. Photo: Fairfax Media FXJ 125429.

Death Syndrome' (SIDS) in his case notes. Kathleen Folbigg had kept a diary of her activities as a young mother, almost obsessively. The last entry, at 2am on 20 February, noted: 'Finally asleep!!' The following day the couple were offered counselling from social workers on SIDS. The autopsy did not provide any conclusive findings, and a case of SIDS was recorded. Dr Springthorpe also took time to talk to the Folbiggs about their loss. Their reactions to Caleb's death contrasted markedly. Craig was depressed and in mourning, while his wife was seemingly cheerful, going back to work at the restaurant where she had been employed before Caleb's birth, and resuming an active social life nightclubbing with friends.

To make sure such a tragedy never happened again, the Folbiggs renovated their house to eliminate any drafts. Craig also agreed never to smoke in the house. When Kathleen fell pregnant again she appeared happy. Patrick Allen David Folbigg was born on 3 June 1990. His mother recorded in her diary: 'I had mixed feelings this day [of Patrick's birth] whether or not I was going to cope as a mother and whether I was going to get stressed out like I did last time. I often regret Caleb and Patrick only because your life changes so much and maybe I'm not the sort of person who likes change, but we will see.'[20] Kathleen Folbigg did not adjust to her maternal role, often appearing angry and resentful, to such an extent that she would growl like an animal, as her husband testified at her trial.

Craig Folbigg dedicated himself to his family, realising that work had to take second place. Patrick was given a newly renovated bedroom. He settled easily into routines, and fed and slept well. After some weeks at home Craig Folbigg began work at a new car dealership. Three days later trouble struck again when Kathleen Folbigg awoke suddenly in the night and went to check on Patrick only to find him not breathing. When Craig Folbigg heard his wife screaming, he ran to Patrick's room to investigate, and called for an ambulance. Officer Hopkins returned again, performing CPR on the little boy, who was struggling for breath. Hopkins noticed pressure marks on the baby's neck.

Patrick was taken to hospital, where multiple tests were conducted that showed he had an abnormal amount of glucose in his urine. He was now epileptic and blind. The additional work required to care for a severely disabled infant proved too much for Kathleen Folbigg. She became depressed and resentful again, although she had a lot of support. Craig's sister, Carole Hewitt, a registered nurse and an experienced mother with a large family, offered a lot of assistance. Around this time, Craig Folbigg read his wife's diary to try to understand her mood swings. He was shocked to find out how deeply resentful she was.

Patrick returned from hospital to Caleb's old room, in retrospect a sign that his days were numbered. On the morning of 13 February 1991, after Craig Folbigg had gone to work, Patrick apparently had another fit, and Kathleen Folbigg believed she then went into 'a trance' as a result. She rang Carole Hewitt, who came to the house to find the little boy dead. Kathleen Folbigg rang her husband at work at 10.30am, saying: 'It's happened again.' An ambulance was summoned and Patrick was taken to hospital even though his lips were blue. Doctors informed his parents that the baby died from asphyxiation. Once again the parents' reactions were completely different: Craig was inconsolable; he lost his job, retreating to his shed and playing a lot with a neighbour's little boy. Kathleen Folbigg, on the other hand, was ready to change jobs and make new friends.

They moved house to Thornton, near Maitland, and Kathleen announced she wanted another baby. Whatever suspicions Craig Folbigg might have had about the deaths of his sons he suppressed for the time being. Sarah Kathleen Folbigg was born on 14 October 1992. The couple installed a sleep apnoea machine to monitor the little girl's breathing through the night but discarded it when it beeped with false alarms. The new baby was a fitful sleeper. Kathleen Folbigg fell back into the patterns laid down in the past: she began growling in anger and frustration. With her husband forced to spend long hours commuting to a new job she was left alone with 'one grouchy little bugger'.[21] The broken sleep patterns of the baby and Folbigg's need for strict routine added to her growing anger and instability. The baby had to be put to bed at 8.30 each night no matter what, an example of Folbigg's rigidity that was the cause of constant arguments between the couple.

Events following a family outing on 29 August 1993 repeated the previous tragedies. When they returned home from a day at the beach, Kathleen Folbigg was tired and frustrated. She accused her husband of 'revvin' up' Sarah, who was too excited and unwilling to go to bed. Craig was disturbed to hear loud growling come from the child's bedroom, a now-familiar warning. 'You fucking deal with her!' he was told as Sarah cried loudly. Later that night he heard screams from the baby's room and discovered an agitated Kathleen there. Sarah was showing no signs of life at 1.34am. Later, a calendar was discovered with 'Sarah left us at 1am' written across the date of 30 August. At this time, by Kathleen Folbigg's account, Sarah had been asleep.

On this occasion, two detectives and a police photographer from Maitland Police Station investigated. There was some discrepancy in the times recorded by the police as to when Sarah had been alive and well. The autopsy revealed no obvious cause of death and SIDS was identified again. It seemed statistically unlikely that three children in one family should perish in this way but the Folbiggs were informed it was 'just bad luck'.

Craig Folbigg suffered such extreme depression and inconsolable grief that his wife ordered him in writing to seek grief counselling. They moved house again, this time to Singleton; Craig spent a lot of his spare time alone in the garage. When his grief did not abate, Kathleen Folbigg left him 'to get on with it on his own'. She returned to Newcastle, enjoying the parties and nightclubs there as much as when she was a child-free, single woman. It wasn't until Kathleen's foster family moved to Darwin that the Folbiggs resumed their marriage. Kathleen Folbigg felt as abandoned as she had been as a toddler.

Craig and Kathleen Folbigg contemplated having another child. They consulted Dr Christopher Seton at the sleep unit at Westmead Children's Hospital for advice. She confided in her diary on 18 June 1996: 'I am ready this time and I know I'll have help and support this time. When I think I am going to lose control like last time I'll just hand the baby over to someone else. Not feel totally alone ... I have learned my lesson this time.'[22] Kathleen Folbigg learned she was pregnant again in November 1996. Yet an entry recorded on 30 October was ominous: 'I pray I'm prepared and ready, mind wise, for this next one. Maybe nature has decided I never will be and it will never happen.' Her feelings of incompetence had not abated, as she revealed in her diary on 4 December 1996: 'I'm ready this time, but have already decided if I get feelings of jealousy or anger too much I will leave Craig and baby rather than being as before ... I know that battling wills and sleep deprivation were the causes last time.' But the causes of *what* was left unexplained in her written thoughts. Hindsight reveals that she meant the death of Sarah. Another diary entry on 1 January 1997 was chilling to contemplate: 'I am going to call for help this time and not attempt to do everything myself anymore. I know that was the main reason for all my stress before, and stress made me do terrible things ...'[23] What these 'terrible things' were was not defined.

Laura Folbigg was born on 7 August 1997. Kathleen Folbigg felt that the nurses forced her to breastfeed, a practice she stopped as soon as she returned home. She did, however, make a seemingly positive move to engage with Sydney researcher Dr Christopher Seton's program on sleep disorders and SIDS. Help was also provided by the David Reed Sleep Unit at the Westmead Children's Hospital. Staff advised the use of a sleep apnoea machine once more to monitor breathing. But all was not well. Folbigg confided again to her diary: 'Sleep? Who needs it? Yes, I am getting a little bit irritable now. This is my punishment for the others, to be continually woken up, because this time we know we have a child with a sleeping disorder ... and I'm getting stressed as I cannot rely on Craig for any real support or help ...' During the day, when Craig Folbigg was away at work, Folbigg turned the monitoring machine off, a source of argument at home and concern at the sleep unit. Within five months, further diary entries revealed her thoughts of running away to rediscover the joys of a single, unencumbered life. That motherhood entailed substituting a 2am departure from a nightclub with a 2am feed never seemed to occur to her, nor that it was something experienced by every parent.

By early 1998 Folbigg's mood had worsened, as she wrote in her diary: '... I've done it. I lost it with her. I yelled at her so angry that it scared her. She hasn't stopped crying ... I knew I was short-tempered and cruel to her [Sarah] and she'd left with a bit of help. I don't want it ever to happen again. I actually seem to have a bond with Laura ... Her moaning, bored, whingey sound drives me up the wall ... '[24] Nightclubbing and going to the gym were her responses to her frustrations. Finally, Folbigg wrote to her husband, even though they lived in the same house, that she wished to leave him due to his 'oppression'. More disturbing was that Laura would leave with her when she terminated the marriage. Almost inexplicably Craig Folbigg continued to love his wife, despite the trauma they had endured and the strains on their relationship. The marriage held tenuously together.

By this time Laura was afraid of her mother and reluctant to stay with her. On 1 March 1999, following a fierce argument at breakfast, during which Folbigg growled and became abusive, Craig Folbigg was summoned from work to learn that their daughter had suddenly stopped breathing. By the time he reached the hospital Laura was dead. Kathleen Folbigg told him that after a morning at the gym – with Laura in childcare – she had put Laura to bed for a nap. She heard the monitor go off but did not go to investigate for around ten minutes. When she got to the bedroom, she discovered Laura had turned blue and did not respond to CPR.

When Craig Folbigg came home, Laura's sandals were on the futon and not in the hallway as Kathleen Folbigg had told him on the telephone. Also the monitor could not be heard from the clothesline, where she reported she had heard it ringing. The police were suspicious, as the likelihood of another SIDS death, especially with a nineteen-month-old child in the daytime, was remote. Detective Senior Constable Bernie Ryan thought it was more than suspicious but lacked evidence to prove otherwise. As he told *Australian Story* on ABC Television: 'Singleton is a small country town. It's not a place that one would go searching for major crime. March 1 1999 was a day that changed my life. It was a very dark day for Singleton that day.' His search of the house revealed anomalies such as the sandals being on the futon rather than in the bedroom. 'Why? Because what Kathleen said didn't happen.'

At the funeral Kathleen Folbigg seemed calm and sedate. In the car going home with her husband, her foster sister, Lea Brown, and her brother-in-law, Michael Folbigg, all she could say was: 'Well, thank fuck that's over. Now I can get on with things.' Even at the wake she was composed and chatting amiably with her gym buddies. One week later, she was back at the gym as if nothing had happened. She returned to work quickly and seemed undisturbed by the tragedy that had engulfed her husband and his family. Rather than showing sympathy for her grieving husband, Folbigg accused him of 'moping'. The marriage ended soon afterwards.

When Craig was sorting through those things of hers remaining in the marital home, he discovered another of her diaries with more chilling entries. One written on 14 October 1996 particularly intrigued him: 'Obviously I am my father's daughter.'[25] His suppressed suspicions were confirmed – his wife had cold-bloodedly killed their four children and there seemed to be evidence of it in her diary. The Crown's case rested upon the entries in the diary, although Folbigg's defence claimed they were mere 'babble books'.[26]

Dr Quang Tuan Au, who conducted Laura's autopsy, informed Detective Ryan that he believed that it was not a SIDS death: her death resulted from murder. Further investigation with Dr Allan Cala at the New South Wales Institute of Forensic Medicine was undertaken. He detected myocarditis (inflammation around the heart) but indicated that this was not the cause of Laura's death. Like Sarah, her lungs were collapsed, although this did not prove suffocation. He left his findings as 'undetermined causes of death'. He did point out, however, that usually SIDS deaths are found in the morning on waking whereas the first three Folbigg children were found with the mother in the early hours of the morning. He contacted Detective Ryan, suggesting a medical review of the four deaths. Only one Folbigg infant had been under six months at death, the customary age by which death by SIDS abates.

Soon after, Craig Folbigg told Detective Ryan that he had read his wife's disturbing diary. From the moment he saw the diary, Ryan decided that it was now a murder investigation. Folbigg spent many hours going over his memories of events with the detective. That same night Kathleen Folbigg went to a ball and brought home a businessman, whom she kissed on her doorstep before undressing in the lounge room, quite visible through the thin curtains. Craig Folbigg confronted her after waiting outside to talk to her. All she could say was: 'You're an arsehole!' She then proceeded to scream at him as she chased him down the driveway, shouting: 'Are you accusing me of Laura's death?' Then she found out the police were investigating all the deaths. He also told her he had read her diary and given it to the police. Kathleen Folbigg's mood changed abruptly as she cajoled and soothed Craig's fears. Despite all that had happened, he agreed to resume their marriage.[27]

To an outsider, the success of Folbigg's emotional manipulation seems unbelievable. Yet it convinced Craig Folbigg to attempt to retract his statement to police. This meant that Detective Ryan could not continue to pursue his investigations with the vigour he required. So he embarked on his own extraordinary quest for justice for Laura and the other three babies.[28] Ryan met with leading international SIDS researchers, such as Dr Susan Beal at the Women's and Children's Hospital in Adelaide, Dr Janice Ophoven in Minneapolis, and pathologists Professor Peter Berry at the Bristol Royal Hospital for Sick Children and Dr Peter Herdson, senior pathologist at the Canberra Hospital, as well as psychological profilers with the FBI and Israel's Mossad.[29] Ryan also investigated Münchausen's syndrome by proxy, a behaviour pattern in which a parent (usually a mother) injures a child in order to get attention and support for herself.

On his return from his extensive research, Detective Ryan arranged for the installation of listening devices in the Folbigg house in July 1999. On 23 July he went to the house and requested that Kathleen Folbigg accompany him to the local police station. The interview was long and detailed, although he did not point out the multiple discrepancies in her stories. This was not a cross-examination. Its purpose was to unnerve her so she would say things at home that could be recorded. He also confronted her with the exact meanings of various suspicious diary entries, all of which she brushed off as if they were of no importance. Her response to the entry about 'stress makes me do terrible things' was merely to indicate she got angry and shouted.[30] After eight hours Folbigg was released and informed that her house would be searched. Police attempted to locate more diaries.

Life for the Folbiggs was tense; Craig was constantly worried he would trigger explosions of rage and abuse if he pressed his wife too hard with his nagging worries about their children's deaths. Alone, Kathleen Folbigg began acting out courtroom scenarios with herself as both defendant and prosecutor, adopting a strange American accent.

Detective Ryan continued to analyse new evidence found in the diaries. Folbigg wrote just before Laura's birth: 'Maybe then he will see when stress of it all is getting to be too much, and save me from feeling like I did before during my dark moods. Hopefully preparing myself will be the end of my dark moods … That will be the key to this baby's survival. It surely will. But enough of dwelling. Things are different this time. It will all work out for sure.'[31]

On 9 November 1997, when Kathleen Folbigg was angry with her husband for getting drunk, she laid out her frustrations in her diary. Her focus was foremost on Laura's crying, a normal part of early infancy, recalling that, 'with Sarah all I wanted was for her to shut up and one day she did'. Ryan continued his research in Canberra as he prepared his brief. The director of public prosecutions at this time believed there was insufficient evidence to proceed.

By mid-2000, the Folbiggs' marriage was finally over, which allowed police to pursue inquiries in more depth. Craig Folbigg was re-interviewed on 19 April 2001; he was now scared when he was arrested for 'hindering an investigation'. Kathleen Folbigg was charged with four counts of murder on 20 April 2001. She was refused bail. Her new partner had no idea that she had had four children let alone what had happened to them. On 18 May 2001 she successfully applied for bail before Justice Robert Hulme of the New South Wales Supreme Court. In the meantime, Detective Ryan went to Melbourne in an attempt to get Folbigg's foster sister, Lea Brown, to act as a witness for the prosecution. She began taping all her conversations with her sister. Brown later told a newspaper that 'if the death penalty was reintroduced she would be the first in line with the injection syringe'.[32]

On 13 February 2003, Folbigg, through her counsel, sought to have each of the four counts of murder dealt with separately rather than concurrently. The New South Wales Court of Appeal dismissed the application.[33] Her barrister took the matter to the High Court of Australia where Justice McHugh in a hearing in chambers dismissed the application for a stay of proceedings.[34] This decision was later examined thoroughly by forensic investigators who argued that it allowed for a Crown argument of similarity and coincidence, as SIDS is a difficult area to diagnose.[35] The trial was conducted in the New South Wales Supreme Court presided over by Justice Graham Barr, with eminent QC Mark Tedeschi, who had prosecuted the case against serial killer Ivan Milat and the killers of Dr Victor Chang, leading for the Crown. Folbigg was defended by Peter Zahra SC. After outlining the circumstances of each of the four deaths, Tedeschi concluded his opening remarks to the jury on 13 May 2003 by reading an excerpt from the defendant's diary of 31 December 1997: 'Getting Laura to be [one] next year ought to be fun. She'll realise a party is going on and that will be it. Wonder if the battle of wills will start with her and I then? We'll actually get to see. She is a fairly good-natured baby. Thank goodness. It will save her from the fate of her siblings, I think she was warned.'

It was alleged that the defendant did not suffer from symptoms of postpartum depression but that this was cold-blooded, premeditated murder. When a video recording of her interview with Detective Ryan was played, as well as another of Laura on the day before she died, Folbigg became hysterical and nearly fell out of the dock. The trial was adjourned while she received medical treatment at nearby St Vincent's Hospital.[36]

When the trial resumed the following day, forensic psychiatrist Dr Rod Milton testified that Folbigg had a narcissistic personality, although she was not insane, an opinion with which other specialists concurred. Folbigg decide not to testify, which common-law systems allow. Justice Barr pointed out to the jury that this is not an admission of guilt since it is up to the prosecution to prove a case beyond reasonable doubt. The jury retired to consider its verdict on the multiple charges. Folbigg was found guilty of the manslaughter of Caleb, the murder of Patrick, Sarah and Laura, as well as inflicting grievous bodily harm upon Patrick. Folbigg was so distressed she could hardly walk past the holding cells below the courtroom to the waiting police van. Craig Folbigg read a short statement to the waiting crowd and media outside, thanking the jury and Detective Bernie Ryan.

In prison, Folbigg received many death threats; even among murderers, killing your own children is unthinkable. In prison she maintained her anger, believing that the Folbigg family were making a fortune by selling the story. On 23 August 2003 Folbigg, dishevelled and unkempt, appeared for sentencing. Detective Ryan, now an expert on child murder, watched from the public gallery. Peter Zahra called psychiatrist Dr Bruce Westmore, who testified that his client was suffering from some deep, unspecified personality disorder and from the effects of her early abuse. Justice Barr attempted to understand the long-term factors that led to Folbigg's convictions, and delivered his statement calmly and methodically.

Kathleen Megan Donovan was born on 14 June 1967. Her Welsh father, Thomas Britton, was a violent man who worked as an enforcer, hit man and debt collector for Sydney underworld crime figure Robert Trimbole. In 1952 he cut his first wife's throat, a crime for which he served just eight months' imprisonment. He fathered several children by different mothers. Britton met Kathleen Donovan in 1965, and spent three years with her before she left him because of his violence. Every morning he would hold a knife to her throat and whisper: 'Will I or won't I?' She abandoned baby Kathleen with him in Balmain, then a rough inner-city suburb. Encountering her out walking one day, Britton begged her to rejoin him. Donovan refused, so he punched her in the face when she took refuge in a butcher's shop. He then stabbed her twenty-five times with a carving knife. She died on the footpath. Britton leaned over and pronounced his final words to her: 'I'm sorry, I had to do it.' He was found guilty of her murder in May 1969 and sentenced to fourteen years' imprisonment. He was later deported to Wales.

As an infant Kathleen Donovan endured prolonged abuse. As a toddler, after the death of her mother and imprisonment of her father, she had first been taken in by an aunt and uncle, but was subsequently sent into care at Bidura Children's Home where she was reportedly a severely troubled and disruptive child. At the age of three she went to live with the Marlboroughs. Her development had been so stunted it was initially feared that she was intellectually handicapped. Under the Marlboroughs' strict care, Kathleen began a calm and stable period of her life. But her adolescence was shattered by constant arguments with her foster mother. Justice Barr noted that during this time there was 'some minor offending but no pattern of violence'.[37] Her husband Craig Folbigg found out some of her past during their marriage when she sought to become reconciled with her natural extended family. Under the circumstances, her potential for good parenting was remote.

But her upbringing, no matter how violent and traumatic, was not a mitigating factor in her sentence. Forensic psychiatrist Dr Michael Giuffrida, who visited her on five occasions during the trial, reported that Folbigg was not psychotic but a deeply troubled and tormented woman who constantly felt abandoned and alone. Her emotional detachment from her own actions and the deaths of her children characterised her demeanour. She had suffered irreparable impairment to her emotional development that manifested itself in lethal consequences. He stated that her attachment to her children was 'a practical and mechanical kind devoid of any sense of loving and passion'. Justice Barr also noted that Folbigg had not physically neglected her children; rather, she was simply incapable of nurturing or caring for them. He sentenced her to forty years' imprisonment with eligibility for parole in 2033.

Represented by David Jackson QC, one of the nation's most eminent lawyers, Folbigg unsuccessfully appealed her conviction on 17 February 2005.[38] Her sentence was, however, reduced to thirty years with parole hearings available in 2029. Folbigg then sought leave to appeal to the High Court of Australia in May 2005 on the grounds that errors in judgment had been made at her trial. She was unsuccessful.[39] On 16 May 2007 she was granted leave to appeal again on the grounds that jurors had access to information from the internet about her mother's murder and also that the jury had been misled about body temperature after infant death. The appeal was heard in the New South Wales Court of Criminal Appeal in November 2007 by Justice Peter McClellan, Justice Carolyn Simpson and Justice Virginia Bell.[40] It was dismissed.

Folbigg has now exercised all her rights to appeal her sentence. Her trials have been lengthy and numerous. But she determinedly maintains her innocence and is convinced of the unfairness of the legal system towards her. In a letter to Lea Brown, Folbigg laid out her case: 'Try to imagine your life spread out, ripped to pieces, examined, opinions cast, character assassinated, your every action, word, thought, doubted, and you're told that you do not know yourself. Add to that, because of all of the above, the most HATED woman alive ... You can't. I live with this every day. I endure all of this knowing that vindication will be mine. This is the last time I'll state – I did not kill my children.'[41]

Folbigg will spend her sentence in isolation for her own protection. This is in stark contrast to Kathy Knight who murdered, skinned and cooked her partner, and was sentenced to life imprisonment 'never to be released' in 2001. Like Folbigg, Knight is incarcerated in Silverwater Women's Correctional Centre (formerly Mulawa Detention Centre), but unlike Folbigg she is able to spend her time sewing amicably with other inmates. Knight is frequently so involved with her craft activities she does not see visiting family members.[42]

CHAPTER 5

A Baffling Case: Keli Lane

There are persistent stereotypes of the type of women who commit infanticide. There's the poverty-stricken, desperate woman with little education and few skills, or the young, frightened single teenager. Such stereotypes are as predictable as they are frequently true. However, neonatal killing can also be driven by severe postpartum depression or psychosis. So how to interpret the actions of a 'golden girl',[1] in the words of Justice Anthony Whealy, who was accused and found guilty of killing her newborn daughter and hiding the body, which was never found? Keli Lane came from a well-respected family in the northern beachside suburb of Manly in Sydney. She was an elite sportswoman with Olympic aspirations who taught at a prestigious private girls' school, and yet in December 2010 she stood convicted of murder.

Born on 21 March 1975, Keli Lane lived in Manly from the time she was four years old. Her father, Robert Lane, was a highly regarded police sergeant and rugby union player and coach. Even though he later switched to rugby league, he remained a core member of the Manly Rugby Union Football Club. Keli's mother, Sandra, was also involved with local sports clubs and was, as well, manager for travelling women's water polo teams. Keli was a keen swimmer who, by adolescence, was a champion water polo player representing the state and the national teams at a junior level.[2] She attended what is now known as Mackellar Girls Campus, where she excelled in water sports. Not academically inclined, Lane was more prominent as a noted sportswoman, well connected to the social and sporting culture of the area, which in Manly conferred prestige.

Her first boyfriend, Aaron Tyack, a surf lifesaver intent upon undertaking trade training, knew the competitiveness of Manly's local culture well: 'Manly can be a very cliquey place. It's like a small town.'[3] In this hierarchical environment, Keli Lane was a star – beautiful, athletic, popular and outwardly charming – from a high-profile local family. At seventeen, though, while she was still a school student, Lane became pregnant and underwent a termination. She told her boyfriend of the pregnancy but not her parents. She had another termination, this time a late-term abortion, again without informing her parents, whom she suspected would be disapproving and unsupportive. And this time she didn't tell Tyack. Her relationship with him, which had been strong and committed, fell apart soon afterwards.[4]

In 1993 Lane was selected for the Under 20s squad to represent New South Wales at the national water polo championships. The team did well, auguring more national and perhaps even international success, although it was not yet an Olympic sport. Yet Keli's teammates Lisa Berry and Taryn Woods were considered more suitable for continuing elite participation.[5]

The following year Lane met Duncan Gillies, whose family included several professional rugby league players. Their mutual commitment to high-level sport, competition and partying were important elements of their relationship. Gillies often spent the night with Lane at her parents' home, where she resided. Robert and Sandra Lane did not entirely approve, though they realised that this was the modern trend and they respected their daughter's choice of boyfriend. Lane began an Arts degree at the University of Newcastle but dropped out fairly quickly.

That year she was deeply disappointed when she was not selected for the Australian women's water polo team, especially when friends and teammates were fortunate in this regard. It spurred her ambitions even more fervently to join the big league of competition. Lane also had a clandestine affair with an older married man in 1994, by whom she became pregnant. This was another secret pregnancy, even though she continued her relationship with Gillies. Rumours circulated about her expanding belly. Witness Allison Cratchley testified at a coronial inquiry in 1995 that 'Manly can be a very toxic place. If you put on a little bit of weight, the next thing you're accused of being pregnant. That's something that happened to me in the past, so I dismissed those rumours.' Barrister David Woods asked the New South Wales head coach Les Kay whether he had broached the subject of pregnancy with Lane at the time. 'It's not a good place to go,' he replied.[6]

On 18 March 1995 Lane and her team from the Balmain Water Polo Club played Sydney University Water Polo Club. Almost unbelievably she gave birth that night at Balmain Hospital after first attending a post-match party at the Bridge Hotel, also in Balmain. Even Gillies' mother, Julie Gillies, an experienced nurse, had no idea that Lane was about to give birth. Incredible as this seems, other contemporary cases show that Lane was not alone in concealing multiple pregnancies. French nurse Dominique Cottrez was accused of murdering eight of her babies in 2010. Her husband had no idea about any of the pregnancies until he found the bodies in their garden.[7]

Lane's newborn daughter was immediately placed for adoption. Social worker Deborah Habib recalled later at the coronial hearing that she advised Lane about the adoption procedures. Lane was emotionally overwrought and sad. As she explained to Habib, she wanted to compete in the Olympics and wouldn't be able to if '... she continued to parent a baby'.[8] On 3 April 1995 Lane swore an affidavit in the adoption proceedings that falsely claimed that Duncan Gillies was willing for his child to be adopted. False, since he knew nothing about the pregnancy and nor was he the father. In a further affidavit Lane swore that Gillies maintained he wanted nothing to do with his daughter and had refused to sign consent forms.[9] Insufficient inquiries were made into her deception.

Lane resumed her life without seeming to miss a beat, representing Australia for a silver medal in the World Championships in Canada. In early 1996 Lane was selected to compete in the New South Wales women's water polo team, which she believed would get her into a future Olympic spot. She was also accepted for study at the Australian College of Physical Education. By this time, Gillies had purchased a home in Gladesville, making their time together even more sporadic.

Yet in December 1995, just nine months after her daughter's birth, Lane became pregnant once again. The father of the baby is unknown.[10] For her twenty-first birthday her parents threw an impressive party in April 1996. Persistent rumours at this time suggested that Lane and Gillies, now a professional football player, were no longer involved. Gillies had been painfully honest with Lane, telling her about a sexual encounter with a teammate and friend of Keli's.[11] His straightforwardness was something she didn't reciprocate.

Other areas of Lane's life progressed. Her career began to take off in 1996 when she became a sports mistress at the prestigious Ravenswood School for Girls on Sydney's North Shore. By this time she was visibly pregnant, although again in secret – or so she thought. Alissa Warren, one of Lane's former students, and later employed as a reporter for Channel Nine News, stated that the students all knew 'Miss Lane was pregnant' in 1996. 'There wasn't much gossip about Miss Lane – but as her belly grew, so did the judging glances and snide remarks between parents. Miss Lane was obviously young, obviously pregnant and not married.'[12]

Her water polo teammates were also highly suspicious that Lane was pregnant. Stacey Gaylard, who had boarded with the Lane family for eight months in 1994, recalled that in 40°C heat at the Sydney International Aquatic Centre at Homebush in 1996 Lane turned up in a heavy tracksuit when everyone else wore shorts and singlet tops. 'I saw her take her towel off and my eyes nearly popped out of my head. I thought, "Oh, my God, there can only be one possible reason for her stomach being so big."' She was so astounded that she and Taryn Woods decided to view Lane from an underwater perspective. She continued: 'We started swimming laps and as we passed her, we looked. She was just so obviously pregnant. How could she think no one would notice? We assumed it was Duncan's baby and that they handled the situation together – maybe arranged for adoption.'

In the past, teammates thought Lane was a 'Keg on Legs', a solidly built woman who partied hard and enjoyed drinking. Coach Les Kay wondered if her weight had been caused by too much 'winter grazing'. He later said that he had heard rumours that Lane was pregnant in 1996 '… but I stay well away from that'.[13] That no one confronted Lane about the pregnancy or even inquired about the possibility indicates that for all her popularity she was emotionally closed and secretive, with no close friends or confidants. In fact, Lane had managed to conceal her pregnancy with her firstborn child not just from her family but also from Gaylard, who had shared a bedroom with her at the time.

On Thursday 12 September 1996, after an induced labour, Lane gave birth to her daughter Tegan at Auburn Hospital in western Sydney. She admitted herself, telling nursing staff that her family was currently away and that her scheduled midwife, 'Julie Melville', could not be located, thus ensuring that staff would be unable to check her medical records. She spun an elaborately concocted story about a desired homebirth, telling the nursing staff that her partner, Duncan Gillies, a professional footballer, was also away. Unlike other new mothers, she had no visitors, no excited relatives, flowers or cards. Even in her hospital room she drew the curtain around her and did not engage in conversation with her fellow new mothers.

At some point a telephone call came from Ryde Hospital inquiring whether a Keli Lane had been admitted since she had presented at Ryde requesting an induced birth.

As it was later revealed, Lane had needed to give birth on the Thursday so she could go to a wedding with Gillies the following Saturday.[14] Lane did allow a hospital social worker to take down case notes: she 'admitted' that Duncan Gillies was her boyfriend, 'currently overseas' before their permanent move to London in a few months.

Lane requested a discharge on Saturday 14 September, and was supplied with Medicare forms that she was pressed to complete. Other medical records were left for her to post back to the hospital. On the form Lane named the newborn Tegan Lee Lane, thus leaving an official paper trail of the baby's existence. When medical staff agreed that both mother and baby were fit for release, Lane left surreptitiously, possibly by the fire exit. Tegan did not have the usual baby capsule or bassinette and was simply carried out in her mother's arms around midday. The nurse on duty recorded in the case notes that Lane's private midwife needed to be contacted to ensure the Guthrie test for congenital illnesses was conducted. By 3pm Lane had arrived home alone seemingly composed and perfectly normal. She and Gillies dressed for the wedding and neither he nor her parents noticed anything different about her appearance. At 4pm she went to the wedding with Gillies, but she seemed a little tired and not as exuberant as usual; she left the festivities unexpectedly early.[15]

On Monday 16 September, Lane rang the Auburn maternity ward informing the duty nurse that she wanted to cancel the standard home visit as she planned to have Tegan's tests and medical procedures done by her homebirth nurse. Lane resumed her normal life as if nothing unusual had happened. Later in the year she was invited to Ben Gillies' wedding and accompanied Duncan as his partner.

The following year Lane faced a series of disappointments. She was not selected for the state women's water polo team and therefore could not participate in the FINA World Cup. The sport was then selected as an Olympic event, raising her hopes for inclusion even though she was not invited to attend the official announcement. When the Australian Institute of Sport released its selection her name was not included. Then in February 1999 she was not selected at the trials in Noosa, and from then any realistic hopes for Olympic glory were gone. Duncan Gillies' career, on the other hand, although not brilliant, was progressing to international level in competitions against Scotland and Fiji. In early 1998 he ended his relationship with Lane. Despite the setbacks, her enthusiasm for her sport did not diminish and she kept alive her hopes that she could be selected to represent her country for the 2000 Summer Olympics in Sydney.

Keli Lane has never been able to adequately explain what happened to her baby Tegan. Photo: Fairfax Media FXJ 40197.

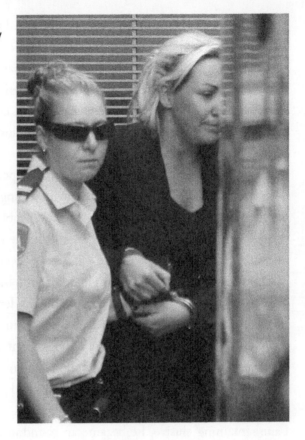

Alarmingly, Keli Lane discovered that she was pregnant again; her attempt to secure a late-term abortion this time was rejected. The father was entirely unaware of this pregnancy, believing Lane was taking contraceptives. As before, Lane informed no one and concealed her pregnancy. She gave birth to a son in Ryde Hospital on 31 May 1999. Again there were no flowers, family or friends to celebrate with her in the maternity ward. And again she indicated to the admission officer that her family and her partner, Duncan Gillies, lived in London, and that she was only back in Australia briefly. When queries about Tegan were made she said that she was in Sydney. Who was minding Tegan while Lane was a maternity patient was not discussed. The little boy was adopted through Anglicare. The adoption officer, Virginia Fung, immediately contacted Lane to sort out the now-complicated procedure for adoption, which had been designed to protect vulnerable women who were relinquishing their babies.

Lane insisted that her baby's father had abandoned her when he found out she was pregnant and that she intended returning to London soon, adding to the confusing web of lies and conflicting stories she had told to different officials and hospital employees. A social worker interviewed Lane, reassuring her that adoption was a discreet process that eliminated as much stigma as humanly possible. Lane left the hospital without the baby and without informing the nursing staff of her departure. The baby had simply been a problem to be solved and then swiftly forgotten about. When the Ryde Hospital postpartum midwife went to Gillies' house in Gladesville to check up on Lane she was informed that Duncan Gillies had not lived there for over eighteen months and that Lane had never been a resident. From that point on Lane made sure she was hard to contact, turning off her mobile telephone. When eventually Virginia Fung caught up with her, she spun another story – that Duncan was emotionally remote and uncaring.

Keli Lane's infant son was initially fostered for a month, and at the end of June his long-term future needed to be decided. With Lane remaining elusive, he became an abandoned baby with no real legal status. And this provoked exactly the kind of attention Lane had wanted to avoid. Her unusual behaviour alerted care workers that here was a complicated and potentially unresolved case. On top of that, Ryde Hospital also had a copy of Tegan's birth records.

At this point Virginia Fung was not yet aware of Tegan's birth or that there was any mystery regarding her whereabouts. She was a thorough and sympathetic adoption officer who, when Lane continued to be elusive, next attempted to contact Duncan Gillies through the Manly Warringah Rugby League Club. When Gillies received the correspondence he was perplexed that anything involving Lane would now concern him, especially since he was engaged to be married. When Gillies spoke to Fung he confirmed he did not live with Lane and he had never been in London with her. Lane's subsequent discussion with him about pregnancies and babies was confused, contradictory and disturbing for him and his fiancée Karen. Tracking down the fax numbers, Fung realised that some had come from Ravenswood School, proving that the story about living in London was a fabrication.

Fung persisted in her hunt for the truth. Lane was deemed to be in no fit state to continue with the adoption process and Fung advised her to seek psychological assistance. Her newborn baby became a ward of the state. A meeting near Ravenswood in mid-1999 proved unsatisfactory, so a few days after that Fung went to visit Lane at the school. Lane told her the name of the father was Aaron Williams, a merchant banker in London with whom she had no further contact. When asked whether her son had any siblings Lane said no, this was her first baby. She requested an access visit with her baby and seemed perfectly happy to be with him. Adoption procedures were resumed. The day that Lane picked potential new parents for the little boy, John Borovnik, a Department of Community Services officer, tracked down the files on Tegan's birth and discovered her absence from any official records.

When confronted by Fung with the fact that she had given birth before, Lane told her that she felt no one would help her if it was revealed she had already been through it previously. The first baby had been adopted, but what of the second, Tegan Lee Lane?

When Borovnik first asked her about Tegan's birth in 1996 Lane denied the baby's existence. On 4 November 1999 Borovnik contacted police in Katoomba, the nearest area to Auburn Hospital.[16] Aaron Williams could not be traced and Julie Melville, although a nurse, did not practise as a midwife.

In late 1999 the Lane file arrived at Manly Police Station and landed on the desk of Matt Kehoe, who was already well regarded for his detective work in the case of Louise Sullivan, the Sydney nanny who had been accused of killing a baby in London. But this new case presented difficulties from the start. Unsuccessfully, Kehoe requested a transfer from the case. In the end it took him more than eighteen months to interview Lane; in that time he did not contact Fung or Borovnik. He did, however, interview Julie Gillies – whose professional name is Julie Melville. Duncan Gillies was as perplexed as his mother to learn about the birth of a baby girl to Keli Lane in 1996.

In late 2000, Keli Lane became pregnant to a young family friend, who had been staying with the Lanes.[17] In February 2001, Kehoe finally interviewed Lane about Tegan's whereabouts. She told him that the baby's father was a man called Andrew Morris, who lived in Balmain with his partner, and that Tegan lived with them. She had lost contact with them years ago. But in her formal interview at Manly Police Station on 13 February 2001, Lane still had Tegan's Medicare card in her possession, hardly likely if the girl lived with her father.[18] Yet, when Kehoe could not locate a birth certificate for Tegan, for another three months nothing was done.

The delays and false starts are understandable, especially since Manly Police Station was under investigation as part of the wider corruption inquiry known as Operation Florida. Kehoe, an officer with an exemplary record, was transferred to another station. In October 2001, Detective Richard Gaut, a new officer to the station, took over the Tegan Lane case.

At first Gaut was concerned to rectify Tegan's legal status and provide her with registration of her birth. Part of this process involved locating her father, Andrew Morris – a frustrating and fruitless task. His interview with Keli Lane was difficult, the interviewee uncooperative. Even the name of Tegan's father was changed – perhaps it was Andrew Norris, who knew? For a woman now with a toddler, from a respected local family and with a position at a prestigious girls' school, Lane hardly appeared on the surface to be a woman who had rather carelessly abandoned an ex-nuptial baby to a man whose name she was not certain of. Inquiries with Medicare revealed that no services had been requested or processed, again unbelievable for a five-year-old urban child. Gaut also contacted Lane's old water polo teammates, who confirmed that Lane had looked pregnant in 1996.

When questioned again in late 2003, Lane admitted she had lied on numerous occasions to social workers and nursing staff regarding her family situation and residence. What is surprising is that she identified real people, like Julie Melville and Duncan Gillies, with whom facts could be later verified or refuted.

Detective Gaut was not about to give up his inquiries concerning what appeared to be a missing child case. He informed Lane the matter would be forwarded to the coroner's office for further investigations.

Rental records did not find an 'Andrew Morris' or 'Andrew Norris' renting in Balmain on the dates Lane had given. On 4 January 2004, Gaut received permission to tap Lane's telephone.

Four days later, Lane was interviewed at Manly Police Station again. By now she had realised that a coroner's inquiry would be a public proceeding and that her parents would find out about the concealed births and the three babies. Lane was distressed and alarmed by the tone of Gaut's questions when he asked why she had wanted Tegan's birth to be induced. An expert psychiatric evaluation of this interview, conducted by Dr Michael Diamond, commented that these questions '… were very close to revealing her true distress at the time when [Lane] was pregnant with Tegan, had kept the pregnancy secret, had no plan for what she might do with Tegan after the birth'.[19] The story that Tegan was given to her father somewhere between Auburn Hospital and Lane's home in Manly was unbelievable.

Lane and her boyfriend intended to marry in February 2004, so she told him about Tegan. She also decided she had better tell her mother.

On 14 March 2004, Tegan's case was referred to the coroner's office as a possible murder. Lane was intensively interviewed again in November 2004, a situation that she found stressful. She was 'in a mess and she was scared', the Supreme Court was later told; this was quite unlike her calm demeanour the day she left Auburn Hospital with Tegan and attended a wedding later that afternoon. Her GP, Dr Jeremy Thompson, treating her at the time, reported that Lane was 'in a distraught state' as she felt she was 'being given a hard time' both by the police investigation team and the journalists who 'hovered around her'. Lane confided in him about the 'compulsions and unhappiness that underlay her prior destructive behaviour' although she strenuously denied having harmed Tegan.[20]

Lane's parents hired a QC to represent her, something far beyond their financial resources. She was advised to say as little as possible, which frustrated the proceedings. With no leads, the court opened up the intriguing case for public scrutiny in newspapers and other forms of media. In June 2005, Coroner John Abernethy, assisted by Sergeant Rebecca Becroft, began the official public inquiry beset by myriad difficulties, given how much time had passed and the inadequate initial police investigations. Gaut, Fung and Borovnik all testified. Robert Lane took the stand, affirming that he could not believe that his daughter would harm a child, regardless of the circumstances of the secret birth. Duncan Gillies and Julie Gillies and a range of friends provided testimony to the coroner. During the proceedings, Sandra Lane did not attend court. She was, however, summoned to appear to answer close questioning about her views on abortion and ex-nuptial birth. She stated that she would have supported her daughter regardless of local negative opinion, contrary to what Lane had assumed.

Keli Lane initially declined to take the witness stand. Coroner Abernethy and her barrister discussed whether she was worried that she could incriminate herself under oath. Eventually she reluctantly took the stand, reminded from the bench that she did not have to answer questions that would incriminate her. When asked about Tegan's birth, she declined to answer. The media outside the court smelt blood and a scoop. From now on Keli Lane was a sensational news item.

On 15 February the coroner's report was released. It canvassed several core questions: that no body had been discovered; that there was no forensic evidence to examine; that Keli Lane had put up her first and third child for adoption; and that Lane may have released Tegan to the care of her natural father in the car park, and that he declined to come forward. However, the coroner concluded by saying that he believed Tegan was dead and that all details of the hearings were to be forwarded to the homicide squad of the New South Wales Police.[21] Lane was admonished for wasting so much police time. When he retired in 2007 after seven years in the Coroner's Court, Abernethy said that 'Tegan Lane was arguably the most frustrating case I did. It was a case I simply could not solve.'[22]

In late 2006, ten years after Tegan's disappearance, the homicide squad assembled a task force with two detectives plus fifteen other police and intelligence officers. Their first task was to check all birth registrations for the relevant period as well as to check records of some 9000 primary schools with white female pupils aged ten. Many parents enrol their children without producing a birth certificate as proof of age, a factor that increased the task force's workload as records were meticulously checked across the nation. DNA samples were taken from over a thousand girls. Men with the name of Andrew Morris or Andrew Norris were also investigated.

Keli Lane's marriage ended in 2007. The strain of the coroner's investigation and her husband's knowledge of the previous three children were no doubt contributing factors. Her employment at Ravenswood School was also terminated.

One by one, Lane's secrets were uncovered. Her medical records revealed that the second pregnancy had been terminated when she was five months' pregnant. Apparently, she had been willing to go through a late-term abortion and might have done so for the other pregnancies had she been able to at the time. Her sexual history exposed other secrets: her friends realised that the mystery father of her firstborn child had attended the wedding on the day that Tegan disappeared, and yet Lane remained untroubled.[23]

In August 2008, the police decided to search and excavate Duncan Gillies' Gladesville property in the hope of finding Tegan's remains. None were found. This was a distressing event for the entire Gillies family, which was reeling not only from the knowledge of Lane's secret births but from the fact that these children had been fathered by other men at a time when Lane was regarded as Duncan Gillies' partner.

In late 2009, after several years of intense police investigation, Keli Lane was arraigned for the murder of Tegan Lane. At her initial hearing on 4 December 2009 before Justice Roderick Howie, Lane – accompanied by her father – was granted bail. On 9 August 2010 she was charged in the New South Wales Supreme Court before Justice Anthony Whealy of three counts of false swearing and one of murder.

The Crown prosecutor, Mark Tedeschi QC, was the most experienced criminal barrister in the state, known for his successful prosecutions of serial killers Ivan Milat and Kathleen Folbigg. Having depleted her financial resources, Lane was represented by an experienced Legal Aid-appointed barrister, Keith Chapple SC.

Tedeschi presented the jury with a withering and damning assessment of Lane's character, revealing that in the eight years from 1992 to 1999 she underwent two abortions and had three ex-nuptial babies, one of whom was now missing. He questioned whether her heavy drinking and partying at pubs, where she kept up with the boys in alcohol consumption, rendered the oral contraceptive she was taking ineffective. The various fathers of her children and her deception towards Gillies were also canvassed, throwing a negative light on her morals. He alleged that the motivations for her callous and in one instance lethal actions were her desire to compete in the Olympics; her desire to maintain an active social and sex life; and her fear of rejection from her family and friends if knowledge of her pregnancies was discovered.

The question of why Tegan was not adopted like the two other children Keli Lane gave birth to remained a vexed one. Attending her friends' wedding several days after Tegan's birth seemed to be imperative to Lane. She could have requested leave of absence from the maternity ward for the evening.

Tedeschi continued his attack: 'Ladies and gentlemen, there is not the slightest suggestion that the accused was suffering from postnatal depression or other mental disturbance after Tegan's birth. Quite the contrary. At 3pm she had an appointment to meet her boyfriend Duncan Gillies at her parents' home so they could get dressed and go to a wedding … The accused was observed having a perfectly good time socialising, drinking, dancing. She was her normal self.' His address took two days to deliver.

Lane's counsel then attempted to dismiss the Crown's contentions. Justice Whealy reminded the jury that telling lies was not evidence of murder.

Various friends, from whom Lane was now estranged, gave evidence, all expressing disbelief as the revelations of secrecy, adoption and the charge of murder rolled out. Listening to their evidence and that of Virginia Fung reduced Lane to tears and despair. Her parents had initially appeared before Justice Whealy without the jury, although they established they were willing to testify in open court. Sandra Lane was confronted with all the information about Tegan and her disappearance. Robert Lane appeared equally uncomfortable in the face of the evidence of his beloved daughter's secret life.

The trial was conducted over four months, much of it consumed with police and forensic evidence. Several men with the name of Andrew Morris or Andrew Norris were called, but none knew Lane. The jury began their deliberations on 6 December 2010 amid intense media coverage and speculation. They took a week to deliver their verdict. The foreman informed the court that they were unanimous in their verdict on the lesser charges of false swearing connected with the two adoptions but divided on the question of murder. Justice Whealy pointed out that a decision of eleven of the twelve was sufficient. When the jury returned after lunch, the foreman informed the court that they had reached a decision and found the accused guilty of murder as charged. Lane was so overcome she collapsed in the dock, requiring medical attention.

Sentencing took place three months later. Unlike many other prisoners guilty of serious criminal acts, and despite the fact that she had been in custody since her conviction, Lane was well dressed and well groomed at her sentencing hearing. Fairfax journalist Jane Cadzow reported that '[s]he looks so wholesome and outdoorsy – so uncomplicated'.[24] With these words Cadzow captured the sentiments of many who had followed and pondered this intriguing case over the years.

Justice Whealy delivered his long and comprehensive sentencing statement on 15 April 2011. Dr Diamond's assessments of Lane's taped interviews with Detective Gaut gave crucial insights into her character and motivations. Lane, he believed, did not have a psychiatric illness but he did describe her behaviour between 1992 and 1999 as 'very destructive [and] repetitive', that of a person with a disordered personality. His Honour addressed the question of premeditation and found that there had been a degree of premeditation, if 'for only a short time', given that Lane had made no provision for Tegan after leaving the hospital. Her history of concealing her pregnancies and births, her multiple deceptions, and her lack of remorse inclined him to a sentence with a non-parole period of thirteen years, to expire on 12 May 2024, after which she was to serve her sentence for the three counts of false swearing: 'A balance of the sentence is to commence on 13 May 2024 and to expire on 12 December 2028.' Justice Whealy expressed his deep regret for the impact this case and sentence would have on the life of the daughter from Lane's marriage, to whom she had been an exemplary mother.

Even at the end of this long trial, despite all the testimony, despite all the press coverage and interviews and speculation, the motives and intentions of the 'golden girl' remained elusive.

Taryn Woods won a gold medal in the 2000 Sydney Summer Olympics.

CHAPTER 6

The Deadly Baby Farmers

'Baby farmer' is a now-forgotten term referring to a long-ago industry in which illegitimate babies were minded – frequently by unscrupulous paid carers who made money at the cost of an infant's welfare and often, too tragically, its survival. In Gilbert and Sullivan's *HMS Pinafore* (1878), the comic figure of Mrs Cripps (Little Butterfly) refers to the practice, a scandal of the day:

> *A many years ago*
> *When I was young and charming*
> *As some of you may know*
> *I practised baby-farming.*

Where unqualified abortionists might 'help out' girls 'in trouble' at the beginning of an illicit pregnancy, baby farmers helped out at the end of it. Often they were the only way a single woman with a dependent child could manage to work and afford to keep herself in the days before social welfare or even legal adoption. Baby farmers acted in a variety of capacities: as permanent baby carers who were paid an initial lump sum plus a weekly allowance by the mother, as day carers, or even as informal adoption agencies. For the more unscrupulous, though, the temptation to take the money and let the infant die was sometimes too lucrative to resist.

In late nineteenth-century England and Wales, six baby farmers were executed for their crimes. English criminologist H. L. Adam characterised a baby farmer as possessing a 'complete lack of maternal feeling'.[1] Yet this was just the point – a baby farmer ran a business, something that depended on cash not sentiment. As the medical journal *The Lancet* affirmed on 24 January 1903: 'The people who relieve parents of their offspring act from sordid and not benevolent motives.'

In the Australian colonies, baby farmers were largely concentrated in the larger urban areas where anonymity prevailed.

For many married working-class women, becoming genuine foster mothers had the benefit of being home-based work.[2] Yet even in such genuine situations, babies still died at alarming rates, particularly those who were bottle-fed since the absence of proper teats on feed bottles and impure milk created significant nutritional and health problems. 'Boarded-out' babies, as they were called, represented a high proportion of all neonatal deaths at the turn of the century. The English magazine *Pall Mall Gazette* noted: 'There is no human creature ... so defenceless as an illegitimate child.'[3]

There had been attempts to regulate the boarding-out trade in the various Australian colonies. In 1873 the New South Wales premier, Henry Parkes, established a Royal Commission to inquire into charities and social welfare. Barrister and later Justice William Windeyer acted as chairman. Educated at The King's School, Parramatta, and the University of Sydney, Windeyer was a liberal thinker with profound Christian sentiments. His wife, Mary Thorley Windeyer (1837–1912), was the daughter of an Anglican priest and was also committed to social justice. In 1874 she supported the establishment of a foundling hospital in Sydney, 'to remove temptation to infanticide' for destitute and single mothers. She also took an active interest in boarded-out children, orphans in church and state institutions and basic education for the poor.

Despite these reforms and institutions, the worst aspects of boarding-out and baby farming persisted. The most lethal and gruesome aspects of baby farming emerged in 1893 in Sydney. Sarah Makin (1845–1918) and John Makin (1845–93) ran a grisly business killing illegitimate babies for profit.

Born to lower middle-class parents in Wollongong, John Makin had established a successful small business as a drayman, carter and butcher. Despite this, Makin served a term of three months' imprisonment in 1881 for stealing a sheep when he killed a lamb he was supposed to be delivering to a customer at Darling Harbour in Sydney.[4] By this time he already had eight children, whose lives were now thrown into extreme poverty by his incarceration and lack of income.

Sarah Makin's past was far less respectable – her father had been transported to Van Diemen's Land from Leeds in 1833, convicted of stealing worsted cloth. He died in Liverpool Asylum for the Destitute and Infirm (New South Wales) in 1885. Her mother was buried in a pauper's grave in Rookwood Cemetery, Sydney, in 1890. At the age of twenty-one and described as a barmaid, midwife and nurse, Sarah Makin married a Scottish sailor, Captain Charles Edwards, in a Presbyterian church in Sydney before marrying again as 'Sarah Edwards, Spinster' five years later to Makin in a Church of England ceremony. She had been neither divorced nor widowed, making her a bigamist. They had ten children, of which seven survived, then a common occurrence because the infant mortality rates were so high.

When John Makin was injured and unable to continue his trade, the couple decided to run a baby farm. The *Infants Protection Act* of 1891 required that all baby farmers, foster parents and lying-in facilities be registered, but this could be sidestepped by categorising the activity as informal adoption over which the Act had no jurisdiction. John Makin would answer newspaper advertisements placed by women seeking care for their babies, and offer bogus adoption agreements, frequently under one of a number of pseudonyms: John Burt, John Maclaughlin or McLaughlan. The prospect of a caring home would have appeared attractive to these desperate mothers, who paid a small fee for the service. Sometimes Makin offered to arrange external adoption for illegitimate babies, also for a fee.[5] These infants never found other homes, instead ending up dead in various gardens around inner Sydney.

A drainer and plumber, James Hanoney, and his offsider, Frances Cooney, were called to a premises at 25 Burren Street, Macdonaldtown, Sydney, on 11 October 1892 to fix some blocked drains. Initially, he thought some foul-smelling baby clothing was the problem until, constructing some trenches, they discovered the decomposing corpses of two babies. The tenants had been John and Sarah Makin and their children, Florence, Clarice, Blanche, Cecil (Tommy) and Daisy, who had lived there from June to late August 1892. They now lived in Botany Street, Redfern. The bodies were removed to the South Sydney Morgue, where government analyst William Hamlet conducted preliminary investigations. He noted in his report the presence of black calico dressing one of the little corpses, a fabric he had seen on one of the Makin daughters.

Two inquests conducted by the Sydney City coroner, J. C. Woore, inquiring into the deaths of the two bodies found in Macdonaldtown, began on 13 October and adjourned for further police investigation.

On 20 October, Sarah Makin allegedly confronted a former neighbour, Mrs Elizabeth Hill, outside the Coroners Court in Chancery Square, screaming at her: 'I have a good mind to ribbon you, bitch. How dare you give evidence against me? You don't know me; you never spoke to me. The child is yours. You took drugs and you put it there.' She raised her umbrella in anger.[6] Hill was the agent for the owner of 25 Burren Street. The Makins strenuously denied any wrongdoing in their testimony, yet when they answered questions, they were evasive, contradictory and confused.

A second inquest opened on 28 October 1892 to assess the circumstances of the death of the second male. Blanche Makin testified that there was only one newborn baby – a girl – in her mother's care. The jury was unable to decide how the baby had died.

During an adjournment in the first inquest, the police continued their grisly business. On 3 November 1892, while digging in 25 Burren Street, constables Thomas Conan and Alexander Brown found another corpse in a shallow grave. Their search was hindered by the large number of spectators who swarmed the street and nearby houses. An hour later they found a further bundle containing the body of a baby; the total by the end of the day came to seven. That afternoon, Sarah, Blanche, Florence and John Makin were taken to Newtown Police Station for further questioning. Protesting, Florence argued that she rarely stayed with her parents as she was in domestic service elsewhere.

The discovery of these small corpses demanded further investigations and inquests, so the previous addresses of the Makins were searched. Three more infant bodies were found at 109 George Street, Redfern, although none were located at 55 Botany Street. On 11 November 1892, the police found two more bodies at 11 Anderson Street, Redfern, where the Makins lived from 7 November 1891 to 28 January 1892. A neighbour, Mrs Williams, told police that she had never seen baby clothes on the washing line. The next day police unearthed the skeleton of a baby at 28 Levey Street, Chippendale.[7] By this time news of the police finds had spread through the community. Despite an unseasonable cold and wet day, a large crowd gathered in Levey and Abercrombie streets in Chippendale, where a tiny body was found buried in the garden. As digging proceeded, another corpse, that of a baby around twelve months of age, was found.

The postmortems carried out by Dr Frederick Milford the following day ascertained they had been dead for between nine and fourteen months. No cause of death could be ascertained after such a long time.

The police began intensive interviewing. The neighbours of the Makins in Levey Street complained of offensive odours and believed babies were buried under the floorboards. At one time the child of these neighbours brought home a bloodstained baby dress and five rusty needles, all wrapped in calico. Senior Constable James Joyce believed those needles had been used to pierce the hearts of the victims. When the floorboards were raised, only dead rats were discovered.[8] The backyards of Kettle Street, Redfern; 6 Wells Street, Redfern; Bay Street in Glebe; Cooks River Road at St Peters; and Harbour Street near Darling Harbour failed to discover more bodies. A body of a baby was found at Zamia Street, Redfern, wrapped in clothing identified by a mother who left her child in the Makins' care.

Jurors at the various inquests were unable to determine the times or causes of these deaths. The police became frustrated and angry as the proceedings continued. Another inquest began on 12 November 1892, again before the coroner, Mr J. C. Woore. Some of the Makins' older children cooperated with the police, who determined that the parents had been conducting their business for around two years. Clarice Makin, aged fourteen, testified that her mother fed babies in her care with condensed milk. They went from healthy to ill in a short time. She recalled a Mr Bottomly coming to the house in Burren Street to inquire about a baby, but which one she was not certain. She could not recall what her mother said about the disappearance of the various babies. Even though her testimony had been terse and vague, Sarah Makin cursed her daughter loudly for cooperating with the proceedings, unlike Florence and Blanche, who stood condemned with their parents.[9] Clarice identified baby clothing that her mother had pawned.

The coroner condemned the Makins for their many confusing and contradictory statements as well as their outright lies. There was a 'chain of circumstances' that connected the multiple deaths on various properties, all where the Makin family had lived. And it was inconceivable that Sarah Makin, who had reared so many of her own children, was ignorant of infant care. After fourteen days, this inquest concluded, with the jury returning a verdict of guilty of manslaughter for John and Sarah Makin and guilty knowledge for daughters Florence and Blanche.

The way the Makins moved constantly meant that mothers, and in one case a father, could not keep track of their boarded child for whom they paid an allowance, collected regularly by John Makin. Coroner Woore turned his attention to the case of baby Mignonetta Lavinia Davis. Her story was unusual since her unmarried parents, Mignonetta (Minnie) Davis and Horace Bottomly, a proofreader at the *Daily Telegraph*, visited her weekly. When she suddenly died, the Makins took money supposedly for the undertaker and said they would arrange the funeral. They simply pocketed the money and buried the little girl in the garden at Burren Street.* The coroner also raised the question of death certificates, which John Makin would fabricate. Pawning the clothes of the dead babies was a particularly repellent aspect of this deliberate trade.

Another inquest was conducted in December 1892, investigating the circumstances of the death of the baby found in Alderson Street, Redfern. Dr Milford and a Dr Marano conducted the autopsy and stated that the baby, aged two to six weeks old, had been dead perhaps six to twelve months. They could not determine the sex or cause of death. The Makins refused to testify and the jury returned an open verdict. Inquests into the deaths of the babies found in George Street, Redfern, were opened. Clara Risby, a single domestic servant, testified that she had placed her daughter with the Makins (who called themselves McLachlan) for the cost of £5 in early May 1892. She identified clothing presented in court as belonging to her baby. Joseph Lopez, a pawnbroker in Waterloo, testified that he had received these items from Daisy Makin on 8 August 1892.

Another single mother, Amber Murray, gave birth to her ex-nuptial son, Horace Amber Murray, in June 1892, arranging for the Makins, then living at 139 George Street in Redfern, to organise his adoption. She was prepared to pay the sum of 10/- per week for his upkeep. This was a considerable amount for an eighteen-year-old domestic servant. It was to be a fateful decision for both Murray and the Makins. Amber Murray gave evidence about the circumstances of the adoption of Horace by a Mrs John Hill (Sarah Makin). Blanche Makin had collected Horace Murray from his mother on 27 June 1892, thus indicating her complicity with the family business. By now there had been fourteen inquests in total. On the order of the coroner, John

---

* Davis and Bottomly married in 1894 and had a son, Harold, born the following year.

and Sarah Makin were ordered to stand trial on 20 February 1893 for the murder of Horace Murray and another baby, name unknown, on 29 June 1892 at 109 George Street, Redfern.

In March 1893 John Makin and Sarah Makin faced proceedings in the New South Wales Supreme Court for the murder of Horace Murray. The trial was heard by Justice Matthew Stephen, the distinguished son of the former chief justice, Sir Alfred Stephen. Mr T. M. Williamson again acted as counsel for the accused, receiving £61 for his services and £70 in expenses, some of which was paid by Makin's brother, Thomas.[10] Amber Murray, the first witness, testified that she wanted a 'kind, motherly woman to adopt her fine baby'. Answering her advertisement in the newspaper, John Makin replied that he and his wife could provide little Horace with such a home for the fee of £3 and a weekly payment of 10/-. She handed over Horace, dressed in a long white gown and a shirt, to their daughter Blanche Makin. She added that she had made the clothes herself and identified exhibits as Horace's outfit.

Other witnesses confirmed the baby was strong and healthy before he left his mother's care. After the testimony of Senior Constable Joyce, counsel for the defendants objected to the further line of questioning which took evidence from premises beyond Burren Street and upon which the Makins were not charged. Justice Stephen, however, ruled that he would allow the scope of the evidence to range wider than Burren Street.[11] Agnes Ward testified that she had entrusted her son aged three months to the Makins, then in Kettle Street, Redfern, in April 1892. She could not locate them when they moved. The next witness, Clara Risby, repeated her evidence from the inquest that she had given £5 to Sarah and John Makin, then living in East Street, Redfern. She sent three baby gowns with the baby. When she went to visit him Sarah Makin told her he was out with her children. After that they moved, and she could not find them. Mary Stacey, another domestic servant, reported that she gave birth to an illegitimate baby in April 1892, whom she gave away in adoption to a 'Mr Ray of

109 George Street, Redfern'. 'Sarah Ray' said they were soon moving to Marrickville and the new address would be forwarded. It never was. Stacey identified the Makins as the Rays. She clearly identified some clothing, which she had made herself with various embellishments.

The Makins' trial is one of the most famous in Australian legal history, for it enshrined the principle of 'similar fact' – meaning in this case that the evidence surrounding the bodies of unidentified babies was allowed alongside that of Horace Murray.[12] This judgment was applied in the British case in 1896 for which Amelia Dyer, Britain's most notorious baby farmer, was executed at Newgate Prison.[13] It was also used as a precedent in the famous 1992 case of serial killer Rodney Cameron, the so-called 'Lonely Hearts Killer', who was convicted in the New South Wales Central Criminal Court.

Neither John nor Sarah Makin testified. They provided no evidence in their defence nor did they call for witnesses.[14] The testimony of their daughter Clarice for the Crown case helped convict them. Both were found guilty of wilful murder. The jury recommended mercy for Sarah Makin. The Makins promptly appealed their sentence on the grounds of the inadmissibility of 'similar facts' evidence. They were represented by a leading Sydney barrister, Sir Julian Salomons (1835–1909), who had stepped down from the bench in 1886 due to the extreme anti-Semitism he experienced from William Windeyer, a progressive on other social issues. The following year Salomons was appointed to the Legislative Council as a Liberal supporter of Sir Henry Parkes.[15]

The Full Court consisting of Justice Windeyer, Justice Innes and Justice William Foster heard the appeal premised upon the question that testimony from other mothers whose babies disappeared in the care of the Makins was not evidence in the death of Horace Murray. It had only served to establish their reputations as disreputable baby farmers and mass murderers. Windeyer, however, got to the heart of the matter when he stated: 'A family might be unfortunate enough to take a house in the backyard of which babies had been buried by a former tenant; but no one could believe that it was a mere coincidence that a person took three houses in the backyards of which former tenants had secretly buried babies.'[16]

The Makins lost their appeal. They reappeared before Justice Stephen to hear their sentences on 30 March 1893. When asked whether they had anything to say before sentence was passed, Sarah Makin remained silent while her husband proclaimed their innocence. Both were sentenced to death, although Justice Stephen stated he would recommend mercy for Sarah Makin to the Executive Council. He concluded: 'You took money from the mother of this child [Horace Murray]: you beguiled her with promises you never meant to perform, having already determined the death of this child ... you buried the child in the yard, I say, like you would bury the carcass of a dog ... carrying on this nefarious and hellish trade ...'[17] The editorial of the *Sydney Morning Herald* for 31 March 1893 praised the decision of the appeal judges, who allowed the evidence of 'similar fact'.

John Makin's family in Wollongong – brothers George, Thomas and Daniel – were devastated by the sentence and refused to believe that he had conducted a career as a deadly baby farmer. They wanted the appeal process to continue and unwisely took it to the Privy Council in London. This would mean a considerable delay in carrying out the sentence if the appeal was lost. Edmund Barton QC, later the new Commonwealth's inaugural prime minister, was then the attorney-general of New South Wales and it was in his hands the appeal was forwarded. On 17 July 1893 the case was heard in the Privy Council funded by the Makin brothers. The appeal was lost. A deputation of citizens from Wollongong met with the premier, to no avail.[18] The Makin family then appealed to Premier Sir George Dibbs for clemency. A large petition from the people of the Illawarra was despatched to the government for consideration. One of John Makin's sisters-in-law took up the cudgels, claiming that Sarah Makin was a violent woman who had struck down her own blind mother in a fit of rage, and that if John 'had got a good woman, he would never have been in the position he was'.[19] The Executive Council reconsidered the appeal for clemency on 14 August. Makin was hanged on 15 August 1893, going to the gallows affirming his innocence and that of his wife.

The Executive Council ruled that Sarah Makin should serve a life sentence. She first went to Bathurst jail, established in 1830, and then to Long Bay State Reformatory for Women in Sydney. Her daughter, Minnie Helby, petitioned for her release in 1907, as did Florence Anderson in 1911. On 11 April 1911, Sarah was released into the care of Florence Anderson, dying in 1918 and buried with the benefit of Anglican rites. Clarice Makin, who had testified against her parents, died in 1951 and was buried in Rookwood Cemetery, far away from her mother's grave.[20] Horace Murray was also buried in this cemetery. The Makin boys all changed their surnames.

On 8 November 1949, a curious little item appeared in the *Sydney Morning Herald* announcing that the threatened railway extension between Redfern and Erskineville would demolish the house where the body of Horace Murray was found. No one protested.

In January 1894, a young married mother of two children, Frances Knorr, convicted of murdering babies in her care, was executed. She was an unregistered baby farmer operating in desperate and chaotic circumstances. How she came to stand on the gallows reveals much about the more vicious aspects of the trade. Evidence of her activities came about by chance, when the new tenants of a modest house in Moreland Road, Brunswick, commercial travellers named William and Francis Clay, decided to make a garden on 4 September 1893. William Clay found the body of a baby some thirty centimetres under the grass. Melbourne's newspaper, the *Argus*, the following day issued an extensive editorial about this 'Traffic in Babies'. In this instance the nude body showed a fractured skull 'almost broken into pieces' and other evidence of violence. The police ascertained that an unnamed woman had occupied the house for a short time in April before moving to Davis Street. While at Moreland Road she borrowed a heavy spade from a neighbour, returning it an hour later. The police, readers were informed, had this woman in their sights for baby farming. She remained elusive, changing address with alarming frequency. The police at this time believed that under various aliases she conducted her trade in Middle Brighton, Coburg, Brunswick, Carlton and Prahran. Former residences were examined in an attempt to locate more bodies of infants after three sets of remains were located in Brunswick at Moreland Road and Davis Street.

At the height of the 1890s Depression, the rate of infanticide in Melbourne had increased. As police and coroners averred, inquiries into the fate of dead babies were a regular and saddening feature of their daily working lives. Most distressing were the babies left alive and abandoned in parks, public gardens and on the doorsteps, many to die slowly. Before the passing of the *Infant Life Protection Act* of 1890, many more would be deliberately killed by poor feeding and neglect. The suburban courts were filled with the cases of neglected babies. In the first eight months of 1893, sixty-seven inquests were held in Melbourne to investigate the deaths of abandoned dead infants. In twenty-five cases the court recorded a finding of 'murder by person or persons unknown'.[21] Yet what the *Argus* editorial failed to grasp was the underground trade in babies that often led to death. The unnamed woman from Moreland Road was soon to capture the country's attention by her lethal exploits.

The police eventually tracked down Frances Knorr, who often went by her birth name, Minnie Thwaites, or by Minnie Knorr, even though she had fled to Sydney with her husband. She was about to give birth quite literally. When Detective Edward Keating informed her as she lay in bed that he was from the Melbourne CIB she immediately said: 'All right, Mr Keating. I know who you have come for. You will not arrest him. Whatever I have done my husband knows nothing about this.' Her young daughter, Gladys Knorr, was left with the Sydney Benevolent Asylum since she had measles and was unfit for the sea journey back to Melbourne.[22]

As the arrest was made public, Knorr was dubbed the 'female Herod'.[23] By 9 September, she was described in the press by Detective

Sergeant Nixon, the investigating officer, as a woman of '… very loose habits, immoral character and hardened nature'.[24] The public was primed for a scandal that promised a catalogue of sexual intrigue, murder and the elimination of unwanted babies. These elements established the basis for a riveting few months of reading.

A month after the discovery of the body in Moreland Road, Coroner Samuel Candler (1827–1911) began inquest proceedings. By now an elderly man, Candler had studied as an apprentice apothecary – the precursors to medical practitioners – before his time as a digger on the goldfields in the 1850s. He was regarded highly by colleagues in his role as a coroner, considered to be 'exacting and austere'.[25] Minnie Knorr (alias Thwaites) and Rudolph Knorr were held in custody over the offence and represented by separate legal counsel. The first witness was Dr James Neild, who had conducted the autopsy on Isaac Marks, the infant found at Moreland Road. He told the court that the skull had fractured due to decay rather than overt violence in the first instance. The baby was about one month old when he died, and had been buried for around three months. The landlady of the premises, Ellen Wood, stated that she had rented the house to a dressmaker, 'Mrs Thwaites', who had explained that her husband was a miner in Broken Hill. Her tenant had then asked if Wood would board her daughter Gladys for several months at the rate of 8s 6d per week. That very evening Thwaites had brought a baby into her new home, but did not divulge his origins. Mrs Thwaites left the premises soon after, moving to Davis Street. Mrs Wood denied that she had cared for the newborn, which she described as 'healthy'. A neighbour, Elizabeth Mullery, recalled that she had seen Mrs Thwaites and Gladys, but saw the baby only once.

Another witness, Mary Drummond of Coburg, testified that Mrs Thwaites had engaged her young daughter Harriet as a nursemaid. Harriet Drummond remembered that Mrs Thwaites had borrowed a spade from a neighbour, but she did not know for what purpose. It was returned with the comment that a pick was required for the heavy digging. Harriet had once also asked her to mind another unnamed newborn baby, who Mrs Thwaites had collected from a young woman at the Melbourne Meat Markets.

This testimony demonstrates the workings of the networks conducted by women to look after babies born to single or deserted mothers who could not care for their child themselves. There was a careless informality to all the proceedings, and it was this outsourcing of maternal attention and its consequences that lay at the heart of the problems with baby farming. Knorr's business was so chaotic that she could not keep track of the various infants in her care and, it was later revealed, sometimes substituted one baby for another when anxious mothers came to visit their boarded infant.[26] At the end of proceedings Coroner Candler ordered that Minnie Knorr stand trial for wilful murder.

Frances Knorr was arraigned in the Supreme Court of Victoria before Justice Sir Edward Dundas Holroyd (1828–1916) in October 1893. Prosecutor Walsh opened the Crown case by detailing Knorr's constant change of address, and her deceptions about her life and the babies placed into her care. The evidence in the backyard and the testimony of the nursery maid were crucial to pointing to the babies' murders. Under oath Knorr revealed the circumstances that had brought her to the dock of the Supreme Court.

She was born to William Thwaites, a respectable and devout hat-maker of Chelsea, London, and his wife Frances in 1867. When her teenage affair with a soldier was discovered, her parents sent her to a reformatory for wayward girls.[27] The superintendent urged her parents to take her back, as Minnie, as she was then called, was not a suitable resident for his institution. Her parents did so, on the proviso that she emigrate to save the family further shame.

At the age of nineteen she arrived in Sydney where she was soon in jail for three months for theft. She married a German waiter – and petty criminal – named Rudolph Knorr at St Philip's Church of England on 2 November 1889. They then moved to Richmond in Melbourne where Rudolph Knorr found work as a waiter at the Oriental Hotel,

and then at Parer's Crystal Cafe in Bourke Street. But with hard
economic times and few restaurant patrons, he lost his job. To make
ends meet Knorr turned to selling furniture he had obtained on hire
purchase. The couple fled to Adelaide to evade prosecution but they
were found and Rudolph was jailed for eighteen months in Pentridge
jail. Frances Knorr took on work as a parlour maid at the Exeter
Hotel in Port Adelaide. She also attempted to establish a business as
a dressmaker but it failed in the economic climate of the Depression,
made worse by her decision to relocate to the small settlement of
Quorn, over three hundred kilometres from Adelaide. She stole from
one of her employees to pay for her fare back to Melbourne.[28]

In 1892 Frances Knorr gave birth to her daughter Gladys in the
Melbourne Women's Hospital. At the time she lived with Mrs Sarah
Walkerden, with whom she was soon entangled in a bitter dispute.
They argued over a little boy she had decided to take in to wet-nurse
along with her own child. Walkerden wanted to orchestrate a lucrative
baby-farming business, which Knorr decided would be her financial
saviour – but not with Walkerden. She left owing her landlady the
large sum of £10 and took to squatting illegally in vacant houses.
As she moved from house to house, Walkerden pursued her, telling
neighbours that Knorr was the wife of a convict and a thief and an
immoral woman 'living in sin'. Knorr had found another means of
survival when she entered into a relationship with the local fish
hawker, Ted Thompson, who supported her and Gladys at a number
of residences in York Street, South Melbourne, and George Street,
Fitzroy. They set up house together at Canning Street until his parents
intervened and forced him home.

Knorr left Gladys in the care of Ted's mother, Ann Thompson, a
seemingly strange choice in her chaotic and increasingly desperate life,
and she and Thompson went to Adelaide together. The lovers parted
after quarrelling, and Knorr went to retrieve Gladys. She begged Ann
Thompson for money but when none was forthcoming she and the
little girl spent the night on the streets. Knorr eventually obtained

work as a dressmaker with a Mrs Gresham in Cardigan Street, Carlton. To make ends meet she also took in Lillian Crichton's baby. Ted Thompson continued to offer 'a few shillings now and again'.

Then in April 1893 she relocated to Brunswick. By the time Knorr arrived in the house in Moreland Road she was exhausted and defeated. She was now only twenty-five, with a small child of her own and one on the way, another child to mind, a husband in jail, a lover who had abandoned her, and a failing business.

She took to her bed with the two children, both of whom were malnourished and crying. As Knorr testified: 'I found the milk had turned quite sour and it was impossible to give either of the children. I had no barley in the house and could not make barley water … the two children continued screaming until morning and at about quarter to four the child Crichton died. It went black in the face and was shaking all over … It died from convulsions … I swear I did it no harm. I thought of going to the police first but got frightened. Then I thought, "I will bury it".' She buried the baby naked, aware that clothing had identified various remains leading to the conviction of the Makins. She said that a man she knew called Wilson helped her bury the body, after which she moved to Davis Street.

Rudolph Knorr rejoined the family in May 1893. His chances of finding gainful employment – as a former convict during a Depression – were slight, forcing Frances Knorr to be the sole breadwinner. Frances Knorr told the court she took in a baby from another young woman, whose name she did not even know. The 'baby was in a dirty filthy state' when she received him, she recalled. 'It died that day and I buried it in the backyard' without her husband's knowledge. This baby, found with a knot around its neck, was, she hinted, murdered by Thompson, although what motive he might have had was never explained, other than on one occasion he had gone to get a baby from its mother for her. Another man, by the name of William Wilson, also assisted her, although he was to remain elusive. She took in another unnamed baby, who also died and was buried without ceremony.[29]

On the witness stand Thompson produced a letter written to him by Knorr during the inquest in October, attempting to establish an alibi for herself. The letter had several passages blacked out, no doubt of an intimate nature. Thompson had showed his mother the letter and on her instigation it was now used as evidence for the prosecution. The contents were frantic attempts to establish false dates for the acceptance of boarded-out babies. On the other hand, the letter could have been dictated by Thompson to clear his own limited involvement in Knorr's business. He may have been what was at the time called a 'fizgig' or police informer.[30]

After a five-day trial Frances Knorr was found guilty of wilful murder and was sentenced to death, the execution to take place on 15 January 1894. Before she collapsed, Knorr shouted out to Ted Thompson, sitting in the public gallery: 'God forgive you your sins, Ted.' The particular sins were not enumerated. It was highly unusual for a woman, particularly the mother of a toddler and a very young baby, to be given a capital sentence. No woman had been executed in Victoria since Elizabeth Scott in 1863. Public opinion was outraged, despite the prurient interest taken in the revelations of adultery, illicit sex and murder heard in the court.

A petition from the 'Women of Victoria' pleaded for mercy, arguing that 'the killing of a woman by any body of men did not accord with the moral sense of the community'.[31] Even the trial judge, Justice Holroyd, said that the evidence was circumstantial, although 'exceedingly strong'.[32] And Sarah Makin, who had killed more babies than Frances Knorr, had been given a commuted life sentence. Over two hundred people held a vigil in Russell Street and marched to nearby Government House to ask for mercy for this young mother. The governor, the seventh Earl of Hopetoun, informed the deputation that, on the advice of the Executive Council, he did not intend to issue a reprieve. Rudolph Knorr begged for clemency, telling the government his wife was an epileptic given to strange irrational behaviour.[33] Her behaviour was at times irrational but whether this was from any mental infirmity or caused by her desperate poverty and circumstances remains open to debate.

While she awaited execution, Knorr became zealously religious, taking to hymn singing day and night at the top of her voice. In this mood of repentance as she sought absolution of her sins, Knorr confessed to killing the three babies and hoped 'that my fate will be a warning for others ... and act as a deterrent to those who are perhaps carrying on the same practice'. The confession appears to have been dictated, as the language does not match that used in her letter to Thompson.[34]

Rudolph Knorr brought Gladys to say goodbye. The *Weekly Times* of 20 January 1894 reported that 'the sight of the mother clinging to the baby was particularly painful ... She heaped kisses on the poor little mite, and prayed she should never know'. Rita Daisy Knorr, the baby she had had with Thompson, ended up in police custody as a neglected child even before her mother's execution. Her chances of survival were slim. Neither Rudolph Knorr nor the Thompsons were willing to take charge of her welfare.[35] Knorr had been correct when she cried out in court at the end of the hearing: 'God help my poor babies!' for she realised Rita might have as short a life as those babies she had killed.

Outside the prison large crowds singing hymns gathered to protest against the proceedings inside. Frances Knorr went to the gallows singing 'Abide with Me' and 'Safe in the Arms of Jesus'. She was calm and dignified. The prison matron collapsed in a fit of hysterical sobbing. Dr Shields, the prison's resident medical officer, was in attendance for the entire ordeal. Usually a member of the clergy or nuns gave comfort to a condemned prisoner but in this case it was Dr Shields who supported the condemned woman.[36] Knorr's last words on this Earth were: 'The Lord is with me. I do not fear what men can do unto me, for I have peace, perfect peace.' Chief Warder Long remarked that she died as 'plucky ... as brave as Ned Kelly'. What more fitting tribute could such a hardened man give to this woman of only twenty-six?[37]

Frances Knorr was convicted of three child murders but there was speculation that she was responsible for more deaths. Photo: Public Records office, Victoria, VPS 5900. Photograph of prisoners sentenced to death and coroner's inquest sheets, PO, Unit 1.

After Knorr's execution many women came forward to police telling them sad stories of babies entrusted to her care, now missing and presumed dead. Knorr may have killed thirteen in all.[38] Along with those of the other three women executed in the Old Melbourne Gaol in Russell Street, now a museum, her death mask is on public display. Her skull is also an exhibit, although it has been wrongly labelled 'Martha Knorr', confusing her with notorious serial poisoner Martha Needle.[39]

In 1907, an even more appalling case of murderous baby farming occurred in Perth. Alice Mitchell was suspected of killing by starvation and neglect up to thirty-seven babies in her care. Her methods were not so much acts of wilful murder like those carried out by Sarah Makin or Frances Knorr, but slow death by negligence.

Despite British settlement since 1829, Western Australia had only attained self-government in 1890. This coincided with the discovery of gold in remote Kalgoorlie (1893) and Coolgardie (1892), substantially aiding the colony's economic development. Yet in the wake of this sudden prosperity came myriad social problems. Government agencies could not provide the public infrastructure and health services required to accommodate the rapidly expanding population. Like Brisbane and Sydney, Perth endured episodes of bubonic plague. The eastern fringes of the city in particular contained noxious industries and places where those who could not find work or success on the goldfields took advantage of cheap accommodation. Alice Mitchell established her business as a baby farmer at various addresses in this area, at Wellington Street, Cavendish Street, Peterson Terrace, Lord Street and Edward Street.[40] Like the Makins and Frances Knorr, she moved constantly, trying to keep one step ahead of any investigation into her deadly trade.

The new colony passed legislation modelled on the English *Infant Life Protection Act* of 1897, which had been enacted in the wake of the Amelia Dyer revelations the previous year. Persons taking in boarded-out children and babies in particular had to be registered and their activities monitored by public health officials. Mitchell, a married woman with a grown family and a husband who kept out of the house from early morning until late at night, registered as an infant carer in January 1901. Every one of the first thirteen children she took in for care died. But no investigation was undertaken even though this was such a suspiciously high number. Between 16 December 1902 and 18 July 1906, Mitchell took in twenty-one infants, and another five from September 1906 to January 1907.[41] Various undertakers at her trial testified that they had taken from her houses thirty-four babies to be buried. More alarming was the fact that, although a medical certificate signed by Dr Officer accompanied each case, there were no inquests into these sudden deaths.[42] Their testimony also indicated that they were not in fact aware that an inquest report was needed before burial.

Alice Mitchell was a greedy woman. When one of her clients, Maud Brown, fell behind in her payments for the upkeep of her infant, Mitchell summoned the police to pursue the debt. Sergeant Patrick

O'Halloran went to visit Mitchell's business, which operated not just as a boarding-out facility but also as a boarding house. He was alarmed by what met his eyes. In his report he said: '[One] child was in an appalling condition. Pus was coming from its eyes, it was fly-specked, extremely wasted, and giving off an offensive odour.' When he summoned a government medical officer, Dr T. G. Davy, the baby was found to be near death and was taken to hospital. This child was Ethel Booth.[43] The death of this previously healthy, thriving baby on 12 February 1907 drew concentrated attention to Alice Mitchell's activities.

Ethel's mother, Elizabeth Booth, told the Coroners Court in April 1907 that:

> I am a single mum and a general servant. I get 15/- per week.
> On 29 September 1906 I was delivered of a female child at
> the [Catholic] House of Mercy, Highgate Hill. It [sic] was a
> healthy baby ... I stayed three months ... and then took the
> baby to Alice Mitchell, who is now in court. I arranged to
> pay her 10/- per week and doctor's fees ... I continued to
> visit the child twice a week ... the father gave me 7/6 per week
> all along ... I gave her 5/- to have the child vaccinated ...
> [Mitchell] did not have the child vaccinated ... [After] three
> weeks I was not allowed to see the child. Mrs Mitchell always
> said it was asleep ... When I did see her I hardly knew her. She
> had sores all over her head, sore eyes, and she was very thin.
> Mrs Mitchell said she was suffering from her teeth ... the next
> night I was going to examine her but she smelt so horribly that
> I put the cover back over ... I told Mrs Mitchell I did not think
> she was getting on well and she replied, 'Yes, she is getting on
> and Dr Officer is very pleased with it.' ... I told her the child
> was very ill ... and I would take it to Perth Hospital ... I got
> the notice of its death on Tuesday around two o'clock. I was
> present when the coroner and the jury viewed the body of the
> child. It was the body of my child, Ethel Booth.[44]

Under these circumstances, the police intervened because medical staff were alarmed by Ethel's condition on admission and her subsequent death.

When the news of Ethel Booth's death – unlike those of the other thirty-six babies who had been buried quietly, unnoticed – reached the newspapers, public attention focused on the various establishments run by Alice Mitchell. The *Western Australian* of 15 February 1907 was confident that 'these rumours … if found to be accurate, will create one of the greatest sensations known in this state and will result in a unanimous demand for more stringent regulations regarding the care of boarded-out infants'. Indeed, this appraisal was prescient; the inquiries surrounding the death of Ethel Booth brought to an end the era of lethal baby farming across the new nation.

The Children's Protection Society, modelled after the Royal Society for the Protection of Children in Great Britain, had been formed only six months previously to address the issues of boarded-out and abandoned children. Confinement for poor women was onerous right from the start – at this time there was no proper midwifery or paediatric training available in Perth. The Fremantle Midwifery Training Centre did not open until 1910 and the King Edward Memorial Hospital in Perth, which catered for confinements, did not open until 1916.[45] Other private concerns – such as the homes run by the Anglican Sisters of the Church, the Catholic House of Mercy, the Salvation Army's Golden Gate, and the Good Shepherd Sisters, as well as the Waifs' Home and the Poor Women's House – could only for a short time assist desperate women with dependent babies and few resources.[46] This is what drove the demand for services like those offered by Alice Mitchell.

On 16 February 1907, the day after the press exposé, Mitchell was arrested and charged with the unlawful killing of Ethel Booth on 12 February 1907. Mitchell was described as being forty-six years of age, 'married, a nurse, able to read and write'. Dr Officer, who Elizabeth Booth had paid for consultations for Ethel, made a public statement defending Mitchell:

> [She] had called him in on several occasions to attend to
> infants who were ailing. Some of them recovered but others
> died ... he instructed Mrs Mitchell on their feeding and
> attention. To the best of my knowledge, his instructions were
> always carried [out]. In the majority of cases death was due to
> bowel complaints following summer diarrhoea.[47]

Diarrhoea was a prolific killer of infants, with Western Australia having the highest infant mortality rate in the new Commonwealth.[48] Sanitation in the burgeoning townships of Kalgoorlie and Coolgardie and in the capital was primitive and too overstretched to cope with the expanding populations. Babies that were not breastfed immediately found themselves in a life-threatening environment. They were frequently given condensed milk, which was full of sugar, or barley water or, the best alternative, Nestlé powdered formula, which had been available in the Australian colonies since the 1870s. It was, however, extremely expensive and far beyond the means of poor women. Even with the best intentions and level of care, bottlefed babies were vulnerable to disease, starvation and death. But Alice Mitchell had no such good intentions.

The inquest into the death of Ethel Booth opened in Perth on 4 March 1907. Registrar and Master of the Supreme Court of Western Australia James Cowan presided over the proceedings with a jury of three. He and his wife Edith Cowan were prominent advocates of children's rights.[49] Inspector Sellenger prosecuted on behalf of the Crown, with barrister R. W. Pennefather KC and N. W. Cowan appearing for the Children's Protection Society. At this stage Mitchell did not have a barrister, but a Jesuit-trained criminal law specialist, Michael G. Lavan (later appointed a KC), watched on her behalf. He did so actively, as evidence from the inquest revealed. On the second day of proceedings, Pennefather for the Children's Protection Society pointed out that baby Brown had died of starvation and that it should be admitted as evidence based on the argument of 'similar facts'. Lavan objected, arguing that only the issue at hand, the death of Ethel Booth, was relevant.

Keith Robertson, an officer with the Perth Local Board of Health, was next called. He stated that Mitchell was registered under requirements of the 1898 *Health Act* to care for babies and infants less than two years of age. Her original licence had been granted for her premises in Wellington Street. He then charted her movements as she set up across various establishments. Her record-keeping was slovenly and inadequate, leading to confusion not just about the name of new arrivals but when they arrived or anything about their history. Elizabeth Booth then gave moving testimony about what she believed had happened to Ethel. Matron Catherine Patterson and the laundress Alice Skinner both confirmed that Ethel was in peak health when she left the House of Mercy to go to Mitchell.[50]

Some thirty-six witnesses were called. The accused did not provide evidence or witnesses for her defence. The inquest concluded on 11 March, with Acting Coroner Cowan declaring that there was sufficient evidence of 'culpable negligence' to go to trial. This commenced on 8 April 1907 before Justice Robert Furse McMillan (later Sir Robert and chief justice) (1858–1931).[51] Mitchell was defended by R. D. Beresford, and the distinguished Scottish-born Crown solicitor, Alexander E. Barker, led the Crown case. Mitchell was charged with wilful murder, an offence that carried the death penalty if convicted. Sergeant O'Halloran gave more details about his examination of the premises where he discovered the condition of Ethel Booth. Maud Brown's baby was similarly emaciated and in a filthy condition. Dr Davy challenged Mitchell's account of her care of the babies.

Two medical staff at the Perth Hospital provided testimony of the state of Ethel Booth on admittance. The chief medical officer, Dr Herbert Tymms, stated that 'she was in a dying condition, extremely emaciated with sunken eyes, and the skin on the body was in folds'. Ethel died the following day, from chronic starvation. He also recalled the similar case of the baby of Susie Turvey, a servant of Mitchell. Dr Saw, another doctor in the Perth Hospital, also confirmed that he saw other starving babies admitted after living with Mitchell. Evidence was submitted that Dr Taaffe had refused to provide further services and home visits as early as 1902 when he saw the state of the premises and the babies. Dr Frederick Hitch also refused further treatment and reported the matter to the police, who did not proceed as Mitchell claimed that she used Dr Officer as her medical practitioner. Dr Hitch had been threatened by legal action for his report.[52]

When Dr Officer took the witness stand he was at pains to establish the difficulties faced by non-breastfed babies. He denied noticing any neglect or filth at Mitchell's home. Justice McMillan was highly sympathetic to this witness, allowing him every opportunity to duck and weave to avoid any taint of negligence on his part. The Crown solicitor also attached no blame to his woeful laxity. Officer frequently attended to the infants boarded with Mitchell at the cost of 5/- per visit and yet baby after baby died of malnutrition and neglect. The health inspector of the Perth City Council, Miss Lenehan, was equally negligent in her duties, testifying that she deferred to Dr Officer's expertise.

Yet other witnesses were not so reticent or willing to hide behind professional formality. Carl and Marion Roux had at one time boarded with Mitchell, and testified that the house was filthy and the babies neglected. Carl Roux stated that Susie Turvey's baby was sadly neglected. He catalogued the vast array of filth on the premises, with babies crawling into the henhouse, babies in soiled nappies covered with flies left in rooms to suffer from starvation. But why didn't they take their concerns to the police or the Board of Health at the time?

The jury found Mitchell guilty of the manslaughter of Ethel Booth after only an hour's deliberation. She was sentenced to five years' hard labour.

In the wake of this judgment, far-reaching reforms into infant welfare and health were enacted in Western Australia. What is surprising is that Mitchell got off so lightly. At least thirty-three babies had died under her negligent care. Although not caused by acts of wilful murder, slow and painful death by starvation and disease was possibly more excruciating. From some perspectives, Alice Mitchell rivals mass killer Martin Bryant, who slaughtered thirty-five people at Port Arthur in 1996. He killed with a gun; Mitchell killed by calculated neglect and a wilful cruelty towards those entrusted to her care.

CHAPTER 7

Child Killers in the Nineteenth Century

In early 1842, hundreds of Sydney residents gathered on the foreshore of Circular Quay awaiting the arrival of the latest ship from England. Since 1840 they had followed the tale of Little Nell Trent and her grandfather published in instalments as part of Charles Dickens's weekly periodical, *Master Humphrey's Clock*. The plot of *The Old Curiosity Shop* was full of pathos as young Nell attempted to aid her ailing and decrepit grandfather. But her struggle to render good made her ill with fatigue. In part seventy-two of the eighty-eight instalments the fate of Little Nell was to be revealed. Would she live? Or, as many eager devotees of Dickens's work secretly feared, would she succumb to exhaustion and die? As the ship docked and the boxes of periodicals came down the gangway, eager readers tore the packaging to find out what had happened. Well-dressed gentlemen cried aloud: 'No! No! She is dead! Little Nell is dead.' Across the wharves and then throughout the city, tears and lamentations were heard as the tragic news spread. Copies of the weekly were auctioned at Moore and Heydon's premises in Pitt Street on Good Friday in 1842, attracting keen bidding.[1]

In this work of fiction the self-sacrificing child dies after a heroic crusade. But the reality of children's deaths in the nineteenth century was far more sombre. The continuing high mortality rate from disease – for example measles, influenza, diphtheria, scarlet fever and chicken pox – was lamentable, but there were also those children who were killed by human hand, and their passing was recorded in the clinical reports of autopsies conducted in morgues, and coronial inquests and trials.

A recurring theme in the nineteenth century, particularly in the 1890s when the world was deeply affected by the economic Depression, is the desperation of impoverished women and particularly those who were mothers. Whether they were unmarried or not, poor women had a hard lot in the Australian colonies. Conditions were so difficult and money so hard to come by that many were forced to live in appalling circumstances of filth and hunger and disease, frequently abandoned by their men, or the recipients of their husband's excessive drinking and violence.

Mary Sullivan was a sixteen-year-old Irish nursemaid sentenced in County Cork to seven years' transportation to Van Diemen's Land for stealing quilts. This was her third offence, with previous convictions for stealing clothes and robbing a workhouse. County Cork was particularly hard hit by the potato blight, which triggered the Irish famine that so devastated the country and was responsible for 1.5 million deaths (almost 20 per cent of the population) between 1845 and 1849. To rob a workhouse where the most destitute of people were sent indicates a desperation that only someone who had lived through the famine could share. What Sullivan had suffered in her early teenage years and whether she lost most of her family to starvation was not recorded in the official records of her crimes.

Sullivan arrived on the *John William Dare* on 22 May 1852 with 171 other female felons. Her stature even for those impoverished times was tiny – she was only 139 centimetres (4 foot 7 inches) in height. Sullivan was described as a 'stout, rough-looking girl of forbidding appearance, and a sullen disposition'.[2] Though her behaviour on board ship had been exemplary, Sullivan was so unruly on arrival that she stayed only four days with her assigned employer. She was returned to the Cascades Female Factory for reprocessing.

Assigned felons had no say in who was to be their employer or the duties they would be expected to perform. Sullivan was next sent to Mrs Emma Langley in Campbell Street, Hobart, to work as a nursery maid. Larret Langley had died in September 1849 leaving his widow with three small children to rear alone. To survive she took in other children as boarders. On 7 July, after just one week in Langley's employ, Sullivan killed Adeline Blackburn Frazer, a two-year-old girl entrusted to her care.[3]

It was not just impoverished single mothers who were forced to give up their children into the care of other women to survive (see Chapter 3). Circumstances could make it necessary for even those who were more affluent. Adeline's father, John Frazer, had formerly served as the assistant superintendent of convicts at Jerusalem, Tasmania, from 6 October 1846 to 12 November 1848, after which he first took up the licence of the Royal Oak Hotel in Macquarie Street and then the Old Commodore Hotel in Brisbane Street.[4] He then left for the goldfields in Victoria, leaving Adeline, aged two, and her brother John, aged four, in the care of Langley because his wife, Elspeth Frazer, was seriously ill in St Mary's Hospital at the time of his departure. Such a disruption to family life was common in the colonies as men ventured to the diggings to make their fortunes – or so they hoped.

On the morning of the killing, described in the *Hobart Town Courier* of 10 July 1852 as 'a cold-blooded and diabolical murder', Sullivan absconded, leaving her fellow convict servant, Mary Ann Farmer, who was employed as a needlewoman, to explain her absence and do her chores. Sullivan had stolen a bonnet, a pair of boots owned by Master Dean, one of Mrs Langley's former boarders, and some tea and sugar. She left behind her government-issued convict garb. Farmer lit the fires and went to wake the children for their breakfast only to find Adeline missing. The boy reported that Sullivan had taken his sister out of her cot into another room. She had not been crying or restless that night. After a search, Farmer discovered Adeline's body, strangled by a strip of calico and hidden in a water-storage unit in the backyard. Dr William Huxtable was called in, but too late for the child had been dead for some time. When District Constable Simpson arrived to investigate he suspected Farmer of the deed and took her into custody.

The inquest into the little girl's murder was held before the coroner and a jury on 14 July in the York Hotel in Brisbane Street. Farmer testified that she had called a neighbour, a Mr Piesse, to assist her before calling for Dr Huxtable. Another boarder at Langley's house, a Miss Hurton, who was blind, reported that even though the children slept in the same room as she did, she did not hear Adeline removed from her cot. Constable Chandler testified that he apprehended Mary Sullivan the next day in Murray Street. As he approached her she said: 'I did not murder the child.' Sullivan also told him that she did 'not care to mind children'. She did not testify at the inquest and was committed for trial in the Supreme Court.[5]

The case with nine counts against Sullivan opened in the criminal sittings of the Supreme Court of Van Diemen's Land on 21 July 1852. The jury was chaired by the wealthy merchant and director of the Van Diemen's Land Bank, George Salier (1813–92).[6] The solicitor-general acted for the Crown and, as was common at the time, the defendant was unrepresented. Sullivan was, however, allowed to question witnesses herself. She took up this opportunity with invective, accusing Farmer of the deed. Sullivan asked for no witnesses in her own defence and offered no explanation of her actions. Proceedings were lengthy and much of the evidence tendered followed that already heard at the inquest. The jury took only a short time to deliver their verdict. Sullivan was found guilty of wilful murder and was given the mandatory sentence of death and dissection.

Yet the case was puzzling. Constable Chandler was at a loss to understand why Sullivan had acted in such a way towards a vulnerable child placed in her care, however unwillingly: 'The motives which could have prompted the girl to such an exercise of her destructive faculty are as yet incomprehensible.'[7] A large petition assembled on her behalf tried to justify her actions as compelled by madness. A medical board examined the prisoner to decide whether or not she was sane but was satisfied that she was merely evil, consumed by an 'utter callousness'. By this time, medical practitioners had increased their professional reputations as expert witnesses able to determine the inner workings of the mind, and therefore going far beyond the primary legal concept of intent. A whole genre of medico-legal literature concerned with women's reproduction, and social and biological functions, had matured in the 1840s and 1850s, influencing procedures even in far-distant Van Diemen's Land.

On 2 August 1852 a warrant was issued by the sheriff for the execution of Mary Sullivan, who 'hitherto manifested an unrelenting obduracy, and nothing seems calculated to bring her to a sense of her enormous guilt'.[8] A large crowd, consisting mainly of women and children, gathered to watch the public execution, which was held in front of the Hobart Town jail in Murray Street three days later. They had waited for hours to get a good viewing spot to watch the terrible spectacle. This was an unusual execution since very few women were hanged in comparison to the large numbers of men in this colony or elsewhere. Moreover, Sullivan was very young. Yet the brutality of her crime and the lack of motive mitigated any real sympathy for her. As Sullivan stood on the scaffold she did not make her confession and nor did she seek forgiveness for her crime. The Roman Catholic vicar-general, the Reverend Dr William Hall (1807–66) attended to her to the last moment of her life. She did pray silently moments before the cap was placed on her head to cover her eyes and then she dropped quickly to her death.[9] After her execution her body was given to the colonial surgeons to dissect under the gaze of various medical staff and apothecaries, as well as assorted gentlemen of the colony.

Emma Courtenay was born into poverty in Launceston in 1873. Until she became pregnant at the age of fourteen, she lived with her mother,

Ann Ross, at 117 Margaret Street. With a degree of unwillingness, Courtenay married twenty-seven-year-old Frederick Williams. Theirs was a 'short and miserable married life',[10] turbulent from the start, exacerbated by her early parenthood and poverty. Their little daughter was at first cared for by Emma's mother. The couple then moved to Melbourne where the child was sent to foster parents who were friends of Frederick Williams. For Emma Williams was now pregnant again. This was disastrous, especially given the long Depression still virulent in 1893. Not only could he not find work or support his family, but Frederick Williams caught typhus from the unsanitary conditions and died in the Melbourne Hospital.[11]

Emma Williams had no skills or resources. Unlike most children born in the 1870s, she was illiterate. With no government benefits even for widows available at the time, she went to live with a man in Port Melbourne. Annoyed by the presence of her little boy, John, who was now about two, the man told Williams to leave and fend for herself. Her only alternative was to engage in prostitution, a heavily crowded industry in this time of severe economic crisis. Constable John Asker of the South Melbourne Police Station commented that: 'I regarded her as a woman of ill fame, having often seen her in the streets at late hours and generally in the company of other women of ill repute. My impression was that she partly, if not wholly, lived on the proceeds of money obtained by illicit means.' This opinion showed no understanding of the series of forces that had propelled the young widow into this desperate way of life. She lived briefly with several men, one called 'Penguin' and another named 'Blizzard'.

At first Williams attempted to care for John. The local fishmonger, Frederick Foster, noticed that she 'took good care of the child'. This was when he was a baby; but as he grew older and learned to walk he proved an impediment to the way she earned a living. Clients not surprisingly objected to his presence. Her solution was to foster him with a baby farmer, Mary Wilson of 105 Ingles Street, Port Melbourne, who took him for the sum of 5/- per week. At Williams' trial, Wilson testified that she ' … appeared fond of the child. She was trying to get work and could not get it. She took the child away because I could not keep it [without payment] any longer.' Williams later brought him back to Wilson and simply left him there for six weeks without notice or payment. When she returned, Wilson forced Williams to take her son back.

With few clients, in early 1895 Williams went to live with a labourer, William Martin, an unsuccessful petty criminal working under various aliases such as Frederick Matthews and William May. He had already served several incarcerations for his crimes including housebreaking, possession of housebreaking tools and vagrancy. His next career move was to act as pimp for Williams. They shared a cottage with John Brown and Mary Costello. Williams' career as a prostitute continued to languish, forcing them to move frequently through the slums of Port Melbourne and South Melbourne without paying their debts or the rent they owed. Williams' life was spiralling further into chaos and desperation. Once, she left the little boy with a stranger for three days after saying she had to run an urgent errand.

In early August 1895, Williams, the child and William Martin moved to 24 Little Park Street in South Melbourne. The place was sparsely furnished – the boy slept in a wooden crate. On 11 August Williams told Martin she had had enough and intended to take her son to a 'Salvation Army woman at the barracks'. This wasn't actually the case for Williams took the child to the Port Melbourne lagoon, placed a bluestone around his neck with part of her petticoat and threw him into the stagnant water, where he drowned. The following day, council worker Neil Oberg found the body. Dr John Brett, who conducted the autopsy, reported the child had died from drowning. He was well fed and well nourished.[12] The news was taken up by the *Herald–Standard*, which featured it on the front page the following day. Martin reported the story to Williams, asking her if it was her son. She said she could not read so she had not heard. He later stated

The brief life of Emma Williams was blighted by poverty and chaos. Photo: Public Records office, Victoria, VPS 5900. Photograph of prisoners sentenced to death and coroner's inquest sheets, PO, Unit 1.

that he tried to get her to go to the police; but all she replied was, 'I am innocent and I won't go ... I will sell the furniture and go to Sydney if you want to go with me ... They can't take us in another colony ...'[13] In this, though, she was misinformed since baby farmer Frances Knorr had been extradited from Sydney to stand trial in Melbourne the previous year.

The police were sure, however, that Emma Williams was the mother of the dead boy. She was arrested and sensational newspaper accounts followed the case. The *Herald–Standard* of 14 August proclaimed 'HEARTLESS MURDER OF A LITTLE CHILD. A CRUEL DEED' next to a drawing of Williams dressed in a hat and a high-collared blouse. She protested her innocence, although when she was in custody she tried to dispose of her petticoat up the police station chimney. William Martin told the police of her actions, no doubt in an attempt to distance himself from the crime. Confronted with the remnants of her petticoat, Williams confessed to killing her son.

Her trial before Justice Sir Henry Hodges (1844–1919), a stern disciplinarian and fervent Christian, took place on 24 September 1895. Williams was defended by William Forlonge, a distinguished barrister from a wealthy pastoral family. He and Alfred Deakin had represented the international serial killer Frederick Deeming in 1892 before Justice Hodges. Williams testified in her own defence. She reported that she had tried to lodge her son with a Catholic home but was refused because they were not Catholics. She then went to Selina Sutherland, a noted philanthropist, but with no success. Sutherland (1839–1909) was a lay 'lady missionary' to the urban poor in Melbourne where her particular concern was with destitute children. Unfortunately, in the two years before this trial there had been dissent in the Melbourne Presbyterian community over the extent of her activities, which were then curtailed.[14] Williams had begged her mother in Launceston to take in the boy, another plea that was refused. She also detailed the various baby farmers who cared for the boy, but without sufficient funds to support him this strategy also failed.

Williams' lover William Martin provided testimony for the prosecution. He had earlier told the police about the hidden petticoat. He also recounted a conversation in which Williams admitted that she had killed John. The court was told there had been arguments in the joint household about John's crying, and that Williams had said she intended giving John into the care of the Salvation Army. Mrs Costello was also unsympathetic to the defence case. Forlonge let matters slip in his cross-examination, as if he already knew he was going to lose.

In his address to the jury William Forlonge asked its members to consider that this had been an act of desperation committed without premeditation, done 'on the impulse of the moment'. In his directions to the jury, however, Justice Hodges was not so inclined to this view. Having sat on the case of serial poisoner Martha Needle the previous year, he believed that society had no responsibility to care for the children of immoral women. He continued by saying that 'all the facts pointed to the one conclusion that the prisoner intentionally took the child's life, when she threw it [sic] into the water with the fixed determination that it should not rise to the surface ... There was not one single question that could be put to the jury on the other side.' The jury took heed of his directions, finding Williams guilty of wilful murder after a deliberation of just twenty minutes. She was sentenced to death by hanging.

Williams claimed she was pregnant and therefore could not be executed. When Dr Andrew Shields, the prison's visiting medical officer, examined her he was not certain whether she was pregnant or not. She was brought before Justice Hodges once more on 18 October 1895. Forlonge again represented her, most likely pro bono since she could not afford his fee or that of his junior, H. S. Cole. She was examined under chloroform in a room adjacent to the courtroom by a team of doctors including the eminent gynaecologist Dr Walter Balls-Headley, J. W. Dunbar Hooper, a fellow of the Royal College of Physicians, and the prison surgeon.[15] This was a unique occurrence in the Australian legal system. Under the law, a woman who was 'quick with child' (that is, more than twenty weeks' pregnant) could not be executed; one under that could be. No impediment to her execution had been found. The jury was informed of this development immediately.

The public was not quite so eager to see a young woman executed even if she had earned a living as a prostitute. Two journalists, Henry Hyde Champion (1859–1928) and Marshall Lyle, took up her case. Champion was an unusual advocate: he had attended Marlborough College and the Royal Military Academy in England, and had seen action in the Afghan War. Although he seemed to be a member of the Establishment, his strong social conscience compelled him to take radical stances. He visited Melbourne in August 1892 before taking up a position in England as the editor of the prestigious literary journal *Nineteenth Century*. But he returned to Melbourne in April 1894 after standing unsuccessfully for the seat of Aberdeen in Scotland. Champion joined the Women's Suffrage League and was a co-founder of the Victorian Social Democratic Federation. In June 1895 he established his own journal, entitled *Champion*, from whose pages he sought support for Emma Williams.[16] The issue dated 26 October 1895 proclaimed that Williams' intended execution 'would exhibit Victoria to the world as the very lowest and most degraded of all civilised communities'. The force of his pen won more sympathy and petitions for the condemned woman.

Another radical advocate, Dr Charles Strong (1844–1942), a founder of the freethinking Australian Church, also sought her reprieve. A well-educated Scotsman with a Calvinist upbringing, Strong originally served as minister to the prestigious Scots Church, Melbourne, from 1875 to 1882. His increasingly radical stance alarmed both the elders and the congregation of this conservative bastion of Presbyterian worship. His new church was determined to change the social system that produced poverty as well as to give more immediate support to its victims.[17] From his pulpit in Flinders Street he urged his congregation to help Emma Williams' cause by petitioning the government for mercy. Three days later a substantial petition was forwarded to the new governor, Lord Brassey (1836–1918), for his consideration.[18] The government decided to determine once more if Williams was pregnant. She was re-examined by the three experts who had already seen her and once again they declared she was not pregnant. The execution was to go ahead. The chaplain at Melbourne jail, the Reverend H. Scott, acted as her spiritual adviser, urging her to become penitent and ask God's forgiveness.

Newspapers carried reports of her last hours. She slept soundly the night before her execution, suggesting she had been administered sedatives, then ate a light breakfast and received counsel from the Reverend Scott. She left a message for Mrs Costello, the landlady who had testified against her at her trial, saying: 'I forgive her.' When the sheriff – the officer of the Supreme Court entrusted with overseeing executions – 'demanded her body in the usual form', Williams was composed, walking 'calmly to the scaffold, on which she maintained her calm demeanour'. When the white cap was drawn over her face, she called out: 'O Lamb of God, I come.' But as the lever of the trapdoor adjusted to her weight she screamed out in fear. She died instantly, or so newspapers reported.[19] This had been the third execution of a woman in Melbourne in two years: Frances Knorr, Martha Needle and now the filicide Emma Williams all died by the noose. The public hounded Sullivan's executioner, Constable Robert Gibbon, to such an extent that he begged the government to allow him to carry firearms for his own protection. His mental health deteriorated under the strain and he was committed to Yarra Bend Asylum as 'a raving lunatic' two years later.[20]

In November 1896, a unique case was heard before the Supreme Court of Queensland. Forty-year-old Marie Christensen, the acting matron at the non-denominational Myora Mission (1891–1942) on Stradbroke Island, stood in the dock accused of the manslaughter of one of the inmates, a five-year-old girl called Cassey.

An earlier mission experiment on Stradbroke Island, conducted by the Italian Passionist fathers in 1825, just a year after the Moreton Bay penal settlement was established, had failed. This new initiative, Myora, had been the brainchild of a group of Brisbane philanthropists who wished to establish a reformatory for Aboriginal children. Under the *Industrial and Reformatory Schools Act* of 1865, magistrates had the power to remove children from neglectful parents. This included any Indigenous children. Children could be sent to missions such as Yarrabah near Cairns, or to this new establishment. Stradbroke Island already housed the state-funded Dunwich Benevolent Asylum where the destitute of the colony – the infirm, the incapacitated and the alcoholic – lived in prison-like conditions.

Myora Mission also contained a state-funded primary school under the leadership of teacher Atkinson Dunnington. With no family, Cassey had been sent to Myora in June 1896. Her health was poor; she was tiny for her age and malnourished. On the morning of

14 September 1896, Christensen took the children down to the sea to bathe. Cassey found the walk from the cottages difficult and resisted entering the water, which suggests she might have come from inland. Christensen forced her into the water anyway, after which Cassey collapsed. She was then forced to walk up the sand dunes. When the little girl lagged and found herself unable to continue, Christensen beat her savagely with a switch, a flogging that went on for several minutes. Cassey was unable to move so the matron roughly dragged her along by the arms. The girl begged a fellow inmate Jackie Gowrie to help her and Christensen responded by finding another switch and beating the little girl again. She then retrieved her cane from her quarters and continued the flogging in earnest. Several older Indigenous people saw the commotion, including seventeen-year-old Topsy McLeod from the kitchen where she worked. One older resident, Budlo Lefu, rushed out of her humpy, gathered Cassey into her arms and went to walk off with her. But Christensen intervened and insisted she put the child down. Lefu reluctantly did so, aware that the power dynamics on the island favoured the acting matron.[21]

Budlo Lefu and her family were not part of the mission but lived a more independent existence. They were not local people but may have been Melanesian islanders brought to Queensland to work in the sugar industry. There were other Melanesians living on the island with the Indigenous people. Lefu's two children attended the mission school but she was concerned by the degree of punishment inflicted on the children by Christensen.[22]

After the acting matron retrieved Cassey, she took her into the dormitory and began to flog her again. Afterwards, Cassey became seriously ill and was unable to eat. Atkinson Dunnington advised Christensen to send for Dr Patrick Mahoney from the Benevolent Asylum, which she did the following day. He prescribed some whisky as a stimulant. The following day Cassey died. Dr Mahoney notified the justice of the peace, arguing he could not issue a death certificate as he had only seen the deceased once.

The justice of the peace, W. R. North, decided to convene a magisterial inquest into Cassey's death, which was held on 19 and 20 September.[23] This was unusual: of the 469 inquests held in Queensland in 1896 very few were conducted into the death of any Indigenous people. Even more unusually for the period, North allowed the sworn testimony of non-Europeans, even though he did not correctly record Budlo Lefu's evidence in the records. Dr Mahoney testified to the thirty contusions on Cassey's buttocks, but he believed these had been insufficient to *cause* death. However, given her weakened and anaemic condition these injuries would have contributed to her death. North filed his report stating: 'Suspect: Marie Christensen. Suspicious circumstances. Flogging child in weak state of health.'[24]

The report of the inquest was forwarded to the attorney-general's office on 25 September, and then to the commissioner of police for his opinion as to whether the matter should go to the Crown prosecutor's office. Sub-inspector James Coathcote and Constable Michael Toomey investigated the case. Toomey went to Stradbroke Island on the government launch *Lucinda*, the vessel on which only five years previously the distinguished members of the Constitutional Convention had worked on the first draft of the Australian Constitution.

On questioning witnesses, Toomey found that North had not recorded the evidence of Christensen's cane. When he spoke to her, she denied owning a cane, although she admitted to using a small switch. Constable Toomey then examined her room and found a cane but Christensen denied using it on Cassey, saying she 'reserved it for the big ones'. Problematically, when he first approached Christensen for questioning, Toomey had not identified himself as a police officer nor did he caution her, issues that were later important at the trial.

A hearing before Philip Pinnock began on 29 September. He was a highly respected old settler who had been appointed police magistrate even before the colony was formed in 1859. Pinnock was considered a fair man ruled by evidence. Christensen was represented by counsel.

The hearing went on for five days with the Crown alone calling twelve witnesses. Constable Toomey had returned to Myora to check the veracity of witness testimony by conducting re-enactments to see, for example, whether Topsy McLeod had indeed been able to see the events from her kitchen window. Evidently, Philip Pinnock was convinced that Christensen had a case to answer and ensured that the proceedings were rigorous.

The case came before the Supreme Court where Christensen pleaded guilty before Justice Patrick Real (1846–1928), a man who had come from the most humble origins to rise to great professional heights. He was considered to be a jurist who favoured the plight of the poor and unfortunate. The Crown case was led by Attorney-General Sir Arthur Rutledge (1843–1917), a former Liberal acting premier with progressive views. Christensen did not have counsel at her trial.[25] Free legal representation for defendants was not available in Queensland until 1903. In her own defence, though, Christensen testified that '[she had] meant no harm to the child'. Dr Mahoney also stated that Cassey had not died from her beatings alone but rather from a series of contributing factors. The Home Secretary presented a report stating that the defendant was a 'woman of good character' but 'not a very strong mind'. None of the material in the proceedings gave any indication of how Christensen came to this point in her life or even what her age was. The position of matron on a poorly funded Aboriginal mission was hardly likely to attract the services of a competent, intelligent person. In such circumstances, employees were often substandard and desperate for work of any sort.

Christensen was given a sentence of two years' imprisonment, which was immediately suspended on payment of a good behaviour bond of £100 for the period of her probation. After the Crown divulged that the Salvation Army had offered to care for Christensen, Justice Real advised that he was willing to apply the new provisions relating to first offenders in the *Offenders' Probation Act 1886*, one of the first such Acts in the world. Whether it was lenient or an appropriate sentence cannot be determined since this was a unique legal case. What the case did reveal was the extreme brutality meted out to Indigenous children in institutions supposedly set up for their care and protection. The fate of removed or 'stolen' children is revealed in this rare and early documented case. Given the racial ideology of that period in Queensland, it is also remarkable that the case ever came to light and was pursued to the highest court in the colony.

CHAPTER 8

The Wicked Stepmother: Martha Rendall

Stepmothers get a bad press; the term 'wicked' is frequently added automatically. Euripides set the stereotype for the next 2500 years when in his play *Alcestis*, written in 483 BC, he declared 'better a serpent than a stepmother'. European folktales are replete with 'wicked stepmothers': they are there in Snow Drop (Snow White), Cinderella, Hansel and Gretel, as well as in the English tale, the Rose Tree. Stepmothers are always jealous of the husbands' children and will do anything to make sure their own get ahead. So say the stereotypes.

Australia had its own notorious stepmother – Martha Rendall – who was executed for the murder of her stepson and the suspected murder of his two sisters in Perth in 1909. In 1932 a feature in the *Western Australian* on 12 May described her as a 'torturer', the perpetrator of 'diabolical cruelty'. She was accused of being 'undoubtedly a sadist who obtained sexual pleasure from inflicting pain on others. She was the most inhumane fiend who ever stood in the dock of the Criminal Court, Perth.' Former Perth CIB detective Aubrey Lamond, who conducted the police investigations into the murders, described Rendall as 'a sadist of the worst kind. Seeing someone in great agony appeared to give her sexual gratification. A queer woman if ever there was one.'[1]

Crime writer Paul B. Kidd describes Rendall as going 'down in history as being among the most sadistic serial killers the world has ever known …'. He compares her reputation to that of Moors

491

murderers Myra Hindley and Ian Brady, and to American child killer and cannibal Albert Fish.[2] More recently, historian Professor Anna Haebich has re-evaluated the extensive evidence to present a far more complex understanding of the deaths of the three children, and the conviction of their stepmother for their murder.[3]

Contemporary assessment of her character debated whether or not Martha Rendall had been born a criminal. From the perspective of pioneer criminologist Cesare Lombroso (1835–1909) and eugenicist Francis Galton (1822–1911), who actually coined the term 'eugenics' as well as the expression 'nature versus nurture', this would certainly have been the case. Five weeks after the inquest into the deaths of the three Morris children, Perth's *Sunday Times* on 19 September 1909 sought answers to this perplexing question. At the outset the journalist pointed out that 'Rendall is her maiden name and is the only one to which she is legally entitled'. This pulled away the facade that she and her de facto husband, Thomas Morris, had so carefully cultivated – that they were a respectable if poor married couple with a large brood of children.

The article revealed that Martha Rendall's father was an English immigrant to South Australia in the 1840s, a respectable man who died when she was twelve years old. Her mother, it was said, then married a man called Moreton who made life 'irksome to the young girl and she soon left home to earn her own living as a domestic servant'. This, the journalist implied, befitted her status as 'an illiterate, uneducated woman, hardly able to write and certainly unable to spell properly'. Rendall met Morris while working as a maid in a hotel in Magill, South Australia, although the year was unknown. Morris and Rendall travelled together to Western Australia in 1905, where she went into service under the name of Mrs Moreton. She had several employers during this period. At the end of the article it was disclosed that she had left two ex-nuptial children back in South Australia. These revelations were published before the trial, creating negative impressions about Rendall's origins and morals. *Truth*, a newspaper devoted to presenting sexual scandal in as many lurid details as possible, also canvassed the outline of Rendall's life and morals. Such exposés of an accused person's life would not be permitted under current media guidelines, but in 1909 sexual innuendo was enough to utterly condemn a woman's reputation and was no impediment to legal proceedings.

Martha Rendall's parents, Thomas and Mary Ann Rendall, arrived in South Australia in 1849 as children, marrying in 1860. He worked as a labourer in the Adelaide foothills. There were thirteen children to the marriage with seven infant deaths. Martha was born in 1871. After her father's death and mother's remarriage Rendall developed an intense and enduring hatred of her stepfather. She went to work as a domestic servant at the age of fifteen and had a son at the age of sixteen. Whether her stepfather strongly disapproved and forced her out, or could indeed have been the father, remains conjecture. The child's father remained anonymous and what happened to it remains a mystery. Rendall entered into a bogus marriage with Alfred Roberts. He was presumably the father of her further two children, Albert who died at the age of three months and Alice, born in 1891.[4] Rendall's life was hard as she continued to work as a servant, barmaid and invalids' nurse. From this evidence we can deduce that she did not rear the children herself since the demands of unskilled manual employment would have prevented her from regular and consistent parenting. Having three illegitimate children by the age of twenty clearly marked Rendall as a 'fallen woman' in the language and sentiments of the era.

Through Alfred Roberts, Martha Rendall met the man who was to control her life and destiny for the next thirteen years, until her execution. Roberts was a cousin to Thomas Morris, born in Melbourne from South Australian parents. Morris was then a married man with a family of seven children, and he was to have two more with his wife before he abandoned her in favour of Rendall. During their early relationship, which commenced around 1896 while he was still living with his wife, Rendall suffered several miscarriages. No doubt these were Morris's children. Rendall followed Morris to Western Australia in 1900 (not 1905 as stated during her arraignment), although he did not leave his wife for another six years. Morris had family already in the west, who secured him work.[5] His wife had urged the move to get him away from his attractive and persistent lover.

Clearly, Rendall was not a woman who cared about the conventions of marriage and motherhood. She already had two living illegitimate children to a man she pretended was her legal husband, another to a different man, and she abandoned them all to follow her married lover to a distant city. There is no evidence that Rendall ever saw them again after she left for Perth in 1900. Although technically 'Miss Rendall', when she sought employment as a domestic servant she called herself 'Mrs Moreton', her mother's name and title. Perhaps she portrayed herself as a young widow.

Or perhaps when Morris and his wife finally parted in April 1906 the opportunity to establish a home with all the appearance of conventionality presented itself. Divorce was expensive and therefore out of the question. Morris was given guardianship of the five younger children from his marriage, which, since the enacting of the various legislations concerning infant and child custody in the 1890s, was no longer the most usual outcome. After Morris threw his wife, Sarah, out of their house because of acrimonious arguments over his liaison with Rendall, she was unable to earn a good living and was forced to take in washing and mending to scrape a meagre existence.[6] In retrospect Rendall would have been better to continue her affair with Morris and leave his wife to care for the family. At first Rendall presented herself to the children as the 'housekeeper', but after she moved to share Morris's bed, she insisted the children – William, Olive, Annie, Arthur and George – call her 'Mother', a term they resisted fiercely. William worked for a living but the other four children were dependent.

Any dreams she may have harboured about domestic felicity and comfort were shattered by their actual location at 23 Robinson Street,

Does Martha Rendall deserve her description as a sadistic serial killer? Photo: Western Australian Police Museum.

in the poorer area of East Perth. To have waited for so long and then to live in a poverty-stricken and dirty neighbourhood along with a brood of resentful children and teenagers was hardly an anticipated romantic outcome. By all accounts, Rendall was a harsh and abusive carer, constantly beating five-year-old Olive and seven-year-old Annie, although this was not uncommon in an era when the rod was never spared, even for minor infractions of discipline. Neighbours such as Lena Carr reported hearing Rendall screeching and screaming at the children for hours on end. This information was used against Rendall in her trial. When he was at home after his long hours at manual labour, Morris apparently chose not to notice.

In April 1907, George, Arthur, Olive and Annie contracted diphtheria, a deadly infectious disease then in epidemic proportions in Perth. Known as the 'strangling angel of children', the disease was easily transmitted. It could reach anyone, no matter how well born or protected: Princess Alice, the third child of Queen Victoria, died when she contracted the infection as an adult. There was no vaccine until 1913.[7] Treatments before this relied on keeping the throat open and neutralising the toxins that gathered at the base of the throat. Various patent remedies were available, such as the dangerous use of quinine and prussic acid (hydrogen cyanide) with emetics. Other home treatments recommended the application to the inside of the throat of sodium benzoate, now used as a food preservative.[8] Before stringent legislation in the 1920s, many patent medicines were deadly. Godfrey's Cordial, which was made for babies, contained lethal doses of laudanum (a by-product of opium) if used incorrectly.[9]

Rendall cared for and nursed the seriously ill children, hampered by the lack of effective treatments. Further care was provided by a Miss Copley from the Silver Chain nursing organisation. The Perth Children's Hospital was not established until 1909 so no residential care was available. Dr James Cuthbert was called in on numerous occasions to provide medical attention. He used the new anti-toxin developed in 1895 as well as strong painkillers. Then Olive, Arthur and George contracted typhus, an often-lethal infection spread in squalid and unhygienic surroundings. Again Dr Cuthbert attended the patients.

Annie was not so fortunate; she died in agony on 27 July 1907. Later evidence revealed that behind closed doors Rendall applied a lotion to her throat that caused her to scream in agony. This was not as suspicious as it might seem; the disease was highly contagious and barriers were necessary to prevent its spread. George Morris later claimed that his stepmother was cruel and heartless, telling him to watch Annie try to get out of bed as Rendall laughed out loud. She was also accused of beating Annie on several occasions when she lay dying.[10] Dr Cuthbert was not alarmed, however, and he provided a death certificate stating that she died of epilepsy and cardiac weakness.

Olive Morris died on 16 October 1907, with Cuthbert certifying death from typhoid and convulsions. At this time the Morris family regularly attended the local Methodist church. The congregation provided considerable support in the wake of the double tragedy. Rendall was also debilitated and constantly ill. During Easter 1908 the family went to Bunbury, where Thomas Morris obtained work.[11] No doubt the temporary relocation was to take advantage of a healthier environment that held no memories of the two dead girls. By this stage, with the revelations of the lethal baby-farming enterprise run by Alice Mitchell documented in all its sordidness, an escape from East Perth was also a flight from the moral contamination of the area. The family returned to Robinson Street on 10 June 1908. When Arthur came home from school one day complaining of a sore throat – the first symptom of diphtheria – he was sent to bed immediately and Dr Cuthbert summoned. Swabbing the patient's throat with a tincture of diluted sulphurous acid in glycerine was ordered. Unlike his sisters, at times the boy appeared to recover before again relapsing.

At the time, Dr Cuthbert had no suspicion that this might be anything but a mysterious ailment that had afflicted children already debilitated by diphtheria and then typhoid fever. He consulted other colleagues for advice. Dr (later Sir) John Cleland (1878–1971) had been trained in tropical medicine in London, arriving in Perth in 1905 to take up the post of government bacteriologist and pathologist. His biographer, R. V. Southcott, notes that the Rendall case made his early reputation.[12] Cuthbert's other distinguished colleague, Dr John Cumpston (1880–1954) had trained in Melbourne and London, becoming an early expert on scarlet fever and diphtheria. He arrived in Western Australia in December 1907.[13] The sensational Rendall case also helped establish his reputation. At the time they visited Arthur Morris they were unable to detect what ailed him and were as puzzled as Dr Cuthbert.[14] Rendall was suspected of suffering from syphilis and the boy was tested in the belief he was her natural son. No results were forthcoming.

The next-door neighbour, Lena Carr, had come to live in the street after the deaths of the two girls. The sound of Arthur screaming alarmed her. She advised sending him to hospital, advice Rendall rejected. Carr claimed at the inquest that she had heard Arthur on several occasions call out 'Murder! Police! Mrs Carr, save me!' Carr did in fact go into the house to investigate. She claimed that she was disturbed by the use of spirit of salts (hydrochloric acid) that Rendall diluted to treat his throat. However, in diluted forms it *was* sometimes used as a home remedy. On one occasion after inhaling the greenish-yellow swabbing liquid that made her eyes sting, Carr said to Rendall, who she believed was the boy's mother: 'Good God, woman! You are not using that for the boy's throat; it is enough to kill a horse.' Carr was also disturbed when Rendall laughed at Arthur's attempts to get out of bed in a weakened condition. As well she alleged that Rendall yanked Arthur out of his bed and threw him onto a couch saying: 'There! Lie there and die!' Another day when Arthur refused treatment Rendall flogged him. Carr did not inform the police because she believed that Rendall was following the regimen ordered by the local doctor.[15] It proved damning testimony at the inquest and trial. On 8 October 1908, Arthur died.

The neighbours were alarmed by the deaths of three children who only two years ago had been so healthy. The Morris household was the talk of East Perth. But the talk did not take into account that they had been afflicted by the deadly infectious diseases diphtheria and typhus. Florence Feakes sent an anonymous letter to Dr Cuthbert expressing her concerns.[16] This may have been what provoked him to test Rendall for syphilis. An autopsy was conducted on Arthur by Cleland, Cumpston and a thoracic specialist, Dr Crouch. Very unusually, Rendall insisted on sitting in on the procedure – relatives never wanted to see their kin dissected and discussed in clinical detail by pathologists. Yet here was a woman, supposedly the child's mother, watching calmly and intently. When the team came to open the chest and throat, she objected and demanded the termination of the autopsy. Since this was not yet a legal case they had no alternative but to acquiesce to her strange request. Dr Cumpston suspected poison, although hydrochloric acid did not occur to him. This is not surprising since poisoners at the time tended to use arsenic, antimony or strychnine. The matter was closed for the time being and no official report was submitted or even kept.

The Morris–Rendall household moved to Edward Street in East Perth. Around April 1909, George, then aged thirteen, alleged that he had been given bitter tea, which burned his throat. Rendall apparently said to him: 'You'll be the next to go.' He later told the inquest that he had heard his father and Rendall quarrelling over the deaths of the children. When Rendall accused Morris of believing she had deliberately murdered his children, he retorted 'So, it is.' This hearsay evidence by a hostile witness was used at the inquest and the trial. George took flight without telling his father. Neighbours who had heard of the deaths of the three children were alarmed when George disappeared, fearing he had been murdered. One male neighbour went to CIB headquarters to discuss the matter with Sergeant Harry Mann. The commissioner of police requested that Thomas Morris be brought in for questioning. Disturbed by the interview, police went to the house in Edward Street to question Rendall, whom they believed to be Morris's wife. There, William Morris also said that he did not know where George had gone.

The day after the police visit, William went to CIB headquarters to speak to detectives away from his father and Rendall. Now he revealed that George had gone to Subiaco to stay with their mother. When asked why George had run away, William told police: 'Mrs Rendall was trying to poison him. She poisoned my two sisters and one of my brothers.' When located and questioned by detectives, George reiterated William's story. The boys' allegation presented the opportunity for further investigations. To divert attention away from her, Rendall said she had had the same symptoms as the dead children had suffered. The distinguished local ear, nose and throat specialist Dr Macaulay reported treating Rendall for a severe sore throat but determined she did not have diphtheria. He suspected she had used a chemical irritant to produce her symptoms.

With the authority of police magistrate Augustus Roe, the police disinterred the bodies of the three Morris children in July 1909. Doctors were present at the exhumation, as were their parents, Sarah and Thomas Morris. Mrs Morris fainted during the grisly proceedings. The remains of the children were tested by a government analyst. Dr Edward Mann conducted the initial investigation, followed by an autopsy by Dr Tymms, the principal medical officer of the Perth Hospital. During the autopsy of Arthur Morris, Tymms found intestinal irritants he believed could have been caused by a poison of some sort. Forensic science was still primitive in Western Australia at the time, so in terms of evidence this was insubstantial and indefinite. Roe still concluded, however, that a coronial inquest was appropriate.

The inquest was followed widely in Perth. Rendall's elaborate fabrication of respectability fell apart as she was revealed to be a woman of questionable morals with illegitimate children; an adulterer who broke up the marriage of a man with nine children and held him in some strange sexual sway. Since the forensic evidence of the prosecution was weak and lacked the rigour usually required in coronial inquiries, the case largely rested on the evidence of Lena Carr and, more importantly, George Morris, who acknowledged he had never seen Rendall use spirit of salt (hydrochloric acid) on any of his siblings, although he had heard them scream because of the gargle they were given for diphtheria. The *Sunday Times* in Perth had to admit that the evidence was 'circumstantial'.[17] Rendall did not help her own case: she remained defiant, unmoved and stoic. A woman in her position was expected to show distress; that she did not seemed to confirm a callous nature that could have easily killed three children.[18] The jury at the inquest was convinced by the flimsy evidence, and found Martha Rendall and Thomas Morris guilty of wilful murder. On 16 August 1909, Augustus Roe ordered they stand trial for wilful murder.

The trial in the Supreme Court of Western Australia opened on 8 September 1909. Acting Chief Justice Robert McMillan (1858–1931), who had presided over the Alice Mitchell case two years earlier, conducted the proceedings. The defendants pleaded not guilty. Crown solicitor Alexander Barker, who had prosecuted the Mitchell case, appeared for the Crown. Morris was represented by F. J. Shaw, while Rendall was represented by James Clydesdale, a University of Glasgow graduate of high calibre. Clydesdale was substantially hindered because his client did not have the resources to obtain her own expert witnesses or request independent forensic tests. Moreover, criminal trials in this era were stacked in favour of the prosecution, given the strength of its resources over those of the much poorer defence. Much of the evidence presented to the coronial inquiry into the death of Arthur Morris was repeated at the five-day hearing. Considerable latitude was given to the admission of hearsay evidence. The prosecution's case was notably weak given that there was no proper forensic evidence, and that various reputable medical men had signed death certificates without demur and had made no official complaints after the first, partial autopsy conducted on Arthur. Still, the Crown had the resources to bring Dr John Cleland back from Sydney where he had taken up a senior position at the Bureau of Microbiology.

Rendall mostly stood condemned as a liar and an adulterer, a heartless mother who had abandoned her own children to run after Thomas Morris.[19] Although Morris was also an adulterer who had abandoned his family, little dirt was cast against his character. He appeared as a shadowy figure in this drama in which Rendall was the protagonist and driver of the fatal events that had befallen the Morris children.

Justice McMillan was clearly convinced of Rendall's guilt as he presented his summation to the jury. She represented a 'moral deformity', although whether lack of morals could be said to lead to mass murder remained unexplained. The jury took less than four hours to reach their verdict: Rendall was found guilty and Morris was found not guilty. Rendall protested her innocence before she was taken away to await execution. In Western Australia at the time there was no court of appeal that could reinvestigate the case. In other states, where this Full Court review existed, the weak prosecuting case should have been sufficient to warrant further examination. McMillan's emotive and biased address to the jury alone would have constituted grounds for appeal. The Court of Criminal Appeal in Western Australia was established in 1911, two years after Rendall's trial. In 1913 the Supreme Court was able to overrule a jury verdict if it was contrary to the facts presented in the case.[20] These reforms were too late to help Martha Rendall.

Her case caused considerable controversy across the state. Few, however, were concerned with Thomas Morris and his role in his children's demise. On 3 October 1909, the *Sunday Times* issued a long feature entitled 'Should We Hang Martha Rendall?'. Surprisingly, the paper, having canvassed most of the legal fraternity in the city, decided that she should not be hanged. The prosecution case in her trial was torn to shreds, revealing its essentially flimsy nature. The article concluded that Rendall stood condemned because leading doctors and other specialists could not discover what had actually killed the children, and therefore they made the assumption that they had been killed by human hand. Unlike cases in Victoria in which women condemned to death for infanticide had been reprieved after public outcry, the incipient feminist moment in Western Australia did not come to Rendall's defence.[21]

Rendall's primary public advocate was a Methodist minister, the Reverend Tom Allan, who had a parish in Fremantle. Reverend Allan was her spiritual adviser from the time of her sentencing on 15 September to her execution on 6 October 1909. He was convinced of her innocence and organised a petition to the attorney-general on her behalf.[22] The radical Labor MLA for the seat of Kanowna, Thomas Walker, himself no stranger to scandal, also spoke in her defence in parliament – to no avail.[23] Thomas Morris visited his longtime lover to say his final farewell. Rendall was executed at 8am on 6 October 1909, protesting her innocence to the last. The attorney-general had ruled that the press could not witness the execution, much to its collective chagrin. Outside the prison gates a large crowd gathered, many protesting the execution of a woman on dubious forensic evidence.[24] She was buried in an unmarked grave in Fremantle Prison.[25]

CHAPTER 9

Child Killers in the Twentieth Century

On 25 October 1994, Susan Smith drove her two young sons, one aged three years and the other fourteen months, into a river in South Carolina and left them to drown. Her initial account was heartrending and tragic: she claimed that she had been carjacked by a black man. Yet as Smith wept in front of an international television audience begging for the return of her boys, the police were investigating the unthinkable – Smith had cold-bloodedly murdered them, leaving them abandoned and trapped in her car to drown. She had disposed of her children believing it would win her the affection and commitment of a well-born and wealthy lover who had told her that the boys stood in the way of any union. Smith sacrificed the lives of her two sons to follow a romantic chimera. She was sentenced to a minimum of thirty years' imprisonment.

Sixty years before this event, Australia too had its own terrible drama in which a young mother killed her son to gain the acceptance of a suitor. On 25 March 1935 Mary Stevens was found guilty in the Supreme Court of Victoria of wilfully murdering her thirteen-month-old son, Leslie. She was sentenced to death.

Stevens was a young domestic servant living in Albury, NSW, who, in November 1932, gave birth to a baby out of wedlock. She relocated to Melbourne in order to find work and a place that could care full-time for Leslie. In January 1934 she asked the Children's Welfare Department to arrange for him to be 'boarded-out'. He went to the City Mission Home in Brunswick, where she paid 10/- a week for his maintenance. This non-sectarian organisation provided residential care for single mothers from 1900 onwards, and had recently taken on the care of toddlers like Leslie Stevens. Later that year Mary Stevens became engaged to Eugene Rollings, a truck driver, also from Albury. At first she was overjoyed that, despite the false step she had taken in life, she seemed assured of a home and financial security. Stevens' happiness was short-lived when Rollings told her that he was unwilling to rear another man's child. Their marriage would only nurture their own children, not, in the colloquial expression of the time, 'someone else's bastard'.

Despite her affection for him, Stevens attempted to have Leslie permanently adopted. This was a hard time to arrange for adoption: marriage and birth rates had plummeted to record lows because of the Depression. As unemployment, evictions and homelessness soared, the possibility of placing a toddler was remote. Leslie's father had taken no responsibility for his welfare and baulked at even providing the slightest payment for his upkeep. On 21 December 1934, Stevens called at the children's home and took Leslie out with her, saying that she intended going to see her family in Albury for the Christmas celebrations. The following morning Leslie was found in the Yarra River, floating face down. Stevens had dressed him in a new blue jumper. Her desire to dress him in new clothes suggests that her initial intention had not been to kill him but indeed take him to Albury with her.

When the police arrested her in Albury, Stevens at first denied having thrown Leslie into the river, concocting a story about a woman who was willing to adopt him. She told Detective F. W. Sickerdick that the woman lived in Lal Lal, near Ballarat, but that she didn't know her name. When pressed further, Stevens admitted that she had murdered her son because he stood in the way of her forthcoming marriage.[1] She told him she had sat on the bank of the river for several hours wondering what she should do. Her only solution, she believed, was to get rid of Leslie for good. How she imagined this would solve her problems when so many people – from her fiancé and parents to people from the children's home and state welfare services – would ask about him is hard to fathom.

Her trial was held before the recently appointed justice to the Supreme Court, Fred Martin (1887–1981), with C. H. Book KC leading the Crown case. Book was a highly experienced and able prosecutor, later appointed to the County Court of Victoria. Stevens was defended by J. M. Cullity. In his testimony Eugene Rollings stated that he had asked Stevens what had become of her son when he saw her in Albury for Christmas. She told him what she told Detective Sickerdick: that Leslie had been adopted but she did not know the woman's name. A labourer, William Henwood from Footscray, testified that he had seen Stevens walking on the north bank of the river near Richmond holding a baby. Later he had seen her alone.

When Stevens entered the witness box she told the court that she loved her son and had done nothing to harm him, a fact clearly at variance with the evidence and her confession to police. The jury deliberated for five and a half hours, returning a guilty verdict, with a strong recommendation for mercy. She was given the statutory death sentence for murder.

The day after her conviction Rollings applied to the governor of Pentridge Prison for permission to visit Stevens. He said he still wished to marry her. He told reporters that he would 'marry her now if they will let me. She has suffered enough already, and my only desire is to give her peace and safety for the rest of her life.'[2] The Executive Council of Victoria considered her sentence in April and commuted her sentence of execution to three years' imprisonment.[3]

The records do not disclose whether Rollings kept his promise and finally married Stevens.

Unaccountably, there was a series of lethal attacks by Australian women armed with axes and knives during the 1930s. Alma Richter of Moonee Ponds killed her nine-year-old son, Allen, with an axe in March 1935. She was found guilty but insane, and was thereafter confined to a psychiatric hospital. In July 1934, Mrs Dominica Guizzardi murdered her neighbour Livia Pinti, the mother of three children, plus her own two-year-old son, William, and five-year-old Alma Giovinazzo, who just happened to be at Mrs Pinti's house delivering a message for her father. There had been no disputes or ill feeling between Guizzardi and Pinti before the attacks with a kitchen knife in Pinti's kitchen. Guizzardi then committed suicide by slashing her own throat. This is one of the worst multiple killings by a woman in Australian history. Police reported that the perpetrator had been treated for 'mental troubles' and was seen just before the murders walking around her neighbourhood of Redcliffe in Perth 'in a very disturbed state of mind'. No one thought to call in a doctor or police at the time.[4] Three years later, at Mount Molloy, near Cairns in Queensland, Isabel Scott West murdered her son George, aged twenty-two; another son, Neil, aged nineteen; and her daughter Ivy, aged fourteen. All were asleep at the time of the attacks by axe. She could offer no explanation for her unprovoked killings.[5] These killings were regarded as particularly traumatic and inexplicable because they had been perpetrated by mothers who had killed their own children.

One of the most intriguing cases of Australian filicide – killing a son or daughter – occurred in Carnegie, a suburb of Melbourne, in 1950. A middle-aged mother, Ivy Cogdon, got out of bed on the night of 11 August, took an axe, and killed her nineteen-year-old daughter, Patricia, as she lay asleep. When arrested by Detective W. W. Mooney, she told him she was 'receiving treatment for a nervous complaint'.[6] In the Coroner's Court on 23 October, Cogdon told Magistrate Burke that she suffered from nightmares. Three medical specialists all presented expert testimony stating that she was 'suffering neurotic troubles and nightmares' and that she had 'not known what she was doing the night her daughter was killed'.[7] Arthur Cogdon revealed that their daughter, Patricia, had been treated for a mental illness and her mother was afraid to the point of obsession that she would never recover.

Sidney Miller, Ivy Cogdon's brother-in-law, testified that she had come to his door, crying hysterically, on the night of 11 August, saying: 'I've had another terrible nightmare. The place was full of soldiers and I was fighting them. Go and see if Pat is all right.' He found his niece dead with dreadful head wounds. Cogdon did not say at the time that she had killed Patricia.

Psychiatrist Dr Henry Stephens of the Prince Alfred Hospital confirmed that Cogdon was troubled by depression and hysteria. 'She is liable to perform certain automatic actions, such as walking in her sleep, and, in such a condition, would have no knowledge of what she was doing and might injure herself or others,' he explained to both the coronial inquest and the criminal trial. Dr John Hurt believed that, while she was not legally insane, Cogdon had no memory of what she did under the blackouts from which she had suffered for twenty years.[8]

The trial for wilful murder was heard in the Supreme Court of Victoria with recently appointed Justice Thomas Sweetman Smith presiding. Her defence team was led by R. V. Monahan KC, who had secured his considerable reputation when he successfully defended Tasmanian Premier Robert Cosgrove in the 1947 inquiry into corruption. Mr M. Cussen, the son of the distinguished jurist Justice Sir Leo Cussen, appeared for the Crown.

The testimony relied upon expert witnesses. Psychologist Edward Campbell believed Cogdon was the 'hysterical type', who could not deal with ordinary life and suffered a low frustration level. Stephens agreed with this diagnosis, adding more details concerning her somnambulism and amnesia. Hysteria and brutal murder, however, are not generally connected in the pattern of mental disorders. Her previous diagnoses and treatment were revealed to be woefully inadequate and inappropriate.

Cogdon's specific fears and delusions manifested themselves in her reaction to current events. She dreamed that Korean Communist soldiers had invaded her suburb and were intent upon 'polluting' her daughter. The Korean War had commenced on 25 June 1950, and Australia readily joined the strong US Allied offensive. Liberal politicians and many citizens believed that this military engagement would be the prelude to a third world war. Australia had not been invaded by the enemy in World War II, but many now believed that a new enemy would realise their long-held fears. Intense anti-Communist feelings heightened this sense of imminent incursion. Cogdon gave no indication of her political beliefs during her trial, although clearly these international developments preyed on her.

The trial concluded on 19 December 1950. The jury acquitted her without even hearing the summation by the Crown and the defence, an event extraordinary in itself. The case was a landmark in common-law jurisdictions, for it was the first time that sleepwalking had been allowed as a defence in an indictment for a capital offence.[9] Cogdon collapsed when she learned she had been found not guilty of wilful murder due to mental impairment. The records do not indicate whether she was confined to a psychiatric hospital.

On 5 December 1980, Helen Moore was sentenced to life imprisonment for the murder of three children. She killed her cousin, sixteen-month-old Susan McIntosh in May 1979, two-year-old Rachel Hay in February 1980, and her half-brother seven-year-old Peter Moore in March 1980, all while babysitting. She also made two attempts on the life of two-year-old Vaughan Nicholson, and severely disabled two-year-old Aaron Crocker. When taken in for questioning, after her brother's death, to the local Sydney police station, Moore readily confessed to Peter's murder. She was just seventeen years old.[10]

Helen Moore was born in 1962 and raised in poor circumstances in western Sydney. Her mother, Jesse Moore, reported that even as a young child her daughter was violent and destructive, tearing her toys apart. At the age of five she was molested by a group of boys at her school. Soon after, a psychiatric patient frightened her with sexual behaviour as she sat on the school bus. Already quite cold and distant in her emotional responses, Moore became more destructive and uncontrollable. Her parents' divorce when she was seven traumatised her further. At the age of thirteen, after she had attacked her brother and nearly tore his hair out by the scalp, Moore was taken to consult a psychiatrist. Rather than addressing the issue of her daughter's violence and anger, Jesse Moore was prescribed Valium to help her cope with her domestic and familial disorders. The implication was that Jesse's mothering and coping skills were at fault, rather than that Helen Moore was a deeply disturbed and possibly psychotic individual.

Five years later Jesse Moore remarried and had two more sons, Peter and Andrew. On 1 March 1979, when he was fourteen months old, Andrew died, apparently from cot death. Helen Moore later said: 'My life started to go wrong when Andrew died. I loved my brother Andrew. I don't know why he was taken away from me but when he was, something happened. Everything in my life went wrong and everything I did went wrong.'[11] She was, however, later charged with his murder before John Hiatt SM on 9 April 1980.[12]

Less than two months later Moore killed Susan McIntosh by holding her hand over the toddler's mouth. Her death was first thought to have also been caused by cot death, even though the syndrome most commonly occurs in infants under six months old. Later at her trial Moore bluntly told the court that 'she [Susan] didn't put up much of a struggle'. She also alleged that her uncle William McIntosh, Susan's father, had sexually abused her regularly from the age of eight until the time of his daughter's death and this was her revenge. He strenuously denied the allegation.

Moore's attempt to suffocate Vaughan Nicholson was not as successful. After her attempt to kill the one-year-old, Moore went back to watching television, only to hear him crying. Alarmed by this unplanned event, she called in a neighbour. Vaughan was admitted to Campbelltown Hospital where he was treated. After these two incidents it is astonishing that anyone could still want Moore's babysitting services. But they did. Two-year-old Aaron Crocker was suffocated in the same manner as Vaughan. Even though he survived the brutal attack, tragically he was in a coma for two weeks and was left blind and crippled. Moore visited him at his bedside. He remained frail and died several years later.

Vaughan Nicholson survived a second attack while Moore was babysitting. By this time, though, people were becoming suspicious. Vaughan's parents started to wonder what pattern was emerging. Yet the thought that a local teenager was deliberately killing children was so unthinkable they put their qualms aside. On 24 February 1980, two-year-old Rachel Hay died suddenly while in Helen Moore's care. The Nicholsons now knew there was 'something very, very wrong going on'.[13] But they still didn't call the police. Five weeks later, on 31 March 1980, Moore rang her mother at work screaming that Peter had fallen down the stairs and killed himself. As soon as she got home, Jesse Moore went straight to the Nicholsons' house across the road in order to call the police. She too had harboured grave concerns about all the sudden and unexplained deaths of previously healthy children. In the police car with Helen after identifying Peter's body, Mrs Moore noticed all the scratches on her daughter's hands confirming her suspicions there had been a struggle before Peter died. She later said: 'Finally, I knew she had done it – she had killed them. I had been facing the terrible truth for so long and finally I knew.'[14]

Moore admitted killing her half-brother immediately. She told the police that she had grabbed him from behind while he was watching his favourite cartoon on television and attempted to suffocate him. He did not die quite as quickly or as easily as the infants. It took a determined struggle of over four minutes to suffocate him before she threw him down the stairs. Moore then went and had a shower before calling her mother and an ambulance, as investigating officer Sergeant D. Worsley testified.[15] The previous day she had taken Peter to the zoo, an event they both enjoyed. She also confessed to the other two murders and two attempted murders.

Her trial was held in the Supreme Court at Parramatta before Justice Adrian Roden in November 1980. Her counsel, John Marsden, was a highly respected and senior barrister. He argued that his client was insane and therefore not responsible for her actions. The eminent forensic psychiatrist Dr William Barclay diagnosed a borderline personality disorder, suggesting that Moore was aware of what she was doing but unaware it was wrong. Dr Greta Goldberg, an experienced clinical and forensic psychologist, offered the opinion that the sexual abuse Moore suffered as a child and teenager had destroyed her normal development.[16]

The prosecution refuted these assessments. Forensic psychiatrist Dr Oscar Schmalzbach OBE, the founder of the Australian Academy of Forensic Sciences, told the court that Moore knew what she was doing and was not mentally ill. Her actions were deliberate, planned – if opportunistic – and persistent.[17] It took the jury just two hours to return a guilty verdict on all three counts of wilful murder and two counts of attempted murder. Helen Moore was sentenced to life imprisonment on each of the three murder counts and ten years for each of the attempted murder counts. After serving only twelve years Moore applied for a sentence review under new 'truth in sentencing' legislation. Justice Loveday reviewed her sentence on 4 September 1992, handing down a term of a minimum of thirteen years and nine months and a maximum of twenty-five years. She was released in 1993, and paroled until 2005 on the proviso she had no contact with any person under sixteen except under the most rigorous supervision. But two years after her release Moore gave birth to a daughter, which put the court in a quandary. Moore and her daughter were placed under twenty-four-hour supervision. There is now a complete media blackout on their current situation and whereabouts.

To contemplate killing one's own healthy, vibrant children with premeditation and deliberation is virtually unimaginable. But what if it is done for revenge? The story of Medea has long fascinated Western culture. The daughter of King Aeëtes of Colchis (modern-day Georgia), the granddaughter of Helios the sun god, she was later the wife of the hero Jason, famed for capturing the Golden Fleece with her wily help. In their decade-long marriage they had two children. They moved to Corinth, where Jason was convinced to abandon Medea for a younger woman, Glauce, King Creon's daughter. Medea not only murdered her rival but she killed her own two children as revenge for Jason's betrayal.[18] The complete Medea story has many more elements of revenge, betrayal, murder and sadism, but at its heart is calculated filicide by an angry, vengeful woman who is prepared to go to unthinkable lengths – a story that continues to resonate in modern culture.

On 5 September 2005, Donna Fitchett made elaborate preparations to murder her two sons, Thomas, aged eleven, and Matthew, aged nine. At first she intended to take sedatives and jump with them off the cliffs at Sorrento in Victoria. Her next abandoned plan was to kill the boys with benzodiazepines and then commit suicide by decapitation with a chain saw. She wrote a long letter to her psychologist explaining what had led to these monstrous thoughts and plans. She posted the letter, and then Donna Fitchett went home and drugged her children. Thomas was then strangled with a sock and left in the marital bedroom, dressed only in a tee shirt. When Matthew woke up confused and groggy, crying because he had wet the bed, Fitchett changed his bed linen and clothes, and settled him down with his teddy bear. She then placed a pillow over his head to kill him. When the family pet, a Rottweiler named Gemma, tried to save his little companion, Fitchett took her outside, tied her up, and returned to the bedroom where she proceeded to strangle Matthew. She then took a non-fatal dose of benzodiazepine and wrote a letter to her husband, David Fitchett. When he returned home later he found his sons dead. Fitchett survived her ingestion of sleeping tablets.[19]

This horror happened in a middle-class suburb of Melbourne; those involved were the most unlikely candidates for such calculated destruction and revenge.

Donna Fitchett was born in the outer Melbourne suburb of Doveton, near Dandenong, in 1959. She attended a Catholic school, leaving in Year 11 to undertake nursing training at St Vincent's Hospital in Melbourne from 1976 to 1978. By the time she met David Fitchett in 1990 she was an experienced and capable nurse. They married in 1993 and had Thomas in 1994 and then Matthew two years later. At first Fitchett continued to work. In 2002 she lost her job at a health clinic in Canterbury and retrained as an options trader. The start-up cost of $150,000 for this risky venture was secured as a loan against equity in the Fitchetts' house in Balwyn North. David Fitchett encouraged his wife's new career move.

After each of her children was born, Fitchett had suffered undiagnosed postnatal depression.[20] Later she was diagnosed with Hashimoto's thyroiditis and an early menopausal hormonal depression. These conditions led to depression, mood swings, tiredness and feelings of confusion. She was prescribed treatment by her local general practitioner, who did not think that psychiatric care was appropriate.[21] The Fitchetts' marriage deteriorated as Fitchett's health and judgment increasingly worsened. Donna Fitchett became obsessed with the relationship her husband had with their sons; she was convinced that he was a lax, uncaring and largely absent father. She blamed his long hours at work and his commitment to playing golf. There was no substantive evidence to support this perception, but the debt on their house was a pressing and constant concern.

In June 2004, Fitchett decided to deal with her problems by consulting psychologist Patra Antonis, which she did on thirty-seven occasions. During the course of her therapy Fitchett came to believe that her husband had a 'passive aggressive' personality and therefore would not change what she believed was selfish, procrastinating behaviour. From early 2005 her depression intensified to such an extent that she spent a lot of time under the blankets in bed. She was not treated for this escalation in her symptoms. David Fitchett was left to eat alone; their sexual life ceased, and they began living in separate bedrooms. On 30 August 2005 Fitchett decided to terminate this unhappy relationship. She told Antonis that she needed to engage in methodical planning, and by this Antonis assumed her client meant financial planning rather than the destructive course she undertook.

When Fitchett informed her husband of her intentions to leave him, their conversation was one-sided. She refused to listen to his point of view or take his feelings into account. When he told her it would be difficult for him to fund two homes, she reacted badly. She had no employment; her job as an options trader was dependent on the line of credit taken out on the marital home, a situation that would be terminated if divorce ensued and the property divided. David Fitchett told her in a moment of anger that 'it would have been better if you had never had the boys'.[22] Many separating couples vent their anger, hurt and disappointment, and what is said is often regretted when tempers cool and more rational judgment is restored, but could this have been the flash point that triggered the lethal attacks?

The next day was Father's Day and Fitchett told her husband that 'he had better ensure he enjoyed it because it would be the last he would have with them as the family'.

With her husband and the children out for the day, Fitchett cleaned the house 'obsessively, including putting some of the boys' clothing into garbage bags'.[23] It was as if the boys had somehow already disappeared and the vestiges of their presence needed to be removed. The following day, she kept the boys home from school to prepare, as they thought, for a wonderful trip. She visited her sister, Louise Mitchell, who described her behaviour as 'distraught' in the later court proceedings. She attributed this to the imminent marriage break-up. On the next morning, at 5.37am Fitchett emailed her other sister, Susan Buckley, declaring her love for her but making disparaging remarks about their father. Eight minutes later she contacted another sister, Marie Ryan, to apologise for not being able to attend their family Christmas lunch although no arrangements had yet been made. Later in the morning Fitchett dropped some things off at Louise Mitchell's house.[24]

Fitchett then wrote to Antonis saying that she 'was determined to lie, to cheat, be selfish and greedy in order to claim whatever I could in order to start a new life with Thomas and Matthew. Who was I kidding? ... I don't know how to be selfish or greedy ... Sadly I am too broken to go on. Today the boys will be given an overdose as I cannot and wouldn't ever abandon them ... They think they are going on an exciting trip today but I've told them they need to take some medicine so they won't get airsick. I'm not a coward – nor am I crazy. I see this as my greatest act of love. I am not punishing David. I pity him.'[25] She ended her letter 'Hugs and kisses, Donna'.

The letter she wrote to David Fitchett was composed after she had murdered their sons. It was equally callous and delusional. She told him: 'I didn't do it because I'm angry with you. I forgive you for whatever hurt you have caused me. You can't help it. I just couldn't abandon our beautiful boys. I have been dead for a few days and I just wanted peace. I overdosed the boys and when they were asleep I suffocated them and then strangled them in case they woke up, they put up a bit of a struggle but said nothing they didn't know it was me or what was happening to each other. They were happy this morning and said they loved you and had a great father's day ... Please take care of the animals especially Gemma ...' Evidence provided at the trial reported that Fitchett had changed Matthew's soiled pyjamas and bed linen before she killed him as she was loath to think anyone would regard her as a 'bad mother'.

David Fitchett returned home on the evening of 6 September 2005 to find his sons dead. He unsuccessfully tried to resuscitate them. Fitchett, who had also cut her arms, neck and groin, went and lay down in Thomas's room until she was taken to Box Hill Hospital under guard for psychiatric assessment. She was committed involuntarily to the Thomas Embling Hospital, where she was considered a high suicide risk. On 17 November, Fitchett was transferred to the women's maximum-security prison. Seven weeks later, Fitchett attempted suicide again and was readmitted to the psychiatric hospital. This pattern recurred, even though she was prescribed heavy antidepressants. Fitchett was victimised by the other prisoners and by

Chillingly, in 2005, on the verge of marital separation, Donna Fitchett warned her husband to make the most of Father's Day. It turned out to be the last time he saw his sons alive. Photo: Newspix NPX1101424.

the correctional staff in prison. Child killers and molesters rank on the lowest level in any prison's hierarchy; a woman who kills her own children is the lowest of the low.

In the trial held in the Supreme Court of Victoria in May 2008, Justice Geoffrey Nettle was on the bench, and Fitchett was defended by Graham Thomas SC, funded by Victoria Legal Aid. Often crying through his ordeal, David Fitchett testified about finding his sons cold and lifeless. He had last seen them happy and playful on Father's Day, a symbolic point that his wife had planned. For the rest of his life, Father's Day would cause him unimaginable pain and grief.

One of the key points of the trial concerned Fitchett's mental state at the time of the offences. The leading expert witness, Professor Paul Mullen, the emeritus professor of Forensic Psychiatry at Monash University, testified that Fitchett was suffering from a major depressive illness that rendered her incapable of understanding the consequences of her actions. Dr Daniel Sullivan, the Assistant Clinical Director of the Victorian Institute of Forensic Mental Health, argued that she was aware of the wrongfulness of her actions but considered that Fitchett was convinced she had acted in her sons' best interests. The expert testimony provided by Dr Yvonne Skinner, a consulting psychiatrist from New South Wales, on the other hand, argued that Fitchett was not seriously depressed at the time of the commission of the crimes – but that her depression had occurred when she realised the enormity and permanence of her crimes afterwards. She asserted that the prisoner fully understood her actions were wrong. The jury inclined towards this opinion in its verdict.

In his sentencing report, Justice Nettle was convinced that Fitchett was 'motivated by spousal revenge which [she] knew to be wrong'. He noted that at no time did the prisoner accept responsibility for her actions, relying totally upon a defence of mental impairment under the Victorian *Crimes (Mental Impairment and Unfitness to be Tried) Act* of 1997. Donna Fitchett was sentenced to seventeen years' imprisonment on each count of murder, with a seven-year sentence imposed on the second count to be served concurrently with count one, thereby reducing the total sentence of incarceration to twenty-four years. A non-parole period was set at eighteen years.[26] Nettle further ordered that Fitchett should be sent to a psychiatric hospital under a security order.

In April 2009, Fitchett appealed her sentence in the Supreme Court of Victoria Court of Appeal. Represented again by a Victoria Legal Aid–appointed barrister Patrick Tehan QC her appeal on the basis of her mental impairment was heard by justices Peter Buchanan, Frank Vincent AO and David Ashley. In the appeal, additional testimony emerged that Thomas had told other people that he wished to live with his father and not his mother, countering his mother's belief that her husband was an aloof and uncaring father. Whether Donna Fitchett was aware of her son's preference was not clear in the testimony.

The Court of Appeal found that the trial judge had erred in his instructions to the jury concerning the defence of mental impairment. A retrial was ordered.[27] The following year, Fitchett was retried before Justice Elizabeth Curtain in the Victorian Supreme Court, again represented by Patrick Tehan. The jury once more found her guilty on both counts of wilful murder. In her sentencing report, Justice Curtain emphasised how Fitchett had told the ambulance officers who came to the murder scene: 'I don't want to go to hospital. I've killed my boys. I just want to die.' While in prison, Fitchett tried to commit suicide four times and was on constant suicide watch. Her counsel reiterated that Fitchett was treated with 'disdain and absolute revulsion by the other prisoners'. She had been constantly bullied, belittled and assaulted. However, Justice Curtain also pointed to Fitchett's 'unfathomable selfishness', saying that her crimes were 'truly appalling and offensive to civilised society'.

Donna Fitchett was once again sentenced to thirty-four years' imprisonment, with a non-parole period of eighteen years. She will be nearly seventy when she is released.

CHAPTER 10

Poisoners of the Nineteenth Century

Rightly or wrongly, over the centuries women have been famed as poisoners – names such as Lucrezia Borgia have echoed through the ages. Poison has been used as a weapon when secrecy is paramount, often in a domestic setting, administered in food, drink and medicine. Family members were frequently the target.

But in nineteenth- and early twentieth-century Britain, the crime was peculiarly dominated by male medical practitioners such as Dr Thomas Cream, who murdered seven prostitutes; Dr Henry Lawson, a morphine addict who killed for financial gain using antimony; Dr George Chapman, who murdered three women, each of whom believed she was his wife; and, most famously, Dr Hawley Crippen, who murdered his wife with hyoscine hydrobromide. Perhaps it wasn't so strange, given the easy and unquestioned access to drugs, poisons and narcotics that doctors have. In weighing the Hippocratic oath against financial gain or psychopathic tendencies, venality might just be the winner. In the late twentieth century, Dr Harold Shipman murdered many of his elderly patients with injections of narcotics. He was convicted of the murder of fifteen patients, although it is possible he murdered 200 more.

It was also not strange that few cases of poisoning were heard in the English courts in the eighteenth century. The symptoms of widespread diseases such as typhoid and cholera are similar to those of poisoning, and the sciences of toxicology and forensic pathology had not yet emerged.[1] This changed in 1803 under Lord Ellenborough's new *Offences Against the Person Act*, which dealt with poisoning as well as proscriptions against induced abortions.[2] Early studies in toxicology had taken some time to appear: Samuel Farr's groundbreaking text, *A Short View of the Extent and Importance of Medical Jurisprudence*, was published in 1798; and George Male's textbook, *Treatise on Judicial or Forensic Medical Medicine; for the use of medical men, coroners and barristers*, first released in 1816, was the first creditable book in the discipline.[3] The isolation of the lethal poison strychnine from an Indian tree in 1819 gave impetus to further research into toxins and poisons.[4]

Two years later, in 1821, three important cases in England, in which the accused were each found guilty of murder by the use of arsenic, were examples of a marked increase in the prevalence of these trials. That year Dr J. G. Smith of the Westminster Hospital in London published a comprehensive textbook. There emerged expert witnesses in the form of chemists, apothecaries and medical practitioners who had some training in forensic medicine.[5]

The first case of poisoning came not long after, in 1824, when Mary Ann Bradley was charged before the Supreme Court of New South Wales with poisoning her husband John Bradley. She was accused of using arsenic to kill him; but despite overwhelming evidence the military jury found her 'not guilty'. Arsenic had been first advertised in the colony in September 1823.[6] Fifty years later, a woman *did* go to the gallows, even though this time she may not have been guilty of poisoning her husband. Elizabeth Woolcock, hanged in Adelaide in 1873, was the only woman ever executed in South Australia, even though thirty-two executions had preceded hers.[7] Woolcock had been convicted of murdering her violent husband, Thomas Woolcock, by mercury poisoning. An examination of the documents suggests that her conviction for murder was tainted because the Woolcocks' drug-addicted medical practitioner, Dr Thomas Bull, may inadvertently have been at fault from incompetence.

Elizabeth Oliver was born to John and Elizabeth Oliver in 1848 in the rough South Australian mining settlement of Burra, 160 kilometres north of Adelaide. The Olivers had arrived in the new colony just five years earlier and lived in extreme poverty in rooms cut into the banks of the Kooringa Creek. Cornish-born John Oliver worked for 'the Monster Mine', one of the copper mines that had opened in 1845. When strikes and loss of production at the mine proved a disappointment for its owners and investors, workers such as Oliver, who had also lost all his possessions in a flash flood, decided they had better prospects when the Victorian goldfields opened in 1851. The family, which now included two other children, relocated to Ballarat, a town Elizabeth Oliver detested, describing it as 'this horrid, sin-stained colony of scoundrels and villains'.[8] The monthly mining licence of 30/- placed immense financial strain on unsuccessful prospectors like John Oliver. After infant daughter Catherine died from the prevalent dysentery, Elizabeth Oliver departed for Adelaide with another man, leaving her daughter Elizabeth to be raised by her father and neighbours. John Oliver moved to the Creswick diggings to try his luck in early 1853, and four-year-old Elizabeth was left on her own with only a kind neighbour, Bridget Darcy, to keep an eye on her.[9]

In the long confession she wrote just before she was executed, Woolcock outlined her chaotic childhood, during which she did not see her mother from the time she was four until she was eighteen. That she was even partially literate was unusual for a poor child living an itinerant life. Her father died from tuberculosis when she was nine, prompting her to earn a living as a maid to a pharmacist in Melbourne. What she did not disclose in her confession was that at just six years old she had witnessed the murder of her father's friend, Henry Powell, by police as an act of retaliation for taking part in the Eureka Rebellion in 1854. Arthur Akehurst, the clerk of the court at Ballarat, along with 'other persons unknown', was accused of murdering Powell by gunshot and sabre cuts. The persons unknown were mounted police who, in a show of the Crown's force, trampled Powell's body as he lay dying.[10]

The following year, when she was seven, Elizabeth Oliver was raped and left for dead by George Shaughshaw, an Indian itinerant. The criminal case was heard before the inaugural Chief Justice of the Supreme Court of Victoria, Sir William à Beckett (1806–69) in sittings in Geelong in January 1855. He described it as 'one of the most atrocious crimes to be brought before me'. The prisoner received the death sentence.[11] Elizabeth Oliver suffered serious and permanent gynaecological damage that rendered her infertile, and she was subject to constant pain for the rest of her life, for which doctors prescribed opium. Working for Mr Lees in his pharmacy since the age of nine, the girl had easy access to strong doses of opium, although it should be remembered that opium was a common ingredient in many patent medicines, as well as being readily available over the counter in Victorian chemist shops at the time.

At the age of fifteen Elizabeth moved back to Ballarat with a large stash of opium. She began working as a maid in a guesthouse, but also supplied opium to prostitutes intent upon robbing their clients. Despite her illegal activities, Elizabeth Oliver continued to attend the Wesleyan Chapel. With the help of William Goldsworthy, a visiting lay preacher who knew her mother in South Australia, she was reunited with her maternal family. Her mother wrote to her in 1865, expressing great sorrow about how she had treated her daughter and begging her to join her at Moonta Mine. Elizabeth Oliver wrote in her confession: 'I thought I should like to see my mother and have a home like other young girls so I gave up my situation and came to Adelaide. My mother and my stepfather received me very kindly and I had a good home for two years ...'[12] She worked as a housekeeper, and taught Sunday school at the Wesleyan Church on the weekends.[13] For a while she weaned herself off her addiction since pure opium was far harder to obtain in South Australia than it had been in Victoria. In South Australia a doctor's prescription was required. Then, when her employers, Mary and Robert Slape, decided to engage a relative, she lost her job.

She met her husband, Cornish miner Thomas Woolcock, in 1866. His wife, Nanny Woolcock, and Francis, one of his sons, had died from fever the previous year and he engaged Oliver as his housekeeper. Hypocritically, given that he had run off with her married mother, Oliver's stepfather, William Williams, was outraged by this arrangement and insisted that Elizabeth and Woolcock marry. She revealed in her confession that he threatened to 'break both my legs. I was afraid he would keep his word as I never knew him to tell a wilful lie …'. This would imply that her stepfather was a violent and abusive man. Thomas Woolcock was also a violent man, addicted to drink and to beating his new wife and his child. Three years later, in 1869, Woolcock's mother and stepfather moved to Adelaide, leaving Elizabeth without a family network to rely upon.

In early 1870 Woolcock left her husband but returned when he promised to stop drinking. The promise was short-lived. Like many perpetrators of domestic violence he 'did not like to part with his money for anything else [but alcohol]'. Her subsequent attempts to leave him were defeated by parental pressure and lack of money. After three years of bad treatment, Woolcock's desperation was so acute she attempted to hang herself. The roof beam broke under the strain and she survived. Unable even to kill herself, Woolcock became still more frustrated and desperate, and started to rely on opium again, despite how difficult it was to obtain.

Thomas Woolcock was illiterate, like most other miners. He supplemented his earnings by diagnosing sick animals, although he left it to his wife to do the actual work. She was constantly at the local chemist obtaining medicines for the animals. Attending to ailing animals was still not sufficient to make ends meet so Thomas Woolcock decided to accept lodgers. A boarder named Thomas Pascoe took up residence in the small home, although the arrangement did not last after Thomas Woolcock became aggressive without provocation. Pascoe was appalled by how Elizabeth Woolcock and her little stepson were treated. Of course, Woolcock decided this was because his lodger had an interest in his young wife. Pascoe had to go. Soon after he left, the family dog was poisoned – believed to be from strychnine – and Pascoe was suspected of the cowardly act.

In her trial the alleged affair was proffered as her motive for eliminating her husband.[14] Despite it constituting no proof of an illicit relationship, the testimony of a neighbour, Frances Carpenter, that Pascoe visited Woolcock during the day when her husband was working at the mine was given credence.[15] That Carpenter was an extremely hostile witness against the young widow at the trial did not provoke concern.

On 23 July 1873, within a month of Pascoe's departure, Thomas Woolcock became seriously ill with severe stomach pains. Elizabeth Woolcock consulted three doctors, who all diagnosed different causes: Dr Thomas Bull prescribed a third of a grain of mercury for Woolcock's 'sore throat'; while Dr John Dickie recommended cream of tartar and rhubarb tablets for stomach problems. At the trial in December 1873, the third, Dr Lloyd Herbert, stated that when he visited Thomas Woolcock on 1 August, the ailing patient was suffering from severe thirst, excessive salivation and a sore throat. Herbert diagnosed 'salivation by mercury'. He continued treatment for thirteen days until Thomas Woolcock informed him that he could no longer afford him and would be returning to his Lodge practitioner, Dr Dickie, who treated him for nothing. (Miners at this time subscribed to medical and pharmaceutical benefits through organisations such as the Oddfellows Lodge.) Dr Herbert also said that Woolcock was already 'not a well man'; he had kidney disease, among other life-threatening complaints including tuberculosis. No doubt his excessive drinking undermined his health.

Elizabeth Woolcock decided to call in Dr Bull once more, despite the resistance of her husband, who said: 'I certainly don't want Dr Bull again, as it was his medicine that made me bad in the first place.' Neighbour Jane Nicholls testified that during his illness Woolcock's tongue became black and that he was vehemently opposed to any further consultation by Dr Bull.[16] This corroborates Dr Herbert's evidence that it was the ingestion of mercury – in other words, Bull's treatment – that had poisoned Thomas Woolcock.

The pharmacist in Moonta, John Opie, testified that he had frequently supplied Elizabeth Woolcock with morphine, which she initially pretended was to clean her curtains and linen. She also sent her young stepson, Thomas, along with notes to request more doses, as well as going herself in the company of a neighbour, Mrs Hannah Blight. Opie told the court that eventually he had to refuse. Then, under a false name, Woolcock sent for laudanum, a tincture of opium.[17] Such hopeless attempts at deceit in a small community where everyone knew everybody else demonstrate her desperation. Charles Rooke, the assistant manager of Birk's Chemist, also testified to her attempts to obtain narcotics. Other witnesses at her trial reported that it was well known that she was a drug addict who would use increasingly bizarre measures to ensure her supply. The testimony of expert witnesses such as these chemists had significant consequences for the outcome of her murder trial.

When Thomas Woolcock died on 4 September 1873, Dr Dickie provided a death certificate that stated he had died from 'pure exhaustion from prolonged vomiting and purging'. Thomas Woolcock's cousin, Elizabeth Snell, believed he had been poisoned and pressured for more investigations. Rumours saying that Elizabeth Woolcock was a drug addict who had poisoned her husband buzzed about the small mining settlement, but so did stories that he was known to be abusive and violent towards her.

An autopsy by doctors Dickie, Gosse and Herbert was conducted in the Woolcocks' house while Elizabeth Woolcock stood outside. Large quantities of mercury were detected in the remains. As well, it appeared that Woolcock had been suffering from tuberculosis and had dysentery at the time of his death. This would account for some of the symptoms he had presented to the three medical practitioners.

Fearful of losing his professional reputation, Dr Dickie ordered an inquest into the death, which was held at Moonta court house before a large panel of fourteen jurors, all of whom were hostile towards the deceased's wife. At the inquest the fact that Dr Bull had prescribed the mercury was completely overlooked. When proceedings concluded, Elizabeth Woolcock was placed under arrest for the wilful murder of her husband, and taken to Wallaroo jail in Adelaide.

The three-day trial in the Supreme Court of South Australia commenced on Wednesday 3 December 1873, and was followed avidly by the public, with large crowds each day skirmishing to get a seat in the gallery. Those who did not, milled outside the courtroom waiting for developments to be relayed outside. The case was presided over by Justice William Wearing QC (1816–75). Prosecuting for the Crown was the solicitor-general, Richard Andrews QC (1823–84), who had served as attorney-general under Premier Sir Robert Torrens.[18] Woolcock was represented pro bono by London-trained barrister Dr James Cholmondeley Kaufmann, who ran a large criminal practice. The first witness was George Francis, an analytical chemist, who testified that he had examined specimens sent to him by Moonta police, and found large quantities of mercury. In a defence far more sophisticated and informed than that of the Crown prosecutor, Dr Kaufmann attempted to refute Francis's claims by consulting the standard textbooks on forensic jurisprudence, *On Poisons in Relation to Medical Jurisprudence and Medicine* (1848) and *The Principles and Practices of Medical Jurisprudence* (1865), both by Alfred Swaine Taylor.

Much of the testimony from the residents of Moonta was highly critical of and antagonistic towards Elizabeth Woolcock, who was, in their eyes, an adulterer and a drug addict. Yet no one had witnessed Woolcock give her husband any mercury preparations other than those prescribed by Dr Bull. A letter to her family in Adelaide dated 10 April, in which Woolcock revealed all the abuse and ill treatment she had endured during her short marriage, was tendered in evidence against her.[19] It was believed to provide a motive for her actions. Until 1898 – twenty-five years into the future – an accused person could not testify in court to defend themselves, so often all a defence counsel could do was try to refute points made by the prosecution rather than presenting a coherent counter-case. In her meagre defence, her stepson testified that 'Mother', as he called her, had tended his father with great care.

It only took twenty minutes for the jury to find Elizabeth Woolcock guilty of the wilful murder of her husband. She was sentenced to death. The sentence caused considerable debate in the colony since no woman – especially one of only twenty-five – had ever been put to death there. Awaiting her execution in Adelaide jail, Woolcock was attended by the Reverend James Bickford (1816–95), a former missionary,[20] whose spiritual counsel and guidance were assiduous. Under his persuasion, Woolcock made her last statement and confession in which she wrote that 'Satan tempted me … I was so ill-treated that I was quite out of my mind and in an evil hour I yielded to the temptation …'. She gave Bickford the sealed letter as she walked calmly to the gallows on 30 December 1873. It was later published verbatim in the newspapers. She wore 'a plain white dress and carried in her hands a bunch of flowers'. The Reverend Bicknell walked to the gallows with her, comforting her with prayers and readings from the Bible.[21]

In her confession, Woolcock wrote that she had given her husband 'powder' that she believed contained poisons. She was most likely referring to a treatment for ringworm that had been procured for the dog, which contained small quantities of mercury. She elaborated that she took the powder herself to no ill effect. At the trial, expert evidence indicated this veterinary preparation was insufficient to kill a person.

At no other time, it appears, did Woolcock dose her husband with mercury drugs other than those prescribed by Thomas Bull. Later, whispers surfaced that the doctor was addicted to atropine, a drug used to treat eye diseases; and that he had regularly overused various other drugs such as chloroform, opium and sulphuric ether. Dr John Dickie testified at the inquest into Bull's demise that the deceased had taken large quantities of belladonna and other narcotics.[22]

At the time he was visiting Woolcock, Bull was confused and muddled. He could certainly have prescribed an incorrect dosage of medication. Although he had studied at the University of Cambridge, Bull had undertaken his licensed medical studies as an apothecary, by then an old-fashioned route to professional qualification. He made up his own medicines for patients rather than providing them with prescriptions to be dispensed by a chemist.[23] Had a pharmacist checked and dispensed his prescription, any errors of dosage would have been noted and verified. Woolcock himself believed that Bull had been the cause of his rapid decline. Because of his addictions Bull was confined to a lunatic asylum after the trial and committed suicide soon afterwards.

Nor did Woolcock ever criticise or accuse his wife of attempting to kill him, even though he had had ample opportunity to do so in front of his family, workmates and neighbours. It is notable that Chief Justice Way wrote to relatives in England that the medical evidence in this capital case was 'unreliable' and even 'mistaken'.[24] Yet once she was found guilty, he had no other choice than to sentence her to death. John Dickie's professional reputation was ruined by the trial and he relocated in shame to Tasmania. Justice Wearing drowned in a shipwreck fifteen months after the trial.

In May 2004 a mock trial by students at the University of Adelaide's Law Week recreated the Woolcock prosecution – and unanimously found her 'not guilty'.[25]

By the 1880s, the expansion of insurance to cover working-class families provided another motive for murder by poison for the more ruthless and mercenary. Friendly societies and lodges began offering small weekly payments to relieve men's unemployment in England from the 1730s. They were slower to establish themselves in the new Australian colonies since there was little potential custom during the convict era. When free settlement began in earnest, however, the friendly societies soon followed. The first, the Oddfellows Lodge, was established in Sydney in 1836 by a far-sighted bookseller and engraver, William Moffitt.[26] Manchester Unity, a breakaway organisation, set up operations in Sydney in 1845. The successful draper David Jones was one of the founders of the Australian Mutual Provident Society in Sydney in 1849. In the absence of welfare benefits, government services, and hospital admission via subscription to the friendly societies and lodges, any severe illness, incapacity or unemployment affecting the breadwinner could plunge working families into dire poverty with alarming speed. At first only tradesmen could afford the premiums. But as relative affluence began to spread with the economic boom that had begun in the goldfields in the 1850s, and extended into the 1880s with a growth in manufacturing and a boom in investment and speculation, workers on more modest wages were able to afford premiums to cover illness, pharmaceuticals, unemployment and death. Life insurance did not simply cover the life of the breadwinner but could be taken out for all family members, including children.

Although it was hardly a novel epithet, Louisa Collins became known as the 'Botany Bay Borgia' when, motivated by passion and financial gain, she killed her two husbands in the late 1880s. In the United States in the 1860s and 1870s, there had been some other husband-murdering 'Borgias': Lydia Sherman progressively murdered three husbands, a stepdaughter and from six to eight of her own children, largely for insurance money. The press dubbed her the 'Borgia of Connecticut'. In the following decade Sarah Jane Robinson poisoned several of her children and relatives for insurance money. Robinson was popularly termed the 'Borgia of Massachusetts'. Like Sherman she died in prison serving a commuted capital sentence because the progressive north-eastern states baulked at executing women, no matter how terrible their crimes.[27] Judicial chivalry was not extended to Australia's own modern Lucrezia Borgia, for Louisa Collins was executed on 8 January 1889 after four separate and controversial trials.

Collins was born in 1849 to Henry and Catherine Hall. The couple worked on 'Belltrees', the profitable pastoral property near Scone in the Hunter Valley in New South Wales run by James White, who had leased the property the previous year from the prominent lawyer and parliamentarian William Charles Wentworth.[28] The Hall family believed they were related to the 'gentleman bushranger' Ben Hall, who had been born in Maitland in 1837 to former convict parents.

Louisa Hall was a beautiful child with blonde curls and big alert eyes. From an early age she was aware of the attention her physical attractiveness brought her. She went into domestic service at Merriwa, a small township to the west of nearby Scone. The men of the district soon noticed her and she was rumoured to be a provocative flirt. Indeed, rumours spread that she was far more than a flirt and offered more than a chaste kiss. Her good looks and teasing personality attracted the attentions of a thirty-six-year-old widower, Charles Andrews, who ran a successful butchering business. Her mother, no doubt fearful of scandal, especially if Louisa produced an illegitimate baby, pressured her to marry this quiet and industrious man with whom she had nothing in common. And so they married on 28 August 1865.

The couple moved to Waterloo in Sydney where Andrews had been raised. He found work initially as a carrier for Lord's Mill until it closed. They then moved into a small cottage at 10 Popple's Terrace in Botany, a rather desolate spot reached by crossing a wooden bridge spanning a fetid swamp. This whole area was deemed a 'noxious trade area', with its wool-scouring factories and tanneries that pumped out hazardous waste. With seven children and no close neighbours or family near her, life for Louisa Andrews became monotonous, lonely and alienating. As the belle of Merriwa she had expected far more, believing her good looks and sex appeal would elevate her from a life of domestic drudgery. She countered the monotony by frequently visiting the Pier Hotel on Botany Road, where she tried to relive her days as a sex siren. By now she was 'pleasantly plump, with bold good looks and a flighty disposition'.[29] But she was more than 'flighty' and flirtatious – she openly engaged in sexual liaisons with hotel patrons, causing gossip around the district. Charles Andrews apparently did nothing about her absences and behaviour, never criticising his wife in public.

Their income had fallen when Andrews left the butchering trade, but, with seven children to support, Louisa Andrews insisted they find ways to supplement the family's resources. The first option was to take in boarders. Rumours began to spread again that the landlady was engaging in sexual encounters while her husband was at work. Charles Andrews continued to maintain his silence, at least in public, wearing the humiliation of being a cuckold to a pretty and much younger wife with considerable dignity.[30]

When Louisa Andrews met labourer Michael (Mick) Collins in 1886 at the Pier Hotel she asked him to come and live at her house as a boarder. He was then twenty-two years old, fourteen years younger than Andrews, handsome and well built. She later described him in a letter to her mother as '... tall and handsome, he was good, loving, attentive, sober and honest ... '.[31] He worked at a local wool-washing shed, earning a small wage. Collins settled in, and around the district became known as Louisa Andrews' accepted paramour. They were seen at the hotel, on the steam tram, and walking along the unpaved roads holding hands, embracing and kissing.[32]

Nine days before Christmas 1886, Charles Andrews reached the end of his tolerance and he vented years of resentment and humiliation when he got into a fight with his young boarder. After the altercation he evicted Collins, throwing all his belongings into the street. Louisa Andrews went straight to the local police station to report her husband's behaviour and seek their assistance. Given the current laws and prevailing attitudes towards the marital home in the 1880s, Constable Jeffs suggested that she calm down, go home and attempt to make peace with her outraged husband.

Louisa Andrews raged against her husband's lack of earning power, forgetting he could earn far more in his trade. He had worked hard to maintain her and their children, although by now the eldest son,

Herbert, lived in Maitland, and Reuben and Arthur were also self-supporting but still living at home.

Louisa Andrews decided to remedy her unhappy situation and forge a new life for herself while she still maintained a semblance of her looks. Around this time, she asked the local draper, a Mr Bullock, about the time lapse between death and an insurance claim.

On Friday 28 January, Charles Andrews told Bullock he would drop some good-quality pork around to him the following day. He failed to show up but the draper thought little of it. By Monday, Andrews was seriously ill, telling his local doctor, Thomas Martin, that he had terrible stomach pains. Gastric complaints and diarrhoea, however, were common in the squalid environment of the Frog's Hollow slum in hot summer. On top of that, his first trade of butchering was known to take place in a dangerous environment because of the poisonous chemicals it used.[33] And the local tanneries used oxalic acid, which was known to be deadly from 1829 when Robert Christison published his landmark textbook on toxicology, *A Treatise on Poisons: In Relation to Medical Jurisprudence, Physiology, and the Practice of Physic*. Arsenic was also used to produce the colour green in wallpapers, a device that Agatha Christie later employed to kill a victim in *The Blue Geranium* (1932). While the rough shanty of the Andrews family did not run to such bourgeois adornment as wallpaper, in his work Andrews dealt extensively with arsenic, and with lead.[34] Despite this combination of factors, Dr Martin did not think that poison was involved when he issued a death certificate for Charles Andrews, who died on Friday 4 February 1887.

Louisa Andrews acted swiftly, catching the tram into the city centre, literally while her husband's body was still warm. With indecent haste, she was intent upon getting his insurance money – the considerable sum of £200 – from the Australian Widows' Fund.

The same lack of emotion was on display when a neighbour, a Mrs Price, asked how her husband was getting on. Andrews replied: 'Oh, he's dead. I'd like you to help me lay him out for the funeral.'[35]

Even though it was normal to wear heavy black mourning clothes for at least a year in the late nineteenth century, her next move was to order some brightly coloured material from the draper. When he expressed his disapproval of this choice for a new widow, she dismissed his concerns, telling him: 'I can mourn Charlie in my heart without having to carry my grief in my clothes.' Three days later Louisa Andrews invited all her friends from the hotel to join her in a wild and noisy all-night party at her home. She had still not told her eldest son, Herbert, about his father's death and nor did she give him any of the insurance money.

Mick Collins moved in again soon after the funeral and became the acknowledged man of the house. On 9 April 1887 Collins and Louisa Andrews married at St Silas Church of England in Waterloo. The bride declared she was twenty-eight years of age instead of the actual thirty-eight. The couple then moved with her children to a small house at Johnson Lane, North Botany. Soon into the marriage, however, she realised she had made a disastrous choice; Collins, unlike her first husband, wasn't keen on working for a living, believing he was entitled to live off her insurance claim. Furthermore, he drank heavily and gambled at every opportunity. He went through her insurance claim with alarming rapidity. She produced a baby seven months into the legal union, presumably conceived while Andrews was still alive – Collins always acknowledged the boy as his child – but he died at the age of five months. Louisa Collins did not appear upset or concerned. She began drinking heavily again at the Pier Hotel and complaining to anyone who would listen that she had tied herself to a 'loafer' and a 'wastrel'. Mick Collins eventually roused himself to get a job, which paid 36/- per week.

A solution to Louisa Collins' disappointments was at hand. Once again poison would be the remedy. Her second husband was not insured, but he undoubtedly knew what had happened to her first husband and therefore she couldn't just leave him. Mick Collins began to suffer extremely painful abdominal seizures. He took to his bed, keeping his trousers on him at all times. Dr George Marshall was called in. He conferred with his colleague Dr Martin, who had treated Charles Andrews, and both attended to the now-dying man. Believing that to have two husbands fall ill with the same symptoms tested credibility, Dr Marshall took samples from the sick man, and the medicine by the bedside, for testing on 4 July 1888.[36] When the police were called in on the doctor's advice, Collins told them he didn't think he was being poisoned. Mick Collins died in agony on 8 July 1888.

This time, there were suspicions that this husband had not died naturally. The police found a glass containing a small amount of arsenic in the sickroom and, in a cupboard, the product 'Rough on Rats', a poison that could be found in any home at the time. Spurred by the information provided by Dr Martin, Dr Marshall refused to provide a death certificate.[37]

An inquest convened at the Sydney morgue before the city coroner Henry Shiell and a jury of twelve men was concluded on 10 July 1888. Doctors Marshall and Martin were key witnesses. Marshall now argued that Charles Andrews might have died from arsenic poisoning. He also testified that Louisa Collins was an 'apathetic nurse', careless and constantly 'the worse for drink'. The government analyst, William Hamlet, testified he had found sufficient arsenic in Collins' stomach to cause death. Contrary evidence was produced that during his short illness Collins had many visitors, some assisting Louisa Collins to nurse her husband. No one saw anything untoward or improper. Collins argued that her husband had been depressed for some time due to a pain in the groin, and took medicine that may have contained poisons. Patent medicines to 'cure' syphilis contained arsenic so what she said may have been true. During the hearing she remained stoical, almost detached, which was used against her to prove she was callous and lacking in womanly feelings.[38]

On 14 July the coroner opened another inquiry, this time into the death of Charles Andrews. After exhumation his body was found to contain faint traces of arsenic. The body of the baby was also disinterred but was not found to contain any poison. Two weeks later the coroner ordered Louisa Collins to stand trial for the wilful murder of her two husbands.[39] She was taken into custody, although not under warrant, later that evening. She was drunk when the police arrived at her home at 6pm when she was feeding the children. With some prescience she told the children: 'I know I am not coming back.'[40]

Her first trial concerned the murder of Mick Collins and commenced on 6 August 1888 before Justice William Foster (1831–1909), a recent appointment to the bench, who had previously served as attorney-general under Henry Parkes. Evidence was presented by neighbours that Collins was often drunk and neglected her home and her children – something that counted against her at a time when gender roles were so rigidly defined. Dr Marshall was less hostile than he had been during the inquest, although he was clearly annoyed she had rejected his advice to admit her husband to hospital. The most damning testimony came from eleven-year-old May Andrews. She stated when asked about the box of 'Rough on Rats': 'I would know a box like it … I have seen it before … It was before my own father got sick – I saw the box first on the top shelf in the house, when we lived in [Popples] Paddock about a year ago.' This testimony linked the deaths of the two husbands together, however circumstantially. The jury could not agree on a verdict, making a second trial necessary. This one began on 5 November 1888 before Justice William Windeyer. The press speculated that Collins might have committed suicide due to illness and poor employment prospects. Perhaps toxic chemicals in wool washing were to blame, Louisa Collins' counsel suggested.[41] Again the jury was split and therefore dismissed.[42]

In the third trial, which opened on 19 November 1888 before Justice Sir Joseph Innes (1834–96), a former Minister of Justice in the New South Wales parliament, Louisa Collins was this time arraigned on the charge of murdering Charles Andrews. Her counsel argued that environmental and employment-related toxicity was to blame for Andrews' death. Again the jury could not agree and was discharged. For her fourth trial, she was again charged with the murder of her second husband, a highly irregular legal proceeding given that the two previous trials concerning Collins had been unsuccessful.[43] It was not until this trial, which commenced on 6 December 1888 before the Chief Justice Sir Frederick Darley (1830–1910), later lieutenant-governor of New South Wales during Federation, that she was found guilty of the wilful murder of Mick Collins. His Honour was savage in his remarks to the convicted prisoner: '… you watched his slow torture and painful death, and this apparently without a moment's remorse. You were indifferent to his pain, and gained his confidence by your simulated affection. There is too much reason to fear that your first husband Andrews also met his death at your hands.'[44] And with that, Louisa Collins was sentenced to death.

Despite her reputation as a drunken, slovenly adulterer there was a degree of sympathy for this mother of seven children now facing the awful finality of the noose. Controversial former undertaker Ninian Melville (1843–97), the member for Northumberland, told the New South Wales Legislative Assembly that the case against Collins was '… an unfortunate exhibition of what was called justice'.[45] Others, like fellow parliamentarian Thomas Walker, however, called her the 'Borgia of Botany Bay', a name that stuck for generations to follow. Premier Sir Henry Parkes canvassed the opinion of the chief justice on the merits of the case, and reported to parliament on 19 December 1888 that the opinion was to proceed with the execution. During that debate there were insistent calls for an appeal.

After four trials an appeal seemed to be a remote possibility. However, it went ahead on 28 December 1888 before the full bench consisting of justices Windeyer and Foster and Chief Justice Darley. At this time judges could sit on appeals even when they had convened earlier proceedings and convictions. Collins again relied on a local lawyer, a Mr Lusk, to represent her pro bono, whereas the Crown had the finest legal minds in the colony at its disposal. Her appeal was rejected.[46] Her daughter May, in an interview with the governor, Lord Carrington, pleaded for her mother's life. He told her he was unable to intervene after the Executive Council confirmed its resolution to see the sentence carried out. He also received many petitions to extend clemency, generally argued on the issue of Collins' possible insanity and the fact that the three initial trials had been unable to convict her.[47] The governor was in a difficult position despite the generosity of spirit and largesse that characterised his term of office. The press was also consumed with opinions for and against the execution of Louisa Collins in early January 1889.

None of the public agitation was successful. Before her execution Collins wrote to Lord Carrington on the cheap blue-lined prison paper she was allotted. In it she begged him to consider that: 'Oh, my Lord. Pray have mercy and pity upon me and spare my life. I beg and implore you ... have mercy on me for my child's [sic] sake. I have seven children ... Spare me my Lord for their sake ... Oh my Lord my life is in your hands.'[48] Supported by the sympathetic and compassionate prison chaplain, Canon C. H. Rich, who was attached to St Andrew's Church of England cathedral, she went to the gallows at Darlinghurst jail on 8 January 1889. Lord Carrington was castigated in the radical and nationalist press as an uncaring chinless wonder.[49] Louisa Collins was the last woman executed in New South Wales.

If there is some measure of doubt in determining the guilt of Louisa Collins, there was none where Martha Needle was concerned. She was a psychopathic, ruthless mass murderer who killed her own children, her husband, and the brother of her naive besotted lover, all for financial gain. She was executed on 22 October 1894 in Melbourne jail.

Martha Needle's early life was chaotic and traumatic. Born Martha Charles in April 1863 to poor parents at Morgan, South Australia, on the Murray River, she was, of the six children born, one of only three children to survive. Despite his meagre existence in the colony, her father, Joseph Charles, was consumed with the fantasy that he was a wealthy heir to a large estate in England. This may have been a sign of mental instability. Her parents parted when Mary Charles accused her husband of attempting to poison her. He did not deny the accusation, replying that since 'they were living so unhappily she could expect nothing else'.

The couple reconciled and moved to Kapunda. But then Mary Charles alleged that he had tried to poison her again. She fled, relocating to North West Bend station where Martha was born some seven months later. Her parents reconciled yet again and moved to Port Lincoln with the other two children.[50] Joseph Charles again abandoned the family. Believing her husband to be dead, in March 1870 Mary Charles married a violent army deserter named Daniel Foran, who had arrived in the colony with the 2nd Somersetshire Regiment of Foot. He wore the detested letter D tattooed on him to indicate his status.

In 1876, Foran was jailed for two years with hard labour for indecently assaulting his twelve-year-old stepdaughter Martha Charles.[51] After the assault on her daughter, Mary Foran began to drink heavily and was constantly before the courts for being drunk in public, using indecent language and neglecting her children. After the attack Martha was sent into domestic service with a Mrs Drew in North Adelaide. That same year Mary Foran was jailed for a month for neglecting her two younger children, who were despatched to the Industrial Home for Neglected Children.[52] She was imprisoned again in 1877 for being a 'habitual drunkard'.[53]

In 1880, at the age of seventeen, Martha Charles married twenty-two-year-old English-born carpenter Henry Needle. The couple had three children: Mabel, born in May 1882, Elsie in October 1884, and lastly May in October 1886.[54] They decided to try their luck in Melbourne, with its booming economy fuelled by construction. At first they were happy together at Cubitt Street, Richmond, but soon the ambitious and beautiful Martha Needle began to resent her modest circumstances. She took to going out at night alone, fuelling domestic arguments. With the sudden death of three-year-old Mabel in December 1885, the marriage further deteriorated. Looking for more money to support his increasingly dissatisfied wife, Henry

Needle went to Sydney; he had little to show for his exertions when he returned.

During this time of stormy reunion, Henry Needle sought medical treatment from the Lodge doctor for severe stomach pains and nausea. Neighbours came in to help, particularly as he refused to take any food or medicines from his wife's hand. This alone should have rung alarm bells but he did not offer any specific allegations against his wife either to the police or to the Lodge doctors. Nor did he voice any concerns about the manner in which Mabel had died. When Henry Needle died on 4 October 1889, the attending doctor issued a death certificate stating he had died of 'subacute hepatitis, enteric fever, and exhaustion.'

Martha Needle had taken out a £200 insurance policy on her husband's life with The Trustees, Executors and Agency Company. She was dismayed when the administrators only paid her £60, keeping the rest in trust for the two minor children. Martha Needle was furious since she had expected to receive the entire amount. She complained about her deceased husband to anyone who would listen, portraying him as a jealous, irritable and violent man.

With her share of the insurance payout Needle began to keep a boarding house in Richmond. It initially proved profitable, although the work involved in running such a business was relentless and arduous, even with servants.[55] Slaving away in a large house, with meals to prepare, laundry to wash and iron, and general duty of care for the boarders was hardly the future Needle envisaged for herself. So in October 1890 she closed the business and went to live in a smaller residence with her two daughters.

Fourteen months later, Elsie died after three weeks of a painful debilitating illness. Like Mabel, the once-healthy little girl suffered terrible stomach pains, emaciation and fever. Again there was no suspicion that foul play might have been involved. The Lodge doctor provided a death certificate stating that the six-year-old had succumbed to 'gangrenous stomatitis and exhaustion'. Needle then applied for, and was given, Elsie's share of her father's insurance claim. Eight months later, on 27 August 1891, May, aged nearly five, suddenly sickened and died. The doctor declared she had succumbed to 'tubercular meningitis'. Again Needle received her share of the insurance claim. To the doctor and neighbours, she was a devoted and grief-stricken mother made distraught by the loss of yet another daughter – on whom she had taken out a separate insurance policy of £60. From this death Needle received around £120 – the payout on May and also May's share of the money held in trust after her father's death. It was the equivalent of three years' wages of an unskilled workingwoman.

Needle decided to look out for another target. She found one when she went to work as the housekeeper to two brothers, saddle makers Otto and Louis Juncken (sometimes called Yuncken), young men from the German community of Lyndoch in South Australia. Within a few months the housekeeper became engaged to marry Otto, despite vehement protests from his family. Brother Louis Juncken was not only alarmed by Needle's outbursts of anger and screaming, but also put out because he had once tried to persuade the young widow to have a sexual liaison with him.

In August 1893, Louis Juncken became desperately ill for a fortnight. While he was sick he finally agreed to the marriage, but as soon as he was well enough he took Otto away to try to knock some sense into him. In response, Martha Needle attempted suicide, leaving a pathetic note that said: 'When my body is found, let me be buried with my children.' Her ruse in combination with her 'tragic' past worked, and Otto became completely devoted to her.

In April 1894 Louis fell ill again, but was reprieved when for a short time he was attended by his sister, Emma Jones. This respite was only short-lived, for he was soon ill again, dying in agony on 15 May 1894. (It was later noted that on 10 May Needle had purchased some 'Rough on Rats' from the local chemist, Mr Richards.[56]) Still, no one at the time was suspicious, and the doctors issued a death certificate saying he had died from 'exhaustion, inflammation of the stomach and membranes of the heart'. This was an extraordinary diagnosis considering that the deceased had been a strong, healthy young man just prior to his sudden illness.

Mrs Juncken and another son, Herman, arrived from South Australia two days after this unexpected death, amazed that Otto still wanted to marry his manipulative housekeeper. The new arrivals insisted that he part from her. In Mrs Juncken's contemptuous view, Needle was nothing but a 'hussy'. With prompting from his mother, Herman convinced his lovestruck younger brother that it was unseemly to live in the same house as an attractive widow. Needle was forced to leave. She left a note to Otto signed 'your cast-off housekeeper'.[57]

Needle moved nearby to a modest home in Richmond. One of her first visitors was Herman Juncken, who attempted to reason with her

Martha Needle was the product of a violent household. W. Mason & Co. Photographers, c. 1880s/90s. Photo: National Trust of Australia (Victoria) Old Melbourne Gaol Collection.

about the unsuitability of her plans to marry Otto. Yet he too became beguiled by her beauty and by her demure and charming manner, and he asked if he could call again. Herman now became Needle's new target. Rather stupidly she attempted to poison him over afternoon tea, serving a cup of decidedly bitter-tasting tea. Dr W. R. Boyd, a local medical practitioner, saved Herman's life with an emetic. After three days in bed, Herman returned to visit Needle, only to be poisoned again. He had just enough strength to crawl to a neighbour's house and once again he was saved by Dr Boyd's ministrations. Not as careless or as gullible as the other doctors, Boyd sent some of the vomit for chemical analysis. It contained a large dose – ten grains – of arsenic, enough to literally kill a horse.

Dr Boyd and Herman Juncken went to see the police with this story and also their suspicions about Louis Juncken's sudden demise. With the evidence of the toxicology report, they decided to set a trap for the suburban femme fatale. On 28 May 1894 Juncken called once more on Needle, who again offered refreshments. Just as he put the cup to his lips, the police stormed the parlour and took the cup and teapot into their possession. The tea was found to contain eleven grains of arsenic, enough to kill five men.

Literally caught in the act, Martha Needle knew she would be arrested and tried, so she attempted to commit suicide by swallowing chloroform in front of the police. Charged with the attempted murder of Herman Juncken, Needle was held in custody while the police continued their intercolonial investigations. Louis Juncken's remains were disinterred in South Australia; they contained thirty-four grains of arsenic. The bodies of Henry, May, Elsie and Mabel were also disinterred but the bodies were too decomposed to give results conclusive enough to stand up to interrogation in court. The amounts of arsenic were minute.

Arresting officers Detective Whitney and Detective Fryer were key witnesses at the police magistrate's inquiry in early August 1894. Dr James E. Neild (1824–1906), the Victorian government's forensic pathologist, and government analyst (and former Conservative parliamentarian) Cuthbert Blackett (1831–1902) provided expert testimony on their forensic investigations. Needle was represented by the disreputable lawyer David Gaunson, a supporter of the notorious, wealthy brothel-keeper Caroline Hodgson, also known as 'Madame Brussels' (see pages 18 and 248). Needle was arraigned for the murder of Louis Juncken.

The trial began in the Supreme Court of Victoria before Justice (later Sir) Henry Hodges (1844–1919) on 24 September 1894. Needle was again represented by Gaunson. The Crown case briefly outlined the accused's marriage and the deaths that had befallen her family. The trial mainly dealt with the circumstances of her association with Louis Juncken and his family; what had happened to her three daughters and her husband was far too circumstantial to go to trial. Justice Hodges cross-examined Otto Juncken for about two hours, an unusual development in a criminal proceeding.[58] Of all the witnesses, only Otto provided any positive testimony about the accused's character. He also told the court that Needle was given to fits and could lapse into deathlike trances for up to five hours. The jury was not convinced by his belief in her good character and her innocence. The all-male jury delivered a guilty verdict after the four-day trial and Needle was sentenced to death. She fainted in utter surprise. For once, her superb figure, pretty face and beguiling smile had not had an impact.

In the Old Melbourne Gaol, she was attended by a Church of England priest, the Reverend H. R. Scott, and a Mrs Hutchinson from the Salvation Army. Unlike condemned baby farmer Frances Knorr (see pages 135–143), who sought salvation in her last days before execution, Needle remained impassive and detached, other than to protest her innocence. Martha Needle was executed on Monday 22 October 1894, refusing any spiritual comfort or prayers. What is surprising is that she had spent most of her insurance money on elaborate graves for her children, which, Otto Juncken testified at the trial, she visited assiduously. She left all her possessions in her will to Otto, to whom she wrote just before her execution: 'Rest assured we will meet again where there is no parting. Your good father, also poor Louis, and my dear little ones will welcome you …'[59]

Almost a century after her execution, Bruce Thompson wrote a play entitled *The Eye of Martha Needle* for La Mama Theatre, which in 1993 was performed at the Adelaide Fringe Festival.[60] The drama centred on the sexual tensions between the three bachelors and the charming widow. Her murderous elimination of her husband and three little girls was overlooked in the drama.

One of the most bizarre poisoning cases ever occurred in Richmond in Melbourne in late 1904. Rosina Hubbard was arrested for the murder of her mother, Sarah Ann Robins, in September that year. At the inquest, held two months later, James Robins testified that he was the third husband of the deceased, who had produced twenty children by her various unions. Only two of these children were still alive. One daughter, Jane, had married 'a coloured man, thereby incurring her mother's displeasure'. The other, Rosina, therefore expected to inherit her mother's estate, valued at £1400. In August 1903 Rosina gave birth to a daughter upon whom old Mrs Robins doted, and who was promised a significant inheritance.

When Mrs Robins had a serious fall from a horse and cart on 29 September 1904,[61] she was taken to hospital where doctors Boyd and Morton believed she had in fact been poisoned. She died the following day, and her autopsy indicated the presence of large amounts of arsenic and mercury.[62]

Rosina Hubbard was arraigned for the wilful murder of her mother before Justice (Sir) Henry Hood in the Victorian Supreme Court on 20 February 1905. She was defended by the notorious David Gauson, while Mr Finlayson KC appeared for the Crown. Dr Morton was the first witness for the prosecution, then Nurse Ellen Fowler stated that she had suspected mercury poisoning when, as well as other symptoms, she saw how sore Mrs Robins' mouth was. In her testimony, Rosina Hubbard said that she thought her mother might have taken the quicksilver (mercury) herself because she believed that Hubbard was having an affair with her stepfather. When Mr Robins testified, he described himself as 'gentleman', which at the time described a man from the gentry with extended resources of money. He was hardly from this background, particularly as he admitted he had 'only a few pounds' to his name when he married Sarah Wilson in 1895. Since that time he had acquired three houses, presumably those of his wife, who, he noted, owned five homes and had money in the bank.

The defence was keen to establish the widower's motive for murdering his wife – arguing he had been driven by simple greed and the opportunity to secure the life of a gentleman. As the trial proceeded, the relationship between Robins and Hubbard came under intense scrutiny. Every salacious detail was reported in newspapers across the nation. Robins admitted that he had registered his stepdaughter's baby, although he denied knowledge of its paternity. He was still the major beneficiary of his wife's will. Frederick Fox, the pharmacist for the Richmond United Friendly Society dispensary, testified that Robins had asked him for arsenic to poison a dog. He gave him thirty grains. The next witness, Dr Crawford Mollinson, testified that Sarah Robins had died from arsenic poisoning.[63]

The evidence of the expert witnesses threw doubt on the actions of the accused and shifted attention to her stepfather for his purchase of the large quantity of arsenic. He also had motive to kill his wife: first, for her money and property, and second, because he was having an affair with her daughter. In his summing up to the jury Justice Hood began his address by pointing out that the accused 'deserved to be pitied for her condition [she was a little person] ...', although what the exact relationship her appearance had to her actions was left unclear. He asked the jury to consider also that Mrs Robins may have committed suicide when she learned of the illicit affair. The jury retired for an hour and then returned a verdict of 'not guilty'.[64] Rosina Hubbard was discharged.

Despite her close call, a few weeks later Hubbard confessed to murdering her mother with arsenic. She told the police that her mother 'often knocked me around, and was jealous of me, and thought my stepfather and I carried on with one another and called me such terrible names. I was determined to do her in'.[65] She was safe to make such an admission since the principle of double jeopardy in common-law jurisdictions meant she could not be charged with the same offence again.

The story had one final twist when it was reported that Rosina Hubbard had been admitted to Melbourne Hospital on 24 May 1905 and died that day from gastroenteric fever.[66] An inquest was conducted before the coroner, Dr R. H. Cole. There were no suspicious circumstances and a finding of 'death by exhaustion' was given.[67]

CHAPTER 11

The Thallium Killers

In 1944 director Frank Capra released his latest comedy, *Arsenic and Old Lace*. In this madcap film, Mortimer Brewster (played by Cary Grant) discovers that his sweet, genteel, 'maiden lady' aunts, Abby and Martha, have extended their charitable activities to relieving old bachelors of their loneliness by hospitably killing them with a recipe of elderberry wine laced with arsenic, strychnine and 'just a touch of cyanide'. Mayhem ensues – and never a touch of reality.

Arsenic continued to be used occasionally as a killer. Although she was never convicted, mother of three children Irene Crofts told the Supreme Court in Melbourne in November 1948 that she had used arsenic to poison her husband, one of the Rats of Tobruk in World War II. She shocked the court when it was revealed she told the investigator, Detective Dent, that she hoped her husband died.[1] He had been violent and often wrecked the furniture in their house in Richmond.[2] Still, arsenic had fallen from favour as the preferred poison for murder since the distinguished star of British forensic pathology, Sir Bernard Spilsbury (1877–1947), had exposed the solicitor Herbert Armstrong of employing arsenic to poison his wife in 1922.

By the 1930s, a new, more insidious poison was available to the killer in the domestic home. In 1938 newspapers in Australia reported the five murders by Martha Marek, another 'modern Lucrezia Borgia', of various family members. She had used a little known metallic poison – thallium.[3] Her motive was financial benefit from insurance claims. The New Zealand detective writer Ngaio Marsh used thallium in the plot of her novel *Final Curtain*, in 1947.

Thallium first came to public attention in Australia in a report in the *Sydney Morning Herald* on 1 August 1862. It described the discovery of a new substance called thallium by chemist and physicist Dr (later Sir) William Crookes. In the previous year *Scientific America* had praised its therapeutic potential.[4] The product was at first used as a depilatory, although its harsh action made razors a far easier and safer alternative. It was also used in preparations to treat ringworm in children but this had disastrous consequences when thirteen children in Spain died in 1930. Three others were left permanently injured. Even after this tragedy, thallium was still used in Australia to treat this common childhood complaint.[5] But its commercial use soon transferred to vermin control.

Even after the bubonic plague epidemics in Australia in the early twentieth century, public officials had still not managed to eliminate rat infestations decades later. In *Kangaroo*, his 1923 novel set in Sydney, D. H. Lawrence remarked on the prevalence of vermin:

> The battle was against rats, fleas and dirt. The plague affects
> the rats first, said the notices, then the fleas and then man ...
> it seemed to his embittered fancy that Sydney harbour, and
> all the coast of New South Wales, was moving with this pest.
> It reminded him of the land of Egypt, under the hand of the
> Lord: plagues of mice and rats and rabbits and snails ... [6]

Despite its reputation since the 1890s as a 'working man's paradise', many people in Australia actually lived in abject poverty. Those in overcrowded inner-city precincts lived in dilapidated housing with few modern amenities. These slums were infested with vermin and diseases. Tuberculosis was prevalent in the post-war period in the inner Sydney suburbs where the thallium dramas were played out. Typhoid and poliomyelitis were also constantly present.

In a survey of 8000 homes in 1945, Melbourne's Slum Abolition Board found that only 1000 of them could be deemed 'tolerably fit'. A

Collingwood family reported that rats 'sit in the kitchen and watch us have dinner'.[7]

In Sydney, in the immediate post-war years, over 250,000 people lived in slums. In 1946 only 13 per cent of homes had refrigerators and only 2 per cent had washing machines.[8] Ashfield Council, which represented inner-city suburbs such as Paddington, Redfern and Rozelle, eradicated 31,000 rats between 1945 and 1947 using 124,000 baits of M109 Rat Paste.[9] This itself was a health hazard since so many unused baits were left in public spaces. Even in middle-class suburbs rats were troublesome in the years just after World War II, often because families had fowls and poultry feed in their back gardens to supplement the meagre government rations.

Rats were certainly attracted to the grain fed to fowls, which in Queensland was often kept in sugarbags, stored under the high, stilted wooden houses. In Brisbane in the early 1950s city council health workers inspected homes for vermin accompanied by packs of excited and vigilant fox terriers.[10] Houses across the nation kept various rat baits readily to hand. The majority of these poisons smelt so disgusting that no one could possibly have used them to lace food or drink undetected. End-o-Rat, M109 Rat Paste, and DDeaTh were far too obvious and noxious to be used on humans – all but 'Thall-Rat', which was sold only in New South Wales, and which had come onto the market in 1939 manufactured by Sayers Allport of North Sydney in convenient 1-, 2-, 4- and 16-ounce sizes.[11]

Between March and October 1952 ten people died and thirty-six were hospitalised in New South Wales from thallium poisoning.[12] In September 1952 the first criminal conviction involving thallium poisoning came before the courts. Four months previously Yvonne Fletcher of Newtown, Sydney, had been arrested for the murder of her two husbands, Desmond George Butler, who died in 1948, and Bertram Fletcher, who died on 23 March 1952. Police prosecutor Sergeant Bush told the central court that investigations had begun when Fletcher was admitted to the Royal Prince Alfred Hospital and his doctors suspected poisoning.[13] Although he never received the sort of publicity that Sir Bernard Spilsbury had received from his expert testimony in criminal cases, the New South Wales government analyst, Thomas McDonald, was instrumental in Yvonne Fletcher's arrest and trial. He suspected thallium had killed Fletcher. Through his investigations of this case, and another in 1953, that of Caroline Grills, McDonald became the world expert on thallium and its effects as a poison on humans. He spent months of research experimenting with thallium in ginger to demonstrate that it was tasteless and odourless. He also established that one-tenth of a grain would be about one-hundredth part of one bottle of Thall-Rat.[14]

Soon after the death of Bertram Fletcher, police ordered the exhumation of Desmond George Butler's remains from Rookwood Cemetery. McDonald undertook the scientific analysis, determining that he had died from thallium poisoning.[15] In the original 1948 inquest conducted by M. J. D. Austin SM, Butler's death was ascribed to natural causes. Peripheral neuritis of unknown origins affecting the heart was cited.[16] He had died in Broughton Hall, part of Callan Park Mental Hospital, suffering extreme depression. He had lost all his hair, the use of his limbs, and much of his eyesight – all symptoms of thallium poisoning. But no one at the time thought of testing for thallium, and tests for arsenic, lead and strychnine all came back negative.

In June 1952, at the request of the attorney-general, the Supreme Court of New South Wales, consisting of the Chief Justice Kenneth Street (1890–1972), Justice William Owen (1899–1972) and Justice Leslie Herron (1902–73), ordered a new inquest into Butler's death. Joint inquest hearings were ordered into both men's deaths. The new coroner's inquest, conducted by E. J. Forrest SM, opened on Monday, 16 June 1952. Thomas McDonald proved to be a star expert witness as he carefully detailed his research on thallium, its effects and its presence in the remains of Butler and Fletcher. Dr H. B. Taylor, also a government analyst, and Dr C. E. Percy, the government medical officer for Sydney, testified that they had carried out tests on the properties of Thall-Rat after Butler's body was exhumed.[17]

Detective R. G. Fergusson testified that when he went to Yvonne Fletcher's house in Ferndale Street, Newtown, she said, 'I have been expecting to see you. I suppose it is about my husband.' Bertram Fletcher was a well-known identity in Newtown; his sister, Florrie Witchard, lived in nearby Susan Street. Yvonne Fletcher openly stated that her new husband, whom she had married in November 1951 after meeting him at a two-up game, was abusive and violent. Three months into the marriage she had had to leave home because of his brutality. She had gone to the Newtown Police Station for a summons for assault. Her husband refused to give her any housekeeping money, he gambled on Saturdays and was 'very moody'. Fletcher soon asked for money to gamble from his new and increasingly angry bride. He also went around the district saying that his new wife was a 'police moll' and that the two children from her previous marriage had TB (tuberculosis). Fletcher was violent to the little boy, beating him 'black and blue' for no cause.[18]

Even more damaging was a report that she had laughed at his funeral, waving to a man in the street. A neighbour, Mrs Edith Roache, stated that Yvonne Fletcher waved at Herbert Wood, known locally as 'Dago Joe', and that he was a frequent visitor to her house. She also confirmed Fletcher's account of the domestic violence that dominated the new home in Ferndale Street. She had heard the accused screaming, 'Don't let him kill my children', as, taking the children with her, she fled the abuse and threats. Fletcher appeared in the street with blood on her face on several occasions. Roache said that Fletcher told her that Bertram Fletcher was telling 'doctors and different people that he was going like Dessie [Butler], and that she had poisoned him'.[19] Roache did not, however, go to the police with this revelation.

In the 1971 play entitled *Mrs Thally F* by John Romeril, the character of Vonny (Yvonne Fletcher) demands of her abusive husband: 'Fancy keeping a girl like me in rags. I don't mean a thing to you, do I? … You're lowering me, Bluey Fletcher, you're dragging me down to your own stinking level.'[20] This implied that Yvonne Fletcher had 'married beneath her', in the parlance of the day. This was not the case. Yvonne Bogan was an uneducated, rough, working-class woman born in 1922 and bred in the inner-city Sydney slums. Desmond George Butler, whom she married in 1943, was employed as a cleaner for Grace Bros department store; Bertram Fletcher worked as a rat baiter for Butler and Norman's bottle factory in the industrial suburb of Alexandria. Neither man served in World War II even though both were of military age.[21] Yvonne Fletcher's desperation was driven not so much by the fact that she did not have a bourgeois home with all modern conveniences, but rather that she had married two violent men who were unable or unwilling to support her and her two children.

In her testimony before the inquest on 25 June 1952, Yvonne Fletcher told the proceedings that she believed her second husband had committed suicide with Thall-Rat 'just to get me into trouble'. Somewhat unadvisedly she also said: 'I had plenty of reason to murder my first husband but not my second.' While 'Butler was an impossible man to live with' she had no idea he would end up 'a mental case' confined to a psychiatric hospital. She called for Jesus to aid her in her dark hour.[22] Jesus did not come to her aid; she was ordered to stand trial for the wilful murders of both her husbands.

The trial commenced on 15 September and was presided over by Justice Edward Kinsella (1893–1967), a man of deep sympathies for ordinary people.[23] The eminent barrister C. V. Rooney QC led the case for the Crown. Only two months previously he had secured the conviction of the notorious gangster 'Chow' Hayes for the murder of an associate.[24] Rooney was a formidable opponent in court. Fletcher was represented by Frederick W. Vizzard, a state-appointed counsel, since she lacked the funds to hire an experienced and therefore expensive barrister. Rooney opened the Crown's accusations by showing how easy it was to purchase deadly rat poison. It only required 2/6 to purchase Thall-Rat at almost any local grocery store.

Rooney dealt first with the death of Desmond Butler, explaining persuasively why no one had been initially suspicious of the presence of thallium. Butler's local doctor had been baffled by his symptoms, and had at first attributed them to severe hysteria. Butler was certified insane and committed in May 1948. At first Yvonne Fletcher refused to take him home, arguing that he was violent towards her, but when he was eventually discharged on 21 July 1948, he was weak, confused and totally debilitated. Rooney argued that Fletcher then administered another dose of thallium to her husband.[25] While he lingered, Yvonne Butler went out at night to enjoy herself, leaving Desmond Butler to be fed and cared for by neighbours.[26] He died on 29 July. Much of the remaining testimony followed that given in the second inquest.

Yvonne Fletcher addressed the jury from the dock, telling its members that 'you know as much about the deaths of these two men as I do. I never poisoned my husbands. I do not know who poisoned them or how they were poisoned. I never bought or handled any poisons at any time.' Despite this, however, evidence was supplied in testimony that Bertram Fletcher had indeed brought home Thall-Rat from his workplace in order to dispose of vermin in their home and yard. He had placed it on bread to tempt the rats in the house. Fletcher also told the jury that she received no benefit from insurance on the deaths of either husband, thereby attempting to refute any implied financial motive. With little clear motive, the Crown's case was based upon circumstantial evidence, for like other instances of poisoning the deed was done in secrecy with the effects only emerging over time. How and when Yvonne Fletcher obtained Thall-Rat to murder Desmond Butler was not so clear. However, Crown prosecutor Rooney painted Yvonne Fletcher as an evil woman, seared by 'black hatred' against her second husband, who was violent and disappointing as a breadwinner.

The jury was not convinced that both men had accidentally ingested thallium and found Yvonne Fletcher guilty of wilful murder on 23 September 1952 after eight days of court deliberations. They took just four hours to reach their verdict that she had poisoned her first husband, Desmond Butler. Justice Kinsella pronounced the death sentence.[27] Yvonne Fletcher collapsed and was admitted to the first offenders section in the hospital at Long Bay jail hospital while her legal counsel decided whether an appeal was appropriate.[28]

For the appeal heard in early December 1952, Fletcher secured the services of J. W. Shand QC for her defence. In the appeal the judges considered the evidence in relation to a recent decision in the House of Lords that quashed a conviction on the grounds that it had been made by wrongfully using one case to substantiate another of similar history.[29] The Court of Criminal Appeal upheld the original judgment against Fletcher, whereupon she requested an appeal to the Privy Council. Her grounds for this were that inadmissible evidence had been used in the trial to wrongfully link two separate incidents. Yvonne Fletcher's appeals were dismissed, but her capital sentence was commuted to a term of life imprisonment. She was assigned to act as cook for the female warders of Long Bay Prison.[30]

Three weeks after the conclusion of Fletcher's criminal trial another case of thallium poisoning came before the Supreme Court of New South Wales. On the advice of the coroner, an illiterate farmer, Ruby Norton, was charged with the wilful murder on 20 July 1952 of her daughter's fiancé, a truck driver named Allen Williams. She was arrested for the offence on 19 August 1952. Williams was a boarder in Norton's house in Cowra, where her daughter Fay, adopted son Boris, and the Worths – her married daughter and son-in-law – also lived. Norton was implacably opposed to Fay's forthcoming marriage and did everything she possibly could to prevent it. She had placed sugar in Williams' petrol tank so he might have an accident, and she had also purchased rat poison from the local pharmacist, Mr D. G. Kritsch.[31] There was nothing sinister in this purchase, however, since most homes, especially in rural areas, kept vermin poison.

Norton's trial began on 10 October 1952. C. V. Rooney QC again led the prosecution team. Norton's son-in-law, George Worth, testified that Norton took an inordinate interest in the outcome of the Fletcher case, although the timing was wrong for this to have been an inspiration for any attempted murder.

Norton was an incipient radical feminist who evinced a dislike of all men and wished to manage 'a woman-run ranch'. Her husband testified that she had previously tried to poison him. She tolerated George Worth only because he was a good farm worker. Norton's sister, Elizabeth Sinclair, and her aunt, Florence Hill, both testified that Norton was a violent woman who had threatened to kill Williams so that Fay would stay single and remain at home. Despite her motive, the stated intention to get rid of Williams, and the opportunity to lace his food with thallium, Ruby Norton was found not guilty and released.[32]

In 1953 thallium had become the poison of choice. Among the thirty-six admissions to hospital since March that year – some of whom were left with permanent injury – were a young man, disappointed in love, who drank a bottle of thallium in front of his former girlfriend in Hurstville, and a seventy-two-year-old pensioner who attempted suicide using thallium because he was 'in pain'. He was kept under observation on the order of the Lunacy Court.[33] Another trial, this time for attempted murder, involved Beryl Haugh of Leichhardt, who had attempted to kill her husband by putting thallium in his cup of tea. She was sentenced to two years' imprisonment in July 1953; Allen Haugh declared he was 'looking forward to a reunion' with his erring wife when she was released from prison and was hopeful 'they could start again'.[34] On 28 June 1953, a dog died in agony outside the Como Hotel in Sutherland, Sydney. It was just one in a spate of thirty-four canines similarly afflicted that day. In the following five days another thirty dogs were poisoned in that same suburb. A reward of £100 was offered to detect and prosecute the cruel perpetrator.[35]

A far more brutal and devastating series of deaths was soon to dominate the pages of national newspapers. Arrested on 12 May,

'Mrs Caroline Grills, sixty-three, of 12 Gerrish Street, Gladesville' was identified as a possible thallium poisoner.

The serial killings by Caroline Grills belied any stereotype of 1950s, plump, middle-aged matrons who liked to bake and serve afternoon tea to family and friends. Feminine talent was then often judged by how well the homemade sponge cake rose and the lightness of its texture. The photographs that appeared in the press showed a woman tiny in stature, only 130 centimetres tall, with a large, comfortable bosom and wide hips, dressed in a cheap flower-print frock, her grey hair in an old-fashioned roll, and wearing unflattering large-rimmed spectacles. She was smiling and lively, revelling in the attention she had attracted. No matter the appearance she gave, Grills was a killer: ruthless, calculating and amused by her power over life and death in the most mundane domestic settings of inner Sydney. Since 1947 she had murdered her stepmother, two relatives by marriage, and a family friend, as well as attempting to kill two other family members in April 1953. Her actions had left another woman, Eveline Lundberg, her husband's sister, blind and disabled.

At her initial hearing before the central court on 12 May 1953, she denied all the charges, protesting her innocence through her solicitor, E. N. Rowley. Though accused of numerous murders Grills was not remanded in custody but was placed on £300 bail, then a substantial amount that represented an unskilled woman's wage for more than two years. Her husband, Richard Grills, was now a real-estate agent with a good income. Moreover, Grills had inherited two houses as a result of her lethal activities.

Caroline Grills had not always lived in comfortable circumstances. Born in 1888 in the working-class industrial suburb of Balmain, her father, George Mickelson, worked as a labourer. At the age of nearly twenty she married Richard Grills, also a labourer, in the local registry office.[36] The Grills went on to have six children, although two sons died. Like many working-class families, the Grills frequently moved from house to house, unable to secure their own home. By the mid-1940s, however, they lived in Randwick, able to afford this more affluent location with Richard Grills's increased earning power as an estate agent. But Caroline Grills hungered for her own home where she could entertain her extended family and wide circle of friends.

Her opportunity to attain the Australian dream of home ownership presented itself in 1947 when she murdered her stepmother, eighty-seven-year-old Christina Mickelson. The old lady was taking an inordinately long time to die so Grills simply decided to hasten the process with thallium-laced food. Her motive was to inherit her father's house in Sydney. Mrs Mickelson was an elderly lady and there was no suspicion that her demise was unusual. Grills later told the court that she was 'old anyway. She used to get pains in her legs. Her legs were all gone. She got that way she could not use her legs at all.' Incapacity in the extremities is a symptom of thallium poisoning.

Not content with this acquisition she then targeted her mother's widowed friend, Angelina Thomas, aged eighty-four, who lived in a comfortable cottage in Leura, in the Blue Mountains. Grills would visit her with fresh fish, then almost impossible to obtain in the Blue Mountains. She made much of the tedious journey and of her expense and effort to obtain only the best and tastiest food for her mother's dear old friend and confidante. The delectable fish dishes were much appreciated by the elderly lonely widow, who died suddenly on 17 January 1948.[37] Richard Grills inherited her house in the will. From being a poor girl in Balmain at the end of the nineteenth century Caroline Grills now had two houses upon which there were no mortgages.

Her husband's brother-in-law, John Lundberg (married to Richard's sister Eveline), aged sixty-seven and living in Sydney, was the next to die suddenly and mysteriously, on 17 October 1948. Before his death he had lost all his hair even though he had had no indications of baldness previously. No property was forthcoming on Lundberg's death; from now on Grills's motive for killing was purely for pleasure – to watch those around her suffer and die in painful lingering circumstances while she was the only one who knew the real truth of their sudden afflictions. There was a hiatus for some years when no one died. This was not because Grills had got bored with her hobby; rather, she had simply been unsuccessful, with only severe illness strangely affecting her extended family and friends. Christine Downey, the daughter of John and Eveline Lundberg, took ill on 1 June 1952 after visiting her aunt and uncle.[38]

On 15 February 1953, Caroline Grills's widowed sister-in-law, Mary Nicholson, aged sixty, also died. Grills had been assiduous in her role of caring, self-sacrificing relative, bringing her food and tending to Mary Nicholson's every need.

On 22 April, John Downey, Christine Downey's husband, unexpectedly came home for lunch. He found Caroline Grills as a guest, alone with his mother-in-law, Eveline Lundberg, aged sixty-seven. Downey was suspicious that death followed Grills's presence at meals. When he thought he saw Grills put something into his mother-in-law's teacup, he made an excuse to take the cup back to the kitchen, where he managed to put some of the contents into a clean jar. Mrs Lundberg soon experienced terrible suffering, losing her sight, her hair and the use of her legs. After she was admitted to hospital, Grills brought her home-cooked food to supplement the hospital diet.[39]

In early May, Downey took the tea he had salvaged to the government analyst, Thomas McDonald, who reported that it contained a large dose of thallium. The assistant medical superintendent of Sydney Hospital, Dr F. M. Farrar, later testified that thallium had been discovered in pathology samples provided by Mrs Downey and Mrs Lundberg.[40]

Several days later, on 11 May 1953, Caroline Grills was arrested by Detective Fergusson, who had also worked on the Fletcher case the previous year. The police disinterred the bodies of Christina Mickelson, John Lundberg and Mary Mickelson, all of which contained large quantities of thallium. Angelina Thomas had been cremated so there were no remains.

Appearing in court on Friday 17 July 1953, on the charges of committing four murders and three attempted murders, Caroline Grills was granted £2000 bail, then the cost of two brand-new Holden sedans. Her counsel, Eric Rowley, argued that his client's health would be adversely affected by incarceration in Long Bay jail and that the case against her was circumstantial. He also argued that Grills '... is known in the district for her philanthropic acts'.[41] Her surface respectability and disarmingly benign appearance belied her cruelty and sadism.

The police searched the Grills's home in Gladesville for evidence, and found one and a half bottles of rat poison on her sideboard. She told Detective Fergusson that 'it is a very good thing to have'. The possession of this product in no way indicated guilt, given that any home would more than likely have rat poison, and Grills had said that she had bought it because one of her neighbours kept fowls, and there were 'always rats and mice where there were fowls'.[42] The police needed to unravel the links between the victims, the motives, the modus operandi and the locations if a conviction was to be assured.

The inquest into the death of Christina Mickelson opened on 11 August 1953. Detective Fergusson detailed the list of victims whom Grills stood accused of killing or attempting to murder. When asked why she would attempt to kill Eveline Lundberg, Grills pointed out that she had no motive, asking: 'Have I got anything to gain by doing a thing like that?' This rather overlooked that she had benefited financially from the first two deaths. When interrogated about a brown wool frock in which traces of thallium were found, the dress that John Downey said she wore when he saw her deposit something into his mother-in-law's tea, Grills denied the accusation. She told the Coroner's Court: 'Well, that is where you are wrong. I only wear that dress in winter.'[43]

The following day John Downey was the star witness. He described the lunch party and how he had retrieved his mother-in-law's tea. Throughout the proceedings, Caroline Grills laughed and smiled. Her counsel warned her to desist as she was creating a very bad impression.[44]

A blind and feeble Eveline Lundberg then took the stand. She recalled a conversation she had had with Grills around Christmas 1951 during which Grills had reported having a dream in which Mrs Lundberg died and left her all her clothes. Eveline Lundberg found this quite chilling in retrospect.[45]

On 13 August 1953, Coroner E. J. Forrest opposed bail at the conclusion of the inquest. Through her lawyer Grills objected to this refusal to prolong her bail. The matter was heard before Justice Maguire, who likewise ordered that no bail be granted. Grills's counsel, Frank Hidden, continued to argue that since no evidence appeared in the Coroner's Court there was no reason to stop bail. When the inquests resumed on 27 August,[46] now also into the death of Angelina Thomas, Alice Hurry testified that she had seen Grills tear up Mrs Thomas's bed within half an hour of her death. At the time she saw nothing sinister in this, although a previous witness, Mrs Isobel Jones, said that Mrs Thomas kept a lot of money around her bed. Both Richard and Caroline Grills knew about the money.[47] John Lundberg suddenly took ill after holidaying with the Grills family before his death. When he became seriously ill, Caroline Grills volunteered to look after him, often bringing over food she had baked for him.[48]

Other witnesses attested to the sinister way in which Grills could behave on occasions. Jean Lane testified that Grills gave her mother, Mary Mickelson, a lolly even though she knew her to be a diabetic. In fact, she had forced it into her mouth. Whether this was cruelty or a desire to kill her mother was not clear. Grills also advised the younger woman to get her mother to 'attend to her will' because two people mentioned in the old one were already dead. This was a strange remark especially since Grills herself was not a beneficiary.[49] Another witness, Noel Lane, Mary Mickelson's son-in-law, told the court that after Mary Mickelson had been involved in a minor car accident in 1948, Grills declared: 'Your mother has not much longer to live. Get your relations from the country down.'[50] Clearly, money, property and

Serial killer Caroline Grills laughed and smiled in court as evidence was heard that the apparent do-gooder had been seen slipping something into an old lady's tea. Photo: Fairfax Media FXT 43229.

real estate were always on her mind, and the relationship between the sick and their estates a preoccupation.

At the conclusion of the inquest on 20 August, Caroline Grills was ordered to stand trial in the Supreme Court of New South Wales on the charge of the murder of her stepmother, Christina Mickelson, and the attempted murder of John Downey, Christine Downey and Eveline Lundberg. More investigations were undertaken into the death of Angelina Thomas in the Katoomba Court of Petty Sessions on 27 August 1953. On 29 August Grills was also charged with Thomas's death.

The trial began on Wednesday 7 October, before Justice Brereton with Charles Rooney QC again leading the case for the prosecution. Grills entered the courtroom with a sheer veil covering her face. Its diaphanous texture could not disguise her cheerful demeanour and laughter despite the seriousness of the proceedings.[51] Rooney opened his case by pointing out that the accused was 'a practised and habitual poisoner who had lost all sense of feeling'.[52] Her counsel refuted the prosecution case, telling the assembled court that this was merely based on evidence of 'similar fact'. It was 'similar fact', however, that had clinched the case against Sarah and John Makin (see pages 126–135).

Rooney proposed that one motive for what seemed to be motiveless crimes lay in Caroline Grills' psychology. She simply loved seeing people suffer; indeed, it was possible she 'experienced a psychological "lift" from administering poison to people and watching its effects'.[53] When he made this observation the accused continued to smile and look around the courtroom cheerily from the prisoner's dock. Detective Fergusson reported that when first questioned, Grills had been defiant, saying: 'Well, you have to prove it, haven't you?'[54]

Much of the evidence at the trial had already been presented at the inquest. One new piece of forensic evidence related to the frocks that Grills had worn in April 1953. The blue dress she wore on 13 April was found not to have any traces of thallium in its pockets; however, the heavy brown dress that John Downey identified as the one she wore the day he removed the teacup for safekeeping did contain thallium in the pockets.[55] In testimony during her trial, Grills denied any knowledge of thallium and its effects, claiming that she had not been aware that Thall-Rat contained thallium until police questioned her. She explained the presence of thallium in the pockets of the brown dress by saying that she had seen a rat in her backyard and taken out some Thall-Rat and bread with which to bait it. When she got some of the poison on her hands she had reached into her pockets to get her handkerchief to wipe them clean. That, she said, was the only way she could explain it.[56]

The jury retired to consider its verdict for a brief twelve minutes. Grills was found guilty of the attempted murder of her sister-in-law, Eveline Lundberg, her friend and confidante for over forty years. When Justice Brereton recorded the death sentence against her, Grills appeared quite unmoved and calm, although the laughter and smiles that had characterised her throughout the trial now ceased. Even Mrs Lundberg was shocked by the verdict despite everything she and her family had endured. In fact, she told the press that no one could be kinder or more helpful than Caroline Grills, particularly to old-age pensioners.[57]

Grills appealed her conviction in April 1954. The appeal was dismissed but her sentence was commuted to life imprisonment.[58] It was expected she would serve fourteen years.[59] In prison Grills became known as 'Aunt Thally' and she took a maternal interest in the younger prisoners, offering them advice and showing concern for their welfare. She died in October 1960 from peritonitis.

The month after Grills' trial and sentence, another salacious case came before the Supreme Court in Sydney. Veronica Monty was charged with attempting to kill her son-in-law, Balmain Rugby League star Bob Ludham, with thallium after the affair they had been conducting while her daughter Judy Ludham attended Mass ended. Prosecutor Charles Rooney played out the dramas connected with all this 'incestuous passion'. Rarely had so much forbidden sex and suffering been publicly aired. The courtroom was packed with eager women awaiting every detail to be exposed and dissected. Monty was acquitted in the Central Criminal Court on 10 December 1953. Her husband promptly sued for divorce, as did Judy Ludham.

As procedures and tests in forensic pathology and toxicology improved, the chances of getting away with murder by using poison or drugs have become increasingly remote – and therefore less frequently attempted. Not until the 1999 conviction of Anu Singh, a young law student in Canberra, for the manslaughter of her partner, Joe Cinque, on 26 October 1997, did another major case grip the public headlines. Singh had injected Cinque with the sleeping drug Rohypnol and then heroin but escaped a murder conviction by reason of diminished responsibility. The case has already entered the annals of international celebrity with Helen Garner's 2004 book, *Joe Cinque's Consolation*; a play by Tom Wright and Lally Katz entitled *Criminology*, performed in 2007; as well as a 2011 episode of former FBI profiler Candice DeLong's popular US cable series *Deadly Women*. Singh completed her master's degree in criminology while on day release from Emu Plains Correctional Centre.[60]

CHAPTER 12

Deadly Manoeuvres in the Nineteenth Century

One of the first cases of husband murder (mariticide) in New South Wales occurred in 1816. Elizabeth Anderson stood accused of the murder of her husband, John Anderson, along with co-defendants James Stock and John Rawlings before Frederick Garling (1775–1848), the newly appointed deputy chief advocate in the Court of Criminal Jurisdiction. This was the superior court in the colony until the Supreme Court was proclaimed in May 1824. And, as was usual at the time, cases were heard with military officers serving as jurors.

At the time of his murder John Anderson was around fifty-five years of age, old for the era. He had arrived as a convict on the *Charlotte*, one of the vessels in the First Fleet. William Bryant and Mary Broad Bryant, the famous absconders who rowed to Timor, were fellow transportees on this vessel. Anderson was a seaman sentenced to seven years' exile and penal servitude for the crime of stealing linen worth £12/2/-. He was convicted in the Exeter Assizes. It's likely that as well as being a sailor his real occupation was as a smuggler, the primary industry in the south-west counties of England in the late eighteenth century. Elizabeth Anderson (née Bruce) was tried and convicted of stealing linen worth 20/- on 10 January 1787. She was transported on the *Lady Penrhyn*, an accompanying First Fleet vessel.

To encourage marriage, social order and sobriety, Governor Arthur Phillip instituted a policy whereby a male convict who married legally would be given a land grant of 30 acres (12 hectares) and no assigned labour. For the economically ambitious this was a way to financial and social elevation, perhaps the start of real independence and autonomy. The Andersons' farm at Pitt Town on the Hawkesbury was long established since Anderson was granted his land on 22 February 1792.

The marriage of Anderson and Bruce had been an expedient one, without the slightest pretence of affection or mutual regard. Assigned convicts were forced to work for these newly emancipated, married former inmates, causing all sorts of tensions, resentments and rivalries.

On the evening of 26 February 1816, John and Elizabeth Anderson quarrelled, as they were wont to do on a daily basis, and John Anderson went to bed early. Early in the evening one of the convict servants, Ralph Melkins, testified he heard his mistress (his employer, Elizabeth Anderson) crying out that she had been robbed. He went into the small farmhouse where he found another convict assignee, James Stock. He also heard the other assigned servant, John Rawlings, call out that his master had been murdered. John Anderson was found outside with an apron around his head and a rope around his throat, barely clinging to life. Stock declared that Mrs Anderson had murdered her husband. Another witness, John Trowell, who worked on another farm, reported that some months previously he had been forced to intervene when Anderson had attempted to stab her husband with a knife.[1]

The accused had no legal representation nor were they allowed to give evidence on their own behalf. The military jury considered the evidence and returned a guilty verdict against Elizabeth Anderson and James Stock, who were sentenced to death, with their bodies to be dissected and anatomised afterwards.[2]

Margaret Galvin, convict number 27924 in Van Diemen's Land, left Dublin on the *Arabian* on 12 October 1846, arriving in Hobart Town on 25 February 1847. Illiterate and without any training or skills, like many transported convicts of the mid-1840s she had survived the terrible Irish Famine. After her sentence expired, Galvin married John Coghlan, a milkman and boarding-house keeper in Hobart. He had arrived as a free man on the brig *Portenia* in 1843, later used in the early 'blackbirding' trade to the islands of Melanesia. How Galvin and Coghlan met is not recorded, although they married on 2 April 1849.[3] For most of their marriage they were teetotal but domestic arguments led them to alcohol. By late 1861 John Coghlan was spending every night with prostitutes at 'Blind Tom's' brothel. Margaret Coghlan was infuriated by this betrayal and public humiliation.

On 6 January 1862 a rumour spread through the area around the Church of St John the Baptist in Goulburn Street that the milkman had been brutally murdered and was lying in his bed with his throat cut. As the Hobart *Mercury* reported, the rumour was all too true. Coghlan had been discovered lying naked on his bed in a pool of blood, his throat cut and his head smashed in. The floor of the small bedroom was covered in blood. Margaret Coghlan and another woman who lived in the house, Catherine Lowe, were taken into custody. They were charged with murder in the presence of Hobart's mayor. After some inquiries Lowe was released. Unlike many other women at the time she was native-born to the colony. Coghlan protested her innocence despite her clothes being soaked with blood.

An inquest was convened the following day at James Cousins' Bull Head Hotel in Goulburn Street before Coroner Algernon Jones and seven jurors. All the witnesses, the jury and the coroner went to view the body and the scene of the crime. This was a common procedure in the days before photography. John Coghlan was positively identified and described as a man of around sixty years of age, holding a razor without bloodstains gently in his left hand. A bloodstained water jug was found in an adjoining room. On returning to the hastily convened jury room, the first witness, Lawrence Benson, who was employed by the Hobart Corporation to light the streetlamps, testified that he had known the deceased for fourteen years. On Sunday night, 5 January, he had seen Coghlan alive in the street having just emerged from the Bull's Head Hotel. He then went into Eliza Hooley's house and that was the last time Benson saw him alive. Benson also reported that

Hooley followed Coghlan into her house, shouting: 'If you will give me some money, I will get you some grog.'

Having obtained some money, Hooley went to St Patrick's public house, returning with rum. By the time he entered Hooley's house, Benson testified, Coghlan was not sober, although neither was he 'dead drunk'. Around three o'clock in the morning, as he went about his rounds of putting out the lamps, Benson saw Margaret Coghlan coming out of her garden, shouting out to her neighbour 'Ellen' across the street. She was drunk and throwing stones. She waited until 6am outside Eliza Hooley's house, becoming increasingly distressed and telling Benson: 'I will murder him. I will have satisfaction.' John Coghlan had publicly humiliated his wife by spending the night with a prostitute in a house directly across the road from his marital home. All their neighbours were able to watch the public spectacle without the slightest bit of difficulty.

Thomas 'Blind Tom' Arnold testified that on the night in question, Mrs Coghlan had bitterly complained to him that 'her husband was away at some of the brothels'. She was visibly upset, and disordered in her appearance and her speech. Constable William Waller stated that the Coghlans had eaten dinner together that night, although there had been trouble between them just before, and Margaret Coghlan had been locked out of her house and caused a public disturbance. He testified that he heard her say: 'Now John, if you give me another chance, I will not drink again for twelve months.' She then 'went onto her knees and called God to witness what she had said'. Waller then confirmed Benson's evidence about Coghlan going to Hooley's house. Constable Waller reported that he had also seen Margaret Coghlan with Constable Cleary around midnight. She had lamented that her husband now chose to spend his nights away from home in brothels. When he saw her again around 3am he inquired why she was not in bed. She demanded he '… get her grog …' followed by 'Oh my God, what will become of me?' She kept repeating the words over and over, he told the coroner's inquest.

He continued that Mary Coghlan had then gone back into her house, only to come out again crying out 'Oh! My God! Coghlan has cut his throat. Oh constable, he has just come home and cut his throat.' When Constable Cleary viewed the body, however, he said in response: 'That could not be, as it has been done some time.' Mrs Coghlan sat on a chair clapping her hands together in distress. Other police and Dr Cairns were sent for to examine the body, which was already quite cold. At the inquest, Dr Cairns deposed his testimony on the state of the body: Coghlan's throat had been cut while he was still alive. The blows on the head had been done with considerable force as the walls and ceiling of the bedroom were splattered with bloodstains.

When Margaret Coghlan addressed the inquest she denied that she had killed her husband and said that she believed he had committed suicide. When Detective Vickers took the stand straight after Mrs Coghlan, he stated that Constable Cleary had reported on Monday morning that John Coghlan had committed suicide, a patently ridiculous proposition given the severity of the head wounds and the clean razor in his hand. Vickers had arrested Margaret Coghlan for the wilful murder of her husband. On being taken to the Female Factory to be housed with the other convict women, Coghlan admitted that she had killed her husband and revealed where the iron bar she had used to beat him was to be found.

In her statement to police, Coghlan outlined the misery of her marriage, which had started with high hopes and amicability. The peace was ruined by their increasing addiction to rum in large quantities. She said that on the evening of the murder her husband had arrived home drunk and behaved aggressively, knocking her over. He then went to bed, only to wake up and threaten her. She said that she 'turned in passion and got the iron bar and struck him on the head'. When she saw he was dying 'she felt so sorry, that she got the razor and cut his throat. That was between twelve and one o'clock.' The timing in her statement does not appear quite correct and she left out the scenes in the street outside Hooley's house, to which other witnesses attested. The coroner and jury recommended she stand trial for wilful murder.

The trial was heard on 28 January 1862 before the Chief Justice Sir Valentine Fleming, a man of sympathy and consideration. Coghlan was represented by a newly admitted barrister, Mr Cansdell, pleading his first case. As was the legal convention at the time, the attorney-general appeared for the Crown. Much of the evidence repeated that heard in the coroner's inquest. Dr Cairns was closely interrogated to remove any possible belief that the victim had committed suicide. The coroner testified how the accused had broken down and stated in writing that she had 'done a terrible wrong and had offended against Almighty God, and must take the consequences'.

In concluding the Crown's case, the attorney-general argued that insufficient provocation in the legal sense had been offered to account for her crime. Outlining the difference between manslaughter and murder he contended that this was a clear case of murder since it had been a deliberate act. The question of premeditation was not considered. In terms of the legal conventions of the time Coghlan received a fair trial. The jury took only ten minutes to find her guilty of the wilful murder of her husband, for which the penalty was death.[4] The chief justice assumed the black cap and read out the sentence, which included dissection and anatomisation even though this practice had ceased in the United Kingdom a full thirty years before.

The citizens of Hobart were sympathetic to Margaret Coghlan; she was a religious woman despite her grievous crime and intemperate habits. A large petition was assembled to plead for mercy for this now elderly woman. The petition stressed the fact that the Coghlans had been teetotallers and for 'years lived happily together, but had broken the pledge and taken up drinking to excess'. Rum was to blame. These entreaties had no effect and the governor and Executive Council were determined to see the sentence carried out.[5] Attended by the Roman Catholic Bishop of Hobart, Robert Willson, as well as the Reverend

G. Hunter, the Sisters of Charity,* and several benevolent ladies of the diocese, the deeply penitent Coghlan awaited execution.

Margaret Coghlan was executed on Friday 7 March 1862 in Hobart Town Gaol. She had been lodged in the Female Factory at the Cascades but was moved to the jail several days before she went to the gallows. Reverend Hunter and the nuns attended her until the under-sheriff arrived at the jail to oversee the Supreme Court's decision, followed by the arrival of the jail governor. Coghlan was clothed in deep mourning, with her eyes bandaged. She was so afraid that she trembled and had to be assisted on the walk from her cell to the gallows. In a loud voice she cried out: 'Lord Jesus have mercy upon me', and then, as newspapers reported, she slipped into the eternal. She had, however, prepared a statement with the assistance of Reverend Hunter to be read after her death. In it Coghlan stated: 'I acknowledge fully the justice of my sentence. I deserve this, and a thousand deaths, if that were possible for the horrible crime I have committed. Drink, the curse upon me, strong drink has caused all my misery ... May God have mercy on my soul, for Jesus' sake, take pity on me. O! May all women be particular, take warning of my awful fate ... O! that I had kept my pledge!'[6]

Though temperance and the avoidance of alcohol was a particularly Protestant preoccupation that gathered strength as the colonies moved from their convict pasts, where alcohol had been used as a basic trading currency, to a more modern progressive free society in the 1850s, Roman Catholics were not immune to its admonitions. Margaret Coghlan was an elderly woman by the standards of the day when she was executed. Her crime had been brutal, a vengeful fury against a husband who had nightly consorted with prostitutes. But her violence had been fuelled by alcohol. And death by hanging was her penalty.

---

* The Irish Sisters of Charity, often highly educated women, had arrived in Hobart in 1842, their first mission to attend to those in prison.

The story of Margaret O'Donohue, who brutally murdered her companion in a brothel in Melbourne in 1872, had an entirely different trajectory from that of her fellow Irishwoman Margaret Coghlan, who was legally married and religious. O'Donohue was born in Brandon, County Cork, around 1850 just after the Irish Famine had officially ended. Cork, in the south, had been severely affected by several seasons of blighted crops that had left millions to starve to death, to migrate, or to be permanently affected, physically and emotionally, by the national trauma.

O'Donohue was slight in build and tiny in height, probably due to the effects of poverty and near starvation in her infancy and childhood. At the age of nineteen, she immigrated to Melbourne on the *Lightning*. She found work as a domestic servant in Williamstown before relocating to a better-paid job as a barmaid at Flanagan's Hotel in North Melbourne. She supplemented her income as a 'privateer', a contemporary term for a woman who undertook prostitution on a part-time basis. Usually it was only a short-term measure as most women soon took up the game permanently.

O'Donohue went to live in the Temperance Hotel in Lonsdale Street, a location that did not match her occupation or aspirations. In 1872 she moved to 'a low brothel frequented by thieves' in Punch Lane. The whole north-eastern section of the CBD in Melbourne was infested with brothels, not just bordellos and luxurious houses of ill fame such as Madame Brussels', but also cheap hotels renting out rooms. A local policeman, Constable Dalton, whose beat encompassed these areas, reported that '[w]hen walking the streets as a prostitute, she [O'Donohue] was bold, and would not be told to go away by the police'.[7] O'Donohue based herself in a brothel run by Mary O'Rourke (alias Hewitt and Hewson). The two were close, although at times terrible fights occurred between the women and their pimps. O'Donohue's life was full of violence. She was assaulted by a Mr Jones, by a German client who claimed she had attempted to rob him, and she was admitted to Melbourne Hospital after a brawl with two

Irish prostitutes on St Patrick's Day in 1872. This level of altercation and violence was not uncommon at the bottom end of prostitution.

On the evening of 18 August 1872, O'Donohue, O'Rourke and another prostitute, Anne Crozier, sat down for an amicable glass of rum before a warming fire. Crozier drank so much she fell unconscious and had to be put to bed. When O'Donohue returned to the front room, O'Rourke became abusive, calling her mother a whore. Incensed, O'Donohue seized an axe used to cut firewood and repeatedly smashed O'Rourke over the head, even after she had fallen to the filthy floor. Not content with this almost demented violence, O'Donohue jumped on her victim's back, breaking her ribs, which punctured her right lung. Coming to her senses after the frenzy, O'Donohue tried to stem the bleeding with bandages.

O'Donohue ran out onto the street and found Constable Flanagan in Bourke Street, telling him what she had done. He was so astounded that he said: 'Nonsense'. 'By God, I have,' she replied. 'I smashed her bloody head in with an axe. Come with me and I will show you.' He accompanied her back to the brothel where he found the dead woman lying near a gin case used as a chair. Constable Flanagan called in Dr James Neild, who conducted the autopsy. He found she had been near death from cancer of the uterus and from advanced syphilis, an occupational hazard of streetwalkers and prostitutes in low-class brothels. It is likely that the constant abuse O'Rourke hurled at her attacker had been fuelled by the syphilis, which often ends in bursts of raving and insanity.

When she was taken into the city watch house for questioning, O'Donohue did not deny her actions. She told police: 'I told her a month ago that I would [kill her] for calling my mother a whore. She was constantly abusing me, and calling me a whore, and my mother a whore; and I told her that if she didn't stop, I would murder her, and I have murdered her.'

On 21 August 1872, Margaret O'Donohue went to trial in the Victorian Supreme Court before Justice Sir Robert Molesworth

(1806–90), an aristocratic Irishman. The Crown case was led by Bryan (later Sir Bryan) O'Loughlen (1828–1905), the attorney-general, who came from a distinguished family of lawyers in County Clare in Ireland. O'Donohue was fortunate to have the pro bono services of the distinguished barrister Henry (later Sir Henry) Wrixon (1839–1913), another Irishman from a legal family. He had served as Victoria's solicitor-general for the previous two years. He was ambitious and talented but this case offered little to test his adversarial skills since his client had already confessed to the commission of the brutal crime. A photograph of O'Donohue shows a pinch-faced young woman with low-set eyes and thick eyebrows, described in newspapers as having 'the cast of vice'. Rather, she looks like a poor, hard-pressed working-woman.

No new evidence was presented at the trial. In this case there had been no coronial inquest, but medical evidence did, however, demonstrate that, because of the 'disease from which she suffered', O'Rourke's bones were brittle. An audience in the 1870s understood the unnamed disease to be syphilis. Wrixon was shaken and emotional as he addressed the jury, begging them to recommend clemency on the basis that O'Donohue had heard her mother called 'an objectionable name'. The jury deliberated for just a short time before returning a verdict of guilty with a strong recommendation for mercy. The gentlemen found it objectionable that a perfectly decent mother, even one whose daughter was a prostitute, should be called a whore. Justice Molesworth pronounced the sentence of death upon the unmoved and silent prisoner.[8]

The premier of the day, James Goodall Francis, was a progressive Liberal. Despite the urgings of Justice Molesworth to hang her, he commuted O'Donohue's sentence to twenty-one years' imprisonment. Given how brutal and savage the crime had been, this was an extraordinary gesture. And lucky for O'Donohue as hers was not the sort of case that aroused public sentiment to petition for mercy. In the end O'Donohue served fourteen years. When she was about to be released, the wardens found that the moths had eaten all her clothes and all that remained was a powdery pile of disintegrating fabric. She was given £5/5/- and a modest set of new clothes, and then the prison gate shut behind her. Her fate outside the walls was left unrecorded.

Born in 1860, Danish immigrant Cecilie Andersen was a naive and trusting woman. Widowed young, she fell for a handsome well-born young man called John Fraser, who lived in her Sydney boarding house. Believing her affection returned, she began to lend him large sums of money and to provide free accommodation and board, as well as the comforts of her bed. Yet he had no intention of marrying her – she was simply a useful convenience. The result? He ended up dead and she ended up on trial for his murder in Melbourne in 1894.

Cecilie Andersen immigrated to Sydney with her husband, a bricklayer, in the boom years of the 1880s. With considerable investment going into urban infrastructure and domestic housing, a skilled tradesman could find ample work at high wages. After her young husband's sudden and untimely death, Andersen set up a boarding house in Surry Hills, taking up to a dozen paying guests at a time. Even with servants the work was strenuous, involving long hours to provide food and lodgings for respectable single men. Many of her paying guests were aspiring professionals, such as accountant John Fraser, who in the 1880s had come to Sydney from his family's large pastoral holding, 'Tallygaroopna', near Shepparton in Victoria. This large sheep property had been opened up in 1841, and ran to 160,000 acres (65,000 hectares). Fraser's father, William Fraser, took over the leasehold on 28 February 1866. The elder Fraser had arrived from Scotland in 1841, locating himself first in Van Diemen's Land. As the best land there was already taken, he moved to Wannon in Victoria's Western Districts. Highly respected for his integrity in business and as the largest landholder in the entire district, William Fraser was active in the community, and was particularly proud of his memberships of the Old Colonists' Association – which celebrated those who had come as free settlers and not as felons – and the Caledonian Club.[9]

John Fraser frequently boasted to his colleagues and his fellow guests at the boarding house that he stood to become a very wealthy man on the death of his father. He expected to inherit around £18,000, more than a small fortune. Little did Fraser know that the National Bank had taken over the property in 1870 and that his father had only managed to wrest back ownership and control in January 1885. Fraser's belief in his expectations blunted his ambitions. Why did he need to work hard in a dreary office when he would become a man of means and leisure? So although he worked, it was only nominal; he valued far more his reputation as a man about town, attending all the best balls and soirées. Money was merely there to spend maintaining his appearance and his lifestyle.

Fraser soon realised that his quiet Danish landlady was gathering a small capital investment as a result of her hard work and dedication. He started doing her books in lieu of paying rent, but soon moved from the study to the bedroom as he eyed her financial resources. Foolishly, Andersen began lending him money on the expectation that they would legitimise their sexual relationship. Over the years she lent him £445, equivalent to ten years' wages for a domestic servant. But Fraser kept putting off the union, even though he must have known that he could take control of Andersen's capital if he married her since the *Married Women's Property Act* had not yet been passed, and so all a woman's property, inheritances and earnings still went automatically to her husband. It is not clear whether Andersen knew that Fraser was a widower. He had married Mary Howe of Hawthorn in 1872 at the age of twenty-eight. They had had two children – Edgar, born in 1873, and Ruby born two years later.[10]

When William Fraser died in October 1892, the *Argus* provided a splendid if small obituary of the old colonist. What they did not mention was that the drought and the severe Depression of the early 1890s had wiped out all the investments he had worked so hard to win back. In fact, 'Tallygaroopna' was almost worthless and needed to be sold to pay existing liabilities. John Fraser and his numerous siblings were left nothing but debts and resentment as their expectations disappeared. The downturn in the economy affected Fraser even further when he lost his job. Still he did not marry Cecilie Andersen. With his high-society lifestyle about to vanish, he set his sights far higher. To Ellen Lee, a wealthy widow living in Melbourne, he repeated the story of his expectations even though he now knew they were groundless. They married on 28 March 1894. By then, the *Married Women's Property Act* had been passed in Victoria, so the new Mrs Fraser could keep control of everything she had inherited from her first marriage. The couple lived in 'Ellengowan', her spacious and elegant home in Malvern.

Andersen soon heard of this betrayal of her purse and her honour. She went to Melbourne to address the situation. With her she took a revolver should mere words not prove sufficiently persuasive to retrieve her money. Money, however, was not the primary objective – Andersen felt righteously insulted, angry and vengeful. When she had heard in late 1893 that Fraser was engaged, she had gone to plead her case and seek the intervention of his brother-in-law, Thomas Stuart, a financial agent. Stuart was not sympathetic, particularly when Andersen swung her revolver around. When she pleaded that 'he is a scoundrel, he has lied and is trying to do me out of my money', Stuart attempted to reason with her. When she said, 'But I'll have it [the money],' he replied: 'It is a pity you should fly off like this and get into such tempers; you will entirely lose your head. I hear you go as far as to threaten Fraser's life and that you carry fire arms ... You are acting like a fool ... going on like a lunatic ...' As they parted, Andersen shouted after him: 'I am not done with him.'[11]

On 1 April 1894 Andersen next visited Fraser's brother Thomas, who lived in comfort in Beaconsfield Parade in St Kilda. Unlike prodigal son John, Thomas had worked hard for his own security rather than rely on expectations. Andersen confronted her lover's brother, telling him: 'This is a fine place for revolver practice.' When Thomas Fraser tried to reason with her, she replied: 'I want John to come back to me. If he comes back I will not ask for the money ... I can mesmerise him and get him to do what I wish ... It is cruel that he should leave me to marry another woman.'[12]

The following day Andersen tracked down the newly wedded couple and insisted that Fraser introduce her to his bride. She was angry and shaking, shouting almost uncontrollably. She asked the new Mrs Fraser whether she knew 'what sort of man she had married'. When Ellen Fraser replied that she did (although this is unlikely in the circumstances), Andersen retorted: 'Then more shame on you!' and walked away feeling more aggrieved than ever. In an attempt to calm her, Fraser went with her to Princes Bridge and did not return home until late that evening.[13]

Determined at least to restore her capital, Andersen consulted a solicitor in order to begin legal action to recover her money. This was likely to be difficult, given Fraser had no money of his own and he had had 'no occupation' when he married Ellen in March. Fraser threatened a countersuit, and Andersen realised she might lose all her capital to the lawyers and still not retrieve her 'loan'.

The matter went to court where Andersen received a better hearing. She was awarded an order of payment of £445 against Fraser on 14 May 1894 even though he had no way of paying it back unless his wife gave him the money or he was declared bankrupt. Rather than pursue this option, Andersen backed off and entered into a solicitor's agreement in which Fraser would pay her off at the rate of 15/- per week, the outstanding balance to accrue interest at 8 per cent. Such a scheme meant that he would be paying off his debt to her forever. Perhaps she thought it would keep them in touch; that she believed he would make the payment himself every Monday shows how addled her thinking was at the time.

In Melbourne, Andersen stayed with her friend Margaret Healy at the Federal Coffee Palace in Collins Street. At the trial Healy testified that her companion talked wildly and obsessively about how she had been betrayed and how she would get her revenge. She related a conversation with the accused:

I kept him in money, food and tobacco for five or six years ...
he said he was coming into a fortune of about £18,000 ...
he has injured my pocket and hurt my heart ... I will have
satisfaction yet or I will take his life ... I knocked him over
when he said he was married, hit him in the mouth and made
it bleed ... it is a pity I had not a revolver. I would have done
the trick then ...

Andersen was so distressed and anxious she could neither sleep nor eat. She complained constantly that her 'brain burned'.

John Fraser was living on an allowance of £3 per week provided by his brothers. Evidently, the new Mrs Fraser was unimpressed by the story of her husband's caddish behaviour, and she was not a woman who liked a man to sponge off her, whatever his relationship to her. Andersen made an appointment to meet Fraser on 19 June 1894 at the Southern Cross Hotel in Bourke Street in order to finalise their financial arrangements. Since Fraser had consistently refused to sign the agreement in the solicitor's office, Andersen took a room with Margaret Healy and insisted that he meet her there. Fraser agreed, no doubt wanting to avoid another public scene. Hyam Winedrawer, an employee at the hotel, later told the court that 'Mrs Andersen was not sober'. He had also noticed that she had a revolver with her – although why he did not then call in the police was a mystery.[14] After all, women did not normally carry revolvers in their purses at respectable hotels in Melbourne.

Hotel guest William Orr, a mining investor, stated that, even though he was a total stranger, Mrs Andersen had spoken to him of her sorrow that Fraser had not married her. He was entirely perplexed by her confidences. Fraser and Andersen came to the hotel several times on the day of the shooting, first at around 2pm and then again at 4pm. Other employees of the hotel – Mary Egan, Patrick Moran and Henry Morphett – reported that Fraser and Andersen arrived together at the hotel at around 8pm and had drinks sent to them. They heard shots about an hour later. On entering the room, Fraser was found dead on the bed with head wounds, while Andersen was alive with self-inflicted head wounds. She was taken to Melbourne Hospital where she was treated by the distinguished surgeon, Mr (later Sir) Charles Ryan, the father of the future Lady Maie Casey, chatelaine of Yarralumla.

The trial for the wilful murder of John Fraser opened in the Victorian Supreme Court on 16 August 1894 before Justice Sir John Madden, a man of deep sympathy and compassion. Andersen arrived in court with her head heavily bandaged, and appeared to be confused and disoriented during the brief one-day hearing. Andersen's barrister, Mr Leon, could only plead mitigating circumstances to account for her actions. Medical experts attested that she was not insane when she shot Fraser and then herself. Andersen did not testify.

In his summing up to the jury, the chief justice pointed out that Fraser did not seem a 'man tired of life', so suicide should be ruled out. He spoke with some insight into the distress that led the prisoner to her actions. The jury deliberated for forty-five minutes before reaching a guilty verdict. Andersen received a death sentence, the full penalty of the law.[15] Justice Madden wrote to the governor, Lord Hopetoun, several days after sentencing, reiterating the various ways the condemned woman 'had suffered at the hands of the deceased'. He asked Hopetoun to exercise his prerogative for mercy.[16]

The public realised that Andersen was not a cruel or vicious killer but a woman who had been wronged and discarded. The Danish residents of Victoria and an additional 20,000 citizens petitioned for clemency through the agency of solicitor Marshall Lyle.[17] The Danish consul-general, F. W. Were, was also active on Andersen's behalf. The owner of a highly respected and influential business in Melbourne, Were was the son of importer Jonathon Were, who had been knighted by the kings of Denmark and Sweden for his commercial and cultural expertise and activities.[18] The petitioners pointed out how badly Andersen had been treated, ending with the emotional plea that 'in the present weak, helpless and disabled condition of the unfortunate woman, such an act [hanging] appears to be particularly revolting'.

The solicitor-general reviewed the circumstances of the case on 16 December after Andersen alleged that she had attempted suicide first and that, in a struggle for the gun, Fraser had then been shot.[19] The Executive Council commuted the sentence to twenty years' imprisonment. Once a strong, robust woman, Andersen was now a wreck: unable to walk, partially paralysed and mentally incompetent.

Even as she served her sentence Andersen had not been forgotten. There was constant pressure to secure her release. A group of ladies were active on her behalf, securing the services of solicitor Waldermar Bannow to act for them. A deputation met with the solicitor-general, Agar Wynne MLC, on 3 July 1901. He told them that he had studied the case and believed Andersen should serve a minimum of ten years in prison.[20] Eighteen months later, the new Danish consul-general, Povl Holdensen, made further representations on Andersen's behalf to Premier William Irvine,[21] a prominent lawyer who would become chief justice when Madden retired in 1918. Irvine promised that this 'unfortunate woman, now sixty years of age' and in ill health, would be released on 30 June 1903.

Cecilie Andersen was indeed released on that date and nothing more is known of a fate that had been so blighted by the passion, vengeance and fury of her life.

CHAPTER 13

Killing of Partners in the Twentieth Century

In 1901 the aspiring novelist Miles Franklin published *My Brilliant Career*, an audacious novel about the emotional struggles of its tomboyish hero, Sybylla Melvyn. When her father's drinking threatens to destroy her family's security and social position, Sybylla travels to her grandmother's homestead in New South Wales. There she meets a handsome and wealthy grazier, Harry Beecham. He proposes marriage, as honourable men did. But Melvyn equivocates. It's not that she doubts his intentions. Rather, her reluctance derives from her ambition to become a writer at a time when marriage and motherhood were likely to compromise her freedom and talent. She prefers to choose the uncertainty of life as a writer rather than the conventional security and social obligations of marriage to a well-connected man.

In real life, as the new century began, this was an unlikely plot. Ethel Herringe and Audrey Jacob clearly had not read *My Brilliant Career*, with its precepts of independence and romantic freedom. Instead, when they believed they had been dishonoured and humiliated, both acted decisively – and permanently – to take revenge for broken promises and sexual betrayal.

On Saturday 22 November 1902, the Melbourne *Argus* reported a strange legal case in New Zealand. The report revealed that a woman, Myra Taylor, had shot her former lover when he refused to marry her, and had instead engaged to marry someone else. On the eve of his wedding, Taylor disguised herself in men's clothing, went to the hotel where he was drinking, and shot him three times. Despite shooting him in front of witnesses, Taylor was acquitted of attempted murder. The paper also reported a case from New South Wales in which a housemaid at the Club House Hotel in Cowra, Ethel Herringe, had shot her employer, a man by the name of Maurice Lee. The tone of the article (subtitled 'A Determined Young Woman') was representative of how this case would be reported in the press. The 'tall and rather prepossessing' Herringe, it revealed, had 'an understanding' with Lee, who had recently returned from serving in the Boer War in South Africa. He had reneged on the marriage, so on the evening of what she thought was to be her wedding night she shot him in front of witnesses. Lee continued to linger in hospital with little hope held for his recovery.[1]

The story might have been presented in a light less favourable to Herringe – she was after all a mere servant who had shot her employer. And there were already hints that she was pregnant, meaning it was a shotgun wedding gone horribly wrong. Furthermore, the victim was a recently returned volunteer for the military engagement in South Africa where the colonies and the recently formed Commonwealth had sent troops as part of an Imperial contingent to fight the rebel Dutch Boers. Lee had served as a sergeant with the West Australian Bushmen's Regiment.

While some saw him as 'a fine stamp of a muscular man', the Reverend Seymour Smith described Lee as 'rather rough and brusque, his language was rough'.[2] Herringe shot her lover in front of this Anglican clergyman, perhaps not the wisest decision on her part. In other circumstances a young single woman in her situation might have borne an ex-nuptial child whose life could have been harsh and even tragic (see early chapters). Yet, by many, Herringe was perceived to be a plucky young woman who had been treated caddishly by a privileged man.

Ethel Herring was born in 1880 to David Herring and Bridget Mary Gray Herring. Several years after her birth her parents decided that plain 'Herring' was too banal, so they added an 'e' to their last name. Before she went to work at the Club House Hotel, Herringe had been employed at 'Melyra', a property near Grenfell in New South Wales, which she left with an excellent character reference.[3]

Many working-class young women of the time did not subscribe to the conventional bourgeois belief in being a virgin when they married, although for this they ran the risk of pregnancy, as Herringe was to discover. Domestic servants also found themselves vulnerable to sexual exploitation by employers and by the sons of the house or establishment where they worked. But from her statements, Herringe did not appear to be a victim but an active agent of her own destiny. Before she became Lee's lover, she had been involved with a friend of her family, another Boer War veteran named Doherty. When he died in South Africa, he left his meagre estate to Herringe. It was later claimed by her supporters that he had been more like a brother than a romantic interest.[4]

When Herringe became pregnant to Lee, she insisted that he marry her – an assertive act for a servant no matter what relationship she had with her employer. Lee gave her an engagement ring, although this might have been to stave off her persistence. Apparently he had been 'engaged' to quite a few other women in the past, perhaps as an enticement into a sexual relationship rather than as a prelude to marriage. A witness at her trial reported that Herringe had stated:

> 'This ring [the engagement ring] has been on a great many
> girls' fingers but I will show him [Lee] a point about it,' she
> said. 'If anyone annoyed me I would have their blood, but I
> am not annoyed with you girls.' On Tuesday I was chaffing
> her; I said, 'There is a pretty girl coming from Victoria, you
> will be losing your boy.' She replied that she 'might take him
> for a while but she will not have him forever'.[5]

Clearly she was determined to secure her rights. On the Thursday 20 November 1902, Herringe arranged for the Reverend Smith to marry her and Lee after the hotel closed. The setting and secrecy in which the drama played out suggests that Lee had not been party to the arrangement.

At the appointed hour, accompanied by her younger sister Kathleen and another witness named Henry Palmer, Herringe waited for her prospective bridegroom. The Herringes were Roman Catholics and therefore not part of the Reverend Smith's parish. He was surprised to learn that the bridegroom was not her Catholic boyfriend Doherty, but an entirely different man – her employer.[6] She knocked on Lee's door and, to his amazement and dismay, was accompanied in by the wedding party. They all then went down to the kitchen – a strange location for a marriage ceremony. When asked point-blank if he intended to marry Herringe as he had promised, Lee replied that he 'declined'. In response, Herringe said that she would 'give him one more chance'.

By now, the Reverend Smith was alarmed and had a quiet word with Lee about the arrangements, saying he would have nothing to do with the legal papers offered to him. Herringe was infuriated and pulled out a concealed revolver. Two shots were fired.[7] Lee sprang at his assailant and, during the struggle, another shot was heard. Henry Palmer also tried to restrain Herringe. By this time Lee had been shot again. He then went calmly to the bar, poured himself a drink, and departed to bed. His nonchalance, at least, has to be admired. But it wasn't a farce. The bullets were real.

When the local police arrived with the doctor it was clear that Lee was seriously injured, despite his bravado. He refused to name his assailant although he did admit '… regarding the girl, that he had wronged her, and had promised to marry, and that he forgave her'.[8] This statement given on his deathbed five days later was important during Herringe's trial since it offered mitigating circumstances and created a degree of sympathy for the wronged woman among the jury. Just before he died from loss of blood and infection, Lee had taken final leave of Herringe: from prison she returned the engagement ring. An inquest was conducted on 26 November 1902 after which Herringe was ordered to stand trial in the circuit sittings of the New South Wales Supreme Court at Young on 15 April the following year.

Herringe was able to secure the services of a top barrister, (later Sir) George Reid KC (1845–1918), who went on to become prime minister in 1905, with a local Cowra solicitor giving instruction. The trial was heard before Sir William Owen (1834–1912), a member of the Scottish gentry who had been educated at Lincoln's Inn. He was regarded as 'a shrewd observer of men and things', an expert on equity and bankruptcy.[9] Reid presented his client as a decent young woman who had been seduced and abandoned by a cad. He pointed out that she had not intended to kill or injure Lee that Thursday night but rather to marry him. Kathleen Herringe, who had given evidence at the inquest, was not called to the stand. Mrs Herringe affirmed that her daughter had been looking forward to marriage and a new life the night before the shootings. At the inquest and the trial Herringe was remorseful, often weeping and sighing. She was so overcome by grief that she was unable to take the stand in her own defence.

Reid was a master tactician in the courtroom. He demonstrated the underlying ruthlessness of Lee's actions, and how the manner in which Herringe had been treated provoked her. Lee's words – 'I won't marry you. You can bloody well shoot!' – were used in evidence for the defence. The purchase of the gun was portrayed as an act of desperation meant to frighten, not injure the deceased. He skipped over the concept of premeditation and calculation – which the jury allowed to slip past as well. Reid concluded his address to the jury by pointing out that the young woman had been 'spurned at the altar' (even though they'd been in the hotel kitchen at the time). There was also some confusion about which shot had killed Lee. It was suggested that it might have been the one that was fired when Palmer intervened, although earlier testimony suggested that this bullet only struck Lee's wrist. The jury retired for a short time and delivered a verdict of manslaughter. Justice Owen sentenced Herringe to only thirty months in prison; in 1894 Cecilie Andersen had been read the death sentence for murdering her absconding lover in Melbourne.

The story did not end with this minimal sentence. The residents of the Cowra and Grenfell districts thought that justice had been heavy-handed and lobbied hard to secure Herringe's early release. This suggests that Lee had not been a popular publican. As the editor of the *Grenfell Vedette*, H. E. Holland, wrote:

> Men of Lee's description are only too common, and every honest man and every honest woman – every brother and sister, every father and mother – should demonstrate their sympathy with this victim – for victim she is. She is not only to face the world; and bear the sorrow that must be hers for the shedding of blood but she has to bear the taunts that will be thrown at her by many less noble than herself.[10]

Harry Holland (1868–1933) was an unusual man to run a small regional newspaper. He was a printer by trade and a militant socialist by inclination. He was a co-founder of the Australian Socialist League in Sydney in 1882. But he wasn't an ideologue, as he demonstrated in the coverage of the Herringe case.[11]

At first the chorus of sympathy and support was locally based. Herringe and her family were popular and respected members of the community. A public meeting was held at Grenfell Council Chambers on 5 May 1903, attended by more people than the venue had ever seen. A large number were women, many deeply moved by Herringe's situation. Despite Herringe's conviction for manslaughter, she was a heroine for the cause of women's rights. Speakers pointed out the double standard that meant only the girl or woman involved bore the public condemnation for premarital sex and pregnancy.[12]

With the support of the Salvation Army, women's activist Anna Hazelton and Holland established the Ethel Herringe Release Committee, with other members helping to circulate petitions in nearby townships. The committee met weekly, keeping up the pressure and publicity. The *Cowra Free Press* opposed this action, concentrating on Herringe's conviction for manslaughter: 'she ... was not entirely blameless' by any means. Cowra Council also refused to allow its buildings to be hired by supporters. But for the most part public opinion swung behind Herringe and the movement to have her released. The local Catholic priest and Protestant ministers endorsed the actions at public meetings.[13]

One important ally was journalist Ada Holman (1869–1949), the new wife of the local member, W. A. Holman (1871–1934), who went on to become the Labor premier during World War I.[14] She had strong links to the influential *Sydney Morning Herald*. Despite her pregnancy and confinement in 1903, Holman worked tirelessly on Herringe's behalf, aided by the feminist and socialist sisters Annie Mackenzie Golding (1855–1934) and Isabella Golding (1864–1940), who were foundation members of the Women's Suffrage League.[15] They were capable and persuasive advocates who organised large petitions, including the signatures of some ten federal MHRs, twenty MLAs and many teachers and other professionals. This was sent to the New South Wales Attorney-General Bernard Wise, close friend and associate of the Holmans, despite the privileged upbringing that saw him educated in England at Rugby School and Oxford University.

The press campaign was not without its obstacles. Wise demanded that Holland retract an editorial of 13 May 1903. He was not convinced that random shootings – which were increasing – should be applauded, however subtly.

Hazelton contacted leading Sydney feminist Rose Scott (1847–1925), who got involved in the Herringe cause, with Hazelton keeping her up to date on local developments. Scott was Australia's best-known and most well connected feminist at the time, and she could bring to bear impressive weight to any issue. On 27 August 1903, Scott, accompanied by other members of the Women's Political Educational League, made representations to Wise, which were ineffective on this occasion. In September a large public meeting was held in Sydney to support Herringe's cause. Still nothing happened.

In June 1904 Wise resigned his portfolio. Herringe's supporters were not confident that she would be released by the new attorney-general, but the order for release was dated 27 July 1904. Herringe had been in custody since her arrest in November 1902. In prison she gave birth to twins whom she named Mary and Patrick Herringe. They were adopted. Herringe then relocated to New Zealand to start her life again without the ignominy of unmarried motherhood and a conviction for manslaughter attached to her name.[16]

Ethel Herringe may have been sentenced to only thirty months' imprisonment for the manslaughter of her lover before reliable witnesses, but Audrey Campbell Jacob, who killed her fiancé in a classic breach of promise tragedy at a charity ball at Government House in Perth, before dozens of witnesses, was found not guilty. Why? She admitted killing him – although she argued the gun went off accidentally – and some of Perth's most prominent citizens in fact saw her ambush her former fiancé. Did she go free because she was young and pretty, an apparently respectable young Catholic woman before a jury of middle-aged Catholic men? The strategy used by her defence counsel was a brilliant case of obfuscation, appeals to gender and religious stereotypes, and sheer bluff.

In 1925 the committee of the St John of God Hospital organised its major fundraising event with a ball held at Government House, a most exclusive setting. The event began at 8.30pm on Wednesday 26 August. It is remembered as one of Western Australia's most famous vice-regal functions because that was the evening Audrey Jacob shot her former fiancé Cyril Gidley through the heart in front of the assembled throng. The ball was suddenly the talk of the town, indeed of the nation, with its story of illicit sex, broken promises, a gorgeous young woman and her handsome intended bridegroom, and the overwhelmingly proper setting. Headlines such as 'SEDUCED,

SCORNED AND SNEERED AT' promised the full catalogue of innuendo, titillation and sex among the young who were throwing off the spirit of Victorianism with their fast and, in this case, deadly ways.

Audrey Campbell Jacob was a twenty-year-old art student, and a privileged member of society. Her father was assistant clerk of the court at Fremantle and therefore had the financial resources to allow her to study rather than go out to work at thirteen as less fortunate young women were forced to in the 1920s. One of eight children, she was educated in a Sisters of St Joseph of the Sacred Heart convent at Norseman, in the goldfields, 190 kilometres south of Kalgoorlie. The Dundas field at Norseman had been discovered in 1894, becoming the second largest goldfield in the colony, and a thriving centre. The Sisters of St Joseph of the Sacred Heart was established as an Australian order by Mother Mary of the Cross (Mother Mary MacKillop). They were an active order of religious sisters committed to good works, education and progressive causes, and by the standards of the day they offered an excellent education for girls. They also encouraged independence, careful thought and charity among their pupils. A talented art student at the convent, Jacob went on to further her career as a painter who apparently was able to sell over two hundred works while she was still at art school.[17]

Jacob was a modern young woman devoted to the latest dance crazes and popular music. The charleston was first performed in 1923 on Broadway, and soon spread across the Western world, fuelled by the new Hollywood musicals screened in cinemas in Australia. The shimmy, which allowed young women to shake in order to make the tassels on their evening dresses move in time with the music, also took hold. Flappers, as such girls were called, were outrageous, full of high spirits and ready to turn their backs on the gloomy years of their youth and childhood, which had been dominated by casualty lists of the dead and injured in World War I. The scandalous tango of the previous decade was also still popular, along with the foxtrot.

Tea dances and dance parties held in the ballrooms of leading hotels were where young people could meet and enjoy themselves freed from the stricter supervision and chaperonage that had existed before the war. Bands that were beginning to get the feel of jazz performed the latest hits, despite the disapproval of the older, pre-war generation. In 1920 the Princeton-educated short-story writer and novelist F. Scott Fitzgerald set the tone for the post-war era, with its 'flaming youth' dedicated to fast cars, fast music, indulgence and sex. His short story 'Bernice Bobs Her Hair', published in 1920, the year his first full-length novel, *This Side of Paradise*, was released, captures the spirit of the modern young woman throwing off her corsets, along with the restrictions and sensible advice of her elders.

When Audrey Jacob became engaged to Cyril Gidley, she was just eighteen. Despite her youth Jacob had already been engaged, to ship's engineer Claude Arundel. She broke it off when the handsome twenty-five-year-old Gidley from Grimsby, in the north of England – and also an engineer but on the MV *Kangaroo* – pressed her to take him on as her recognised suitor.

Jacob had known Gidley for about two years before they became engaged, having met him when his ship was in port. They became officially engaged without immediately telling her parents, and it was announced in three newspapers, including the *West Australian* on 8 October 1924.

Gidley was highly sexually experienced, with a girl in every port of the Far East (as it was then called) – diversions when his vessel docked. He also romanced other women quite openly in Perth, still a small community, where news travelled fast. Jacob was far too naive to realise what she was contending with. She admitted in her testimony that Gidley 'seduced' her and then 'used violence towards her' within six weeks of their engagement. This was clearly a troubled relationship built on threats and recriminations. Later there were hints that Gidley had raped Jacob. But still she continued her engagement. She left home and moved into a flat with another girl in 'Surrey Chambers' on

Audrey Jacob had been seduced and thrown off; in a sensational crime of passion, she shot dead her lover at a ball. Photo: *Sunday Times*, 30 August 1925.

St George's Terrace, near Government House, allowing her to escape her parents' watchfulness and disapproval.

At some point the engagement was broken off. On 25 August 1925, Jacob had threatened to shoot Gidley, and then kill herself. Only days earlier, Cyril Gidley had written a letter in which he declared that Jacob had 'threatened me with my life'.[18]

On the evening of 26 August 1925, the band at the St John of God Hospital fundraising ball played all the fashionable melodies and a little jazz, despite the presence of Catholic Archbishop Clune. The dance floor filled with couples dancing the foxtrot. Audrey Jacob, dressed in a Pierrot costume, danced only with her friend Annie Humphreys, who was dressed as Pierrette. Fancy-dress parties had become popular after the war, antidotes to the years of mourning black worn by widows and mothers, and the khaki worn by those who had served. In fancy-dress, people could assume new identities and behave in ways markedly different from the rigidity required by the black and khaki.

At first Jacob did not see Gidley among the crowd of revellers, but at around 9pm Humphreys spied him and his companion and pointed them out to Jacob. Her reaction was one of amazement since she had been led to believe he had departed for Singapore when the *Kangaroo* left port a few days earlier. He had, however, been unwell and unable to travel or work. Gidley had visited an old school friend of his father, Wilford Mitchell, and his family. Mrs Maude Mitchell was the organiser of the ball and president of the St John of God Hospital Free Ward Committee, and she asked Gidley to attend.[19] He took their daughter Maude Mitchell as his partner to the event.[20]

Audrey Jacob told the court in testimony at her trial that Gidley 'refused to recognise me. He passed me three or four times – more, in fact – but he was very cold. Sometimes he would look at me and put his chin up. Several times as he passed me he gave me a bit of a sneer and then turned away and laughed.' Around midnight Humphreys decided that she would accept the invitation of a young man to dance, leaving Jacob alone to brood. For some time she simply disappeared.[21] As Jacob told the court:

> I was feeling very upset and ill, and my head was aching. I went to
> my room and I lay down on my bed. I cried about half an hour,
> I think. I then started to undress. When I opened the drawer I
> saw a revolver [given to her previously for protection by Claude
> Arundel] and then I decided to end my life. So I started to dress
> again. I meant to go to the foreshore to end my life. I didn't put
> on the Pierrot costume because I didn't want to do it in fancy
> dress. I picked up the first dress handy, which happened to be
> a blue costume hanging over the end of the bed. I wrapped the
> revolver in a handkerchief and went out intending to go down
> to the foreshore. But on the Terrace I changed my mind and
> decided to go to the Catholic cathedral first and say my rosary ...
> I passed the ballroom on the way. They were still dancing. The
> thought came to me to go and ask Cyril what was the matter ...

A woman about to commit suicide does not normally change into a ball gown and worry that she might appear ridiculous in fancy-dress.

When Jacob returned to Government House she had changed into a 'peacock blue frock' and settled herself on the balcony where she could watch the movements of the people downstairs. Humphreys wanted to leave the ball because she had to catch the 2am transport back to Fremantle where she lived, but Jacob refused to go. She asked her friend to tell Gidley she wanted to see him. Humphreys did as she was asked.

A reporter attending the event for the Perth *Mirror* outlined what happened next:

> I don't think anyone particularly noticed the tallish, slim young girl ... who threaded her way through the dancers as the music was dying away and the crowd was demanding an encore. She made no display of her intentions, gave no sign of rage or hysteria. Near the centre of the hall slightly to the left, a well-dressed young man, dark, nicely featured and attired in full evening dress, was standing chatting to his partner. Until then all the actions of the developing drama had been commonplace. She was noticed by only a few as she approached the man ... The report of the revolver woke the dancers to the horror of what had happened. The man was slipping to the floor. They hurried over; believing there had been a joke somewhere; that a cracker had exploded or some humorist was seeking to cause a stir ... Someone bent to feel his pulse. The two young men lifted him up and then I saw a dreadful smear of blood on his lips, increasing as I looked, to a trickle ... then his face had that grey-green pallor that speaks only one thing. His eyes were open, and there was a look of wondering terror in them ...[22]

The band stopped playing the foxtrot, 'Follow Yvette'. A police officer, Constable Wood, was summoned quickly, no doubt from duty in the vice-regal residence. He testified at the inquest that he had heard a shot at around 1.30am. On proceeding to the ballroom, he saw a man lying on the dance floor with blood on his face. He went over to Audrey Jacob and took her by the arm. As he told the inquest: 'As I did so, she said, "I did it", and I then took the revolver from her.'[23]

Witness Claude Kingston covered the dead man with his dinner jacket out of a sense of decency to preserve the dignity of the dead. Many of the young men attending the ball had seen far too much death in all its indignities when they served in the army during the war.

Another witness to the tragedy, Frederick Crowder, stated that he had seen Jacob standing alone and then making her way across the throng on the dance floor: '… with that a shot rang out … as I knelt by his side I heard her say, "Well, I've got you now." She had a revolver in her right hand, at the side of her dress. A policeman arrived and I heard her say, "Get me out quietly and quickly."'[24] Gidley was carried into the cloakroom, where he died very soon after. The proceedings stopped just as he died. The band still concluded the evening by playing 'God Save the King'. Revellers left the scene after giving statements to the police, many unsure of what they had seen happen in such an unlikely venue.

Audrey Jacob was taken into protective custody. While Sergeant Brodie was waiting for the matron of the lock-up, he testified, the prisoner asked: 'Is he dead?' Brodie confirmed that Gidley had died within 'four or five minutes'. Jacob replied that 'he only got what he deserved! … Everybody who knows him will say the same.' Brodie's colleague, Constable Timms, corroborated Jacob's admissions. He stated that when asked why she had 'done such a thing', she replied: 'He had plenty of warning but he took no notice.'[25]

Jacob appeared before Police Magistrate A. B. Kidson the following morning amid a frenzy of press reporters and eager spectators. Remanded in custody, given this was a capital offence, she was charged with wilful murder. Beginning on 3 September, Kidson also conducted the three-day inquest into the circumstances surrounding

Cyril Gidley's death. The lives of both the victim and his alleged killer were laid bare during the proceedings. The stories were sordid and recriminatory, touching on rape, parental abuse, smuggling, blackmail and sexual promiscuity – all paraded before an eager public.[26] Coroner Kidson returned the verdict that Jacob had wilfully murdered Cyril Gidley, and she was ordered to stand trial in the Supreme Court of Western Australia.

The Supreme Court trial opened on 8 October with Hubert Parker (1883–1966), the son of Justice Sir Stephen Parker, presenting the case for the Crown before Justice John Northmore (1865–1968). Both were devoutly religious with his Honour known for leading prayers and Bible readings in his chambers.[27] Jacob was defended by Arthur Haynes, who proved to be a brilliant choice as he skilfully played on the prejudices and sympathies of the jury. He carefully rehearsed his client on how to dress, act and behave in this courtroom drama where reputations would be sullied and defended. Jacob dressed in the 'height of fashion' as a modern middle-class woman – but not as a flapper. Her calm demeanour and self-possession were commented on in the numerous newspaper accounts. She never wavered from her claim that this had all been a terrible accident, unplanned and unforeseen. This was the core legal issue: what had been her intent? Were there sufficient grounds for a plea of provocation, or was it wilful and meditated murder? There was no doubt that she had killed her former lover; the jury had to decide the circumstances behind it. Was it an accidental killing or deliberate?

Jacob told her story in the witness box calmly. She spoke in a clear, low tone, never raising her voice or displaying histrionics. The key part of her testimony involved going to say the rosary in the cathedral after she decided not to commit suicide. When her barrister asked her whether she had any intention to kill Gidley, she simply replied: 'No, none whatsoever.' When further asked whether she intended to harm Gidley, again she was resolute and direct in her response: 'No. If I could I would undo what has been done.' The Crown prosecutor was not so beguiled. He inquired how well she had practised using her revolver, to which Jacob replied that the event had been her first shot.

Not letting go of the crucial question of the revolver and whether it was accidentally discharged, Parker attempted to force Jacob to re-enact the death scene. This was a tactical mistake in terms of proving her guilt; Jacob appeared before the jury as a fumbling young woman unaccustomed to firearms and their use. When her counsel returned to cross-examine her, the jury began to sympathise with this solid young woman in the witness stand on trial for her life. In the scenario presented by Haynes, Gidley was a promiscuous, cruel and deceitful young man who had seduced and injured the reputation of an innocent convent-educated girl. Haynes' closing address to the jury was brilliant in its conception and execution:

> He would ask them to remember the tumult, which ran
> through the girl's brain. What did the future hold for her; to
> be thrown over by the object of her love and for whom she had
> the closest attachment and between whom there were ties. Life
> and her outlook presented an emptiness to her; and one could
> well understand her going home and lying on the bed and
> sobbing for half an hour; then seeing the revolver and walking
> out into the night to end her days.

The jury retired to consider its verdict and was back in less than three hours, returning at 8.45pm on 9 October 1925 after they had enjoyed their dinner break. They found the defendant not guilty and she was discharged.

Accompanied by her mother, Jessie Jacob, and a medical practitioner, she returned to her parents' home. The news of the verdict was flashed across the screens at various cinemas. Jacob left Perth and Australia for good, soon after marrying a wealthy New Yorker.[28]

CHAPTER 14

Eugenia Falleni, the 'Man–Woman' Killer

Eugenia Falleni, or, as she was mostly known, Harry Crawford, murdered her 'wife' Annie Birkett Crawford in 1917, dumping her body in Chatswood, Sydney, bushland on or about 1 October, the New South Wales Eight-Hour Day public holiday. When the story of the 'man–woman' murderer eventually came to light in 1920, the press had a field day with the titillating revelations that unfolded.* Not only had the accused 'married' and murdered one woman, but since had 'married' another unsuspecting woman two and a half years later. Rather than focusing on the murder and the callous way the victim had been discarded and buried, much of the coverage took the form of ribald speculation about the 'sex pervert' who had married two women, one of whom was a widow with a son.[1]

On 2 October 1917, Ernest Howard, a young employee of Cumberland Paper Mills at Lane Cove, saw what he thought were human remains on his way to work. The body was that of a woman. With the remains were a hatpin, part of a hat, a table knife, an empty whisky flagon, an enamel mug, a glass, a suitcase, a piece of greenstone and some cheap costume jewellery. The body appeared to have been burned alive. Police at first postulated that it was an alcoholic who had had an accident, hit her head and then fallen into a campsite fire.

---

* The terminology used in this chapter varies. When Falleni is in female apparel I call her 'she' otherwise as Harry Crawford I use 'he'.

The body remained unidentified despite investigations to discover the victim's name. But it was wartime, and enlistments in the army meant that police resources were scarce. The death of an itinerant or homeless person was simply not regarded as important. Newspapers did, however, run stories about the case, and pictures of some of the items found at the scene were included in an attempt to help identify the victim. No relatives came forward to make inquiries or claim the charred remains. Despite the autopsy finding that the woman had ended up in the fire while she was still alive – although unconscious – the inquest delivered an open verdict.

That month, in a cheap boarding house in rough maritime Woolloomooloo, on Sydney Harbour, the landlady, Mrs Henrietta Schieblich, was attempting to eject a troublesome boarder, Harry Crawford, an illiterate, unkempt man who was often drunk and abusive. Crawford told Schieblich that his wife had deserted him and that it was her teenage son, Harry Birkett, who was now residing with him. The boy, who was about fifteen, was harshly treated by his stepfather, constantly abused and humiliated. What the landlady didn't know was that Crawford had attempted to get rid of the boy, quite literally, not long before, going out one night to dig a grave in a remote spot along Bellevue Road. They had taken a ferry out to Watsons Bay with Crawford carrying a shovel for the occasion. When they came to a likely spot, Crawford made the boy dig a substantial hole. This was to be Harry Birkett's grave, dug himself under threat from his stepfather. But Crawford had second thoughts, and so the pair returned to the boarding house, arriving the following morning soaking wet and exhausted. Crawford told his landlady: 'I am going to kill the bastard.'

Crawford's behaviour was often weird and unsettling: he claimed that his rooms were haunted; drunken rages and shouting were common. One day, unwittingly, Mrs Schieblich said to him: 'Perhaps it is your wife that is haunting you. I think perhaps that you killed her.' She decided that the quickest way to make him leave was to tell him that the police had called around making inquiries about him. Crawford disappeared during the night.

She had in fact at one time considered contacting the police; Crawford, who was entirely illiterate, had become agitated when she read him the story of the mysterious charred body. The *Evening News* on 3 October 1917 ran a feature about the mysterious burned woman under the heading 'Was it Murder?'. The article mentioned her black lace stockings and her home-patched shoes. The sight of the shoes made Crawford especially agitated. He had muttered: 'That's her. That's her.' Neighbours also told the police that Crawford had often asked them to read out any articles about murders but not about any other news.[2] Young Harry Birkett was also, Schieblich stated later, upset when he saw the newspaper accounts, crying out: 'Oh, Mother! Mother! Mother! I don't know. I don't know.' This newspaper kept the story running, asking thirteen days later, 'Who Patched the Shoes?'. No one came forward and the case went cold. Yet no one found Crawford. Why Birkett did not go to the police and report his fears about his mother's safety is puzzling. But he was young and frightened of Crawford, which might have made him keep his fears to himself.

On 13 June 1920, Harry Birkett, now an apprentice tailor in the southern Sydney suburb of Sans Souci, and his aunt Lily Nugent reported to the police that his mother had been missing since October 1917. Birkett explained that he had believed she was living with Lily in Kogarah. It was the greenstone found in the fire that finally identified her. Nugent recognised it as belonging to her sister, and dental surgeons John McManus and H. G. Vernon at last confirmed that the set of dentures worn by the woman matched those supplied to a Mrs Birkett. Three weeks later, Detective Sergeant Stewart Robson and constables Walsh and Watkins took Harry Crawford in for questioning about the disappearance of his wife. He had been hard to track down since he frequently changed jobs and name, but they had located him working at the Empire Hotel in Annandale.

By this time the police knew that Crawford had been born in Italy. Detective Robson said to Crawford: 'You say your name is Harry Crawford and you were born in Scotland ... Have you any marks on your body that will assist in identifying you as a Scotsman and where you say you were born? ... I believe you are Italian.' When Crawford replied: 'No, I am a Scotsman from Edinburgh,' Robson continued his line of interrogation: 'Strip off a little and let me see.' Crawford objected.[3] The ploy was transparent; Robson was not looking for tattoos or ethnic markings. He was looking for something else. Members of the small Italian community in Sydney would undoubtedly have been aware of Crawford's longstanding masquerade and of the existence of a daughter named Josephine Falleni. Despite this, when Crawford suddenly admitted to being a woman during the police interrogation, the police were astounded as they surveyed the stocky, short, unkempt man before them. He told them his name was Eugenia Falleni.

Not only did Crawford come from a national group that many Australians of the time looked down on, but he was now marked as a 'sex pervert', and one who was crafty, secretive and perhaps even murderous.

By the end of the nineteenth century, the new field of sexology had emerged, investigating the basic categorisations of sex, sexual preferences and identity. Richard von Krafft-Ebing's innovative 1886 text, *Pyschopathia Sexualis*, had done much to formulate the concept of homosexuality, thereby forging the connection between practice and preference into a whole identity that defined a person. A cross-dressing woman such as Falleni, who did her utmost to act, dress and live as a man, was believed to belong to the most intractable level of degenerative homosexuality. Havelock Ellis, who had spent time in Australia, also studied sexuality and believed that homosexuality was a congenital abnormality bordering on deformity. Australian jurists, journalists and medical practitioners were aware of these new concepts which began to influence their discourse on sexuality and identity by the 1920s.[4]

The press had previously enjoyed reporting on the criminal cases of the likable larrikin and flamboyant cross-dresser Marion (Bill) Edwards, a mannish woman who enjoyed teasing out all the possibilities of gender alignment and display.[5] Other women who took on male roles were applauded. Flora Sandes, who served in the Serbian Army during World War I, was congratulated by the *Argus* newspaper as 'A Modern Amazon'. A woman called Maud Butler had enlisted in the AIF as a man and she too was praised for serving God, King and Empire.[6] But Harry Crawford/ Eugenia Falleni was not such a loveable character; indeed, she was to prove vicious and devious, determined to preserve her male gender identification at all costs, even murder.

Detective Robson searched Crawford's home at 47 Durham Street, Stanmore, where Crawford now lived with his new wife, Elizabeth Allison, an older woman in her first marriage. On searching the premises the police found a dildo in a locked leather trunk. Marked as Exhibit G1 – and called 'The Article' in the press – it was to be the central feature in the trial.[7] Presumably Crawford had already remarked on its existence to the police to explain how she could pass as a sexually active man. Robson reported that:

> I opened the bag. I got the article from it and asked the accused … 'Did your first wife know that you were using anything like this?' The accused said, 'No, not until the latter stages of our married life' … I said to the accused, 'Is this what you referred to as having used on your first wife?' I then took the accused to the Central Police Station where she [sic] was charged [with murder].

'The Article' also caught the medical profession's attention. At a lecture to the British Medical Association Branch in Sydney in 1921, a Dr Palmer brought along the dildo as a 'show and tell', explaining:

'This article was an artificial penis which Falleni had used in her various sexual adventures.'[8]

Its existence suggests that Falleni regarded herself as a man rather than a lesbian, exhibiting gender realignment rather than the desire to become a transvestite. Unlike Marion Edwards, who could play with gender identity for good effect, Crawford/Falleni possessed a transgender identity.

After he was arrested and charged with the murder of Annie Birkett, Crawford attended the Central Police Court on 6 July 1920, where he was refused bail. The press and public were also in attendance, interested to see how the accused would appear in what might be the solution to a longstanding unsolved murder. The next evening the *Evening News* revealed that Crawford was a woman masquerading as a man, sensationalising the case with the headline, 'The Man–Woman'. The public was hooked, eager for further salacious developments and sordid details. The issue of the murder rather paled into insignificance as the sexual elements of the case came to dominate both the court proceedings and the public's appetite for exposure and titillation.

The following day the newspaper carried the bare outlines of the drama, beginning with Harry Birkett's recent report to police that he was concerned about his mother's whereabouts. That she had disappeared nearly three years before did not seem to strike anyone as particularly strange. Nor did the fact that the boy had said he thought she was with her sister, although other evidence suggests that he had told his Aunt Lily that his mother had gone missing years ago. In the midst of the drama, the *Truth* pointed out a universal one on 11 July when it said that Falleni was 'better off as a man', able to earn far more for fewer hours work than as a female in low-paid unskilled labour.[9]

On 14 July 1920 the *Evening Sun* illustrated an article with a full-length photograph of 'Harry Crawford' dressed in a man's suit with shirt, tie and a man's hat. He was short and slightly built, with a rough weather-beaten and wrinkled face that was set into hard lines. The *Truth* on 11 July described the accused as having hollow cheeks, with a 'jaw square and masculine. The features generally are those of a man rather than a woman ... the face is lined and wrinkled and has the appearance of having been shaved.' The crowds gathered for Falleni/Crawford's second appearance at the Central City Court were eager to view this strange person accused of a grotesque crime. Daughter Josephine Falleni, who now worked in a jam factory in Pyrmont, had made statements to the police that day about her mother whom she rarely saw. She had gone to live with her 'father' and Annie Birkett when she was about fourteen but meetings were infrequent after Mrs Birkett disappeared.

Truth, a tabloid newspaper, provided more details about Eugenia Falleni's strange life on 18 July 1920, reporting that she had been married in Italy to a ship's captain named Martello. They had had a daughter, Josephine, who had been sent away by her harsh and uncaring mother. The truth actually was that Falleni had never been legally married to anyone, male or female.

When Falleni/Crawford appeared again in court on 28 July, the room was filled with spectators, most of them women. The *Sun* reported on 29 July 1920 that: 'She was still in male attire, and did not appear to heed what was going on in court. She fixed her eyes on the ceiling.'

Eugenia Falleni was born in Livorno, Italy, around 1875, her family moving to the unlikely destination of New Zealand when she was a toddler. Her gender inversion apparently started early. It was possible she was dyslexic since she was unable to concentrate or learn to read and write. In childhood she dressed as a boy and as a teenager sought work in male occupations such as bricklaying. Following the pattern of many disaffected adolescents, at least in their fantasies, Falleni ran away to sea on a cargo vessel plying the South Pacific routes. While on board she became pregnant, to whom and in what circumstances she never revealed. She left her life at sea around 1898, moving first with her little daughter, Josephine, born on 19 September 1898, to Newcastle. Josephine later testified that her mother 'was very cruel to me when I was a child. And used to frighten me ... my mother tried

The public pored over every salacious detail in the case of Eugenia Falleni (left), born a woman but living as a man. Eugenia killed her first wife to prevent the exposure of her secret. Photo: *Daily Telegraph*, 7 July 1920.

to smother me when I was a baby.' She was eventually fostered to a Mr and Mrs De Anglis, who lived in Double Bay. They were attached to the child and brought her up with care and affection. In the days before legal adoption these informal arrangements were commonplace.

Falleni resumed her male identity, now with the name 'Harry Crawford', and took on casual work, often in pubs, living in boarding houses for single men. At the age of twelve Josephine was sent out to work as a domestic servant and encouraged to become independent. At first she went out with Mrs De Anglis to clean the large houses in the area.[10] The girl had no idea that her 'father' was her mother until she was much older. She believed that her mother had died and this was the reason her father had had to have her fostered. Mrs De Anglis had apparently tried to protect her charge from too much knowledge.

Crawford started working as a coachman for a Dr Clarke whose practice was located in Lane Cove Road, Wahroonga, on Sydney's North Shore, in 1912. He lived above the stables and generally kept to himself, his leisure time spent in drinking bouts when he was known to become loquacious and a nuisance. Here he met a widow, thirty-two-year-old Annie Bell Birkett who worked as a cook–housekeeper for the doctor's family. Her son Harry, aged around ten, lived with her. Her husband, an English tailor named Harry Birkett, had died in 1906 leaving her few financial resources. Wahroonga was a sparsely settled, quiet area at this time, and the two servants were thrown into each other's company. Initially, Birkett was not impressed by the badly spoken, uncouth and frequently drunk coachman. She had ambitions – to set up a small business for herself – and regarded her work as a domestic as a means to social and economic improvement.

In 1913 Birkett purchased a confectionery shop in Balmain in inner Sydney. Crawford followed her, obtaining work at the local meatworks. He started a campaign to woo the young widow with constant gifts and offers to do odd jobs around the shop. Before long Crawford had moved in. They were married by a Methodist minister in Balmain that year. Crawford then refused to go out to work for a living. Due to his intemperate habits, inability to earn a wage and hostility to his stepson, tensions soon emerged in the household.

There were more surprises when Josephine Falleni, by then sixteen, turned up to see her 'father'. There had been no mention of a previous marriage or a child. She simply came to live with them. By this stage, Josephine was aware her 'father' was her mother and she reminded him that Mrs Birkett could not be deceived forever. She told 'her': 'She'll find out one of these days. My mother said, "Oh, I will watch it. I would rather do away with myself than let the police find out anything about me."'[11] At the trial there was considerable speculation about how the widow had not realised that her lover was a woman rather than a man.

Josephine started running around with men and became pregnant. This became too much for Birkett, who already disliked her cheeky, disrespectful stepdaughter. Tensions grew so much that Birkett sold her shop and went to live with her sister, Lily Nugent, in Kogarah. For a year or so she went to work for a Dr Binns as his housekeeper in Belgrave Street, Kogarah. Crawford started another romantic campaign to win her back and they were reunited. They went to live in Drummoyne, a suburb not far from Balmain, where the respectable, sober and conservatively dressed 'Mrs Daisy Crawford' contrasted to her short, bad-tempered, uncouth and often drunken husband, who spoke only broken English.

Lily Nugent wrote to her sister: 'I have found out something queer about Harry. I don't know what to do, but I'll tell you about it when I see you and get your advice ...'[12]

'There's something queer about Harry' is a phrase that has stuck to Crawford/Falleni to the present day. Without doubt, this was when Mrs Birkett discovered her husband was really a woman. She told her sister she intended seeking an annulment, without realising that she didn't need one since she was not actually married. But such an action meant public revelation, something Crawford deeply feared. Neighbours reported at the trial that Crawford and Birkett were a deeply unhappy couple, often arguing. The exact nature of their heated arguments and altercations was not revealed. 'Daisy' Crawford (as Annie Birkett was known) was certainly not a meek, subservient woman, however respectable her aspirations. Even though it was humiliating for her, 'Mrs Crawford' took in washing to make ends meet, with her young son running messages.

The day before the Eight-Hour Day holiday, a neighbour, Mrs Jane Wig, saw Crawford carrying a suitcase and dressed in a gabardine raincoat, although it was not raining. On the day of the public holiday, Crawford went to see another neighbour, Mrs Lydia Parnell, saying that his wife had not come home all night. He was apparently distressed that she might have run off with another man. Quite out of the blue he asked her son, George Parnell, if there had been anything about a murder or a dead woman in the papers.

On the Monday afternoon of the holiday, Harry Birkett returned home from work to find that his mother had gone without leaving a note, which was unlike her since the pair were close. Crawford, who sat drinking whisky at the kitchen table, told him: 'She's gone away with some friends – Mrs Murray and her daughter – to North Sydney.' Harry Birkett had never heard of these friends. Crawford soon arranged for everything in the house to be sold. Had he been more astute, young Harry Birkett would have realised then that something was drastically wrong. Why would his mother not tell him where she was and why would her husband simply sell all her furniture and belongings? They then relocated to Mrs Schieblich's boarding house at Woolloomooloo.

The trial in the Criminal Court before Chief Justice Sir William Cullen (1855–1935) began on 5 October 1920, three years after the disappearance of Annie Birkett. The accused was represented by an inexperienced barrister, A. McDonnell, who was instructed by Maddocks Cohen, while the Crown case was led by the highly experienced W. T. Coyle. Such unequal situations frequently occurred when the accused could not afford good representation or when no barrister was prepared to act pro bono. Crawford appeared in women's clothes, no doubt on the advice of her counsel. The Crown prosecutor opened his address by saying:

> I find it difficult to refrain from referring to the accused as
> he, but when I do you will understand that I mean the accused,
> who posed as a man, and definitely stated she was a man, and
> married two women as a man … all her actions since have been
> characterised by cunning and deceit.

This was a damning statement; yet a life of utmost deceit does not mean an individual has a proclivity to murder. Much of the trial was concerned with 'The Article' and its use, the source of much amusement on the part of many women in the public gallery. The

English operetta star Dame Marie Tempest and her husband Graham Brown attended the proceedings. Coyle apologised that he had to refer to such indelicate matters. But of course the public could not get enough. Falleni disliked the public and judicial gaze, and insisted on being shielded by a blue screen.

The Crown called twenty-seven witnesses, whereas the defence had only Josephine Falleni, whose mother had now been exposed by newspapers across the country not only as a freak of nature but as a potential murderer. Josephine often cried and was inarticulate throughout most of her testimony. Crawford/Falleni made no admissions or confessions, and even though by the 1920s the accused did at last have the right to testify in his or her own defence, Falleni did not take the stand. She would have made a poor advocate for herself in any case: her English was broken despite living all but two years of her life within the British Empire; she was rough, inarticulate and stubborn. The secrecy and deception that had been her way of life since adolescence could not now be broken even to save her own life. Researchers therefore have no direct evidence of how Falleni perceived herself or viewed the world.

The Crown had a body of circumstantial evidence. An orchardist, James Hicks from North Ryde, testified that he had seen a man coming down Lane Cove Road to the Cumberland Mills where he worked at about 5.30am on Eight Hour Day in 1917. He had identified Crawford in a police line-up. Sergeant Gorman reported under oath that kerosene had been found at the scene of the crime. Government Medical Officer Dr A. A. Palmer, who conducted the autopsy, gave his findings about the cruel and violent way the deceased had died. No one else had a motive to kill Annie Birkett, by all accounts a quiet and modest woman, and given the element of disfiguration nor was it the modus operandi of a killing done by a stranger.

Crawford had a strong motive to kill his 'wife' – Birkett had intended to expose him. This is a strange element of the case. Generally the threat of exposure most affects individuals with a public reputation; but Crawford/Falleni was an illiterate person with a low-paid, casual labouring job with no public reputation to speak of. With little else to go on, it can only be assumed that her identity as a man was so strongly embedded that she would do anything – including murder – to preserve it. Police also discovered that Crawford was in the habit of having affairs with other married women whose husbands were away, often on active service during the war. This occurred while he was married to Birkett as well as afterwards. Dr Palmer, who was fascinated by sexual inversion and its practices, later told the British Medical Association that:

> Each of these women had become aware that Falleni visited the other. One of them, actuated by ill-feeling and jealousy, had made a hole in the weatherboard wall of the other woman's bedroom and, looking through this hole, had witnessed cohabitation between Falleni and the second woman.[13]

The trial reeked of this kind of voyeurism. Yet some people were sympathetic to Falleni. Surgeon Herbert Moran, who wrote about the case in 1939, believed that '[s]ociety had been hunting her all these furtive years and she had become like a creature which when cornered turns with savage claws on the pursuer'.[14] But this overlooks the basic fact that Crawford was largely 'hunted' for murder, and a highly brutal callous one.

The jury was out for some two hours before delivering a verdict of guilty. Eugenia Falleni was sentenced to death, which was commuted to life imprisonment. An appeal was dismissed since there was no new evidence to assess and no one else came forward to confess. Falleni served just ten years before her release. She assumed the identity of 'Mrs Jean Ford' and kept a boarding house in Paddington. She was run over by a car in Oxford Street on 9 June 1938 and buried with Anglican rites at Rookwood Cemetery.[15]

CHAPTER 15

Fighting Back

How the legal system in Australia dealt with women brutalised and tyrannised by violent partners shows surprising sympathy and insight into the motivation of women who fight back. In November 1834, Ann Walsh (alias Smith) stood before the Supreme Court of New South Wales charged with inflicting a mortal wound on her de facto husband, John Taylor. A convicted felon, she had arrived from Cork in 1824 on the *Almorah*. Since the trial was conducted during the still-early days of the colony, the case was heard before a military jury and the chief justice, Sir Francis Forbes (1784–1841). Smith was undefended even though this was a serious offence, but she *was* able to produce witnesses on her behalf. A shoemaker, Charles Daniels, who owned a boarding house in George Street, Sydney, told the court that Smith and Taylor had lived together in his house. Their relationship was volatile, characterised by 'angry words' and violence.[1] On the morning of the fatal assault, 23 October, the couple had argued. In the course of the dispute, Smith got a knife and stabbed Taylor. He was taken to Sydney Hospital where he died a week later. Smith alleged that Taylor threatened her, was constantly violent and had recently struck her with a heavy door bolt. When asked by a juror whether she was drunk on the morning of the attack, she replied that she was not.

Taylor's employer, Gabriel Thompson, a bricklayer of Ultimo, testified that he had visited Taylor in hospital. He was a sober man, unlike most of his other employees, he reported. He told Thompson that on the day of the assault Smith had asked him to go to the public house and get her half a pint of rum, which he did. She consumed this before 8am and then ordered him to get another. When he refused, she knifed him. Thompson believed they had argued about her constant drunkenness, a common problem in Sydney in this period among both men and working-women.

For a woman who allegedly drank heavily and possessed no education, Smith showed herself to be adept at calling and examining witnesses. The chief justice recognised the mitigating circumstances that 'the deceased had previously used violence'. He believed 'a sudden impulse of passion had prevailed over discretion and one which did not call for the extreme severity of the law'. Even in the early nineteenth century, and in what was essentially still a penal colony, rather than give the full weight of punishment, Forbes understood the dynamics that had led to the woman's retaliatory violence.[2] Smith was convicted of the lesser charge of manslaughter – which did not have the mandatory death penalty – and sentenced to transportation for seven years. She died in the harsh secondary detention centre, Moreton Bay Penal Settlement, in January 1839, just prior to its closure.[3]

In the Saturday edition of *Bell's Life in Sydney and Sporting Reviewer*, on 9 April 1859, an unusual article was featured. Murders and domestic assaults were common fare much documented in newspapers. This particular article, though, featured a series of drawings, then uncommon. They depicted a thin depressed-looking middle-aged woman sitting in the dock of a courtroom dressed modestly in a bonnet and a cloak. Her hands were crossed demurely upon her lap. Mary Ann Perry was accused of the brutal murder of her husband, John Perry. The more astounding images were the drawings of the dead man in his bed, and one of the deceased's employers, painting contractor Henry Crane. Mary Ann Perry appeared the epitome of quiet respectability, a far cry from the drunken, riotous, emancipist female defendants more common in court in previous decades.

The couple lived in a small rented house in Burwood, where the Longbottom Government Farm had been established in 1821, and small farms were allocated initially to former soldiers in the New South Wales Corps. In 1855 Burwood was one of four inaugural railway stations in the colony. At the murder trial Sergeant William Grimmel testified that Perry was often drunk and abusive towards his wife: they '... lived very unhappily together'. Grimmel had frequently observed Perry drunk in public places, particularly in his current employment of painting the local public house. The local baker, John Blassett, stated that when he went to collect an outstanding payment around Christmas 1858, Mary Ann Perry came to the door, appearing 'very low spirited and melancholy ... but not as if she were drunk ... She had had words with her husband that morning ...'. When Blassett insisted on payment, Mrs Perry said to her morose husband: 'Here's the baker, and he wants his money.' Perry called out from inside the cottage that he would pay on Thursday to which his wife shouted in response: 'Come and tell him yourself.' After that incident the house was always closed.

The butcher, Alexander McCallum, told the court that on Christmas Eve Mary Ann Perry suddenly arrived at his house and asked to be allowed indoors. He offered her a glass of wine. She told him that her husband had 'turned her out' and she wanted to stay the night there. He responded that he could not allow a married woman to stay the night under his roof even in these circumstances. Obviously, Mary Ann Perry was desperate. To go to a tradesman whom she hardly knew and ask for shelter shows that. Some time later she said her husband had gone to Sydney, leaving her destitute. She asked McCallum to buy her pig and some of her furniture. When he went to the house he found it 'topsy-turvy' as if there had been a struggle. He purchased the pig for 30/-.

Other witnesses outlined the tensions within the marriage that had been keenly observed by the small community. A Mrs Elizabeth Menzies said she had spoken to Perry on 28 December and asked about her husband. Perry had replied that he had 'gone away that morning'. When asked for further details, she'd replied: 'Good bye,

God bless you!' She spoke of him as 'her poor dear husband …
When I asked her where he had supposed to have gone, she gave me
a long sigh, and said he had gone to heaven …' At this point the
police should have been called in to investigate John Perry's sudden
disappearance.

Mrs Chitley said that Mary Ann Perry arrived on her doorstep
unexpectedly on 29 December saying that her husband had stolen the
wages he was to pay the painters and had absconded to Sydney. She
asked to be allowed to stay the night even though the two women
were not close friends. She came back on New Year's Day, 'dejected
and crying', asking again to stay. She did not say at this time what was
bothering her or what specifically had occurred. Two days earlier, on
30 December, Perry had tried to sell a black bag, for which she was
given 4/-. Later, there was found to be blood inside the leather bag.
On 15 January 1859, Perry also tried to sell her furniture to a local
builder, William Lucas, and to the pawnbroker, Mrs Barnes. Still the
police had not been called.

Finally, on 10 February 1859, Sergeant Grimmel, accompanied
by Mr Linden, the owner of the cottage, went to the closed-up house
because of a number of complaints of a foul odour. On entering the
premises the detective found a man's body on a bed covered by a sheet.
It was the decomposing corpse of John Perry. The fully dressed body
was by now almost black, with a large gash across his temple. Grimmel
later said that he never noticed any smells coming from the cottage,
which he generally passed three or four times a day.

An inquest was convened to establish the cause of death. The jury,
as was common at this time, visited the scene of the crime and viewed
the body themselves. Mary Ann Perry was arrested and committed
to stand trial in the Central Criminal Court in April before Justice
Samuel Milford (1797–1865), who had served a disastrous term as
the inaugural resident judge in the Moreton Bay District in 1857. An
aloof, cold man more interested in equity, this sort of case hardly suited
his temperament. Perry was too poor to afford counsel. The court

Demure and respectable Mary Ann Perry was found guilty of killing her husband – 'a drunken character'. She received the death sentence but it was commuted to fifteen years in jail. Image: *Bell's Life in Sydney and Sporting Reviewer*, 9 April 1859.

appointed Charles Blakeney (1802–78), who had served as a barrister on the Moreton Bay Circuit of the New South Wales Supreme Court and went on that year to become its first resident barrister.

The case was prosecuted by the attorney-general, Sir William Montagu Manning QC (1811–95), as was the convention in the mid-nineteenth century. He had trained at Lincoln's Inn and was considered highly competent and with excellent judgment. He opened the Crown's case by stating that he believed the murder was committed on 27 December between 10am and 10pm but allowed that this could be disputed. With such a putrefying body the forensic science of the time would have found it difficult to ascertain the time of death. Discussing the issue of motive, Manning believed that the deceased was 'a drunken character', an indication that the Crown intended to be merciful in this case of domestic homicide. Even though this had been a brutal crime, with the victim killed with an axe as he lay asleep on the bed, it was implied that John Perry's drunken and abusive behaviour had contributed to his demise. Abused and battered women, then as now, often killed their assailants when they were asleep or drunk and incapable of retaliating.

The jury retired for an hour, returning with a guilty verdict. Perry was given the death sentence. Justice Milford informed her that he 'held out no hope to you of the commendation of your sentence. You must prepare yourself for death …' Mary Ann Perry had sat with a degree of depression and resignation throughout the trial and continued to keep her composure. She showed no emotion at all. Criminal cases at this time could not be appealed. Her only hope lay with the Executive Council. The premier, Sir Stuart Donaldson (1812–67), was a man of conservative principles, but even so his Executive Council did commute Mary Ann Perry's sentence to fifteen years' imprisonment.[4]

In March 1928, Norah Schieb was arrested for the murder of her husband, farmer Thomas Schieb from Bingera, near Bundaberg. The case hardly seemed to warrant a long investigation or lengthy trial, for Norah Schieb told the police: 'When I hit my husband with an axe I meant to kill him … I am glad I killed my husband. I am not one bit sorry.' Queensland had abolished capital punishment in 1922 but Schieb could still have spent the rest of her life in prison if found guilty. What happened in the course of her trial and the judge's sentence, though, indicates that the legal system was able to discern the impact of domestic violence, and to understand that the murder proceeded from prolonged and frequent spousal abuse.

Norah Schieb revealed that on 9 November 1927, Thomas Schieb arrived back at the farm around midday. He had been drinking that morning but was still sober. Later, she saw him drinking from a bottle of gin. When questioned about it, she said they 'began rowing all the time, [with him] wanting me to sign the farm over to him'. They jointly owned the farm and Thomas Schieb wanted full possession, then no doubt to eject his wife. Incessant arguments about his consumption of alcohol characterised this stormy marriage. Later on that day, after constant altercations, he struck her on the face and around the body.

Around 7pm he and one of the workers on the farm, John Barrett, drove off without saying where they were going. Returning an hour later both were 'paralytic drunk'.

Going down into the cane fields to be alone, Norah Schieb thought she would avoid the violence that usually attended these drunken episodes, but her husband followed her and 'started bashing me straight away ... and knocked me down and kicked me on the hip, and screwed my left arm'. A farm worker, Tom Burns, came to her assistance after he heard her screaming. He asked if she would like to be taken into town, presumably for her own safety. Around 10pm, Thomas Schieb had fallen fully clothed onto the bed to sleep off his drunkenness. Norah Schieb told the police:

> Seeing my husband Thomas Schieb was asleep I sneaked
> away down the veranda and down the steps and walked to the
> woodheap at the back of the house, picked up the axe from the
> woodheap and walked up the stairs and sneaked around the
> veranda to my husband's room and stood alongside the bed
> and I hit him three blows on the head with the back of the axe.
> I hit him so he would not wake up. When I hit my husband
> Thomas Schieb with the axe he never moved or spoke ...
> after I planted the axe I came back to my bedroom and laid
> on the bed and went to sleep and woke up about four o'clock
> this morning and about five o'clock I had a wash and went to
> inform Constable Dwyer of South Kolan Police that I had
> killed my husband ...

Like Mary Ann Perry, Norah Schieb waited until her husband was asleep and unlikely to wake before she killed him. This was her defence against constant brutality witnessed by staff and neighbours.

Schieb was arrested for the wilful murder of her husband, standing trial in the circuit sittings of the Supreme Court of Queensland at Bundaberg on 5 March 1928 before Justice Frank

Brennan (1884–1949). The elevation in March 1925 of this former Labor parliamentarian, solicitor and Minister for Health and Public Instruction had been controversial. His was an inherently political appointment; moreover Brennan was initially not a barrister. Brennan had applied to become a barrister in 1924 using the amendment to legislation allowing solicitors of five years' standing to practise at the bar.[5] What he lacked in courtroom experience was more than compensated for by his deep understanding and sympathy for ordinary people, largely arising from his abiding Catholic faith.

The accused could have pleaded guilty since she had confessed to the police that she had killed her husband. But at the trial she pleaded not guilty. Schieb was represented by Edwin J. D. Stanley, the nephew of the chief justice, Sir James Blair. He had begun his career in the Crown Law Office before entering private practice in 1923. Like his uncle, he was a man possessed of an enormous social conscience, as well as a competency that saw him elevated to the bench in 1944.[6] Given the personal characteristics of the presiding judge and her counsel, Schieb could not have been more fortunate in her trial. Justice Brennan soon ascertained through his cross-examination that the defendant had suffered what appeared to be brain damage from the brutality she suffered during her marriage. The police also reported her rambling speech, although this could be accounted for by the stress and trauma brought on by her actions.

During his cross-examination of Dr Egmont Schmidt, who had conducted the postmortem, Stanley questioned closely about the physical and mental state of the accused and the deceased. Dr Schmidt reported that Thomas Schieb was a powerful man physically, unsurprising since he owned a cane farm, which required considerable manual labour. He also believed that while the accused was 'just an ordinary woman ... she was subnormal' in intelligence. The question of whether she was insane or suffering 'mental depression' was canvassed. Dr Schmidt believed – although he was not a psychiatrist and nor did he examine the accused immediately after the offence – that she might have been temporarily insane, and that was what had given her the extraordinary physical power to kill a strong man with an axe; parts of Thomas Schieb's skull had been found two metres from his body.[7]

The all-male jury found Norah Schieb guilty of the lesser offence of manslaughter, and made a strong recommendation for mercy. In his sentencing statement Justice Brennan stated that this had been a violent marriage where the prisoner could quite easily have been killed by her husband. There was no evidence presented in the Magistrate's or Supreme Court that she had been violent, except during the lethal attack. The testimony of witnesses was that the deceased could indeed have killed his wife that day, had it not been for their intervention. Schieb was released since Justice Brennan 'saw no good reason for sending the woman to gaol'.[8]

Although in the late 1920s there was no formal idea of 'battered woman syndrome' or legal apprehension of the cycle of domestic violence, some jurists, members of juries and legal counsel understood the dynamics that led women, so often described as 'perfectly ordinary', to murder their brutal husbands by stealth and with immense savagery.

A violent perpetrator of domestic violence was not always killed by the victim. Sometimes a child acted to end perpetual terror and abuse, often in defence of her mother. In April 1909, teenager Esther Salon, who lived with her family in the regional district of Marengo, near Young in New South Wales, shot her father with a revolver as he tried to choke her mother. Henry Salon had previously attempted to kill his wife in 1903, and had been bound over to keep the peace for six months. He often threatened to kill his wife, causing her to live in constant fear. The coroner reported that Esther's actions had been in protection of another's life and the children's court discharged her.[9] Patricide and matricide are rare crimes, usually only committed in such extreme circumstances.

In 1937 Kathleen Burnes was brought to trial in Charleville for the wilful murder of her stepfather, Anthony Trioly. Sergeant H. J. Kirk told the Magistrate's Court in the committal hearing that he had gone to the local bowling green where he found the deceased, Mary, his wife, and Kathleen Burnes, his married stepdaughter. Burnes told Kirk: 'I shot him. He came home drunk and was trying to choke Mum. My little sister Nettie came running to my house and told me that Dad was drunk and was trying to kill them all. I got my husband's rifle and I saw him trying to choke my mother. I called out for him to let her go. He then rushed at me and I lifted the rifle and fired …'[10] Burnes was committed to stand trial for wilful murder.

The case was heard before Justice Edward Archibald Douglas (1877–1947) in the circuit sittings of the Supreme Court of Queensland held in Charleville, a small regional community north-west of Brisbane. Douglas was the son of a Scottish aristocrat, John Douglas, a former premier of Queensland. He brought years of living and working on Thursday Island (where at various times his father had been a magistrate), mixing with a rough multi-ethnic community, to the bench. This had equipped him with an experience of life unusual in the judiciary.

Burnes pleaded not guilty to the charge despite her confession to the police. Evidence at the trial revealed that Trioly was frequently violent towards his family, especially when he was drunk. Mary Trioly's sister, Bonnie Campbell, testified that Mary and the youngest daughter, Anthonette (Nettie), lived in constant fear for their wellbeing, safety and lives. Neighbours verified the accounts of the extreme and frequent domestic violence in the Trioly household. On one occasion the deceased had chased Kathleen Burnes and another young woman with a knife, intending to harm them. The defendant was so terrified of her stepfather that she would wake up screaming in the night, terrified that he would enter her marital home and kill her.

Mary Trioly testified that her husband had tried to kill her younger daughter and that when she intervened he had 'kicked her in the stomach'. When she fell over, he 'lifted her to her feet by her hair. He then seized her throat and threatened to choke her.' On the day of his death, Trioly tried to kill his wife and only stopped when he was confronted by his stepdaughter, Kathleen Burnes. Justice Douglas recorded in his notebook that the deceased 'was a dangerous man when under the influence'.

The all-male jury selected from Charleville considered their verdict for just three minutes before entering a not-guilty verdict. To a man, they fully accepted that on the day of his death, the deceased was intent upon violence and perhaps murder against his wife and ten-year-old daughter, and that the defendant had acted to protect them and herself. Kathleen Burnes was discharged.[11]

Since Mary Ann Perry's case, a new century had brought a different and more enlightened perspective to cases argued as self-defence. The judges and juries in the cases of Norah Schieb and Kathleen Burnes understood that in both instances the man who had been killed was a violent abuser who terrorised his family, often in the full sight of others. A broader conceptualisation of self-defence was accepted in the case of Schieb, who had killed her abuser when he was drunk and sound asleep.

Both cases were still unusual because, in general, neighbours and employees rarely intervened in marital disputes, even those that appeared rancorous or even dangerous, driven by the customary wisdom that no one should 'come between a man and his wife'. Marriage was a private domain where a man could rule wife and family, literally without inference. The longstanding tradition of a man's 'ownership' of his wife and children was still enshrined in common-law doctrines. Even in the late 1890s everything a woman brought into a marriage passed into the ownership of her husband, as did everything she might receive afterwards; a wife also had no rights over her children at all. These archaic and intolerant laws concerning a woman's right to divorce, legally separate, own property and keep bequests, and to keep her wages, were challenged in the later nineteenth century.

In 1857, the United Kingdom passed legislation allowing divorce by petition. South Australia followed with its legislation the following year.

By 1863, all the Australian colonies now allowed husbands to petition for divorce on the grounds of a wife's adultery. Late amendments allowed women to petition on the grounds of adultery with cruelty, drunkenness and criminality.[12] Justice William Windeyer in New South Wales led the reform movement to increase women's rights with regard to matrimony.[13] Women's Property Acts allowing married women to retain their own property and earnings were passed in the 1890s along with rights of custody of their children.[14] Yet, in spite of the immense gains in women's political rights as enfranchised citizens, the informal rule of a husband within the internal dynamics of the family persisted. Indeed, it has persisted into the twenty-first century.

Norah Schieb's case was unusual: women who killed abusive partners when they were asleep, drunk or unconscious were, in general, considered to have committed wilful murder rather than to have been acting in self-defence. This was because the offences were not committed in a moment of imminent threat – for example, the conventional scenario of a 'pub brawl' – instead, they waited until the abuser was unable to retaliate. So of course their actions appear premeditated and the women appear vengeful, sneaky and vicious.

Then in 1979, American researcher Dr Lenore E. Walker published a landmark study entitled *The Battered Woman*. This study sought to understand the complex cycles of violence that characterised a considerable number of domestic environments. Walker specifically focused on why women who experience severe domestic violence persist in a relationship that humiliates, brutalises and sometimes even kills them. The defence was first tested in Australia in the Erika Kontinnen trial in 1991 in South Australia, and, accepted in the appeal, the 'battered woman syndrome' has now become a more widely used explanatory argument for defence counsel in common-law jurisdictions.[15]

Erika Kontinnen never denied that she killed Edward Hill. At 7.30am on 28 March 1991, she went to the Angas Street Police Station accompanied by Hill's de facto wife, Olga Runjanjic, to say as much. The levels of sadism, terror, violence and deprivation of liberty the deceased man perpetrated on the two women are almost unbelievable.

Kontinnen was a poorly educated woman with few life or employment skills. She had been involved with Hill's cousin Ronald for nearly a decade before he left her for another woman. However sympathetic he at first appeared, Edward Hill hated women, allegedly because he had contracted syphilis at the age of eighteen. By the time he was just twenty-five, he had thirteen convictions for violence, including assault upon a homosexual with whom he lived in a predatory relationship.[16] His upbringing had been troubled, with an aggressive and violent father. He spent much of his youth in reformatories and boys' homes, and was an avid follower of the mass murderer Charles Manson. At one time, Hill had admitted himself to hospital fearing his violent urges were out of control.[17]

Erika Kontinnen alleged she was forced into a sexual relationship with Hill in 1988. He was then living with his common-law wife, Olga Runjanjic, with whom he later had a son, Archie. Like Kontinnen, Runjanjic had little formal education and was forced to work as a prostitute to supplement the couple's unemployment benefits. With this income they purchased a property at Swan Reach in north-west Victoria. Soon after Kontinnen moved in with the couple, Hill pressured her to purchase the adjoining property in order to start a firewood business. Since she had a job at the local Bridgestone factory and could go guarantor on the loan, Kontinnen was in a position to further the threesome's interests. She agreed.

Almost as soon as the ink had dried, Hill began to be abusive and violent towards her, contending that she now threatened his financial security by taking out a loan which he had no means of servicing. His solution was to force both women to become prostitutes as well as running a telephone sex business. Initially, Kontinnen refused, but the beatings endured by Runjanjic escalated so quickly and became so horrific that she consented.

Hill treated his two 'wives' as slaves – at his beck and call, administering to every whim and fantasy, no matter how abhorrent. He ran a regime of terror, not allowing them to sleep for any extended period or to have any personal autonomy. His physical violence was so severe that both women frequently ended up in hospital. Even then Hill forced them to leave before adequate treatment was completed. On one occasion, Runjanjic had a wound on her head that became infested with maggots, which Hill found highly amusing. He was cruel to Archie in front of the women, throwing him against the wall and even holding his head underwater. Another time he held a shotgun to the little boy's head to terrorise his mother.

Kontinnen and Runjanjic formed a close bond, united by their fear of Hill and their concern for each other, and for Archie. Hill was inordinately proud of his sexual prowess and often brought other women to the house, as well as forcing Runjanjic to have sex with other men so he could watch. This would in turn lead to accusations of infidelity, for which Runjanjic would then be beaten so severely that she would have to be hospitalised. Hill brought gay lovers to the house sometimes. He threatened the women that if either left him, or if he was sent to prison, he would ensure they were both 'executed'. Hill also frequently beat the two women in public, yet no one attempted to intervene or reported the incidents to the police. As in most cases of domestic violence, at certain parts of the cycle Hill could be charming, contrite and easygoing. But these periods became increasingly rare.

Kontinnen and Runjanjic appeared in the Supreme Court of South Australia in May 1991 on the charges of falsely imprisoning Patricia Hunter and causing her grievous bodily harm. Hill, who had also been charged with this crime, was by this time dead. The victim was a longstanding friend of Kontinnen who had been critical of her relationship with Hill. It was alleged that some articles had been stolen from a house in Adelaide where Kontinnen, Hill and Runjanjic lived when they came into Adelaide. Hill alleged that the thief was Hunter. On a pretext devised by Hill, Kontinnen lured her to the Swan Reach property, where Hill beat her with a shotgun. He then handcuffed her to a bed and cut the rings from her fingers even though she had a broken arm that required medical attention. Hunter was then moved to another property and held there against her will for almost a week, from 29 May 1989 to 3 June 1989.

In the original trial, the defendants Kontinnen and Runjanjic denied they knew that violence would be used against Hunter. Yet, at the same time, they contended that they were so terrorised by Hill they had to go along with his plan. The pair were found guilty. In their appeal in 1992, their counsel, K. V. Borick, argued that the case was a notable instance of the 'battered woman syndrome'. He outlined Kontinnen's and Runjanjic's lives with Hill and described how he had terrorised them, keeping them in mortal fear. The work of Lenore Walker, as well as cases in the United States and Canada that had tested the assumptions, were cited by defence counsel in the appeal. Chief Justice Leonard King, Justice Christopher Legoe and Justice Derek Bollen accepted the veracity of the syndrome that led women to act abhorrently when they are completely under the control of another person.[18] Kontinnen and Runjanjic were retried in early 1993 and sentenced to three and a half years' jail, which was suspended on payment of a three-year good behaviour bond.

Before being retried for the Hunter case, Kontinnen was tried for the murder of Edward Hill on Monday 28 January 1991. The story emerged that the day before, Hill had been particularly aggressive, and had been threatening and attacking Runjanjic with a broom. Her face and legs were injured. The two women took Archie and fled the house, hiding in a park. Since they had no money, they were forced by necessity to return home, where they knew they would be punished. Kontinnen later left the house to service one of her clients. When she returned that night, she decided to read a magazine but when Hill saw her reading without his permission he made her stand at the back of the room. When Archie started to cry, Hill became even more infuriated.

Hill then proceeded to beat Kontinnen. When he finished, he said quietly and matter-of-factly: 'I'm tired. I'm going to get some sleep and all yous [sic] will be dead when I wake up.' Kontinnen got a gun and shot him, although she could not recall these events. The two women fled with the baby and went to a local service station, where Kontinnen called a friend, who urged them to go to the police. Hill was known to the police. The women were reportedly so concerned about their own safety that, on returning to the scene, Kontinnen climbed in through a window to see if Hill was still alive.[19]

Kontinnen's trial outlined the level of violence, terror and threats to which Hill had subjected Kontinnen, Runjanjic and Archie Hill on an almost daily basis. The jury accepted that Kontinnen had acted in defence of herself and the others, and she was acquitted.

When asked by the police: 'How could you still love him?' Runjanjic replied: 'Love is strange, love is blind.' Kontinnen also added: 'Sometimes I felt I loved him.'

Three years later, in 1994, Margaret Raby was charged with the wilful murder of her husband, Keith, who, she testified, had defecated, urinated and vomited on her. She was subject to constant sexual torture and humiliation. He left firearms around their marital home that he threatened to use on a constant basis. In her trial before Justice Bernard Teague in the Victorian Supreme Court she testified that, 'I loved Keith very much, with all my heart, and I thought what I could give him, sir, with my love and psychiatric help, we could overcome what he did to me.'[20] Like Kontinnen and Runjanjic, Raby exhibited a common response of women in violent domestic relationships. They love their partner and feel responsible for his behaviour and the subsequent abuse. This sense of responsibility, as well as the attrition of autonomy and escalation of fear, goes some way to explaining why women in such relationships are unable to leave their abuser.

Raby's trial was the first time the battered woman syndrome had been successfully used as part of a defence in Victoria.

CHAPTER 16

Deadly Lovers' Pacts in the Nineteenth Century

Marriage was the bedrock upon which society was founded, and men were in sole charge of the union. Until 1923 in the United Kingdom, the only grounds for divorce was adultery – and the only person who could sue for divorce was a husband. Before that time, a man could be as unfaithful, cruel and violent as he liked. If his wife left him, he kept everything – all her property, all her money ... and the children. It was possible after 1878 for a woman to legally separate from her husband, but she could not divorce and therefore could not marry again. After 1923, adultery became grounds for both husbands and wives to divorce, and in 1937 the additional reasons of cruelty and desertion were added. It was not until the 1970s that no-fault divorce became a reality, with a more equal approach to sharing property and care of any children. The very fact that women could be trapped in loveless, cruel or squalid marriages with no recourse or support meant that sometimes the desire for escape could take on a deadly form.

Lucretia Dunkley and her lover, Martin Beech, were executed in 1843 for the wilful murder of Lucretia's husband Henry Dunkley, a successful farmer from Goulburn. He had been killed with such force that his face had been almost obliterated. Situated 200 kilometres from Sydney, Goulburn was the first regional inland town in the colony of New South Wales. British settlement had been permitted from 1825, although few then ventured so far into this remote and dangerous place. In 1827 William Pitt Faithfull (1806–96) was granted land on the Goulburn plains. The first legal land sales were conducted in 1839. Soon the authorities in Sydney despatched convicts to the area to work in road gangs, many of whom were housed in the Towrang Stockade. Others, like Tom Shepherd transported from Southampton in 1830, worked as 'ticket of leave' (paroled) convicts for private settlers such as Henry Dunkley.

The courts had become accustomed to dealing with disgruntled convicts who took up arms against their assigned masters and injured or killed them. But the circumstance of the wife of a respectable free farmer who appeared to have conspired with her convict lover was particularly unsettling. Her origins were far from respectable as she had been transported from Wales.[1] Suspicions were aroused when Dunkley tried to sell some wheat without her husband's presence. When questioned later at her farm, Dunkley told police that her husband had been murdered by Martin Beech, a ticket-of-leave convict in their employ. On 19 September 1842, almost a week after the crime was later revealed to have taken place, Sergeant John Cook went to the farm and found the body of Henry Dunkley. Beech was arrested and taken to the lock-up in Goulburn.

Dunkley was taken to see Beech where she said that she had no idea why he would kill his master. His clothes were stained with blood, but this, Beech said, came from a bullock he had killed. The police took Beech to the farm to view the body, which he initially denied could be that of Henry Dunkley and obdurately refused to touch when he was asked to. Meanwhile Henry's widow threw herself onto the corpse, which she kissed with a great show of affection and grief.

The story she told was unbelievable. Dunkley alleged that she was asleep with her husband on the night of 13 September 1842, when Beech entered their bedroom and murdered the sleeping man with an axe. She hid under the bed but then helped him conceal the crime. She did not call out for the other convicts and servants to come to her aid or to call the police. This and the fact that the day before her husband's murder she had told people that he was going to Goulburn the next morning point to her as a willing accomplice. At the inquest on 28 September both Dunkley and Beech were held over for the wilful murder of Henry Dunkley.[2]

The trial in the Supreme Court of New South Wales was held before the chief justice, Sir James Dowling (1784–1844), and a civilian jury in Berrima on 5 September 1843. Servants on the farm testified that Mrs Dunkley had conducted a sexual liaison with Beech.[3] Dunkley alleged that her co-accused was solely responsible for the murder, although a report of the inquest says that they had planned to sell Henry Dunkley's property, marry, and move hundreds of kilometres away 'where no one knew what they had done'.[4] It may also have been that she had set Beech up, using their sexual liaison and promises for the future. In any case, Dunkley denounced Beech to police right from the start of the investigation. During the trial she shouted abuse at him, at the Crown prosecutor, and at the jury and judge. She frequently laughed and called every witness a liar and a perjurer. By contrast, Beech was composed and calm.

The jury took just five minutes to find the pair guilty of wilful murder. They were both sentenced to be hanged 'without the least hope of human mercy'. Chief Justice Dowling's sentencing remarks are worth examination. Even though he was accustomed to dealing with loud, aggressive and violent behaviour from convict women, Dowling still felt compelled to tell Dunkley that she was 'the Devil in female form ... a drunken polluter of the rites of Hymen, the violator of every tie by which the sacred institution of marriage can unite in holy wedlock, yielding to brutal lust and with her paramour, consummating her guilty passion in the blood of her husband'. He also invoked the medieval concept of *petit treason*, now no longer in use in common-law jurisdictions. But in those days, wives and servants were beholden to their 'masters'. If either one took up arms against their lawful master, then the penalty was severe. Dowling also accused Beech of violating his duty to his master by 'murderous treason'.

Dowling was disappointed that 'the humane spirit of the modern age forbids the dreadful severity ... by which the treasons of a murderous wife was expiated by burning alive'; Lucretia Dunkley was lucky that burning at the stake had been outlawed in England in 1790. What had not been known at the trial was that Dunkley was pregnant. She and Beech were executed in Berrima jail on Monday 9 October 1843[5] and later 'anatomised' and dissected by the local surgeon James Ramsay. Their skulls and the skeleton of the foetus were donated by Dr Ramsay in November 1854 to the Australian Museum, where they were placed on public display.[6]

Sometimes lust and greed produce a volatile mixture that prompts murder. In 1855 Bridget Hurford became the first woman executed in Western Australia. Her supposed lover, Enoch Dodd, was also hanged. Philip Dixon, who had forged the last will of John Hurford, was found guilty of forgery and sentenced to transportation to Van Diemen's Land for the term of his natural life.[7] He was only pardoned because he had turned queen's evidence. At first the accomplices had got away with murder, for the medical practitioner conducting the autopsy, Hannibal Bryan, was later found to be neither qualified nor registered. He was so incompetent he did not know the most basic procedure and could not even use a stethoscope, which, invented in France in 1816, was by then, forty years later, a widespread medical instrument. Bryan found nothing suspicious about the elderly man's sudden death.

John Hurford had arrived as a free man soon after the Swan River Colony was established in 1829. He first went to Augusta and then moved to Wonnerup Inlet near Busselton, where he took up farming. Most of his workers were former convicts, frequently those who found it difficult to find employment, even with significant labour shortages in the new settlement. Hurford was described as an eccentric who worked hard and kept company with vagabonds and tough former felons. In 1851, at the age of sixty-five — then considered ancient — he married. By this stage he was a wealthy man who had accrued a small fortune of £2000. His new wife, Bridget Larkin, was a young widow with three children: Thomas, Bridget and Neddy Larkin.[8] Her husband, a soldier in the 21st Regiment, had recently drowned in Bunbury, and she was desperate to secure her family's security.

From the start Hurford was allegedly abusive and aggressive towards her husband. Not only verbally abusive but on one occasion she had knocked him down, dislodging some of his teeth. After just four years he tired of the constant quarrelling and violence. He went to live with his neighbours, the Greens, after his wife had pushed him out of his bed and onto the floor, this being the final straw. At the Greens, Hurford lived in one room, being forced to share it with a servant, George Jones.[9] Despite how substantial his own house was – with a separate kitchen, several bedrooms and dairy – sharing with Jones was, for Hurford, far preferable to living with his wife. At the end of six weeks, however, his neighbour explained they needed the room to store barley, and so Hurford was obliged to return home. He was so afraid of his wife that he asked Jones to come and share his bedroom.

On 8 April 1855, Hurford complained of feeling unwell with a severe sore throat. Bridget Hurford gave him some mulled wine. She also asked Jones to sleep in another room to give her husband a chance to rest. Later that night John Hurford was found dead in his bed; his eyes were open and protruding and there were red marks on his neck. The inquest found, on the evidence of 'Dr' Hannibal Bryan, that he had died of natural causes. Witnesses confirmed that the old man had indeed complained of a sore throat, which was swollen. Hurford's will was probated and Bridget Hurford became a wealthy woman.

Later in April, Enoch Dodd confessed to Philip Dixon that he had killed John Hurford and that the whole plot had been Bridget Hurford's idea. On the night of the murder she had urged Dodd to act, with the inducements of a horse and £10 – and the influence of large quantities of alcohol. When he baulked, she stood over him until he had strangled her husband to death. Dodd and Dixon were both ticket-of-leave convicts and hardened men. Yet both found this callous murder of the elderly man who employed them under good conditions repugnant. But that didn't stop Dodd ransacking the dead man's belongings with Bridget Hurford.[10]

In September 1855, a lengthy magisterial inquiry was held in Vasse to reconsider the death of John Hurford. On 24 August, Hurford and Dodd had been charged with murder and Dixon with forgery. It was revealed at the inquiry that Bridget Hurford maintained her own home on the property, which had several subdivisions, some with tenant farmers. Several witnesses testified that Hurford had said he would never leave his wife a farthing, and also that the signature on the will was not that of the deceased. A highly literate employee, Andrew Norman, told the magistrates' hearing that he customarily did all correspondence for Hurford and had not been asked to arrange a new will.[11] Neighbour John Green revealed that Hurford had been prepared to sell his property to get away from his wife and that 'several people' had come to view it.[12]

On 4 October 1855, Bridget Hurford and Enoch Dodd appeared before Justice William Mackie (1799–1860), a highly competent jurist trained at Trinity College, Cambridge, and the Inner Temple. He was one of the first free settlers to arrive in the Swan River Colony in October 1829.[13] In this trial he was assisted by a bench of magistrates, but not a jury. His health was poor and there was speculation that he might not be able to take on such a complicated case. Richard Birnie (1808–88) was the advocate-general. He came from a distinguished legal family; his father, (Sir) Richard Birnie, had identified the Cato Street conspirators in the 1820 plot to assassinate the British prime minister and cabinet, the last time in British history that prisoners convicted of high treason were hanged, drawn and quartered.[14] Hurford was defended by Nathaniel Howell, who had arrived in Western Australia in 1853 at the age of twenty-one. Despite his youth and inexperience, Howell was an able counsel, skilled in cross-examination. It was to no avail – Hurford and Dodd were found guilty of wilful murder and sentenced to death.

On Monday 15 October 1855, Bridget Hurford and Enoch Dodd were publicly executed in the new Fremantle jail along with a convict, George Williams, who had attempted to murder a warder. The public eagerly awaited the well-publicised event. Just before 7am a military and police escort took the male prisoners on open carts to the place of execution, where they had to wait some ten minutes before Hurford arrived in a closed cart. Dodd appeared to be very distressed but Hurford was quiet and weak. She had confessed to the crime before her death. A Roman Catholic priest accompanied her to the gallows saying prayers as they walked along. He took charge of her body when it was cut down after hanging for thirty minutes. After Hurford's body was removed from the gallows the two men were hanged. The newspapers commented that many women had attended the executions.[15]

Elizabeth Scott was hanged in 1863 for killing her husband with the help of her lover and another accomplice. She was the first woman to be executed in the colony of Victoria. Her life had been marred by tragedy and brutality that belied a genteel upbringing in England. Scott was born in 1840 in Twickenham, a settlement identified in the Domesday Book of 1086, on the southern side of the Thames River near the beautiful royal parks of Richmond. When she was twelve, her parents moved to Canterbury in New Zealand before deciding to try their luck on the Victorian goldfields.

For a young girl with a sensitive disposition the goldfields were a rude shock. They were rough, dirty and violent. Most people lived in tents that could be easily transported as the goldfields expanded and moved. Dysentery and cholera were constant reminders of the lack of public health facilities; there were few resources or public infrastructure of any kind. People who came to make their fortunes often became desperate when their rewards did not match their hopes. Robert Scott was one who had initially been fortunate; he had accumulated a considerable financial asset from his prospecting. But as a severe alcoholic he had drunk much of it away. In 1854, believing he was far wealthier than he was, and when she was just fourteen, Elizabeth's parents forced her to marry this uncouth, drunken man of thirty-six. Their daughter did not end up in the life of gentility and luxury they had anticipated.

By the time she was twenty she had borne four children, two of whom had died in the unsanitary conditions. Robert Scott set up a grog shanty between Mansfield and Devil's River in the north-east of the colony, an area later famous as the stomping ground of the Kelly Gang. The Scott shanty was on the stock route and isolated from other dwellings. With Elizabeth Scott's fine looks and good manners it soon became a popular meeting place offering food, accommodation and alcohol for the many lonely single men working in the district.[16] Scott was also a shrewd businesswoman who knew how to grow the small business. Before long she fell in love with a nineteen-year-old farm labourer, David Gedge, who was kind, shy and adoring. Like her he was English, having been born at Deptford in Kent, and was accustomed to finer things than the Devil's River grog shanty.

Despite Robert Scott's obsessive watchfulness over his pretty young wife's movements, Gedge and Elizabeth Scott became lovers. They often met when Robert Scott lay drunk and unconscious at night. At other times they met in the nearby stringybark forest. Elizabeth began to plan a life away from the squalor and crudeness, although a quiet young man with no ambition was unlikely to be able to give her a comfortable new life. Elizabeth Scott also had another ardent admirer in the form of their Macao-born general servant, Julian Cross, who despised his employer and the manner in which he treated his wife. Cross was not aware of Elizabeth Scott's liaison with Gedge, and evidence suggests that his attentions towards his mistress remained platonic.

On 13 April 1863, a merchant named Ellias Ellis and his wife, Ellen, stayed at the Scotts' establishment for the night on their way to Melbourne. They had already stayed there three days earlier, on their way to Jamieson, then a small goldfield supply settlement. On that occasion they both saw Elizabeth Scott and Gedge leave the bar at around 5pm, go to the stables and lock the door, and then return again an hour later, coming inside hand in hand. The middle-aged couple said nothing, since it was hardly their business to monitor other people's morals.

During their second stay, on 13 April, the Ellises pitched their tent about 20 metres from the Scotts' house. Elizabeth Scott was starved of feminine company and confided to Ellen Ellis how troubled and unhappy her marriage was. She explained how her parents had forced her to marry when she was still practically a child, and how worried she was that her husband drank so frequently and so much that he was ruining his health and their livelihood. He was suicidal, constantly telling anyone who would listen that he intended to end his misery with a shotgun.

That night Elizabeth Scott asked Mrs Ellis to help her with her husband, who was suffering from delirium tremens. He lay shivering, his teeth chattering, complaining that he was freezing. Mrs Ellis rubbed his feet and suggested that it was time to call in a doctor. Even though there was none nearby, she insisted, in case Elizabeth was later called to account for her husband's death, which seemed imminent. Mrs Ellis stayed to have a nobbler of whisky with him. When she went into the kitchen, she saw Elizabeth Scott and David Gedge huddled at the table deep in conversation. Then Gedge left the two women to talk. After she returned to her tent, Mrs Ellis later heard Robert Scott violently retching.

Around midnight, Ellias and Ellen Ellis were woken by the sound of a single gunshot. Gedge came to their tent and told them that Scott had killed himself. Mr Ellis rushed to the house, where he found Elizabeth Scott in the kitchen. On entering the bedroom he saw the deceased; smoke was still lingering from the gunfire. Scott was lying on his right side, with a pistol near his right knee. Ellis stayed there for about ten minutes, taking note of all the arrangements and conditions in the room, which he later sketched for the trial.[17] He noticed a wound near Scott's left ear. When Ellis returned to the kitchen, Gedge and Julian Cross were there, together with Mrs Ellis. He told them: 'This is a bad job. There'll be a coroner's inquest over this ... it is impossible for a man to have shot himself from the position in which he is lying.' He then said he had attended several inquests and was familiar with the procedures. He believed that this had been a particularly inept attempt to make murder look like suicide. That a right-handed man could shoot himself near his left ear and then lie on his right side was always going to lead to questions. Had he been shot in his right ear, the killers might have got away with murder, given the standards of rural policing and forensic science in 1863.

Ellis berated Elizabeth Scott for leaving a pistol near her husband's reach when she knew he was morose and suicidal.

Cross was sent off on horseback to find help from the police. What Gedge and Scott didn't know was that Cross immediately confessed to them.

The Ellises returned to their tent to try to sleep. Around 4am Gedge went to see Ellias Ellis, claiming that it was the 'blackfellow [meaning Cross] that shot Bob'. What is not clear is whether Cross was part of the plot from the start or brought in only when Gedge bungled the first attempt. Ellis said he would take charge until the police came. When they arrived at around 10am, Ellis conducted them to the room where Robert Scott lay dead.

Elizabeth Scott, David Gedge and Julian Cross were arrested for the wilful murder of Robert Scott and stood before the Chief Justice of Victoria, Sir William Stawell (1815–89), in Supreme Court sittings at Beechworth on 28 October 1863. An aristocratic Irishman, Stawell had been trained at Trinity College, Dublin, and Lincoln's Inn before arriving in the colony in 1843. Scott was represented by barrister George Stephen, the brother of Sir Alfred Stephen, Chief Justice of New South Wales. Dogged by a scandal very early in his career, he eventually set up a practice in Beechworth before embarking on a career as a faith healer.[18]

Julian Cross provided crucial evidence for the prosecution case when he testified that Gedge had told him that he had shot at Scott but the pistol failed to fire. At first Cross did not know what to do but Elizabeth Scott had pleaded with him to kill her husband. So he swallowed some brandy and went into the bedroom and shot the almost comatose man. The men had to later fit the bullet to the pistol while Elizabeth Scott calmly watched. In the trial she denied any involvement in the murder, pleading that it was undertaken entirely without her knowledge or consent by her two admirers. The jury was not convinced, and all three were found guilty and sentenced to death.

No woman had been executed in the colony before then, and this was an uncomfortable start. Elizabeth Scott was a young mother, attractive and personable, a woman who had been married to a drunken brute who had humiliated and belittled her. She could have waited until he drank himself to death, given he was already suffering delirium tremens. Instead, she conspired with her lover, David Gedge, and admirer, Julian Cross, to murder him. As an accessory, she was equally guilty of the capital crime. The three prisoners were kept in Melbourne jail to await their public execution. The sheriff, the official of the Supreme Court who oversaw the punishments handed down, was concerned there would be a considerable crowd to witness this unprecedented act, so he ordered that only forty-five spectators be admitted, much to the disappointment of many Melbourne residents.

On 11 November 1863, the three prisoners were brought from the cells to the scaffold by the jailer, led by Julian Cross. The Anglican Dean of Melbourne, the Very Reverend Hussey Macartney, had attended Scott in her final days and accompanied her to the gallows, saying prayers. Cross was a Roman Catholic from Portuguese Macao and attended by two priests. The Reverend G. Stoddard attended Gedge. Scott was executed first. Her dying words were: 'David, will you not clear me?' He remained silent. She had dressed smartly for her execution in widows' black and carefully arranged and braided hair.[19]

Judges and juries were tough on married women who were found guilty of killing an unwanted husband. Ellen Thomson was the only woman ever executed in Queensland. The case remains contentious since the circumstances of her husband's death by gunshot in 1886 at Port Douglas in far northern Queensland are open to multiple interpretations. The remarks to the jury by the presiding judge, Justice (later Sir) Pope Cooper, were inflammatory and worded in such a way that a guilty verdict for Thomson and her lover John Harrison was inevitable. Before her death Thomson dictated an extraordinary confession that revealed that her youngest child was illegitimate, fathered by a man who was not her husband, and that this was her 'guilty secret'. She denied ever plotting to kill William Thomson, although she admitted she hated him.[20]

Ellen Lynch was born in poverty in Cork in southern Ireland in 1846 at the height of the Famine. She and her family endured the full brunt of the disaster since they did not leave Ireland until 1857. Her father died, leaving Ellen, her mother, and Mary, a sister two years her junior, to fend for themselves. The deprivations of her childhood were marked on Ellen's body: she was only 145 centimetres (4 foot 9 inches) in height, tiny even for the mid-nineteenth century. Her mother, Mary Murphy Lynch, had a sister, Honora Heffernan, who lived in Goulburn in New South Wales. She had been transported to New South Wales from Cork in 1839 and issued with her 'certificate of freedom' in 1846 after serving her entire seven-year sentence. In Goulburn, Mary Murphy Lynch married another former convict from Ireland. James Heffernan had arrived in the colony in 1840 from County Meath.[21] Although the Lynch family now had a support network and some form of income, the girls did not attend school; Ellen Thomson was almost illiterate when she died.

In 1862, when she was just sixteen, Ellen Lynch married William Wood, then aged thirty-five years old. They stayed in Goulburn where they had five children, one of whom, Victoria, died in 1867. William Wood died in 1871, leaving his family with few resources. Ellen

Wood therefore in 1873 decided to try her luck in Cooktown, a small northern port in Queensland that was the entry point for miners and goods destined for the newly opened Palmer River goldfields.

This was a wild and violent environment where several frontiers operated at the same time. Settlers waged war upon the Indigenous peoples for the control of the land, and intense animosity was directed towards the 18,000 to 20,000 Chinese miners who had come from Canton, Pekin and Macao intent upon acquiring wealth from this single mining field. There were few facilities and little infrastructure in such mining centres and their ports. For the few British women that ventured into these remote and largely lawless places there was always plenty of work as servants, cooks, barmaids – and prostitutes. Cooktown supported some sixty-five registered hotels and over thirty general stores at the height of the gold rush.

How Ellen Wood earned a living for herself and her four children isn't known since she did not refer to it in her confession. After five years in Cooktown the family moved to Port Douglas, the small port near the Daintree River and the Hodgkinson River goldfields. These had opened up in 1876 when British miners left the Palmer River site searching for richer pickings.[22] Wood obtained the post of housekeeper to the elderly William Thomson, who had been the first farmer in the district, taking up a selector's block in October 1877. He also employed Chinese tenant farmers and labourers to produce maize, coffee and coconuts for the expanding population. Under discriminatory legislation, Chinese people were not permitted to own or take out selections.

In late 1880, Wood gave birth to a daughter whom she named Ellen, and who took the surname Wood. Soon after, she married her employer. This child was later the subject of litigation over her guardianship after her mother's execution. The putative father was William Owen Jones, a resident of Port Douglas and the executor of William Thomson's will.[23] In her deathbed statement she reported that Jones convinced her to make Thomson believe he was the child's father.

The marriage was a disaster from the start. A widower with an adult family, Thomson was then aged fifty-six and he loathed the noise the five children made. Just before her execution in June 1887, Ellen Thomson dictated a letter to the governor, Sir Anthony Musgrave, begging for mercy. In this sad epistle she explained that she had previously asked him and the then premier, Sir Samuel Griffith, during their tour of Port Douglas to provide a school 'to bring my children up the right way, as my husband was so cranky. I banished all the children so that they would not annoy the poor old man ...'[24]

Before her execution she detailed what had happened to some of her children: Eve married young and Thomson refused to attend his stepdaughter's wedding; Jemmy had been taken in by the clerk of the court in Port Douglas as 'an act of charity'; and Bob had been despatched to his grandmother in Goulburn. William Thomson resented Nellie (Ellen) because of the speculation about her paternity. She favoured his friend William Jones in looks. So the little girl was often left in the township, although Ellen Thomson did not say with whom.

The couple worked the farm together, labouring hard in the tropical climate, battling constant rain and ever-encroaching vegetation. William owned cattle, and Ellen brought some pigs into the marriage. The farm was not going well financially; Thomson told his wife that the Bank of New South Wales was pressing him for a debt of £100. Arguments were so frequent and menacing that Ellen Thomson stayed in the marital house while William Thomson slept in a smaller building next door. It is not clear when she met John Harrison, a worker on the neighbouring farm 'Bonnie Doon', or when they became lovers. He was an Englishman, fourteen years her junior, and a blacksmith by trade who had deserted the British Army. His photograph in the prison records showed him to be a handsome man with a fresh complexion and fair hair, rather like Heath Ledger. Ellen Thomson was careworn, with grey hair and rough blunt hands that had seen hard work all her life. Her complexion was pitted and deeply ravaged, as if she had suffered smallpox.

William Thomson's second marriage – to Ellen Lynch, a widow with four children – was disastrous. Convicted for her role in his violent death, Ellen was the only woman executed in Queensland. Photo: Queensland State Archives.

There were varying accounts about how William Thomson died on the evening of 22 October 1886. Ellen Thomson stated in her confession that she believed her husband had committed suicide with a bullet to the head. He had said to her that morning he was 'disappointed and miserable for want of money … and did not want to live … the bank would soon foreclose'. She suggested they sell their respective livestock. He was also distressed about the unruly behaviour of his Chinese tenants, whom he could no longer manage. Perhaps his son Bill could come as manager, he wondered. 'The yellow dogs have ruined me and [I] will be putting a bullet through some of them or burning down their humpies about them …' he told his wife.

Ellen Thomson dictated in her jail confession that she went to bed that night around 8pm and was awakened by the sound of a gunshot. She got out of bed and said: 'God Almighty, what's up? I sang out, "Daddy, what is up?" But I got no answer … I went to Marshall's [the

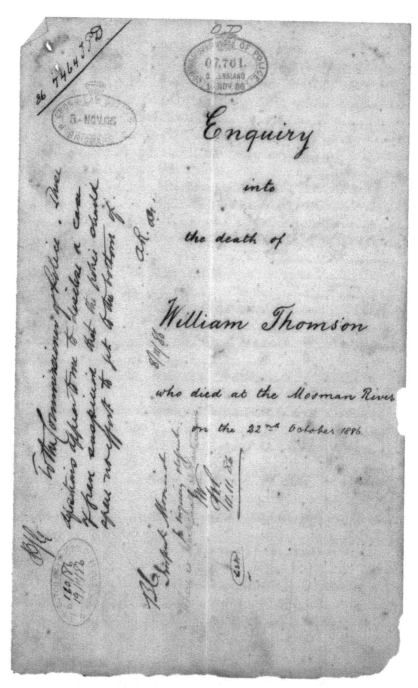

Notes from the statements used as evidence in the trial of Ellen Thomson.
Image: Queensland State Archives.

farm where Harrison worked] as there was something wrong with Billy and [asked them] to come on down at once ...' She saw Harrison there and spoke to him: 'Is it not a dreadful thing if anything has happened to Billy?' He replied: 'I hope, Mrs Thompson [sic] it is not as bad as you think.' At this time she did not say she had seen her husband lying injured or dead. Marshall and Harrison came to her selection, where they found Thomson dying, too late for medical treatment.

In the trial held in Townsville on 10 and 11 May 1887, a different version of events was presented. Patrick Moran, who worked on the Thomsons' farm, testified that the evening of the shooting he was playing his harmonica when Harrison arrived and started a verbal altercation with Thomson, who said to him: 'I thought you had gone away.' He then accused the young man of 'hawking' (having sex) with his wife, whom he called 'the old woman'. He laughed about her having a 'fancy man'. (It was true enough – for the period she *was* old, since many women died in their mid-forties from the long-term effects of multiple childbirths and rough conditions.) Ellen Thomson had been sitting on the verandah during this argument. When her husband put his hand in his shirt, she called out: 'Look out, Jack, he has got a revolver; you don't know what the old bastard might do.' Harrison then shot him. He said later at the trial that it had been in self-defence.[25] A careful reading of all the testimony favours this version of events.

When other witnesses were called, they stated that there had been two shots. Ah Wing, Ah Loy and Jane Le Ong, a British woman married to Chinese tenant farmer Le Ong, all testified there were two shots, which ruled out suicide. Dr Marley, who at first thought there had only been one shot – through the head – later told both the police inquiry and the Supreme Court trial there were two shots. The Crown prosecutor, Virgil Power, brought in another witness, Henry Oubridge, who had shared a cell with Harrison in the lock-up in Townsville. He alleged that the prisoner confided in him that he hoped to get 'the sugar' – meaning the Thomson farm – by killing the owner and marrying his widow. Given that the farm was almost bankrupt, something Ellen Thomson knew well, and that the property had been left to the deceased man's brother, Thomas Thomson, this seems unlikely.

Both accused were represented at their joint trial by a Townsville solicitor, not a barrister. Except for Indigenous defendants, there was no public defence for criminal matters until 1903, nor was the accused allowed to speak in his or her own defence. Witnesses could, however, be called. Recently admitted solicitor Jacob Lue was competent and also fully conversant with advances in medical jurisprudence and the particularities of shattered gunshot wounds. In fact, he was more competent on this matter than Dr Marley who, he reminded the court, had changed his mind about the deceased's injuries. But his arguments were to no avail, with so many witnesses testifying that they had heard two shots.

Justice Pope Cooper, a vain and opinionated man who had trained at the University of Sydney with the future inaugural prime minister, Edmund Barton, was resentful that his career remained stuck in northern Queensland.[26] In his address to the jury, Justice Cooper said that 'in every case of murder the law assumes that murder has been committed until the contrary is proven'. This was completely incorrect; in common law, the accused is considered innocent until proven guilty beyond reasonable doubt. His words gave the jury an indication of Cooper's own opinion. They took some time to consider their verdict, some ten hours before declaring that they found both the accused guilty as charged. Thomson and Harrison were both sentenced to death. Unfortunately, no appeals were allowed for criminal cases in Queensland until 1903, even though, given the judge's partiality and misdirection to the jury, in this case there should have been one.

Thomson and Harrison were taken to Brisbane and housed in Boggo Road jail. Despite her lack of education and her inexperience with legal matters, Ellen Thomson had been perceptive enough to realise she had not been given a fair trial. What she had really been found guilty of was adultery. She wrote to the governor saying that witnesses had given false testimony and asking that 'Pope Cooper may never be allowed to sentence another woman in Queensland without first having heard both sides of the story'. She also demanded considerable compensation for her children and that Father Denis Fouhy be given guardianship of her daughter Ellen.[27]

On 2 June 1887 the Executive Council did consider the convictions and sentences but did not recommend mercy – the executions were to proceed. In the press there had been considerable agitation about these imminent executions, strengthened because one was the mother of a large family. Many citizens were outraged when the Executive Council decided to release Lewis Shaw, who had been convicted of kidnapping and killing New Guineans bound for the colony's sugar plantations in 1885. With a conservative government sympathetic to the sugar planters in power, Shaw's fate had altered. Also a black American, Jacob Stevenson, who had been convicted of rape, then a capital offence, was pardoned.[28] Yet in the Harrison–Thomson case, despite the conflicting evidence and testimony, the executions proceeded.

At 8am on the morning of Monday, 13 June 1887, the prisoners were taken from their cells and escorted to the gallows. This was not a public execution, which Queensland had banned as early as 1851. Right to the last minute Thomson was confident that she would be reprieved. Accompanied by the Sisters of Mercy and Father Fouhy, she continued to protest her innocence. On the gallows she said: 'I never shot my husband and I am dying like an angel.' Her sole concern was for her little daughter Ellen.

Various accounts of the execution were printed in newspapers. The most graphic was on 17 June by William Lane, who wrote under the pseudonym 'The Sketcher' for the radical newspaper *The Boomerang*. He later went on to edit *The Worker* and found a utopian colony in Paraguay. Lane believed that Thomson was guilty but was impressed that she had died 'game'. Dressed in black, looking pale and gaunt, Ellen Thomson carried her crucifix. Lane then went on to detail the horrors of the procedure. The rope had cut into Thomson's neck, severing her jugular vein. Those around her were spattered with her blood. All the officials, doctors, jail staff and clergy were 'sickened' by the grotesque spectacle. After this, John Harrison was executed, and to the distress of all present, the same thing happened.

Queensland had never permitted the dissection or anatomising of the bodies of those executed. Yet in this unique case in the colony's history, 'Professor' Gustav de Blumenthal, a German-born phrenologist, was permitted to examine the skulls of Thomson and Harrison; this, despite the fact that phrenology (a method of ascertaining a person's character by examining the structure of the skull) had by now been largely discredited. Without any medical or scientific qualifications, de Blumenthal pronounced that Ellen Thomson had been combative and destructive, with 'the moral propensities small and the sexual love–amativeness, exceedingly large'. Her lover was apparently also possessed of these qualities, as well as selfishness, and had wanted 'old Thomson dead far more than he did old Thomson's wife'.[29]

The following week, the largest newspaper in the colony, the *Brisbane Courier*, reported in full the decision of the Supreme Court in the matter of the guardianship of Ellen Wood, described as illegitimate. Father Fouhy sought guardianship in line with her mother's dying wish, yet William Thomson's will stated that she should be given into his brother's care. He was entitled by law to do this because, until new legislation was passed four years later, women had no custody rights even to their legitimate children. Thomson's actions were simply driven by spite. However, since the child was illegitimate – the biological daughter of William Jones – and bore her mother's first married name, the court decided that Ellen Wood should be given into the care of Father Fouhy, who then sent the little girl back to Port Douglas to be cared for by Father Brady. She was to be raised in the Roman Catholic faith as her mother had wished.[30]

Acknowledgments

I should like to acknowledge my debt of gratitude to all those at HarperCollins who laboured on my manuscript to turn it into a book.

The archivists at the State Archives of Tasmania were helpful in sending electronic records of several cases. Jane Wassell at the Queensland State Archives helped me track down several significant Queensland cases.

Librarians at the University of Queensland Library, most notably those in the Law Library, helped me locate relevant sources and legal commentaries.

Trudy Cowley, part of the splendid team at the Female Factory Research Group in Hobart, interrupted her honeymoon to send me records she had collected. This generosity to a fellow historian goes beyond the call of duty.

Endnotes

Introduction

1. Nancy Gray, 'Dumaresq, William John (1793–1866)', http://adb.anu.edu. au/biography/dumaresq-william-john-2239; refer also to Alan Atkinson, *The Europeans in Australia: A History, Volume 2: Democracy*, Oxford University Press, Melbourne, 2004, pp. 140–141.

2. Charlotte Anley, *Prisoners of Australia: A Narrative*, J. Hatchard, London, 1841, pp. 25–26. [Viewed online. Italics are in the original document.]

3. Brenda R. Weber, 'Situating Exceptional Women', *Nineteenth-Century Gender Studies*, Vol. 5, No. 1, 2009. [Viewed online.]

4. Clothilde Rougé-Maillart et. al., 'Women who kill their children', *American Journal of Forensic Medicine and Pathology*, Vol. 26, No. 4, 2005, p. 320 [viewed online]; Geoffrey R. McKee, *Why Mothers Kill: A Forensic Psychologist's Casebook*, Oxford University Press, New York, 2006. McKee suggests that many suffered from mental illness or substance abuse.

5. Martin Daly and Margo Wilson, *Homicide*, Aldine de Gruyter, New York, 1988. This deals with the issue at length.

6. P. R. Wilson, *Murder of the Innocents: Child-Killers and Their Victims*, Rigby, Adelaide, 1985, p. 52.

7. M. P. Wilkins, 'A Comfortable Evil: Female Serial Murderers in American Culture', PhD thesis, Penn State University, 2004, p. 5. [Viewed online.]

8. Kathy Laster, 'Arbitrary Chivalry: Women and Capital Punishment in Victoria, 1842–1967' in David Phillips and Susanne Davies, *A Nation of Rogues: Crime, Law and Punishment in Colonial Australia*, Melbourne University Press, Carlton, 1994, p. 169.

9. Peter Vronsky, *Serial Female Killers: How and Why Women Become Monsters*, Berkley Books, New York, 2007; Michael Kelleher and C. L. Kelleher, *Murder Most Rare: The Female Serial Killer*, Praeger,

Westport, Connecticut, 1998; Martin Daly and Margo Wilson, *Homicide*, Aldine de Gruyter, New York, 1988.

10. Lindy Cameron and Ruth Wykes, *Women Who Kill: Chilling Portraits of Australia's Worst Female Murderers*, The Five Mile Press, Scoresby, 2010, p. 3.

11. Judith Knelman, 'Women Murderers in Victorian Britain', *History Today*, Vol. 48, No. 8, 1998, p. 14.

Chapter 1 Lethal Abortion in the Nineteenth Century

1. John Keown, *Abortion, Doctors and the Law: Some Aspects of the Legal Regulation of Abortion in England, 1803–1982*, Cambridge University Press, Cambridge, 2002.

2. Viewed in online version of *The Sydney Gazette and New South Wales Advertiser*, 8 August 1828.

3. *British Medical Journal*, Vol. 1, 1868, pp. 127, 175 and 197.

4. Gideon Haigh, *The Racket: How Abortion Became Legal in Australia*, Melbourne University Press, Melbourne, 2008, pp. 14–15.

5. Shurlee Swain and Renate Howe, *Single Mothers and Their Children: Disposal, Punishment and Survival in Australia*, Cambridge University Press, Melbourne, 1995, p. 45.

6. *South Australian Register*, 12 December 1882.

7. *Argus*, 30 July 1886.

8. *Ibid.*

9. David Dunstan, 'Gillott, Sir Samuel', http://adb.anu.edu.au/biography/gillott-sir-samuel-6390.

10. *Queanbeyan Age*, 29 September 1886; refer also to Lynn Finch and Jon Stratton, 'The Australian Working Class and the Practice of Abortion, 1880–1940', *Journal of Australian Studies*, No. 23, 1988, pp. 45–64.

11. A. M. Mitchell, 'Youl, Dr Richard (1821–1897)', http://adb.anu.edu.au/biography/youl-richard-4900/text 8201.

12. *Argus*, 30 July 1886.

13. R. G. De B. Griffith, 'Holroyd, Sir Edward Dundas (1828–1916)', http://adb.anu.edu.au/biography/holroyd-sir-edward-dundas-3784/text5983.

14. Robert Miller, 'Williams, Sir Hartley (1843–1929)', http://adb.anu.edu.au/biography/williams-sir-hartley-4856/text8111.

15. Marian Aveling, 'Purves, James Liddell (1843–1910)', http://adb.anu.edu. au/biography/purves-james-liddell-4419/text7215.

16. *Argus*, 5 November 1886; Ruth Campbell, 'Madden, Sir John (1844– 1918), http://adb.anu.edu.au/biography/madden-sir-john-7453/text12981. Sir John Madden, later the Chief Justice of Victoria, was the second most expensive QC.

17. *Argus*, 26 November 1886.

18. Cited in Ruth Teale, *Colonial Eve: Sources on Women in Australia 1788–1914*, OUP, Melbourne, 1978, p. 134.

19. *Gippsland Times*, 1 July 1891.

20. *Portland Guardian*, 1 July 1891.

21. *Adelaide Advertiser*, 25 May 1898; 27 October 1898.

22. *Argus*, 26 November 1895.

23. Patricia Sumerling, 'The Darker Side of Motherhood: Abortion and Infanticide in South Australia, 1870–1910', *Journal of the History Society of South Australia*, Vol. 13, 1985. [Viewed online.]

24. South Australian Archives, Police Department GRG5/2/160, 25 February 1897, cited in Sumerling, *op. cit.*

25. *Ibid.*

26. Peter Bartlett, 'Downer, Sir John William (1843–1915)', http://adb.anu. edu.au/biography/downer-sir-john-william-6007/text10261.

27. *Barrier Miner*, 6 March 1897.

28. Ronald Elmslie and Susan Nance, 'Smith, William Ramsay (1859–1937)', http://adb.anu.edu.au/biography/smith-william-ramsay-8493/text4941.

29. *South Australian Register*, 9 March 1897.

30. W. D. Refshauge, 'Shepherd, Arthur Edmund (1867–1942)', http://adb. anu.edu.au/biography/shepherd-arthur-edmund-8412/text14775.

31. *Adelaide Register*, 11 April 1908.

32. *Adelaide Register*, 15 April 1908.

33. *Barrier Miner*, 16 August 1908.

34. *Brisbane Courier*, 19 December 1898.

35. *Argus*, 19 January 1899.

36. *Argus*, 3 February 1923.

37. *Argus*, 13 January 1899.

38. *Argus*, 13 January 1899.
39. Bryan Gandevia, 'Neild, James Edward (1824–1906)', http://adb.anu.edu.au/biography/neild-james-edward-4288/text6939.
40. *Argus*, 14 January 1899.
41. Haigh, *op. cit.,* p. 19.
42. *Bathurst Free Press and Mining Journal*, 17 January 1899, p. 2.
43. *Western Mail*, 3 January 1899.
44. *Ibid*, p. 20.
45. *Argus*, 23 January 1899.
46. Argus, 26 January 1899.
47. *Argus*, 26 January 1899.
48. *Argus*, 26 January 1899.
49. *Argus*, 26 January 1899.
50. *The West Australian*, 3 February 1899.
51. *Western Mail*, 3 February 1899.
52. *The West Australian*, 3 February 1899.
53. *The West Australian*, 3 February 1899.
54. *The West Australian*, 23 February 1899.
55. *South Australian Register*, 23 February 1899.
56. *South Australian Register*, 24 February 1899.
57. *The North Western Advocate and Emu Bay Times*, 27 February 1899.
58. *The West Australian*, 28 February 1899.
59. *Argus*, 13 March 1899.
60. *Morwell Advertiser*, 27 April 1900.
61. Haigh, *op. cit.*, p. 21.

Chapter 2 Lethal Abortion in the Twentieth Century

1. C. A. von Oppeln, 'Crowther, Sir William Edward Lodewyk Hamilton (1887–1981)', http://adb.anu.edu.au/biography/crowther-william-edward-lodewyk-hamilton-12374/text22237.
2. *Examiner* (Launceston), 30 August 1905; *Hobart Mercury*, 24 August 1905 and 28 August 1905.
3. *Sydney Morning Herald*, 21 September 1905.
4. *Sydney Morning Herald*, 20 September 1905.
5. *Sydney Morning Herald*, 15 November 1905.

6. Katie Spearritt and Kay Saunders, 'Is There Life after Birth? Childbirth, death and danger for settler women in colonial Queensland', *Journal of Australia Studies*, No. 29, 1991, pp. 64–75.

7. *Attorney-General (NSW) v Jackson* [1906] HCA 90; (1906) 3 CLR 730 (12 April 1906).

8. J. M. Bennett, 'Blacket, Wilfred (1859–1937)', http://adb.anu.edu.au/ biography/blacket-wilfred-5260/text8865.

9. *Sydney Morning Herald*, 11 May 1906.

10. Neville Hicks and E. J. Lea-Scarlett, 'Beale, Octavius Charles (1850–1930)', http://adb.anu.edu.au/biography/beale-octavius-charles-5165/ text8675.

11. *Western Mail* (Perth), 19 December 1908.

12. *Argus*, 11 December 1909.

13. Geoffrey Serle, 'Schutt, William John (1868–1933)', http://adb.anu.edu. au/biography/schutt-william-john-8362/text14673.

14. *Hope v R* [1909] HCA 6; (1909) 9 CLR 257 (15 March 1909).

15. *Argus*, 20 March 1909.

16. *Adelaide Advertiser*, 23 May 1910.

17. J. McI. Young, 'Hood, Sir Joseph Henry (1846–1922)', http://adb.anu. edu.au/biography/hood-sir-joseph-henry-6725/text11615.

18. Norma Marshall, 'Maxwell, George Arnot (1859–1935)', http://adb.anu. edu.au/biography/maxwell-george-arnot-7533/text13139.

19. *Argus*, 21 June 1910; *Hobart Mercury*, 23 June 1910.

20. *Adelaide Register*, 22 July 1910; *Argus*, 24 April 1912.

21. *Barrier Miner*, 13 January 1923.

22. Zoe Carthew, '"She had not a Baby Face": The death of Bertha Coughlan', *Provenance: The Journal of the Public Record Office of Victoria*, No. 5, 2006, p. 44.

23. *Barrier Miner*, 3 February 1923.

24. Cited in Gideon Haigh, *The Racket: How Abortion Became Legal in Australia,* Melbourne University Press, Melbourne, 2008, p. 35.

25. Janet McCalman, *Struggletown: Public and Private Life in Richmond, 1900–1965*, Melbourne University Press, Melbourne, 1984, p. 131.

26. *Argus*, 5 February 1923; Carthew, *op. cit.*, pp. 31–46.

27. Haigh, *op. cit.*, pp. 33–34.

28. Carthew, *op. cit.*, p. 33.

29. *Ibid.*

30. *Ibid.*, p. 39.

31. *Ibid.*, pp. 38–39.

32. *Sydney Morning Herald*, 2 March 1923.

33. Carthew, *op. cit.*, pp. 33, 41–42.

34. *Sydney Morning Herald*, 2 March 1923.

35. *Cairns Post*, 8 March 1923.

36. *Barrier Miner*, 9 March 1923.

37. *Sunday Times* (Perth), 11 March 1923.

38. Elise B. Histed, 'Mann, Sir Frederick Wollaston (1869–1958)', http://adb. anu.edu.au/biography/mann-sir-frederick-wollaston-7473/text13023.

39. *Argus*, 21 April 1923.

40. *Adelaide Advertiser*, 17 September 1924.

41. *Argus*, 24 January 1924.

42. *Adelaide Advertiser*, 20 February 1924.

43. *Brisbane Courier*, 10 March 1925.

44. *Cairns Post*, 26 March 1925.

45. *Burnie Advocate*, 12 January 1928.

46. *Barrier Miner*, 20 February 1928.

47. *Argus*, 12 January 1928.

48. *Launceston Examiner*, 18 January 1928.

49. *Hobart Mercury*, 18 February 1928.

50. *Advocate*, 12 January 1928.

51. *Argus*, 17 November 1928.

52. *Adelaide Mail*, 23 November 1929.

53. *Cairns Post*, 25 May 1923.

54. *Brisbane Courier*, 4 August 1928.

55. Cited in *Western Argus* (Kalgoorlie), 29 December 1931.

56. Ann Farmer, *By Their Fruits: Eugenics, Population Control, and the Abortion Debate*, Catholic University of America Press, Washington DC, 2008, pp. 90–91.

57. Meredith Foley, 'Goodisson, Lillie Elizabeth (1860–1947)', http://adb.anu. edu.au/biography/goodisson-lillie-elizabeth-6422/text10983.

58. Stephen Garton, 'Jones, Reginald Stuart (1902–1961)', http://adb.anu.edu.au/biography/jones-reginald-stuart-10641.htm

59. *Argus*, 5 January 1915; 24 March 1915.

60. W. M. Hughes, 'Can Motherhood Deaths be Prevented?', *Australian Women's Weekly*, 27 August 1935.

61. *Canberra Times*, 5 March 1935; Heather Radi, 'D'Arcy, Dame Constance Elizabeth (1869–1950)', http://adb.anu.edu.au/biography/d'arcy-dame-constance-elizabeth-5880/text10005. She was a devout Roman Catholic, which may have also informed her strong opinions.

62. *Age*, 7 August 2004. Refer also to 'Billy Hughes's Family Secret', *Rewind*, ABC Television, 8 August 2004.

63. Cited in Haigh, *op. cit.*, p. 48.

64. *Argus*, 3 August 1938.

65. *Morning Bulletin* (Rockhampton), 18 April 1938.

66. Haigh, *op. cit.*, pp. 40–43.

67. *Courier Mail*, 7 March 1945.

68. Deposition submitted in Case 40, Supreme Court of Queensland, Criminal Depositions, Queensland State Archives (QSA), CC 399: case of Vera Humphries, 22 February 1943.

69. *Courier Mail*, 7 April 1943.

70. *Ibid.*; *Cairns Post*, 2 June 1943.

71. Cited in Haigh, *op. cit.*, pp. 43–44.

72. *Hobart Mercury*, 23 August 1944.

73. Ross Johnston, *History of the Queensland Bar*, Bar Association of Queensland, Toowong, 1984, p. 91.

74. QSA SCT/CC 417 depositions 46–70, 1946, case 52 of 1946; *Courier Mail*, 27 March 1946.

75. *Courier Mail*, 27 April 1946.

76. *Western Australian*, 2 March 1949.

77. *Courier Mail*, 4 May 1949.

78. *Hobart Mercury*, 5 March 1949.

79. *Burnie Advocate*, 4 May 1949.

80. *Canberra Times*, 27 January 1950.

81. *Sydney Morning Herald*, 11 March 1950.

Chapter 3 Baby Killers in the Nineteenth Century

1. www.capitalpunishmentuk.org/fempublic.html.

2. Annette Ballinger, *Dead Women Walking: Executing Women in England and Wales, 1900–1955*, Ashgate, Aldershot, 2000, p. 1.

3. Judith A. Allen, *Sex and Secrets: Crimes Involving Australian Women Since 1880*, Oxford University Press, Melbourne, 1990, pp. 29–30.

4. 'Luttrell, Edward (1756–1824)', http://adb.anu.edu.au/biography/luttrell-edward-2381/text3135.

5. Paula Byrne, *Criminal Law and Colonial Subject, New South Wales 1810–1830*, Cambridge University Press, Melbourne, 1993, p. 255.

6. William Hunter, 'On the Uncertainty of the Signs of Murder in the Case of Bastard Children', *Medical Observations and Inquiries by a Society of Physicians in London*, Vol. 6, 1784, reproduced as an eBook.

7. K. J. Kramar and W. D. Watson, 'The Insanities of Reproduction: Medico–Legal Knowledge and the Development of Infanticide Law', *Social and Legal Studies*, Vol. 15, No. 2, 2006, p. 241.

8. Byrne, *op. cit.*, pp. 255–56.

9. Helen MacDonald, *Human Remains: Episodes in Human Dissection*, Melbourne University Press, Melbourne, 2005, p. 54. I have consistently used the spelling McLauchlan as reported in the press. In the official archival record of executions in Hobart in 1830 she is called Mary McLaughlin alias Sutherland, though other records call her McLaughlan. TSAL EC4/1. The Tasmanian State Archives and Library kindly sent me all the records concerned with her case electronically.

10. Helen MacDonald, 'A Dissection in Reverse: Mary McLaughlan, Hobart Town, 1830', *Lilith*, Vol. 13, 2004, p. 16.

11. MacDonald, *Human Remains*, pp. 54–55.

12. MacDonald, 'A Dissection in Reverse', p. 17.

13. G. H. Stancombe, 'Scott, James (1790–1837)', http://adb.anu.edu.au/biography/scott-james-2641/text3671.

14. MacDonald, *Human Remains*, pp. 59–62.

15. *Hobart Town Gazette and Van Diemen's Land Advertiser*, 2 March 1822.

16. Female Factory Research Group, *Convict Lives: Women at Cascades Female Factory*, Research Tasmania, Hobart, 2009; Kay Daniels, *Convict Lives*, Allen and Unwin, Sydney, 1999; Joy Damousi, *Depraved and Disorderedly:*

Female Convicts, Sexuality and Gender in Colonial Australia, Cambridge University Press, Melbourne, 1997.

17. MacDonald, *Human Remains*, pp. 65–68.
18. Peter Crisp, 'Hone, Joseph (1784–1861)', http://adb.anu.edu.au/biography/hone-joseph-2195/text2833.
19. E. R. Pretyman, 'Baylee, Pery (1784–?)', http://adb.anu.edu.au/biography/baylee-pery-1757/text1957.
20. R. P. Davis, *The Tasmanian Gallows: A Study in Capital Punishment*, Cat and Fiddle Press, Hobart, 1974, pp. xii–xiii; James Boyce, *Van Diemen's Land*, Black Inc., Melbourne, 2008, pp. 168–69.
21. *Hobart Town Courier*, 4 April 1829. This announced his appointment as assistant surgeon to the colony.
22. M. Clark and C. Crawford (eds), *Legal Medicine in History*, Cambridge University Press, Cambridge, 1994, p. 174.
23. MacDonald, *Human Remains*, pp. 73–76.
24. A. Alison, *Principles of the Criminal Law of Scotland*, Blackwell, Edinburgh, 1832, p. 159.
25. Roger Smith, *Trial by Medicine: Responsibility in Victorian Trials*, Edinburgh University Press, Edinburgh, 1981, pp. 148–50.
26. H. R. Thomas, 'Thomas, Jocelyn Henry Connor (1780–1862)', http://adb.anu.edu.au/biography/thomas-jocelyn-henry-connor-2726/text3843; P. R. Eldershaw, 'Burnett, John (1781–1860)', http://adb.anu.edu.au/biography/burnett-john-1855/text1826.
27. MacDonald, *Human Remains*, p. 77.
28. MacDonald, 'A Dissection in Reverse', p. 19.
29. 'Bedford, William (1781–1852)', http://adb.anu.edu.au/biography/bedford-william-1760/text1963.
30. Ida McAuley, 'Bisdee, John (1796–1862)', http://adb.anu.edu.au/biography/bisdee-john-1786/text2013.
31. *Tasmanian and Austral–Asiatic Review*, 23 April 1830.
32. MacDonald, 'A Dissection in Reverse', p. 20.
33. *The Sydney Gazette and New South Wales Advertiser*, 6 April 1833.
34. *Hobart Colonial Times*, 31 July 1857.
35. *Ballarat Star*, 4 August 1864; *The Australian Advertiser* (Adelaide), 9 August 1864, has a long article on the incident.

36. MacDonald, *Human Remains*, pp. 49–51.

37. MacDonald, 'A Dissection in Reverse', pp. 13–15.

38. *Hobart Town Courier*, 15 May 1835.

39. Details of the case are contained in Decisions of the Nineteenth Century Tasmanian Superior Court, *R v Masters*; *Hobart Town Courier*, 12 May 1838.

40. Peter Bolger, 'Bedford, Edward Samuel Pickard (1809–1876)', http://adb. anu.edu.au/biography/bedford-edward-samuel-pickard-2962/text4311.

41. For more details refer to Kramar and Watson, *op. cit.*; Hilary Marland, *Dangerous Motherhood: Insanity and Childbirth in Victorian Britain*, Palgrave Macmillan, London, 2000.

42. Smith, *op. cit.*, pp. 146–47; Tony Ward, 'The Sad Subject of Infanticide: Law, Medicine and Child Murder', *Social and Legal Studies*, Vol. 8, No. 2, 1999, pp. 163–80.

43. J. M. Bennett, 'Hargrave, John Fletcher (1815–1885)', http://adb.anu.edu. au/biography/hargrave-john-fletcher-3718/text5835.

44. *Sydney Morning Herald*, 26 November 1867.

45. M. Carter and A. A. Morrison, 'Harding, George Rogers (1838–1895)', http://adb.anu.edu.au/biography/harding-george-rogers-3712/text5825.

46. A. Rahmentula, 'Real, Sir Patrick (1846–1928)', http://adb.anu.edu.au/ biography/real-sir-patrick-8169/text14281.

47. *R v Judge*, Queensland State Archives (QSA) Supreme Court Records, CCT 7/N42.

48. *Brisbane Courier*, 2 May 1885.

49. *Brisbane Courier*, 30 April 1885.

50. Ross Johnston, *History of the Queensland Bar*, The Bar Association of Queensland, Toowong, 1984, p. 99.

51. *Queensland Law Journal*, Vol. 1, 1885, pp. 61–62.

52. Cited in Ruth Teale (ed.), *Colonial Eve: Sources on Women in Australia 1788–1914*, Oxford University Press, Melbourne, 1978, pp. 142–43.

53. *Ibid.*, p. 137.

54. *Argus*, 21 December 1870.

55. S. M. Ingram, 'O'Loghlen, Sir Bryan (1828–1905)', http://adb.anu.edu. au/biography/o'loghlen-sir-bryan-4331/text7028.

56. Petition on behalf of Maggie Heffernan, *Women's Sphere*, December 1900, cited in Teale, pp. 139–40.

57. J. McI. Young, 'Hodges, Sir Henry Edward Agincourt (1844–1919)', http://adb.anu.edu.au/biography/hodges-sir-henry-edward-agincourt-1092/text11549.

58. The case is detailed in *Women's Sphere*, December 1900, and reprinted in Teale, *op. cit.*, pp. 139–40.

59. Letter to the editor by Marshall Lyle (dated 22 February), *Argus*, 23 February 1900.

60. *Bendigo Advertiser*, 21 December 1901, p. 3.

Chapter 4 Baby Killers in the Twentieth Century

1. Senate debates, 18 March 2010.

2. *Sydney Morning Herald*, 11 February 2009.

3. *Brisbane Courier*, 4 March 1901.

4. C. T. Beck and J. W. Driscoll, *Post-partum Mood and Anxiety Disorders*, Jones and Bartlett, Sudbury, 2006.

5. Judith Wheelwright, 'Nothing in Between: Modern Cases of Infanticide', in Mark Jackson (ed.), *Infanticide: Historical perspectives on child murder and concealment, 1550–2000*, Ashgate, Aldershot, 2002, pp. 270–72.

6. *Adelaide Advertiser*, 11 May 1910.

7. Norma Marshall, 'Maxwell, George Arnot (1859–1935)', http://adb.anu.edu.au/biography/maxwell/george/arnot-7533/text13139.

8. R. G. DeB. Griffith, 'à Beckett, Sir Thomas (1836–1919)', http://adb.anu.edu.au/biography/a-beckett-sir-thomas-2860/text4073.

9. *Brisbane Courier*, 23 April 1913.

10. *Argus*, 18 April 1915.

11. *Argus*, 16 June 1915.

12. Queensland State Archives (QSA) Supreme Court Criminal Sittings SCT/CC 297, item ID 95745, trial of Nellie Spiers for concealing a birth, 7 July 1924.

13. Robert Likeman, *'Tis but the Time: The life of Lieut-Col. Espie Dods, DSO MC AAMC*, Slouch Hat Publications, McCrea, Victoria, 2007, for more details.

14. *Cairns Post*, 14 January 1952.

15. *Age*, 28 April 2005.
16. *The Mail* (Adelaide), 13 October 1951.
17. *Adelaide Advertiser*, 22 December 1951. The files in this type of case are not opened for scrutiny by researchers for 65 years.
18. Readers are advised to consult Matthew Benns, *When the Bough Breaks: The True Story of Child Killer Kathleen Folbigg*, Bantam Books, Sydney, 2003. This is the most well documented account of this case, apart from the record of the trials and appeals.
19. *R v Folbigg* [2008] NSWSC, 24 October 2003.
20. *Ibid.*, refer also to Malcolm Brown (ed.), *Cold-blooded Murder: True Crimes that Rocked Australia*, Hachette, Sydney, 2008, p. 166; Paul B. Kidd, *The Australian Crime File*, Five Mile Press, Rowville, Victoria, 2005, pp. 39–44.
21. *R v Folbigg* [2008] NSWSC, 24 October 2003.
22. *Ibid.*
23. *Ibid.*
24. *Ibid.*
25. *Ibid.*
26. Belinda Morrisey, 'Monstrous Semantics: The Case of Criminal Diaries', *Australian Feminist Studies*, No. 65, 2010, p. 301.
27. *Ibid.*, pp. 137–47.
28. 'Of Woman Born', *Australian Story*, ABC Television, 15 March 2004.
29. *Ibid.*
30. *R v Folbigg* [2008] NSWSC, 24 October 2003.
31. *Ibid.*
32. *Ibid.*
33. *Ibid.*
34. *Folbigg v R*, HCA Transcripts S59/2003.
35. Sharmila Betts and Jane Goodman-Delahunty, 'The Case of Kathleen Folbigg: How Did Justice and Medicine Fare?', *Australian Journal of Forensic Sciences*, Vol. 39, No. 1, 2007, pp. 10–24. [Accessed online 1 December 2011.] The authors are both psychologists.
36. *Ibid.*, pp. 246–68 for summary of the trial; Brown, *op. cit.*, pp. 177–80. Key points of the original trial can be read in the 2007 appeal: *Folbigg v R* [2007] NSWCCA 371.
37. *R v Folbigg* [2003] NSWSC, 24 October 2003.

38. *R v Folbigg* [2005] NSWCCA 23 judgment, delivered 17 February 2005 before Sully JA, Dunford J and Hidden J.

39. *Folbigg v R* [2005] HCA trans 657, 2 September 2005.

40. *Folbigg v R* [2007] NSWCCA 371.

41. *Daily Telegraph*, 9 July 2003; Benns, *op. cit.*, p. 287.

42. Peter Lalor, *Blood Stain: The True Story of Katherine Knight, the Mother and Abattoir Worker who Became Australia's Worst Female Killer*, Allen and Unwin, Sydney, 2002, p. 305.

Chapter 5 A Baffling Case: Keli Lane

1. *R v Keli Lane* [2011] NSWSC 289, 15 April 2011. Much of the material on this case can be located in the court records online.

2. *Ibid.*

3. Article by Jane Cadzow, *Newcastle Herald*, 15 April 2011.

4. *Ibid.*

5. Rachael Jane Chin, *Good Girl: The Story of Keli Lane and Her Missing Baby, Tegan*, Simon and Schuster, Sydney, 2011, p. 25. Readers are advised to consult this excellent book for more details, along with Justice Whealy's sentencing, which is available online.

6. Chin, *op. cit.*, p. 45 and pp. 53–54.

7. *Australian*, 31 August 2010.

8. *Newcastle Herald*, 15 April 2011.

9. *R v Keli Lane* [2011]

10. *Ibid.*

11. Chin, *op. cit.*, p. 48.

12. *Sunday Telegraph*, 17 April 2011.

13. Emma Martin, 'We knew she was hiding something', *Who* magazine, 25 April 2011.

14. *Manly Daily*, 10 August 2010.

15. *R v Keli Lane* [2011], *ibid.*

16. *Ibid.*

17. To protect his identity and that of his daughter with Lane, I have not used his name.

18. Refer to Chin, *op. cit.*, Chapter 9.

19. *R v Keli Lane* [2011].

20. *Ibid.*
21. Chin, *op. cit.*, Chapter 17.
22. *Ibid.*, p. 259.
23. *Ibid.*, p. 255.
24. *Newcastle Herald*, 15 April 2011.

Chapter 6 The Deadly Baby Farmers
1. H. L. Adam, *Women and Crime*, T. W. Laurie, London, 1911, p. 176.
2. Kathy Laster, 'Frances Knorr: She killed babies, didn't she?' in M. Lake and F Kelly (eds), *Double Time*, Penguin, Melbourne, 1985, p. 18.
3. *Pall Mall Gazette*, 19 December 1899.
4. Carol Herben, *From Burren Street to the Gallows: The John and Sarah Makin Story*, J. and C. Herben, Fairy Meadow, 1997, p. 3.
5. Heather Radi, 'Makin, Sarah Jane (1845–1918)', http://adb.anu.edu.au/bioggraphy/makin-sarah-jane-13271.
6. Herben, *op. cit.*, p. 11.
7. *Australian Town and Country Journal*, 19 November 1892.
8. *Ibid.*
9. *Bathurst Free Press and Mining Journal*, 17 November 1892. This provides a word-for-word account of Clarice Makin's testimony.
10. Herben, *op. cit.*, p. 87.
11. *Sydney Morning Herald*, 7 March 1893.
12. G. D. Woods, *The Baby Farmers: A History of Criminal Law in New South Wales: The Colonial Period 1788–1900*, Federation Press, Annandale, 2002, p. 396.
13. Judith Rowbotham and Kim Stevenson (eds), *Criminal Conversations: Victorian Crimes, Social Panic and Moral Outrage*, University of Ohio Press, Athens, 2005, p. 214, available as an eBook.
14. *Sydney Morning Herald*, 24 March 1893.
15. Suzanne Edgar and Bede Nairn, 'Salomons, Sir Julian Emanuel (1835–1909)', http://adb.anu.edu.au/biography/salomons-sir-julian-emanuel-4532/text7423.
16. *R v Makin and Wife* [1893] NSWLR 1 at 22; *Sydney Morning Herald*, 31 March 1893.
17. Quoted in Woods, *op. cit.*, p. 399.

18. *Sydney Morning Herald*, 13 August 1892.

19. *Sydney Morning Herald*, 12 August 1893.

20. Herben, *op. cit.*, p. 173.

21. Alan Sharpe, *Crime and Punishment: Fifty Crimes that Shocked Australia*, Kingsclear Books, Crows Nest, 1997, p. 116.

22. *Ibid.*, p. 116.

23. *Age*, 6 September 1893.

24. *Age*, 9 September 1893.

25. Simon Cooke, 'Candler, Samuel Curtis (1827–1911)', http://adb.anu.edu.au/biography/candler-samuel-curtis-12839/text23177.

26. Lucy Sussex, '"God Help My Poor Baby!" The Case of Frances Knorr' in K. Greenwood (ed.), *The Thing She Loves: Why Women Kill*, Allen and Unwin, Sydney, 1996, p. 100.

27. *Herald*, 6 December 1893. 'The home was a religious organisation in Chelsea', Sharpe, *op. cit.*, p. 115.

28. *Ibid.*

29. *South Australian Register*, 2 December 1893.

30. Sussex, *op. cit.*, p. 102.

31. Kathy Laster, 'Knorr, Frances Lydia Alice (Minnie) (1867–1894)', http://adb.anu.edu.au/biography/knorr-frances-lydia-alice-minnie-13030/text23559.

32. Barbara Yazbeck, '"Deviant Motherhood" in the Late Nineteenth Century: A case study of the trial and execution of Frances Knorr and Emma Williams for child murder', MA thesis, University of Melbourne, 2002, Chapter 2, p. 36.

33. Sussex, *op. cit.*, p. 104.

34. *Ibid.*

35. *Argus*, 4 January 1894.

36. *Argus*, 16 January 1894, gives a full account of the execution.

37. Sussex, *op. cit.*, p. 105.

38. P. R. Kidd, *The Australian Crime File: The 'Best of' Collection of Notorious True Crime Stories*, The Five Mile Press, Rowville, Victoria, 2005, p. 165.

39. The author visited the Old Melbourne Gaol Museum in September 2011. Women killers are disproportionately represented among the exhibits.

40. Penelope Hetherington, 'Baby Farming in Western Australia: The case against Alice Mitchell, 1907', *Studies in Western Australian History*,

Vol. 25, 2007, pp. 88–89. Readers are advised to consult this article for more details concerning this case and its aftermath; refer also to Jennifer Worrall, 'Baby Farming' in Jenny Gregory and Jan Gothard (eds), *Historical Encyclopedia of Western Australia*, UWAP, Perth, 2009, p. 118.

41. *Western Australian*, 6 March 1907.

42. *Western Australian*, 9 March 1907.

43. P. B. Kidd, *Australia's Serial Killers: The Definite History of Serial Multicide in Australia*, Macmillan, Sydney, 2000, p. 42.

44. *Western Australian*, 9 April 1907.

45. Hetherington, *op. cit.*, p. 78.

46. Hetherington, *op. cit.*, pp. 76–79.

47. *Western Australian*, 18 February 1907.

48. Hetherington, *op. cit.*, p. 80; S. Thompson, 'Infant Mortality' in Gregory and Gothard, *op. cit.*, pp. 478–79.

49. Margaret Brown, 'Cowan, Edith Dircksey (1861–1932)', http://adb.anu. edu.au/biography/cowan-edith-dircksey-5791/text9823. She was the first woman elected to a house of parliament in Australia in 1921.

50. *Western Australian*, 6 March 1907.

51. E. J. Edwards, 'McMillan, Sir Robert Furse (1858–1931)', http://adb.anu. edu.au/biography/mcmillan-sir-robert-furse-7424/text12919; G. C. Bolton and G. Byrne, *May It Please Your Honour: A History of the Supreme Court of Western Australia from 1861–2005*, Supreme Court of Western Australia, Perth, 2005, pp. 104–105, 137, 167–68.

52. *Western Australian*, 11 and 13 April 1907.

Chapter 7 Child Killers in the Nineteenth Century

1. *Sydney Herald*, 24 March 1842.

2. *Colonial Times*, 16 July 1852.

3. *Hobart Town Courier*, 10 July 1852.

4. Archives Office Tasmania (AOT) CSO 50/21 and 50/22. [These sources were kindly sent to me by historian Trudy Cowley.]

5. *Hobart Town Courier*, 16 July 1852.

6. Peter Bogner, 'Salier, George (1813–1892)', http://adb.anu.edu.au/ biography/salier-george-4531/text7421.

7. *Hobart Town Courier*, 4 August 1852; Trudy Cowley, 'Mary Sullivan, murderer' in Female Factory Research Group, *Convict Lives: Women at Cascades Female Factory*, Research Tasmania, Hobart, 2009, pp. 157–60.

8. *Colonial Times*, 3 August 1852.

9. *Argus*, 14 August 1852.

10. *South Australian Register*, 5 November 1895.

11. Michael Cannon, 'Emma Williams: The prostitute compelled to drown her own child' in *The Woman as Murderer: Five who paid with their lives*, Today's Australian Publishing Company, Mornington, Victoria, 1994, p. 127.

12. *South Australian Register*, 5 November 1895.

13. Cannon, *op. cit.*, p. 112; Barbara Yazbeck, '"Deviant Motherhood" in the Late Nineteenth Century: A case study of the trial and execution of Frances Knorr and Emma Williams for child murder', MA thesis, University of Melbourne, Melbourne, 2002, Chapter 3.

14. Ruth Hoban, 'Sutherland, Sulina Murray McDonald (1839–1909)', http://adb.anu.edu.au/biography/sutherland-selina-murray-4674/text7727.

15. *Argus*, 19 October 1895.

16. G. Serle, 'Champion, Henry Hyde (1859–1928)', http://adb.anu.edu.au/biography/champion-henry-hyde-5548/text9457.

17. C. R. Badger, 'Strong, Charles (1844–1942)', http://adb.anu.edu.au/biography/strong-charles-4658/text7697

18. *Barrier Miner*, 30 October 1895.

19. *Barrier Miner*, 5 November 1895; *Argus*, 5 November 1895.

20. Cannon, *op. cit.*, p. 145.

21. Details of the case are taken from the trial contained in *The Queen v Marie Christensen*, November 1896, Supreme Court of Queensland, Queensland State Archives (QSA) SCT/CC 127; Sean Gouglas and J. C. Weaver, 'A Postcolonial Understanding of Law and Society: Exploring criminal trials in colonial Queensland', *Australian Journal of Legal History*, Vol. 14, 2003. [Viewed e-Journal online.]

22. Evidence of Budlo Lefu in *R v Christensen*.

23. *Brisbane Courier*, 26 September 1896.

24. Details of the inquest may be found at QSA JUS/N245, File 370/96. My thanks to archivist Jane Wassel for locating these files.

25. Gouglas and Weaver, *op. cit.*

Chapter 8 The Wicked Stepmother: Martha Rendall

1. *Sunday Times* (Perth), 17 December 1950.

2. Paul B. Kidd, *Australia's Serial Killers: The Definitive History of Serial Multicide in Australia*, Pan Macmillan, Sydney, 2000, p. 58.

3. Anna Haebich, *Murdering Stepmothers: The Execution of Martha Rendell*, UWAP, Nedlands, 2010. In the contemporary documents the executed woman is often called Martha Rendall and I have followed this name through my text.

4. *Ibid.*, p. 141.

5. *Ibid.*, pp. 183–88.

6. *Ibid.*, p. 49; Sarah Morris described her life after her marriage ended at the inquest into the deaths of her three children, cited in the *Western Australian*, 11 August 1909.

7. S. T. Shulman, 'The History of Pediatric Infectious Diseases', *Pediatric Research*, Vol. 55, No. 1, 2004, pp. 163–76.

8. *The Australian Home Companion*, 7 April 1860; *Adelaide Advertiser*, 9 February 1895.

9. Lionel Rose, *The Massacre of the Innocents: Infanticide in Britain 1800–1939*, Routledge & Kegan Paul, London, 1986, pp. 10–12.

10. *West Australian*, 21 May 1932.

11. *West Australian*, 21 May 1909.

12. R. V. Southcott, 'Cleland, Sir John Burton (1878–1971)', http://adb.anu. edu.au/biography/cleland-sir-john-burton-5679/text9595.

13. M. Roe, 'Cumpston, John Howard Lidgett (1880–1954)', http://adb. anu.edu.au/biography/cumpston-john-howard-lidgett-5846/text9935. He became the inaugural Director-General of Federal Health.

14. *Sydney Morning Herald*, 17 August 1909.

15. *West Australian*, 11 August 1909.

16. *Sydney Morning Herald*, 17 August 1909.

17. *Sunday Times*, 12 September 1909.

18. *West Australian*, 11 August 1909.

19. Haebich also concurs with this interpretation in her book, *op. cit.*

20. G. C. Bolton and G. Byrne, *May It Please Your Honour: A History of the Supreme Court of Western Australia 1861–2005*, Supreme Court of Western Australia, Perth, 2005, p. 135; Jenny Gregory and Jan Gothard (eds),

Historical Encyclopedia of Western Australia, Perth, UWAP, 2009, *op. cit.*, p. 525.

21. Haebich, *op. cit.*, p. 1. [e-Journal edition].
22. *West Australian*, 2 October 1909.
23. Haebich, *op. cit.*, p. 11.
24. *West Australian*, 7 October 1909.
25. Kidd, *op. cit.*, p. 55.

Chapter 9 Child Killers in the Twentieth Century

1. *Adelaide Advertiser*, 26 March 1935.
2. *West Australian*, 27 March 1935.
3. *Age*, 12 April 1935.
4. *Western Argus*, 17 July 1934.
5. *Adelaide Advertiser*, 18 December 1937.
6. *Sydney Morning Herald*, 13 August 1950.
7. *Canberra Times*, 24 October 1950.
8. *Argus*, 24 October 1950.
9. *Argus*, 20 December 1950.
10. Paul B. Kidd, *Australia's Serial Killers: The Definitive History of Multicide in Australia*, Pan Macmillan, Sydney, 2000, pp. 200–201; P. R. Wilson, *Murder of the Innocents: Child Killers and Their Victims*, Rigby, Adelaide, 1985, pp. 48–52.
11. *Ibid*, p. 200.
12. *Sydney Morning Herald*, 10 April 1980.
13. Kidd, *op. cit.*, p. 230.
14. *Ibid.*, p. 231.
15. 'Babysitter "was killer"', *Age*, 2 April 1980.
16. Wilson, *op. cit.*, p. 50.
17. *Ibid.*, p. 51.
18. Michael Grant and John Hazel, *Who's Who in Classical Mythology*, Routledge, London, 2002, pp. 212–14.
19. *R v Fitchett* [2008] VSC 258 (18 July 2008). All statements and evidence are taken from the court records.
20. *Ibid.*, from Justice Nettle's sentencing statement.
21. *Ibid.*, from section entitled 'Moral Culpability'.

22. *Ibid.*, *op. cit.*
23. Justice Nettle's sentencing statement, *op. cit.*
24. *R v Fitchett* [2010] VSC 393.
25. *R v Fitchett* [2008] VSC 258 (18 July 2008).
26. *Ibid.*
27. *R v Fitchett* [2009] VSCA 150 (25 June 2009).

Chapter 10 Poisoners of the Nineteenth Century
1. Katherine Watson, *Poisoned Lives: English Poisoners and Their Victims 1750 to 1914*, Hambledon, London, 2004, p. 7.
2. *Ibid.*, p. 190.
3. Sir Sydney Smith, 'The History and Development of Forensic Medicine', *British Medical Journal*, 24 March 1951, p. 604.
4. *Ibid.*, p. 34.
5. See Katherine Watson, 'Medical and Chemical Expertise in English Trials for Criminal Poisoning, 1750–1914', *Medical History*, Vol. 50, No. 3, 2006, pp. 373–90 for further details.
6. *Sydney Gazette and New South Wales Advertiser*, 25 September 1823.
7. *Adelaide Register*, 23 June 1920.
8. Allan Peters, *Dead Woman Walking: Was an Innocent Woman Hanged?* Bas Publishing, Seaford, Victoria, 2008, p. 23. Readers are advised to consult this fascinating and well-researched account.
9. *Ibid.*, pp. 28–30.
10. *Worker*, 19 October 1895.
11. Peters, *op. cit.*, pp. 61–64.
12. 'The Last Statement and Confession of Elizabeth Woolcock to Mr Bickford', 16 December 1873 in J. Towler and T. J. Porter, *The Hempen Collar: Executions in South Australia 1838–1964*, Wednesday Press, Parafield Gardens, 1999, pp. 72–73. It was originally published in the *Adelaide Observer*, 3 January 1874.
13. *Ibid.*
14. *South Australian Advertiser*, 3 December 1873.
15. *South Australian Register*, 5 December 1873.
16. *Ibid.*
17. *Ibid.*

18. Robin Milhouse, 'Andrews, Richard Bullock (1823–1884)', http://adb. anu.edu.au/biography/andrews-richard-bullock-2889/text4139.

19. *South Australian Register*, 5 December 1873.

20. Renate Howe, 'Bicknell, James (1816–1895)', http://adb.anu.edu.au/ biography/bickford-james-2993/text4375.

21. *South Australian Advertiser*, 31 December 1873.

22. *Yorke's Peninsular Advertiser and Miners' News*, 25 May 1874.

23. Peters, *op. cit.*, pp. 291–94.

24. 'Elizabeth Woolcock', http://en.wikipedia.org.wki.Elizabeth_Woolcock; Peters, *op. cit.*

25. Peters, *op. cit.*, p. 301.

26. *Australian*, 18 May 1841.

27. Ann Jones, *Women Who Kill*, The Feminist Press, New York, NY, 2009, pp. 145–57.

28. Martha Rutledge, 'White, James (1828–1890)', http://adb.anu.edu.au/ biography/white-james-4837/text8073.

29. Cited in Alan Sharpe, *Crime and Punishment: Fifty Crimes That Shocked Australia*, Kingsclear Books, Crows Nest, 1997, p. 100.

30. The coronial inquiry was concerned with Louisa Collins' character. Refer to Wendy Kukulies-Smith and Susan Priest, '"No Hope for Mercy" for the Borgia of Botany Bay: Louisa May Collins, the last woman executed in NSW, 1889', *Canberra Law Review*, Vol. 10, No. 2, 2010.

31. Sharpe, *op. cit.*, p. 102.

32. *Ibid.*, p. 100.

33. William Guy and David Ferrier, *Principles of Forensic Medicine*, fourth edition (first published in 1844), p. 177 [read as an e-Book]. Guy was the inaugural professor of forensic medicine at King's College, London.

34. Smith, *op. cit.*, p. 605.

35. Sharpe, *op. cit.*, p. 101.

36. This was reported in Central Criminal Court papers, July 1888, inquest no. 786, cited in Kukulies-Smith and Priest, *op. cit.*, p. 148.

37. *Argus*, 24 July 1888.

38. Kukulies-Smith and Priest, *op. cit.*, p. 148.

39. *Sydney Morning Herald*, 18 July 1888.

40. Cited in Kukulies-Smith and Priest, *op. cit.*, p. 144.

41. *Sydney Morning Herald*, 6 November 1888; 9 November 1888.

42. *Sydney Morning Herald*, 9 November 1888.

43. Kukulies-Smith and Priest, *op. cit.*, provide an excellent coverage of the legal issues on this matter.

44. *R v Collins* [1888] NSWSupC2. The full judgment can be read in the *Brisbane Courier*, 10 December 1888.

45. *NSW Parliamentary Debates* (LA), 19 December 1888. His biography can be read at http://adb.anu.edu.au/biography/melville-ninian-4184/text6725.

46. Kukulies-Smith and Priest, *op. cit.*, pp. 154–55.

47. *Ibid.*, p. 155.

48. *Ibid.*, p. 157.

49. *The Bulletin*, 12 January 1889.

50. Mrs Foran gave this long interview to the *South Australian Register*, 20 June 1894.

51. *South Australian Register*, 4 April 1876.

52. *South Australian Register*, 13 July 1876.

53. *South Australian Register*, 15 March 1877.

54. www.victoria.mypeoplepuzzle.net/familygroup.php?/familyID=F47.

55. Kidd, *op. cit.*, p. 23.

56. Much of this evidence comes from the court proceedings. Refer to the *Argus*, 3 August 1894, for an account of the police court hearing.

57. *Argus*, 16 June 1894. This issue contains a series of letters written by Martha Needle and Otto Juncken.

58. *Argus*, 25 September 1894.

59. Cited in www.familytreecircles.com/martha-needle-34559.html.

60. Kidd, *op. cit.*, p. 30.

61. *Northern Miner*, 15 November 1894.

62. *Sydney Morning Herald*, 18 November 1904.

63. *Argus*, 21 February 1905.

64. *Ibid.*

65. *Western Australian*, 10 March 1905.

66. *Barrier Miner*, 24 May 1905.

67. *Kalgoorlie Western Argus*, 18 July 1905.

Chapter 11 The Thallium Killers

1. *Canberra Times*, 5 November 1948.
2. *Western Australian*, 7 December 1948.
3. *Courier Mail*, 10 May 1938.
4. *Courier Mail*, 27 March 1929; *Townsville Daily Bulletin*, 2 April 1919.
5. Noel Sanders, *The Thallium Enthusiasms and Other Australian Outrages*, Local Consumption Publications, Sydney, 1995, p. 45. Readers should consult this wide-ranging account.
6. D. H. Lawrence, *Kangaroo* (1923) [read as an e-Book].
7. Kate Darian-Smith, *On the Homefront: Melbourne in wartime, 1939–1945*, Oxford University Press, Melbourne, 1990, p. 102.
8. Kay Saunders and Raymond Evans (eds), *Gender Relations in Australia: Domination and negotiation*, Harcourt Brace Jovanovich, Sydney, 1992, p. 185.
9. Sanders, *op. cit.*, Chapter 1.
10. I lived in the middle-class northern Brisbane suburb of The Grange in the early 1950s and remember the excitement for local children when the pack of yapping fox terriers made its way around the area looking for rats. Our parents were not quite so enthusiastic about this implied slur on bourgeois standards of respectability. The fox terrier was then not a suitable pet, given its reputation as a working animal doing dirty jobs.
11. Sanders, *op. cit.*, pp. 18–19.
12. *Sydney Morning Herald*, 19 June 1953.
13. *Courier Mail*, 20 May 1952.
14. Richard Hall, 'Clues Under the Microscope: Great Sydney crimes', *Sydney City Monthly*, 28–31 August 1982, pp. 29–30.
15. *Courier Mail*, 20 May 1952.
16. *Sydney Morning Herald*, 11 June 1952.
17. *Sydney Morning Herald*, 21 June 1952.
18. *Sydney Morning Herald*, 17 June 1952.
19. *Adelaide Advertiser*, 18 June 1952.
20. John Romeril, *Mrs Thally F* in R. Fisher (ed.), *Seven One-Act Plays*, Currency Press, Sydney, 1983.
21. Their names do not appear on the Australian War Memorial Service records for World War II.

22. *Adelaide Advertiser*, 26 June 1952.

23. Martha Rutledge, 'Kinsella, Edward Parnell (Ted) (1893–1967)', http://adb.anu.edu.au/biography/kinsella-edward-parnell-ted-1074/text19051.

24. *Sydney Morning Herald*, 29 May 1952.

25. *Argus*, 17 September 1952.

26. James Holledge, *Australia's Wicked Women*, Horwitz, London, 1968, p. 36.

27. *Argus*, 24 September 1952.

28. *Canberra Times*, 29 September 1952.

29. *Courier Mail*, 10 December 1952.

30. *Courier Mail*, 30 August 1954.

31. *Sydney Morning Herald*, 20 August 1952.

32. Archive Office, NSW: CP, Supreme Court and Courts, *R v Ruby May Norton*, 10/10484, cited in Clair Scrine, '"More Deadly Than the Male" – The Sexual Politics of Female Poisoning: Trials of the thallium women', *Limina*, Vol. 8, 2002, p. 130. Testimony of witnesses is taken from the court case.

33. *Sydney Morning Herald*, 19 June 1953.

34. *Courier Mail*, 31 July 1953.

35. Cited in Sanders, *op. cit.*, pp. 9–10.

36. Stephen Garton, 'Grills, Caroline (1888?–1960)', http://adb.anu.edu.au/biography/grills-caroline-10371/text1837.

37. *Sydney Morning Herald*, 15 August 1953.

38. *Argus*, 9 July 1953.

39. *Sydney Morning Herald*, 15 August 1953; *Burnie Advocate*, 8 October 1953.

40. *Burnie Advocate*, 13 August 1953.

41. *Canberra Times*, 8 July 1953.

42. *Sydney Morning Herald*, 12 August 1953.

43. *Argus*, 12 August 1953.

44. *Argus*, 11 August 1953.

45. *Courier Mail*, 14 August 1953.

46. *Argus*, 21 August 1953, reported the inquest would resume the following week on that date.

47. *Argus*, 15 August 1953.

48. *Launceston Examiner*, 20 August 1953.

49. *Argus*, 19 August 1953.

50. *Launceston Examiner*, 18 August 1953.

51. *Truth*, 16 August 1953, cited in Scrine, *op. cit.*, p. 132.

52. *Sydney Morning Herald*, 8 October 1953.

53. *Sydney Morning Herald*, 9 October 1953.

54. *Courier Mail*, 13 October 1953.

55. *Sydney Morning Herald*, 8 October 1953.

56. *Sydney Morning Herald*, 14 October 1953.

57. *Adelaide Advertiser*, 16 October 1953.

58. *Adelaide Advertiser*, 10 April 1954.

59. *Argus*, 24 September 1954.

60. Miranda Devine, 'Her new career's to die for', *Sydney Morning Herald*, 4 June 2005.

Chapter 12 Deadly Manoeuvres in the Nineteenth Century

1. *Sydney Gazette and New South Wales Advertiser*, 22 June 1816.

2. *R v Anderson* [1816] NSWKR 5; *Sydney Gazette*, 22 June 1816.

3. Tasmanian State Archives. Marriage of Margaret Galvin and John Coghlin (sic) CON 52/1/3, researched from online records.

4. *Hobart Mercury*, 29 January 1862.

5. *Brisbane Courier*, 15 March 1862.

6. *Bell's Life in Sydney and Sporting Chronicle*, 8 March 1862.

7. Michael Cannon, *The Woman as Murderer*, Today's Publishing Company, Mornington, Victoria, 1994, p. 42.

8. *Sydney Morning Herald*, 27 August 1872. Cannon writes that the jury did not recommend mercy. Newspaper accounts of the time attest that it did.

9. *Argus*, 17 October 1892. Obituary of William Fraser.

10. *Traralgon Record*, 22 June 1894. This article provided a good deal of background information.

11. *Argus*, 1 August 1894.

12. Cannon, *op. cit.*, p. 87.

13. *Argus*, 1 August 1894.

14. *Ibid.*

15. *Argus*, 17 August 1894.

16. Cannon, *op. cit.*, pp. 91–92.

17. *South Australian Register*, 12 December 1894.

18. Weston Bate, 'Were, Jonathon Binns (1809–1885)', http://adb.anu.edu. au/biography/were-jonathon-binns-2783/text3963.

19. *Barrier Miner*, 17 December 1894.

20. *Argus*, 4 July 1901.

21. *Barrier Miner*, 23 June 1903.

Chapter 13 Killing of Partners in the Twentieth Century

1. *Adelaide Advertiser*, 21 November 1902.

2. *Evening News*, 21 November 1902.

3. Cited in Juliet Peers, 'The Case of Ethel Herringe' in Kerry Greenwood (ed.), *The Thing She Loves: Why Women Kill*, Allen and Unwin, Sydney, 1996, p. 56.

4. *Ibid.*, p. 57.

5. Cited in *ibid.*, pp. 57–58.

6. *Grenfell Vedette*, 6 May 1903, cited in *ibid.*, p. 59.

7. *Adelaide Advertiser*, 21 November 1902.

8. *Kalgoorlie Western Argus*, 25 November 1902.

9. Martha Rutledge, 'Owen, Sir Langer Meade Loftus (1862–1935)', http:// adb.anu.edu.au/biography/owen-sir-langer-meade-loftus-8499/text13813. Sir Langer was the son of Sir William Owen.

10. *Grenfell Vedette*, 29 April 1903, cited in Peers, *op. cit.*, p. 62.

11. AWSS, 'Holland, Henry Edmund (Harry) (1868–1933)', http://adb.anu. edu.au/biography/holland-henry-edmund-harry-6708/text11579.

12. Peers, *op. cit.*, pp. 62–63.

13. *Ibid.*, pp. 63–64.

14. Heather Radi, 'Holman, Ada Augusta (1869–1949)', http://adb.anu.edu. au/biography/holman-ada-augusta-666710/text11583.

15. Beverley Kingston, 'Golding, Annie Mackenzie (1855–1934)', http:// adb.anu.edu.au/biography/golding-annie-mackenzie-6416/text10971; J. A. Allen, *Rose Scott: Vision and Revision in Feminism*, Oxford University Press, Melbourne, 1994 [read as an e-Book].

16. Peers, *op. cit.*, p. 68. This chapter provides more details on the aftermath of this intriguing case.

17. Jacob made this statement in her testimony in the courtroom at her trial.

18. Testimony of William Murphy, customs officer, Perth; letter written by Cyril Gidley on 16 August 1925, cited in the *Mirror*, 12 September 1925.

19. Jill Matthews, 'Ballroom Tragedy, Courtroom Drama' in Greenwood, *op. cit.*, p. 32; Claude Kingston, *It Don't Seem a Day Too Much*, Rigby, Adelaide, 1971.

20. *Mirror*, 12 September 1925, reporting on the evidence of Maude Mitchell at the inquest.

21. Matthews, *op. cit.*, pp. 32–33.

22. *Mirror* (Perth), 27 August 1925.

23. *Mirror*, 12 September 1925.

24. Reported in *Western Australian*, 4 September 1925. This newspaper reported the trial. References from these proceedings come from this newspaper.

25. *Mirror*, 12 September 1925.

26. Matthews, *op. cit.*, p. 34.

27. G. C. Bolton and G. Byrne, *May It Please Your Honour: A History of the Supreme Court of Western Australia 1861–2005*, Supreme Court of Western Australia, Perth, 2011, p. 135; , *op. cit.*, p. 99.

28. *Ibid.*, p. 154.

Chapter 14 Eugenia Falleni, The 'Man–Woman' Killer

1. Ruth Ford, 'The Man–Woman Murderer: Sex fraud, sexual inversion and the unmentionable "Article" in 1920s Australia', *Gender and History*, Vol. 12, No. 1, 2000, pp. 158–95.

2. Alan Sharpe, *Crime and Punishment: Fifty Crimes That Shocked Australia*, Milsons Point, Currawong Press, 1982, pp. 174–76.

3. *Barrier Miner*, 20 August 1920. Evidence before C. H. Gale SM at Central Police Court, Sydney.

4. Ford, *op. cit.*, pp. 163–64.

5. Kay Saunders, *Notorious Australian Women*, ABC Books, Sydney, 2011, Chapter 5.

6. Ford, *op. cit.*, p. 175.

7. Herbert Moran, 'Portrait of an Invert' in *Viewless Winds: Being the Recollections and Digressions of an Australian Surgeon*, Peter Davies, London, 1939, pp. 230–36.

8. Cited in Ford, *op. cit.*, p. 180.

9. Suzanne Falkiner, *Eugenia: A Man*, Pan Books, Sydney, 1988, pp. 6–17. Readers are recommended to consult this well-researched account; Carolyn Strange, 'Falleni, Eugenia (c. 1875–1938)', http://adb.anu.edu.au/biography/falleni-eugenia-12911/text23325. Cited in Falkiner, *op. cit.*, p. 40. The details of the court case can be found in newspapers such as the *Sydney Morning Herald*.

10. *Ibid.*

11. *Kalgoorlie Western Argus*, 24 August 1920, reporting evidence at the last day of the hearing at Central Police Court.

12. Cited in *ibid.*, p. 23.

13. Cited in Ford, *op. cit.*, p. 181.

14. Moran, *op. cit.*, pp. 230–36.

15. Strange, *op. cit.*

Chapter 15 Fighting Back

1. Testimony of Charles Daniels at the trial of Ann Smith, *Sydney Gazette and New South Wales Advertiser*, 5 November 1834.

2. *R v Smith* (no. 2) [1834] NSWSupC 124; *Sydney Herald*, 17 November 1834 and 20 November 1834.

3. Convict Records NSW, 4/4549, Reel 690, p. 024.

4. This case can be followed in the *Sydney Morning Herald* account of the trial of 5–7 April 1859. The coverage is particularly detailed. Notice of commutation of sentence is contained in a list of sentences 3 May 1860.

5. Malcolm Cope, 'Brennan, Frank Tenison (1884–1949)', http://adb.anu.edu.au/biography/brennan-frank-tenison-5348/text9043.

6. Ross Johnston, *History of the Queensland Bar*, Queensland Bar Association, Toowong, 1984, pp. 91–92.

7. All testimony is taken from the transcript of the trial. Queensland State Archives (QSA) Supreme Court Trial Records, ID 787407.

8. *Rockhampton Bulletin*, 7 March 1928.

9. *Kalgoorlie Western Argus*, 13 April 1909.

10. *Argus*, 27 November 1936.

11. QSA Justice E. A. Douglas Notebook 11/3/1937-20/5/1937 ID 18554; *Courier Mail*, 18 May 1937.

12. Ruth Teale, *Colonial Eve: Sources on Australian Women in Australia 1788–1914*, OUP, Melbourne, 1978, pp. 166–68.

13. Hilary Golder, *Divorce in 19th-Century New South Wales*, University of New South Wales Press, Sydney, 1985, page 215.

14. Katie Spearritt, 'New Dawns: First wave feminism 1880–1914' in Kay Saunders and Raymond Evans (eds), *Gender Relations in Australia: Domination and Negotiation*, Harcourt Brace Jovanovich, Sydney, 1992, pp. 325–47.

15. B. F. Bartal, 'Battered Wife Syndrome Evidence: The Australian experience', British Society of Criminology Conference, July 1995, published September 1998 and available online; E. A. Sheehy et. al., 'Defending Battered Women on Trial: The Battered Wife Syndrome and its limitations', *Criminal Law Journal*, Vol. 16, 1992.

16. Details of this complicated case can be located in court records available online; refer to *The Queen v Runjanjic The Queen v Kontinnen*, Nos 226 and 227 of 1991 Judgment No. 2951 [1991] SASC 2951; (1992) 56 SASR 114; Joanna Brodie, '"All Yous Will be Dead in the Morning": The Kontinnen case' in Kerry Greenwood (ed.), *The Thing She Loves: Why Women Kill*, Allen and Unwin, Sydney, 1996, pp. 44–53; Nan Seuffert, 'Domestic Violence, Discourses of Romantic Love and Complex Personhood in the Law', *Melbourne University Law Review*, Vol. 8, 1999.

17. Nigel Hunt, *Sunday Herald Sun*, 12 April 1992.

18. *The Queen v Runjanjic The Queen v Kontinnen*, Nos 226 and 227, *op. cit.*

19. Belinda Morrisey, *When Women Kill: Questions of Agency and Subjectivity*, Routledge, London, 2003, p. 85.

20. *R v Raby*, Supreme Court of Victoria (unreported), 17 October 1994, cited in Seuffert, *op. cit.*, p. 1.

Chapter 16 Deadly Lovers' Pacts in the Nineteenth Century

1. *Sydney Morning Herald*, 5 October 1842.

2. *Australasian Chronicle*, 4 October 1842.

3. Details of the widely reported case can be read in the *Sydney Morning Herald*, 9 September and 15 September 1843.

4. *Sydney Morning Herald*, 5 October 1842.

5. *Morning Chronicle*, 21 October 1843.

6. *Empire*, 6 November 1854.
7. G. C. Bolton and G. Byrne, *May It Please Your Honour: A History of the Supreme Court of Western Australia from 1861–2005*, Supreme Court of Western Australia, Perth, 2005, p. 29.
8. *Ibid.*
9. *Perth Gazette and Independent Journal of Politics and News*, 14 September 1855.
10. *Sunday Times* (Perth), 19 September 1909; Alan Sharpe and Vivien Encel, *Murder! Twenty-five True Crimes*, Kingsclear Books, Crows Nest, 1997.
11. *Perth Gazette and Independent Journal of Politics and News*, 14 September 1855.
12. *Ibid.*
13. J. H. M. Honniball, 'Mackie, William Henry (1799–1860)', http://adb.anu.edu.au/biography/mackie-william-henry-2410/text3191.
14. Ann-Mari Jordens, 'Birnie, Richard (1808–1888)', http://adb.anu.edu.au/biography/birnie-richard/2997/text4385.
15. *Perth Gazette and Independent Journal of Politics and News*, 19 October 1855.
16. Paul B. Kidd, *The Australian Crime File: The 'Best' of Collection of Notorious True Crime Stories*, The Five Mile Press, Rowville, Victoria, 2005, pp. 189–95.
17. *Maitland Mercury and Hunter River General Advertiser*, 7 November 1863. This is a lengthy account of the trial.
18. 'Stephen, George Milner (1812–1894)', http://adb.anu.edu.au/biography/stephen-george-milner-1294/text 3771.
19. *South Australian Advertiser*, 26 November 1863.
20. Ellen Thomson, Brisbane Gaol, 23 May 1887, Queensland State Archives (QSA) PRI/6 01/01/87–31/12/1907, Prisoners under sentence of death, Sheriff's Office, Prison Department.
21. NSW Convict Index, 4/4404 reel 1022, 950.
22. Raymond Evans, Kay Saunders and Kathryn Cronin, *Race Relations in Colonial Queensland*, University of Queensland Press, St Lucia, 1988 (first published 1975), pp. 282–84.

23. The case in Criminal Jurisdiction of the Supreme Court of Queensland in October 1887 was fully reported in the *Brisbane Courier*, 22 October 1887.

24. QSA Justice Department File A/18487 01/01/87-31/12/87, Supreme Court of Northern District, Townsville.

25. *Brisbane Courier*, 11 May 1887.

26. Ross W. Johnston, *History of the Queensland Bar*, Bar Association of Queensland, Toowong, 1984, pp. 65–68.

27. Cited in Marion Purnell, 'Ellen Lynch (1841 [sic]–1887), the only woman to have been legally hanged in Queensland', www.easystreetretreat.com.au/lynch_ellen.html.

28. *Sydney Morning Herald*, 3 June 1887.

29. *The Boomerang*, 17 June 1887.

30. *Brisbane Courier*, 22 June 1887.